MACROECONOMICS

CANADA IN THE GLOBAL ENVIRONMENT

MACROECONOMICS

CANADA IN THE GLOBAL ENVIRONMENT

SIXTH EDITION

MICHAEL PARKIN ✦ ROBIN BADE

University of Western Ontario

PEARSON

Addison
Wesley

Toronto

Library and Archives Canada Cataloguing in Publication

Parkin, Michael, 1939–
    Macroeconomics : Canada in the global environment / Michael Parkin, Robin Bade.—6th ed.

Includes index.
ISBN 0-321-41842-5

1. Macroeconomics—Textbooks. 2. Canada—Economic conditions—1991–
—Textbooks. I. Bade, Robin II. Title.

HB172.5.P363 2006   339   C2005-905354-2

0-321-41842-5

Vice President, Editorial Director: Michael J. Young
Editor in Chief, Business and Economics: Gary Bennett
Director of Marketing, Business and Economics: Bill Todd
Associate Editor: Stephen Broadbent
Production Editor: Jennifer Handel
Copy Editor: Lu Cormier
Proofreader: Edie Franks
Production Coordinator: Deborah Starks
Page Layout: Carolyn E. Sebestyen
Technical Illustrator: Richard Parkin
Indexer: Belle Wong
Permissions and Photo Research: Lisa Brant
Art Director: Julia Hall
Interior and Cover Design: Anthony Leung
Cover Image: Background, Ron Stroud/Masterfile; Centre, Greg Stott/Masterfile

Statistics Canada information is used with the permission of the Minister of Industry, as Minister responsible for Statistics Canada. Information on the availability of the wide range of data from Statistics Canada can be obtained from Statistics Canada's Regional Offices, its World Wide Web site at http://www.statcan.ca, and its toll-free access number 1-800-263-1136. The Statistics Canada CANSIM II database can be accessed at http://cansim2.statcan.ca/cgi-win/CNSMCGI.EXE.

2 3 4 5   10 09 08 07 06

Printed and bound in the United States of America.

The cover depicts a Canadian urban scene viewed through the lens of the Parkin–Bade icon. You can look at this cover in many different ways. Here is what we see.

First, we see a metaphor for what our text, Web site, and other supplements seek to be—a window that gives students a sharply focused view of the world based on a clear and compelling account of timeless principles.

Second, we see a symbol of what economics (and all scientific endeavour) is about. The Parkin–Bade icon is like an economic model. We use models to understand reality. The model is abstract, like the diamond shape and its hole or aperture. The model distorts our view of the world by omitting some details. But it permits us to see the focus of our interest in the brightest and clearest possible light.

To our students

Michael Parkin received his training as an economist at the Universities of Leicester and Essex in England. Currently in the Department of Economics at the University of Western Ontario, Professor Parkin has held faculty appointments at Brown University, the University of Manchester, the University of Essex, and Bond University. He is a past president of the Canadian Economics Association and has served on the editorial boards of the *American Economic Review* and the *Journal of Monetary Economics* and as managing editor of the *Canadian Journal of Economics*. Professor Parkin's research on macroeconomics, monetary economics, and international economics has resulted in over 160 publications in journals and edited volumes, including the *American Economic Review*, the *Journal of Political Economy*, the *Review of Economic Studies*, the *Journal of Monetary Economics*, and the *Journal of Money, Credit and Banking*. He became most visible to the public with his work on inflation that discredited the use of wage and price controls. Michael Parkin also spearheaded the movement towards European monetary union.

Robin Bade earned degrees in mathematics and economics at the University of Queensland and her Ph.D. at the Australian National University. She has held faculty appointments in the business schools at the University of Edinburgh and Bond University and in the economics departments at the University of Manitoba, the University of Toronto, and the University of Western Ontario. Her research on international capital flows appears in the *International Economic Review* and the *Economic Record*.

Professor Parkin and Dr. Bade are the joint authors of *Modern Macroeconomics* (Pearson Education Canada), an intermediate text, and *Foundations of Economics* (Pearson Education Canada), and have collaborated on many research and textbook writing projects. They are both experienced and dedicated teachers of introductory economics.

PREFACE

This book presents economics as a serious, lively, and evolving science. Its goal is to open students' eyes to the "economic way of thinking" and to help them gain insights into how the economy works and how it might be made to work better.

We provide a thorough and complete coverage of the subject, using a straightforward, precise, and clear writing style.

We are conscious that many students find economics hard, so we place the student at centre stage and write for the student. We use language that doesn't intimidate and that allows the student to concentrate on the substance.

We open each chapter with a clear statement of learning objectives, a real-world student-friendly vignette to grab attention, and a brief preview. We illustrate principles with examples that are selected to hold the student's interest and to make the subject lively. And we put principles to work by using them to illuminate current real-world problems and issues.

We present some advanced topics, such as game theory, the modern theory of the firm, public choice theory, rational expectations, and new growth theory. But we explain these topics with familiar core ideas and tools.

Today's course springs from today's issues—the information revolution, the Asian economic boom, the Kyoto debate, and the expansion of international trade and investment. But the principles that we use to understand these issues remain the core principles of our science.

Governments and international agencies place renewed emphasis on long-term fundamentals as they seek to sustain economic growth. This book reflects this emphasis.

To help promote a rich, active learning experience, we have developed MyEconLab, a comprehensive online learning environment that features tests, personalized study plans, a dynamic eText, interactive tutorials, frequent news updates, and more.

The Sixth Edition Revision

ECONOMICS, SIXTH EDITION, RETAINS ALL OF the improvements achieved in its predecessor with its thorough and detailed presentation of modern economics, emphasis on real-world examples and critical thinking skills, diagrams renowned for pedagogy and precision, and path-breaking technology.

We organize our description of what is new in the sixth edition in four sections:

- Refocused and revised introductory chapters
- Revised and updated microeconomics content
- Revised and updated macroeconomics content
- MyEconLab

Refocused and Revised Introductory Chapters

1. We have refocused Chapter 1 to place greater emphasis on the role of incentives in influencing people's choices and on the question: Can choices made in the pursuit of self-interest also serve the social interest? This central question of economics is introduced through eight pressing issues in today's world that are explored further at various later points in the text. They are central planning versus the market, globalization, the new economy, the post 9/11 economy, corporate scandals, HIV/AIDS, disappearing tropical rainforests, and water shortages.

   These issues grab the student's attention and provide an early signal that economics is not a narrow business oriented subject but one that addresses issues of major social concern.

2. We have heavily revised our explanation of the gains from trade (Chapter 2), which we now begin with a numerical example and follow with a graphical analysis. The example has absolute advantage built into it so that the role of comparative advantage is demonstrated more vividly.

Revised and Updated Microeconomics Content

In addition to thorough and extensive updating, the microeconomics chapters feature the following eight revisions, some of them major:

1. Efficiency and Equity (Chapter 5) has been extensively revised. We have deleted the short refresher on efficiency and now refer the reader back to Chapter 2, where this topic is introduced and explained.

   We have added a new section that describes the eight alternative methods that might be used to allocate scarce resources: market price, command, majority rule, contest, first-come-first-served, lottery, personal characteristics, and force. By laying out these alternatives, we are better able to evaluate the ability of the market to achieve an efficient outcome. We return to these alternatives later in the chapter and ask whether there are situations in which one of them might improve on the market allocation.

   The sections that show the equivalence of demand and marginal social benefit and supply and marginal social cost have been rewritten to place the emphasis on moving from the individual to society. Consequently, we now derive the market demand and supply curves in this chapter. We also explain the connections between individual and economy-wide consumer surplus and producer surplus.

   We have rewritten the case study on a water shortage in a natural disaster to review the fairness and efficiency of the market compared with its alternatives.

2. Markets in Action (Chapter 6) has an expanded discussion of the inequity of rent ceilings, which also examines the equity implications of the alternative allocation methods. We have added an explicit graphical analysis of the inefficiency of the minimum wage and added brief discussion of living wage laws. A new section explicitly (and graphically) analyzes taxes levied on the seller and the buyer to demonstrate their equivalence.

3. Utility and Demand (Chapter 7) now opens with an explanation of how a change in income or prices changes the budget line (similar to what is done in the parallel indifference curve chapter, Chapter 8, but less technically and without equations. The section on individual demand and market demand has been removed from this chapter because it is now covered in Chapter 5—see above).

4. A new appendix to Chapter 8 explains the connection between marginal utility theory and indifference

curve theory for those wishing to teach both approaches to consumer theory.

5. Perfect Competition (Chapter 11) has a new explanation of the efficiency of perfect competition illustrated graphically with a figure of both the market and the individual firm in long-run equilibrium.

6. Monopolistic Competition and Oligopoly (Chapter 13) has an expanded discussion of short-run loss (as well as profit) and exit (as well as entry). It also has an expanded comparison of monopolistic competition and perfect competition covering both the markup over marginal cost and the excess capacity result. We have expanded the discussions of the efficiency of monopolistic competition and advertising. We also explain advertising as a signal and the role of brand names.

  A new introduction to oligopoly explains the cost and demand conditions in which it arises and gives some examples. The game theory section now includes an R&D game of chicken, which we contrast with the prisoners' dilemma.

7. Competition Policy (Chapter 14) includes new material on price cap regulation, which shows that a price cap with monopoly can lower the price and increase output.

8. Public Goods and Common Resources (Chapter 16) has a new introduction on classifying goods and resources and identifies common resources—rival and nonexcludable resources. It also notes that nonrival and excludable goods and services are produced by natural monopoly. The chapter now explores the tragedy of the commons (along with the free-rider problem). We have removed the section on taxes from this chapter and now cover them only in Chapter 6.

Revised and Updated Macroeconomics Content

In addition to thorough and extensive updating, the macroeconomics chapters feature the following eight major revisions:

1. A First Look at Macroeconomics (Chapter 19) has new material on the Lucas wedge and Okun gap—the wedge created by growth slowdown and the gap created by recession. This description serves to emphasize the vital importance of economic growth and the ability of small changes to make a big difference.

2. Fiscal Policy (Chapter 24) has been revised to explain the government expenditures multiplier and autonomous tax/transfer payments multiplier more generally in terms of the slope of the aggregate expenditure curve rather than the marginal propensity to consume. We have also improved our explanation of the role of induced taxes and transfer payments in affecting the multipliers and of the distinction between cyclical and structural budget balance.

3. Money, Banking, and Interest Rates (Chapter 25) is now the first of three chapters that pave the way towards an explanation of how the Bank of Canada conducts its monetary policy. The section on the banking system is broader than in the previous editions. As before, it describes the functions of the depository institutions. But it now also provides a brief description of the role played in the banking system by the Bank of Canada. It describes and explains of the functions of the Large Value Transfer System (LVTS) and the Automated Clearing Settlement System (ACCS), which lay an institutional foundation for a later (new) description and analysis of the Bank of Canada's monetary policy.

  Substantially rewritten material on how banks create money now unifies two sections of the fifth edition to explain the money multiplier. (The separate deposits multiplier is gone.)

4. The Exchange Rate (Chapter 26) is now placed before the discussion of monetary policy. This placement serves to emphasize the role of a flexible exchange rate as a foundation for the conduct of monetary policy. The chapter has a new section on exchange rate policy that reviews the four options: flexible, fixed, crawling peg, and currency union, and explains that only a flexible exchange rate leaves monetary policy free to pursue domestic goals.

5. Monetary Policy (Chapter 28) is the most heavily revised chapter in the new edition. It begins with a new discussion of the Bank of Canada's monetary policy objective, its achievement, and its rationale. A new description and analysis of the conduct of monetary policy explains how the overnight rate target is set and how it is achieved using the operating band between

bank rate and the settlements balances rate and open market operations. This section includes an explanation of the crucial distinction between an instrument rule and a targeting rule for the conduct of monetary policy. We have written a new explanation of the monetary policy transmission mechanism (building on that of the fifth edition but in the context of the Bank's current operating procedures) that includes the explanation of the interest-sensitive expenditure curve from the fifth edition Chapter 25. We also provide a new discussion of alternative approaches to monetary policy including Taylor and McCallum rules, exchange rate targeting, and money stock targeting and we explain why a rule for monetary policy is necessary.

6. Fiscal and Monetary Interactions (Chapter 29) has a new section on "Policy Coordination, Conflict, and Risk" that explains the risks of using an interest rate instrument if the response of the interest rate is too little or too slow and the difficulty of determining the appropriate level for the interest rate when fiscal policy changes.

7. The fifth edition chapters on the Business Cycle, Policy Challenges, and the Stock Market have been removed. (Web-based versions of these chapters are available for those who want to cover them).

8. Trading with the World (Chapter 32) now has a section on the balance of payments (from Chapter 34 in the previous edition).

MyEconLab

MyEconLab is a turnkey, online solution for your economics course. Featuring a new and powerful graphing engine and testing bank, students are able to self-test and generate a study plan, and instructors are able to assign homework and capture grades. With a tight, everything-in-one-place organization around the new testing tool, questions include true and false, fill-in-the-blank, multiple-choice, numerical, and complete-the-graph. Because questions are generated algorithmically, there are about 40,000 questions per chapter!

Users of our previous Web site will find MyEconLab an exciting and powerful resource. Practice Tests for each section of the textbook enable students to test their ability and identify the areas in which they need further work. Based on a student's performance on a practice test, a personalized study plan shows where further study needs to focus. Once students have received their study plan, additional practice exercises, keyed to the textbook, provide extensive practice and link directly to the eText, with animated graphs and other resources.

Users of MyEconLab will revel in the powerful graphing tool integrated into both the practice tests and practice exercises. This tool enables students to manipulate graphs and see how the concepts, numbers, and graphs are connected. A new, powerful feature is that questions using the graphing tool (like all other questions) can be submitted and graded.

For review and self-assessment, MyEconLab provides tutorials launched directly from the practice exercises. Using the tutorial instruction, students can see a demonstration of step-by-step solutions to practice problems, or they can participate in guided, step-by-step tutorials that promote self-discovery.

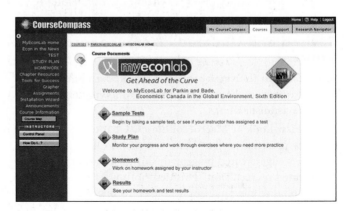

Features to Enhance Teaching and Learning

HERE, WE DESCRIBE THE CHAPTER FEATURES THAT are designed to enhance the learning process. Each chapter contains the following learning aids.

Chapter Opener

Each chapter opens with a one-page student-friendly, attention-grabbing vignette. The vignette raises questions that both motivate the student and focus the chapter. The sixth edition carries this story into the main body of the chapter, and relates it to the chapter-ending *Reading Between the Lines* feature.

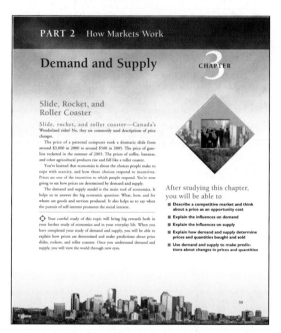

Chapter Objectives

A list of learning objectives enables students to see exactly where the chapter is going and to set their goals before they begin the chapter. We link the objectives directly to the chapter's major headings.

> After studying this chapter, you will be able to
> - Describe a competitive market and think about a price as an opportunity cost
> - Explain the influences on demand
> - Explain the influences on supply
> - Explain how demand and supply determine prices and quantities bought and sold
> - Use demand and supply to make predictions about changes in prices and quantities

In-Text Review Quizzes

A review quiz at the end of most major sections enables students to determine whether a topic needs further study before moving on. The review quiz includes the corresponding Study Plan in MyEconLab.

> ### REVIEW QUIZ
> 1 What is the distinction between a money price and a relative price?
> 2 Why is a relative price an opportunity cost?
> 3 Can you think of an example of a good whose money price and relative price have risen?
> 4 Can you think of an example of a good whose money price and relative price have fallen?
>
> **myeconlab** Study Plan 3.1

Key Terms

Highlighted terms within the text simplify the student's task of learning the vocabulary of economics. Each highlighted term appears in an end-of-chapter list and an end-of-book glossary with page numbers, boldfaced in the index, and on Flashcards on MyEconLab.

> ffee by the price of a pack of gum and find of one price to the other. The ratio of one nother is called a **relative price**, and a *relative opportunity co*

> ### KEY TERMS
> Change in demand, 62
> Change in supply, 67
> ~~Change in~~ demanded, 65

> **Above full-employment equilibrium** A macroeconomic equilibrium in which real GDP exceeds potential GDP. (p. 519)
>
> **Absolute advantage** A person has an absolute advantage if that person is more productive than another person. (p. 42)

Diagrams That Show the Action

This book has set new standards of clarity in its diagrams. Our goal has always been to show "where the economic action is." The diagrams in this book continue to generate an enormously positive response, which confirms our view that graphical analysis is the most powerful tool available for teaching and learning economics. But many students find graphs hard to work with. For this reason, we have developed the entire art program with the study and review needs of the student in mind. The diagrams feature

■ Shifted curves, equilibrium points, and other important features highlighted in red

■ Colour-blended arrows to suggest movement

■ Graphs paired with data tables

■ Diagrams labelled with boxed notes

■ Extended captions that make each diagram and its caption a self-contained object for study and review

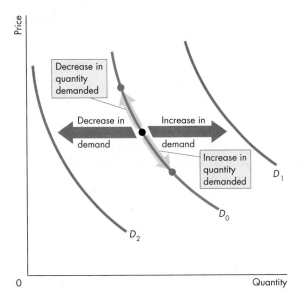

Reading Between the Lines

Each chapter ends with an economic analysis of a significant news article from the popular press together with a thorough economic analysis of the issues raised in the article. The sixth edition features 22 new *Reading Between the Lines* articles and analysis along with 8 classics from the fifth edition that remain relevant today. We chose each article because it sheds additional light on the questions first raised in the chapter opener.

Special "You're the Voter" sections in selected chapters invite students to analyze typical campaign topics and to probe their own stances on key public policy issues. Critical thinking questions about the article appear with the end-of-chapter questions and problems.

End-of-Chapter Study Material

Each chapter closes with a concise summary organized by major topics, lists of key figures, tables, and terms (all with page references), problems, critical thinking questions, and Web exercises. The problems are arranged in parallel pairs with solutions to the odd-numbered problems provided in MyEconLab.

Each problem also appears on MyEconLab, where it can be worked online in the chapter Test and Study Plan. We also provide the links needed for the Web exercises in MyEconLab.

---

50   CHAPTER 2   THE ECONOMIC PROBLEM

SUMMARY

KEY POINTS

Production Possibilities and Opportunity Cost (pp. 34–36)

- The production possibilities frontier, *PPF*, is the boundary between production levels that are attainable and those that are not attainable when all the available resources are used to their limit.
- Production efficiency occurs at points on the *PPF*.
- Along the *PPF*, the opportunity cost of producing more of one good is the amount of the other good that must be given up.
- The opportunity cost of a good increases as production of the good increases.

Using Resources Efficiently (pp. 37–39)

- The marginal cost of a good is the opportunity cost of producing one more unit.
- The marginal benefit from a good is the maximum amount of another good that a person is willing to forgo to obtain more of the first good.
- The marginal benefit of a good decreases as the amount of the good available increases.
- Resources are used efficiently when the marginal cost of each good is equal to its marginal benefit.

Economic Growth (pp. 40–41)

- Economic growth, which is the expansion of production possibilities, results from capital accumulation and technological change.
- The opportunity cost of economic growth is forgone current consumption.

Gains from Trade (pp. 42–45)

- A person has a comparative advantage in producing a good if that person can produce the good at a lower opportunity cost than everyone else.
- People gain by specializing in the activity in which they have a comparative advantage and trading with others.
- Dynamic comparative advantage arises from learning-by-doing.

Economic Coordination (pp. 45–47)

- Firms coordinate a large amount of economic activity, but there is a limit to the efficient size of a firm.
- Markets coordinate the economic choices of people and firms.
- Markets can work efficiently only when property rights exist.
- Money makes trading in markets more efficient.

KEY FIGURES

Figure 2.1	Production Possibilities Frontier, 34
Figure 2.4	Efficient Use of Resources, 39
Figure 2.7	The Gains from Trade, 44
Figure 2.8	Circular Flows in the Market Economy, 47

KEY TERMS

Absolute advantage, 42
Allocative efficiency, 39
Capital accumulation, 40
Comparative advantage, 42
Dynamic comparative advantage, 45
Economic growth, 40
Firm, 45
Learning-by-doing, 45
Marginal benefit, 38
Marginal benefit curve, 38
Marginal cost, 37
Market, 46
Money, 46
Preferences, 38
Production efficiency, 35
Production possibilities frontier, 34
Property rights, 46
Technological change, 40

PROBLEMS   51

PROBLEMS

Go to [myeconlab] for solutions to odd-numbered problems and additional exercises.

1. Calculate Wendell's opportunity cost of one hour of tennis when he increases the time he plays tennis from
   a. 6 hours a week.
   b. 8 hours a week.

2. Calculate Tina's opportunity cost of a day of skiing when she increases her time spent skiing from
   a. 2 to 4 days a month.
   b. 4 to 6 days a month.

3. Wendell, in problem 1, has the following marginal benefit curve:

   a. If Wendell is efficient, what is his grade?
   b. Why would Wendell be worse off getting a higher grade?

4. Tina in problem 2, has the following marginal benefit curve:

   a. If Tina is efficient, how much does she ski?
   b. Why would Tina be worse off spending more days a month skiing?

5. Sunland's production possibilities are

Food (kilograms per month)		Sunscreen (litres per month)
300	and	0
200	and	50
100	and	100
0	and	150

   a. Draw a graph of Sunland's *PPF*.

---

52   CHAPTER 2   THE ECONOMIC PROBLEM

   b. What are Sunland's opportunity costs of producing food and sunscreen at each output?

6. Jane's Island's production possibilities are

Corn (kilograms per month)		Cloth (metres per month)
6	and	0
4	and	2
2	and	4
0	and	6

   a. Draw a graph of the *PPF* on Jane's Island.
   b. What are Jane's opportunity costs of producing corn and cloth at each output in the table?

7. In problem 5, to get a litre of sunscreen the people of Sunland are willing to give up 5 kilograms of food if they have 25 litres of sunscreen, 2 kilograms of food if they have 75 litres of sunscreen, and 1 kilogram of food if they have 125 litres of sunscreen.
   a. Draw a graph of Sunland's marginal benefit from sunscreen.
   b. What is the efficient quantity of sunscreen?

8. In problem 6, to get a metre of cloth Jane is willing to give up 1.5 kilograms of corn if she has 2 metres of cloth; 1.0 kilogram of corn if she has 4 metres of cloth; and 0.5 kilograms of corn if she has 6 metres of cloth.
   a. Draw a graph of Jane's marginal benefit from cloth.
   b. What is Jane's efficient quantity of cloth?

9. Busyland's production possibilities are

Food (kilograms per month)		Sunscreen (litres per month)
150	and	0
100	and	100
50	and	200
0	and	300

   Calculate Busyland's opportunity costs of food and sunscreen at each output in the table?

10. Joe Island's production possibilities are

Corn (kilograms per month)		Cloth (metres per month)
12	and	0
8	and	1
4	and	2
0	and	3

   What are Joe's opportunity costs of producing corn and cloth at each output in the table?

11. In problems 5 and 9, Sunland and Busyland each produce and consume 100 kilograms of food and 100 litres of sunscreen per month, and they do not trade. Now the countries begin to trade with each other.
   a. What good does Sunland sell to Busyland and what good does it buy from Busyland?
   b. If Sunland and Busyland divide the total output of food and sunscreen equally, what are the gains from trade?

12. In problems 6 and 10, Jane's Island and Joe's Island each produce and consume 4 kilograms of corn and 2 metres of cloth and they do not trade. Now the islands begin to trade.
   a. What good does Jane sell to Joe and what good does Jane buy from Joe?
   b. If Jane and Joe divide the total output of corn and cloth equally, what are the gains from trade?

CRITICAL THINKING

1. After you have studied *Reading Between the Lines* on pp. 48–49, answer the following questions:
   a. At what point on the blue *PPF* in Fig. 1 on p. 49 is the combination of education goods and services and consumption goods and services efficient? Explain your answer.
   b. Students are facing rising tuition. How does higher tuition change the opportunity cost of education and how does it change the *PPF*s in Fig. 1 and Fig. 2?
   c. Who receives the benefits from education? Is the marginal cost of education equal to the marginal benefit of education? Is resource use in the market for education efficient?

WEB EXERCISES

Use the links on [myeconlab] to work the following exercise.

1. Obtain data on the tuition and other costs of enrolling in the MBA program at a school that interests you.
   a. Draw a *PPF* that shows the tradeoff that you would face if you decided to enroll in the MBA program.
   b. Do you think the marginal benefit of an MBA exceeds the marginal cost?

For the Instructor

THIS BOOK ENABLES YOU TO ACHIEVE THREE objectives in your principles course:

■ Focus on the economic way of thinking

■ Explain the issues and problems of our time

■ Choose your own course structure

Focus on the Economic Way of Thinking

You know how hard it is to encourage a student to think like an economist. But that is your goal. Consistent with this goal, the text focuses on and repeatedly uses the central ideas: choice; tradeoff; opportunity cost; the margin; incentives; the gains from voluntary exchange; the forces of demand, supply, and equilibrium; the pursuit of economic rent; and the effects of government actions on the economy.

Explain the Issues and Problems of Our Time

Students must use the central ideas and tools if they are to begin to *understand* them. There is no better way to motivate students than by using the tools of economics to explain the issues that confront today's world. Issues such as central planning versus the market; globalization and the emergence of China as a major economic force; the new economy with new near monopolies such as eBay and the widening income gap between rich and poor; the post-9/11 economy and the reallocation of resources towards counterterrorism and the defence that it entails; corporate scandals and the principal-agent problems and incentives faced by corporate managers; HIV/AIDS and the enormous cost of drugs for treating it; the disappearing tropical rainforests and the challenge that this tragedy of the commons creates; the challenge of managing the world's water resources.

Choose Your Own Course Structure

You want to teach your own course. We have organized this book to enable you to do so. We demonstrate the book's flexibility in the flexibility chart and alternative sequences table that appear on pp. xxiv–xxv. You can use this book to teach a traditional course that blends theory and policy or a current policy issues course. Your micro course can emphasize theory or policy. You can structure your macro course to emphasize long-term growth and supply-side fundamentals. Or you can follow a traditional macro sequence and emphasize short-term fluctuations. The choices are yours.

Instructor's Manual

The Instructor's Manual, written by Torben Drewes of Trent University, integrates the teaching and learning package and is a guide to all the supplements. Each chapter contains a chapter outline, what's new in the sixth edition, teaching suggestions, a look at where we have been and where we are going, descriptions of the electronic supplements, and additional discussion questions. The chapter outline and teaching suggestions sections are keyed to the PowerPoint lecture notes. Solutions to end-of-chapter problems are provided in a separate section.

New Lecture Notes This edition of the Instructor's Manual offers two new exciting features. Extensive lecture notes that incorporate alternative teaching examples—"Points of Interest"—enable a new user of Parkin and Bade to walk into the classroom well armed with engaging stories and explanations and a seasoned user to access a whole new set of fresh examples.

New Worksheets Another new and innovative feature is a set of worksheets. These Worksheets ask the student to contemplate real-world problems that illustrate economic principles. Examples include showing the effect of the catastrophic events of 9/11 using a marginal cost/marginal benefit diagram and calculating the effects of funding social security for the huge number of baby-boomer retirees. Instructors can assign these as in-class group projects or as homework. There is a Worksheet for every chapter.

Two Test Banks

To provide lots of choice when preparing tests and exams, we offer two Test Banks in TestGen with a total of more than 8,700 questions. Test Bank 1, prepared by Morteza Haghiri of Mount Allison University and Wilson Wong of Champlain College, contains over 4,500 multiple-choice questions. Test Bank 2, prepared by Sigrid Ewender of Kwantlen University College and Ariel Lade of the University of Victoria, contains about 4,200 multiple-choice, true-false, and short-answer questions. Both testbanks are thoroughly revised, upgraded, and improved.

Personal Response System Questions

Gauge your students' course progress with clicker questions that enable instructors to pose questions, record results, and display those results instantly in the classroom. Questions are provided in PowerPoint® format.

Image Library

Nearly all of the tables and figures from the text are available for viewing in the Image Library included on the Instructor's Resource CD-ROM.

PowerPoint® Resources

We have developed a full-colour Microsoft PowerPoint Lecture Presentation for each chapter that includes all the figures from the text, animated graphs, and speaking notes. The slide outlines are based on the chapter outlines in the Instructor's Manual, and the speaking notes are based on the Instructor's Manual teaching suggestions. The presentations can be used electronically in the classroom or can be printed to create hard-copy transparency masters, and they can be accessed using Windows or Macintosh. We have also prepared a set of PowerPoint lecture notes for students. Students can download these from MyEconLab, print them, and bring them to class. The instructor's set contains the option to present full-screen-size graphs.

Instructor's Resource CD-ROM with Computerized Test Banks

This CD contains Computerized Test Bank files, Personal Response System questions, Instructor's Manual files in Microsoft Word, PowerPoint files, and an Image Library. Our two test banks are available in Test Generator Software (TestGen-EQ with QuizMaster-EQ). Fully networkable, they are available for Windows and Macintosh. TestGen-EQ's new graphical interface enables instructors to view, edit, and add questions; transfer questions to tests; and print different forms of tests. Tests can be formatted with varying fonts and styles, margins, and headers and footers, as in any word-processing document. Search and sort features let the instructor quickly locate questions and arrange them in a preferred order. QuizMaster-EQ, working with your school's computer network, automatically grades the exams, stores the results on disk, and allows the instructor to view or print a variety of reports.

Course Management Systems

We offer three alternative course management systems—CourseCompass, Blackboard, and WebCT. Each system provides a dynamic, interactive, content-rich, and flexible online course management tool that enables instructors to easily and effectively customize online course materials to suit their needs. Instructors can track and analyze student performance on an array of Internet activities. Please contact your Pearson Education Canada representative for more details.

MyEconLab

The Web site that accompanies *Economics*, Sixth Edition, breaks new ground by providing a structured environment in which students can practice what they learn and test their understanding and then pursue a study plan that is generated from their performance on practice tests. Every new copy of Parkin/Bade, *Economics: Canada in the Global Environment*, Sixth Edition, comes with a student code to access the power of MyEconLab.

MyEconLab provides rich content resources keyed to the eText as well as flexible tools that enable instructors to easily and effectively customize online course materials to suit their needs.

Instructors can create and assign tests, quizzes, or graded homework assignments that incorporate graphing questions and online versions of the end-of-chapter problems in the textbook. MyEconLab saves instructors time by automatically grading all questions and tracking results in an online grade book. Now available from within MyEconLab is the added testing capability of over 4,000 multiple-choice questions derived from the sixth edition of the Parkin/Bade Test Bank 1.

Once registered for MyEconLab, instructors have access to downloadable supplements such as Instructor's Manuals, PowerPoint lecture notes, and Test Banks. Instructors also have access to a "Consult the Author" feature that allows them to ask questions of and make suggestions to the author via e-mail and receive a response within 24 hours.

For more information about MyEconLab, or to request an Instructor Access Code, visit **http://www.myeconlab.com.**

For the Student

Study Guide

The sixth edition Study Guide by Avi Cohen of York University and Harvey King of the University of Regina is carefully coordinated with the main text. Each chapter of the Study Guide contains

- Key concepts
- Helpful hints
- True-false questions that ask students to explain their answers
- Multiple-choice questions
- Short-answer questions

Each part allows students to test their cumulative understanding with questions that go across chapters and work a sample midterm examination.

MyEconLab

MyEconLab—the online homework and tutorial system that is packaged with every new copy of *Economics*—puts students in control of their own learning through a suite of study and practice tools correlated with the online, interactive version of the textbook and other media tools. Every new copy of Parkin/Bade, *Economics: Canada in the Global Environment*, Sixth Edition, comes with a student code to access the power of MyEconLab.

Within MyEconLab's structured environment, students practice what they learn, test their understanding, and then pursue a Study Plan that MyEconLab generates for them based on their performance on practice tests.

At the core of MyEconLab are the following features:

- **Practice Tests**—Practice tests for every chapter section enable students to test their understanding and identify the areas in which they need to do further work. Practice Test questions based directly on the review quizzes and end-of-chapter problems ask students to work with graphs: interpreting them, manipulating them, and even drawing them. Instructors can let students use the supplied pre-built tests or create their own tests.

- **Personalized Study Plan**—Based on a student's performance on a practice test, MyEconLab generates a Personalized Study Plan that shows where further study is needed. The correlation between the text and MyEconLab is perfect and seamless.

- **Additional Practice Exercises**—The Personalized Study Plans direct students to additional exercises for each topic. Additional practice exercises are keyed to each section of the textbook and link students to the eText with animated graphs.

- **Tutorial Instruction**—Launched from the additional practice exercises, tutorial instruction is provided in the form of solutions to problems, step-by-step explanations, and other media-based explanations.

- **Powerful Graphing Tool**—Integrated into the practice tests and additional practice exercises, the graphing tool lets students manipulate and even draw graphs so that they grasp how the concepts, numbers, and graphs are connected.

- Three types of graphing problems:

    1. Draw Graphs—MyEconLab's Draw Graph problems automatically grade the graphs students draw.

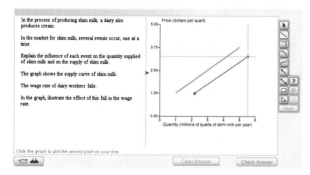

    2. Model-based Graphs—Students can change data inputs and watch curves shift. Multiple-choice, true-false, and short-answer questions quiz students on their interpretations of the graph.

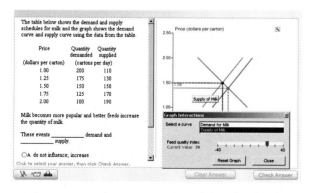

3. Data Graphs—Students can plot up to five variables against each other to give a clear picture of how economic indicators relate to each other.

MyEconLab Study Plan links to the following resources:

- **eText**—Quick reference to specific pages of the textbook that correspond to each Study Plan exercise.

- **Animated Figures**—Step-by-step animations of every figure from the textbook with audio explanations of the action.

- **Glossary**—A searchable version of the textbook glossary with additional examples and links to related terms.

Additional MyEconLab Resources

- **Ask the Authors**—Virtual office hours with Robin Bade and Michael Parkin.

- **Glossary Flashcards**—Every key term available as a flashcard, allowing students to quiz themselves on vocabulary from one or more chapters at a time.

- **Economics in the News**—Updated every week during the school year, news items with links to sources for further reading and discussion questions.

- **Links for Web Exercises**—All the links needed for answering the Web Exercises in the textbook—checked and updated regularly so that they don't disappear.

PowerPoints Lecture Notes

We have prepared a full set of PowerPoint lecture notes for students. These notes contain an outline of each chapter with the textbook figures animated. Students can downloaded these lecture notes from MyEconLab, print them, and bring them to class or use them in creating their own set of notes for use when preparing for tests and exams.

Acknowledgments

WE THANK OUR CURRENT AND FORMER COLLEAGUES AND friends at the University of Western Ontario who have taught us so much. They are Jim Davies, Jeremy Greenwood, Ig Horstmann, Peter Howitt, Greg Huffman, David Laidler, Phil Reny, Chris Robinson, John Whalley, and Ron Wonnacott. We also thank Doug McTaggart and Christopher Findlay, co-authors of the Australian edition, and Melanie Powell and Kent Matthews, co-authors of the European edition. Suggestions arising from their adaptations of earlier editions have been helpful to us in preparing this edition.

We thank the several thousand students whom we have been privileged to teach. The instant response that comes from the look of puzzlement or enlightenment has taught us how to teach economics.

It is an especial joy to thank the many outstanding managers, editors, and others at Pearson Education Canada who have contributed to the concerted publishing effort that brought this edition to completion. Allan Reynolds, President and CEO, and Steve O'Hern, President of Higher Education, have once again provided outstanding corporate direction. They have worked hard to build a corporate culture that brings the best out of its editors and authors. Michael Young, Vice President and Editorial Director for Higher Education, has been a devoted contributor through his appointment and management of the outstanding editors with whom we've worked. Gary Bennett, now Editor in Chief of Business and Economics, has played a major role in bringing this revision to completion and in finding and managing a team of outstanding supplements authors. Stephen Broadbent brought his experience and dedicated professionalism to the development effort. Matthew Christian and Laura Canning built MyEconLab. Bill Todd, Marketing Manager, provided inspired marketing direction. His brochures and, more important, his thoughtful questions and prodding for material had a significant impact on the shape of the text. Anthony Leung, Designer, designed the cover, text, and package and surpassed the challenge of ensuring that we meet the highest design standards. Jennifer Handel, our Production Editor, worked miracles on a tight production schedule and coped calmly with late-changing content. Lu Cormier copyedited the text manuscript and Edie Franks proofread the final pages. We thank all of these wonderful people. It has been inspiring to work with them and to share in creating what we believe is a truly outstanding educational tool.

We thank our supplements authors, Avi Cohen, Harvey King, Torben Drewes, Sigrid Ewender, Morteza Haghiri, Ariel Lade, and Wilson Wong. And we thank Kit Pasula for the extraordinarily careful accuracy review of near-final pages. Kit caught many slips and even some errors of substance that we are relieved to have had the opportunity of correcting.

We thank the people who work directly with us. Jeannie Gillmore provided outstanding research assistance on many topics, including the *Reading Between the Lines* news articles and worked long and diligently to create the MyEconLab test questions and guided solutions. Jane McAndrew provided excellent library help. Richard Parkin created the electronic art files and offered many ideas that improved the figures in this book. And Laurel Davies managed an ever-growing and more complex coding of draw-graph objects, feedback, and many other features of the MyEconLab question database.

As with the previous editions, this one owes an enormous debt to our students. We dedicate this book to them and again thank them for their careful reading and critical comments on the previous edition.

Classroom experience will continue to test the value of this book. We would appreciate hearing from instructors and students about how we can continue to improve it in future editions.

Michael Parkin
Robin Bade
London, Ontario, Canada
michael.parkin@uwo.ca
robin@econ100.com

Reviewers

Ather H. Akbari, Saint Mary's University
Iris Au, University of Toronto
Bogdan Buduru, Concordia University
Beverly J. Cameron, University of Manitoba
Jason Childs, University of New Brunswick, Saint John
Marilyn Cottrell, Brock University
Livio Di Matteo, Lakehead University
Torben Drewes, Trent University
Oliver Franke, Athabasca University
Bruno Fullone, George Brown College
Philippe Ghayad, Dawson College and Concordia University
David Gray, University of Ottawa
Eric Kam, Ryerson University
Cevat Burc Kayahan, University of Guelph
Eva Lau, University of Waterloo
Anastasia M. Lintner, University of Guelph
Christian Marfels, Dalhousie University
Roberto Martínez-Espiñeira, St. Francis Xavier University
Rob Moir, University of New Brunswick Saint John
Saeed Moshiri, University of Manitoba
Derek Pyne, Memorial University of Newfoundland
Jim Sentance, University of Prince Edward Island
Lance Shandler, Kwantlen University College
Peter W. Sinclair, Wilfrid Laurier University
Glen Stirling, University of Western Ontario
Irene Trela, University of Western Ontario
Jane Waples, Memorial University of Newfoundland
Andrew Wong, Grant MacEwan College
Peter Wylie, University of British Colombia, Okanagan
Ayoub Yousefi, University of Western Ontario

Macroeconomics Flexibility Chart

Core	Policy	Optional
19. A First Look at Macroeconomics **20.** Measuring GDP and Economic Growth **21.** Monitoring Cycles, Jobs, and the Price Level	These chapters provide a solid introduction to the issues of macroeconomics and the measurement of the key macro variables.	
22. Aggregate Supply and Aggregate Demand Provides a complete overview of the determination of real GDP and the price level, which subsequent chapters cover in greater depth.		**23.** Expenditure Multipliers This chapter may be covered before chapter 22 or omitted.
25. Money, Banking, and Interest Rates A comprehensive account of what money is, how the banking system creates it, and how the payments system works.	**24.** Fiscal Policy	**26.** The Exchange Rate Repositioned in this edition to provide underpinning for discussion of monetary policy. The chapter may be delayed or omitted.
	28. Monetary Policy A new chapter that explains what the Bank of Canada does and how its actions influence the economy. **29.** Fiscal and Monetary Interactions	**27.** Inflation Repositioned in this edition to provide underpinning for discussion of monetary policy. The chapter may be delayed or omitted because the *AS–AD* chapter (22) provides an outline of the inflation process.
30. The Economy at Full Employment A unique chapter that explains the forces that determine potential GDP. **31.** Economic Growth Although optional, this chapter is crucial for understanding Canada's productivity growth slowdown.	These chapters may be covered before Chapter 22.	
		32. Trading with the World

Four Alternative Macro Sequences

BRIEF CONTENTS

CONTENTS

Summary (Key Points, Key Figures and Tables, and Key Terms), Problems, Critical Thinking, and Web Exercises appear at the end of each chapter.

CREDITS

What Is Economics?

Understanding Our Changing World

You are studying economics at a time of enormous change and uncertainty. Much of the change is for the better. The information age of laptop computers with wireless connection to the Internet, MP3 music, DVD movies, cell phones, Palm Pilots, iPods, and a host of other gadgets and toys have transformed the way we work and play.

But some change is for the worse. After the hype of the new millennium, the global economy slipped into recession. The September 11 terrorist attacks slashed business and vacation travel, shrank our airlines, and tightened security at the Canada-U.S. border and at airports and seaports. SARS, mad cow disease, and disputes with the United States about softwood lumber, all sent shockwaves through the Canadian economy.

◆ The information age, global recession, and the effects of terrorism are just some of the forces that are changing today's world. Your course in economics will help you to understand how these powerful forces shape our world. This chapter takes the first step. It describes the questions that economists try to answer, the way they think about those questions, and the methods they use in the search for answers. Economics makes extensive use of graphs, and an appendix provides a guide to these graphical methods.

After studying this chapter, you will be able to

- **Define economics and distinguish between microeconomics and macroeconomics**
- **Explain the big questions of economics**
- **Explain the key ideas that define the economic way of thinking**
- **Explain how economists go about their work as social scientists**

Definition of Economics

ALL ECONOMIC QUESTIONS ARISE BECAUSE WE want more than we can get. We want a peaceful and secure world. We want clean air, lakes, and rivers. We want long and healthy lives. We want good schools, colleges, and universities. We want spacious and comfortable homes. We want an enormous range of sports and recreational gear from running shoes to jet skis. We want the time to enjoy sports, games, novels, movies, music, travel, and hanging out with our friends.

What each one of us can get is limited by time, by the income we earn, and by the prices we must pay. Everyone ends up with some unsatisfied wants. What as a society we can get is limited by our productive resources. These resources include the gifts of nature, human labour and ingenuity, and tools and equipment that we have produced.

Our inability to satisfy all our wants is called **scarcity**. The poor and the rich alike face scarcity. A child wants a $1.00 can of pop and two 50¢ packs of gum but has only $1.00 in his pocket. He faces scarcity. A millionaire wants to spend the weekend playing golf *and* spend the same weekend at the office attending a business strategy meeting. She faces scarcity. A society wants to provide improved health care, install a computer in every classroom, explore space, clean polluted lakes and rivers, and so on. Society faces scarcity. Even parrots face scarcity!

Not only do I want a cracker—we all want a cracker!

© The New Yorker Collection 1985, Frank Modell from cartoonbank.com. All Rights Reserved.

Faced with scarcity, we must *choose* among the available alternatives. The child must *choose* the pop *or* the gum. The millionaire must *choose* the golf game *or* the meeting. As a society, we must *choose* among health care, national defence, and the environment.

The choices that we make depend on the incentives that we face. An **incentive** is a reward that encourages or a penalty that discourages an action. If the price of pop falls, the child has an *incentive* to choose more pop. If a profit of $10 million is at stake, the millionaire has an *incentive* to skip the golf game. As computer prices tumble, school boards have an *incentive* to connect more classrooms to the Internet.

Economics is the social science that studies the *choices* that individuals, businesses, governments, and entire societies make as they cope with *scarcity* and the *incentives* that influence and reconcile those choices. The subject divides into two main parts:

- Microeconomics
- Macroeconomics

Microeconomics

Microeconomics is the study of the choices that individuals and businesses make, the way these choices interact in markets, and the influence of governments. Some examples of microeconomic issues are: Why are people buying more SUVs and fewer minivans? How would a tax on e-commerce affect Amazon.com?

Macroeconomics

Macroeconomics is the study of the performance of the national economy and the global economy. Some examples of macroeconomic issues are: Why did production and jobs shrink in 2001? Why has Japan's economy stagnated? Can the government bring prosperity by cutting tax rates?

REVIEW QUIZ

1 List some examples of choices being made in Canada today.
2 Use the headlines in today's news to provide some examples of scarcity around the world.
3 Use today's news to illustrate the distinction between microeconomics and macroeconomics.

myeconlab   Study Plan 1.1

Two Big Economic Questions

TWO BIG QUESTIONS SUMMARIZE THE SCOPE OF economics:

- How do choices end up determining *what*, *how*, and *for whom* goods and services get produced?
- When do choices made in the pursuit of *self-interest* also promote the *social interest*?

What, How, and For Whom?

Goods and services are the objects that people value and produce to satisfy human wants. Goods are physical objects such as basketballs. Services are tasks performed for people such as haircuts. By far the largest part of what Canada produces today is services such as retail and wholesale trade, health care, and education. Goods are a small part of total production.

What? What we produce changes over time. Sixty years ago, almost 20 percent of Canadians worked on farms. That number has shrunk to less than 3 percent today. Over the same period, the number of people who produce goods—in mining, construction, and manufacturing—has shrunk from 60 percent to less than 25 percent. The decrease in farming and manufacturing is reflected in an increase in services. Sixty years ago, 20 percent of the population produced services. Today, more than 75 percent of working Canadians have service jobs. Figure 1.1 shows these trends.

What determines the quantities of corn, DVDs, and haircuts and all the other millions of items that we produce?

How? Goods and services are produced by using productive resources that economists call **factors of production**. Factors of production are grouped into four categories:

- Land
- Labour
- Capital
- Entrepreneurship

Land The "gifts of nature" that we use to produce goods and services are called **land**. In economics, land

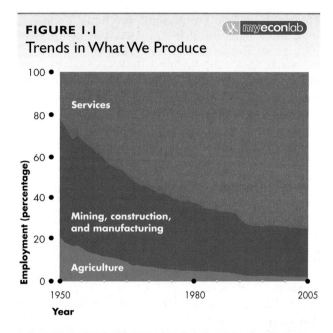

FIGURE 1.1
Trends in What We Produce

myeconlab

Services have expanded and agriculture, mining, construction, and manufacturing have shrunk.

Source of data: Statistics Canada.

is what in everyday language we call *natural resources*. It includes land in the everyday sense together with metal ores, oil, gas and coal, water, and air.

Our land surface and water resources are renewable and some of our mineral resources can be recycled. But the resources that we use to create energy are nonrenewable—they can be used only once.

Labour The work time and work effort that people devote to producing goods and services is called **labour**. Labour includes the physical and the mental efforts of all the people who work on farms and construction sites and in factories, shops, and offices.

The *quality* of labour depends on **human capital**, which is the knowledge and skill that people obtain from education, on-the-job training, and work experience. You are building your own human capital right now as you work on your economics course, and your human capital will continue to grow as you become better at your job.

Human capital expands over time. Today, more than 85 percent of the population of Canada has completed high school and more than 43 percent have a college or university degree. Figure 1.2 shows a measure of the growth of human capital in Canada over the past few decades.

Capital The tools, instruments, machines, buildings, and other items that businesses now use to produce goods and services are called **capital**.

In everyday language, we talk about money, stocks, and bonds as being capital. These items are financial capital. They play an important role in enabling people to lend to businesses and provide businesses with financial resources, but they are not used to produce goods and services. Because they are not productive resources, they are not capital.

Entrepreneurship The human resource that organizes labour, land, and capital is called **entrepreneurship**. Entrepreneurs come up with new ideas about what and how to produce, make business decisions, and bear the risks that arise from these decisions.

How do the quantities of factors of production that get used to produce the many different goods and services get determined?

For Whom? Who gets the goods and services that are produced depends on the incomes that people earn. A large income enables a person to buy large quantities of goods and services. A small income leaves a person with few options and small quantities of goods and services.

People earn their incomes by selling the services of the factors of production they own:

- Land earns **rent**.
- Labour earns **wages**.
- Capital earns **interest**.
- Entrepreneurship earns **profit**.

Which factor of production earns the most income? The answer is labour. Wages and fringe benefits are around 70 percent of total income. Land, capital, and entrepreneurship share the rest. These percentages have been remarkably constant over time.

Knowing how income is shared among the factors of production doesn't tell us how it is shared among individuals. You know of lots of people who earn very large incomes. The average baseball salary in 2005 was about $3 million, and some stars such as Roy Halladay of the Toronto Blue Jays get a bit more than $13 million.

You know of even more people who earn very small incomes. Servers at McDonald's average around $7 an hour; checkout clerks, gas station attendants, and textile and leather workers all earn less than $10 an hour.

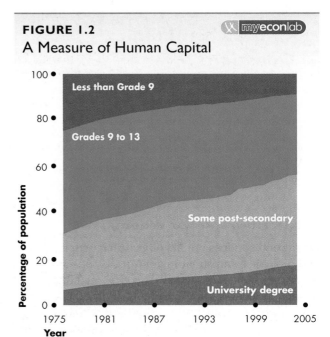

FIGURE 1.2
A Measure of Human Capital

Today, more than 43 percent of the Canadian population has post-secondary certificates, diplomas, or university degrees. A further 42 percent have completed high school.

Source of data: Statistics Canada.

You probably know about other persistent differences in incomes. Men, on the average, earn more than women; university and college graduates, on the average, earn more than high school graduates.

We can get a good sense of who consumes the goods and services produced by looking at the percentages of total income earned by different groups of people. The 20 percent of people with the lowest incomes receive 5 percent of total income, while the richest 20 percent receive 45 percent of total income. So on the average, people in the top 20 percent earn almost 9 times the incomes of those in the 20 percent who earn the least.

Why is the distribution of income so unequal? Why do women earn less than men?

Economics provides some answers to these questions about what, how, and for whom goods and services get produced.

The second big question of economics that we'll now examine is a harder question both to appreciate and to answer.

When Is the Pursuit of Self-Interest in the Social Interest?

Every day, you and 32 million other Canadians, along with 6.5 billion people in the rest of the world, make economic choices that result in "What," "How," and "For Whom" goods and services get produced.

Are the goods and services produced, and the quantities in which they are produced, the right ones? Do the factors of production employed get used in the best possible way? And do the goods and services that we produce go to the people who benefit most from them?

You know that your own choices are the best ones for you—or at least you think they're the best at the time that you make them. You use your time and other resources in the way that makes most sense to you. But you don't think much about how your choices affect other people. You order a home delivery pizza because you're hungry and want to eat. You don't order it thinking that the delivery person or the cook needs an income. You make choices that are in your self-interest. Choices made in **self-interest** are choices that are best for the person making them.

When you act on your economic decisions, you come into contact with thousands of other people who produce and deliver the goods and services that you decide to buy or who buy the things that you sell. These people have made their own decisions— what to produce and how to produce it, whom to hire or whom to work for, and so on. Like you, everyone else makes choices that they think are best for them. When the pizza delivery person shows up at your home, he's not doing you a favour. He's earning his income and hoping for a nice tip.

Could it be possible that when each one of us makes choices that are in our own best interest, it turns out that these choices are also the best for society as a whole? Choices that are the best for society as a whole are said to be in the **social interest**.

Economists have been trying to find the answer to this question since 1776, the year in which Adam Smith's monumental book, *An Inquiry into the Nature and the Causes of the Wealth of Nations*, was published. The question is a hard one to answer, but a lot of progress has been made. Much of the rest of this book helps you to learn what we know about this question and its answer. To help you start thinking about the question, we're going to illustrate it with eight topics that generate heated discussion in today's world. You're already at least a little bit familiar with each one of them. They are

- Central planning versus the market
- Globalization
- The new economy
- The post 9/11 economy
- Corporate scandals
- HIV/AIDS
- Disappearing tropical rainforests
- Water shortages

Central Planning Versus the Market The Soviet Union was founded in 1924 and the People's Republic of China in 1948. These two nations operated the world's largest centrally planned economies.

The antithesis of central planning is the market economy in which resources are privately owned and people are free to trade in markets at prices that are determined by market forces.

From the 1920s until the 1980s, many people believed that self-interest and the social interest could be reconciled only by central economic planning and that the Soviet Union and China had adopted a superior economic system.

As it turned out these economies performed only modestly and China's decade-long so-called "Cultural Revolution" (1966–1976) was an economic disaster.

China began to transform its economy in 1978 when Deng Xiaoping succeeded Mao Zedong. Deng's dictum was to "seek truth from facts" and do what works. He could see Canada, the United States, Europe, Japan, Australia, and Taiwan and Hong Kong, the latter two of which he regarded as part of China, growing richer and richer while China stagnated. He had no time for poverty and said (he has many memorable sayings): "Poverty is not socialism. To be rich is glorious." And in line with his basic outlook: "It doesn't matter if a cat is black or white so long as it catches mice."

In the almost 30 years since China began developing markets and private enterprise, the Chinese economy has performed like no other. Output has grown at an average rate of around 8 percent a year, with living standards doubling every decade or so. All the expansion has occurred in the private market sector of the economy. The market economy continues to be a resounding success for China.

The experiment with central economic planning in the Soviet Union and Eastern Europe lasted a bit longer. But not much longer. On November 9, 1989, a date that will long be written about in economic history books, the Berlin Wall tumbled and with its destruction, two Germanys embarked on a path towards unity.

West Germany had a market economy and East Germany a centrally planned economy. The integration of the economies of the two Germanys took the form of converting the East German economy to capitalism. State-owned enterprises were sold and markets were freed. People previously completely banned from moving between East and West Germany became free to move to any part of Germany (and indeed to any part of the European Union).

Part of Germany's economic problem today stems from a heavy dose of socialism in the form of extraordinarily high wages and benefits as well as rigid employment regulations that make it hard for firms to fire workers (and so firms are cautious to hire them).

Soon after the collapse of the Berlin Wall, the Soviet Union collapsed. It splintered into a number of independent states, each of which embarked on a process of building free markets and the development of the ethics needed to operate an efficient capitalist economy.

Most Chinese and Eastern Europeans are in no doubt that despite a long and difficult adjustment process from central planning to a market economy, the move is worthwhile.

But are they correct? And if they are correct, how do markets manage to do a better job than central economic planning?

Globalization Whenever world leaders hold summit meetings, anti-globalization protests accompany them. Globalization—the expansion of international trade and investment—has been going on for centuries, but during the 1990s, advances in microchip, satellite, and fibre-optic technologies brought a dramatic fall in the cost of communication and accelerated the process. A phone call or even a video conference between people on different continents has become an everyday and easily affordable event. Every day, 20,000 people travel by air between North America and East Asia, and close to that number travel between North America and Europe.

The result of this explosion of communication is a globalization of production decisions. When Nike decides to increase the production of sports shoes, people who live in China, Indonesia, or Malaysia get

more work. As more and more people use credit cards, people in Barbados get hired to key in the data from sales slips. When Sony wants to create a new game for PlayStation 2, or when Steven Spielberg wants a movie animation sequence, programmers in India or New Zealand write the code. And when China Airlines wants some new regional jets, it is most likely that Canadians who work for Bombardier will build them.

As part of the process of globalization, Canada produces more services and fewer manufactured goods. And China and the small economies in East Asia produce an expanding volume of manufactures.

The economies of Asia are also growing more rapidly than are those of North America and Europe. China is already the world's second largest economy in terms of production and, on current trends, by 2013 it will be the world's largest economy. This rapid economic expansion in Asia will bring further changes to the global economy as the wealthier Chinese and other Asians begin to travel and buy more of the goods and services that Canada and other parts of the world produce. Globalization will proceed at an accelerated pace.

But globalization is leaving some behind. The nations of Africa and parts of South America are not sharing in the prosperity that globalization is bringing to other parts of the world.

Is globalization a good thing? Whom does it benefit? Globalization is pretty clearly in the interest of the owners of multinational firms that profit by producing in low-cost regions and selling in high-price regions. But is globalization in your interest and the interest of the young worker in Malaysia who sews your new running shoes? Is it in the social interest?

The New Economy The 1980s and 1990s were years of extraordinary economic change that have been called the *Information Revolution*. Economic revolutions don't happen very often. The previous one, the *Industrial Revolution*, occurred between 1760 and 1830 and saw the transformation from rural farm life to urban industrial life for most people. The revolution before that, the *Agricultural Revolution*, occurred around 10,000 years ago and saw the transformation from a life of hunting and gathering to a life of settled farming.

Placing the events of the last 20 years of the twentieth century on the status of those two previous revolutions might be a stretch. But the changes that occurred during those years were incredible. And they were based on one major technology: the microprocessor or computer chip. Moore's law predicted that the number of transistors that could be placed on one integrated chip would double every 18 months. This prediction turned out to be remarkably accurate. In 1980, a PC chip had 60,000 transistors. By 2000, chips with more than 40 million transistors were in machines like the one that sits on your lap.

The spinoffs from faster and cheaper computing were widespread. Telecommunications became much faster and cheaper, music and movie recording became more realistic and cheaper, millions of routine tasks that previously required human decision and action were automated. You encounter these automated tasks every day when you check out at the supermarket, call directory assistance, or call a government department or large business.

All the new products and processes and the low-cost computing power that made them possible were produced by people who made choices in the pursuit of self-interest. They did not result from any grand design or government economic plan.

When Gordon Moore set up Intel and started making chips, no one had told him to do so, and he wasn't thinking how much easier it would be for you to turn in your essay on time if you had a faster PC. When Bill Gates quit Harvard to set up Microsoft, he wasn't trying to create the best operating system and improve people's computing experience. Moore and Gates and thousands of other entrepreneurs were in hot pursuit of the big payoffs that many of them achieved. Yet their actions did make everyone else better off. They did advance the social interest.

But could more have been done? Were resources used in the best possible way during the information revolution? Did Intel make the best possible chips and sell them in the right quantities for the right prices? Or was the quality of the chips too low and the price too high? And what about Microsoft? Did Bill Gates have to be paid $US46 billion to produce the successive generations of Windows and Word? Were these programs developed in the social interest?

The Economic Response to 9/11 The awful events of September 11, 2001 created economic shockwaves that will last for some years and changed "What," "How," and "For Whom."

The biggest changes in production occurred in the travel, accommodation, and security industries. Much business travel was replaced by teleconferencing. Much vacation travel left the air and went onto the highway. Foreign trips were cut back. Airlines lost business and cut back on their orders for new airplanes. Banks that had lent money to airlines wrote off millions of dollars in losses.

But sales of SUVs and RVs increased. And airports, although operating at lower capacity, beefed up their security services. Thousands of new security agents were hired and state-of-the-art scanners were installed.

Thousands of people made choices in pursuit of their self-interest that led to these changes in production. But were these changes also in the social interest?

Corporate Scandals In 2000, the names Enron and WorldCom meant corporate integrity and spectacular success. But today, they are tainted with scandal.

Founded in 1985, Enron expanded to become the seventh largest U.S. business by 2001. But its expansion was built on an elabourate web of lies, deceit, and fraud. In October 2001, after revelations by one of its former executives, Enron's directors acknowledged that by inflating reported income and hiding debts, they had made the firm appear to be worth considerably more than it actually was. One Enron executive, Michael Kopper, pleaded guilty to charges of money laundering and wire fraud and helped federal investigators uncover the fraud that made millions of dollars for the firm's executives and wiped out its stockholders' wealth.

Scott Sullivan, a highly respected financial officer, joined WorldCom in 1992 and helped turn it into one of the world's telecommunications giants. In his last year with the company, Sullivan's salary was $US700,000 and his bonus (in stock options) was $US10 million. But just ten years after joining the company, Sullivan was fired and arrested for allegedly falsifying the company's accounts, inflating its book profits by almost $US4 billion, and inflating his own bonus in the process. Shortly after these events, WorldCom filed for bankruptcy protection in the largest bankruptcy filing in U.S. history, laid off 17,000 workers, and, like Enron, wiped out its stockholders' wealth.

These cases illustrate the fact that sometimes, in the pursuit of self-interest, people break the law. Such behaviour is not in the social interest. Indeed, the law was established precisely to limit such behaviour.

But some corporate behaviour is legal yet regarded by some as inappropriate. For example, many people think that top executive salaries are out of control. In some cases, executives who have received huge incomes have brought ruin to the companies that they manage.

The people who hired the executives acted in their own self-interest and appointed the best people they could find. The executives acted in their own self-interest. But what became of the self-interest of the stockholders and the customers of these firms? Didn't they suffer? Aren't these glaring examples of conflict between self-interest and the social interest?

HIV/AIDS The World Health Organization and United Nations estimate that 42 million people were suffering from HIV/AIDS in 2002. During that year, 3 million died from the disease and there were 5 million new cases. Most of the HIV/AIDS cases—30 million of them in 2002—were in Africa, where incomes average around $7 a day. The most effective treatment for this disease is an antiretroviral drug made by the large multinational drug companies. The cost of this treatment is around $2,700 a year—more than $7 a day. For sales to poor countries, the cost has been lowered to around $1,200 a year—$3.30 a day.

Developing new drugs is a high-cost and high-risk activity. And if the activity were not in the self-interest of the drug companies, they would stop the effort. But once developed, the cost of producing a drug is just a few cents a dose. Would it be in the social interest for drugs to be made available at the low cost of producing them?

Disappearing Tropical Rainforests Tropical rainforests in South America, Africa, and Asia support the lives of 30 million species of plants, animals, and insects—approaching 50 percent of all species on the planet. These rainforests provide us with the ingredients for many goods including soaps, mouthwashes, shampoos, food preservatives, rubber, nuts, and fruits. The Amazon rainforest alone converts about 450 million tonnes of carbon dioxide into oxygen each year.

Yet tropical rainforests cover less than two percent of the Earth's surface and are heading for extinction. Logging, cattle ranching, mining, oil extraction, hydroelectric dams, and subsistence farming are destroying the equivalent of two football fields every second or an area larger than New York City every day. At the current rate of destruction, almost all the tropical rainforest ecosystems will be gone by 2030.

Each one of us makes economic choices that are in our self-interest to consume products, some of which are destroying this natural resource. Are our choices damaging the social interest? And if they are, what can be done to change the incentives we face and change our behaviour?

Water Shortages The world is awash with water—it is our most abundant resource. But 97 percent of it is seawater. Another 2 percent is frozen in glaciers and ice. The 1 percent of the earth's water that is available for human consumption would be sufficient if only it were in the right places. Canada, Finland, and a few other places have more water than they can use, but Australia, Africa, and California (and many other places) could use much more water than they can get. Some people pay less for water than others. California farmers, for example, pay less than California households. Some of the highest prices for water are faced by people in the poorest countries who must either buy from a water dealer's truck or carry water in buckets over long distances.

In the United Kingdom, water is provided by private water companies. In Canada, public enterprises deliver the water.

In India and Bangladesh, plenty of rain falls, but it falls during a short wet season and the rest of the year is dry. Dams could help to reduce the shortage in the dry season, but not enough have been built in those countries.

Are the nations' and the world's water resources being managed properly? Are the decisions that we each make in our self-interest to use, conserve, and transport water also in the social interest?

We've just looked at eight topics that illustrate the big question: Do choices made in the pursuit of self-interest also serve the social interest?

You'll discover, as you work through this book, that much of what we do in the pursuit of our self-interest does indeed further the social interest. But there are areas in which the social interest and self-interest come into conflict. You'll discover the principles that help economists to figure out when the social interest is being served, when it is not, and what might be done when it is not.

REVIEW QUIZ

1 Describe the broad facts about "What," "How," and "For Whom" goods and services get produced.
2 Use headlines from the recent news to illustrate the potential for conflict between self-interest and the social interest.

myeconlab Study Plan 1.2

The Economic Way of Thinking

THE DEFINITION OF ECONOMICS AND THE questions that you've just reviewed tell you about the *scope of economics*. But they don't tell you how economists *think* about these questions and go about seeking answers to them.

You're now going to begin to see how economists approach economic questions. First, in this section, we'll look at the ideas that define the *economic way of thinking*. This way of thinking needs practice, but it is powerful and as you become more familiar with it, you'll begin to see the world around you with a new and sharp focus.

Choices and Tradeoffs

Because we face scarcity, we must make choices. And when we make a choice, we select from the available alternatives. For example, you can spend the weekend studying for your next economics test and having fun with your friends, but you can't do both of these activities at the same time. You must choose how much time to devote to each. Whatever choice you make, you could have chosen something else instead.

You can think about your choice as a tradeoff. A **tradeoff** is an exchange—giving up one thing to get something else. When you choose how to spend your weekend, you face a tradeoff between studying and hanging out with your friends.

Guns Versus Butter The classic tradeoff is between guns and butter. "Guns" and "butter" stand for any pair of goods. They might actually be guns and butter. Or they might be broader categories such as national defence and food. Or they might be any pair of specific goods or services such as cola and bottled water, baseball bats and tennis rackets, universities and hospitals, realtor services and career counselling.

Regardless of the specific objects that guns and butter represent, the guns-versus-butter tradeoff captures a hard fact of life: If we want more of one thing, we must trade something else in exchange for it.

The idea of a tradeoff is central to the whole of economics. We'll look at some examples, beginning with the big questions: What, How, and For Whom? We can view each of these questions about the goods and services that get produced in terms of tradeoffs.

What, How, and For Whom Tradeoffs

The questions what, how, and for whom goods and services are produced all involve tradeoffs that are similar to that between guns and butter.

"What" Tradeoffs What goods and services get produced depends on choices made by each one of us, by our government, and by the businesses that produce the things we buy.

Each of these choices involves a tradeoff. Each one of us faces a tradeoff when we choose how to spend our income. You go to the movies this week, but you forgo a few cups of coffee to buy the ticket. You trade off coffee for a movie.

The federal government faces a tradeoff when it chooses how to spend our tax dollars. Parliament votes for more hospitals but cuts back on educational programs. The federal government trades off education for hospitals.

Businesses face a tradeoff when they decide what to produce. Nike hires Tiger Woods and allocates resources to designing and marketing a new golf ball but cuts back on its development of a new running shoe. Nike trades off running shoes for golf balls.

"How" Tradeoffs How goods and services get produced depends on choices made by the businesses that produce the things we buy. These choices involve a tradeoff. For example, Tim Hortons opens a new doughnut store with an automated production line and closes an older store with a traditional kitchen— Tim Hortons trades off labour for capital.

"For Whom" Tradeoffs For whom goods and services are produced depends on the distribution of buying power. Buying power can be redistributed —transferred from one person to another—in three ways: by voluntary payments, by theft, or through taxes and benefits organized by governments. Redistribution brings tradeoffs.

Each of us faces a "for whom" tradeoff when we choose how much to contribute to the United Nations' famine relief fund. You cut your spending and donate $50. You trade off your own spending for a small increase in economic equality.

We make choices that influence redistribution by theft when we vote to make theft illegal and devote resources to law enforcement. We trade off some goods and services for an increase in the security of our property.

We also vote for taxes and social programs that redistribute buying power from the rich to the poor. Government redistribution confronts society with what has been called the **big tradeoff**—the tradeoff between equality and efficiency. Taxing the rich and making transfers to the poor bring greater economic equality. But taxing productive activities such as running a business, working hard, and saving and investing in capital discourages these activities. So taxing productive activities means producing less. A more equal distribution means there is less to share.

You can think of the big tradeoff as being the problem of how to share a pie that everyone contributes to baking. If each person receives a share of the pie that reflects the size of her or his effort, everyone will work hard and the pie will be as large as possible. But if the pie is shared equally, regardless of contribution, some talented bakers will slacken off and the pie will shrink. The big tradeoff is one between the size of the pie and how equally it is shared. We trade off some production for increased equality.

Choices Bring Change

What, how, and for whom goods and services are produced changes over time. And choices bring change. The quantity and range of goods and services available today in Canada is much greater than that in Africa. And the economic condition of Canada today is much better than it was a generation ago. But the quality of economic life (and its rate of improvement) doesn't depend purely on nature and on luck. It depends on many of the choices made by each one of us, by governments, and by businesses. And these choices involve tradeoffs.

One choice is that of how much of our income to consume and how much to save. Our saving can be channelled through the financial system to finance businesses and to pay for new capital that increases production. The more we save and invest, the more goods and services we'll be able to produce in the future. When you decide to save an extra $1,000 and forgo a vacation, you trade off the vacation for a higher future income. If everyone saves an extra $1,000 and businesses invest in more equipment that increases production, the average consumption per person rises. As a society, we trade off current consumption for economic growth and higher future consumption.

A second choice is how much effort to devote to education and training. By becoming better educated and more highly skilled, we become more productive

and are able to produce more goods and services. When you decide to remain in school for another two years to complete a professional degree and forgo a huge chunk of leisure time, you trade off leisure today for a higher future income. If everyone becomes better educated, production increases and income per person rises. As a society, we trade off current consumption and leisure time for economic growth and higher future consumption.

A third choice, usually made by businesses, is how much effort to devote to research and the development of new products and production methods. Ford Motor Company can hire engineers to do research on a new robotic assembly line or to operate the existing plant and produce cars. More research brings greater productivity in the future but means smaller current production—a tradeoff of current production for greater future production.

Seeing choices as tradeoffs emphasizes the idea that to get something, we must give up something. What we give up is the cost of what we get. Economists call this cost the opportunity cost.

Opportunity Cost

The highest-valued alternative that we give up to get something is the **opportunity cost** of the activity chosen. "There's no such thing as a free lunch" is not just a clever throwaway line. It expresses the central idea of economics: that every choice involves a cost.

You can quit school, or you can remain in school. If you quit school and take a job at McDonald's, you earn enough to buy some CDs, go to the movies, and spend lots of free time with your friends. If you remain in school, you can't afford these things. You will be able to buy these things and more when you graduate, and that is one of the payoffs from being in school. But for now, when you've bought your books, you have nothing left for CDs and movies. And doing assignments leaves no time for hanging around with your friends. The opportunity cost of being in school is the highest-valued alternative that you would have done if you had quit school.

All the "what," "how," and "for whom" tradeoffs that we've just considered involve opportunity cost. The opportunity cost of some guns is the butter forgone; the opportunity cost of a movie ticket is the number of cups of coffee forgone.

And the choices that bring change also involve opportunity cost. The opportunity cost of more goods and services in the future is less consumption today.

Choosing at the Margin

You can allocate the next hour between studying and e-mailing your friends. But the choice is not all or nothing. You must decide how many minutes to allocate to each activity. To make this decision, you compare the benefit of a little bit more study time with its cost—you make your choice at the **margin**.

The benefit that arises from an increase in an activity is called **marginal benefit**. For example, suppose that you're spending four nights a week studying and your grade point average is 3.0. You decide that you want a higher grade and decide to study an extra night each week. Your grade now rises to 3.5. The marginal benefit from studying for one additional night a week is the 0.5 increase in your grade. It is *not* the 3.5 grade. The reason is that you already have the benefit from studying for four nights a week, so we don't count this benefit as resulting from the decision you are now making.

The cost of an increase in an activity is called **marginal cost**. For you, the marginal cost of increasing your study time by one night a week is the cost of the additional night not spent with your friends (if that is your best alternative use of the time). It does not include the cost of the four nights you are already studying.

To make your decision, you compare the marginal benefit from an extra night of study with its marginal cost. If the marginal benefit exceeds the marginal cost, you study the extra night. If the marginal cost exceeds the marginal benefit, you do not study the extra night.

By evaluating marginal benefits and marginal costs and choosing only those actions that bring greater benefit than cost, we use our scarce resources in the way that makes us as well off as possible.

Responding to Incentives

Our choices respond to incentives. A change in marginal cost or a change in marginal benefit changes the incentives that we face and leads us to change our choice.

For example, suppose your economics instructor gives you a problem set and tells you that all the problems will be on the next test. The marginal benefit from working these problems is large, so you diligently work them all. In contrast, if your math instructor gives you a problem set and tells you that none of the problems will be on the next test, the marginal benefit from working these problems is lower, so you skip most of them.

The central idea of economics is that we can predict how choices will change by looking at changes in incentives. More of an activity is undertaken when its marginal cost falls or marginal benefit rises; less of an activity is undertaken when its marginal cost rises or marginal benefit falls.

Incentives are also the key to reconciling self-interest and the social interest. When our choices are *not* in the social interest, it is because we face the wrong incentives. One of the central challenges for economists is to figure out the incentive systems that result in self-interested choices leading to the social interest.

Human Nature, Incentives, and Institutions

Economists take human nature as given and view people as acting in their self-interest. All people—consumers, producers, politicians, and public servants—pursue their self-interest.

Self-interested actions are not necessarily *selfish* actions. You might decide to use your resources in ways that bring pleasure to others as well as to yourself. But a self-interested act gets the most value for *you* based on *your* view about value.

If human nature is given and if people act in their self-interest, how can we take care of the social interest? Economists answer this question by emphasizing the crucial role that institutions play in influencing the incentives that people face as they pursue their self-interest.

The key institution is a legal system that protects personal security and private property and enables people to specialize and trade in markets. You will learn as you progress with your study of economics that where these institutions exist, self-interest can indeed promote the social interest.

REVIEW QUIZ

1 Provide three examples of a tradeoff and describe the opportunity cost involved in each.
2 Provide an everyday example to illustrate what we mean by choosing at the margin.
3 What is the main factor that influences choices?
4 What do economists say about the role of institutions in promoting the social interest?

myeconlab **Study Plan 1.3**

Economics: A Social Science

ECONOMICS IS A SOCIAL SCIENCE (ALONG WITH political science, psychology, and sociology). Economists try to discover how the economic world works, and in pursuit of this goal (like all scientists), they distinguish between two types of statements:

- What *is*
- What *ought to be*

Statements about what *is* are called *positive* statements and they might be right or wrong. We can test a positive statement by checking it against the facts. When a chemist does an experiment in her laboratory, she is attempting to check a positive statement against the facts.

Statements about what *ought to be* are called *normative* statements. These statements depend on values and cannot be tested. When Parliament debates a motion, it is ultimately trying to decide what ought to be. It is making a normative statement.

To see the distinction between positive and normative statements, consider the controversy over global warming. Some scientists believe that centuries of the burning of coal and oil are increasing the carbon dioxide content of the earth's atmosphere and leading to higher temperatures that eventually will have devastating consequences for life on this planet. "Our planet is warming because of an increased carbon dioxide buildup in the atmosphere" is a positive statement. It can (in principle and with sufficient data) be tested. "We ought to cut back on our use of carbon-based fuels such as coal and oil" is a normative statement. You can agree with or disagree with this statement, but you can't test it. It is based on values. Health-care reform provides an economic example of the distinction. "Universal health care cuts the amount of work time lost to illness" is a positive statement. "All Canadians should have equal access to health care" is a normative statement.

The task of economic science is to discover positive statements that are consistent with what we observe and that help us to understand the economic world. This task can be broken into three steps:

- Observation and measurement
- Model building
- Testing models

Observation and Measurement

Economists observe and measure data on such things as the quantities of natural and human resources, wages and work hours, the prices and quantities of the different goods and services produced, taxes and government spending, and the quantities of goods and services bought from and sold to other countries.

Model Building

The second step towards understanding how the economic world works is to build a model. An **economic model** is a description of some aspect of the economic world that includes only those features of the world that are needed for the purpose at hand. A model is simpler than the reality it describes. What a model includes and what it leaves out result from assumptions about what is essential and what are inessential details.

You can see how ignoring details is useful—even essential—to our understanding by thinking about a model that you see every day: the TV weather map. The weather map is a model that helps to predict the temperature, wind speed and direction, and precipitation over a future period. The weather map shows lines called isobars—lines of equal barometric pressure. It doesn't show the highways. The reason is that our theory of the weather tells us that the pattern of air pressure, not the location of the highways, determines the weather.

An economic model is similar to a weather map. For example, an economic model of a cell phone network might tell us the effects of the development of a new low-cost technology on the number of cell phone subscribers and the volume of cell phone use. But the model would ignore such details as the colours of the covers on people's cell phones and the tunes they use for ring tones.

Testing Models

The third step is testing the model. A model's predictions might correspond to the facts or be in conflict with them. By comparing the model's predictions with the facts, we can test a model and develop an economic theory. An **economic theory** is a generalization that summarizes what we think we understand about the economic choices that people make and the performance of industries and entire economies. Economic theory is a bridge between an economic model and the real economy.

The process of building and testing models creates theories. For example, meteorologists have a theory that if the isobars form a particular pattern at a particular time of the year (a model), then it will snow (reality). They have developed this theory by repeated observation and by carefully recording the weather that follows specific pressure patterns.

Economics is a young science. It was born in 1776 with the publication of Adam Smith's *Wealth of Nations* (see p. 54). Over the years since then, economists have discovered many useful theories. But in many areas, economists are still looking for answers. The gradual accumulation of economic knowledge gives most economists some faith that their methods will, eventually, provide usable answers to the big economic questions.

But progress in economics comes slowly. Let's look at some of the obstacles to progress in economics.

Obstacles and Pitfalls in Economics

We cannot easily do economic experiments. And most economic behaviour has many simultaneous causes. For these two reasons, it is difficult in economics to unscramble cause and effect.

Unscrambling Cause and Effect
By changing one factor at a time and holding all the other relevant factors constant, we isolate the factor of interest and are able to investigate its effects in the clearest possible way. This logical device, which all scientists use to identify cause and effect, is called *ceteris paribus*. **Ceteris paribus** is a Latin term that means "other things being equal" or "if all other relevant things remain the same." Ensuring that other things are equal is crucial in many activities, and all successful attempts to make scientific progress use this device.

Economic models (like the models in all other sciences) enable the influence of one factor at a time to be isolated in the imaginary world of the model. When we use a model, we are able to imagine what would happen if only one factor changed. But *ceteris paribus* can be a problem in economics when we try to test a model.

Laboratory scientists, such as chemists and physicists, perform experiments by actually holding all the relevant factors constant except for the one under investigation. In non-experimental sciences such as economics (and astronomy), we usually observe the outcomes of the simultaneous operation of many factors. Consequently, it is hard to sort out the effects of each individual factor and to compare them with what a model predicts. To cope with this problem, economists take three complementary approaches.

First, they look for pairs of events in which other things were equal (or similar). An example might be to study the effects of unemployment insurance on the unemployment rate by comparing the United States with Canada on the presumption that the people in the two economies are sufficiently similar. Second, economists use statistical tools—called econometrics. Third, when economists can, they perform experiments. This relatively new approach puts real subjects (usually students) in a decision-making situation and varies their incentives in some way to discover how they respond to a change in one factor at a time.

Economists try to avoid fallacies—errors of reasoning that lead to a wrong conclusion. But two fallacies are common, and you need to be on your guard to avoid them. They are the

- Fallacy of composition
- *Post hoc* fallacy

Fallacy of Composition
The fallacy of composition is the (false) statement that what is true of the parts is true of the whole or that what is true of the whole is true of the parts. There are many everyday examples of this fallacy. Standing at a ball game to get a better view works for one person but not for all—what is true for a part of a crowd is not true for the whole crowd.

The fallacy of composition arises in many economic situations that stem from the fact that the parts interact with each other to produce an outcome for the whole that might differ from the intent of the parts.

For example, a firm fires some workers to cut costs and improve its profits. If all firms take similar actions, income falls and so does spending. The firm sells less, and its profits don't improve.

Or suppose that a firm thinks it can gain market share by cutting its price and mounting a large advertising campaign. Again, if the one firm takes these actions they work. But if all the firms in an industry take the same actions, they all end up with the same market share as before and lower profits.

Post Hoc Fallacy
Another Latin phrase—*post hoc ergo propter hoc*—means "after this, therefore because of this." The *post hoc* fallacy is the error of reasoning

that a first event *causes* a second event because the first occurred before the second. Suppose you are a visitor from a far-off world. You observe lots of people shopping in early December, and then you see them opening gifts and partying in the holiday season. "Does the shopping cause the holiday season?" you wonder. After a deeper study, you discover that the holiday season causes the shopping. A later event causes an earlier event.

Unravelling cause and effect is difficult in economics. And just looking at the timing of events often doesn't help. For example, the stock market booms, and some months later the economy expands—jobs and incomes grow. Did the stock market boom cause the economy to expand? Possibly, but perhaps businesses started to plan the expansion of production because a new technology that lowered costs had become available. As knowledge of the plans spread, the stock market reacted to *anticipate* the economic expansion. To disentangle cause and effect, economists use economic models and data and, to the extent that they can, perform experiments.

Economics is a challenging science. Does the difficulty of getting answers in economics mean that anything goes and that economists disagree on most questions? Perhaps you've heard the joke "If you laid all the economists in the world end to end, they still wouldn't reach a conclusion." Surprisingly, perhaps, the joke does not describe reality.

Agreement and Disagreement

Economists have reached conclusions and agree on a wide range of questions. And often the agreed-upon view of economists disagrees with the popular and sometimes politically correct view. When Bank of Canada Governor David Dodge testifies before Parliament, his words are rarely controversial among economists, even when they generate endless debate in the media and Parliament.

Here are 12 propositions with which at least 7 out of every 10 economists broadly agree:

- Tariffs and import restrictions make most people worse off.
- A large budget deficit has an adverse effect on the economy.
- A minimum wage increases unemployment among young workers and low-skilled workers.

- Cash payments to welfare recipients make them better off than do transfers-in-kind of equal cash value.
- A tax cut can help to lower unemployment when the unemployment rate is high.
- The distribution of income should be more equal.
- Inflation is primarily caused by a rapid rate of money creation.
- The government should restructure welfare along the lines of a "negative income tax."
- Rent ceilings cut the availability of housing.
- Pollution taxes are more effective than pollution limits.
- The redistribution of income is a legitimate role for the government.
- The federal budget should be balanced on the average over the business cycle but not every year.

Which of these propositions are positive and which are normative? Notice that economists are willing to offer their opinions on normative issues as well as their professional views on positive questions. Be on the lookout for normative propositions dressed up as positive propositions.

REVIEW QUIZ

1 What is the distinction between a positive statement and a normative statement? Provide an example (different from those in the chapter) of each type of statement.
2 What is a model? Can you think of a model that you might use (probably without thinking of it as a model) in your everyday life?
3 What is a theory? Why is the statement "It might work in theory, but it doesn't work in practice" a silly statement?
4 What is the *ceteris paribus* assumption and how is it used?
5 Try to think of some everyday examples of the fallacy of composition and the *post hoc* fallacy.

myeconlab Study Plan 1.4

SUMMARY

KEY POINTS

A Definition of Economics (p. 2)

- All economic questions arise from scarcity—from the fact that wants exceed the resources available to satisfy them.
- Economics is the social science that studies the choices that people make as they cope with scarcity.
- The subject divides into microeconomics and macroeconomics.

Two Big Economic Questions (pp. 3–8)

- Two big questions summarize the scope of economics:
  1. How do choices end up determining *what*, *how*, and *for whom* goods and services get produced?
  2. When do choices made in the pursuit of *self-interest* also promote the *social interest*?

The Economic Way of Thinking (pp. 9–11)

- Every choice is a tradeoff—exchanging more of something for less of something else.
- The classic guns-versus-butter tradeoff represents all tradeoffs.
- All economic questions involve tradeoffs.
- The big social tradeoff is that between equality and efficiency.
- The highest-valued alternative forgone is the opportunity cost of what is chosen.
- Choices are made at the margin and respond to incentives.

Economics: A Social Science (pp. 12–14)

- Economists distinguish between positive statements—what is—and normative statements—what ought to be.

- To explain the economic world, economists develop theories by building and testing economic models.
- Economists use the *ceteris paribus* assumption to try to disentangle cause and effect and are careful to avoid the fallacy of composition and the *post hoc* fallacy.
- Economists agree on a wide range of questions about how the economy works.

KEY TERMS

Big tradeoff, 10
Capital, 4
Ceteris paribus, 13
Economic model, 12
Economics, 2
Economic theory, 12
Entrepreneurship, 4
Factors of production, 3
Goods and services, 3
Human capital, 3
Incentive, 2
Interest, 4
Labour, 3
Land, 3
Macroeconomics, 2
Margin, 11
Marginal benefit, 11
Marginal cost, 11
Microeconomics, 2
Opportunity cost, 10
Profit, 4
Rent, 4
Scarcity, 2
Self-interest, 5
Social interest, 5
Tradeoff, 9
Wages, 4

PROBLEMS

Go to (myeconlab) **for solutions to odd-numbered problems and additional exercises.**

1. Your friends go the movies one evening and you decide to stay home and do your economics assignment and practice test. You get 80 percent on your next economics exam compared with the 70 percent that you normally score. What is the opportunity cost of your extra points?

2. You go to the movies one evening instead of studying for your economics test. You get 50 percent on your next economics test rather than the 70 percent that you usually get. What is the opportunity cost of going to the movies?

3. You plan to go to school this summer. If you do, you won't be able to take your usual job that pays $6,000 for the summer, and you won't be able to live at home for free. The cost of tuition is $2,000 and textbooks is $200, and living expenses are $1,400. What is the opportunity cost of going to summer school?

4. You plan to go skiing next weekend. If you do, you'll have to miss doing your usual weekend job that pays $100. You won't be able to study for 8 hours and you won't be able to use your prepaid college meal plan. The cost of travel and accommodations will be $350, the ski rental will cost $60, and your food will cost $40. What is the opportunity cost of the ski trip?

5. The local mall has free parking, but the mall is always very busy, and it usually takes 30 minutes to find a parking space. Today when you found a vacant spot, Harry also wanted it. Is parking really free at this mall? If not, what did it cost you to park today? When you parked your car today, did you impose any costs on Harry? Explain your answers.

6. The university has built a new movie house. Admission for students is free and there are always plenty of empty seats. But when the movie house screened *Lord of the Rings*, the lines were long. So the movie house decided to charge $4 per student. Cadbury Schweppes offered students a free soft drink. Compare the student's opportunity cost of seeing the movie *Lord of the Rings* with that of any other movie screened in the year. Which is less costly and by how much?

CRITICAL THINKING

1. Use the two big questions of economics and the economic way of thinking to organize a short essay about the economic life of a homeless man. Does he face scarcity? Does he make choices? Can you interpret his choices as being in his own best interest? Can either his own choices or the choices of others make him better off? If so, how?

WEB EXERCISES

Use the links on (myeconlab) **to work the following exercises.**

1. Visit the CBC.
   a. What is the top economic news story today?
   b. With which of the big questions does it deal? (It must deal with at least one of them and might deal with more than one.)
   c. What tradeoffs does the news item discuss?
   d. Write a brief summary of the news item in a few bulleted points using as much as possible of the economic vocabulary that you have learned in this chapter and that is in the key terms list on p. 15.

2. Visit *Resources for Economists on the Internet*. This site is a good place from which to search for economic information on the Internet.
   a. Scroll down the page and click on General Interest.
   b. Visit the "general interest" sites and become familiar with the types of information they contain.

3. Visit Statistics Canada.
   a. What is the number of people employed (nonfarm employment) in your area?
   b. Has employment increased or decreased?
   c. What is income per person (per capita income) in your area?

APPENDIX

Graphs in Economics

After studying this appendix, you will be able to

- **Make and interpret a time-series graph, a cross-section graph, and a scatter diagram**

- **Distinguish between linear and nonlinear relationships and between relationships that have a maximum and a minimum**

- **Define and calculate the slope of a line**

- **Graph relationships among more than two variables**

Graphing Data

A GRAPH REPRESENTS A QUANTITY AS A DISTANCE on a line. Figure A1.1 shows two examples. Here, a distance on the horizontal line represents temperature, measured in degrees Celsius. A movement from left to right shows an increase in temperature. The point marked 0 represents zero degrees Celsius. To the right of 0, the temperature is positive. To the left of 0 (as indicated by the minus sign), the temperature is negative. A distance on the vertical line represents altitude or height, measured in thousands of metres above sea level. The point marked 0 represents sea level. Points above 0 represent metres above sea level. Points below 0 (indicated by a minus sign) represent metres below sea level.

By setting two scales perpendicular to each other, as in Fig. A1.1, we can visualize the relationship between two variables. The scale lines are called *axes*. The vertical line is the *y-axis*, and the horizontal line is the *x-axis*. Each axis has a zero point, which is shared by the two axes. This zero point, common to both axes, is called the *origin*.

To show something in a two-variable graph, we need two pieces of information: the value of the *x*-variable and the value of the *y*-variable. For example, off the coast of British Columbia on a winter's day, the temperature is 10 degrees—the value of *x*. A fishing boat is located at 0 metres above sea level—the value of *y*. These two bits of information appear as point *A* in Fig. A1.1. A climber at the top of Mt. McKinley on a cold day is 6,194 metres above sea level in a zero-degree gale. These two pieces of information appear as point *B*. The position of the

FIGURE A1.1
Making a Graph

Graphs have axes that measure quantities as distances. Here, the horizontal axis (*x*-axis) measures temperature, and the vertical axis (*y*-axis) measures height. Point *A* represents a fishing boat at sea level (0 on the *y*-axis) on a day when the temperature is 10°C. Point *B* represents a climber on Mt. McKinley, 6,194 metres above sea level, at a temperature of 0°C. Point *C* represents a climber on Mt. McKinley, 6,194 metres above sea level, at a temperature of 10°C.

climber on a warmer day might be at the point marked *C*. This point represents the peak of Mt. McKinley at a temperature of 10 degrees.

We can draw two lines, called *coordinates*, from point *C*. One, called the *y-coordinate*, runs from *C* to the horizontal axis. Its length is the same as the value marked off on the *y*-axis. The other, called the *x-coordinate*, runs from *C* to the vertical axis. Its length is the same as the value marked off on the *x*-axis. We describe a point in a graph by the values of its *x*-coordinate and its *y*-coordinate.

Graphs like that in Fig. A1.1 can show any type of quantitative data on two variables. Economists use three types of graphs based on the principles in Fig. A1.1 to reveal and describe the relationships among variables. They are

- Time-series graphs
- Cross-section graphs
- Scatter diagrams

17

Time-Series Graphs

A **time-series graph** measures time (for example, months or years) on the x-axis and the variable or variables in which we are interested on the y-axis. Figure A1.2 is an example of a time-series graph. It provides some information on the average price of unleaded gasoline across Canada.

In Fig. A1.2, we measure time in years running from 1990 to 2005. We measure the price of gasoline (the variable that we are interested in) on the y-axis.

The point of a time-series graph is to enable us to visualize how a variable has changed over time and how its value in one period relates to its value in another period.

A time-series graph conveys an enormous amount of information quickly and easily, as this example illustrates. It shows

- The *level* of the price of gasoline—when it is *high* and *low*. When the line is a long way from the x-axis, the price is high. When the line is close to the x-axis, the price is low.
- How the price *changes*—whether it *rises* or *falls*. When the line slopes upward, as in 2000, the price is rising. When the line slopes downward, as in 1993, the price is falling.
- The *speed* with which the price changes—whether it rises or falls *quickly* or *slowly*. If the line is steep, then the price rises or falls quickly. If the line is not steep, the price rises or falls slowly. For example, the price rose quickly from 2003 to 2004 and slowly from 1995 to 1996. The price fell quickly from 2001 to 2002 and slowly from 1991 to 1994.

A time-series graph also reveals whether there is a trend. A trend is a general tendency for a variable to move in one direction. A **trend** might be upward or downward. In Fig. A1.2, you can see that the price of gasoline had a general tendency to rise from the mid-1990s to 2005. That is, although the price rose and fell, the general tendency was for it to rise—the price had an upward trend.

A time-series graph also helps us detect cycles in variables. You can see some peaks and troughs in the price of gasoline in Fig. A1.2. You can see a trough in 1998 and a peak in 2001.

Finally, a time-series graph also lets us compare the variable in different periods quickly. Figure A1.2 shows that the 1990s were different from the 2000s. The

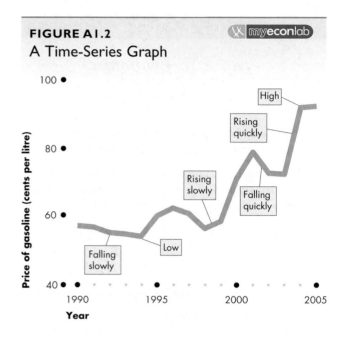

FIGURE A1.2
A Time-Series Graph

A time-series graph plots the level of a variable on the y-axis against time (day, week, month, or year) on the x-axis. This graph shows the average price of gasoline each year from 1990 to 2005. It shows us when the price of gasoline was *high* and when it was *low*, when the price *increased* and when it *decreased*, and when it changed *quickly* and when it changed *slowly*.

price of gasoline fluctuated more in the 2000s than it did in the 1990s.

You can see that a time-series graph conveys a wealth of information. And it does so in much less space than we have used to describe only some of its features. But you do have to "read" the graph to obtain all this information.

Cross-Section Graphs

A **cross-section graph** shows the values of an economic variable for different groups in a population at a point in time. Figure A1.3, called a *bar chart*, is an example of a cross-section graph.

The bar chart in Fig. A1.3 shows the number of visitors to each province in 2004. The length of each bar indicates the number of visitors. This figure enables you to compare the number of visitors across the provinces. And you can do so much more quickly and clearly than you could by looking at a list of numbers.

FIGURE A1.3
A Cross-Section Graph

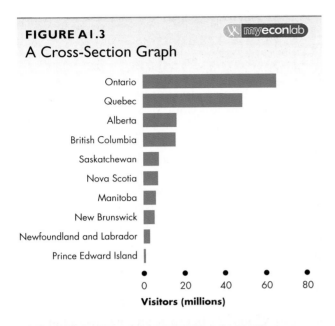

A cross-section graph shows the level of a variable across the members of a population. This bar chart shows the number of visitors to each province in 2004.

Scatter Diagrams

A **scatter diagram** plots the value of one variable against the value of another variable. Such a graph reveals whether a relationship exists between two variables and describes their relationship. Figure A1.4(a) shows the relationship between expenditure and income. Each point shows expenditure per person and income per person in a given year from 1990 to 2004. The points are "scattered" within the graph. The point labelled *A* tells us that in 1999, income per person was $19,610 and expenditure per person was $18,448. The dots in this graph form a pattern, which reveals that as income increases, expenditure increases.

Figure A1.4(b) shows the relationship between the number of international phone calls and the price of a call. This graph shows that as the price per minute falls, the number of calls increases.

Figure A1.4(c) shows a scatter diagram of inflation and unemployment in Canada. Here, the dots show no clear relationship between these two variables. The dots in this graph reveal that there is no simple relationship between these variables.

FIGURE A1.4
Scatter Diagrams

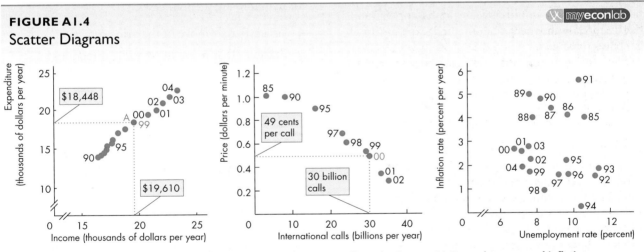

(a) Expenditure and income   **(b) International phone calls and prices**   **(c) Unemployment and inflation**

A scatter diagram reveals the relationship between two variables. Part (a) shows the relationship between expenditure and income. Each point shows the values of the two variables in a specific year. For example, point A shows that in 1999, average income was $19,610 and average expenditure was $18,448. The pattern formed by the points shows that as income increases, expenditure increases.

Part (b) shows the relationship between the price of an international phone call and the number of calls made. This graph shows that as the price of a phone call falls, the number of calls made increases. Part (c) shows the inflation rate and unemployment rate in Canada. This graph shows that the inflation rate and the unemployment rate are not closely related.

Breaks in the Axes Two of the graphs you've just looked at, Fig. A1.4(a) and Fig. A1.4(c), have breaks in their axes, as shown by the small gaps. The breaks indicate that there are jumps from the origin, 0, to the first values recorded.

In Fig. A1.4(a), the breaks are used because the lowest value of expenditure exceeds $13,000 and the lowest value of income exceeds $17,000. With no breaks in the axes of this graph, there would be a lot of empty space, all the points would be crowded into the top right corner, and we would not be able to see whether a relationship exists between these two variables. By breaking the axes, we are able to bring the relationship into view.

Putting a break in the axes is like using a zoom lens to bring the relationship into the centre of the graph and magnify it so that it fills the graph.

Misleading Graphs Breaks can be used to highlight a relationship. But they can also be used to mislead— to make a graph that lies. The most common way of making a graph lie is to use axis breaks either to stretch or to compress a scale. For example, suppose that in Fig. A1.4(a), the *y*-axis ran from zero to $45,000 while the *x*-axis was the same as the one shown. The graph would now create the impression that despite a huge increase in income, expenditure had barely changed.

To avoid being misled, it is a good idea to get into the habit of always looking closely at the values and the labels on the axes of a graph before you start to interpret it.

Correlation and Causation A scatter diagram that shows a clear relationship between two variables, such as Fig. A1.4(a) or Fig. A1.4(b), tells us that the two variables have a high correlation. When a high correlation is present, we can predict the value of one variable from the value of the other variable. But correlation does not imply causation.

Sometimes a high correlation is a coincidence, but sometimes it does arise from a causal relationship. It is likely, for example, that rising income causes rising expenditure (Fig. A1.4a) and that the falling price of a phone call causes more calls to be made (Fig. A1.4b).

You've now seen how we can use graphs in economics to show economic data and to reveal relationships between variables. Next, we'll learn how economists use graphs to construct and display economic models.

Graphs Used in Economic Models

THE GRAPHS USED IN ECONOMICS ARE NOT ALWAYS designed to show real-world data. Often they are used to show general relationships among the variables in an economic model.

An *economic model* is a stripped down, simplified description of an economy or of a component of an economy, such as a business or a household. It consists of statements about economic behaviour that can be expressed as equations or as curves in a graph. Economists use models to explore the effects of different policies or other influences on the economy in ways that are similar to the use of model airplanes in wind tunnels and models of the climate.

You will encounter many different kinds of graphs in economic models, but there are some repeating patterns. Once you've learned to recognize these patterns, you will instantly understand the meaning of a graph. Here, we'll look at the different types of curves that are used in economic models, and we'll see some everyday examples of each type of curve. The patterns to look for in graphs are the four cases:

- Variables that move in the same direction
- Variables that move in opposite directions
- Variables that have a maximum or a minimum
- Variables that are unrelated

Let's look at these four cases.

Variables That Move in the Same Direction

Figure A1.5 shows graphs of the relationships between two variables that move up and down together. A relationship between two variables that move in the same direction is called a **positive relationship** or a **direct relationship**. A line that slopes upward shows such a relationship.

Figure A1.5 shows three types of relationships: one that has a straight line and two that have curved lines. But all the lines in these three graphs are called curves. Any line on a graph—no matter whether it is straight or curved—is called a *curve*.

A relationship shown by a straight line is called a **linear relationship**. Figure A1.5(a) shows a linear rela-

FIGURE A1.5

Positive (Direct) Relationships

(a) Positive, linear relationship   **(b) Positive, becoming steeper**   **(c) Positive, becoming less steep**

Each part of this figure shows a positive (direct) relationship between two variables. That is, as the value of the variable measured on the x-axis increases, so does the value of the variable measured on the y-axis. Part (a) shows a linear relationship—as the two variables increase together, we move along a straight line. Part (b) shows a positive relationship such that as the two variables increase together, we move along a curve that becomes steeper. Part (c) shows a positive relationship such that as the two variables increase together, we move along a curve that becomes less steep.

tionship between the number of kilometres travelled in 5 hours and speed. For example, point *A* shows that we will travel 200 kilometres in 5 hours if our speed is 40 kilometres an hour. If we double our speed to 80 kilometres an hour, we will travel 400 kilometres in 5 hours.

Figure A1.5(b) shows the relationship between distance sprinted and recovery time (the time it takes the heart rate to return to its normal resting value). This relationship is an upward-sloping one that starts out quite flat but then becomes steeper as we move along the curve away from the origin. The reason this curve slopes upward and becomes steeper is because the additional recovery time needed from sprinting an additional 100 metres increases. It takes less than 5 minutes to recover from the first 100 metres, but it takes more than 10 minutes to recover from the second 100 metres.

Figure A1.5(c) shows the relationship between the number of problems worked by a student and the amount of study time. This relationship is an upward-sloping one that starts out quite steep and becomes flatter as we move away from the origin. Study time becomes less productive as the student spends more hours studying and becomes more tired.

Variables That Move in Opposite Directions

Figure A1.6 shows relationships between things that move in opposite directions. A relationship between variables that move in opposite directions is called a **negative relationship** or an **inverse relationship**.

Figure A1.6(a) shows the relationship between the number of hours available for playing squash and the number of hours for playing tennis when the total is 5 hours. One extra hour spent playing tennis means one hour less playing squash and vice versa. This relationship is negative and linear.

Figure A1.6(b) shows the relationship between the cost per kilometre travelled and the length of a journey. The longer the journey, the lower is the cost per kilometre. But as the journey length increases, the cost per kilometre decreases, and the fall in the cost is smaller, the longer the journey. This feature of the relationship is shown by the fact that the curve slopes downward, starting out steep at a short journey length and then becoming flatter as the journey length increases. This relationship arises because some of the costs are fixed (such as auto insurance), and the fixed cost is spread over a longer journey.

FIGURE A1.6

Negative (Inverse) Relationships

(a) Negative, linear relationship   **(b) Negative, becoming less steep**   **(c) Negative, becoming steeper**

Each part of this figure shows a negative (inverse) relationship between two variables. That is, as the value of the variable measured on the *x*-axis increases, the value of the variable measured on the *y*-axis decreases. Part (a) shows a linear relationship. The total time spent playing tennis and squash is 5 hours. As the time spent playing tennis increases, the time spent playing squash decreases, and we move along a straight line. Part (b) shows a negative relationship such that as the journey length increases, the curve becomes less steep. Part (c) shows a negative relationship such that as leisure time increases, the curve becomes steeper.

Figure A1.6(c) shows the relationship between the amount of leisure time and the number of problems worked by a student. Increasing leisure time produces an increasingly large reduction in the number of problems worked. This relationship is a negative one that starts out with a gentle slope at a small number of leisure hours and becomes steeper as the number of leisure hours increases. This relationship is a different view of the idea shown in Fig. A1.5(c).

Variables That Have a Maximum or a Minimum

Many relationships in economic models have a maximum or a minimum. For example, firms try to make the maximum possible profit and to produce at the lowest possible cost. Figure A1.7 shows relationships that have a maximum or a minimum.

Figure A1.7(a) shows the relationship between rainfall and wheat yield. When there is no rainfall, wheat will not grow, so the yield is zero. As the rainfall increases up to 10 days a month, the wheat yield increases. With 10 rainy days each month, the wheat

yield reaches its maximum at 2 tonnes per hectare (point *A*). Rain in excess of 10 days a month starts to lower the yield of wheat. If every day is rainy, the wheat suffers from a lack of sunshine and the yield decreases to zero. This relationship is one that starts out sloping upward, reaches a maximum, and then slopes downward.

Figure A1.7(b) shows the reverse case—a relationship that begins sloping downward, falls to a minimum, and then slopes upward. Most economic costs are like this relationship. An example is the relationship between the cost per kilometre and speed for a car trip. At low speeds, the car is creeping in a traffic jam. The number of kilometres per litre is low, so the cost per kilometre is high. At high speeds, the car is travelling faster than its efficient speed, using a large quantity of gasoline, and again the number of kilometres per litre is low and the cost per kilometre is high. At a speed of 100 kilometres an hour, the cost per kilometre is at its minimum (point *B*). This relationship is one that starts out sloping downward, reaches a minimum, and then slopes upward.

FIGURE A1.7
Maximum and Minimum Points

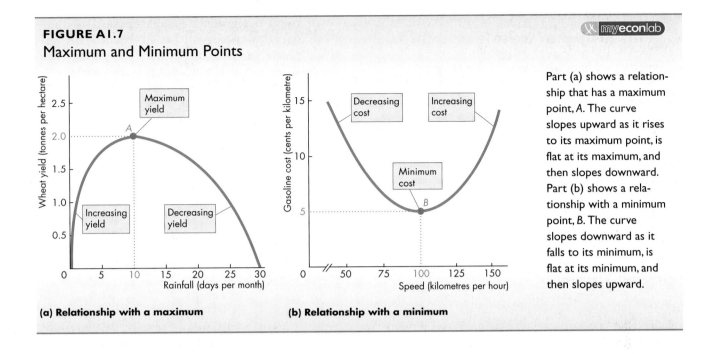

Part (a) shows a relationship that has a maximum point, *A*. The curve slopes upward as it rises to its maximum point, is flat at its maximum, and then slopes downward. Part (b) shows a relationship with a minimum point, *B*. The curve slopes downward as it falls to its minimum, is flat at its minimum, and then slopes upward.

(a) Relationship with a maximum   **(b) Relationship with a minimum**

Variables That Are Unrelated

There are many situations in which no matter what happens to the value of one variable, the other variable remains constant. Sometimes we want to show the independence between two variables in a graph, and Fig. A1.8 shows two ways of achieving this.

In describing the graphs in Figs. A1.5 through A1.7, we have talked about curves that slope upward and downward, and curves that become less steep or steeper. Let's spend a little time discussing exactly what we mean by slope and how we measure the slope of a curve.

FIGURE A1.8
Variables That Are Unrelated

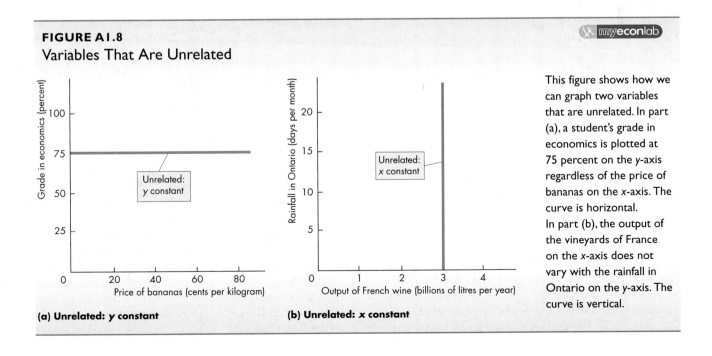

This figure shows how we can graph two variables that are unrelated. In part (a), a student's grade in economics is plotted at 75 percent on the *y*-axis regardless of the price of bananas on the *x*-axis. The curve is horizontal.
In part (b), the output of the vineyards of France on the *x*-axis does not vary with the rainfall in Ontario on the *y*-axis. The curve is vertical.

(a) Unrelated: *y* constant   **(b) Unrelated: *x* constant**

The Slope of a Relationship

WE CAN MEASURE THE INFLUENCE OF ONE variable on another by the slope of the relationship. The **slope** of a relationship is the change in the value of the variable measured on the y-axis divided by the change in the value of the variable measured on the x-axis. We use the Greek letter Δ (*delta*) to represent "change in." Thus Δy means the change in the value of the variable measured on the y-axis, and Δx means the change in the value of the variable measured on the x-axis. Therefore the slope of the relationship is

$$\Delta y / \Delta x$$

If a large change in the variable measured on the y-axis (Δy) is associated with a small change in the variable measured on the x-axis (Δx), the slope is large and the curve is steep. If a small change in the variable measured on the y-axis (Δy) is associated with a large change in the variable measured on the x-axis (Δx), the slope is small and the curve is flat.

We can make the idea of slope sharper by doing some calculations.

The Slope of a Straight Line

The slope of a straight line is the same regardless of where on the line you calculate it. The slope of a straight line is constant. Let's calculate the slopes of the lines in Fig. A1.9. In part (a), when x increases from 2 to 6, y increases from 3 to 6. The change in x

---

FIGURE A1.9
The Slope of a Straight Line

(a) Positive slope

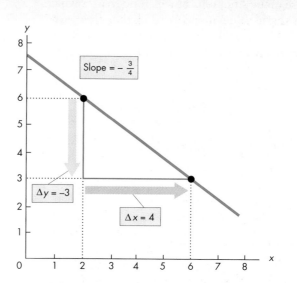

(b) Negative slope

To calculate the slope of a straight line, we divide the change in the value of the variable measured on the y-axis (Δy) by the change in the value of the variable measured on the x-axis (Δx), as we move along the curve. Part (a) shows the calculation of a positive slope. When x increases from 2 to 6, Δx equals 4. That change in x brings about an increase in y from 3 to 6, so Δy equals 3. The slope ($\Delta y/\Delta x$) equals 3/4. Part (b) shows the calculation of a negative slope. When x increases from 2 to 6, Δx equals 4. That increase in x brings about a decrease in y from 6 to 3, so Δy equals -3. The slope ($\Delta y/\Delta x$) equals $-3/4$.

is +4—that is, Δx is 4. The change in y is +3—that is, Δy is 3. The slope of that line is

$$\frac{\Delta y}{\Delta x} = \frac{3}{4}.$$

In part (b), when x increases from 2 to 6, y decreases from 6 to 3. The change in y is *minus* 3—that is, Δy is –3. The change in x is *plus* 4—that is, Δx is 4. The slope of the curve is

$$\frac{\Delta y}{\Delta x} = \frac{-3}{4}.$$

Notice that the two slopes have the same magnitude (3/4) but the slope of the line in part (a) is positive (+3/+4 = 3/4), while that in part (b) is negative (–3/+4 = –3/4). The slope of a positive relationship is positive; the slope of a negative relationship is negative.

The Slope of a Curved Line

The slope of a curved line is trickier. The slope of a curved line is not constant. Its slope depends on where on the line we calculate it. There are two ways to calculate the slope of a curved line: You can calculate the slope at a point, or you can calculate the slope across an arc of the curve. Let's look at the two alternatives.

Slope at a Point To calculate the slope at a point on a curve, you need to construct a straight line that has the same slope as the curve at the point in question. Figure A1.10 shows how this is done. Suppose you want to calculate the slope of the curve at point A. Place a ruler on the graph so that it touches point A and no other point on the curve, then draw a straight line along the edge of the ruler. The straight red line is this line, and it is the tangent to the curve at point A. If the ruler touches the curve only at point A, then the slope of the curve at point A must be the same as the slope of the edge of the ruler. If the curve and the ruler do not have the same slope, the line along the edge of the ruler will cut the curve instead of just touching it.

Now that you have found a straight line with the same slope as the curve at point A, you can calculate the slope of the curve at point A by calculating the slope of the straight line. Along the straight line, as x

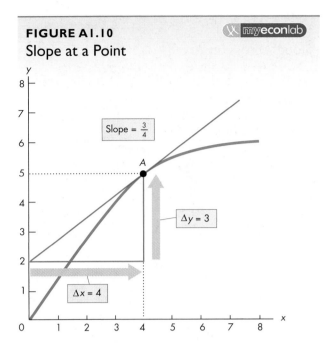

FIGURE A1.10
Slope at a Point

To calculate the slope of the curve at point A, draw the red line that just touches the curve at A—the tangent. The slope of this straight line is calculated by dividing the change in y by the change in x along the red line. When x increases from 0 to 4, Δx equals 4. That change in x is associated with an increase in y from 2 to 5, so Δy equals 3. The slope of the red line is 3/4. So the slope of the curve at point A is 3/4.

increases from 0 to 4 ($\Delta x = 4$) y increases from 2 to 5 ($\Delta y = 3$). Therefore the slope of the line is

$$\frac{\Delta y}{\Delta x} = \frac{3}{4}.$$

Thus the slope of the curve at point A is 3/4.

Slope Across an Arc An arc of a curve is a piece of a curve. In Fig. A1.11, you are looking at the same curve as in Fig. A1.10. But instead of calculating the slope at point A, we are going to calculate the slope across the arc from B to C. You can see that the slope at B is greater than the slope at C. When we calculate the slope across an arc, we are calculating the average slope between two points. As we move along the arc from B to C, x increases from 3 to 5 and y increases from 4 to 5.5. The change in x is 2 ($\Delta x = 2$), and the

FIGURE A1.11   myeconlab
Slope Across an Arc

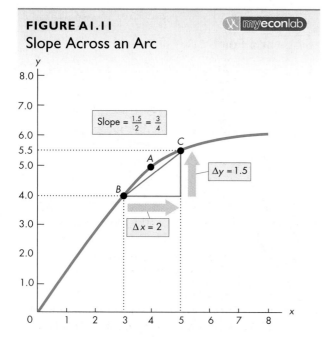

To calculate the average slope of the curve along the arc *BC*, draw a straight line from *B* to *C*. The slope of the line *BC* is calculated by dividing the change in *y* by the change in *x*. In moving from *B* to *C*, Δ*x* equals 2 and Δ*y* equals 1.5. The slope of the line *BC* is 1.5 divided by 2, or 3/4. So the slope of the curve across the arc *BC* is 3/4.

change in *y* is 1.5 (Δ*y* = 1.5). Therefore the slope of the line is

$$\frac{\Delta y}{\Delta x} = \frac{1.5}{2} = \frac{3}{4}.$$

Thus the slope of the curve across the arc *BC* is 3/4.

This calculation gives us the slope of the curve between points *B* and *C*. The actual slope calculated is the slope of the straight line from *B* to *C*. This slope approximates the average slope of the curve along the arc *BC*. In this particular example, the slope across the arc *BC* is identical to the slope of the curve at point *A*. But the calculation of the slope of a curve does not always work out so neatly. You might have some fun constructing some more examples and some counter-examples.

You now know how to make and interpret a graph. But so far, we've limited our attention to graphs of two variables. We're now going to learn how to graph more than two variables.

Graphing Relationships Among More Than Two Variables

WE HAVE SEEN THAT WE CAN GRAPH THE relationship between two variables as a point formed by the *x*- and *y*-coordinates in a two-dimensional graph. You may be thinking that although a two-dimensional graph is informative, most of the things in which you are likely to be interested involve relationships among many variables, not just two. For example, the amount of ice cream consumed depends on the price of ice cream and the temperature. If ice cream is expensive and the temperature is low, people eat much less ice cream than when ice cream is inexpensive and the temperature is high. For any given price of ice cream, the quantity consumed varies with the temperature; and for any given temperature, the quantity of ice cream consumed varies with its price.

Figure A1.12 shows a relationship among three variables. The table shows the number of litres of ice cream consumed each day at various temperatures and ice cream prices. How can we graph these numbers?

To graph a relationship that involves more than two variables, we use the *ceteris paribus* assumption.

Ceteris Paribus   We noted in the chapter (see p. 13) that every laboratory experiment is an attempt to create *ceteris paribus* and isolate the relationship of interest. We use the same method to make a graph when more than two variables are involved.

Figure A1.12(a) shows an example. There, you can see what happens to the quantity of ice cream consumed when the price of ice cream varies and the temperature is held constant. The line labelled 21°C shows the relationship between ice cream consumption and the price of ice cream if the temperature remains at 21°C. The numbers used to plot that line are those in the third column of the table in Fig. A1.12. For example, if the temperature is 21°C, 10 litres are consumed when the price is 60¢ a scoop and 18 litres are consumed when the price is 30¢ a scoop. The curve labelled 32°C shows consumption as the price varies if the temperature remains at 32°C.

We can also show the relationship between ice cream consumption and temperature when the price of ice cream remains constant, as shown

FIGURE A1.12

Graphing a Relationship Among Three Variables

(a) Price and consumption at a given temperature

(b) Temperature and consumption at a given price

(c) Temperature and price at a given consumption

Price	Ice cream consumption (litres per day)			
(cents per scoop)	–10°C	10°C	21°C	32°C
15	12	18	25	50
30	10	12	18	37
45	7	10	13	27
60	5	7	10	20
75	3	5	7	14
90	2	3	5	10
105	1	2	3	6

The quantity of ice cream consumed depends on its price and the temperature. The table gives some hypothetical numbers that tell us how many litres of ice cream are consumed each day at different prices and different temperatures. For example, if the price is 60¢ a scoop and the temperature is 21°C, 10 litres of ice cream are consumed. This set of values is highlighted in the table and each part of the figure.

To graph a relationship among three variables, the value of one variable is held constant. Part (a) shows the relationship between price and consumption when temperature is held constant. One curve holds temperature at 32°C and the other at 21°C. Part (b) shows the relationship between temperature and consumption when price is held constant. One curve holds the price at 60¢ a scoop and the other at 15¢ a scoop. Part (c) shows the relationship between temperature and price when consumption is held constant. One curve holds consumption at 10 litres a day and the other at 7 litres a day.

in Fig. A1.12(b). The curve labelled 60¢ shows how the consumption of ice cream varies with the temperature when ice cream costs 60¢ a scoop, and a second curve shows the relationship when ice cream costs 15¢ a scoop. For example, at 60¢ a scoop, 10 litres are consumed when the temperature is 21°C and 20 litres when the temperature is 32°C.

Figure A1.12(c) shows the combinations of temperature and price that result in a constant consumption of ice cream. One curve shows the combination that results in 10 litres a day being consumed, and

the other shows the combination that results in 7 litres a day being consumed. A high price and a high temperature lead to the same consumption as a lower price and a lower temperature. For example, 10 litres of ice cream are consumed at 21°C and 60¢ a scoop, 32°C and 90¢ a scoop, and at 10°C and 45¢ a scoop.

With what you have learned about graphs, you can move forward with your study of economics. There are no graphs in this book that are more complicated than those that have been explained in this appendix.

Mathematical Note
Equations to Straight Lines

IF A STRAIGHT LINE IN A GRAPH DESCRIBES THE relationship between two variables, we call it a *linear relationship*. Figure 1 shows the linear relationship between a person's expenditure and income. This person spends $100 a week (by borrowing or spending previous savings) when income is zero. And out of each dollar earned, this person spends 50 cents (and saves 50 cents).

All linear relationships are described by the same general equation. We call the quantity that is measured on the horizontal (or x-axis) x and we call the quantity that is measured on the vertical (or y-axis) y. In the case of Fig. 1, x is income and y is expenditure.

A Linear Equation

The equation that describes a straight-line relationship between x and y is

$$y = a + bx.$$

In this equation, a and b are fixed numbers and they are called constants. The values of x and y vary so these numbers are called variables. Because the equation describes a straight line, it is called a *linear equation*.

The equation tells us that when the value of x is zero, the value of y is a. We call the constant a the y-axis intercept. The reason is that on the graph the straight line hits the y-axis at a value equal to a. Figure 1 illustrates the y-axis intercept.

For positive values of x, the value of y exceeds a. The constant b tells us by how much y increases above a as x increases. The constant b is the slope of the line.

Slope of Line

As we explain in the chapter, the *slope* of a relationship is the change in the value of y divided by the change in the value of x as we move along the line. We use the Greek letter Δ (*delta*) to represent "change in." Thus Δy means the change in the value of the variable measured on the y-axis, and Δx means the change in the value of the variable measured on the x-axis. Therefore the slope of the relationship is

$$\Delta y / \Delta x.$$

To see why the slope is b, suppose that initially the value of x is x_1, or $200 in Fig. 2. The corresponding value of y is y_1, also $200 in Fig. 2. The equation to the line tells us that

$$y_1 = a + bx_1. \tag{1}$$

Now the value of x increases by Δx to $x_1 + \Delta x$ (or $400 in Fig. 2). And the value of y increases by Δy to $y_1 + \Delta y$ (or $300 in Fig. 2).

Figure 1 Linear relationship

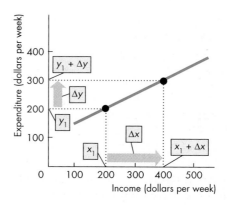

Figure 2 Calculating slope

The equation to the line now tells us that

$$y_1 + \Delta y = a + b(x_1 + \Delta x). \qquad (2)$$

To calculate the slope of the line, subtract equation (1) from equation (2) to obtain

$$\Delta y = b\Delta x \qquad (3)$$

and now divide equation (3) by Δx to obtain

$$\frac{\Delta y}{\Delta x} = b.$$

So, the slope of the line is b.

Position of Line

The y-axis intercept determines the position of the line on the graph. Figure 3 illustrates the relationship between the y-axis intercept and the position of the line on the graph. The y-axis measures saving and the x-axis measures income. When the y-axis intercept, a, is positive, the line hits the y-axis at a positive value of y—as the blue line does. When the y-axis intercept, a, is zero, the line hits the y-axis at the origin—as the purple line does. When the y-axis intercept, a, is negative, the line hits the y-axis at a negative value of y—as the red line does. As the equations to the three lines show, the value of the y-axis intercept does not influence the slope of the line.

Positive Relationships

Figure 1 shows a positive relationship—the two variables x and y move in the same direction. All positive relationships have a slope that is positive. In the equation to the line, the constant b is positive. In this example, the y-axis intercept, a, is 100. The slope b equals $\Delta y/\Delta x$, which is 100/200 or 0.5. The equation to the line is

$$y = 100 + 0.5x.$$

Negative Relationships

Figure 4 shows a negative relationship—the two variables x and y move in the opposite direction. All negative relationships have a slope that is negative. In the equation to the line, the constant b is negative. In the example in Fig. 4, the y-axis intercept, a, is 30. The slope, b, equals $\Delta y/\Delta x$, which is $-20/2$ or -10. The equation to the line is

$$y = 30 + (-10)x$$

or,

$$y = 30 - 10x.$$

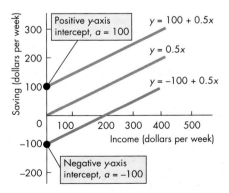

Figure 3 The y-axis intercept

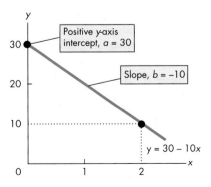

Figure 4 Negative relationship

SUMMARY

KEY POINTS

Graphing Data (pp. 17–20)

- A time-series graph shows the trend and fluctuations in a variable over time.

- A cross-section graph shows how variables change across the members of a population.

- A scatter diagram shows the relationship between two variables. It shows whether two variables are positively related, negatively related, or unrelated.

Graphs Used in Economic Models (pp. 20–23)

- Graphs are used to show relationships among variables in economic models.

- Relationships can be positive (an upward-sloping curve), negative (a downward-sloping curve), positive and then negative (have a maximum point), negative and then positive (have a minimum point), or unrelated (a horizontal or vertical curve).

The Slope of a Relationship (pp. 24–26)

- The slope of a relationship is calculated as the change in the value of the variable measured on the y-axis divided by the change in the value of the variable measured on the x-axis—that is, $\Delta y/\Delta x$.

- A straight line has a constant slope.

- A curved line has a varying slope. To calculate the slope of a curved line, we calculate the slope at a point or across an arc.

Graphing Relationships Among More Than Two Variables (pp. 26–27)

- To graph a relationship among more than two variables, we hold constant the values of all the variables except two.

- We then plot the value of one of the variables against the value of another.

KEY FIGURES

Figure A1.1   Making a Graph, 17
Figure A1.5   Positive (Direct) Relationships, 21
Figure A1.6   Negative (Inverse) Relationships, 22
Figure A1.7   Maximum and Minimum Points, 23
Figure A1.9   The Slope of a Straight Line, 24
Figure A1.10 Slope at a Point, 25
Figure A1.11 Slope Across an Arc, 26

KEY TERMS

Cross-section graph, 18
Direct relationship, 20
Inverse relationship, 21
Linear relationship, 20
Negative relationship, 21
Positive relationship, 20
Scatter diagram, 19
Slope, 24
Time-series graph, 18
Trend, 18

REVIEW QUIZ

1. What are the three types of graphs used to show economic data?

2. Give an example of a time-series graph.

3. List three things that a time-series graph shows quickly and easily.

4. Give examples, not those in the chapter, of scatter diagrams that show a positive relationship, a negative relationship, and no relationship.

5. Draw some graphs to show the relationships between two variables that
   a. Move in the same direction.
   b. Move in opposite directions.
   c. Have a maximum.
   d. Have a minimum.

6. Which relationship in question 5 is a positive relationship and which is a negative relationship?

7. What are the two ways of calculating the slope of a curved line?

8. How do we graph a relationship among more than two variables?

 Study Plan 1.5

PROBLEMS

Go to ⓧ **myeconlab** for solutions to odd-numbered problems and additional exercises.

The spreadsheet provides data on the Canadian economy: Column A is the year, column B is the inflation rate, column C is the interest rate, column D is the growth rate, and column E is the unemployment rate. Use this spreadsheet to answer problems 1, 2, 3, and 4.

	A	B	C	D	E
1	1995	2.2	7.2	2.9	9.6
2	1996	1.6	4.3	1.6	9.7
3	1997	1.6	3.6	4.2	9.2
4	1998	0.9	5.0	4.1	8.4
5	1999	1.7	4.9	5.6	7.6
6	2000	3.1	5.7	5.2	6.8
7	2001	2.1	3.9	1.8	7.2
8	2002	2.1	2.7	3.1	7.7
9	2003	3.0	2.9	2.1	7.6
10	2004	1.7	2.3	2.8	7.2

1. Draw a time-series graph of the inflation rate.
   a. In which year(s) (i) was inflation highest, (ii) was inflation lowest, (iii) did it increase, (iv) did it decrease most?
   b. What was the main trend in inflation?

2. Draw a time-series graph of the interest rate.
   a. In which year(s) (i) was the interest rate lowest, (iii) did it increase, (iv) did it increase most?
   b. What was the main trend in the interest rate?
   c. Draw a scatter diagram to show the relationship between the inflation rate and the interest rate. Describe the relationship.

3. Draw a scatter diagram to show the relationship between the inflation rate and the interest rate. Describe the relationship.

4. Draw a scatter diagram to show the relationship between the growth rate and the unemployment rate. Describe the relationship.

5. Draw a graph to show the relationship between the two variables x and y:

x	0	1	2	3	4	5	6	7	8
y	0	1	4	9	16	25	36	49	64

   a. Is the relationship positive or negative?
   b. Does the slope of the relationship increase or decrease as the value of x increases?
   c. Think of some economic relationships that might be similar to this one.

6. Draw a graph that shows the relationship between the two variables x and y:

x	0	1	2	3	4	5
y	25	24	22	16	8	0

   a. Is the relationship positive or negative?
   b. Does the slope of the relationship increase or decrease as the value of x increases?
   c. Think of some economic relationships that might be similar to this one.

7. In problem 5, calculate the slope of the relationship between x and y when x equals 4.

8. In problem 6, calculate the slope of the relationship between x and y when x equals 3.

9. In problem 5, calculate the slope of the relationship across the arc when x increases from 3 to 4.

10. In problem 6, calculate the slope of the relationship across the arc when x increases from 4 to 5.

11. Calculate the slope of the relationship shown at point A in the following figure.

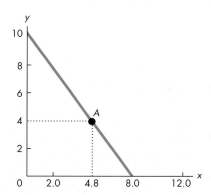

12. Calculate the slope of the relationship shown at point A in the following figure.

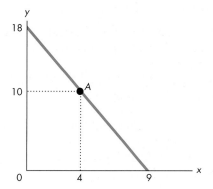

13. Calculate the slope of the relationship:

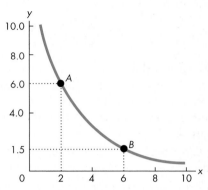

a. At points *A* and *B*.
b. Across the arc *AB*.

14. Calculate the slope of the relationship:

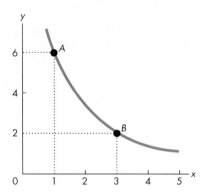

a. At points *A* and *B*.
b. Across the arc *AB*.

15. The table gives the price of a balloon ride, the temperature, and the number of rides a day.

Price	Balloon rides (number per day)		
(dollars per ride)	10°C	20°C	30°C
5.00	32	40	50
10.00	27	32	40
15.00	18	27	32
20.00	10	18	27

Draw graphs to show the relationship between

a. The price and the number of rides, holding the temperature constant.
b. The number of rides and temperature, holding the price constant.
c. The temperature and price, holding the number of rides constant.

16. The table gives the price of an umbrella, the amount of rainfall, and the number of umbrellas purchased.

Price	Umbrellas (number per day)		
(dollars per umbrella)	0	2	10
		(mm of rainfall)	
10	7	8	12
20	4	7	8
30	2	4	7
40	1	2	4

Draw graphs to show the relationship between

a. The price and the number of umbrellas purchased, holding the amount of rainfall constant.
b. The number of umbrellas purchased and the amount of rainfall, holding the price constant.
c. The amount of rainfall and the price, holding the number of umbrellas purchased constant.

WEB EXERCISES

Use the links on **myeconlab** to work the following exercises.

1. Find the Consumer Price Index (CPI) for the latest 12 months. Make a graph of the CPI. During the most recent month, was the CPI rising or falling? Was the rate of rise or fall increasing or decreasing?
2. Find the unemployment rate for the latest 12 months. Graph the unemployment rate. During the most recent month, was it rising or falling? Was the rate of rise or fall increasing or decreasing?
3. Use the data that you obtained in exercises 1 and 2. Make a graph to show whether the CPI and the unemployment rate are related.
4. Use the data that you obtained in exercises 1 and 2. Calculate the percentage change in the CPI each month. Make a graph to show whether the percentage change in the CPI and the unemployment rate are related to each other.

The Economic Problem

CHAPTER 2

Good, Better, Best!

We live in a style that surprises our grandparents and would have astonished our great-grandparents. MP3s, video games, cell phones, gene splicing, personal computers, and iPods, which did not exist even 25 years ago, have transformed our daily lives. For most of us, life is good and getting better. But we still make choices and face costs.

Perhaps the biggest choice that you will make is when to quit school and begin full-time work. When you've completed your current program, will you remain in school and work towards a postgraduate degree or a professional degree? What are the costs and consequences of this choice? We'll return to this question in *Reading Between the Lines* at the end of this chapter.

We see an incredible amount of specialization and trade in the world. Each one of us specializes in a particular job—as a lawyer, a journalist, a homemaker. Why? How do we benefit from specialization and trade?

Over many centuries, social institutions have evolved that we take for granted. They include firms, markets, and a political and legal system that protects private property. Why have these institutions evolved?

◆ These are the questions that we study in this chapter. We begin with the core economic problem—scarcity and choice—and the concept of the production possibilities frontier. We then learn about the central idea of economics: using resources efficiently. We also discover how we can expand production by accumulating capital, expanding our knowledge, and specializing and trading with each other. What you will learn in this chapter is the foundation on which all economics is built.

After studying this chapter, you will be able to

■ **Define the production possibilities frontier and calculate opportunity cost**

■ **Distinguish between production possibilities and preferences and describe an efficient allocation of resources**

■ **Explain how current production choices expand future production possibilities**

■ **Explain how specialization and trade expand our production possibilities**

■ **Explain why property rights and markets have evolved**

Production Possibilities and Opportunity Cost

EVERY WORKING DAY, IN MINES, FACTORIES, SHOPS, and offices and on farms and construction sites across Canada, 138 million people produce a vast variety of goods and services valued at $50 billion. But the quantities of goods and services that we can produce are limited by both our available resources and by technology. And if we want to increase our production of one good, we must decrease our production of something else—we face tradeoffs. You are going to learn about the production possibilities frontier, which describes the limit to what we can produce and provides a neat way of thinking about and illustrating the idea of a tradeoff.

The **production possibilities frontier** *(PPF)* is the boundary between those combinations of goods and services that can be produced and those that cannot. To illustrate the *PPF*, we focus on two goods at a time and hold the quantities produced of all the other goods and services constant. That is, we look at a *model* economy in which everything remains the same *(ceteris paribus)* except for the production of the two goods we are considering.

Let's look at the production possibilities frontier for CDs and pizza, which stand for *any* pair of goods or services.

Production Possibilities Frontier

The *production possibilities frontier* for CDs and pizza shows the limits to the production of these two goods, given the total resources available to produce them. Figure 2.1 shows this production possibilities frontier. The table lists some combinations of the quantities of pizzas and CDs that can be produced in a month given the resources available. The figure graphs these combinations. The *x*-axis shows the quantity of pizzas produced, and the *y*-axis shows the quantity of CDs produced.

The *PPF* illustrates *scarcity* because we cannot attain the points outside the frontier. They are points that describe wants that can't be satisfied. We can produce at all the points *inside* the *PPF* and *on* the *PPF*. They are attainable points. Suppose that in a typical month, we produce 4 million pizzas and 5 million CDs. Figure 2.1 shows this combination as point *E* and as possibility *E* in the table. The figure also shows

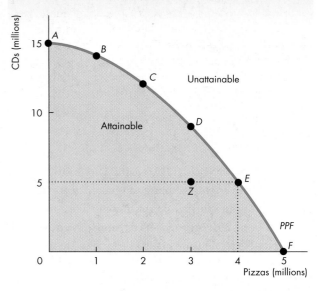

FIGURE 2.1
Production Possibilities Frontier

Possibility	Pizzas (millions)		CDs (millions)
A	0	and	15
B	1	and	14
C	2	and	12
D	3	and	9
E	4	and	5
F	5	and	0

The table lists six points on the production possibilities frontier for CDs and pizza. Row *A* tells us that if we produce no pizza, the maximum quantity of CDs we can produce is 15 million. Points *A*, *B*, *C*, *D*, *E*, and *F* in the figure represent the rows of the table. The line passing through these points is the production possibilities frontier (*PPF*). The *PPF* separates the attainable from the unattainable. Production is possible at any point *inside* the orange area or *on* the frontier. Points outside the frontier are unattainable. Points inside the frontier such as point *Z* are inefficient because resources are wasted or misallocated. At such points, it is possible to use the available resources to produce more of either or both goods.

other production possibilities. For example, we might stop producing pizza and move all the people who produce it into producing CDs. Point *A* in the figure and possibility *A* in the table show this case. The quantity of CDs produced increases to 15 million, and pizza production dries up. Alternatively, we might close the CD factories and switch all the resources into producing pizza. In this situation, we produce 5 million pizzas. Point *F* in the figure and possibility *F* in the table show this case.

Production Efficiency

We achieve **production efficiency** if we cannot produce more of one good without producing less of some other good. When production is efficient, we are at a point *on* the *PPF*. If we are at a point *inside* the *PPF*, such as point *Z*, production is *inefficient* because we have some *unused* resources or we have some *misallocated* resources or both.

Resources are unused when they are idle but could be working. For example, we might leave some of the factories idle or some workers unemployed.

Resources are *misallocated* when they are assigned to tasks for which they are not the best match. For example, we might assign skilled pizza makers to work in a CD factory and skilled CD makers to work in a pizza shop. We could get more pizza *and* more CDs from these same workers if we reassigned them to the tasks that more closely match their skills.

If we produce at a point inside the *PPF* such as *Z*, we can use our resources more efficiently to produce more pizzas, more CDs, or more of *both* pizzas and CDs. But if we produce at a point *on* the *PPF*, we are using our resources efficiently and we can produce more of one good only if we produce less of the other. That is, along the *PPF*, we face a *tradeoff*.

Tradeoff Along the *PPF*

Every choice *along* the *PPF* involves a *tradeoff*—we must give up something to get something else. On the *PPF* in Fig. 2.1, we must give up some CDs to get more pizza or give up some pizza to get more CDs.

Tradeoffs arise in every imaginable real-world situation, and you reviewed several of them in Chapter 1. At any given point in time, we have a fixed amount of labour, land, capital, and entrepreneurship. By using our available technologies, we can employ these resources to produce goods and services. But we are limited in what we can produce. This limit defines a boundary between what we can attain and what we cannot attain. This boundary is the real-world's production possibilities frontier, and it defines the tradeoffs that we must make. On our real-world *PPF*, we can produce more of any one good or service only if we produce less of some other goods or services.

When doctors say that we must spend more on AIDS and cancer research, they are suggesting a tradeoff: more medical research for less of some other things. When the prime minister says that he wants to spend more on education and health care, he is suggesting a tradeoff: more education and health care for less national defence or less private spending (because of higher taxes). When an environmental group argues for less logging, it is suggesting a tradeoff: greater conservation of endangered wildlife for less paper. When your parents say that you should study more, they are suggesting a tradeoff: more study time for less leisure or sleep.

All tradeoffs involve a cost—an opportunity cost.

Opportunity Cost

The *opportunity cost* of an action is the highest-valued alternative forgone. The *PPF* helps us to make the concept of opportunity cost precise and enables us to calculate it. Along the *PPF*, there are only two goods, so there is only one alternative forgone: some quantity of the other good. Given our current resources and technology, we can produce more pizzas only if we produce fewer CDs. The opportunity cost of producing an additional pizza is the number of CDs we *must* forgo. Similarly, the opportunity cost of producing an additional CD is the quantity of pizzas we *must* forgo.

For example, at point *C* in Fig. 2.1, we produce fewer pizzas and more CDs than at point *D*. If we choose point *D* over point *C*, the additional 1 million pizzas *cost* 3 million CDs. One pizza costs 3 CDs.

We can also work out the opportunity cost of choosing point *C* over point *D* in Fig. 2.1. If we move from point *D* to point *C*, the quantity of CDs produced increases by 3 million and the quantity of pizzas produced decreases by 1 million. So if we choose point *C* over point *D*, the additional 3 million CDs *cost* 1 million pizzas. One CD costs 1/3 of a pizza.

Opportunity Cost Is a Ratio Opportunity cost is a ratio. It is the decrease in the quantity produced of one good divided by the increase in the quantity produced of another good as we move along the production possibilities frontier.

Because opportunity cost is a ratio, the opportunity cost of producing an additional CD is equal to the *inverse* of the opportunity cost of producing an additional pizza. Check this proposition by returning to the calculations we've just worked through. When we move along the *PPF* from *C* to *D*, the opportunity cost of a pizza is 3 CDs. The inverse of 3 is 1/3, so if we decrease the production of pizza and increase the production of CDs by moving from *D* to *C*, the opportunity cost of a CD must be 1/3 of a pizza. You can check that this number is correct. If we move from *D* to *C*, we produce 3 million more CDs and 1 million fewer pizzas. Because 3 million CDs cost 1 million pizzas, the opportunity cost of 1 CD is 1/3 of a pizza.

Increasing Opportunity Cost The opportunity cost of a pizza increases as the quantity of pizzas produced increases. Also, the opportunity cost of a CD increases as the quantity of CDs produced increases. This phenomenon of increasing opportunity cost is reflected in the shape of the *PPF*—it is bowed outward.

When a large quantity of CDs and a small quantity of pizzas are produced—between points *A* and *B* in Fig. 2.1—the frontier has a gentle slope. A given increase in the quantity of pizzas *costs* a small decrease in the quantity of CDs, so the opportunity cost of a pizza is a small quantity of CDs.

When a large quantity of pizzas and a small quantity of CDs are produced—between points *E* and *F* in Fig. 2.1—the frontier is steep. A given increase in the quantity of pizzas *costs* a large decrease in the quantity of CDs, so the opportunity cost of a pizza is a large quantity of CDs.

The *PPF* is bowed outward because resources are not all equally productive in all activities. People with several years of experience working for Sony are good at producing CDs but not very good at making pizzas. So if we move some of these people from Sony to Domino's, we get a small increase in the quantity of pizzas but a large decrease in the quantity of CDs.

Similarly, people who have spent years working at Domino's are good at producing pizzas, but they have no idea how to produce CDs. So if we move some of these people from Domino's to Sony, we get a small increase in the quantity of CDs but a large decrease in the quantity of pizzas. The more of either good we try to produce, the less productive are the additional

resources we use to produce that good and the larger is the opportunity cost of a unit of that good.

Increasing Opportunity Costs Are Everywhere
Just about every activity that you can think of is one with an increasing opportunity cost. We allocate the most skillful farmers and the most fertile land to the production of food. And we allocate the best doctors and the least fertile land to the production of health-care services. If we shift fertile land and tractors away from farming to hospitals and ambulances and ask farmers to become hospital porters, the production of food drops drastically and the increase in the production of health-care services is small. The opportunity cost of a unit of health-care services rises. Similarly, if we shift our resources away from health care towards farming, we must use more doctors and nurses as farmers and more hospitals as hydroponic tomato factories. The decrease in the production of health-care services is large, but the increase in food production is small. The opportunity cost of a unit of food rises.

This example is extreme and unlikely, but these same considerations apply to any pair of goods that you can imagine.

REVIEW QUIZ

1 How does the production possibilities frontier illustrate scarcity?
2 How does the production possibilities frontier illustrate production efficiency?
3 How does the production possibilities frontier show that every choice involves a tradeoff?
4 How does the production possibilities frontier illustrate opportunity cost?
5 Why is opportunity cost a ratio?
6 Why does the *PPF* for most goods bow outward so that opportunity cost increases as the quantity produced of a good increases?

myeconlab Study Plan 2.1

We've seen that what we can produce is limited by the production possibilities frontier. We've also seen that production on the *PPF* is efficient. But we can produce many different quantities on the *PPF*. How do we choose among them? How do we know which point on the *PPF* is the best one?

Using Resources Efficiently

YOU'VE SEEN THAT WE ACHIEVE PRODUCTION efficiency at every point on the *PPF*. But which point is best? What quantities of CDs and pizzas best serve the social interest?

This question is an example of real-world questions of enormous consequence such as: How much should we spend on treating AIDS and how much on cancer research? Should we expand education and health-care programs or cut taxes? Should we spend more on the preservation of rainforests and the conservation of endangered wildlife?

To answer these questions, we must find a way of measuring and comparing costs and benefits.

The *PPF* and Marginal Cost

The **marginal cost** of a good is the opportunity cost of producing *one more unit* of it. We calculate marginal cost from the *slope* of the *PPF*. As the quantity of pizza produced increases, the *PPF* gets steeper and marginal cost increases. Figure 2.2 illustrates the calculation of the marginal cost of a pizza.

Begin by finding the opportunity cost of pizza in blocks of 1 *million* pizzas. The first million pizzas cost 1 million CDs, the second million pizzas cost 2 million CDs, the third million pizzas cost 3 million CDs, and so on. The bars in part (a) illustrate these calculations.

The bars in part (b) show the cost of an average pizza in each of the 1 million pizza blocks. Focus on the 3rd million pizzas—the move from *C* to *D* in part (a). Over this range, because the 1 million pizzas cost 3 million CDs, one of these pizzas, on the average, costs 3 CDs—the height of the bar in part (b).

Next, find the opportunity cost of *each* additional pizza—the marginal cost of a pizza. The marginal cost of a pizza is increasing as the quantity of pizza produced increases. The marginal cost at point *C* is less than it is at point *D*. On the average over the range from *C* to *D*, the marginal cost of a pizza is 3 CDs. But it exactly equals 3 CDs only in the middle of the range between *C* and *D*. The red dot in part (b) indicates that the marginal cost of a pizza is 3 CDs when 2.5 million pizzas are produced. Each black dot in part (b) is interpreted in the same way. The orange curve that passes through these dots, labelled *MC*, is the marginal cost curve. It shows the marginal cost of a pizza at each quantity of pizza as we move along the *PPF*.

FIGURE 2.2
The *PPF* and Marginal Cost

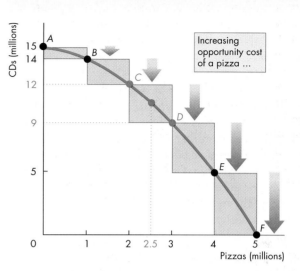

(a) *PPF* and opportunity cost

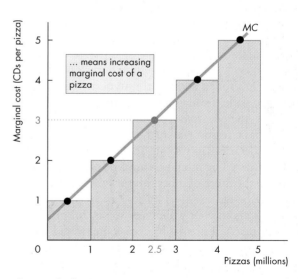

(b) Marginal cost

Marginal cost is calculated from the slope of the *PPF*. As the quantity of pizza produced increases, the *PPF* gets steeper and the marginal cost of a pizza increases. The bars in part (a) show the opportunity cost of pizza in blocks of 1 million pizzas. The bars in part (b) show the cost of an average pizza in each of these 1 million blocks. The orange curve, *MC*, shows the marginal cost of a pizza at each point along the *PPF*. This curve passes through the centre of each of the bars in part (b).

Preferences and Marginal Benefit

Look around your classroom and notice the wide variety of shirts, caps, pants, and shoes that you and your fellow students are wearing today. Why is there such a huge variety? Why don't you all wear the same styles and colours? The answer lies in what economists call preferences. **Preferences** are a description of a person's likes and dislikes.

You've seen that we have a concrete way of describing the limits to production: the *PPF*. We need a similarly concrete way of describing preferences. To describe preferences, economists use the concept of marginal benefit. The **marginal benefit** of a good or service is the benefit received from consuming one more unit of it.

We measure the marginal benefit of a good or service by the most that people are *willing to pay* for an additional unit of it. The idea is that you are not willing to pay more for a good than it is worth to you. But you are willing to pay an amount up to what it is worth. So the willingness to pay for something measures its marginal benefit.

Economists use the marginal benefit curve to illustrate preferences. The **marginal benefit curve** shows the relationship between the marginal benefit of a good and the quantity of that good consumed. It is a general principle that the more we have of any good or service, the smaller is its marginal benefit and the less we are willing to pay for an additional unit of it. This tendency is so widespread and strong that we call it a principle—the *principle of decreasing marginal benefit.*

The basic reason why marginal benefit of a good or service decreases as we consume more of it is that we like variety. The more we consume of any one good or service, the more of other things we see that we would like better.

Think about your willingness to pay for pizza (or any other item). If pizza is hard to come by and you can buy only a few slices a year, you might be willing to pay a high price to get an additional slice. But if pizza is all you've eaten for the past few days, you are willing to pay almost nothing for another slice.

In everyday life, we think of what we pay for goods and services as the money that we give up—dollars. But you've learned to think about cost as other goods or services forgone, not a dollar cost. You can think about willingness to pay in the same terms. The price you are willing to pay for something is the quantity of other goods and services that you are willing to forgo. Let's continue with the example of CDs and pizzas and illustrate preferences this way.

FIGURE 2.3 myeconlab
Preferences and the Marginal Benefit Curve

Possibility	Pizzas (millions)	Willingness to pay (CDs per pizza)
A	0.5	5
B	1.5	4
C	2.5	3
D	3.5	2
E	4.5	1

The smaller the quantity of pizzas produced, the more CDs people are willing to give up for an additional pizza. If pizza production is 0.5 million, people are willing to pay 5 CDs per pizza. But if pizza production is 4.5 million, people are willing to pay only 1 CD per pizza. Willingness to pay measures marginal benefit. And decreasing marginal benefit is a universal feature of people's preferences.

Figure 2.3 illustrates preferences as the willingness to pay for pizza in terms of CDs. In row *A*, pizza production is 0.5 million, and at that quantity, people are willing to pay 5 CDs per pizza. As the quantity of pizza produced increases, the amount that people are willing to pay for it falls. When pizza production is 4.5 million, people are willing to pay only 1 CD per pizza.

Let's now use the concepts of marginal cost and marginal benefit to describe the efficient quantity of pizzas to produce.

Efficient Use of Resources

When we cannot produce more of any one good without giving up some other good, we have achieved *production efficiency*, and we're producing at a point on the *PPF*. When we cannot produce more of any good without giving up some other good that we *value more highly*, we have achieved **allocative efficiency** and we are producing at the point on the *PPF* that we prefer above all other points.

Suppose in Fig. 2.4, we produce 1.5 million pizzas at point *A* on the *PPF*. The marginal cost of a pizza is 2 CDs and the marginal benefit from a pizza is 4 CDs. Because someone values an additional pizza more highly than it costs to produce, we can get more value from our resources by moving some of them out of producing CDs and into producing pizzas.

Now suppose we produce 3.5 million pizzas at point *C* on the *PPF*. The marginal cost of a pizza is now 4 CDs but the marginal benefit is only 2 CDs. Because the additional pizza costs more to produce than anyone thinks it is worth, we can get more value from our resources by moving some of them away from producing pizzas and into producing CDs.

But suppose we produce 2.5 million pizzas at point *B* on the *PPF*. Marginal cost and marginal benefit are now equal at 3 CDs. This allocation of resources is efficient. If more pizzas are produced, the forgone CDs are worth more than the additional pizzas. If fewer pizzas are produced, the forgone pizzas are worth more than the additional CDs.

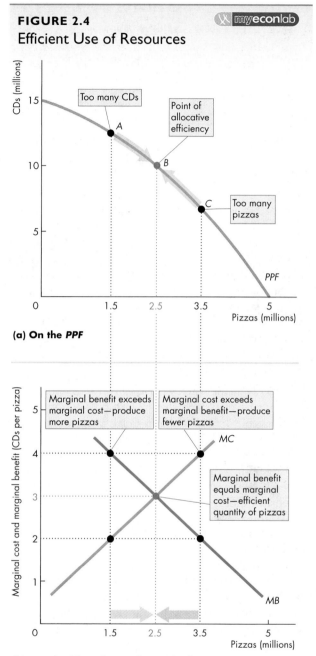

FIGURE 2.4
Efficient Use of Resources

(a) On the PPF

(b) Marginal benefit equals marginal cost

The greater the quantity of pizzas produced, the smaller is the marginal benefit (*MB*) from pizza—the fewer CDs people are willing to give up to get an additional pizza. But the greater the quantity of pizzas produced, the greater is the marginal cost (*MC*) of pizza—the more CDs people must give up to get an additional pizza. When marginal benefit equals marginal cost, resources are being used efficiently.

REVIEW QUIZ

1 What is marginal cost? How is it measured?
2 What is marginal benefit? How is it measured?
3 How does the marginal benefit from a good change as the quantity of that good increases?
4 What is production efficiency and how does it relate to the production possibilities frontier?
5 What conditions must be satisfied if resources are used efficiently?

myeconlab **Study Plan 2.2**

You now understand the limits to production and the conditions under which resources are used efficiently. Your next task is to study the expansion of production possibilities.

Economic Growth

ĐURING THE PAST 30 YEARS, PRODUCTION PER person in the Canada has doubled. Such an expansion of production is called **economic growth.** Economic growth increases our *standard of living*, but it doesn't overcome scarcity and avoid opportunity cost. To make our economy grow, we face a trade-off—the faster we make production grow, the greater is the opportunity cost of economic growth.

The Cost of Economic Growth

Two key factors influence economic growth: technological change and capital accumulation. **Technological change** is the development of new goods and of better ways of producing goods and services. **Capital accumulation** is the growth of capital resources, which includes *human capital.*

As a consequence of technological change and capital accumulation, we have an enormous quantity of cars that enable us to produce more transportation than was available when we had only horses and carriages; we have satellites that make global communications possible on a scale that is much larger than that produced by the earlier cable technology. But new technologies and new capital have an opportunity cost. To use resources in research and development and to produce new capital, we must decrease our production of consumption goods and services. Let's look at this opportunity cost.

Instead of studying the *PPF* of pizzas and CDs, we'll hold the quantity of CDs produced constant and examine the *PPF* for pizzas and pizza ovens. Figure 2.5 shows this *PPF* as the blue curve *ABC.* If we devote no resources to producing pizza ovens, we produce at point *A.* If we produce 3 million pizzas, we can produce 6 pizza ovens at point *B.* If we produce no pizza, we can produce 10 ovens at point *C.*

The amount by which our production possibilities expand depends on the resources we devote to technological change and capital accumulation. If we devote no resources to this activity (point *A*), our *PPF* remains at *ABC*—the blue curve in Fig. 2.5. If we cut the current production of pizza and produce 6 ovens (point *B*), then in the future, we'll have more capital and our *PPF* will rotate outward to the position shown by the red curve. The fewer resources we devote to producing pizza and the more resources we

FIGURE 2.5 (X) myeconlab

Economic Growth

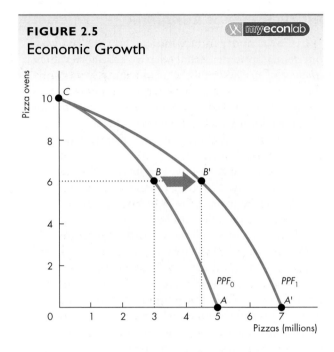

PPF_0 shows the limits to the production of pizza and pizza ovens, with the production of all other goods and services remaining the same. If we devote no resources to producing pizza ovens and produce 5 million pizzas, we remain at point A. But if we decrease pizza production to 3 million and produce 6 ovens, at point B, our production possibilities expand. After one period, the PPF rotates outward to PPF_1 and we can produce at point B', a point outside the original PPF. We can rotate the PPF outward, but we cannot avoid opportunity cost. The opportunity cost of producing more pizzas in the future is fewer pizzas today.

devote to producing ovens, the greater is the expansion of our production possibilities.

Economic growth is not free. To make it happen, we devote resources to producing new ovens and less to producing pizza. In Fig. 2.5, we move from *A* to *B.* There is no free lunch. The opportunity cost of more pizzas in the future is fewer pizzas today. Also, economic growth is no magic formula for abolishing scarcity. On the new production possibilities frontier, we continue to face a tradeoff and opportunity cost.

The ideas about economic growth that we have explored in the setting of the pizza industry also apply to nations. Let's look at two examples.

Economic Growth in Canada and Hong Kong

If as a nation we devote all our resources to producing consumption goods and none to research and capital accumulation, our production possibilities in the future will be the same as they are today. To expand our production possibilities in the future, we must devote fewer resources to producing consumption goods and some resources to accumulating capital and developing technologies so that we can produce more consumption goods in the future. The decrease in today's consumption is the opportunity cost of an increase in future consumption.

The experiences of Canada and Hong Kong make a striking example of the effects of our choices on the rate of economic growth. In 1965, the production possibilities per person in Canada were three times those in Hong Kong (see Fig. 2.6). Canada devoted one-fifth of its resources to accumulating capital and the other four-fifths to consumption. In 1965, Canada was at point *A* on its *PPF*. Hong Kong devoted one-third of its resources to accumulating capital and two-thirds to consumption. In 1965, Hong Kong was at point *A* on its *PPF*.

Since 1965, both countries have experienced economic growth, but growth in Hong Kong has been more rapid than that in Canada. Because Hong Kong devoted a bigger fraction of its resources to accumulating capital, its production possibilities have expanded more quickly.

By 2005, the production possibilities per person in Hong Kong and Canada were similar. If Hong Kong continues to devote more resources to accumulating capital than we do (at point *B* on its 2005 *PPF*), Hong Kong will continue to grow more rapidly than Canada. But if Hong Kong increases consumption and decreases capital accumulation (moving to point *D* on its 2005 *PPF*), then its rate of economic growth will slow.

Canada is typical of the rich industrial countries, which include the United States, Western Europe, and Japan. Hong Kong is typical of the fast-growing Asian economies, which include Taiwan, Thailand, South Korea, and China. Growth in these countries slowed during the Asia crisis of 1998 but quickly rebounded. Production possibilities expand in these countries by between 5 and almost 10 percent a year. If these high growth rates are maintained, these other Asian countries will eventually close the gap on Canada as Hong Kong has done.

FIGURE 2.6   myeconlab
Economic Growth in Canada and Hong Kong

Capital goods (per person)

Hong Kong in 2005

Canada in 2005

B

Hong Kong in 1965

D   *C*

A   *A*   Canada in 1965

0   Consumption goods (per person)

In 1965, the production possibilities per person in Canada were much larger than those in Hong Kong. But Hong Kong devoted more of its resources to accumulating capital than did Canada, so Hong Kong's production possibilities frontier has shifted outward more quickly than has that of Canada. In 2005, Hong Kong's production possibilities per person were similar to those in Canada.

REVIEW QUIZ

1 What are the two key factors that generate economic growth?

2 How does economic growth influence the production possibilities frontier?

3 What is the opportunity cost of economic growth?

4 Why has Hong Kong experienced faster economic growth than Canada has?

 Study Plan 2.3

Next, we're going to study another way in which we expand our production possibilities—the amazing fact that *both* buyers and sellers gain from specialization and trade.

Gains from Trade

PEOPLE CAN PRODUCE FOR THEMSELVES ALL THE goods that they consume, or they can concentrate on producing one good (or perhaps a few goods) and then trade with others—exchange some of their own goods for those of others. Concentrating on the production of only one good or a few goods is called *specialization*. We are going to discover how people gain by specializing in the production of the good in which they have a *comparative advantage* and trading with each other.

Comparative Advantage and Absolute Advantage

A person has a **comparative advantage** in an activity if that person can perform the activity at a lower opportunity cost than anyone else. Differences in opportunity costs arise from differences in individual abilities and from differences in the characteristics of capital and land.

No one excels at everything. One person is an outstanding pitcher but a poor catcher; another person is a brilliant lawyer but a poor teacher. In almost all human endeavours, what one person does easily, someone else finds difficult. The same applies to land and capital. One plot of land is fertile but has no mineral deposits; another plot of land has outstanding views but is infertile. One machine has great precision but is difficult to operate; another is fast but often breaks down.

Although no one excels at everything, some people excel and can outperform others in a large number of activities—and perhaps even in all activities. A person who is more productive than others has an **absolute advantage**.

Absolute advantage involves comparing productivities—production per hour—while comparative advantage involves comparing opportunity costs.

Notice that a person who has an absolute advantage does not have a *comparative* advantage in every activity. John Grisham is a better lawyer and a better writer of fast-paced thrillers than most people. He has an absolute advantage in these two activities. But compared to others, he is a better writer than lawyer, so his *comparative* advantage is in writing.

Because people's abilities and the quality of their resources differ, they have different opportunity costs of producing various goods. These differences in opportunity cost are the source of comparative advantage.

Let's explore the idea of comparative advantage by looking at two smoothie bars: one operated by Liz and the other operated by Joe.

Liz's Smoothie Bar Liz produces smoothies and salads. In Liz's high-tech bar, she can turn out either a smoothie or a salad every 90 seconds. If she spends all her time making smoothies, she produces 40 an hour. And if she spends all her time making salads, she also produces 40 an hour. If she splits her time equally between the two, she can produce 20 smoothies and 20 salads an hour. For each additional smoothie Liz produces, she must decrease her production of salads by one and for each additional salad she produces, she must decrease her production of smoothies by one. So

Liz's opportunity cost of producing 1 smoothie is 1 salad,

and

Liz's opportunity cost of producing 1 salad is 1 smoothie.

Liz's customers buy smoothies and salads in equal quantities, so she splits her time equally between the two items and produces 20 smoothies and 20 salads an hour.

Joe's Smoothie Bar Joe also produces both smoothies and salads. But Joe's bar is smaller than Liz's. Also, Joe has only one blender and it's a slow old machine. Even if Joe uses all his resources to produce smoothies, he can produce only 6 an hour. But Joe is pretty good in the salad department so if he uses all his resources to make salads, he can produce 30 an hour.

TABLE 2.1	Liz's Production Possibilities	
Item	**Minutes to produce 1**	**Quantity per hour**
Smoothies	1.5	40
Salads	1.5	40

TABLE 2.2	Joe's Production Possibilities	
Item	Minutes to produce 1	Quantity per hour
Smoothies	10	6
Salads	2	30

Joe's ability to make smoothies and salads is the same regardless of how he splits an hour between the two tasks. He can make a salad in 2 minutes or a smoothie in 10 minutes. For each additional smoothie Joe produces, he must decrease his production of salads by 5. And for each additional salad he produces, he must decrease his production of smoothies by 1/5 of a smoothie. So

Joe's opportunity cost of producing 1 smoothie is 5 salads,

and

Joe's opportunity cost of producing 1 salad is 1/5 of a smoothie.

Joe's customers, like Liz's, buy smoothies and salads in equal quantities. So Joe spends 50 minutes of each hour making smoothies and 10 minutes of each hour making salads. With this division of his time, Joe produces 5 smoothies and 5 salads an hour.

Liz's Absolute Advantage You can see from the numbers that describe the two smoothie bars that Liz is four times as productive as Joe—her 20 smoothies and salads an hour are four times Joe's 5. Liz has an absolute advantage—she is more productive than Joe in producing both smoothies and salads. But Liz has a comparative advantage in only one of the activities.

Liz's Comparative Advantage In which of the two activities does Liz have a comparative advantage? Recall that comparative advantage is a situation in which one person's opportunity cost of producing a good is lower than another person's opportunity cost of producing that same good. Liz has a comparative advantage in producing smoothies. Her opportunity cost of a smoothie is 1 salad, whereas Joe's opportunity cost of a smoothie is 5 salads.

Joe's Comparative Advantage If Liz has a comparative advantage in producing smoothies, Joe must have a comparative advantage in producing salads. His opportunity cost of a salad is 1/5 of a smoothie, while Liz's opportunity cost of a salad is 1 smoothie.

Achieving the Gains from Trade

Liz and Joe run into each other one evening in a singles bar. After a few minutes of getting acquainted, Liz tells Joe about her amazingly profitable smoothie business that is selling 20 smoothies and 20 salads an hour. Her only problem, she tells Joe, is that she wishes she could produce more because potential customers leave when her lines get too long.

Joe isn't sure whether to risk spoiling his chances by telling Liz about his own struggling business. But he takes the risk. When he explains to Liz that he spends 50 minutes of every hour making 5 smoothies and 10 minutes making 5 salads, Liz's eyes pop. "Have I got a deal for you!" she exclaims.

Here's the deal that Liz sketches on a table napkin. Joe stops making smoothies and allocates all his time to producing salads. And Liz increases her production of smoothies to 35 an hour and cuts her production of salads to 5 an hour—see Table 2.3(a).

TABLE 2.3	Liz and Joe Gain from Trade	
(a) Production	**Liz**	**Joe**
Smoothies	35	0
Salads	5	30
(b) Trade	**Liz**	**Joe**
Smoothies	sell 10	buy 10
Salads	buy 20	sell 20
(c) After trade	**Liz**	**Joe**
Smoothies	25	10
Salads	25	10
(d) Gains from trade	**Liz**	**Joe**
Smoothies	+5	+5
Salads	+5	+5

They then trade. Liz sells Joe 10 smoothies and Joe sells Liz 20 salads—the price of a smoothie is 2 salads—see Table 2.3(b).

After the trade, Joe has 10 salads—the 30 he produces minus the 20 he sells to Liz. And he has the 10 smoothies that he buys from Liz. So Joe doubles the quantities of smoothies and salads he can sell—see Table 2.3(c).

Liz has 25 smoothies— the 35 she produces minus the 10 she sells to Joe. And she has 25 salads— the 5 she produces plus the 20 she buys from Joe—see Table 2.3(c). Both Liz and Joe gain 5 smoothies and 5 salads—see Table 2.3(d).

Liz draws a graph (Fig. 2.7) to illustrate her suggestion. The blue *PPF* in part (a) shows Joe's production possibilities. He is producing at 5 smoothies and 5 salads an hour at point *A*. The blue *PPF* in part (b)

shows Liz's production possibilities. She is producing at 20 smoothies and 20 salads an hour at point *A*.

Liz's proposal is that they each produce more of the good in which they have a comparative advantage. Joe produces 30 salads and no smoothies at point *B* on his *PPF*. Liz produces 35 smoothies and 5 salads at the point *B* on her *PPF*.

Liz and Joe then trade— exchange—smoothies and salads at a price of 2 salads per smoothie, or 1/2 of a smoothie per salad. Joe gets smoothies for 2 salads each, which is less than the 5 salads it costs him to produce a smoothie. And Liz gets salads for 1/2 a smoothie each, which is less than the 1 smoothie that it costs her to produce a salad.

With trade, Joe has 10 smoothies and 10 salads at point *C*—a gain of 5 smoothies and 5 salads. Joe moves to a point *outside* his *PPF*.

FIGURE 2.7
The Gains from Trade

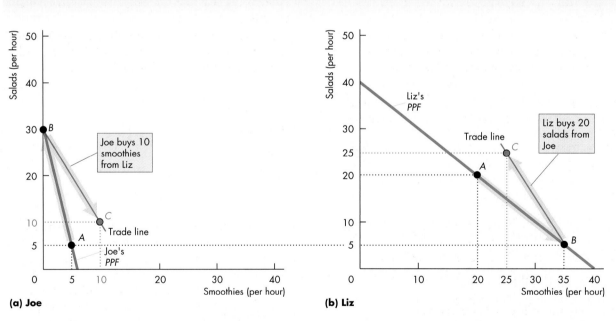

(a) Joe

(b) Liz

Joe initially produces at point *A* on his *PPF* in part (a), and Liz initially produces at point *A* on her *PPF* in part (b). Joe's opportunity cost of producing a salad is less than Liz's, so Joe has a comparative advantage in producing salad. Liz's opportunity cost of producing a smoothie is less than Joe's, so Liz has a comparative advantage in producing smoothies. If Joe specializes in salad, he produces 30 salads and no smoothies at point *B* on his *PPF*. If Liz produces 35 smoothies

and 5 salads, she produces at point *B* on her *PPF*. They exchange salads for smoothies along the red "Trade line." Liz buys salads from Joe for less than her opportunity cost of producing them, and Joe buys smoothies from Liz for less than his opportunity cost of producing them. Each goes to point *C*—a point outside his or her *PPF*. Both Joe and Liz increase production by 5 smoothies and 5 salads with no change in resources.

With trade, Liz has 25 smoothies and 25 salads at point *C*—a gain of 5 smoothies and 5 salads. Liz moves to a point *outside* her *PPF.*

Despite Liz's absolute advantage in producing smoothies and salads, both Liz and Joe gain from producing more of the good in which they have a comparative advantage and trading.

The gains that we achieve from international trade are similar to those achieved by Joe and Liz in this example. When Canadians buy T-shirts from China and when China buys regional jets from Canada, both countries gain. We get our shirts at a lower cost than that at which we can produce them, and China gets its regional jets at a lower cost than that at which it can produce them.

Dynamic Comparative Advantage

At any given point in time, the resources and technologies available determine the comparative advantages that individuals and nations have. But just by repeatedly producing a particular good or service, people become more productive in that activity, a phenomenon called **learning-by-doing**. Learning-by-doing is the basis of *dynamic* comparative advantage. **Dynamic comparative advantage** is a comparative advantage that a person (or country) possesses as a result of having specialized in a particular activity and, as a result of learning-by-doing, having become the producer with the lowest opportunity cost.

Singapore, for example, pursued dynamic comparative advantage vigorously when it decided to begin a bio-technology industry in which it initially didn't have a comparative advantage.

REVIEW QUIZ

1   What gives a person a comparative advantage?
2   Distinguish between comparative advantage and absolute advantage.
3   Is production still efficient when people specialize?
4   Why do people specialize and trade?
5   What are the gains from specialization and trade?
6   What is the source of the gains from trade?
7   How does dynamic comparative advantage arise?

myeconlab **Study Plan 2.4**

Economic Coordination

PEOPLE GAIN BY SPECIALIZING IN THE PRODUCTION of those goods and services in which they have a comparative advantage and then trading with each other. Liz and Joe, whose production of salads and smoothies we studied earlier in this chapter, can get together and make a deal that enables them to enjoy the gains from specialization and trade. But for billions of individuals to specialize and produce millions of different goods and services, their choices must somehow be coordinated.

Two competing economic coordination systems have been used—central economic planning and decentralized markets.

Central economic planning might appear to be the best system because it can express national priorities. But when this system was tried, as it was for 60 years in Russia, and for 30 years in China, it was a miserable failure. Today, these and most other previously planned economies are adopting a decentralized market system.

To make decentralized coordination work, four complementary social institutions that have evolved over many centuries are required. They are

- Firms
- Property rights
- Markets
- Money

Firms

A **firm** is an economic unit that hires factors of production and organizes those factors to produce and sell goods and services. Examples of firms are your local gas station, Wal-Mart, and Roots.

Firms coordinate a huge amount of economic activity. The coffee shop Second Cup, for example, might buy the machines and labour services of Liz and Joe and start to produce salads *and* smoothies at all its outlets.

But if a firm gets too big, it can't keep track of all the information that is needed to coordinate its activities. For this reason, firms themselves specialize and trade with each other. For example, Wal-Mart could produce all the things that it sells in its stores. And it could produce all the raw materials that are used to produce the things that it sells. But Sam Walton would not have become one of the wealthiest people in the world if he had followed that path. Instead, Wal-Mart buys from other firms that specialize in the production of a narrow range of items. And this trade takes place in markets.

Property Rights

The social arrangements that govern the ownership, use, and disposal of resources, goods, and services are called **property rights**. *Real property* includes land and buildings—the things we call property in ordinary speech—and durable goods such as plant and equipment. *Financial property* includes stocks and bonds and money in the bank. *Intellectual property* is the intangible product of creative effort. This type of property includes books, music, computer programs, and inventions of all kinds and is protected by copyrights and patents.

Where property rights are enforced, people have the incentive to specialize and produce the goods in which each person has a comparative advantage. Where people can easily steal the production of others, then time, energy, and resources are devoted not to production but to protecting possessions. If we had not developed property rights, we would still be hunting and gathering like our Stone Age ancestors.

Markets

In ordinary speech, the word *market* means a place where people buy and sell goods such as fish, meat, fruits, and vegetables. In economics, a *market* has a more general meaning. A **market** is any arrangement that enables buyers and sellers to get information and to do business with each other. An example is the market in which oil is bought and sold—the world oil market. The world oil market is not a place. It is the network of oil producers, oil users, wholesalers, and brokers who buy and sell oil. In the world oil market, decision makers do not meet physically. They make deals throughout the world by telephone, fax, and direct computer link.

Markets have evolved because they facilitate trade. Without organized markets, we would miss out on a substantial part of the potential gains from trade. Enterprising individuals and firms, each pursuing their own self-interest, have profited from making markets—standing ready to buy or sell the items in which they specialize. But markets can work only when property rights exist.

Money

Money is any commodity or token that is generally acceptable as a means of payment. Liz and Joe didn't use money in the example above. They exchanged salads and smoothies. In principle, trade in markets can exchange any item for any other item. But you can perhaps imagine how complicated life would be if we exchanged goods for other goods. The "invention" of money makes trading in markets much more efficient.

Circular Flows Through Markets

Figure 2.8 shows the flows that result from the choices that households and firms make. Households specialize and choose the quantities of labour, land, capital, and entrepreneurship to sell or rent to firms. Firms choose the quantities of factors of production to hire. These (red) flows go through the *factor markets*. Households choose the quantities of goods and services to buy, and firms choose the quantities to produce. These (red) flows go through the *goods markets*. Households receive incomes and make expenditures on goods and services (green flows). These green flows are payments for the corresponding real (red) flows.

How do markets coordinate all these decisions?

Coordinating Decisions

Markets coordinate individual decisions through price adjustments. To see how, think about your local market for hamburgers. Suppose that some people who want to buy hamburgers are not able to do so. To make the choices of buyers and sellers compatible, buyers must scale down their appetites or more hamburgers must be offered for sale (or both must happen). A rise in the price of a hamburger produces this outcome. A higher price encourages producers to offer more hamburgers for sale. It also encourages some people to change their lunch plans. Fewer people buy hamburgers, and more buy hot dogs. More hamburgers (and more hot dogs) are offered for sale.

Alternatively, suppose that more hamburgers are available than people want to buy. In this case, to make the choices of buyers and sellers compatible, more hamburgers must be bought or fewer hamburgers must be offered for sale (or both). A fall in the price of a hamburger achieves this outcome. A lower price encourages firms to produce fewer hamburgers. It also encourages people to buy more hamburgers.

FIGURE 2.8
Circular Flows in the Market Economy

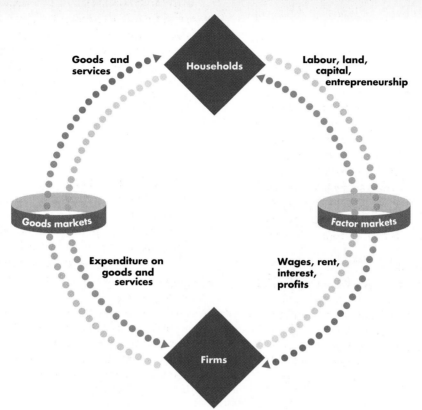

Households and firms make economic choices and markets coordinate these choices.

Households choose the quantities of labour, land, capital, and entrepreneurship to sell or rent to firms in exchange for wages, rent, interest, and profit. Households also choose how to spend their incomes on the various types of goods and services available.

Firms choose the quantities of factors of production to hire and the quantities of the goods and services to produce.

Goods markets and factor markets coordinate these choices of households and firms. The clockwise red flows are real flows—the flows of factors of production from households to firms and the flows of goods and services from firms to households. The counterclockwise green flows are the payments for the red flows—the flow of income for the factors of production and the flow of expenditure on goods and services.

REVIEW QUIZ

1 Why are social institutions such as markets and property rights necessary?
2 What are the main functions of markets?
3 What are the flows in the market economy that go from firms to households? Which of these flows is a money flow and which is a real flow?

myeconlab **Study Plan 2.5**

◆ You have now begun to see how economists approach economic questions. Scarcity, choice, and divergent opportunity costs explain why we specialize and trade and why firms, property rights, markets, and money have developed. You can see all around you the lessons you've learned in this chapter. *Reading Between the Lines* on pp. 48–49 gives an example. It explores the *PPF* of a student like you and the choices that students must make that influence their own economic growth—the growth of their incomes.

The Cost and Benefit of Education

GLOBE AND MAIL, AUGUST 28, 2002

Academics leap to defence of the MBA

They don't come with a guarantee, but business degrees offer students well-paying jobs with reputable companies, say many of Canada's top business schools, throwing coldwater on a new study questioning the value of an MBA. ...

After surveying decades of research, Jeffrey Pfeffer and Christina Fong of Stanford's graduate school of business have concluded that, with the possible exception of the most elite programs, master's degrees in business administration teach little that would be of real use in the business world. ...

The salaries for these graduates are a telling story. At Queen's University's School of Business, for example, the average starting salary is $95,000. Before joining the program, the average salary of students is $59,750. And at the Rotman School of Management at the University of Toronto, students entering the two-year program have salaries in the $50,000 [range] on average. But the average starting salary for this year's graduate was $89,000. ...

Brian Bemmels, associate dean for academic programs at the University of British Columbia's faculty of commerce, said the research article forces schools to evaluate their programs. He added that the article is based on a lot of opinion.

UBC's business school made a major change in 1995, restructuring its MBA program and reducing it to 15 months from two years to minimize losses of income to students. The average age of students in the program is 31.

Mr. Bemmels said the demand for an MBA degree speaks for itself. UBC had well over 700 applicants for 100 seats this year. Only 17 per cent of the incoming class has a business degree, he said. The rest are graduates of medicine, engineering and general arts.

"All these people wouldn't be doing it if they didn't think it was valuable," Mr. Bemmels said.

"I don't believe the notion that they have been fooled and tricked into something that's no good for them," he added.

Reprinted with permission from *The Globe and Mail.*

Essence of the Story

■ Jeffrey Pfeffer and Christina Fong of the Stanford Graduate School of Business say that MBA programs teach little of use in the business world.

■ The salaries earned by MBA graduates tell a different story.

■ The average starting salary for an MBA is $95,000, up from $59,750 before the MBA.

■ At the Rotman School of Management at the University of Toronto, students entering the two-year program have an average salary of $50,000 and an average starting salary of $89,000 after graduation.

■ Brian Bemmels said the UBC business school had over 700 applicants for 100 places and most were graduates of medicine, engineering, and general arts.

Economic Analysis

■ Education increases human capital and expands production possibilities.

■ The opportunity cost of a degree is forgone consumption. The payoff is an increase in lifetime production possibilities.

■ Figure 1 shows the choices facing a high school graduate who can consume education goods and services and consumption goods and services on the blue *PPF*.

■ Working full time, this person can consume at point *A* on the blue *PPF* in Fig. 1.

■ By attending university, the student moves from point *A* to point *B* along her *PPF*, forgoes current consumption (the opportunity cost of education), and increases the use of educational goods and services.

■ On graduating from university, earnings jump, so production possibilities expand to the red *PPF* in Fig. 1.

■ Figure 2 shows a university graduate's choices. The blue curve is the same *PPF* as the red *PPF* in Fig. 1.

■ Working full time, this person earns enough to consume at point *C* on the blue *PPF* in Fig. 2.

■ By pursuing an MBA, the student moves from point *C* to point *D* along her *PPF*, forgoes current consumption (the opportunity cost of an MBA), and increases the use of educational goods and services.

■ With an MBA, a person's earnings jump again, so production possibilities expand to the red *PPF* in Fig. 2.

■ For people who have the required ability, the benefits of post-secondary and post-graduate education exceed the costs.

You're the Voter

■ The Canada Millennium Scholarship Foundation, funded by the federal government, provides $4,000 a year to 900 young Canadians.

■ Do you think the Canada Millennium Scholarship Foundation should be expanded so that more students can benefit from it?

■ With the huge return from post-secondary and post-graduate education, why don't more people remain in school for longer?

■ Would you vote for or against a tax increase to provide greater funding for the Canada Millennium Scholarship Foundation? Why?

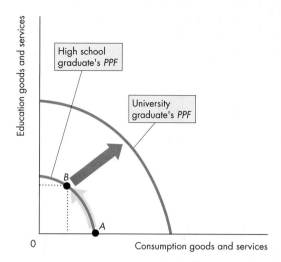

Figure 1　High school graduate's choices

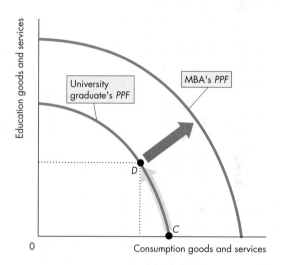

Figure 2　University graduate's choices

SUMMARY

KEY POINTS

Production Possibilities and Opportunity Cost (pp. 34–36)

- The production possibilities frontier, *PPF*, is the boundary between production levels that are attainable and those that are not attainable when all the available resources are used to their limit.
- Production efficiency occurs at points on the *PPF*.
- Along the *PPF*, the opportunity cost of producing more of one good is the amount of the other good that must be given up.
- The opportunity cost of a good increases as production of the good increases.

Using Resources Efficiently (pp. 37–39)

- The marginal cost of a good is the opportunity cost of producing one more unit.
- The marginal benefit from a good is the maximum amount of another good that a person is willing to forgo to obtain more of the first good.
- The marginal benefit of a good decreases as the amount of the good available increases.
- Resources are used efficiently when the marginal cost of each good is equal to its marginal benefit.

Economic Growth (pp. 40–41)

- Economic growth, which is the expansion of production possibilities, results from capital accumulation and technological change.
- The opportunity cost of economic growth is forgone current consumption.

Gains from Trade (pp. 42–45)

- A person has a comparative advantage in producing a good if that person can produce the good at a lower opportunity cost than everyone else.
- People gain by specializing in the activity in which they have a comparative advantage and trading with others.
- Dynamic comparative advantage arises from learning-by-doing.

Economic Coordination (pp. 45–47)

- Firms coordinate a large amount of economic activity, but there is a limit to the efficient size of a firm.
- Markets coordinate the economic choices of people and firms.
- Markets can work efficiently only when property rights exist.
- Money makes trading in markets more efficient.

KEY FIGURES

KEY TERMS

PROBLEMS

Go to **myeconlab** for solutions to odd-numbered problems and additional exercises.

1. Calculate Wendell's opportunity cost of one hour of tennis when he increases the time he plays tennis from
   a. 6 hours a week.
   b. 8 hours a week.

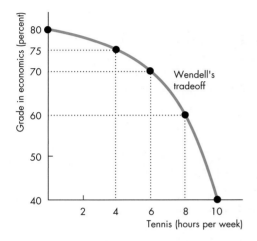

2. Calculate Tina's opportunity cost of a day of skiing when she increases her time spent skiing from
   a. 2 to 4 days a month.
   b. 4 to 6 days a month.

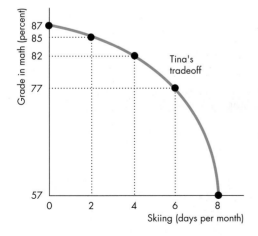

3. Wendell, in problem 1, has the following marginal benefit curve:

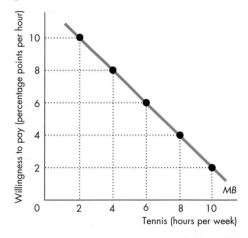

   a. If Wendell is efficient, what is his grade?
   b. Why would Wendell be worse off getting a higher grade?

4. Tina in problem 2, has the following marginal benefit curve:

   a. If Tina is efficient, how much does she ski?
   b. Why would Tina be worse off spending more days a month skiing?

5. Sunland's production possibilities are

Food (kilograms per month)		Sunscreen (litres per month)
300	and	0
200	and	50
100	and	100
0	and	150

   a. Draw a graph of Sunland's *PPF.*

b. What are Sunland's opportunity costs of producing food and sunscreen at each output?

6. Jane's Island's production possibilities are

Corn (kilograms per month)		Cloth (metres per month)
6	and	0
4	and	2
2	and	4
0	and	6

a. Draw a graph of the *PPF* on Jane's Island.
b. What are Jane's opportunity costs of producing corn and cloth at each output in the table?

7. In problem 5, to get a litre of sunscreen the people of Sunland are willing to give up 5 kilograms of food if they have 25 litres of sunscreen, 2 kilograms of food if they have 75 litres of sunscreen, and 1 kilogram of food if they have 125 litres of sunscreen.
a. Draw a graph of Sunland's marginal benefit from sunscreen.
b. What is the efficient quantity of sunscreen?

8. In problem 6, to get a metre of cloth Jane is willing to give up 1.5 kilograms of corn if she has 2 metres of cloth; 1.0 kilogram of corn if she has 4 metres of cloth; and 0.5 kilogram of corn if she has 6 metres of cloth.
a. Draw a graph of Jane's marginal benefit from cloth.
b. What is Jane's efficient quantity of cloth?

9. Busyland's production possibilities are

Food (kilograms per month)		Sunscreen (litres per month)
150	and	0
100	and	100
50	and	200
0	and	300

Calculate Busyland's opportunity costs of food and sunscreen at each output in the table.

10. Joe Island's production possibilities are

Corn (kilograms per month)		Cloth (metres per month)
12	and	0
8	and	1
4	and	2
0	and	3

What are Joe's opportunity costs of producing corn and cloth at each output in the table?

11. In problems 5 and 9, Sunland and Busyland each produce and consume 100 kilograms of food and 100 litres of sunscreen per month, and they do not trade. Now the countries begin to trade with each other.
a. What good does Sunland sell to Busyland and what good does it buy from Busyland?
b. If Sunland and Busyland divide the total output of food and sunscreen equally, what are the gains from trade?

12. In problems 6 and 10, Jane's Island and Joe's Island each produce and consume 4 kilograms of corn and 2 metres of cloth and they do not trade. Now the islands begin to trade.
a. What good does Jane sell to Joe and what good does Jane buy from Joe?
b. If Jane and Joe divide the total output of corn and cloth equally, what are the gains from trade?

CRITICAL THINKING

1. After you have studied *Reading Between the Lines* on pp. 48–49, answer the following questions:
a. At what point on the blue *PPF* in Fig. 1 on p. 49 is the combination of education goods and services and consumption goods and services efficient? Explain your answer.
b. Students are facing rising tuition. How does higher tuition change the opportunity cost of education and how does it change the *PPF*s in Fig. 1 and Fig. 2?
c. Who receives the benefits from education? Is the marginal cost of education equal to the marginal benefit of education? Is resource use in the market for education efficient?

WEB EXERCISES

Use the links on (X) myeconlab **to work the following exercise.**

1. Obtain data on the tuition and other costs of enrolling in the MBA program at a school that interests you.
a. Draw a *PPF* that shows the tradeoff that you would face if you decided to enroll in the MBA program.
b. Do you think the marginal benefit of an MBA exceeds the marginal cost?

Your Economic Revolution

You are making progress in your study of economics. You've already encountered the big questions and big ideas of economics. And you've learned about the key insight that specialization and exchange create economic wealth.

You are studying economics at a time that future historians might call the *Information Revolution*. We reserve the word *Revolution* for big events that influence all future generations.

During the *Agricultural Revolution*, which occurred 10,000 years ago, people learned to domesticate animals and plant crops. They stopped roaming in search of food and settled in villages and eventually towns and cities, where they developed markets in which to exchange their products.

During the *Industrial Revolution*, which began 240 years ago, people used science to create new technologies. This revolution brought extraordinary wealth for some but created conditions in which others were left behind. It brought social and political tensions that we still face today.

During today's *Information Revolution*, people who embraced the new technologies prospered on an unimagined scale. But the incomes and living standards of the less educated are falling behind, and social and political tensions are increasing. Today's revolution has a global dimension. Some of the winners live in previously poor countries in Asia, and some of the losers live here in North America.

So you are studying economics at an interesting time. Whatever *your* motivation is for studying economics, *our* objective is to help you do well in your course, to enjoy it, and to develop a deeper understanding of the economic world around you.

Three reasons why we hope that we both succeed: First, a decent understanding of economics will help you to become a full participant in the Information Revolution. Second, an understanding of economics will help you play a more effective role as a citizen and voter and enable you to add your voice to those who are looking for solutions to our social and political problems. Third, you will enjoy the sheer fun of *understanding* the forces at play and how they are shaping our world.

If you are finding economics interesting, think seriously about majoring in the subject. A degree in economics gives the best training available in problem solving, offers lots of opportunities to develop conceptual skills, and opens doors to a wide range of graduate courses, including the MBA, and to a wide range of jobs. You can read more about the benefits of an economics degree in the essay by Robert Whaples and Harvey King in your *Study Guide*.

Economics was born during the Industrial Revolution. We'll look at its birth and meet its founder, Adam Smith. Then we'll talk about the progress that economists have made and some of the outstanding policy problems of today with one of today's most distinguished economists, Lawrence H. Summers, President of Harvard University.

The Sources of Economic Wealth

> "It is not from the benevolence of the butcher, the brewer, or the baker that we expect our dinner, but from their regard to their own interest."
>
> ADAM SMITH
> *The Wealth of Nations*

THE FATHER OF ECONOMICS

Adam Smith *was a giant of a scholar who contributed to ethics and jurisprudence as well as economics. Born in 1723 in Kirkcaldy, a small fishing town near Edinburgh, Scotland, Smith was the only child of the town's customs officer (who died before Adam was born).*

His first academic appointment, at age 28, was as Professor of Logic at the University of Glasgow. He subsequently became tutor to a wealthy Scottish duke, whom he accompanied on a two-year grand European tour, following which he received a pension of £300 a year— ten times the average income at that time.

With the financial security of his pension, Smith devoted ten years to writing An Inquiry into the Nature and Causes of the Wealth of Nations, *which was published in 1776. Many people had written on economic issues before Adam Smith, but he made economics a science. Smith's account was so broad and authoritative that no subsequent writer on economics could advance ideas without tracing their connections to those of Adam Smith.*

THE ISSUES

Why are some nations wealthy while others are poor? This question lies at the heart of economics. And it leads directly to a second question: What can poor nations do to become wealthy?

Adam Smith, who is regarded by many scholars as the founder of economics, attempted to answer these questions in his book *The Wealth of Nations*, published in 1776. Smith was pondering these questions at the height of the Industrial Revolution. During these years, new technologies were invented and applied to the manufacture of cotton and wool cloth, iron, transportation, and agriculture.

Smith wanted to understand the sources of economic wealth, and he brought his acute powers of observation and abstraction to bear on the question. His answer:

- The division of labour
- Free markets

The division of labour—breaking tasks down into simple tasks and becoming skilled in those tasks—is the source of "the greatest improvement in the productive powers of labour," said Smith. The division of labour became even more productive when it was applied to creating new technologies. Scientists and engineers, trained in extremely narrow fields, became specialists at inventing. Their powerful skills accelerated the advance of technology, so by the 1820s, machines could make consumer goods faster and more accurately than any craftsman could. And by the 1850s, machines could make other machines that labour alone could never have made.

But, said Smith, the fruits of the division of labour are limited by the extent of the market. To make the market as large as possible, there must be no impediments to free trade both within a country and among countries. Smith argued that when each person makes the best possible economic choice, that choice leads as if by "an invisible hand" to the best outcome for society as a whole. The butcher, the brewer, and the baker each pursue their own interests but, in doing so, also serve the interests of everyone else.

THEN

Adam Smith speculated that one person, working hard, using the hand tools available in the 1770s, might possibly make 20 pins a day. Yet, he observed, by using those same hand tools but breaking the process into a number of individually small operations in which people specialize —by the *division of labour*—ten people could make a staggering 48,000 pins a day. One draws out the wire, another straightens it, a third cuts it, a fourth points it, a fifth grinds it. Three specialists make the head, and a fourth attaches it. Finally, the pin is polished and packaged. But a large market is needed to support the division of labour: one factory employing ten workers would need to sell more than 15 million pins a year to stay in business.

NOW

If Adam Smith were here today, the computer chip would fascinate him. He would see it as an extraordinary example of the productivity of the division of labour and of the use of machines to make machines that make other machines. From a design of a chip's intricate circuits, cameras transfer an image to glass plates that work like stencils. Workers prepare silicon wafers on which the circuits are printed. Some slice the wafers, others polish them, others bake them, and yet others coat them with a light-sensitive chemical. Machines transfer a copy of the circuit onto the wafer. Chemicals then etch the design onto the wafer. Further processes deposit atom-sized transistors and aluminum connectors. Finally, a laser separates the hundreds of chips on the wafer. Every stage in the process of creating a computer chip uses other computer chips. And like the pin of the 1770s, the computer chip of today benefits from a large market—a global market—to buy chips in the huge quantities in which they are produced efficiently.

Many economists have worked on the big themes that Adam Smith began. One of these is Lawrence H. Summers, President of Harvard University and a distinguished economist.

Lawrence H. Summers *is President of Harvard University. Born in 1954 in New Haven, Connecticut, into a family of distinguished economists, he was an undergraduate at the Massachusetts Institute of Technology and a graduate student at Harvard University. While still in his 20s, he became one of the youngest tenured economics professors at Harvard University. In Washington, he has held a succession of public service jobs at the World Bank and in the U.S. government, culminating in 1999 with his appointment as Secretary of the Treasury—the chief financial officer of the United States and the president's highest-ranking advisor.*

Dr. Summers's research has covered an enormous range of macroeconomic and public policy issues that include capital taxation, unemployment, global financial crises, the transition to a market economy in Eastern Europe, and the problem of speeding progress in the developing countries.

Michael Parkin and Robin Bade talked with Lawrence Summers about his career and the progress that economists have made since the pioneering days of Adam Smith.

Lawrence H. Summers

How does Adam Smith's assessment of the "nature and causes of the wealth of nations" look today in light of the lessons that economists have learned over the past two centuries?

Adam Smith is looking very good today. I think one of the most important insights of the social sciences of the last several centuries is Smith's idea that good things can come from the invisible hand—from decentralization rather than from central planning and direction. But Smith is also prescient in recognizing the various qualifications to the argument for the invisible hand, whether involving fairness, externalities, or monopoly.

What do we know today that Adam Smith didn't know?

We know today much more than Smith did about economic fluctuations and about the role of money—about what we today call macroeconomics. We know more today about economic situations that involve bargaining, whether between two individuals or between small numbers of firms in an industry, or between a buyer and a seller. We know much more today about markets without perfect information. I know how good my used car is when I sell it—you don't when you buy it. I know whether I'm sick when I buy medical insurance, but the insurance company has to try to figure it out. The role of information in markets, which turns out to be quite profound, is something we understand much better today. And we also understand much better today the role of politics and governments in shaping the economy, which is far larger than it was in Smith's day.

Coincidentally, a few days before we're holding this conversation, a new nation was born— East Timor. What advice can economists offer a new and extremely poor nation as it takes its first steps?

Much of economic success involves strong rights to property. Has anyone ever washed a rented car or taken as good care of their hotel room as their home? When people own their farmlands, they're much more likely to farm them sustainably. When businesses own their machinery, they're much more likely to take care of it. When individuals own what they produce, they're much more likely to work hard.

Strong property rights and the framework of laws that support them are profoundly important to the market-based exchanges that are essential to economic success. So also is stable money that can be a basis for exchange. So also is an educated and capable population. But if there is a single lesson that is important for a starting economy, it is that strong property rights can motivate individuals.

One lesson that we've learned from your work at the World Bank is that the return to educating girls in developing countries is very high. What did you discover in that work?

Primary education, and especially for girls, may be the highest return investment available in the developing world. Those who read produce more and therefore earn more. Girls who are educated grow up to be better mothers who have smaller, happier, healthier families. Women who are educated are empowered with greater career options. They are less likely to fall into prostitution, and that reduces the spread of AIDS.

Women who are educated are much more likely to take care of the environment. So it is in many respects that primary education, and especially that of girls, generates very large returns.

Are there any other activities that yield comparable returns for developing countries?

Maybe some investments in health care that generate very large returns—it's a difficult evaluation to make. The really crucial lesson is that a country's most precious assets are its people, and investments in people are likely to be the most important investments of all.

Some of your earliest research was on taxing the income from capital. Why isn't the income from capital just like the income from labour?

Think about it this way: Two individuals both earn a hundred dollars. One spends it all this year; the other saves half of it and earns 10 percent interest next year. Who should pay more total taxes? Plausibly, for fairness, both should pay the same tax. A tax on income will lead to the same taxes in the first year for the two individuals; and higher taxes in the second year for the individual who saved.

In effect, taxes on capital income are taxes on future consumption, and it is far from clear why a society should want to tax future consumption more highly than present consumption.

On the other hand, very large fortunes often show up as capital income, and so designing a workable and fair tax system that doesn't tax investment income is something that is very difficult to do.

> " *The really crucial lesson is that a country's most precious assets are its people, and investments in people are likely to be the most important investments of all.* "

Would you say that we have not yet managed to figure this one out?

We'll all be working on finding the best tax systems for a long time to come. And it may mean that the income tax is, as Churchill said of democracy, terrible but the best alternative.

The United States has a large and persistent current account deficit, a low personal saving rate, and a projected deficit in the Social Security and Medicare trust funds. Are you concerned about these problems?

Herb Stein, who was a leading American policy economist, once said that the unsustainable cannot be sustained and must surely end!

This is a concern, given that U.S. national debt to foreigners is rising faster than U.S. income. And it's a concern in terms of the financing of Social Security and Medicare as our population ages. In a way, the solution to both these problems is more American saving, because that will put us in a stronger position as our population ages, and will allow us to have investment in the United States without incurring debts to foreigners.

Probably the most potent way of increasing a country's national savings is to improve the position of its budget. Whether to increase taxes or cut expenditures is a judgment for the congress to debate. My guess is that some combination would be appropriate. There are aspects of expenditures that are going to be hard to control. On the other hand, there are other aspects in terms of transfer payments and terms of various subsidies where economies probably are possible. And one virtue of a strong fiscal position is that it reduces interest expense down the road.

Did you always want to be an economist? How did you choose economics?

I thought I would be a mathematician or a physicist, but found myself very interested in questions of public policy. I was very involved in debate when I was in college. So I found myself wanting very much to combine an interest in public policy issues with an analytical approach, and economics gave me a way to do that. I also found that I had some aptitude, relative to my aptitude for pure mathematics or physics, so I gravitated to economics.

What led a brilliant academic economist to Washington? What did you want to achieve?

I hoped to put to use some of what I had learned in my studies in a direct way and to enhance my understanding of the way actual economies work by seeing how the policy process operated. I had a great time in Washington and feel that my economics training made a huge difference in everything I did. Whether it was thinking about how to respond to the Mexican and Asian financial crises or working on financial deregulation. Whether it was choosing optimal investments for the Customs Department in protecting our borders or designing tax incentives to promote saving. Whether it was supporting the protection of the Social Security trust fund or thinking about enforcement policies against corporate tax shelters. Principles of economics—in terms of maximizing benefits relative to costs, in terms of always thinking of the margin, in terms of always recognizing the opportunity cost of choices taken, in terms of always needing to see things add up—was quite valuable.

And what insights does economics bring to the task of running a major university?

I came to Harvard because I thought after my time in government the two most important resources that were going to shape the economies of the future were leaders and new ideas, and those are the two things that a university produces.

Successful leadership in a university is all about what economists think about all the time—incentives—whether it's for professors to do a good job teaching, attracting the best scholars in a particular area, or motivating concern and research about the most important problems.

Leadership and management for the university are very much about economics because they're very much about incentives. Some of them are pecuniary and involve money, but other incentives come from people's feelings of being appreciated; they come from the teams in which people have an opportunity to work; they come from the way in which the university is organized. If working at the treasury was heavily about applied macroeconomics, leadership in the university is heavily about applied microeconomics.

What is your advice to a student who is just setting out to become an economist? What other subjects work well with economics?

The best advice to students is, don't be a commodity that's available in a perfectly competitive market. Stand out by developing your own distinctive expertise in something you care deeply about. It matters much less what it is and much more that it be yours and it not be a hundred other people's.

I think there is enormous potential in almost every area of economics, but I think that the people who will contribute the most to economics over the next quarter century will be those who have some keen understanding of the context in which economics is playing out—the international context, the technological context, and the political context. So my hope would be that those interested in economics would understand that economics is very different from physics in that it is tracking a changing reality and that in order to do the best economics in a given period, you have to be able to track that changing reality, and that means understanding international, technological, and political contexts.

Demand and Supply

CHAPTER 3

Slide, Rocket, and Roller Coaster

Slide, rocket, and roller coaster—Canada's Wonderland rides? No, they are commonly used descriptions of price changes.

The price of a personal computer took a dramatic slide from around $3,000 in 2000 to around $500 in 2005. The price of gasoline rocketed in the summer of 2005. The prices of coffee, bananas, and other agricultural products rise and fall like a roller coaster.

You've learned that economics is about the choices people make to cope with scarcity, and how those choices respond to incentives. Prices are one of the incentives to which people respond. You're now going to see how prices are determined by demand and supply.

The demand and supply model is the main tool of economics. It helps us to answer the big economic question: What, how, and for whom are goods and services produced. It also helps us to say when the pursuit of self-interest promotes the social interest.

◆ Your careful study of this topic will bring big rewards both in your further study of economics and in your everyday life. When you have completed your study of demand and supply, you will be able to explain how prices are determined and make predictions about price slides, rockets, and roller coasters. Once you understand demand and supply, you will view the world through new eyes.

After studying this chapter, you will be able to

- ■ **Describe a competitive market and think about a price as an opportunity cost**
- ■ **Explain the influences on demand**
- ■ **Explain the influences on supply**
- ■ **Explain how demand and supply determine prices and quantities bought and sold**
- ■ **Use demand and supply to make predictions about changes in prices and quantities**

Markets and Prices

WHEN YOU NEED A NEW PAIR OF RUNNING SHOES, want a bagel and a latte, plan to upgrade your stereo system, or need to fly home for Thanksgiving, you must find a place where people sell those items or offer those services. The place in which you find them is a *market*. You learned in Chapter 2 (p. 46) that a market is any arrangement that enables buyers and sellers to get information and to do business with each other.

A market has two sides: buyers and sellers. There are markets for *goods* such as apples and hiking boots, for *services* such as haircuts and tennis lessons, for *resources* such as computer programmers and earth-movers, and for other manufactured *inputs* such as memory chips and auto parts. There are also markets for money such as Japanese yen and for financial securities such as Yahoo! stock. Only our imagination limits what can be traded in markets.

Some markets are physical places where buyers and sellers meet and where an auctioneer or a broker helps to determine the prices. Examples of this type of market are the wholesale fish, meat, and produce markets and car auction markets.

Some markets are groups of people spread around the world who never meet and know little about each other but are connected through the Internet or by telephone and fax. Examples are the e-commerce markets and currency markets.

But most markets are unorganized collections of buyers and sellers. You do most of your trading in this type of market. An example is the market for basketball shoes. The buyers in this $3 billion-a-year market are the 45 million North Americans who play basketball (or who want to make a fashion statement). The sellers are the tens of thousands of retail sports equipment and footwear stores. Each buyer can visit several different stores, and each seller knows that the buyer has a choice of stores.

Markets vary in the intensity of competition that buyers and sellers face. In this chapter, we're going to study a **competitive market**—a market that has many buyers and many sellers, so no single buyer or seller can influence the price.

Producers offer items for sale only if the price is high enough to cover their opportunity cost. And consumers respond to changing opportunity cost by seeking cheaper alternatives to expensive items.

We are going to study the way people respond to *prices* and the forces that determine prices. But to pur-

sue these tasks, we need to understand the relationship between a price and an opportunity cost.

In everyday life, the *price* of an object is the number of dollars that must be given up in exchange for it. Economists refer to this price as the **money price**.

The *opportunity cost* of an action is the highest-valued alternative forgone. If, when you buy a coffee, the highest-valued thing you forgo is some gum, then the opportunity cost of the coffee is the *quantity* of gum forgone. We can calculate the quantity of gum forgone from the money prices of coffee and gum.

If the money price of coffee is $1 a cup and the money price of gum is 50¢ a pack, then the opportunity cost of one cup of coffee is two packs of gum. To calculate this opportunity cost, we divide the price of a cup of coffee by the price of a pack of gum and find the *ratio* of one price to the other. The ratio of one price to another is called a **relative price**, and a *relative price is an opportunity cost*.

We can express the relative price of coffee in terms of gum or any other good. The normal way of expressing a relative price is in terms of a "basket" of all goods and services. To calculate this relative price, we divide the money price of a good by the money price of a "basket" of all goods (called a *price index*). The resulting relative price tells us the opportunity cost of the good in terms of how much of the "basket" we must give up to buy it.

The theory of demand and supply that we are about to study determines *relative prices,* and the word "price" means *relative* price. When we predict that a price will fall, we do not mean that its *money* price will fall—although it might. We mean that its *relative* price will fall. That is, its price will fall *relative* to the average price of other goods and services.

REVIEW QUIZ

1 What is the distinction between a money price and a relative price?
2 Why is a relative price an opportunity cost?
3 Can you think of an example of a good whose money price and relative price have risen?
4 Can you think of an example of a good whose money price and relative price have fallen?

myeconlab **Study Plan 3.1**

Let's begin our study of demand and supply, starting with demand.

Demand

IF YOU DEMAND SOMETHING, THEN YOU

1. Want it,
2. Can afford it, and
3. Plan to buy it.

Wants are the unlimited desires or wishes that people have for goods and services. How many times have you thought that you would like something "if only you could afford it" or "if it weren't so expensive"? Scarcity guarantees that many—perhaps most—of our wants will never be satisfied. Demand reflects a decision about which wants to satisfy.

The **quantity demanded** of a good or service is the amount that consumers plan to buy during a given time period at a particular price. The quantity demanded is not necessarily the same as the quantity actually bought. Sometimes the quantity demanded exceeds the amount of goods available, so the quantity bought is less than the quantity demanded.

The quantity demanded is measured as an amount per unit of time. For example, suppose that you buy one cup of coffee a day. The quantity of coffee that you demand can be expressed as 1 cup per day, 7 cups per week, or 365 cups per year. Many factors influence buying plans and one of them is price. We look first at the relationship between the quantity demanded of a good and its price. To study this relationship, we keep all other influences on buying plans the same and we ask: How, other things remaining the same, does the quantity demanded of a good change as its price changes?

The law of demand provides the answer.

The Law of Demand

The **law of demand** states

Other things remaining the same, the higher the price of a good, the smaller is the quantity demanded; and the lower the price of a good, the greater is the quantity demanded.

Why does a higher price reduce the quantity demanded? For two reasons:

■ Substitution effect
■ Income effect

Substitution Effect When the price of a good rises, other things remaining the same, its *relative* price—its opportunity cost—rises. Although each good is unique, it has *substitutes*—other goods that can be used in its place. As the opportunity cost of a good rises, people buy less of that good and more of its substitutes.

Income Effect When a price rises and all other influences on buying plans remain unchanged, the price rises *relative* to people's incomes. So faced with a higher price and an unchanged income, people cannot afford to buy all the things they previously bought. They must decrease the quantities demanded of at least some goods and services, and normally, the good whose price has increased will be one of the goods that people buy less of.

To see the substitution effect and the income effect at work, think about the effects of a change in the price of a recordable compact disc—a CD-R. Several different goods are substitutes for a CD-R. For example, an audiotape and prerecorded CD provide services similar to those of a CD-R.

Suppose that a CD-R initially sells for $3.00 and then its price falls to $1.50. People now substitute CD-Rs for audiotapes and prerecorded CDs—the substitution effect. And with a budget that now has some slack from the lower price of a CD-R, people buy more CD-Rs—the income effect. The quantity of CD-Rs demanded increases for these two reasons.

Now suppose that a CD-R initially sells for $3.00 and then the price doubles to $6.00. People now substitute prerecorded CDs and audiotapes for CD-Rs—the substitution effect. And faced with a tighter budget, people buy fewer CD-Rs—the income effect. The quantity of CD-Rs demanded decreases for these two reasons.

Demand Curve and Demand Schedule

You are now about to study one of the two most used curves in economics: the demand curve. And you are going to encounter one of the most critical distinctions: the distinction between *demand* and *quantity demanded.*

The term **demand** refers to the entire relationship between the price of the good and the quantity demanded of the good. Demand is illustrated by the demand curve and the demand schedule. The term *quantity demanded* refers to a point on a demand curve—the quantity demanded at a particular price.

Figure 3.1 shows the demand curve for CD-Rs. A **demand curve** shows the relationship between the quantity demanded of a good and its price when all other influences on consumers' planned purchases remain the same.

The table in Fig. 3.1 is the demand schedule for CD-Rs. A *demand schedule* lists the quantities demanded at each price when all the other influences on consumers' planned purchases remain the same. For example, if the price of a CD-R is 50¢, the quantity demanded is 9 million a week. If the price is $2.50, the quantity demanded is 2 million a week. The other rows of the table show the quantities demanded at prices of $1.00, $1.50, and $2.00.

We graph the demand schedule as a demand curve with the quantity demanded of CD-Rs on the *x*-axis and the price of a CD-R on the *y*-axis. The points on the demand curve labelled *A* through *E* correspond to the rows of the demand schedule. For example, point *A* on the graph shows a quantity demanded of 9 million CD-Rs a week at a price of 50¢ a disc.

Willingness and Ability to Pay Another way of looking at the demand curve is as a willingness-and-ability-to-pay curve. And the willingness and ability to pay is a measure of *marginal benefit.*

If a small quantity is available, the highest price that someone is willing and able to pay for one more unit is high. But as the quantity available increases, the marginal benefit of each additional unit falls and the highest price that someone is willing and able to pay also falls along the demand curve.

In Fig. 3.1, if only 2 million CD-Rs are available each week, the highest price that someone is willing to pay for the 2 millionth CD-R is $2.50. But if 9 million CD-Rs are available each week, someone is willing to pay 50¢ for the last CD-R bought.

A Change in Demand

When any factor that influences buying plans other than the price of the good changes, there is a **change in demand**. Figure 3.2 illustrates an increase in demand. When demand increases, the demand curve shifts rightward and the quantity demanded is greater at each and every price. For example, at a price of $2.50, on the original (blue) demand curve, the quantity demanded is 2 million discs a week. On the new (red) demand curve, the quantity demanded is 6 million discs a week. Look closely at the numbers in the table in Fig. 3.2 and check that the quantity demanded is greater at each price.

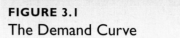

FIGURE 3.1
The Demand Curve

	Price (dollars per disc)	Quantity demanded (millions of discs per week)
A	0.50	9
B	1.00	6
C	1.50	4
D	2.00	3
E	2.50	2

The table shows a demand schedule for CD-Rs. At a price of 50¢ a disc, 9 million a week are demanded; at a price of $1.50 a disc, 4 million a week are demanded. The demand curve shows the relationship between quantity demanded and price, everything else remaining the same. The demand curve slopes downward: As price decreases, the quantity demanded increases.

The demand curve can be read in two ways. For a given price, the demand curve tells us the quantity that people plan to buy. For example, at a price of $1.50 a disc, the quantity demanded is 4 million discs a week. For a given quantity, the demand curve tells us the maximum price that consumers are willing and able to pay for the last disc available. For example, the maximum price that consumers will pay for the 6 millionth disc is $1.00.

Six main factors bring changes in demand. They are changes in

1. The prices of related goods
2. Expected future prices
3. Income
4. Expected future income
5. Population
6. Preferences

1. Prices of Related Goods The quantity of CD-Rs that consumers plan to buy depends in part on the prices of substitutes for CD-Rs. A **substitute** is a good that can be used in place of another good. For example, a bus ride is a substitute for a train ride; a prerecorded CD is a substitute for a CD-R, and a hamburger is a substitute for a hot dog. If the price of a substitute for a CD-R rises, people buy less of the substitute and more CD-Rs. For example, if the price of a prerecorded CD rises, people buy fewer CDs and more CD-Rs. The demand for CD-Rs increases.

The quantity of CD-Rs that people plan to buy also depends on the prices of complements with CD-Rs. A **complement** is a good that is used in conjunction with another good. Hamburgers and fries are complements. So are spaghetti and meat sauce, and so are CD-Rs and CD burners. If the price of a CD burner falls, people buy more CD burners *and more* CD-Rs. A fall in the price of a CD burner increases the demand for CD-Rs in Fig. 3.2.

2. Expected Future Prices If the price of a good is expected to rise in the future and if the good can be stored, the opportunity cost of obtaining the good for future use is lower today than it will be when the price has increased. So people retime their purchases—they substitute over time. They buy more of the good now before its price is expected to rise (and less after), so the current demand for the good increases. For example, suppose that Florida is hit by a frost that damages the season's orange crop. You expect the price of orange juice to rise in the future. So you fill your freezer with enough frozen juice to get you through the next six months. Your current demand for frozen orange juice has increased, and your future demand has decreased.

Similarly, if the price of a good is expected to fall in the future, the opportunity cost of buying the good today is high relative to what it is expected to be in the future. So again, people retime their purchases. They buy less of the good now before its price

FIGURE 3.2

An Increase in Demand

A change in any influence on buyers' plans other than the price of the good itself results in a new demand schedule and a shift of the demand curve. A change in the price of a CD burner changes the demand for CD-Rs. At a price of $1.50 a disc, 4 million discs a week are demanded when a CD burner costs $300 (row C of the table) and 8 million CD-Rs a week are demanded when a CD burner costs $100. A *fall* in the price of a CD burner *increases* the demand for CD-Rs. The demand curve shifts *rightward*, as shown by the shift arrow and the resulting red curve.

Original demand schedule CD burner $300			New demand schedule CD burner $100		
	Price (dollars per disc)	Quantity demanded (millions of discs per week)		Price (dollars per disc)	Quantity demanded (millions of discs per week)
A	0.50	9	A'	0.50	13
B	1.00	6	B'	1.00	10
C	1.50	4	C'	1.50	8
D	2.00	3	D'	2.00	7
E	2.50	2	E'	2.50	6

falls, so the demand for the good decreases today and increases in the future.

Computer prices are constantly falling, and this fact poses a dilemma. Will you buy a new computer now, in time for the start of the school year, or will you wait until the price has fallen some more? Because people expect computer prices to keep falling, the current demand for computers is less (the future demand is greater) than it otherwise would be.

3. Income Consumers' income influences demand. When income increases, consumers buy more of most goods, and when income decreases, consumers buy less of most goods. Although an increase in income leads to an increase in the demand for *most* goods, it does not lead to an increase in the demand for *all* goods. A **normal good** is one for which demand increases as income increases. An **inferior good** is one for which demand decreases as income increases. Long-distance transportation has examples of both normal goods and inferior goods. As incomes increase, the demand for air travel (a normal good) increases and the demand for long-distance bus trips (an inferior good) decreases.

4. Expected future income When expected future income increases, demand might increase. For example, a sales person gets the news that she will receive a big bonus at the end of the year, so she decides to buy a new car right now.

5. Population Demand also depends on the size and the age structure of the population. The larger the population, the greater is the demand for all goods and services; the smaller the population, the smaller is the demand for all goods and services.

For example, the demand for parking spaces or movies or CD-Rs or just about anything that you can imagine is much greater in the Greater Toronto Area (population 4.6 million) than it is in North Bay (population 110,000).

Also, the larger the proportion of the population in a given age group, the greater is the demand for the goods and services used by that age group.

For example, in 2001, there were 2.1 million 20–24-year-olds in Canada compared with 2.5 million in 1981. As a result, the demand for university places decreased during those years. During those same years, the number of Canadians aged 85 years and over increased by 235,000. As a result, the demand for nursing home services increased.

TABLE 3.1   The Demand for CD-Rs

The Law of Demand

The quantity of CD-Rs demanded

Decreases if:	Increases if:
■ The price of a CD-R rises	■ The price of a CD-R falls

Changes in Demand

The demand for CD-Rs

Decreases if:	Increases if:
■ The price of a substitute falls	■ The price of a substitute rises
■ The price of a complement rises	■ The price of a complement falls
■ The price of a CD-R is expected to fall in the future	■ The price of a CD-R is expected to rise in the future
■ Income falls*	■ Income rises*
■ Expected future income falls	■ Expected future income rises
■ The population decreases	■ The population increases

*A CD-R is a normal good.

6. Preferences Demand depends on preferences. *Preferences* are an individual's attitudes towards goods and services. For example, a rock music fanatic has a much greater preference for CD-Rs than does a tone-deaf technophobe. As a consequence, even if they have the same incomes, their demands for CD-Rs will be very different.

Table 3.1 summarizes the influences on demand and the direction of those influences.

A Change in the Quantity Demanded Versus a Change in Demand

Changes in the factors that influence buyers' plans cause either a change in the quantity demanded or a change in demand. Equivalently, they cause either a movement along the demand curve or a shift of the demand curve. The distinction between a change in the quantity demanded and a change in demand is the same as that between a movement along the demand curve and a shift of the demand curve.

A point on the demand curve shows the quantity demanded at a given price. So a movement along the demand curve shows a **change in the quantity demanded**. The entire demand curve shows demand. So a shift of the demand curve shows a *change in demand*. Figure 3.3 summarizes these distinctions.

Movement Along the Demand Curve If the price of a good changes but everything else remains the same, there is a movement along the demand curve. Because the demand curve slopes downward, a fall in the price of a good increases the quantity demanded of it and a rise in the price of the good decreases the quantity demanded of it—the law of demand.

In Fig. 3.3, if the price of a good falls when everything else remains the same, the quantity demanded of that good increases and there is a movement down the demand curve D_0. If the price rises when everything else remains the same, the quantity demanded of that good decreases and there is a movement up the demand curve D_0.

A Shift of the Demand Curve If the price of a good remains constant but some other influence on buyers' plans changes, there is a change in demand for that good. We illustrate a change in demand as a shift of the demand curve. For example, if the price of a CD burner falls, consumers buy more CD-Rs regardless of the price of a CD-R. That is what a rightward shift of the demand curve shows—more CD-Rs are bought at each and every price.

In Fig. 3.3, when any factor that influences buying plans, other than the price of the good, changes, there is a *change in demand* and the demand curve shifts. Demand *increases* and the demand curve *shifts rightward* (to the red demand curve D_1) if the price of a substitute rises, the price of a complement falls, the expected future price of the good rises, income increases (for a normal good), expected future income increases, or the population increases. Demand *decreases* and the demand curve *shifts leftward* (to the red demand curve D_2) if the price of a substitute falls, the price of a complement rises, the expected future price of the good falls, income decreases (for a normal good), expected future income decreases, or the population decreases.(For an inferior good, the effects of changes in income are in the direction opposite to those described above.)

FIGURE 3.3 myeconlab

A Change in the Quantity Demanded Versus a Change in Demand

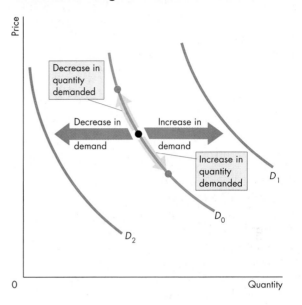

When the price of the good changes, there is a movement along the demand curve and *a change in the quantity demanded,* shown by the blue arrows on demand curve D_0. When any other influence on buyers' plans changes, there is a shift of the demand curve and a *change in demand.* An increase in demand shifts the demand curve rightward (from D_0 to D_1). A decrease in demand shifts the demand curve leftward (from D_0 to D_2).

REVIEW QUIZ

1 What is the law of demand and how do we illustrate it?
2 If a fixed amount of a good is available, what does the demand curve tell us about the price that consumers are willing to pay for that fixed quantity?
3 List all the influences on buying plans that change demand, and for each influence say whether it increases or decreases demand.
4 What happens to the quantity of Palm Pilots demanded and the demand for Palm Pilots if the price of a Palm Pilot falls and all other influences on buying plans remain the same?

myeconlab **Study Plan 3.2**

Supply

IF A FIRM SUPPLIES A GOOD OR SERVICE, THE FIRM

1. Has the resources and technology to produce it,
2. Can profit from producing it, and
3. Plans to produce it and sell it.

A supply is more than just having the *resources* and the *technology* to produce something. *Resources and technology* are the constraints that limit what is possible.

Many useful things can be produced, but they are not produced unless it is profitable to do so. Supply reflects a decision about which technologically feasible items to produce.

The **quantity supplied** of a good or service is the amount that producers plan to sell during a given time period at a particular price. The quantity supplied is not necessarily the same amount as the quantity actually sold. Sometimes the quantity supplied is greater than the quantity demanded, so the quantity bought is less than the quantity supplied.

Like the quantity demanded, the quantity supplied is measured as an amount per unit of time. For example, suppose that GM produces 1,000 cars a day. The quantity of cars supplied by GM can be expressed as 1,000 a day, 7,000 a week, or 365,000 a year. Without the time dimension, we cannot tell whether a particular number is large or small.

Many factors influence selling plans and again, one of them is price. We look first at the relationship between the quantity supplied of a good and its price. And again, as we did when we studied demand, to isolate this relationship, we keep all other influences on selling plans the same and we ask: How, other things remaining the same, does the quantity supplied of a good change as its price changes?

The law of supply provides the answer.

The Law of Supply

The **law of supply** states:

Other things remaining the same, the higher the price of a good, the greater is the quantity supplied; and the lower the price of a good, the smaller is the quantity supplied.

Why does a higher price increase the quantity supplied? It is because *marginal cost increases*. As the quantity produced of any good increases, the marginal cost of producing the good increases. (You can refresh your memory of increasing marginal cost in Chapter 2, p. 37.)

It is never worth producing a good if the price received for it does not at least cover the marginal cost of producing it. So when the price of a good rises, other things remaining the same, producers are willing to incur a higher marginal cost and increase production. The higher price brings forth an increase in the quantity supplied.

Let's now illustrate the law of supply with a supply curve and a supply schedule.

Supply Curve and Supply Schedule

You are now going to study the second of the two most used curves in economics: the supply curve. And you're going to learn about the critical distinction between *supply* and *quantity supplied*.

The term **supply** refers to the entire relationship between the quantity supplied and the price of a good. Supply is illustrated by the supply curve and the supply schedule. The term *quantity supplied* refers to a point on a supply curve—the quantity supplied at a particular price.

Figure 3.4 shows the supply curve of CD-Rs. A **supply curve** shows the relationship between the quantity supplied of a good and its price when all other influences on producers' planned sales remain the same. The supply curve is a graph of a supply schedule.

The table in Fig. 3.4 sets out the supply schedule for CD-Rs. A *supply schedule* lists the quantities supplied at each price when all the other influences on producers' planned sales remain the same. For example, if the price of a CD-R is 50¢, the quantity supplied is zero—in row *A* of the table. If the price of a CD-R is $1.00, the quantity supplied is 3 million CD-Rs a week—in row *B*. The other rows of the table show the quantities supplied at prices of $1.50, $2.00, and $2.50.

To make a supply curve, we graph the quantity supplied on the *x*-axis and the price on the *y*-axis, just as in the case of the demand curve. The points on the supply curve labelled *A* through *E* correspond to the rows of the supply schedule. For example, point *A* on the graph shows a quantity supplied of zero at a price of 50¢ a CD-R.

FIGURE 3.4
The Supply Curve

The table shows the supply schedule of CD-Rs.

	Price (dollars per disc)	Quantity supplied (millions of discs per week)
A	0.50	0
B	1.00	3
C	1.50	4
D	2.00	5
E	2.50	6

The table shows the supply schedule of CD-Rs. For example, at a price of $1.00, 3 million discs a week are supplied; at a price of $2.50, 6 million discs a week are supplied. The supply curve shows the relationship between the quantity supplied and price, everything else remaining the same. The supply curve usually slopes upward: As the price of a good increases, so does the quantity supplied.

A supply curve can be read in two ways. For a given price, it tells us the quantity that producers plan to sell at that price. And for a given quantity, it tells us the minimum price that producers are willing to accept for that quantity.

Minimum Supply Price Just as the demand curve has two interpretations, so too does the supply curve. The demand curve can be interpreted as a willingness-and-ability-to-pay curve. The supply curve can be interpreted as a minimum-supply-price curve. It tells us the lowest price at which someone is willing to sell another unit.

If a small quantity is produced, the lowest price at which someone is willing to sell one more unit is low. But if a large quantity is produced, the lowest price at which someone is willing to sell one more unit is high.

In Fig. 3.4, if 6 million CD-Rs a week are produced, the lowest price that a producer is willing to accept for the 6 millionth disc is $2.50. But if only 4 million CD-Rs are produced each week, the lowest price that a producer is willing to accept for the 4 millionth disc is $1.50.

A Change in Supply

When any factor that influences selling plans other than the price of the good changes, there is a **change in supply**. Five main factors bring changes in supply. They are changes in

1. The prices of resources used to produce the good
2. The prices of related goods produced
3. Expected future prices
4. The number of suppliers
5. Technology

1. Prices of Productive Resources The prices of productive resources influence supply. The easiest way to see this influence is to think about the supply curve as a minimum-supply-price curve. If the price of a productive resource rises, the lowest price a producer of a good that uses that resource is willing to accept rises, so supply of the good decreases. For example, during 2005, the price of jet fuel increased and the supply of air transportation decreased. Similarly, a rise in the minimum wage decreases the supply of hamburgers. If the wages of disc producers rise, the supply of CD-Rs decreases.

2. Prices of Related Goods Produced The prices of related goods and services that firms produce influence supply. For example, if the price of a prerecorded CD rises, the supply of CD-Rs decreases. CD-Rs and prerecorded CDs are *substitutes in production*—goods that can be produced by using the same resources. If the price of beef rises, the supply of cowhide increases. Beef and cowhide are *complements in production—* goods that must be produced together.

3. Expected Future Prices If the price of a good is expected to rise, the return from selling the good in the future is higher than it is today. So supply of the good decreases today and increases in the future.

4. The Number of Suppliers The larger the number of firms that produce a good, the greater is the supply of the good. And as firms enter an industry, the supply in that industry increases. As firms leave an industry, the supply in that industry decreases.

5. Technology The term "technology" is used broadly to mean the way that factors of production are used to produce a good. Technology changes both positively and negatively. A positive technology change occurs when a new method is discovered that lowers the cost of producing a good. An example is new methods used in the factories that make CDs. A negative technology change occurs when an event such as extreme weather or natural disaster increases the cost of producing a good. A positive technology change increases supply, and a negative technology change decreases supply.

Figure 3.5 illustrates an increase in supply. When supply increases, the supply curve shifts rightward and the quantity supplied is larger at each and every price. For example, at a price of $1, on the original (blue) supply curve, the quantity supplied is 3 million discs a week. On the new (red) supply curve, the quantity supplied is 6 million discs a week. Look closely at the numbers in the table in Fig. 3.5 and check that the quantity supplied is larger at each price.

Table 3.2 summarizes the influences on supply and the directions of those influences.

A Change in the Quantity Supplied Versus a Change in Supply

Changes in the factors that influence sellers' plans cause either a change in the quantity supplied or a change in supply. Equivalently, they cause either a movement along the supply curve or a shift of the supply curve.

A point on the supply curve shows the quantity supplied at a given price. A movement along the supply curve shows a **change in the quantity supplied**. The entire supply curve shows supply. A shift of the supply curve shows a *change in supply*.

FIGURE 3.5

An Increase in Supply

Original supply schedule Old technology			New supply schedule New technology		
	Price (dollars per disc)	Quantity supplied (millions of discs per week)		Price (dollars per disc)	Quantity supplied (millions of discs per week)
A	0.50	0	A'	0.50	3
B	1.00	3	B'	1.00	6
C	1.50	4	C'	1.50	8
D	2.00	5	D'	2.00	10
E	2.50	6	E'	2.50	12

A change in any influence on sellers' plans other than the price of the good itself results in a new supply schedule and a shift of the supply curve. For example, if Imation Enterprises invents a new, cost-saving technology for producing CD-Rs, the supply of CD-Rs changes. At a price of $1.50 a disc, 4 million discs a week are supplied when producers use the old technology (row *C* of the table) and 8 million CD-Rs a week are supplied when producers use the new technology. An advance in technology *increases* the supply of CD-Rs. The supply curve shifts *rightward*, as shown by the shift arrow and the resulting red curve.

Figure 3.6 illustrates and summarizes these distinctions. If the price of a good falls and everything else remains the same, the quantity supplied of that good decreases and there is a movement down the supply curve S_0. If the price of a good rises and everything else remains the same, the quantity supplied increases and there is a movement up the supply curve S_0. When any other influence on selling plans changes, the supply curve shifts and there is a *change in supply*. If the supply curve is S_0 and if production costs fall, supply increases and the supply curve shifts to the red supply curve S_1. If production costs rise, supply decreases and the supply curve shifts to the red supply curve S_2.

TABLE 3.2   The Supply of CD-Rs

The Law of Supply

The quantity of CD-Rs supplied

Decreases if:	*Increases if:*
■ The price of a CD-R falls	■ The price of a CD-R rises

Changes in Supply

The supply of CD-Rs

Decreases if:	*Increases if:*
■ The price of a resource used to produce CD-Rs rises	■ The price of a resource used to produce CD-Rs falls
■ The price of a substitute in production rises	■ The price of a substitute in production falls
■ The price of a complement in production falls	■ The price of a complement in production rises
■ The price of a CD-R is expected to rise in the future	■ The price of a CD-R is expected to fall in the future
■ The number of CD-R producers decreases	■ The number of CD-R producers increases
■ A less efficient technology for producing CD-Rs is used	■ A more efficient technology for producing CD-Rs is used

FIGURE 3.6

A Change in the Quantity Supplied Versus a Change in Supply

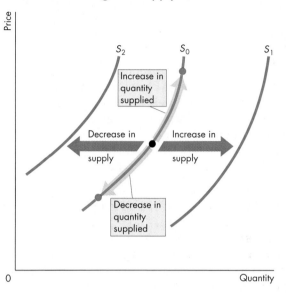

When the price of the good changes, there is a movement along the supply curve and *a change in the quantity supplied,* shown by the blue arrows on supply curve S_0. When any other influence on selling plans changes, there is a shift of the supply curve and a *change in supply.* An increase in supply shifts the supply curve rightward (from S_0 to S_1), and a decrease in supply shifts the supply curve leftward (from S_0 to S_2).

REVIEW QUIZ

1 What is the law of supply and how do we illustrate it?
2 What does the supply curve tell us about the price at which firms will supply a given quantity of a good?
3 List all the influences on selling plans, and for each influence say whether it changes supply.
4 What happens to the quantity of Palm Pilots supplied and the supply of Palm Pilots if the price of a Palm Pilot falls?

 Study Plan 3.3

Your next task is to use what you've learned about demand and supply and understand how prices and quantities are determined.

Market Equilibrium

WE HAVE SEEN THAT WHEN THE PRICE OF A GOOD rises, the quantity demanded *decreases* and the quantity supplied *increases*. We are now going to see how prices coordinate the plans of buyers and sellers and achieve an equilibrium.

An *equilibrium* is a situation in which opposing forces balance each other. Equilibrium in a market occurs when the price balances the plans of buyers and sellers. The **equilibrium price** is the price at which the quantity demanded equals the quantity supplied. The **equilibrium quantity** is the quantity bought and sold at the equilibrium price. A market moves towards its equilibrium because

- Price regulates buying and selling plans.
- Price adjusts when plans don't match.

Price as a Regulator

The price of a good regulates the quantities demanded and supplied. If the price is too high, the quantity supplied exceeds the quantity demanded. If the price is too low, the quantity demanded exceeds the quantity supplied. There is one price at which the quantity demanded equals the quantity supplied. Let's work out what that price is.

Figure 3.7 shows the market for CD-Rs. The table shows the demand schedule (from Fig. 3.1) and the supply schedule (from Fig. 3.4). If the price of a disc is 50¢, the quantity demanded is 9 million discs a week, but no discs are supplied. There is a shortage of 9 million discs a week. This shortage is shown in the final column of the table. At a price of $1.00 a disc, there is still a shortage, but only of 3 million discs a week. If the price of a disc is $2.50, the quantity supplied is 6 million discs a week, but the quantity demanded is only 2 million. There is a surplus of 4 million discs a week. The one price at which there is neither a shortage nor a surplus is $1.50 a disc. At that price, the quantity demanded is equal to the quantity supplied: 4 million discs a week. The equilibrium price is $1.50 a disc, and the equilibrium quantity is 4 million discs a week.

Figure 3.7 shows that the demand curve and the supply curve intersect at the equilibrium price of $1.50 a disc. At each price *above* $1.50 a disc, there is a surplus of discs. For example, at $2.00 a disc, the surplus

FIGURE 3.7
Equilibrium

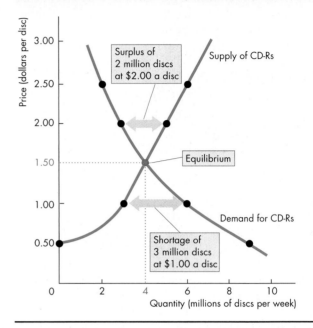

Price (dollars per disc)	Quantity demanded	Quantity supplied	Shortage (–) or surplus (+)
	(millions of discs per week)		
0.50	9	0	–9
1.00	6	3	–3
1.50	4	4	0
2.00	3	5	+2
2.50	2	6	+4

The table lists the quantities demanded and quantities supplied as well as the shortage or surplus of discs at each price. If the price is $1.00 a disc, 6 million discs a week are demanded and 3 million are supplied. There is a shortage of 3 million discs a week, and the price rises.

If the price is $2.00 a disc, 3 million discs a week are demanded and 5 million are supplied. There is a surplus of 2 million discs a week, and the price falls.

If the price is $1.50 a disc, 4 million discs a week are demanded and 4 million are supplied. There is neither a shortage nor a surplus. Neither buyers nor sellers have any incentive to change the price. The price at which the quantity demanded equals the quantity supplied is the equilibrium price.

is 2 million discs a week, as shown by the blue arrow. At each price *below* $1.50 a disc, there is a shortage of discs. For example, at $1.00 a disc, the shortage is 3 million discs a week, as shown by the red arrow.

Price Adjustments

You've seen that if the price is below equilibrium, there is a shortage and that if the price is above equilibrium, there is a surplus. But can we count on the price to change and eliminate a shortage or surplus? We can, because such price changes are beneficial to both buyers and sellers. Let's see why the price changes when there is a shortage or a surplus.

A Shortage Forces the Price Up Suppose the price of a CD-R is $1. Consumers plan to buy 6 million discs a week, and producers plan to sell 3 million discs a week. Consumers can't force producers to sell more than they plan, so the quantity that is actually offered for sale is 3 million discs a week. In this situation, powerful forces operate to increase the price and move it towards the equilibrium price. Some producers, noticing lines of unsatisfied consumers, raise the price. Some producers increase their output. As producers push the price up, the price rises towards its equilibrium. The rising price reduces the shortage because it decreases the quantity demanded and increases the quantity supplied. When the price has increased to the point at which there is no longer a shortage, the forces moving the price stop operating and the price comes to rest at its equilibrium.

A Surplus Forces the Price Down Suppose the price of a CD-R is $2. Producers plan to sell 5 million discs a week, and consumers plan to buy 3 million discs a week. Producers cannot force consumers to buy more than they plan, so the quantity that is actually bought is 3 million discs a week. In this situation, powerful forces operate to lower the price and move it towards the equilibrium price. Some producers, unable to sell the quantities of CD-Rs they planned to sell, cut their prices. In addition, some producers scale back production. As producers cut the price, the price falls towards its equilibrium. The falling price decreases the surplus because it increases the quantity demanded and decreases the quantity supplied. When the price has fallen to the point at which there is no longer a surplus, the forces moving the price stop operating and the price comes to rest at its equilibrium.

The Best Deal Available for Buyers and Sellers When the price is below equilibrium, it is forced up towards the equilibrium. Why don't buyers resist the increase and refuse to buy at the higher price? Because they value the good more highly than the current price and they cannot satisfy all their demands at the current price. In some markets—for example, the auction markets that operate on eBay— the buyers might even be the ones who force the price up by offering to pay higher prices.

When the price is above equilibrium, it is bid down towards the equilibrium. Why don't sellers resist this decrease and refuse to sell at the lower price? Because their minimum supply price is below the current price and they cannot sell all they would like to at the current price. Normally, it is the sellers who force the price down by offering lower prices to gain market share from their competitors.

At the price at which the quantity demanded and the quantity supplied are equal, neither buyers nor sellers can do business at a better price. Buyers pay the highest price they are willing to pay for the last unit bought, and sellers receive the lowest price at which they are willing to supply the last unit sold.

When people freely make offers to buy and sell and when demanders try to buy at the lowest possible price and suppliers try to sell at the highest possible price, the price at which trade takes place is the equilibrium price—the price at which the quantity demanded equals the quantity supplied. The price coordinates the plans of buyers and sellers, and no one has an incentive to change it.

REVIEW QUIZ

1 What is the equilibrium price of a good or service?
2 Over what range of prices does a shortage arise?
3 Over what range of prices does a surplus arise?
4 What happens to the price when there is a shortage?
5 What happens to the price when there is a surplus?
6 Why is the price at which the quantity demanded equals the quantity supplied the equilibrium price?

 myeconlab **Study Plan 3.4**

Predicting Changes in Price and Quantity

└─ THE DEMAND AND SUPPLY THEORY THAT WE HAVE just studied provides us with a powerful way of analyzing influences on prices and the quantities bought and sold. According to the theory, a change in price stems from a change in demand, a change in supply, or a change in both demand and supply. Let's look first at the effects of a change in demand.

A Change in Demand

What happens to the price and quantity of CD-Rs if the demand for CD-Rs increases? We can answer this question with a specific example. Between 1998 and 2001, the price of a CD burner fell from $300 to $100. Because the CD burner and CD-R discs are complements, the demand for discs increased, as is shown in the table in Fig. 3.8. The original demand schedule and the new one are set out in the first three columns of the table. The table also shows the supply schedule for CD-Rs.

When demand increases, there is a shortage at the original equilibrium price of $1.50 a disc. To eliminate the shortage, the price must rise. The price that makes the quantity demanded and quantity supplied equal again is $2.50 a disc. At this price, 6 million discs are bought and sold each week. When demand increases, both the price and the quantity increase.

Figure 3.8 shows these changes. The figure shows the original demand for and supply of CD-Rs. The original equilibrium price is $1.50 a disc, and the quantity is 4 million discs a week. When demand increases, the demand curve shifts rightward. The equilibrium price rises to $2.50 a disc, and the quantity supplied increases to 6 million discs a week, as highlighted in the figure. There is an *increase in the quantity supplied* but *no change in supply*—a movement along, but no shift of, the supply curve.

We can reverse this change in demand. Start at a price of $2.50 a disc with 6 million discs a week being bought and sold, and then work out what happens if demand decreases to its original level. Such a decrease in demand might arise from a fall in the price of an MP3 player (a substitute for CD-R technology). The decrease in demand shifts the demand curve leftward. The equilibrium price falls to $1.50 a disc, and the equilibrium quantity decreases to 4 million discs a week.

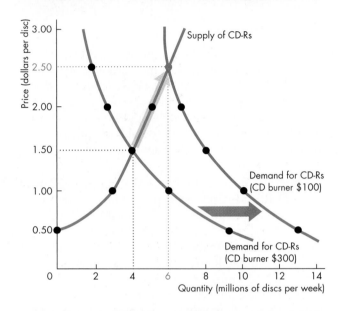

FIGURE 3.8 ⓧ myeconlab

The Effects of a Change in Demand

Price	Quantity demanded (millions of discs per week)		Quantity supplied
(dollars per disc)	CD burner $300	CD burner $100	(millions of discs per week)
0.50	9	13	0
1.00	6	10	3
1.50	**4**	**8**	**4**
2.00	3	7	5
2.50	2	6	6

With the price of a CD burner at $300, the demand for CD-Rs is the blue demand curve. The equilibrium price is $1.50 a disc, and the equilibrium quantity is 4 million discs a week. When the price of a CD burner falls from $300 to $100, the demand for CD-Rs increases and the demand curve shifts rightward to become the red curve.

At $1.50 a disc, there is now a shortage of 4 million discs a week. The price of a disc rises to a new equilibrium of $2.50. As the price rises to $2.50, the quantity supplied increases—shown by the blue arrow on the supply curve—to the new equilibrium quantity of 6 million discs a week. Following an increase in demand, the quantity supplied increases but supply does not change—the supply curve does not shift.

We can now make our first two predictions:

1. When demand increases, both the price and the quantity increase.
2. When demand decreases, both the price and the quantity decrease.

A Change in Supply

When Imation and other producers introduce new cost-saving technologies in their CD-R production plants, the supply of CD-Rs increases. The new supply schedule (the same one that was shown in Fig. 3.5) is presented in the table in Fig. 3.9. What are the new equilibrium price and quantity? The answer is highlighted in the table: The price falls to $1.00 a disc, and the quantity increases to 6 million a week. You can see why by looking at the quantities demanded and supplied at the old price of $1.50 a disc. The quantity supplied at that price is 8 million discs a week, and there is a surplus of discs. The price falls. Only when the price is $1.00 a disc does the quantity supplied equal the quantity demanded.

Figure 3.9 illustrates the effect of an increase in supply. It shows the demand curve for CD-Rs and the original and new supply curves. The initial equilibrium price is $1.50 a disc, and the quantity is 4 million discs a week. When the supply increases, the supply curve shifts rightward. The equilibrium price falls to $1.00 a disc, and the quantity demanded increases to 6 million discs a week, highlighted in the figure. There is an *increase in the quantity demanded* but *no change in demand*—a movement along, but no shift of, the demand curve.

We can reverse this change in supply. If we start out at a price of $1.00 a disc with 6 million discs a week being bought and sold, we can work out what happens if supply decreases to its original level. Such a decrease in supply might arise from an increase in the cost of labour or raw materials. The decrease in supply shifts the supply curve leftward. The equilibrium price rises to $1.50 a disc, and the equilibrium quantity decreases to 4 million discs a week.

We can now make two more predictions:

1. When supply increases, the quantity increases and the price falls.
2. When supply decreases, the quantity decreases and the price rises.

FIGURE 3.9   myeconlab

The Effects of a Change in Supply

Price (dollars per disc)	Quantity demanded (millions of discs per week)	Quantity supplied (millions of discs per week)	
		Old technology	New technology
0.50	9	0	3
1.00	6	3	6
1.50	4	4	8
2.00	3	5	10
2.50	2	6	12

With the old technology, the supply of CD-Rs is shown by the blue supply curve. The equilibrium price is $1.50 a disc, and the equilibrium quantity is 4 million discs a week. When the new technology is adopted, the supply of CD-Rs increases and the supply curve shifts rightward to become the red curve.

At $1.50 a disc, there is now a surplus of 4 million discs a week. The price of a CD-R falls to a new equilibrium of $1.00 a disc. As the price falls to $1.00, the quantity demanded increases—shown by the blue arrow on the demand curve—to the new equilibrium quantity of 6 million discs a week. Following an increase in supply, the quantity demanded increases but demand does not change—the demand curve does not shift.

A Change in Both Demand and Supply

You can now predict the effects of a change in either demand or supply on the price and the quantity. But what happens if *both* demand and supply change together? To answer this question, we look first at the case in which demand and supply move in the same direction—either both increase or both decrease. Then we look at the case in which they move in opposite directions—demand decreases and supply increases or demand increases and supply decreases.

Demand and Supply Change in the Same Direction We've seen that an increase in the demand for CD-Rs raises its price and increases the quantity bought and sold. And we've seen that an increase in the supply of CD-Rs lowers its price and increases the quantity bought and sold. Let's now examine what happens when both of these changes occur together.

The table in Fig. 3.10 brings together the numbers that describe the original quantities demanded and supplied and the new quantities demanded and supplied after the fall in the price of the CD burner and the improved CD-R production technology. These same numbers are illustrated in the graph. The original (blue) demand and supply curves intersect at a price of $1.50 a disc and a quantity of 4 million discs a week. The new (red) supply and demand curves also intersect at a price of $1.50 a disc but at a quantity of 8 million discs a week.

An increase in either demand or supply increases the quantity. So when both demand and supply increase, so does the equilibrium quantity.

An increase in demand raises the price, and an increase in supply lowers the price, so we can't say whether the price will rise or fall when demand and supply increase together. In this example, the price does not change. But notice that if demand increases by slightly more than the amount shown in the figure, the equilibrium price will rise. And if supply increases by slightly more than the amount shown in the figure, the equilibrium price will fall.

We can now make two more predictions:

1. When *both* demand and supply increase, the quantity increases and the price might increase, decrease, or remain the same.
2. When *both* demand and supply decrease, the quantity decreases and the price might increase, decrease, or remain the same.

FIGURE 3.10
The Effects of an Increase in Both Demand and Supply

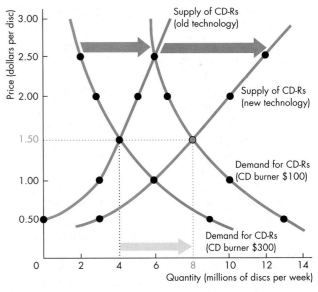

Price (dollars per disc)	Original quantities (millions of discs per week)		New quantities (millions of discs per week)	
	Quantity demanded CD burner $300	Quantity supplied old technology	Quantity demanded CD burner $100	Quantity supplied new technology
0.50	9	0	13	3
1.00	6	3	10	6
1.50	4	4	8	8
2.00	3	5	7	10
2.50	2	6	6	12

When a CD burner costs $300 and firms use the old technology to produce discs, the price of a disc is $1.50 and the quantity is 4 million discs a week. A fall in the price of the CD burner increases the demand for CD-Rs, and improved technology increases the supply of CD-Rs. The new supply curve intersects the new demand curve at $1.50 a disc, the same price as before, but the equilibrium quantity increases to 8 million discs a week. These increases in demand and supply increase the quantity but leave the price unchanged.

Demand and Supply Change in Opposite Directions Let's now see what happens when demand and supply change together in *opposite* directions. A new production technology increases the supply of CD-Rs as before. But now the price of an MP3 download rises. An MP3 download is a *complement* of a CD-R. With more costly MP3 downloads, some people switch from buying CD-Rs to buying prerecorded CDs. The demand for CD-Rs decreases.

The table in Fig. 3.11 describes the original and new demand and supply schedules and the original (blue) and new (red) demand and supply curves. The original equilibrium price is $2.50 a disc, and the quantity is 6 million discs a week. The new supply and demand curves intersect at a price of $1.00 a disc and at the original quantity of 6 million discs a week.

A decrease in demand or an increase in supply lowers the price. So when a decrease in demand and an increase in supply occur together, the price falls.

A decrease in demand decreases the quantity, and an increase in supply increases the quantity, so we can't say for sure which way the quantity will change when demand decreases and supply increases at the same time. In this example, the quantity doesn't change. But notice that if demand had decreased by slightly more than is shown in the figure, the quantity would have decreased. And if supply had increased by slightly more than is shown in the figure, the quantity would have increased. So

1. When demand decreases and supply increases, the price falls and the quantity might increase, decrease, or remain the same.
2. When demand increases and supply decreases, the price rises and the quantity might increase, decrease, or remain the same.

REVIEW QUIZ

1 What is the effect on the price of a CD-R and the quantity of CD-Rs if (a) the price of a PC falls or (b) the price of an MP3 download rises or (c) more firms produce CD-Rs or (d) CD-R producers' wages rise or (e) any two of these events occur together? (Draw the diagrams!)

myeconlab **Study Plan 3.5**

To complete your study of demand and supply, take a look at *Reading Between the Lines* on pp. 76–77, which looks at the rocketing price of gasoline in the summer of 2005.

FIGURE 3.11   **myeconlab**

The Effects of a Decrease in Demand and an Increase in Supply

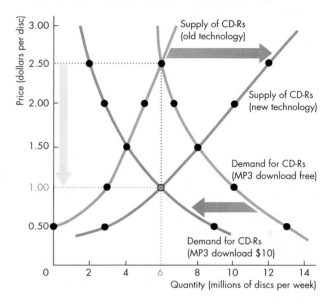

Price (dollars per disc)	Original quantities (millions of discs per week)		New quantities (millions of discs per week)	
	Quantity demanded MP3 download free	**Quantity supplied** old technology	**Quantity demanded** MP3 download $10	**Quantity supplied** new technology
0.50	13	0	9	3
1.00	10	3	6	6
1.50	8	4	4	8
2.00	7	5	3	10
2.50	6	6	2	12

When MP3 downloads are free and firms use the old technology to produce discs, the price is $2.50 a disc and the quantity is 6 million discs a week. A rise in the price of an MP3 download decreases the demand for CD-Rs, and improved technology increases the supply of CD-Rs. The new equilibrium price is $1.00 a disc, a lower price, but in this case the quantity remains constant at 6 million discs a week. This decrease in demand and increase in supply lower the price but leave the quantity unchanged.

Demand and Supply:
The Price of Oil

BLOOMBERG, AUGUST 23, 2005

Crude Oil Prices Rise on Concern Demand May Outstrip Supply

Crude oil rose above $66 a barrel in New York on concern that refiners will struggle to meet increased fuel demand during the Northern Hemisphere winter.

Kuwait Petroleum Corp. late yesterday said it shut its 85,000 barrel-a-day Europoort refinery near Rotterdam because of a failure in its steam boilers. More than 20 U.S. and European refineries have had unplanned unit shutdowns since early July.

"There is a perception that supply will be insufficient to meet demand later this year," said Steve Bellino, a trader at Fimat USA Inc. in New York. "The fact remains that there are no shortages, but the concern is there. Prices continue to be bid up just about every morning." ...

Essence of the Story

■ The price of crude oil reached $US66 a barrel in August 2005.

■ The reported reason for the price rise was an expected increase in demand for oil during the winter.

■ Another reported reason was a decrease in supply that resulted from shutdowns of refineries.

■ One trader said that there is a perception that supply will be insufficient to meet demand.

■ The trader also noted that there were no shortages.

Economic Analysis

■ The price of crude oil increased from an average of $US38 a barrel in 2004 to $66 a barrel in August 2005.

■ The quantity of oil produced increased from 83 million barrels a day in 2004 to 84 million barrels a day in 2005.

■ The most significant factor at work in the oil market in 2005 was an increasing awareness that the global demand for oil is going to increase at a much faster rate than previously thought.

■ The main source of the increase in demand is a rapid expansion in the economies of China and India, which is increasing the demand for oil in these countries. (China and India account for two-fifths of the world's population.)

■ The decrease in production by a refinery near Rotterdam reported in the news article is not significant. The production of this refinery is only one-tenth of one percent of world production and the shutdown is temporary.

■ Figure 1 illustrates the global market for oil in 2004 and 2005.

■ The supply of oil was constant and represented by the supply curve S.

■ In 2004, the demand for oil was D_{04}.

■ The equilibrium price was $US38 a barrel and the equilibrium quantity was 83 million barrels a day.

■ The demand for oil increased in 2005 and the demand curve shifted rightward to D_{05}.

■ The equilibrium price increased to $US66 a barrel and the equilibrium quantity increased to 84 million barrels a day.

■ There was no shortage of oil because the rise in the equilibrium price kept the quantity demanded equal to the quantity supplied.

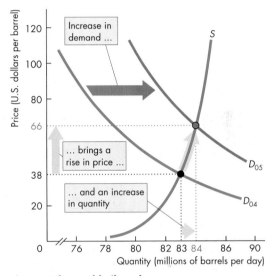

Figure 1 The world oil market

77

Mathematical Note
Demand, Supply, and Equilibrium

Demand Curve

The law of demand says that as the price of a good or service falls, the quantity demanded of that good or service increases. We illustrate the law of demand by setting out a demand schedule, drawing a graph of the demand curve, or writing down an equation. When the demand curve is a straight line, the following linear equation describes it:

$$P = a - bQ_D$$

where P is the price and Q_D is the quantity demanded. The a and b are positive constants.

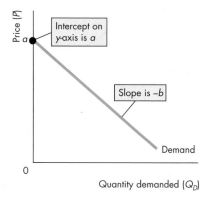

The demand equation tells us three things:

1. The price at which no one is willing to buy the good (Q_D is zero). That is, if the price is a, then the quantity demanded is zero. You can see the price a on the graph. It is the price at which the demand curve hits the y-axis—what we call the demand curve's "intercept on the y-axis."

2. As the price falls, the quantity demanded increases. If Q_D is a positive number, then the price P must be less than a. And as Q_D gets larger, the price P becomes smaller. That is, as the quantity increases, the maximum price that buyers are willing to pay for the good falls.

3. The constant b tells us how fast the maximum price that someone is willing to pay for the good falls as the quantity increases. That is, the constant b tells us about the steepness of the demand curve. The equation tells us that the slope of the demand curve is $-b$.

Supply Curve

The law of supply says that as the price of a good or service rises, the quantity supplied of that good or service increases. We illustrate the law of supply by setting out a supply schedule, drawing a graph of the supply curve, or writing down an equation. When the supply curve is a straight line, the following linear equation describes it:

$$P = c + dQ_S$$

where P is the price and Q_S is the quantity supplied. The c and d are positive constants.

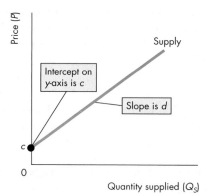

The supply equation tells us three things:

1. The price at which sellers are not willing to supply the good (Q_S is zero). That is, if the price is c, then no one is willing to sell the good. You can see the price c on the graph. It is the price at which the supply curve hits the y-axis—what we call the supply curve's "intercept on the y-axis."

2. As the price rises, the quantity supplied increases. If Q_S is a positive number, then the price P must be greater than c. And as Q_S increases, the price P gets larger. That is, as the quantity increases, the minimum price that sellers are willing to accept rises.

3. The constant d tells us how fast the minimum price at which someone is willing to sell the good rises as the quantity increases. That is, the constant d tells us about the steepness of the supply curve. The equation tells us that the slope of the supply curve is d.

Market Equilibrium

Demand and supply determine market equilibrium. The figure shows the equilibrium price (P^*) and equilibrium quantity (Q^*) at the intersection of the demand curve and the supply curve.

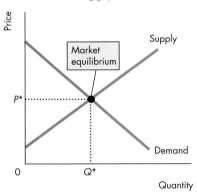

We can use the equations to find the equilibrium price and equilibrium quantity. The price of a good adjusts until the quantity demanded equals the quantity supplied. That is,

$$Q_D = Q_S.$$

So at the equilibrium price (P^*) and equilibrium quantity (Q^*),

$$Q_D = Q_S = Q^*.$$

To find the equilibrium price and equilibrium quantity, substitute Q^* for Q_D in the demand equation and Q^* for Q_S in the supply equation. Then the price is the equilibrium price (P^*), which gives

$$P^* = a - bQ^*$$

$$P^* = c + dQ^*.$$

Notice that

$$a - bQ^* = c + dQ^*.$$

Now solve for Q^*:

$$a - c = bQ^* + dQ^*$$

$$a - c = (b + d)Q^*$$

$$Q^* = \frac{a - c}{b + d}.$$

To find the equilibrium price, (P^*), substitute for Q^* in either the demand equation or the supply equation.

Using the demand equation, we have

$$P^* = a - b\left(\frac{a - c}{b + d}\right)$$

$$P^* = \frac{a(b + d) - b(a - c)}{b + d}$$

$$P^* = \frac{ad + bc}{b + d}.$$

Alternatively, using the supply equation, we have

$$P^* = c + d\left(\frac{a - c}{b + d}\right)$$

$$P^* = \frac{c(b + d) + d(a - c)}{b + d}$$

$$P^* = \frac{ad + bc}{b + d}.$$

An Example

The demand for ice cream cones is

$$P = 800 - 2Q_D.$$

The supply of ice cream cones is

$$P = 200 + 1Q_S.$$

The price of a cone is expressed in cents, and the quantities are expressed in cones per day.

To find the equilibrium price (P^*) and equilibrium quantity (Q^*), substitute Q^* for Q_D and Q_S and P^* for P. That is,

$$P^* = 800 - 2Q^*$$

$$P^* = 200 + 1Q^*.$$

Now solve for Q^*:

$$800 - 2Q^* = 200 + 1Q^*$$

$$600 = 3Q^*$$

$$Q^* = 200.$$

And

$$P^* = 800 - 2(200) = 400.$$

The equilibrium price is $4 a cone, and the equilibrium quantity is 200 cones per day.

SUMMARY

KEY POINTS

Markets and Prices (p. 60)

- A competitive market is one that has so many buyers and sellers that no one can influence the price.
- Opportunity cost is a relative price.
- Demand and supply determine relative prices.

Demand (pp. 61–65)

- Demand is the relationship between the quantity demanded of a good and its price when all other influences on buying plans remain the same.
- The higher the price of a good, other things remaining the same, the smaller is the quantity demanded—the law of demand.
- Demand depends on the prices of substitutes and complements, expected future prices, income, expected future income, population, and preferences.

Supply (pp. 66–69)

- Supply is the relationship between the quantity supplied of a good and its price when all other influences on selling plans remain the same.
- The higher the price of a good, other things remaining the same, the greater is the quantity supplied—the law of supply.
- Supply depends on the prices of resources used to produce a good, the prices of related goods produced, expected future prices, the number of suppliers, and technology.

Market Equilibrium (pp. 70–71)

- At the equilibrium price, the quantity demanded equals the quantity supplied.
- At prices above equilibrium, there is a surplus and the price falls.
- At prices below equilibrium, there is a shortage and the price rises.

Predicting Changes in Price and Quantity (pp. 72–75)

- An increase in demand brings a rise in the price and an increase in the quantity supplied. (A decrease in demand brings a fall in the price and a decrease in the quantity supplied.)

- An increase in supply brings a fall in the price and an increase in the quantity demanded. (A decrease in supply brings a rise in the price and a decrease in the quantity demanded.)
- An increase in demand and an increase in supply bring an increased quantity, but the price might rise, fall, or remain the same. An increase in demand and a decrease in supply bring a higher price, but the quantity might increase, decrease, or remain the same.

KEY FIGURES

KEY TERMS

PROBLEMS

Go to **myeconlab** for solutions to odd-numbered problems and additional exercises.

1. What is the effect on the price of an audiotape and the quantity of audiotapes sold if
   a. The price of a CD rises?
   b. The price of a Walkman rises?
   c. The supply of CD players increases?
   d. Consumers' incomes increase?
   e. Workers who make audiotapes get a pay raise?
   f. The price of a Walkman rises at the same time as the workers who make audiotapes get a pay raise?
2. What is the effect on the price of a DVD player and the quantity of DVD players sold if
   a. The price of a DVD rises?
   b. The price of a DVD falls?
   c. The supply of DVD players increases?
   d. Consumers' incomes decrease??
   e. The wage rate of workers who produce DVD players increases?
   f. The wage rate of workers who produce DVD players rises and at the same time the price of a DVD falls?
3. The following events occur one at a time:
   i. The price of crude oil rises.
   ii. The price of a car rises.
   iii. All speed limits on highways are abolished.
   iv. Robot technology cuts the cost of producing a car.
   Which of these events will increase or decrease (state which)
   a. The demand for gasoline?
   b. The supply of gasoline?
   c. The quantity of gasoline demanded?
   d. The quantity of gasoline supplied?
4. The following events occur one at a time:
   i. The price of airfares halve.
   ii. The price of beef falls.
   iii. A cheap new strong cloth, a close substitute for leather, is invented.
   iv. A new high-speed technology for cutting leather is invented.
   Which of these events will increase or decrease (state which)
   a. The demand for leather bags?
   b. The supply of leather bags?
   c. The quantity of leather bags demanded?
   d. The quantity of leather bags supplied?

5. The figure illustrates the market for pizza.
   a. Label the curves in the figure.
   b. What are the equilibrium price of a pizza and the equilibrium quantity of pizza?

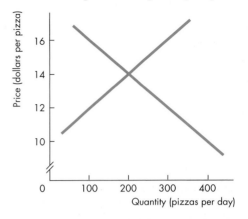

6. The figure illustrates the market for fish.
   a. Label the curves in the figure.
   b. What are the equilibrium price of a fish and the equilibrium quantity of fish?

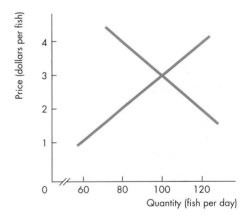

7. The demand and supply schedules for gum are

Price (cents per pack)	Quantity demanded	Quantity supplied
	(millions of packs per week)	
20	180	60
30	160	80
40	140	100
50	120	120
60	100	140
70	80	160
80	60	180

   a. Draw a graph of the gum market and mark in the equilibrium price and quantity.

b. Suppose that gum is 70¢ a pack. Describe the situation in the gum market and explain how the price of gum adjusts.

8. The demand and supply schedules for potato chips are

Price (cents per bag)	Quantity demanded	Quantity supplied
	(millions of bags per week)	
50	160	130
60	150	140
70	140	150
80	130	160
90	120	170
100	110	180

a. Draw a graph of the potato chip market and mark in the equilibrium price and quantity.
b. Suppose that chips are 60¢ a bag. Describe the situation in the market for chips and explain how the price adjusts.

9. In problem 7, suppose that a fire destroys some gum-producing factories and the supply of gum decreases by 40 million packs a week.
a. Has there been a shift of or a movement along the supply curve of gum?
b. Has there been a shift of or a movement along the demand curve for gum?
c. What are the new equilibrium price and equilibrium quantity of gum?

10. In problem 8, suppose a new dip comes onto the market, which is very popular and the demand for potato chips increases by 30 million bags per week.
a. Has there been a shift of or a movement along the supply curve of potato chips?
b. Has there been a shift of or a movement along the demand curve for gum?
c. What are the new equilibrium price and equilibrium quantity of potato chips?

11. In problem 9, suppose an increase in the teenage population increases the demand for gum by 40 million packs per week at the same time as the fire occurs. What are the new equilibrium price and quantity of gum?

12. In problem 10, suppose that a virus destroys several potato farms with the result that the supply of potato chips decreases by 40 million bags a week at the same time as the dip comes onto the market. What are the new equilibrium price and quantity of potato chips?

CRITICAL THINKING

1. After you have studied *Reading Between the Lines* on pp. 76–77, answer the following questions:
a. What happened to the price of oil between 2004 and 2005?
b. Why did the supply-side event reported in the news article have almost no effect on the supply of oil?
c. Why did the demand for oil increase in 2005?
d. Why did the equilibrium quantity of oil increase in 2005?
e. What might eventually decrease the demand for oil and lower its equilibrium price?

WEB EXERCISES

Use the links on (X) myeconlab to work the following exercises.

1. Obtain data on the prices and quantities of wheat.
a. Make a figure similar to Fig. 3.7 on p. 70 to illustrate the market for wheat since 2001.
b. Show the changes in demand and supply and the changes in the quantity demanded and the quantity supplied that are consistent with the price and quantity data.
2. Obtain data on the price of oil.
a. Describe how the price of oil has changed over the past five years.
b. Draw a demand-supply graph to explain what happens to the price when there is an increase or a decrease in supply and no change in demand.
c. What do you predict would happen to the price of oil if a new drilling technology permitted deeper ocean sources to be used?
d. What do you predict would happen to the price of oil if a clean and safe nuclear technology were developed?
e. What do you predict would happen to the price of oil if automobiles were powered by batteries instead of by internal combustion engines?

The Amazing Market

The four chapters that you've just studied explain how markets work. The market is an amazing instrument. It enables people who have never met and who know nothing about each other to interact and do business. It also enables us to allocate our scarce resources to the uses that we value most highly. Markets can be very simple or highly organized.

A simple market is one that the American historian Daniel J. Boorstin describes in *The Discoverers* (p. 161). In the late fourteenth century,

> *The Muslim caravans that went southward from Morocco across the Atlas Mountains arrived after twenty days at the shores of the Senegal River. There the Moroccan traders laid out separate piles of salt, of beads from Ceutan coral, and cheap manufactured goods. Then they retreated out of sight. The local tribesmen, who lived in the strip mines where they dug their gold, came to the shore and put a heap of gold beside each pile of Moroccan goods. Then they, in turn, went out of view, leaving the Moroccan traders either to take the gold offered for a particular pile or to reduce the pile of their merchandise to suit the offered price in gold. Once again the Moroccan traders withdrew, and the process went on. By this system of commercial etiquette, the Moroccans collected their gold.*

An organized market is the Toronto Stock Exchange, which trades many millions of stocks each day. Another is an auction at which the government sells rights to broadcasters and cellular telephone companies for the use of the airwaves.

All of these markets determine the prices at which exchanges take place and enable both buyers and sellers to benefit.

Everything and anything that can be exchanged is traded in markets. There are markets for goods and services; for resources such as labour, capital, and raw materials; for dollars, pounds, and yen; for goods to be delivered now and for goods to be delivered in the future. Only the imagination places limits on what can be traded in markets.

You began your study of markets in Chapter 3 by learning about the laws of demand and supply. There, you discovered the forces that make prices adjust to coordinate buying plans and selling plans.

The laws of demand and supply that you've learned and used in these four chapters were discovered during the nineteenth century by some remarkable economists. We conclude our study of demand and supply and markets by looking at the lives and times of some of these economists and by talking to a leading Canadian economist who studies labour markets.

Discovering the Laws of Demand and Supply

> "The forces to be dealt with are... so numerous, that it is best to take a few at a time. ... Thus we begin by isolating the primary relations of supply, demand, and price."
>
> ALFRED MARSHALL
> *The Principles of Economics*

THE ECONOMIST

Alfred Marshall *(1842–1924) grew up in an England that was being transformed by the railroad and by the expansion of manufacturing. Mary Paley was one of Marshall's students at Cambridge, and when Alfred and Mary married, in 1877, celibacy rules barred Alfred from continuing to teach at Cambridge. By 1884, with more liberal rules, the Marshalls returned to Cambridge, where Alfred became Professor of Political Economy.*

Many others had a hand in refining the theory of demand and supply, but the first thorough and complete statement of the theory as we know it today was set out by Alfred Marshall, with the acknowledged help of Mary Paley Marshall. Published in 1890, this monumental treatise, The Principles of Economics, *became the textbook on economics on both sides of the Atlantic for almost half a century. Marshall was an outstanding mathematician, but he kept mathematics and even diagrams in the background. His supply and demand diagram appears only in a footnote.*

THE ISSUES

The laws of demand and supply that you studied in Chapter 3 were discovered during the 1830s by Antoine-Augustin Cournot (1801–1877), a professor of mathematics at the University of Lyon, France. Although Cournot was the first to use demand and supply, it was the development and expansion of the railroads during the 1850s that gave the newly emerging theory its first practical applications. Railroads then were at the cutting edge of technology just as airlines are today. And as in the airline industry today, competition among the railroads was fierce.

Dionysius Lardner (1793–1859), an Irish professor of philosophy at the University of London, used demand and supply to show railroad companies how they could increase their profits by cutting rates on long-distance business on which competition was fiercest and by raising rates on short-haul business on which they had less to fear from other transportation suppliers.

Today, economists use the principles that Lardner worked out during the 1850s to calculate the freight rates and passenger fares that will give airlines the largest possible profit. And the rates calculated have a lot in common with the railroad rates of the nineteenth century. On local routes on which there is little competition, fares per kilometre are highest, and on long-distance routes on which the airlines compete fiercely, fares per kilometre are lowest.

Known satirically among scientists of the day as "Dionysius Diddler," Lardner worked on an amazing range of problems from astronomy to railway engineering to economics. A colourful character, he would have been a regular guest on late-night talk shows if they had been around in the 1850s. Lardner visited the École des Ponts et Chaussées (School of

Bridges and Roads) in Paris and must have learned a great deal from Jules Dupuit.

In France, Jules Dupuit (1804–1866), a French engineer/economist, used demand to calculate the benefits from building a bridge and, once the bridge was built, for calculating the toll to charge for its use. His work was the forerunner of what is today called *cost-benefit analysis*. Working with the principles invented by Dupuit, economists today calculate the costs and benefits of highways and airports, dams, and power stations.

NOW

Today, using the same principles that Dupuit devised, economists calculate whether the benefits of expanding airports and air-traffic control facilities are sufficient to cover their costs. Airline companies use the principles developed by Lardner to set their prices and to decide when to offer "seat sales." Like the railroads before them, the airlines charge a high price per kilometre on short flights, for which they face little competition, and a low price per kilometre on long flights, for which competition is fierce.

THEN

Dupuit used the law of demand to determine whether a bridge or canal would be valued enough by its users to justify the cost of building it. Lardner first worked out the relationship between the cost of production and supply and used demand and supply theory to explain the costs, prices, and profits of railroad operations. He also used the theory to discover ways of increasing revenue by raising rates on short-haul business and lowering them on long-distance freight.

Markets do an amazing job. The laws of demand and supply help us to understand how markets work. But in some situations, a market must be designed and institutions must be created to enable the market to function well. Also, the item traded often makes a crucial difference to how the market works. One market that has some special features is the labour market, as you will discover in the conversation on the following pages with Paul Beaudry, one of Canada's leading economists.

TALKING WITH

Paul Beaudry is a Professor of Economics at the University of British Columbia and currently holds the Canada Research Chair in Economics. He is also a Faculty Research Fellow at the National Bureau of Economic Research in the United States. He was born in Québec City in 1960. He obtained a bachelor's degree in Economics at the Université Laval, a master's degree at the University of British Columbia, and a doctoral degree at Princeton University. Professor Beaudry's research is concerned with the functioning of markets, particularly the labour market. Professor Beaudry was granted the Bank of Canada's Research Fellowship for 2005.

Paul Beaudry

Benoît Carmichael and Patrick González (co-authors of our French Canadian edition) talked with Paul Beaudry about his work and the progress economists have made since the time of Alfred Marshall in understanding how markets work.

Professor Beaudry, what attracted you to economics?

Several factors influenced my choice. During my secondary education and at the beginning of the CEGEP, I was mostly interested in mathematics and science. Then, at the university, I was introduced to philosophy and to philosophical questions. Philosophy classes deeply moved me. In fact, they changed my vision of the world. I became passionate about fundamental questions such as: Why do I exist? What is the notion of good and evil? What is a just society?

All these questions started to make me doubt. Initially, I thought that I would follow a career in science or engineering, but all these questions put me in a state of uncertainty. So I decided to stop my studies and travel. I worked in construction, so I could afford a big trip for myself. I travelled through all of Europe, North Africa, and Turkey. While on these trips, I talked a lot about philosophical and social questions with the people that I met. It was a fabulous experience!

During these talks economic questions were often raised: Why are certain countries rich and others poor? What should we do to reduce these inequalities? I quickly realized that the questions I understood the least were those related to the economics, and I thought that these question were important ones. Moreover, I was beginning to believe that several of the fundamental philosophical questions I was thinking about were impossible to solve. But this was not the case for economic questions. So I decided to get back to my studies and to study economics. I found that studies in economics allowed me both to address important social and human questions and to use formal mathematics tools that I liked.

What do we know today about the functioning of markets that Alfred Marshall ignored?

In the classical framework of Alfred Marshall, prices play an important role, but quite a simple one. When the price of a good rises, consumers want to consume less of it, and producers want to produce more of it. In Marshall's world, economic market participants do not try to extract information from prices, they react in a mechanical way.

On the other hand, in several markets, prices play a much more complex role than that envisioned by Marshall. Let's take the example of the stock market. The holder of a share listed on the stock exchange won't necessarily want to sell it when its price increases. Indeed, the increase in the share price can signify that the underlying company is in a good position to make profits; the holder will then want to wait for the share price to increase again. Let's take another example. When we buy a bottle of wine, we often think that its price is an indication of the quality of the wine. The information role of prices did not appear in Marshall's work.

In your research work, you are very interested in labour markets. What are the characteristics of labour markets that make them different from other markets?

When a company hires someone, it must ensure that the person is sufficiently motivated to perform the required tasks diligently and not shirk. In contrast, when a company buys a tonne of steel to build a bridge, it needn't wonder about the steel's motivation to do its work. A labour market is therefore very different from other markets because it is made up of individuals who have their own motivations and objectives. That is why one of the roles of a good employer is to find a way to reconcile the interests of an employee with those of the company.

For most goods, this kind of problem doesn't exist. Buying a good at the lowest possible price often proves to be the best strategy. However, an employer has to recognize that his employees want to be treated fairly and impartially. If he doesn't pay them enough, it is most probable that they won't put in much effort or show very much enthusiasm for their work.

> " *... when a company buys a tonne of steel to build a bridge, it needn't wonder about the steel's motivation to do its work. A labour market is ... different ... because it is made of individuals who have their own motivations and objectives.* "

Marshall believed that the market would direct young people towards the jobs they do best. But he believed that taxes should cover the cost of education. Today, some people see education as an investment in human capital that should be paid for by the families who benefit. What is your view on this issue?

Education has two aspects. It increases the skills of an individual in the labour market, and therefore also increases a person's earnings. Also, thanks to education, people are more informed, and that is important for the functioning of a democracy. In the first case, the gain is essentially private, so it seems reasonable to ask young people or their families to contribute to the costs of education. However, in the second case, the gain obtained through education is a social gain, so it seems fair that the state should cover a part of costs of education. This is, in fact, what we now observe. It remains very difficult to make decisions about what percentage of university fees students should pay? 75 percent? 50 percent? 25 percent? This question is open to debate.

Over the past 25 years in North America, we have observed a deterioration in the relative compensation of low-skilled workers. However, in European countries such as Germany, this decrease hasn't been as large. What explains this difference?

It is a very good question, and a topic that still raises lots of discussion. My own research puts forward the important role of demography. In North America, the baby boom of the 1950s and 1960s considerably increased the work force at the end of the 1970s and the beginning of the 1980s. On the other hand, during the same period, neither private savings nor

151

investment in physical capital increased. Thus, the increase in labour supply and the absence of an increase in the supply of physical capital created a relative shortage of physical capital.

The economy reacted to this shortage in several ways. We have observed a strong tendency towards the adoption of new methods of production which use physical capital in an efficient way, as well as an increase in imports of goods that use physical capital in an intensive way. These two changes have resulted in a reduction of the demand for labour, in particular among less-qualified workers. This, in turn, has

> " *What we have to remember is that the labour market is principally a market of long-term relations.* "

resulted in an increase of the gap in income between qualified and less-qualified workers. In Germany, where the baby boom was not so importance, the problem of a relative shortage of physical capital did not occur. The structure of employment remained stable and the income of less-qualified workers did not decrease.

Through your work, you have demonstrated that people who enter the labour market during a time of recession have less interesting career prospects than those who enter it during a period of expansion. Why is this so?

In spite of the fact that the labour market does not function exactly as the apple market does, it still is a market which reflects the strengths of the supply and demand model. In times of recession, the demand for labour is weak and people who enter the labour market in such times receive less attractive job offers.

What we have to remember is that the labour market is principally a market of long-term relations. Thus, if a worker enters the labour market during a good period, he will generally manage to negotiate a job that will offer him promising career prospects. Conversely, a worker who enters the labour market during a time of recession will generally obtain a badly paid job which offers mediocre career prospects. This is in fact what the analytical frame-

work of supply and demand predicts in the case of a market based on long-term relations.

How should the government intervene in the labour market when it is undergoing profound structural change? Are the usual policies (such as employment insurance) still appropriate?

First, we have to understand that the labour market is in a state of continuous flux. It is very difficult for a government to make the distinction between a structural change and cyclical change (the latter being more temporary). Government intervention is therefore limited. At best, the state can help individuals absorb the many ups and downs of the labour market without having to determine whether the change is structural or not. This is precisely the role played by employment insurance.

Unfortunately, employment insurance programs are not perfect, and they often do not help people adapt to change. Employment insurance must be flexible and allow people to go back to university or to experiment with new types of jobs. Too often, employment insurance incites people to the status quo and in so doing does not fulfill its primary function: that of helping workers to adapt to a labour market in perpetual flux.

How do you recognize a good economics student? Are there any particular skills that you are looking for?

A good economics student is a student who likes history and politics and who is not afraid of mathematics. A good economic student is one who observes society and who asks why things are the way they are.

A characteristic that I always look for in an economics student is open-mindedness. A student must not have too many preconceived ideas or be too politically committed. If he or she is too involved in a social cause, he or she often loses some sense of objectivity. That said, the student must be passionate about social issues but shouldn't believe that he or she already knows all the answers and risks becoming the champion of a cause instead of an economics researcher.

Emotions and principles have their place, but facts and scientific methods are the very essence of the rigorous economic research that provides answers about the functioning of the economy.

A First Look at Macroeconomics

CHAPTER 19

What Will Your World Be Like?

During the past 100 years, the quantity of goods and services produced in Canada's farms, factories, shops, and offices has expanded more than twentyfold. As a result, we have a much higher standard of living than our grandparents had. Will production always expand?

For most of us, a high standard of living means finding a good job. What kind of job will you find when you graduate? Will you have lots of choice, or will you face a labour market with a high unemployment rate in which jobs are hard to find?

A high standard of living means being able to afford to buy life's necessities and have some fun. If prices rise too quickly, some people get left behind and must trim what they buy. What will the dollar buy next year; in ten years when you are paying off your student loan; and in 50 years when you are spending your life's savings in retirement?

Since 1997, the federal government has collected more in taxes than it has spent on public services. But for the 26 years before 1997, the government ran a deficit. How will government budget deficits and surpluses affect your future?

To keep production expanding and prevent an economic slowdown, the federal government and the Bank of Canada—the nation's financial managers—take policy actions. How do their actions influence production, jobs, prices, and the ability of Canadians to compete in the global marketplace?

◆ These are the questions of macroeconomics that you are about to study. In *Reading Between the Lines* at the end of the chapter, we'll take a quick look at Canada's macroeconomic performance in 2005.

After studying this chapter, you will be able to

- ■ **Describe the origins and issues of macroeconomics**
- ■ **Describe the trends and fluctuations in economic growth**
- ■ **Describe the trends and fluctuations in jobs and unemployment**
- ■ **Describe the trends and fluctuations in inflation**
- ■ **Describe the trends and fluctuations in government and international deficits**
- ■ **Identify the macroeconomic policy challenges and describe the tools available for meeting them**

Origins and Issues of Macroeconomics

ECONOMISTS BEGAN TO STUDY ECONOMIC growth, inflation, and international payments as long ago as the 1750s, and this work was the origin of macroeconomics. But modern macroeconomics did not emerge until the **Great Depression**, a decade (1929–1939) of high unemployment and stagnant production throughout the world economy. In the Depression's worst year, 1933, the production of Canada's farms, factories, shops, and offices was only 70 percent of its 1929 level and 20 percent of the labour force was unemployed. These were years of human misery on a scale that is hard to imagine today. They were also years of extreme pessimism about the ability of the market economy to work properly. Many people believed that private ownership, free markets, and democratic political institutions could not survive.

The science of economics had no solutions to the Great Depression. The major alternative system of central planning and socialism seemed increasingly attractive to many people. It was in this climate of economic depression and political and intellectual turmoil that modern macroeconomics emerged with the publication in 1936 of John Maynard Keynes' *The General Theory of Employment, Interest, and Money* (see pp. 530–531).

Short-Term Versus Long-Term Goals

Keynes' theory was that depression and high unemployment result from insufficient private spending and that to cure these problems, the government must increase its spending. Keynes focused primarily on the *short term*. He wanted to cure an immediate problem almost regardless of the *long-term* consequences of the cure. "In the long run," said Keynes, "we're all dead."

But Keynes believed that after his cure for depression had restored the economy to a normal condition, the long-term problems of inflation and slow economic growth would return. And he suspected that his cure for depression, increased government spending, might trigger inflation and might lower the long-term growth rate of production. With a lower long-term growth rate, the economy would create fewer jobs. If this outcome did occur, a policy aimed at lowering unemployment in the short run might end up increasing it in the long run.

By the late 1960s and through the 1970s, Keynes' predictions became a reality. Inflation increased, economic growth slowed, and in some countries unemployment became persistently high. The causes of these developments are complex. But they point to an inescapable conclusion: The long-term problems of inflation, slow growth, and persistent unemployment and the short-term problems of economic fluctuations intertwine and are most usefully studied together. So although macroeconomics was reborn during the Great Depression, it has now returned to its older tradition. Today, macroeconomics is a subject that tries to understand long-term economic growth and inflation as well as short-term business fluctuations and unemployment.

The Road Ahead

There is no unique way to study macroeconomics. Because its rebirth was a product of depression, the common practice for many years was to pay most attention to short-term output fluctuations and unemployment, but never to completely lose sight of the long-term issues. When a rapid inflation emerged during the 1970s, this topic returned to prominence. During the 1980s, when long-term growth slowed in Canada and other rich industrial countries but exploded in East Asia, economists redirected their energy towards economic growth. During the 1990s, as information technologies further shrank the globe, the international dimension of macroeconomics became more prominent. The result of these developments is that modern macroeconomics is a broad subject that studies all the issues we've just identified: economic growth and fluctuations, unemployment, inflation, and government and international deficits.

Over the past 40 years, economists have developed a clearer understanding of the forces that determine macroeconomic performance and have devised policies that they hope will improve this performance. Your main goal is to become familiar with the theories of macroeconomics and the policies that they make possible. To set you on your path towards this goal, we're going to take a first look at economic growth, jobs and unemployment, inflation, and surpluses and deficits, and learn why these macroeconomic phenomena merit our attention.

myeconlab   **Study Plan 19.1**

Growth and Fluctuations

YOUR PARENTS ARE RICHER THAN YOUR GRAND-parents were when they were young. But are you going to be richer than your parents are? And are your children going to be richer than you? The answers depend on the rate of economic growth.

Economic growth is the expansion of the economy's production possibilities. It can be pictured as an outward shift of the production possibilities frontier (*PPF*)—see Chapter 2, pp. 40–41.

We measure economic growth by the increase in real gross domestic product. **Real gross domestic product** (also called **real GDP**) is the value of the total production of all the nation's farms, factories, shops, and offices measured in the prices of a single year. Real GDP in Canada is currently measured in the prices of 1997 (called 1997 dollars). We use the dollar prices of a single year to eliminate the influence of *inflation*—the increase in the average level of prices—and determine how much production has grown from one year to another. (Real GDP is explained more fully in Chapter 20 on pp. 466–470.)

Real GDP is not a perfect measure of total production because it does not include everything that is produced. It excludes the things we produce for ourselves at home (preparing meals, doing laundry, house painting, gardening, and so on). It also excludes production that people hide to avoid taxes or because the activity is illegal—the underground economy. But despite its shortcomings, real GDP is the best measure of total production available. Let's see what it tells us about economic growth.

Growth and Fluctuations in Canada

Figure 19.1 shows real GDP in Canada since 1961 and highlights two features of economic growth:

- The growth of potential GDP
- Fluctuations of real GDP around potential GDP

The Growth of Potential GDP When all the economy's labour, capital, land, and entrepreneurial ability are fully employed, the value of production is called **potential GDP**. Real GDP fluctuates around potential GDP and the rate of long-term economic growth is measured by the growth rate of potential GDP. It is shown by the steepness of the potential GDP line (the black line) in Fig. 19.1.

From 1960 through 1973, potential GDP grew at an unusually rapid rate of 5.1 percent a year. But the growth rate slowed from the mid-1970s to the mid-1990s. The growth rate of output per person sagged during these years in a phenomenon called the **productivity growth slowdown**. The growth rate of potential GDP increased during the late 1990s and 2000s, but it is too soon to tell whether this increase is the beginning of a new phase of more rapid growth.

Why did the productivity growth slowdown occur? This question is controversial. We explore the causes of the productivity growth slowdown in Chapter 31. Whatever its cause, the slowdown means that we all have smaller incomes today than we would have had if the economy had continued to grow at its 1960s rate.

Let's now look at real GDP fluctuations around potential GDP.

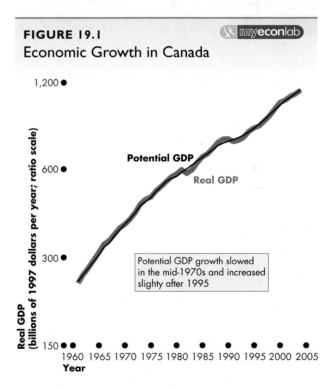

FIGURE 19.1
Economic Growth in Canada

Potential GDP growth slowed in the mid-1970s and increased slighty after 1995

The growth rate of potential GDP was 5.1 percent a year from 1960 through 1973. Growth slowed from the mid-1970s to the mid-1990s but sped up slightly after 1995. Real GDP fluctuates around potential GDP.

Sources of data: Real GDP, Statistics Canada, Table 380–0017. Potential GDP, calculated from Bank of Canada and International Monetary Fund estimates of the gap between actual real GDP and potential GDP.

Fluctuations of Real GDP Around Potential GDP
Real GDP fluctuates around potential GDP in a
business cycle. A **business cycle** is the periodic but
irregular up-and-down movement in production.

Business cycles are not regular, predictable, or
repeating cycles like the phases of the moon. Their
timing changes unpredictably. But cycles do have some
things in common. Every business cycle has two
phases:

1. A recession
2. An expansion

and two turning points:

1. A peak
2. A trough

Figure 19.2 shows these features of the most
recent business cycle in Canada. A **recession** is a
period during which real GDP decreases—the growth
rate of real GDP is negative—for at least two successive quarters. The most recent recession, which is
highlighted in the figure, began in the first quarter of
1990 and ended in the first quarter of 1991. This
recession lasted for four quarters. An **expansion** is a
period during which real GDP increases. The most
recent expansion began in the second quarter of 1991.
This expansion is the longest expansion on record. An
earlier expansion ended in the first quarter of 1990.

When a business cycle expansion ends and a recession begins, the turning point is called a *peak*. The
most recent peak occurred in the first quarter of 1990.
When a business cycle recession ends and an expansion
begins, the turning point is called a *trough*. The most
recent trough occurred in the first quarter of 1991.

Recessions are rare. But real GDP sometimes
sinks below potential GDP without a recession,
when the growth rate remains positive. A **growth
recession** occurs when the real GDP growth rate
remains positive but slows so that real GDP falls
below potential GDP. Three growth recessions
occurred during the long expansion of the 1990s
and 2000s: from the beginning of 1995 to the first
quarter of 1996, from mid-2000 to mid-2001, and
for most of 2003.

FIGURE 19.2
The Most Recent Canadian Business Cycle

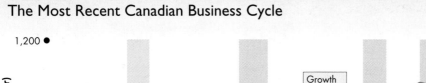

A business cycle has two
phases: recession and expansion. The most recent recession (highlighted) ran from
the first quarter of 1990
through the first quarter of
1991. Then a new expansion
began in the second quarter
of 1991. A business cycle has
two turning points, a peak and
a trough. In the most recent
business cycle, the peak
occurred in the first quarter
of 1990 and the trough
occurred in the first quarter
of 1991. Growth recessions
occurred in 1995–1996,
2000–2001, and 2003.

Sources of data: Real GDP, Statistics Canada, Table 380–0017. Potential GDP, calculated from Bank of Canada and International Monetary Fund estimates of the gap
between real GDP and potential GDP.

The Most Recent Recession in Historical Perspective Compared with earlier recessions, the 1991 recession was mild. You can see how mild by looking at Fig. 19.3, which shows a longer history of Canadian economic growth. The biggest decrease in real GDP occurred during the Great Depression of the 1930s. A decrease also occurred in 1946 and 1947, after a huge World War II expansion. A serious recession also occurred during the early 1980s, when the Bank of Canada and the Federal Reserve Board in the United States hiked interest rates to previously unimagined levels.

Each of these economic downturns was more severe than that in 1991. But you can see that the Great Depression was much more severe than anything that followed it. This episode was so extreme that we call it a *depression*.

This last truly great depression occurred before governments started taking policy actions to stabilize the economy. It also occurred before the birth of modern macroeconomics. Is the absence of another great depression a sign that macroeconomics has contributed to economic stability? Some people believe it is. Others doubt it. We'll evaluate these opinions on a number of occasions in this book.

We've looked at real GDP growth and fluctuations in Canada. But is the Canadian experience typical? Do other countries share our experience? Let's see whether they do.

Economic Growth Around the World

All countries experience economic growth, but the growth rate varies both over time and across countries. The fluctuations in economic growth rates over time tend to be correlated across countries, but some countries experience greater volatility in growth rates than others. And some growth rate differences across countries persist over a number of years.

We'll compare Canada's economic growth over time with that in other countries. And we'll look at longer term differences in economic growth rates among countries and groups of countries.

Growth Rates over Time First, we'll compare the growth rate of real GDP per person in Canada with that in the three largest economies: the United States, Japan, and Germany.

FIGURE 19.3
Long-Term Economic Growth in Canada

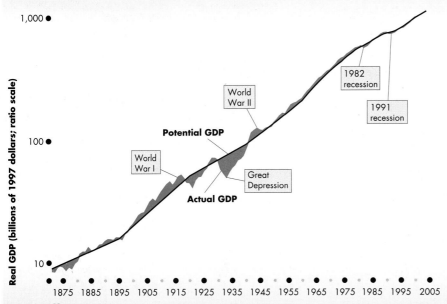

The thin black line shows potential GDP. Along this line, real GDP grew at an average rate of 3.7 percent a year between 1870 and 2001. The blue areas show when real GDP was above potential GDP, and the red areas show when it was below potential GDP. During some periods, such as World War II, real GDP expanded quickly. During other periods, such as the Great Depression and more recently in 1982 (following interest rate hikes) and 1991, real GDP declined.

Sources of data: 1870–1925, Angus Maddison, *Dynamic Forces in Capitalist Development*, Oxford University Press, New York, 1991. 1926–2001, and Statistics Canada, *Historical Statistics of Canada*, series F 55 and CANSIM series v1992292.

Figure 19.4(a) shows these four growth rates from 1960 to 2000 (from 1970 for Germany). You can see three striking facts in the figure. First, during the 1960s Japan's growth rate was much faster than that in the other countries. Second, after 1970 all four growth rates were similar. And third, Canada's growth rate has been a bit less that that of the United States so the gap between Canada and the United States has widened slightly.

Persistent Differences in Growth Rates Second, we'll look at longer term persistent differences across countries. Figure 19.4(b) compares the growth of the Canadian economy with that of several other countries and regions from 1980 through 2004. Among the advanced economies (the red bars), the European Union has grown the slowest and the U.S. economy has grown fastest. Canada is just behind the United States.

Among the developing economies (the green bars) the most rapid growth has occurred in Asia, where the average growth rate was more than 7 percent a year. The slowest growing developing countries are in the Western Hemisphere (Central and South America) and Africa.

The transition economies (purple bar) include those of Russia and the countries of Central and Eastern Europe that are making a transition from a state-managed economy to a market economy. Growth in Central and Eastern Europe averaged 2 percent a year. But production in Russia has shrunk.

World average growth (the blue bar) has been 3.4 percent a year, somewhat greater than the Canadian growth rate.

Consequences of Persistent Differences The persistent differences in growth rates are bringing dramatic change in how world real GDP is shared across economies. Because Canada and the United States are growing more slowly than the world, the North American economy's share of world real GDP is falling. But some fast-growing nations such as China and India are becoming significantly bigger parts of the global economy. China's share of world real GDP increased from 4 percent in 1980 to 13 percent in 2004 and India increased from 2 percent in 1980 to 6 percent in 2004. And the share of these large Asian economies continues to expand. If the current trends persist, the Asian economy will be larger than that of North America by around 2020.

FIGURE 19.4 *myeconlab*
Economic Growth Around the World

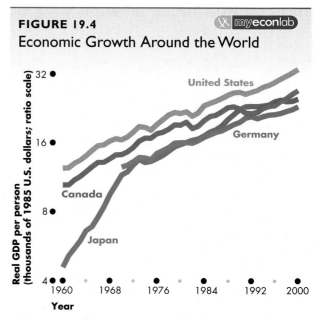

(a) Canada and three large economies

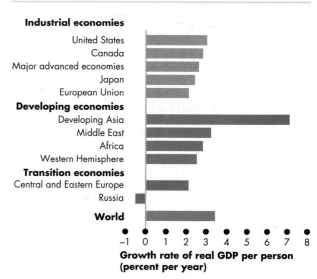

(b) Average growth rates: 1980–2004

In part (a), Japan grew fastest during the 1960s. Canadian economic growth has been a bit slower than that of the United States. In part (b), growth rate differences persist. Between 1980 and 2004, Asian economies grew fastest and the Russian economy shrank. The Canadian growth rate is a bit lower than the world average growth rate.

Source of data: Alan Heston, Robert Summers, and Bettina Aten, Penn World Table Version 6.1, Center for International Comparisons at the University of Pennsylvania (CICUP), October 2002. and International Monetary Fund, *World Economic Outlook,* September 2005, Washington, D.C.

The Lucas Wedge and the Okun Gap

You've seen that productivity growth slowed during the 1970s. And you've seen that real GDP growth fluctuates so that real GDP falls below potential GDP from time to time. How costly are the growth slowdown and lost output over the business cycle?

The answers are provided by two measures:

- The Lucas wedge
- The Okun gap

The Lucas Wedge The **Lucas wedge** is the accumulated loss of output that results from a slowdown in the growth rate of real GDP per person. It is given this name because Robert E. Lucas Jr., a leading macroeconomist, drew attention to it and remarked that once you begin to think about the benefits of faster economic growth, it is hard to think about anything else!

Figure 19.5(a) shows the Lucas wedge that arises from the productivity growth slowdown of the 1970s. The black line in the figure tracks the path that potential GDP would have followed if its 1960s growth rate had been maintained through the next 35 years to 2005.

The Lucas wedge is a staggering $11.5 trillion—10 years' real GDP at the 2005 level. This incredibly large number is a measure of the cost of slower productivity growth.

The Okun Gap Real GDP minus potential GDP is called the **output gap**. The output gap can be positive (real GDP exceeds potential GDP) or negative (potential GDP exceeds real GDP). When the output gap is negative, it is sometimes called the *Okun gap* because Arthur M. Okun, an economic adviser to President Lyndon Johnson, drew attention to it as a source of loss from economic fluctuations.

Figure 19.5(b) shows the Okun gap from the recessions that occurred over the same years as those for which we've just calculated the Lucas wedge.

The Okun gap is $173 billion—about two months of real GDP in 2005. This number is a measure of the cost of business cycle fluctuations.

You can see that the Lucas wedge is a much bigger deal than the Okun gap—*66 times* as big a deal! Smoothing the business cycle saves spells of high unemployment and lost output. But maintaining a high rate of productivity growth makes a dramatic difference to the standard of living.

FIGURE 19.5 myeconlab

The Lucas Wedge and the Okun Gap

(a) The Lucas wedge

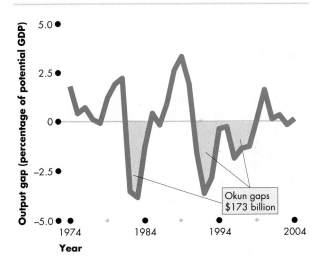

(b) The Okun gap

In part (a), the Lucas wedge that arises from the productivity growth slowdown of the 1970s is a staggering $11.5 trillion or ten times the real GDP of 2005.

In part (b), the Okun gap that arises from the lost production in recessions since the early 1970s amount to $173 billion or about two months of real GDP in 2005.

Over this 35-year period, the Lucas wedge is 66 times as large as the Okun gap.

Sources of data: Real GDP, Statistics Canada, Table 380–0017. Potential GDP calculated from Bank of Canada and International Monetary Fund estimates of the gap between actual and potential GDP. Growth projections are authors' calculations.

Benefits and Costs of Economic Growth

The Lucas wedge is a measure of the dollar value of lost real GDP if the growth rate slows. But this cost translates into real goods and services. It is a cost in terms of an inferior Canadian health-care system, fewer child-care services, worse roads, and less housing. We even have less to spend on cleaner lakes, more trees, and cleaner air.

But fast growth is also costly. Its main cost is forgone *current* consumption. To sustain a high growth rate, resources must be devoted to advancing technology and accumulating capital rather than to *current* consumption. This cost cannot be avoided. But it brings the benefit of greater consumption in the future. (See Chapter 2, p. 38.)

Two other possible costs of faster growth are a more rapid depletion of exhaustible natural resources such as oil and natural gas and increased pollution of the air, rivers, and oceans. But neither of these two costs is inevitable. The technological advances that bring economic growth help us to economize on natural resources and to clean up the environment. For example, more efficient auto engines cut gasoline use and tailpipe emissions.

REVIEW QUIZ

1 What is economic growth and how is the long-term economic growth rate measured?
2 What is the distinction between real GDP and potential GDP?
3 What is a business cycle and what are its phases?
4 What is a recession?
5 In what phase of the business cycle was the Canadian economy during 2005?
6 What happened to economic growth in Canada and other countries during the 1970s?
7 What are the benefits and the costs of long-term economic growth?

myeconlab Study Plan 19.2

We've seen that real GDP grows and that it fluctuates over the business cycle. The business cycle brings fluctuations in the number of jobs available and in unemployment. Let's now examine these macroeconomic problems.

Jobs and Unemployment

WHAT KIND OF LABOUR MARKET WILL YOU ENTER when you graduate? Will there be plenty of good jobs to choose from, or will there be so much unemployment that you will be forced to take a low-paying job that doesn't use your education? The answer depends, to a large degree, on the total number of jobs available and on the unemployment rate.

Jobs

The Canadian economy is an incredible job-creating machine. In 2005, 16 million Canadians or 62 percent of those aged 15 years and older had jobs. That number is 2.7 million more than in 1995 and 4.4 million more than in 1985. Every year, on the average, since the mid-1970s, the Canadian economy has created about 220,000 *additional* jobs. Since 2000, it has created 1.6 million additional jobs.

The pace of job creation and destruction fluctuates over the business cycle. More jobs are destroyed than created during a recession, so the number of jobs decreases. For example, during the 1991 recession, Canadian production shrank and 260,000 jobs disappeared. But through the expansion that followed, the number of jobs created expanded quickly and many more jobs were created during the expansion than the number destroyed in the recession. By the beginning of 1995, there were more people at work than before the recession began.

Unemployment

Not everyone who wants a job can find one. On any one day in a normal or average year, more than 1 million people are unemployed, and during a recession or depression, unemployment rises above this level. For example, in November 1992, the worst month for unemployment in recent times, 1,740,000 people were looking for jobs.

Unemployment is defined as a state in which a person does not have a job but is available for work, willing to work, and has made some effort to find work within the previous four weeks. The total number of people who are employed and unemployed is called the **labour force**. The **unemployment rate** is the percentage of the people in the labour force who are unemployed. (The concepts of the labour force and unemployment are explained more fully in Chapter 21 on pp. 488–489.)

The unemployment rate is not a perfect measure of the underutilization of labour for several reasons. We'll review two of the main ones.

First, the unemployment rate excludes discouraged workers. A **discouraged worker** is a person who does not have a job, is available for work, and is willing to work but who has given up the effort to find work. Many people switch between the unemployed and discouraged worker categories in both directions every month. Second, the unemployment rate measures unemployed people rather than unemployed labour hours. As a result, the unemployment rate excludes part-time workers who want full-time jobs.

These limitations of unemployment tend to underestimate the amount of labour market slack. But despite them, the unemployment rate is the best available measure of underused labour resources. Let's look at some facts about unemployment.

Unemployment in Canada

Figure 19.6 shows the unemployment rate in Canada from 1926 through 2005. Three features stand out. First, during the Great Depression of the 1930s, the unemployment rate climbed to an all-time high of almost 20 percent during 1933 and remained high throughout the 1930s.

Second, the unemployment rate reached an all-time low of 1.2 percent during World War II.

Third, although in recent years we have not experienced anything as devastating as the Great Depression, we have seen some high unemployment rates during recessions. The figure highlights two of them—the 1982 recession and the 1991 recession.

Fourth, the unemployment rate never falls to zero. In the period since World War II, the average unemployment rate has been 6.7 percent.

How does Canadian unemployment compare with unemployment in other countries?

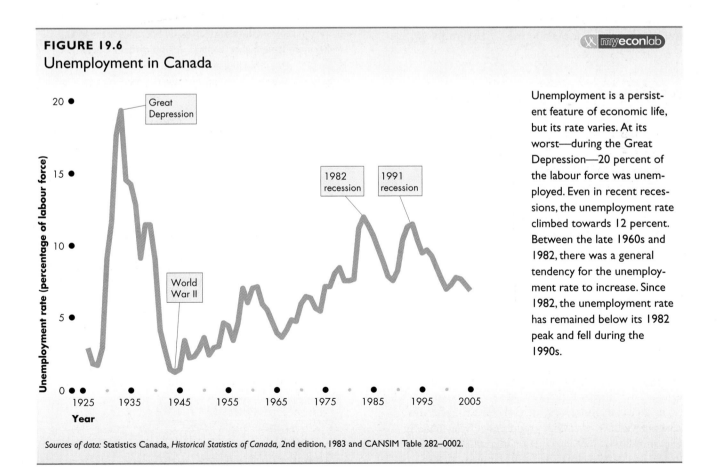

FIGURE 19.6
Unemployment in Canada

Unemployment is a persistent feature of economic life, but its rate varies. At its worst—during the Great Depression—20 percent of the labour force was unemployed. Even in recent recessions, the unemployment rate climbed towards 12 percent. Between the late 1960s and 1982, there was a general tendency for the unemployment rate to increase. Since 1982, the unemployment rate has remained below its 1982 peak and fell during the 1990s.

Sources of data: Statistics Canada, *Historical Statistics of Canada,* 2nd edition, 1983 and CANSIM Table 282–0002.

Unemployment Around the World

Figure 19.7 compares the unemployment rate in Canada with those in Western Europe, Japan, and the United States. Over the period shown in this figure, Canadian unemployment averaged 9 percent, much higher than Japanese unemployment (which averaged 3.3 percent), and higher than U.S. unemployment (which averaged 6.2 percent) and UK unemployment (which averaged 7.8 percent). Only the average of France, Italy, and Germany (9.2 percent) exceeded that of Canada.

Unemployment rates in all the countries fluctuate over the business cycle, increasing during a recession and decreasing during an expansion. The cycles in Canadian unemployment are similar to those in U.S. unemployment, but the European cycle is out of phase with the North American cycle.

During the past 25 years, the trend in U.S. unemployment has been downward and during the past 15 years, the trend in Japanese unemployment has been upward. The unemployment rates of Canada and Western Europe display no trends.

Let's now look at some of the consequences of unemployment that make it the serious problem that it is.

Why Unemployment Is a Problem

Unemployment is a serious economic, social, and personal problem for two main reasons:

- Lost production and incomes
- Lost human capital

Lost Production and Incomes The loss of a job brings an immediate loss of income and production. These losses are devastating for the people who bear them and make unemployment a frightening prospect for everyone. Employment insurance creates a safety net, but it does not provide the same living standard that having a job provides.

Lost Human Capital Prolonged unemployment can permanently damage a person's job prospects. For example, a manager loses his job when his employer downsizes. Short of income, he becomes a taxi driver. After a year in this work, he discovers that he can't compete with new MBA graduates. He eventually gets hired as a manager but in a small firm and at a low wage. He has lost some of his human capital.

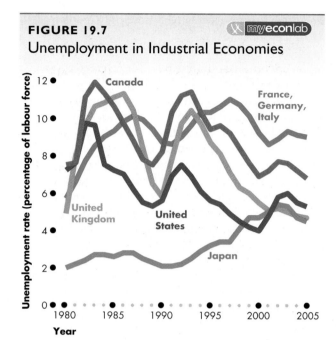

FIGURE 19.7
Unemployment in Industrial Economies

The unemployment rate in Canada has been higher, on the average, than the unemployment rates of the United States, the United Kingdom, and Japan. Only France, Italy, and Germany have higher average unemployment rates than Canada. The cycle in Canadian unemployment is similar to that in U.S. unemployment but out of phase with that in Western Europe.

Source of data: International Monetary Fund, *World Economic Outlook*, September 2005, Washington, D.C.

The costs of unemployment are spread unequally, which makes unemployment a highly charged political problem as well as a serious economic problem.

REVIEW QUIZ
1 What have been the main trends and cycles in the unemployment rate in Canada since 1926?
2 Compare unemployment in Canada, the United States, Western Europe, and Japan.
3 What are the main costs of unemployment that make it a serious problem?
myeconlab Study Plan 19.3

Let's now turn to the third major macroeconomic issue: inflation.

Inflation

PRICES ON THE AVERAGE CAN BE RISING, FALLING, or stable. **Inflation** is a process of rising prices. We measure the *inflation rate* as the percentage change in the *average* level of prices or the **price level**. A common measure of the price level is the *Consumer Price Index* (CPI). The CPI tells us how the average price of all the goods and services bought by a typical urban household changes from month to month. (The CPI is explained in Chapter 21, p. 498.)

So that you can see how the inflation rate is measured, let's do a calculation. In December 2003, the CPI was 122.3, and in December 2004, it was 124.6, so the inflation rate during 2004 was

$$\text{Inflation rate} = \frac{124.6 - 122.3}{122.3} \times 100$$

$$= 1.9 \text{ percent.}$$

Inflation in Canada

Figure 19.8 shows the Canadian inflation rate from 1960 through 2005. During the early 1960s, the inflation rate was low. It began to increase during the late 1960s at the time of the Vietnam War. But the largest increases occurred in 1974 and 1980, years in which the actions of the Organization of Petroleum Exporting Countries (OPEC) resulted in exceptionally large increases in the price of oil. Inflation was brought under control in the early 1980s when Bank of Canada Governor Gerald Bouey and U.S. Federal Reserve Chairman Paul Volcker pushed interest rates up and people cut back on their spending. Since the early 1990s, inflation has been kept inside an announced target range of between 1 percent and 3 percent a year.

The inflation rate rises and falls over the years, but it rarely becomes negative. If the inflation rate is negative, the price *level* is falling and we have **deflation**. Since the 1930s, the price level has generally increased—the inflation rate has been positive.

FIGURE 19.8
Inflation in Canada

Inflation is a persistent feature of economic life in Canada. The inflation rate was low in the first half of the 1960s, but it increased during the late 1960s at the time of the Vietnam War. The inflation rate increased further with the OPEC oil price hikes but eventually declined in the early 1980s because of policy actions taken by the Bank of Canada. Since the early 1990s the Bank of Canada has kept the inflation rate inside a target range of 1 to 3 percent a year.

Source of data: Statistics Canada, CANSIM Table 326–0002.

Inflation Around the World

Figure 19.9 shows inflation around the world since 1970. It also shows the Canadian inflation rate in a broader perspective. Part (a) shows that the other industrial countries shared Canada's burst of double-digit inflation during the 1970s and the decline in inflation during the 1980s and 1990s. But Canada has achieved a lower inflation rate than most countries. Part (b) shows that the average inflation rate of industrial countries has been very low compared with that of developing counties. Among the developing countries, the most extreme inflation in recent times occurred in the Democratic Republic of Congo, where the inflation rate was 23,773 percent a year in 1994!

Is Inflation a Problem?

A very low inflation rate is not a problem. But a high inflation rate is a serious problem. It makes inflation hard to predict, and unpredictable inflation makes the economy behave a bit like a casino in which some people gain and some lose and no one can predict where the gains and losses will fall. Gains and losses occur because of unpredictable changes in the value of money. Money is used as a measuring rod of value in the transactions that we undertake. Borrowers and lenders, workers and employers, all make contracts in terms of money. If the value of money varies unpredictably over time, then the amounts *really* paid and received—the quantity of goods that the money will buy—also fluctuate unpredictably. Measuring value with a measuring rod whose units vary is a bit like trying to measure a piece of cloth with an elastic ruler. The size of the cloth depends on how tightly the ruler is stretched.

In a period of rapid, unpredictable inflation, resources get diverted from productive activities to forecasting inflation. It becomes more profitable to forecast the inflation rate correctly than to invent a new product. Doctors, lawyers, accountants, farmers—just about everyone—can make themselves better off, not by specializing in the profession for which they have been trained but by spending more of their time dabbling as amateur economists and inflation forecasters and managing their investment portfolios.

From a social perspective, this diversion of talent resulting from inflation is like throwing scarce resources onto the garbage heap. This waste of resources is a cost of inflation.

FIGURE 19.9
Inflation Around the World

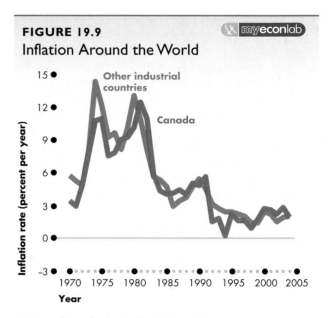

(a) Canada and other industrial countries

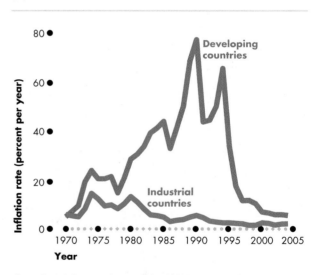

(b) Industrial countries and developing countries

Inflation in Canada is similar to that in other industrial countries. Compared with developing countries, inflation in Canada and the other industrial countries is low.

Sources of data: International Monetary Fund, *International Financial Statistics Yearbook*, Washington, D.C., 2004.

The most serious type of inflation is called *hyperinflation*—an inflation rate that exceeds 50 percent a month. At the height of a hyperinflation, workers are often paid twice a day because money loses its value so quickly. As soon as workers are paid, they rush out to spend their wages before they lose too much value.

Hyperinflation is rare but there have been some spectacular examples of it. Several European countries experienced hyperinflation during the 1920s after World War I and again during the 1940s after World War II. During these episodes, money became utterly worthless and the financial system collapsed.

But hyperinflation is more than just a historical curiosity. It can occur at any time. In 1994, when the Democratic Republic of Congo had an inflation rate of 23,773 percent a year, its price level was rising by 58 percent a month! Bolivia, Nicaragua, and Peru have had inflation rates in exess of 10,000 percent a year—close to 50 percent a month—during the past 20 years.

Inflation imposes costs, but getting rid of inflation is also costly. Policies that lower the inflation rate increase the unemployment rate. Most economists think the increase in the unemployment rate that accompanies a fall in the inflation rate is temporary. But some economists say that higher unemployment is a permanent cost of low inflation. The cost of lowering inflation must be evaluated when an anti-inflation policy is pursued. You will learn more about inflation and the costs of curing it in Chapter 28.

REVIEW QUIZ

1 What is inflation and how does it influence the value of money?
2 How is inflation measured?
3 What has been Canada's inflation record since 1961?
4 How does inflation in Canada compare with inflation in other industrial countries and in developing countries?
5 What are some of the costs of inflation that make it a serious economic problem?

myeconlab Study Plan 19.4

Now that you've studied economic growth and fluctuations, unemployment, and inflation, let's turn to the fourth macroeconomic issue: surpluses and deficits. What happens when a government spends more than it collects in taxes? And what happens when a nation buys more from other countries than it sells to them? Do governments and nations face the problem that you and I would face if we spent more than we earned? Do they run out of funds? Let's look at these questions.

Surpluses and Deficits

IN 1998, FOR THE FIRST TIME IN ALMOST 30 YEARS, the federal government had a budget surplus. For 26 years, it had a deficit. And most years, Canada has an international deficit. What is the government budget surplus and deficit? What is an international deficit?

Government Budget Surplus and Deficit

If a government collects more in taxes than it spends, it has a surplus—a **government budget surplus**. If a government spends more than it collects in taxes, it has a deficit—a **government budget deficit**. The federal government had a surplus in 2004.

Figure 19.10(a) shows the federal government and total government budget surplus and deficit from 1960 to 2005. (Total government is federal, provincial, and local governments.) So that we can compare the surplus or deficit in one year with that in another year, we measure the surplus or deficit as a percentage of GDP. (The concept of GDP, which is explained more fully in Chapter 20, pp. 466–470, equals total income in the economy.) You can think of this measure as the number of cents of surplus or deficit per dollar of income earned by an average Canadian.

The total government had a budget deficit every year from 1975 through 1996. The government deficit fluctuated and swelled during recessions. From 1982 through 1996, the deficit was never less than 2 percent of GDP.

Since 1993, the federal government deficit has shrunk, and in 1998, a surplus emerged. Since 1998, the federal budget surplus has become larger. In 2004, the federal government surplus was 1.5 percent of GDP.

International Surplus and Deficit

When we import goods and services from the rest of the world, we make payments to foreigners. When we export goods and services to the rest of the world, we receive payments from foreigners. If our imports exceed our exports, we have an international deficit.

Figure 19.10(b) shows the history of Canada's international balance from 1960 to 2004. The figure shows the balance on the **current account**, which includes our exports minus our imports but also takes into account interest payments paid to and received from the rest of the world. To compare

FIGURE 19.10
Government Budget and International Surpluses and Deficits

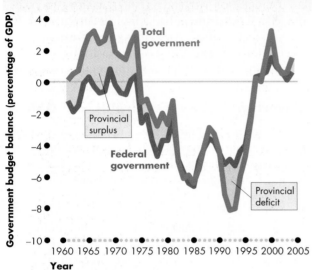

(a) Canadian government budget balance

(b) Canadian international balance

In part (a), the federal government had a large and persistent deficit from 1970 to 1996. The provincial governments had a large deficit during the early 1990s.

In part (b), the Canadian current account shows the balance of our exports minus our imports. In most years since

1970, Canada has had an international deficit. The deficit became large during the mid-1970s and early 1980s. It persisted at around 3 to 4 percent of GDP through the mid-1990s. From 1999 to 2004, Canada had an international surplus.

Source of data: Statistics Canada, CANSIM Tables 376–0001, 380–0002, and 380–0007.

one year with another, the figure shows the current account as a percentage of GDP. In 2001, Canada had a current account surplus of 2.8 percent of GDP. But in most years, Canada has had a current account deficit and it has fluctuated. From 1986 to 1995, the deficit was persistently around 3 percent to 4 percent of GDP. Our imports have exceeded our exports during these years. In 1996 and between 1999 and 2004, Canada had a current account surplus.

Do Surpluses and Deficits Matter?

Why do deficits cause anxiety? What happens when a government cannot cover its spending with taxes, or when a country buys more from other countries than it sells to them?

If you spend more than you earn, you have a deficit. And to cover your deficit, you go into debt. But when you borrow, you must pay interest on your

debt. Just like you, if a government or a nation has a deficit, it must borrow. And like you, the government and the nation must pay interest on their debts.

Whether borrowing and paying out huge amounts of interest is a good idea depends on what the borrowed funds are used for. If you borrow to finance a vacation, you must eventually tighten your belt, cut spending, and repay your debt as well as pay interest on the debt. But if you borrow to invest in a business that earns a large profit, you might be able to repay your debt and pay the interest on it while continuing to increase your spending. It is the same with a government and a nation. A government or a nation that borrows to increase its consumption might be heading for trouble later. But a government or a nation that borrows to buy assets that earn a profit might be making a sound investment.

You will learn more about the government's budget surplus in Chapter 24 and about the international current account in Chapter 32.

Macroeconomic Policy Challenges and Tools

FROM THE TIME OF ADAM SMITH'S *Wealth of Nations* in 1776 until the publication of Keynes' *General Theory of Employment, Interest, and Money* in 1936, it was widely believed that the only economic role for government was to enforce property rights. The economy behaved best, it was believed, if the government left people free to pursue their own best interests. The macroeconomics of Keynes challenged this view. Keynes' central point was that the economy will not fix itself and that government actions are needed to achieve and maintain full employment. The Canadian government declared full employment as a policy goal soon after World War II ended.

Policy Challenges and Tools

Today, the five widely agreed challenges for macroeconomic policy are to

1. Reduce unemployment
2. Boost economic growth
3. Stabilize the business cycle
4. Keep inflation low
5. Reduce government and international deficits

But how can we do all these things? What are the tools available to pursue the macroeconomic policy challenges? Macroeconomic policy tools are divided into two broad categories:

- Fiscal policy
- Monetary policy

Fiscal Policy Making changes in tax rates and in government spending programs is called **fiscal policy**. This range of actions is under the control of the federal government. Fiscal policy can be used to try to boost long-term growth by creating incentives that encourage saving, investment, and technological change. Fiscal policy can also be used to try to smooth out the business cycle. When the economy is in a recession, the government might cut taxes or increase its spending. Conversely, when the economy is in a rapid expansion, the government might increase taxes or cut its spending in an attempt to slow real GDP growth and prevent inflation from increasing. Fiscal policy is discussed in Chapter 24.

Monetary Policy Changing interest rates and changing the amount of money in the economy is called **monetary policy**. These actions are under the control of the Bank of Canada. The principal aim of monetary policy is to keep inflation in check. To achieve this objective, the Bank prevents the quantity of money from expanding too rapidly. Monetary policy can also be used to smooth the business cycle. When the economy is in recession, the Bank might lower interest rates and inject money into the economy. And when the economy is in a rapid expansion, the Bank might increase interest rates in an attempt to slow real GDP growth and prevent inflation from increasing. We study monetary policy in Chapter 28.

◆ In your study of macroeconomics, you will learn what is currently known about the causes of unemployment, economic growth, business cycles, inflation, and government and international surpluses and deficits. You will also learn more about the policy choices and challenges that the government and the Bank of Canada face. *Reading Between the Lines* on pp. 460–461 examines unemployment, inflation, and economic growth in Canada in 2005.

Unemployment, Inflation, and Growth

THE GLOBE AND MAIL, OCTOBER 8, 2005

As unemployment rate declines, spectre of worker shortage raised

Canada's unemployment rate dropped back to a three-decade low in September, and a survey suggests companies are having increasing difficulty finding the right kinds of workers to support their growing businesses.

The unemployment rate fell 0.1 percentage points to 6.7 per cent last month, tying with June, 2005, for the lowest rate since March, 1976.

"There just isn't a huge supply of available and qualified workers," said Douglas Porter, deputy chief economist at BMO Nesbitt Burns. ...

About 19,200 full-time jobs were added to the economy in September, offset by a loss of about 21,400 part-time jobs, Statscan said.

While its report suggests companies weren't hiring much in September, firms told the Bank of Canada that they had strong intentions of hiring in the future.

In the central bank's quarterly Business Outlook Survey, 50 per cent of the companies surveyed said they intended to hire more people in the next 12 months.

And a whopping 51 per cent said they are facing labour shortages that restrict their ability to meet demand. That's up from 36 per cent in the bank's summer survey.

Regional differences in the Canadian economy are becoming more pronounced, the central bank said, with energy-rich Western Canada very optimistic about sales growth over the next year. About three-quarters of Western companies said they expect to hire more workers in the next year. ...

The central bank survey also pointed to signs of rising inflation expectations.

About one-quarter of the companies said they expect inflation to rise above the 3-per-cent ceiling on the bank's target band. And 60 per cent expect annual inflation to be in the top end of the target range.

The Statistics Canada jobs report also revealed some signs of inflation, with average hourly earnings rising 3.5 per cent from a year earlier — higher than in August, and higher than the national inflation rate of 2.6 per cent. ...

Reprinted with permission from *The Globe and Mail.*

Essence of the Story

■ In September 2005, Canada's unemployment rate was 6.7 percent.

■ This unemployment rate was the lowest since 1976.

■ Full-time jobs replaced part-time jobs.

■ Surveys showed that businesses were expected serious labour shortages in the near future.

■ A survey by the Bank of Canada revealed that more people were expecting the inflation rate to rise.

■ Regional differences existed with the strongest growth occurring in the energy sector of Western Canada.

Economic Analysis

■ The Canadian economy experienced a falling unemployment rate throughout 2004 and 2005.

■ Figure 1 shows this unemployment record.

■ When the unemployment rate falls too low, labour shortages arise that might make wage rates rise more rapidly.

■ If wage rates do rise more rapidly, inflation might increase.

■ The Bank of Canada survey of inflation expectations reported in the news article found some signs that people were beginning to think a higher inflation rate was coming.

■ There was little evidence in the actual inflation performance of 2004 and 2005 to support the expectation of higher inflation.

■ Figure 2 shows the inflation rate in 2004 and 2005. Despite a rising inflation rate during 2005, the rate remained firmly inside the Bank of Canada's target range of 1 percent to 3 percent a year.

■ The news article says that the Canadian economy is experiencing differnt rates of growth in different sectors.

■ In particular, it points to more rapid growth in the energy sectors of Western Canada.

■ Figure 3 provides some perspective on this observation.

■ The figure shows the growth rates of production in various industries in the year from July 2004 to July 2005 (the most recent data available at the time of writing.)

■ The sectors that are growing fastest are *not* those associated with energy. Mining and oil and gas extraction expanded more slowly than the national average.

■ It was retail trade, wholesale trade, information and cultural industries, utilities, education services, construction, finance, insurance and real estate, administrative and waste management services, transportation and warehousing—all services, that expanded the most quickly.

■ It is because sectors expand at different rates with some sectors shrinking that labour is reallocated and that unemployment arises.

Figure 1 Unemployment rate

Figure 2 Inflation rate

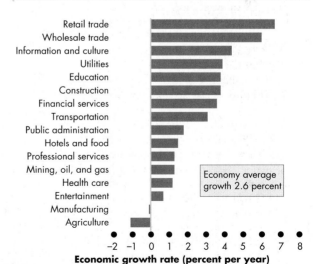

Figure 3 Growth rates July 2004 to July 2005

461

SUMMARY

KEY POINTS

Origins and Issues of Macroeconomics (p. 446)

- Macroeconomics studies economic growth and fluctuations, jobs and unemployment, inflation, and surpluses and deficits.

Growth and Fluctuations (pp. 447–452)

- Economic growth is the expansion of potential GDP. Real GDP fluctuates around potential GDP in a business cycle.
- The main benefit of long-term economic growth is higher future consumption, and the main cost is lower current consumption.
- Slow productivity growth (the Lucas wedge) is more costly than the business cycle (the Okun gap).

Jobs and Unemployment (pp. 452–454)

- The Canadian economy creates about 200,000 jobs a year but unemployment persists.
- Canadian unemployment increases during a recession and decreases during an expansion.
- The Canadian unemployment rate is higher than that in the United States and Japan.
- Unemployment can permanently damage a person's job prospects.

Inflation (pp. 455–457)

- Inflation, a process of rising prices, is measured by the percentage change in the CPI.
- Inflation is a problem because it lowers the value of money and makes money less useful as a measuring rod of value.

Surpluses and Deficits (pp. 457–459)

- When the government collects more in taxes than it spends, the government has a budget surplus. When the government spends more than it collects in taxes, the government has a budget deficit.

- When imports exceed exports, a nation has an international deficit.
- Deficits are financed by borrowing.

Macroeconomic Policy Challenges and Tools (p. 459)

- The macroeconomic policy challenge is to use fiscal policy and monetary policy to boost long-term growth, stabilize the business cycle, lower unemployment, tame inflation, and prevent large deficits.

KEY FIGURES

KEY TERMS

PROBLEMS

Go to <X> myeconlab **for solutions to odd-numbered problems and additional exercises.**

1. In which country in 1992 was
   a. The growth rate of real GDP highest: Canada, Japan, or the United States?
   b. The unemployment rate highest: Canada, Japan, the United Kingdom, or the United States?
   c. The inflation rate lowest: Canada, Germany, the United Kingdom, or the United States?
   d. The government budget deficit (as a percentage of GDP) largest: Canada, Japan, the United Kingdom, or the United States?

2. In which country in 2000 was
   a. The growth rate of real GDP highest: Canada, Japan, or the United States?
   b. The unemployment rate lowest: Canada, Japan, the United Kingdom, or the United States?
   c. The inflation rate lowest: Canada, the United Kingdom, Japan, or the United States?
   d. The government budget surplus (as a percentage of GDP) smallest: Canada, the United Kingdom, or the United States?
   e. Is it possible to say in which country consumption possibilities are growing fastest? Why or why not?

3. The figure shows the real GDP growth rates in India and Pakistan from 1989 to 1996.

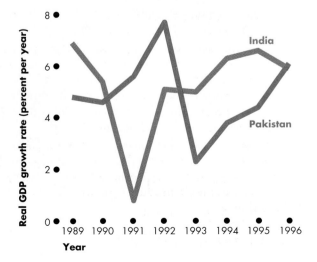

   a. In which years did economic growth in
      i. India increase? And in which year was growth the fastest?
      ii. Pakistan decrease? And in which year was growth the slowest?
   b. Compare the paths of economic growth in India and Pakistan during this period.

4. The figure shows the growth rate of real GDP per person in Australia and Japan from 1989 to 1996.

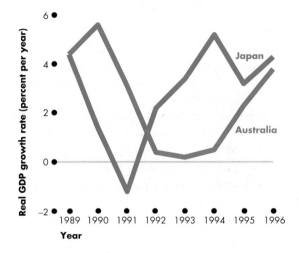

   a. In which years did economic growth in
      i. Australia increase? And in which year was growth the fastest?
      ii. Japan decrease? And in which year was growth the slowest?
   b. Compare the paths of economic growth in Australia and Japan during this period.

5. The figure shows real GDP in Germany from the first quarter of 1991 to the second quarter of 1994.

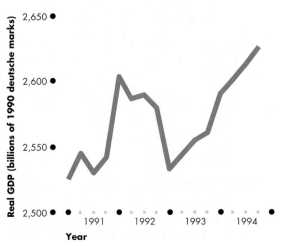

a. How many recessions did Germany experience during this period?

b. In which quarters, if any, did Germany experience a business cycle peak?

c. In which quarters, if any, did Germany experience a business cycle trough?

d. In which quarters, if any, did Germany experience an expansion?

6. The table shows Canada's rate of economic growth during 2004 and the first two quarters of 2005.

	2004	2005
First quarter	0.6	0.5
Second quarter	1.2	0.8
Third quarter	0.9	
Fourth quarter	0.5	

a. Did Canada experience a recession during this period?

b. Did the economic growth rate speed up or slow down during 2004 and 2005?

c. Which of the two years had the highest average economic growth rate?

7. Use Data Graphing on **MyEconLab** to answer the following questions. In 1998, which country—Canada, Japan, the United Kingdom, or the United States—had

a. The largest budget deficit?

b. A current account surplus?

8. Use Data Graphing on **MyEconLab** to answer the following questions. In 2002, which country—Canada, Japan, the United Kingdom, or the United States—had

a. The largest budget surplus?

b. The largest current account deficit?

9. Use Data Graphing on **MyEconLab** to make a scatter diagram of the inflation rate and the unemployment rate in Canada.

a. Describe the relationship.

b. Do you think that low unemployment brings an increase in the inflation rate?

10. Use Data Graphing on **MyEconLab** to make a scatter diagram of the government budget deficit as a percentage of GDP and the unemployment rate in Canada.

a. Describe the relationship.

b Do you think that low unemployment brings a decrease in the budget deficit?

CRITICAL THINKING

1. Study *Reading Between the Lines* on pp. 460–461 and then answer the following questions

a. What happened to Canada's unemployment rate during 2004 and 2005?

b. What happened to Canada's inflation rate during 2004 and 2005?

c. Which sectors of the Canadian economy experienced the fastest growth during 2004 and 2005?

d. Which sectors of the Canadian economy experienced the slowest growth or even shrank during 2004 and 2005?

WEB EXERCISES

Use the links on (X) myeconlab **to work the following exercises.**

1. Get the latest data on real GDP, unemployment, and inflation in Canada.

a. Update Figs. 19.2, 19.6, and 19.8.

b. What dangers does the Canadian economy face today?

c. What actions, if any, do you think might be needed to keep the economy strong?

2. Get data on the unemployment rate in your home province.

a. Compare unemployment in your home province with that in Canada as a whole.

b. Why do you think your province might have a higher or a lower unemployment rate than the Canadian average?

3. Get data on the Consumer Price Index for the capital city in your home province.

a. Compare the inflation rate in the capital city of your home province with that in Canada as a whole.

b. Compare the inflation rate in the capital city of your home province with that of the capital cities in neighbouring provinces.

4. Get data on the following variables for Canada for the most recent period. Describe how the following variables have changed over the last year.

a. The unemployment rate

b. The inflation rate

c. The government budget surplus or deficit

d. The international deficit

Measuring GDP and Economic Growth

CHAPTER 20

An Economic Barometer

Will our economy keep expanding through 2006 and 2007? And will the expansion be rapid or slow? Or are we going to slip into recession? Many Canadian companies wanted to know the answer to this question. Nortel wanted to know whether to hire more workers or delay the hirings for a while. Bombardier wanted to know whether to expand its capacity to build railroad engines. To assess the state of the economy and to make big decisions about business expansion and contraction, firms such as Nortel and Bombardier use forecasts of GDP. What exactly *is* GDP and how can we use it to tell us how rapidly our economy is expanding or if we are headed towards recession?

To reveal the growth or shrinkage of GDP, we must remove the effects of inflation and assess how *real* GDP is changing. How do we remove the inflation component of GDP to reveal *real* GDP?

Some countries are rich while others are poor. How do we compare economic well-being in one country with that in another? How can we make international comparisons of GDP?

◆ In this chapter, you will find out how economic statisticians measure GDP, real GDP, and the economic growth rate. You will also learn about the limitations of these measures. In *Reading Between the Lines* at the end of the chapter, we'll look at Canadian real GDP during 2005.

After studying this chapter, you will be able to

- **Define GDP and use the circular flow model to explain why GDP equals aggregate expenditure and aggregate income**
- **Explain the two ways of measuring GDP**
- **Explain how we measure *real* GDP and the GDP deflator**
- **Explain how we use real GDP to measure economic growth and describe the limitations of our measure**

Gross Domestic Product

WHAT EXACTLY IS GDP, HOW IS IT CALCULATED, what does it mean, and why do we care about it? You are going to discover the answers to these questions in this chapter. First, what *is* GDP?

GDP Defined

GDP, or **gross domestic product**, is the market value of all the final goods and services produced within a country in a given time period. This definition has four parts:

- Market value
- Final goods and services
- Produced within a country
- In a given time period

We'll examine each in turn.

Market Value To measure total production, we must add together the production of apples and oranges, computers and popcorn. Just counting the items doesn't get us very far. For example, which is the greater total production: 100 apples and 50 oranges, or 50 apples and 100 oranges?

GDP answers this question by valuing items at their *market values*—at the prices at which each item is traded in markets. If the price of an apple is 10¢, the market value of 50 apples is $5. If the price of an orange is 20¢, the market value of 100 oranges is $20. By using market prices to value production, we can add the apples and oranges together. The market value of 50 apples and 100 oranges is $5 plus $20, or $25.

Final Goods and Services To calculate GDP, we value the *final goods and services* produced. A **final good** (or service) is an item that is bought by its final user during a specified time period. It contrasts with an **intermediate good** (or service), which is an item that is produced by one firm, bought by another firm, and used as a component of a final good or service.

For example, a Ford SUV is a final good, but a Firestone tire on the SUV is an intermediate good. A Dell computer is a final good, but an Intel Pentium chip inside the computer is an intermediate good.

If we were to add the value of intermediate goods and services produced to the value of final goods and services, we would count the same thing many times—a problem called *double counting*. The value of an SUV already includes the value of the tires, and the value of a Dell PC already includes the value of the Pentium chip inside it.

Some goods can be an intermediate good in some situations and a final good in other situations. For example, the ice cream that you buy on a hot summer day is a final good, but the ice cream that a café buys and uses to make sundaes is an intermediate good. The sundae is the final good. So whether a good is an intermediate good or a final good depends on what it is used for, not on what it is.

Some items that people buy are neither final goods nor intermediate goods. Examples of such items include financial assets—stocks and bonds—and second-hand goods—used cars and existing homes. These items are not part of GDP. But a used car and an existing home were part of GDP in the year in which they were produced.

Produced Within a Country Only goods and services that are produced *within a country* count as part of that country's GDP. Roots Canada Limited, a Canadian firm, produces T-shirts in Taiwan, and the market value of those T-shirts is part of Taiwan's GDP, not part of Canada's GDP. Toyota, a Japanese firm, produces automobiles in Cambridge, Ontario, and the value of this production is part of Canada's GDP, not part of Japan's GDP.

In a Given Time Period GDP measures the value of production *in a given time period*—normally either a quarter of a year (called the quarterly GDP data) or a year (called the annual GDP data).

GDP measures not only the value of total production but also total income and total expenditure. The equality between the value of total production and total income is important because it shows the direct link between productivity and living standards. Our standard of living rises when our incomes rise and we can afford to buy more goods and services. But we must produce more goods and services if we are to be able to buy more goods and services.

Rising incomes and a rising value of production go together. They are two aspects of the same phenomenon—increasing productivity. To see why, we study the circular flow of expenditure and income.

GDP and the Circular Flow of Expenditure and Income

Figure 20.1 illustrates the circular flow of expenditure and income. The economy consists of households, firms, governments, and the rest of the world (the diamonds), which trade in factor markets, goods (and services) markets, and financial markets. We focus first on households and firms.

Households and Firms Households sell and firms buy the services of labour, capital, and land in factor markets. For these factor services, firms pay income to households: wages for labour services, interest for the use of capital, and rent for the use of land. A fourth factor of production, entrepreneurship, receives profit.

Firms' retained earnings—profits that are not distributed to households—are part of the household sector's income. You can think of retained earnings as

being income that households save and lend back to firms. Figure 20.1 shows the total income—*aggregate income*—received by households, including retained earnings, by the blue dots labelled *Y*.

Firms sell and households buy consumer goods and services—such as inline skates and haircuts—in the markets for goods and services. The total payment for these goods and services is **consumption expenditure**, shown by the red dots labelled *C*.

Firms buy and sell new capital equipment—such as computer systems, airplanes, trucks, and assembly line equipment—in the goods market. Some of what firms produce is not sold but is added to inventory. For example, if GM produces 1,000 cars and sells 950 of them, the other 50 cars remain in GM's inventory of unsold cars, which increases by 50 cars. When a firm adds unsold output to inventory, we can think of the firm as buying goods from itself. The purchase of new plant, equipment, and buildings and

---

FIGURE 20.1

The Circular Flow of Expenditure and Income

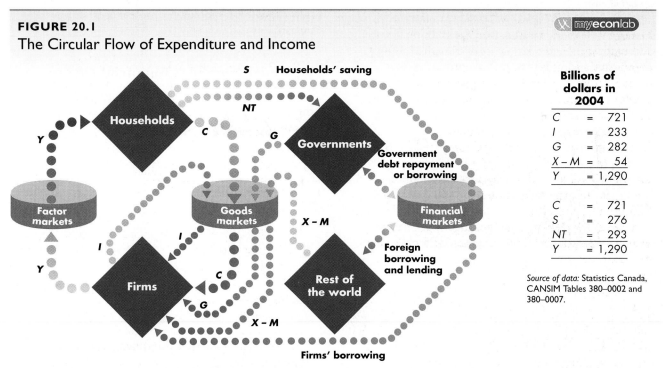

Billions of dollars in 2004		
C	=	721
I	=	233
G	=	282
X – M	=	54
Y	=	1,290

C	=	721
S	=	276
NT	=	293
Y	=	1,290

Source of data: Statistics Canada, CANSIM Tables 380–0002 and 380–0007.

In the circular flow of expenditure and income, households make consumption expenditures (*C*); firms make investment expenditures (*I*); governments purchase goods and services (*G*); and the rest of the world purchases net exports (*X* – *M*)—(red flows). Households receive incomes (*Y*) from firms (blue flow).

Aggregate income (blue flow) equals aggregate expenditure (red flows). Households use their income to consume (*C*), save (*S*), and pay net taxes (*NT*). Firms borrow to finance their investment expenditures, and governments and the rest of the world borrow to finance their deficits or lend their surpluses (green flows).

the additions to inventories are **investment**, shown by the red dots labelled *I*.

Governments Governments buy goods and services, called **government expenditures**, from firms. In Fig. 20.1, government expenditures on goods and services are shown as the red flow *G*. Governments use taxes to pay for their purchases. Figure 20.1 shows taxes as net taxes by the green dots labelled *NT*. **Net taxes** are equal to taxes paid to governments minus transfer payments received from governments. *Transfer payments* are cash transfers from governments to households and firms, such as social security benefits, unemployment compensation, and subsidies, and interest payments on the governments' debt.

Rest of the World Firms sell goods and services to the rest of the world, **exports**, and buy goods and services from the rest of the world, **imports**. The value of exports minus the value of imports is called **net exports**, which Fig. 20.1 shows by the red flow *X* – M.

If net exports are positive, there is a net flow from the rest of the world to Canadian firms. If net exports are negative, there is net flow from Canadian firms to the rest of the world.

GDP Equals Expenditure Equals Income Gross domestic product can be determined in two ways: by the total expenditure on goods and services or by the total income earned producing goods and services.

The total expenditure—*aggregate expenditure*—is the sum of the red flows in Fig. 20.1. Aggregate expenditure equals consumption expenditure plus investment plus government expenditures plus net exports.

Aggregate income earned producing goods and services is equal to the total amount paid for the factors used—wages, interest, rent, and profit. This amount is shown by the blue flow in Fig. 20.1. Because firms pay out as incomes (including retained profits) everything they receive from the sale of their output, income (the blue flow) equals expenditure (the sum of the red flows). That is,

$$Y = C + I + G + X - M.$$

The table in Fig. 20.1 shows the numbers for 2004. You can see that the sum of the expenditures is $1,290 billion, which also equals aggregate income.

Because aggregate expenditure equals aggregate income, these two methods of valuing GDP give the same answer. So

GDP equals aggregate expenditure and equals aggregate income.

The circular flow model is the foundation on which the national economic accounts are built.

Financial Flows

The circular flow model also enables us to see the connection between the expenditure and income flows and flows through the financial markets that finance deficits and pay for investment. These flows are shown in green in Fig. 20.1. Household **saving** (*S*) is the amount that households have left after they have paid their net taxes and bought their consumption goods and services. Government borrowing finances a government budget deficit. (Government lending arises when the government has a budget surplus.) And foreign borrowing pays for a deficit with the rest of the world. These financial flows are the sources of the funds that firms use to pay for their investment in new capital. Let's look a bit more closely at how investment is financed.

How Investment Is Financed

Investment adds to the stock of capital and is one of the determinants of the rate at which production grows. Investment is financed from three sources:

1. Private saving
2. Government budget surplus
3. Borrowing from the rest of the world

Private saving is the green flow labelled *S* in Fig. 20.1. Notice that households' income is consumed, saved, or paid in net taxes. That is,

$$Y = C + S + NT.$$

But you've seen that *Y* also equals the sum of the components of aggregate expenditure. That is,

$$Y = C + I + G + X - M.$$

By using these two equations, you can see that

$$I + G + X - M = S + NT$$

Now subtract *G* and *X* from both sides of the last equation and add *M* to both sides to obtain

$$I = S + (NT - G) + (M - X).$$

In the last equation, $(NT - G)$ is the government budget surplus and $(M - X)$ is borrowing from the rest of the world.

If net taxes (NT) exceed government expenditures (G), the government has a budget surplus equal to $(NT - G)$, and this surplus contributes towards paying for investment. If net taxes are less than government expenditures, the government has a budget deficit equal to $(NT - G)$, which is now negative. This deficit subtracts from the sources that finance investment.

If we import more than we export, we borrow an amount equal to $(M - X)$ from the rest of the world. So part of the rest of the world's saving finances investment in Canada. If we export more than we import, we lend an amount equal to $(X - M)$ to the rest of the world. So part of Canadian saving is used to finance investment in other countries.

The sum of private saving (S) and government saving $(NT - G)$ is called **national saving**. So investment is financed by national saving and foreign borrowing. In 2004, Canadian investment was $233 billion. National saving was $287 billion and $X - M$ was $54 billion. Canada lent $54 billion to the rest of the world.

Gross and Net Domestic Product

What does the "gross" in GDP mean? *Gross* means *before* accounting for the depreciation of capital. The opposite of gross is *net*, which means *after* accounting for the depreciation of capital. To understand what the depreciation of capital is and how it affects aggregate expenditure and income, we need to expand the accounting framework that we use and distinguish between flows and stocks.

Flows and Stocks in Macroeconomics A **flow** is a quantity per unit of time. The water that is running from an open faucet into a bathtub is a flow. So is the number of CDs you buy during a month and the amount of income that you earn during a month. GDP is a flow—the value of the final goods and services produced in a country *during a given time period.* Saving and investment are also flows.

A **stock** is a quantity that exists at a point in time. The water in a bathtub is a stock. So are the number of CDs that you own and the amount of money in your savings account. The two key stocks in macroeconomics are wealth and capital. And the flows of saving and investment change these stocks.

Wealth and Saving The value of all the things that people own is called **wealth**. What people own (a stock) is related to what they earn (a flow). People earn an income, which is the amount they receive during a given time period from supplying the services of factors of production. Income that is left after paying net taxes is either consumed or saved. *Consumption expenditure* is the amount spent on consumption goods and services. *Saving* is the amount of income remaining after consumption expenditures are met. So saving adds to wealth.

For example, suppose that at the end of the school year, you have $250 in a savings account and some textbooks that are worth $300. That's all you own. Your wealth is $550. Suppose that you take a summer job and earn an income after taxes of $5,000. You are extremely careful and spend only $1,000 through the summer on consumption goods and services. At the end of the summer, when school starts again, you have $4,250 in your savings account. Your wealth is now $4,550. Your wealth has increased by $4,000, which equals your saving of $4,000. Your saving of $4,000 equals your income after taxes of $5,000 minus your consumption expenditure of $1,000.

National wealth and national saving work just like this personal example. The wealth of a nation at the start of a year equals its wealth at the start of the previous year plus its saving during the year. Its saving equals its income after taxes minus its consumption expenditure.

Capital and Investment *Capital* is the plant, equipment, buildings, and inventories of raw materials and semi-finished goods that are used to produce other goods and services. The amount of capital in the economy exerts a big influence on GDP.

Two flows change the stock of capital: investment and depreciation. *Investment*, the purchase of new capital, increases the stock of capital. (Investment includes additions to inventories.) **Depreciation** is the decrease in the stock of capital that results from wear and tear and obsolescence. Another name for depreciation is **capital consumption**. The total amount spent on purchases of new capital and on replacing depreciated capital is called **gross investment**. The amount by which the stock of capital increases is called **net investment**.

Net investment = Gross investment − Depreciation.

Figure 20.2 illustrates these concepts. On January 1, 2006, Cindy's CDs, Inc., had 3 machines. This quantity was its initial capital. During 2006, Cindy's scrapped an older machine. This quantity is its depreciation. After depreciation, Cindy's stock of capital was down to 2 machines. But also during 2006, Cindy's bought 2 new machines. This amount is its gross investment. By December 31, 2006, Cindy's CDs had 4 machines, so its capital had increased by 1 machine. This amount is Cindy's net investment. Cindy's net investment equals its gross investment (the purchase of 2 new machines) minus its depreciation (1 machine scrapped).

The example of Cindy's CDs can be applied to the economy as a whole. The nation's capital stock decreases because capital depreciates and increases because of gross investment. The change in the nation's capital equals its net investment.

Back to the Gross in GDP We can now see the distinction between gross domestic product and net domestic product. On the income side of the flows that measure GDP, a firm's *gross* profit is its profit *before* subtracting *depreciation*. A firm's gross profit is part of aggregate income, so depreciation is counted as part of gross income and GDP. Similarly, on the expenditure side of the flows that measure GDP, *gross investment* includes depreciation, so depreciation is counted as part of aggregate expenditure, and total expenditure is a gross measure.

Net domestic product excludes depreciation. Like GDP, net domestic product can be viewed as the sum of incomes or expenditures. Net income includes firms' *net* profits—profits *after* subtracting depreciation. And net expenditure includes *net* investment, which also excludes depreciation.

The Short Term Meets the Long Term The flows and stocks that you've just studied influence GDP growth and fluctuations. One of the reasons why GDP grows is that the capital stock grows. Investment adds to capital, so investment leads to GDP growth. But investment fluctuates, which brings fluctuations to GDP. So capital and investment along with wealth and saving are part of the key to understanding both GDP growth and fluctuations.

Investment and saving interact with income and consumption expenditure in a circular flow of expenditure and income. In this circular flow, income equals expenditure, which also equals the value of production. This equality is the foundation on which a nation's economic accounts are built and from which its GDP is measured.

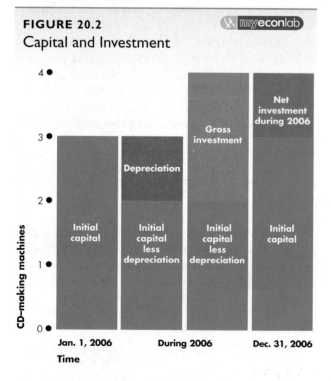

FIGURE 20.2
Capital and Investment

Cindy's CDs has a capital stock at Dec. 31, 2006 that equals its capital stock at Jan. 1, 2006 plus its net investment during 2006. Net investment is equal to gross investment less depreciation. Cindy's gross investment is the 2 new machines bought during the year, and its depreciation is the 1 machine that Cindy's scrapped during the year. Cindy's net investment is 1 machine.

REVIEW QUIZ

1 Define GDP. Distinguish between a final good and an intermediate good. Provide examples.
2 Why does GDP equal aggregate income and also equal aggregate expenditure?
3 How is Canadian investment financed? What determines national saving?
4 What is the distinction between gross and net?

myeconlab **Study Plan 20.1**

Let's now see how the ideas that you've just studied are used in practice. We'll see how GDP and its components are measured in Canada today.

Measuring Canada's GDP

STATISTICS CANADA USES THE CONCEPTS THAT YOU met in the circular flow model to measure GDP and its components in the *National Income and Expenditure Accounts*. Because the value of aggregate output equals aggregate expenditure and aggregate income, there are two approaches available for measuring GDP, and both are used. They are

- The expenditure approach
- The income approach

The Expenditure Approach

The *expenditure approach* measures GDP as the sum of consumption expenditure (C), investment (I), government expenditures on goods and services (G), and net exports of goods and services ($X - M$), corresponding to the red flows in the circular flow model in Fig. 20.1. Table 20.1 shows the result of this approach for 2004. The table uses the terms in the *National Income and Expenditure Accounts*.

Personal expenditures on consumer goods and services are the expenditures by households on goods and services produced in Canada and in the rest of the world. They include goods such as CDs and books and services such as banking and legal advice. They do *not* include the purchase of new homes, which Statistics Canada counts as part of investment. But they do include the purchase of other consumer durable goods such as cars and microwave ovens.

Business investment is expenditure on capital equipment and buildings by firms and expenditure on new homes by households. It also includes the change in business inventories.

Government expenditures on goods and services are the purchases of goods and services by all levels of government. This item includes expenditures on national defence and garbage collection. But it does *not* include *transfer payments* because they are not purchases of goods and services.

Net exports of goods and services are the value of exports minus the value of imports. This item includes telephone equipment that Nortel sells to AT&T in the United States (a Canadian export), and Japanese DVD players that Sears buys from Sony (a Canadian import).

Table 20.1 shows the relative magnitudes of the four items of aggregate expenditure.

TABLE 20.1   GDP: The Expenditure Approach

Item	Symbol	Amount in 2004 (billions of dollars)	Percentage of GDP
Personal expenditures on consumer goods and services	C	721	56.0
Business investment	I	233	18.0
Government expenditures on goods and services	G	282	21.8
Net exports of goods and services	$X - M$	54	4.2
Gross domestic product	Y	1,209	100.0

The expenditure approach measures GDP as the sum of personal expenditures on consumer goods and services (C), business investment (I), government expenditures on goods and services (G), and net exports ($X - M$). In 2004, GDP measured by the expenditure approach was $1,290 billion. Personal expenditures on consumer goods and services is the largest expenditure item.

Source of data: Statistics Canada, CANSIM Table 380–0002.

The Income Approach

The *income approach* measures GDP by summing the incomes that firms pay households for the factors of production they hire—wages for labour, interest for capital, rent for land, and profits for entrepreneurship. Let's see how the income approach works.

The *National Income and Expenditure Accounts* divide incomes into five categories:

1. Wages, salaries, and supplementary labour income
2. Corporate profits
3. Interest and miscellaneous investment income
4. Farmers' income
5. Income from non-farm unincorporated businesses

Wages, salaries, and supplementary labour income is the payment for labour services. It includes net wages and salaries (called "take-home pay") plus taxes withheld plus benefits such as pension contributions.

Corporate profits are the profits of corporations, some of which are paid to households in the form of dividends and some of which are retained by corporations as undistributed profits. They are all income.

Interest and miscellaneous investment income is the interest households receive on loans they make minus the interest households pay on their own borrowing.

Farmers' income and *income from non-farm unincorporated businesses* are a mixture of the previous three items. They include compensation for labour, payment for the use of capital, and profit, lumped together in these two catch-all categories.

Table 20.2 shows these five incomes and their relative magnitudes.

The sum of the incomes is called *net domestic income at factor cost*. The term *factor cost* is used because it is the cost of the *factors of production* used to produce final goods and services. When we sum all the expenditures on final goods and services, we arrive at a total called *domestic product at market prices*. Market prices and factor cost would be the same except for indirect taxes and subsidies.

An *indirect tax* is a tax paid by consumers when they buy goods and services. (In contrast, a *direct tax* is a tax on income.) Provincial sales taxes, GST, and taxes on alcohol, gasoline, and tobacco products are indirect taxes. Because of indirect taxes, consumers pay more for some goods and services than producers receive. Market price exceeds factor cost. For example, if the sales tax is 7 percent, when you buy a $1 chocolate bar you pay $1.07. The factor cost of the chocolate bar including profit is $1. The market price is $1.07.

A *subsidy* is a payment by the government to a producer. Payments made to grain growers and dairy farmers are subsidies. Because of subsidies, consumers pay less for some goods and services than producers receive. Factor cost exceeds market price.

To get from factor cost to market price, we add indirect taxes and subtract subsidies. Making this adjustment brings us one step closer to GDP, but it does not quite get us there.

The final step is to add depreciation (or capital consumption). You can see the reason for this adjustment by recalling the distinction between gross and net profit and between gross and net investment. Total income is a net number because it includes firms' net profits, which exclude depreciation. Total expenditure is a gross number because it includes gross investment. So to get from total income to GDP, we must add depreciation to total income.

TABLE 20.2   GDP: The Income Approach

Item	Amount in 2004 (billions of dollars)	Percentage of GDP
Wages, salaries, and supplementary labour income	644	49.9
Corporate profits	187	14.5
Interest and miscellaneous investment income	55	4.3
Farmers' income	3	0.2
Income from non-farm unincorporated businesses	81	6.3
Indirect taxes *less* subsidies	148	11.5
Capital consumption (depreciation)	172	13.3
Gross domestic product	1,290	100.0

The sum of all incomes equals net domestic income at factor cost. GDP equals net domestic income at factor cost plus indirect taxes less subsidies plus capital consumption (depreciation). In 2004, GDP measured by the income approach was $1,290 billion. Wages, salaries, and supplementary labour income was by far the largest part of aggregate income.

Source of data: Statistics Canada, CANSIM Table 380–0001.

REVIEW QUIZ

1 What is the expenditure approach to measuring GDP?
2 What is the income approach to measuring GDP?
3 What adjustments must be made to total income to make it equal GDP?

myeconlab **Study Plan 20.2**

You now know how GDP is defined and measured. The dollar value of GDP can change because either prices change or the volume of goods and services produced changes. You are next going to learn how we unscramble these two sources of change in GDP to reveal changes in the volume of goods and services produced—changes in what we call *real* GDP.

Real GDP and the Price Level

YOU'VE SEEN THAT GDP MEASURES TOTAL expenditure on final goods and services in a given period. In 2004, GDP was $1,290 billion. The year before, in 2003, GDP was $1,216 billion. Because GDP in 2004 was greater than in 2003, we know that one or two things must have happened during 2004:

■ We produced more goods and services in 2004 than in 2003.

■ We paid higher prices for our goods and services in 2004 than we paid in 2003.

Producing more goods and services contributes to an improvement in our standard of living. Paying higher prices means that our cost of living has increased but our standard of living has not. So it matters a great deal why GDP has increased.

You're now going to learn how economists at Statistics Canada split GDP into two parts. One part tells us the change in production, and the other part tells us the change in prices. The method that is used has changed in recent years, and you are going to learn about the new method.

We measure the change in production by using a number that we call real GDP. **Real GDP** is the value of final goods and services produced in a given year when valued at constant prices. By comparing the value of the goods and services produced at constant prices, we can measure the change in the volume of production.

Calculating Real GDP

Table 20.3 shows the quantities produced and the prices in 2005 for an economy that produces only two goods: balls and bats. The first step towards calculating real GDP is to calculate **nominal GDP**, which is the value of the final goods and services produced in a given year valued at the prices that prevailed in that same year. Nominal GDP is just a more precise name for GDP that we use when we want to be emphatic that we are not talking about real GDP.

Nominal GDP Calculation To calculate nominal GDP in 2005, sum the expenditures on balls and bats in 2005 as follows:

Expenditure on balls = 100 balls × $1 = $100.

Expenditure on bats = 20 bats × $5 = $100.

Nominal GDP in 2005 = $100 + $100 = $200.

Table 20.4 shows the quantities produced and the prices in 2006. The quantity of balls produced increased to 160, and the quantity of bats produced increased to 22. The price of a ball fell to 50¢, and the price of a bat increased to $22.50. To calculate nominal GDP in 2006, we sum the expenditures on balls and bats in 2006 as follows:

Expenditure on balls = 160 balls × $0.50 = $80.

Expenditure on bats = 22 bats × $22.50 = $495.

Nominal GDP in 2006 = $80 + $495 = $575.

To calculate real GDP, we choose one year, called the *base year*, against which to compare the other years. In Canada today, the base year is 1997. The choice of the base year is not important. It is just a common reference point. We'll use 2005 as the base year. By definition, real GDP equals nominal GDP in the base year. So real GDP in 2005 is $200.

Base-Year Prices Value of Real GDP The base-year prices method of calculating real GDP, which is the traditional method, values the quantities produced in each year at the prices of the base year. Table 20.5 shows the prices in 2005 and the quantities in 2006 (based on the information in Tables 20.3 and

---

TABLE 20.3 GDP Data for 2005

Item	Quantity	Price
Balls	100	$1.00
Bats	20	$5.00

TABLE 20.4 GDP Data for 2006

Item	Quantity	Price
Balls	160	$ 0.50
Bats	22	$22.50

TABLE 20.5   2006 Quantities and 2005 Prices

Item	Quantity	Price
Balls	160	$1.00
Bats	22	$5.00

20.4). The value of the 2006 quantities at the 2005 prices is calculated as follows:

Expenditure on balls = 160 balls × $1.00 = $160.

Expenditure on bats = 22 bats × $5.00 = $110.

Value of the 2006 quantities at 2005 prices = $270.

Using the traditional base-year prices method, $270 would be recorded as real GDP in 2006.

Chain-Weighted Output Index Calculation The **chain-weighted output index** method, which is the new method of calculating real GDP, uses the prices of two adjacent years to calculate the real GDP growth rate. So to find the real GDP growth rate in 2006, we compare the quantities produced in 2005 and 2006 by using both the 2005 prices and the 2006 prices. We then average the two sets of numbers in a special way that we'll now describe.

To compare the quantities produced in 2005 and 2006 at 2006 prices, we need to calculate the value of 2005 quantities at 2006 prices. Table 20.6 summarizes these quantities and prices. The value of the 2005 quantities at the 2006 prices is calculated as follows:

Expenditure on balls = 100 balls × $0.50 = $50.

Expenditure on bats = 20 bats × $22.50 = $450.

Value of the 2005 quantities at 2006 prices = $500.

We now have two comparisons between 2005 and 2006. At the 2005 prices, the value of production increased from $200 in 2005 to $270 in 2006.

TABLE 20.6   2005 Quantities and 2006 Prices

Item	Quantity	Price
Balls	100	$ 0.50
Bats	20	$22.50

The increase in value is $70, and the percentage increase is ($70 ÷ $200) × 100, which is 35 percent.

At the 2006 prices, the value of production increased from $500 in 2005 to $575 in 2006. The increase in value is $75, and the percentage increase is ($75 ÷ $500) × 100, which is 15 percent.

The new method of calculating real GDP uses the average of these two percentage increases. The average of 35 percent and 15 percent is (35 + 15) ÷ 2, which equals 25 percent. Real GDP is 25 percent greater in 2006 than in 2005. Real GDP in 2005 is $200, so real GDP in 2006 is $250.

Chain Linking The calculation that we've just described is repeated each year. Each year is compared with its preceding year. So in 2007, the calculations are repeated but using the prices and quantities of 2006 and 2007. Real GDP in 2007 equals real GDP in 2006 increased by the calculated percentage change in real GDP for 2007. For example, suppose that real GDP for 2007 is calculated to be 20 percent greater than that in 2006. You know that real GDP in 2006 is $250. So real GDP in 2007 is 20 percent greater and is $300. In every year, real GDP is valued in base-year dollars (in this example, 2005 dollars).

By applying the calculated percentage change to the real GDP of the preceding real GDP, each year is linked back to the dollars of the base year like the links in a chain.

Calculating the Price Level

You've seen how real GDP is used to reveal the change in the quantity of goods and services produced. We're now going to see how we can find the change in prices that increases our cost of living.

The average level of prices is called the **price level**. One measure of the price level is the **GDP deflator**, which is an average of current-year prices expressed as a percentage of base-year prices. We calculate the GDP deflator by using nominal GDP and real GDP in the formula:

GDP deflator = (Nominal GDP ÷ Real GDP) × 100.

You can see why the GDP deflator is a measure of the price level. If nominal GDP rises but real GDP remains unchanged, it must be that the price level has risen. The formula gives a higher value for the GDP deflator. The larger the nominal GDP for a given real GDP, the higher is the price level and the larger is the GDP deflator.

TABLE 20.7 Calculating the GDP Deflator

Year	Nominal GDP	Real GDP	GDP deflator
2005	$200	$200	100
2006	$575	$250	230

Table 20.7 shows how the GDP deflator is calculated. In 2005, the base year, the deflator is 100. In 2006, it is 230, which equals nominal GDP of $575 divided by real GDP of $250 and then multiplied by 100.

Deflating the GDP Balloon

You can think of GDP as a balloon that is blown up by growing production and rising prices. In Fig. 20.3, the GDP deflator lets the inflation air out of the nominal GDP balloon—the contribution of rising prices—so that we can see what has happened to *real* GDP. The red balloon for 1984 shows real GDP in that year. The green balloon shows *nominal* GDP in

2004. The red balloon for 2004 shows real GDP for that year. To see real GDP in 2004, we *deflate* nominal GDP using the GDP deflator.

REVIEW QUIZ

1 What is the distinction between nominal GDP and real GDP?
2 What is the traditional method of calculating real GDP?
3 What is the new method of calculating real GDP?
4 How is the GDP deflator calculated?

myeconlab   Study Plan 20.3

You now know how to calculate real GDP and the GDP deflator. Your next task is to learn how to use real GDP to calculate economic growth and to make economic welfare comparisons. We also look at some limitations of real GDP as a measure of economic welfare and as a tool for comparing living standards across countries.

FIGURE 20.3
The Canadian GDP Balloon

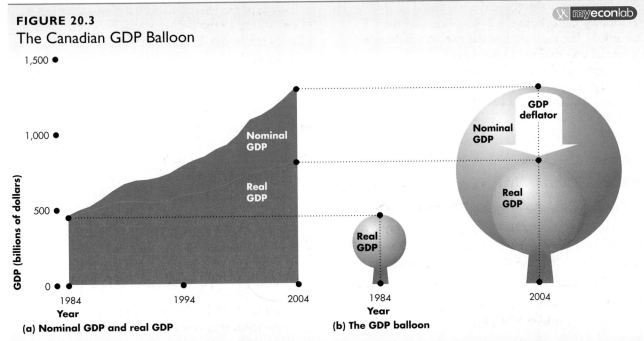

(a) Nominal GDP and real GDP

(b) The GDP balloon

Part of the rise in GDP comes from inflation and part from increased production—an increase in real GDP. The GDP deflator lets some air out of the GDP balloon so that we can see the extent to which production has increased.

Source of data: Statistics Canada, CANSIM Table 380–0002.

Measuring Economic Growth

WE USE ESTIMATES OF REAL GDP TO CALCULATE the economic growth rate. The **economic growth rate** is the percentage change in the quantity of goods and services produced from one year to the next. To calculate the economic growth rate, we use the formula:

$$\text{Economic growth rate} = \frac{\text{Real GDP this year} - \text{Real GDP last year}}{\text{Real GDP last year}} \times 100.$$

For example, real GDP was $1,124 billion in 2004 and $1,092 billion in 2003. So the economic growth rate (percent per year) during 2004 was

$$\text{Economic growth rate} = \frac{\$1,124 - \$1,092}{\$1,092} \times 100$$

$$= 2.93 \text{ percent.}$$

We want to measure the economic growth rate so that we can make

- Economic welfare comparisons
- International comparisons
- Business cycle forecasts

Although the real GDP growth rate is used for these three purposes, it is not a perfect measure for any of them. Nor is it a totally misleading measure. We'll evaluate the limitations of real GDP and its growth rate in each of the three cases.

Economic Welfare Comparisons

Economic welfare is a comprehensive measure of the general state of economic well-being. Economic welfare improves when the production per person of *all* the goods and services grows. The goods and services that make up real GDP growth are only a part of all the items that influence economic welfare.

Today, because of real GDP growth, real GDP per person in Canada of $33,000 is 80 percent higher that it was in 1971. But are we 80 percent better off? Does this growth of real GDP provide a full and accurate measure of the change in economic welfare?

It does not. The reason is that economic welfare depends on many factors that are not measured by real GDP or that are not measured accurately by real GDP. Some of these factors are

- Overadjustment for inflation
- Household production
- Underground economic activity
- Health and life expectancy
- Leisure time
- Environment quality
- Political freedom and social justice

Overadjustment for Inflation The price indexes that are used to measure inflation give an upward-biased estimate of true inflation. (You will learn about the sources of this bias on p. 501.) If we overestimate the rise in prices, we underestimate the growth of real GDP. When car prices rise because cars have gotten better (safer, more fuel efficient, more comfortable), the GDP deflator counts the price increase as inflation. So what is really an increase in production is counted as an increase in price rather than an increase in real GDP. It is deflated away by the wrongly measured higher price level. The magnitude of this bias is probably less than 1 percentage point a year, but its exact magnitude is not known.

Household Production An enormous amount of production takes place every day in our homes. Preparing meals, cleaning the kitchen, changing a light bulb, cutting the grass, washing the car, doing the laundry, and helping a high school student with homework are all examples of productive activities that do not involve market transactions and are not counted as part of GDP.

If all these activities grew at the same rate as real GDP, then not measuring them would not be a problem. But it is likely that market production, which is part of GDP, is increasingly replacing household production, which is not part of GDP. Two trends point in this direction. One is the number of people who have jobs, which has increased from 58 percent in 1970 to 65 percent in 2001. The other is the trend in the purchase of traditionally home-produced goods and services in the market. For example, more and more families now eat in fast-food restaurants—one of the fastest-growing industries in Canada today—and use day-care services. This trend means that an increasing proportion of food preparation and child care that were part of household production are now measured as part of GDP. So real GDP grows more rapidly than does real GDP plus home production.

Underground Economic Activity The *underground economy* is the part of the economy that is purposely hidden from the view of the government to avoid taxes and regulations or because the goods and services being produced are illegal. Because underground economic activity is unreported, it is omitted from GDP.

The underground economy is easy to describe, even if it is hard to measure. It includes the production and distribution of illegal drugs, production that uses illegal labour that is paid less than the minimum wage, and jobs done for cash to avoid paying income taxes. This last category might be quite large and includes tips earned by cab drivers, hairdressers, and hotel and restaurant workers.

Estimates of the scale of the underground economy range between 5 and 15 percent of GDP ($60 billion to $180 billion) in Canada and much more in some countries. It is particularly large in some Eastern European countries that are making a transition from communist economic planning to a market economy.

If the underground economy is a constant proportion of the total economy, the growth rate of real GDP provides a useful estimate of *changes* in economic welfare. But production can shift from the underground economy to the rest of the economy, and can shift the other way. The underground economy expands relative to the rest of the economy if taxes rise sharply or if regulations become especially restrictive. And the underground economy shrinks relative to the rest of the economy if the burdens of taxes and regulations ease.

During the 1980s, when tax rates were cut, there was an increase in the reporting of previously hidden income and tax revenues increased. So some part (but probably a small part) of the expansion of real GDP during the 1980s represented a shift from the underground economy rather than an increase in production.

Health and Life Expectancy Good health and a long life—the hopes of everyone—do not show up in real GDP, at least not directly. A larger real GDP does enable us to spend more on medical research, health care, a good diet, and exercise equipment. And as real GDP has increased, our life expectancy has lengthened—from 70 years at the end of World War II to approaching 80 years today. Infant deaths and death in childbirth, two fearful scourges of the nineteenth century, have almost been eliminated.

But we face new health and life expectancy problems every year. AIDS and drug abuse are taking young lives at a rate that causes serious concern. When we take these negative influences into account, we see that real GDP growth overstates the improvements in economic welfare.

Leisure Time Leisure time is an economic good that adds to our economic welfare. Other things remaining the same, the more leisure we have, the better off we are. Our working time is valued as part of GDP, but our leisure time is not. Yet from the point of view of economic welfare, leisure time must be at least as valuable to us as the wage that we earn for the last hour worked. If it were not, we would work instead of taking the leisure. Over the years, leisure time has steadily increased. The workweek has become shorter, more people take early retirement, and the number of vacation days has increased. These improvements in economic well-being are not reflected in real GDP.

Environmental Quality Economic activity directly influences the quality of the environment. The burning of hydrocarbon fuels is the most visible activity that damages our environment. But it is not the only example. The depletion of exhaustible resources, the mass clearing of forests, and the pollution of lakes and rivers are other major environmental consequences of industrial production.

Resources that are used to protect the environment are valued as part of GDP. For example, the value of catalytic converters that help to protect the atmosphere from automobile emissions are part of GDP. But if we did not use such pieces of equipment and instead polluted the atmosphere, we would not count the deteriorating air that we were breathing as a negative part of GDP.

An industrial society possibly produces more atmospheric pollution than an agricultural society does. But pollution does not always increase as we become wealthier. Wealthy people value a clean environment and are willing to pay for one. Compare the pollution in East Germany in the late 1980s with pollution in Canada. East Germany, a poor country, polluted its rivers, lakes, and atmosphere in a way that is unimaginable in Canada or in wealthy West Germany.

Political Freedom and Social Justice Most people value political freedoms such as those provided by the Canadian Charter of Rights and Freedoms and the

Constitution of Canada. And they value social justice or fairness—equality of opportunity and social security safety nets that protect people from the extremes of misfortune.

A country might have a very large real GDP per person but have limited political freedom and equity. For example, an elite might enjoy political liberty and extreme wealth while the vast majority are effectively enslaved and live in abject poverty. Such an economy would generally be regarded as having less economic welfare than one that had the same amount of real GDP but in which political freedoms were enjoyed by everyone. Today, China has rapid real GDP growth but limited political freedoms, while Russia has slow real GDP growth and an emerging democratic political system. Economists have no easy way to determine which of these countries is better off.

The Bottom Line Do we get the wrong message about the growth in economic welfare by looking at the growth of real GDP? The influences that are omitted from real GDP are probably important and could be large. Developing countries have a larger underground economy and a larger amount of household production than do developed countries. So as an economy develops and grows, part of the apparent growth might reflect a switch from underground to regular production and from home production to market production. This measurement error overstates the rate of economic growth and the improvement in economic welfare.

Other influences on living standards include the amount of leisure time available, the quality of the environment, the security of jobs and homes, and the safety of city streets. It is possible to construct broader measures that combine the many influences that contribute to human happiness. Real GDP will be one element in those broader measures but by no means the whole of them.

International Comparisons

All the problems we've just reviewed affect the economic welfare of every country, so to make international comparisons of economic welfare, factors additional to real GDP must be used. But real GDP comparisons are major components of international welfare comparisons, and two special problems arise in making these comparisons. First, the real GDP of one country must be converted into the same currency units as the real GDP of the other country.

Second, the same prices must be used to value the goods and services in the two countries. Let's look at these two problems by using a striking example: a comparison of China and the United States.

In 2003, real GDP per person in the United States was $39,000. The official Chinese statistics published in the International Monetary Fund's (IMF) World Economic Outlook (WEO) say that real GDP per person in China in 2003 was 9,500 yuan. (The yuan is the currency of China.) On the average, during 2003, $US1 was worth 8.276 yuan.

If we use this exchange rate to convert Chinese yuan into U.S. dollars, we get a value of $1,150. This comparison of China and the United States makes China look extremely poor. In 2003, GDP per person in the United States was 34 times that in China.

Figure 20.4 shows the story of real GDP in China from 1983 to 2003 based on converting the yuan to the U.S. dollar at the market exchange rate

Figure 20.4 also shows another story based on an estimate of real GDP per person that is much larger than the official measure. Let's see how this alternative measurement is made. GDP in the United States is measured by using prices that prevail in the United States. China's GDP is measured by using prices that prevail in China. But the relative prices in the two countries are very different. Some goods that are expensive in the United States cost very little in China. These items have a small weight in China's real GDP. If, instead of using China's prices, all the goods and services produced in China are valued at the prices prevailing in the United States, then a more valid comparison can be made of GDP in the two countries. Such a comparison uses prices called *purchasing power parity prices* or PPP.

Alan Heston, Robert Summers, and Bettina Aten, economists in the Center for International Comparisons at the University of Pennsylvania, have used PPP prices to construct real GDP data for more than 100 countries. The IMF now uses methods similar to those of Heston, Summers, and Aten to calculate PPP estimates of GDP in all countries. The PPP comparisons tell a remarkable story about China.

According to the PPP comparisons, GDP per person in the United States in 2003 was 6 times that of China, not the 34 times shown at the market exchange rate. Figure 20.4 shows the PPP view of China's real GDP and compares it with the market exchange rate view.

A prominent China scholar, Thomas Rawski of the University of Pittsburgh, doubts both sets of data

FIGURE 20.4

Two Views of Real GDP in China

myeconlab

Valuing GDP at the market exchange rate (MER), China is a poor developing country in which income per person is less than 3 percent of the U.S. level. But valuing GDP at purchasing power parity (PPP) prices, China's real GDP is 16 percent of the U.S. level. Some China scholars think that even the market exchange rate numbers are too big. So there is much uncertainty about China's real GDP.

Sources of data: International Monetary Fund, World Economic Outlook database, April, 2005, and Alan Heston, Robert Summers, and Bettina Aten, Penn World Table Version 6.1, Center for International Comparisons at the University of Pennsylvania (CICUP), October 2002.

shown in Fig. 20.4. He believes that the growth rate of China's real GDP has been exaggerated for some years and that even the market exchange rate data overstate real GDP in China.

U.S. real GDP is measured pretty reliably. But China's is not. The alternative measures of China's real GDP are unreliable, and the truth about real GDP in China is not known. But China is growing, and many businesses are paying close attention to the prospects of expanding their activities in China and other fast-growing Asian economies.

Business Cycle Forecasts

If policymakers plan to raise interest rates to slow an expansion that they believe is too strong, they look at the latest estimates of real GDP. But suppose that for the reasons we've just discussed, real GDP is mismeasured. Does this mismeasurement hamper our ability to identify the phases of the business cycle? It does

not. The reason is that although the omissions from real GDP do change over time, they probably do not change in a systematic way with the business cycle. So inaccurate measurement of real GDP does not necessarily cause a wrong assessment of the phase of the business cycle.

The fluctuations in economic activity measured by real GDP tell a reasonably accurate story about the phase of the business cycle that the economy is in. When real GDP grows, the economy is in a business cycle expansion; when real GDP shrinks (for two successive quarters), the economy is in a recession. Also, as real GDP fluctuates, so do production and jobs.

But real GDP fluctuations probably exaggerate or overstate the fluctuations in total production and economic welfare. The reason is that when business activity slows in a recession, household production increases and so does leisure time. When business activity speeds up in an expansion, household production and leisure time decrease. Because household production and leisure time increase in a recession and decrease in an expansion, real GDP fluctuations tend to overstate the fluctuations in total production and in economic welfare. But the directions of change of real GDP, total production, and economic welfare are probably the same.

REVIEW QUIZ

1 Does real GDP measure economic welfare? If not, why not?
2 Does real GDP measure total production of goods and services? If not, what are the main omissions?
3 How can we make valid international comparisons of real GDP?
4 Does the growth of real GDP measure the economic growth rate accurately?
5 Do the fluctuations in real GDP measure the business cycle accurately?

myeconlab **Study Plan 20.4**

◆ You've now studied the methods used to measure GDP, economic growth, and the price level. And you've learned about some of the limitations of these measures. *Reading Between the Lines* on pp. 480–481 looks at Canadian real GDP during 2005.

Your next task is to learn how we measure employment and unemployment and inflation.

The Quarterly GDP Report

GLOBE AND MAIL, 1 SEPTEMBER 2005

Economy on a roll in second quarter

The Canadian economy picked up steam in the second quarter, expanding at a greater-than-expected 3.2-per-cent annual pace, and economists say that makes an interest rate rise next week a done deal.

Strong retail sales and home building, combined with a decline in imports, underpinned second-quarter activity, Statistics Canada said yesterday. The number was well above economists' expectations of a 2.7-per-cent gain and surpassed the Bank of Canada's 2.3-per-cent forecast. Growth in the first quarter, meantime, was revised down to 2.1 per cent.

The report reinforced the view that interest rates will rise next week. The central bank meets on Wednesday and is widely expected to raise its key rate for the first time in 11 months, to 2.75 per cent from 2.5 per cent, to keep inflation in check as the economy grows. ...

Yesterday's Statscan report showed imports fell 0.9 per cent while exports edged up 0.2 per cent. Retail trade rose 1.1 per cent in the quarter, while wholesale trade gained 2.3 per cent, boosted by strong demand for durable and semi-durable goods. Personal expenditures grew 0.6 per cent. Investment in housing rose 1.9 per cent, after declining in the first quarter. As a result, the finance and insurance and the real estate sectors gained 0.9 per cent. The output of real estate agents and brokers jumped 4.4 per cent in the quarter amid a strong home resale market.

Reprinted with permission from The Globe and Mail.

Essence of the Story

■ Statistics Canada reported that real GDP grew at an annual rate of 3.2 percent in the second quarter of 2005.

■ Real GDP had grown at an annual rate of 2.1 percent in the first quarter of 2005, so the growth rate sped up in the second quarter.

■ The component of aggregate expenditure that grew quickly during the second quarter of 2005 was consumer expenditure.

■ Imports decreased, which also helped speed growth of domestic production during the second quarter.

Economic Analysis

■ Statistics Canada reports the nation's GDP numbers every three months.

■ To make the quarterly numbers easy to compare with annual numbers, growth rates are reported at annual rates.

■ An annual growth rate is calculated from quarterly data by using the formula:

$$g = [(x_t/x_{t-1})^4 - 1] \times 100,$$

where g is the annualized growth rate, x_t is the value of the variable in the current quarter, and x_{t-1} is the value of the variable in the preceding quarter.

■ The change in real GDP in a quarter is equal to

$$\Delta C + \Delta I + \Delta G + \Delta X - \Delta M$$

■ Figure 1 shows the composition of the increase in real GDP in the second quarter of 2005 with the change in inventories, a component of investment, shown separately from the rest of investment.

■ You can see in the left column of Fig. 1 that the increase in consumption expenditure and the decrease in imports made larger contributions to the change in real GDP than did the other components.

■ You can also see that the increase in real GDP coming from the decrease in imports was almost offset by the decrease in inventories.

■ The news article compares the second quarter with the first quarter, and Fig. 2 shows the composition of the increase in real GDP in the first quarter of 2005.

■ You can see in the right column of Fig. 2 that in the first quarter, the increase in imports and the decrease in inventories offset most of the increases in the other components of real GDP and made the increase in real GDP small.

■ So real GDP increased by more in the second quarter of 2005 than it did in the first quarter because imports fell and inventories fell less in the second quarter than in the first quarter.

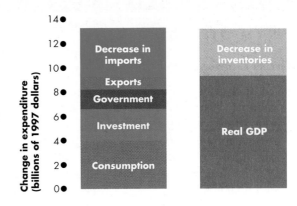

Figure 1 Changes in second quarter of 2005

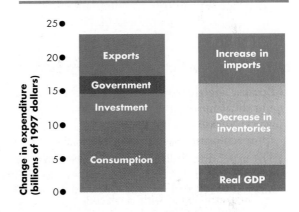

Figure 2 Changes in first quarter of 2005

481

SUMMARY

KEY POINTS

Gross Domestic Product (pp. 466–470)

- GDP, or gross domestic product, is the market value of all the final goods and services produced in a country during a given period.
- A final good is an item that is bought by its final user during a specified time period, and contrasts with an intermediate good, which is a component of a final good.
- GDP is calculated by using the expenditure and income totals in the circular flow of expenditure and income.
- Aggregate expenditure on goods and services equals aggregate income and GDP.

Measuring Canada's GDP (pp. 471–472)

- Because aggregate expenditure, aggregate income, and the value of aggregate production are equal, we can measure GDP by using the expenditure approach or the income approach.
- The expenditure approach sums consumption expenditure, investment, government expenditures on goods and services, and net exports.
- The income approach sums wages, interest, rent, and profit (and indirect taxes and depreciation).

Real GDP and the Price Level (pp. 473–475)

- Real GDP is measured by a chain-weighted output index that compares the value of production each year with its value at the previous year's prices.
- The GDP deflator measures the price level based on the prices of the items that make up GDP.

Measuring Economic Growth (pp. 476–479)

- We measure the economic growth rate as the percentage change in real GDP.

- Real GDP growth is not a perfect measure of economic growth because it excludes quality improvements, household production, the underground economy, environmental damage, health and life expectancy, leisure time, political freedom, and social justice.
- The growth rate of real GDP gives a good indication of the phases of the business cycle.

KEY FIGURES AND TABLES

KEY TERMS

PROBLEMS

Go to 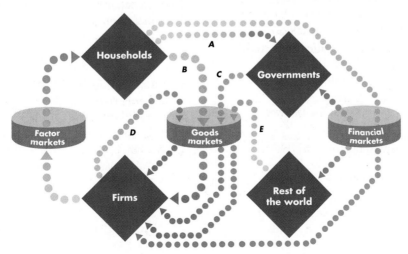 myeconlab for solutions to odd-numbered problems and additional exercises.

1. The figure at the bottom of the page shows the flows of expenditure and income on Lotus Island. During 2005, *A* was $20 million, *B* was $60 million, *C* was $24 million, *D* was $30 million, and *E* was $6 million. Calculate
   a. Aggregate expenditure.
   b. Aggregate income.
   c. GDP.
   d. Government budget deficit.
   e. Household saving.
   f. Government saving.
   g. National saving.
   h. Borrowing from the rest of the world.

2. In problem 1, during 2006, *A* was $25 million, *B* was $450 million, *C* was $30 million, *D* was $30 million, and *E* was –$10 million. Calculate the quantities in problem 1 during 2006.

3. Martha owns a copy shop that has 10 copiers. One copier wears out each year and is replaced. In addition, this year Martha will expand her business to 14 copiers. Calculate Martha's initial capital stock, depreciation, gross investment, net investment, and final capital stock.

4. Wendy operates a weaving shop with 20 looms. One loom wears out each year and is replaced. But this year, Wendy will expand her business to 24 looms. Calculate Wendy's initial capital stock, depreciation, gross investment, net investment, and final capital stock.

5. The transactions in Ecoland last year were

Item	Dollars
Wages paid to labour	800,000
Consumption expenditure	600,000
Taxes	250,000
Transfer payments	50,000
Profits	200,000
Investment	250,000
Government expenditures	200,000
Exports	300,000
Saving	300,000
Imports	250,000

   a. Calculate Ecoland's GDP.
   b. Did you use the expenditure approach or the income approach to make this calculation?
   c. How is investment financed?

6. The transactions in Highland last year were

Item	Dollars
Wages paid to labour	400,000
Consumption expenditure	350,000
Net taxes	125,000
Profits	140,000
Investment	150,000
Government expenditures	130,000
Exports	120,000
Saving	135,000
Imports	140,000

   a. Calculate Highland's GDP.
   b. What extra information do you need to calculate net domestic product at factor cost?
   c. Where does Highland get the funds to finance its investment?

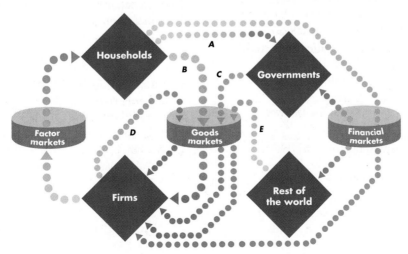

7. Bananaland produces only bananas and sunscreen. The base year is 2005, and the tables give the quantities produced and prices.

	Quantity	
Good	**2005**	**2006**
Bananas	1,000 bunches	1,100 bunches
Sunscreen	500 bottles	525 bottles

	Price	
Good	**2005**	**2006**
Bananas	$2 a bunch	$3 a bunch
Sunscreen	$10 a bottle	$8 a bottle

a. Calculate nominal GDP in 2005 and 2006.
b. Calculate real GDP in 2006 using the base-year prices method.

8. Sea Island produces only lobsters and crabs. The base year is 2006, and the tables give the quantities produced and the prices.

	Quantity	
Good	**2006**	**2007**
Lobsters	1,000	1,450
Crabs	500	525

	Price	
Good	**2006**	**2007**
Lobsters	$20 each	$25 each
Crabs	$10 each	$12 each

a. Calculate nominal GDP in 2006 and 2007.
b. Calculate real GDP in 2007 using the base-year prices method.

9. Bananaland (in problem 7) decides to use the chain-weighted output index method to calculate real GDP. Using this method,
a. Calculate the growth rate of real GDP in 2006.
b. Calculate the GDP deflator in 2006.
c. Compare and comment on the differences in real GDP using the base-year prices and chain-weighted output index methods.

10. Sea Island (in problem 8) decides to use the chain-weighted output index method to calculate real GDP. Using this method,
a. Calculate the growth rate of real GDP in 2007.
b. Calculate the GDP deflator in 2007.
c. Compare and comment on the differences in real GDP using the base-year prices and chain-weighted output index methods.

CRITICAL THINKING

1. Study *Reading Between the Lines* on pp. 480–481 and then answer the following questions:
a. In the first and second quarters of 2005, which components of aggregate expenditure increased most?
b. According to the news article, which components of aggregate income increased most during the first and second quarters of 2005?
c. What happened to net exports during the first two quarters of 2005? Did they increase or decrease? Did Canada increase or decrease its net lending to the rest of the world during those two quarters?
d. Was Canada in a recession, growth recession, or expansion during the first half of 2005?
e. What happened to total investment during the first two quarters of 2005?
f. Where, in the circular flow model, do changes in business inventories appear?

WEB EXERCISES

Use the links on (X myeconlab) **to work the following exercise.**

1. Visit Statistics Canada. There you can obtain all the available data on GDP and the components of aggregate expenditure and aggregate income. You will find data in current prices (nominal GDP) and constant prices (real GDP).
a. What is the value of nominal GDP in the current quarter?
b. What is the value of real GDP in the current quarter using the chain-weighted index method?
c. What is the GDP deflator in the current quarter?
d. What was the value of real GDP in the same quarter of the previous year?
e. By how much has real GDP changed over the past year? (Express your answer as a percentage.)
f. Did real GDP increase or decrease and what does the change tell you about the state of the economy over the past year?

Monitoring Cycles, Jobs, and the Price Level

CHAPTER 21

Vital Signs

Our economy ebbs and flows like a tide between strong expansion, slow down, and recession. What exactly is a recession, who decides when one begins and ends, and what criteria are used to make these decisions?

Each month, we chart the unemployment rate as a measure of Canadian economic health. How do we measure the unemployment rate? What does it tell us? Is it a reliable vital sign for the economy?

Every month, we also chart the number of people working, the number of hours they work, and the wages they receive. Are most new jobs full time or part time? And are they high-wage jobs or low-wage jobs?

As the Canadian economy has expanded over the past few years, the unemployment rate has trended downward. But even in the boom times of 2005, more than 1 million Canadians were unemployed. Questions about the health of the labour market are of vital importance to these unemployed workers and to the millions of others who fear the risk of unemployment.

Having a good job that pays a decent wage is only half of the equation that translates into a good standard of living. The other half is the cost of living. We track the cost of the items that we buy with another number that is published every month—the Consumer Price Index, or CPI. What is the CPI? How is it calculated? And does it provide a reliable guide to the changes in our cost of living?

◆ These are the questions we study in this chapter. We begin by looking at the way in which a recession is identified and dated. And we end, in *Reading Between the Lines,* by putting the spotlight on the CPI in 2005.

After studying this chapter, you will be able to

- **Explain how we date the business cycle**
- **Define the unemployment rate, the labour force participation rate, the employment-to-population ratio, and aggregate hours**
- **Describe the sources and types of unemployment and define full employment and the natural rate of unemployment**
- **Explain how we measure the price level and the inflation rate using the CPI**

The Business Cycle

THE BUSINESS CYCLE IS A PERIODIC BUT IRREGU-
lar up-and-down movement in production and jobs
(see p. 448). There is no official, government-spon-
sored record of the dating of business cycles. Instead,
business cycles are identified by two private agencies:
the Economic Cycle Research Institute (ECRI) and
the National Bureau of Economic Research (NBER).
The ECRI identifies and dates the business cycles in
Canada and 17 other countries and the NBER dates
the U.S. business cycle. The working definition of
the business cycle used by the ECRI is as follows:

> ... pronounced, pervasive and persistent
> advances and declines in aggregate economic
> activity, which cannot be defined by any single
> variable, but by the consensus of key measures
> of output, income, employment and sales.[1]

A business cycle has two phases—expansion and
recession—and two turning points—peak and
trough. The NBER, whose methods the ECRI uses,
defines the phases and turning points of the cycle as
follows.

> A *recession* is a significant decline in activity
> spread across the economy, lasting more than a
> few months, visible in industrial production,
> employment, real income, and wholesale-retail
> trade. A recession begins just after the economy
> reaches a *peak* of activity and ends as the economy
> reaches its *trough*. Between trough and peak, the
> economy is in an *expansion*.[2]

Real GDP is the broadest measure of economic
activity, and another popular working definition of a
recession is a decrease in real GDP that lasts for at
least two quarters. But we don't measure real GDP
each month, so the ECRI and NBER do not use the
real GDP numbers. Instead, they look at employment, which is the broadest *monthly* indicator of economic activity, along with other monthly measures
that include personal income, sales of goods, and
industrial production.

Business Cycle Dates

Figure 21.1(a) provides a quick summary of the
Canadian business cycle since 1926. The figure shows
the percentage deviation of real GDP from potential
GDP.

The Great Depression, which began with a recession that ran from August 1929 to March 1933, was
the most severe contraction of economic activity ever
experienced. Over a 43-month period, real GDP
shrank by 33 percent. Canada has had only four other
recessions: at the end of World War II, 1954, 1982,
and 1990–1991. The ECRI identified one other recession during 1957, but it was so mild that it doesn't
show up in the real GDP data.

Expansion is the normal state of the economy, and
the biggest expansion occurred during World War II.
But the longest expansion ran from 1954 to 1982
(except for a mild stop in 1957). There is no correlation between the length of an expansion and the
length of the preceding recession.

Growth Rate Cycles

Because recessions are rare, just looking at expansions
and recessions misses a lot of the volatility in our
economy. An alternative and more sensitive approach
is to examine growth rate cycle downturns. A **growth
rate cycle downturn** is a

> ... pronounced, pervasive and persistent
> decline in the *growth rate* of aggregate economic
> activity. The procedures used to identify peaks
> and troughs in the growth rate cycle are analo-
> gous to those used to identify business cycle turn-
> ing points, except that they are applied to the
> growth rates of the same time series, rather than
> their levels.[3]

Figure 21.1(b) shows the growth rate cycles since
1961 (the first year for which we have quarterly real
GDP data).

REVIEW QUIZ

1 What are the phases of the business cycle?
2 Have recessions been getting worse?

 Study Plan 21.1

---

[1] You can find this definition and the dates of the business cycles
in 18 countries at the ECRI Web site (www.businesscycle.com).

[2] "The NBER's Business Cycle Dating Procedure," January 10,
2002, NBER Web site (www.nber.org). (Italics added.)

[3] This definition is from the ECRI Web site (with small changes).

FIGURE 21.1
Two Views of Canadian Business Cycles

(a) Deviations from potential GDP since 1926

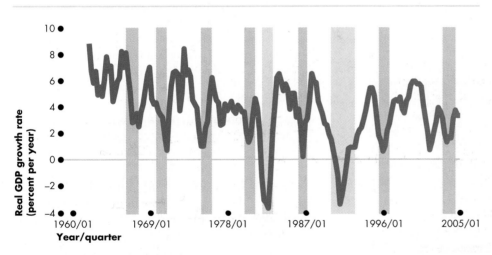

(b) Growth rate cycles since 1961

Part (a) shows the patterns of recession and expansion since the mid-1920s using real GDP as the measuring rod. Recessions have lasted from almost four years during the Great Depression, when real GDP fell by 33 percent, to a year in 1953–1954, when real GDP fell by 1.2 percent. Canada has had only four recessions since World War II.

Part (b) shows the higher frequency growth rate cycles since 1961, again using real GDP as the measuring rod of economic activity. The two deepest growth rate recessions occurred during 1982 and 1991, the periods in which real GDP shrank and the economy was in recession in part (a). The other growth rate recessions identified by the shading in the figure were milder and did not take real GDP growth into negative territory.

Sources of data: Business cycle dates and growth rate cycle dates: The Economic Cycle Research Institute. Real GDP: Statistics Canada, *Historical Statistics of Canada*, Catalogue 11-516-XIE (1926–1960) and Table 380–0002 (1961–2004).

Jobs and Wages

YOU HAVE SEEN THAT EMPLOYMENT IS ONE OF THE key features of the economy that helps the ECRI and NBER to determine the onset of recession. The state of the labour market has a large impact on our incomes and our lives. We become concerned when jobs are hard to find and more relaxed when they are plentiful. But we want a good job, which means that we want a well-paid and interesting job.

You are now going to learn how economists track the health of the labour market.

Population Survey

Every month, Statistics Canada surveys 54,000 households and asks a series of questions about the age and job market status of their members. This survey is called the Labour Force Survey. Statistics Canada uses the answers to describe the anatomy of the labour force.

Figure 21.2 shows the population categories used by Statistics Canada and the relationships among the categories in 2004. It divides the population into two groups: the working-age population and others who are too young to work. The **working-age population** is the total number of people aged 15 years and over. Statistics Canada divides the working-age population into two groups: those in the labour force and those not in the labour force. It also divides the labour force into two groups: the employed and the unemployed. So the **labour force** is the sum of the employed and the unemployed.

To be counted as employed in the Labour Force Survey, a person must have either a full-time job or a part-time job. To be counted as *un*employed, a person must be available for work and must be in one of three categories:

1. Without work but has made specific efforts to find a job within the previous four weeks
2. Laid off from a job and waiting to be called back to work
3. Waiting to start a new job within four weeks

Anyone surveyed who satisfies one of these three criteria is counted as unemployed. People in the working-age population who are neither employed nor unemployed are classified as not in the labour force.

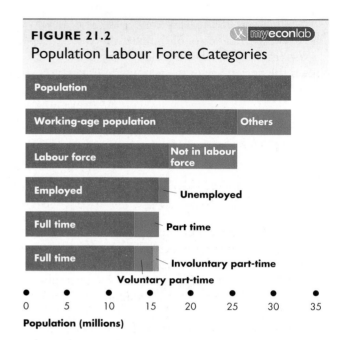

FIGURE 21.2
Population Labour Force Categories

The population is divided into the working-age population and others. The working-age population is divided into those in the labour force and those not in the labour force. The labour force is divided into those employed and those unemployed. The people employed are divided into full-time and part-time workers. And part-time workers are divided into those who are voluntary and involuntary part-time workers.

Source of data: Statistics Canada, CANSIM Tables 282–0002 and 051–0001.

In 2004, the population of Canada was 31.95 million of which 6.52 million were under 15 years of age. The working-age population was 25.43 million and of these 8.25 million were not in the labour force. Most of them were either in school full time or retired. The remaining 17.18 million people made up the Canadian labour force. Of these, 15.95 million were employed and 1.23 million were unemployed.

Four Labour Market Indicators

Statistics Canada calculates four indicators of the state of the labour market:

- The unemployment rate
- The involuntary part-time rate
- The labour force participation rate
- The employment-to-population ratio

The Unemployment Rate The amount of unemployment is an indicator of the extent to which people who want jobs can't find them. The **unemployment rate** is the percentage of the people in the labour force who are unemployed. That is,

$$\text{Unemployment rate} = \frac{\text{Number of people unemployed}}{\text{Labour force}} \times 100$$

and

$$\text{Labour force} = \text{Number of people employed} + \text{Number of people unemployed.}$$

In 2004, the number of people employed was 15.95 million and the number unemployed was 1.23 million. So the labour force was 17.18 million (15.95 million plus 1.23 million) and the unemployment rate was 7.2 percent (1.23 million ÷ 17.18 million × 100).

Figure 21.3 shows the unemployment rate (the orange line and plotted on the right-hand scale) and three other labour market indicators between 1961 and 2004. The average unemployment rate has been 7.8 percent, and it reached peak values at the ends of the 1982 and 1990–1991 recessions.

The Involuntary Part-Time Rate Part-time workers who want full-time work do not get counted as being unemployed. To measure this type of underemployment, Statistics Canada counts the number of involuntary part-time workers—part-time workers who want full-time jobs. The *involuntary part-time rate* is the percentage of the people in the labour force who work part time but want full-time jobs.

$$\text{Involuntary part-time rate} = \frac{\text{Number of involuntary part-time workers}}{\text{Labour force}} \times 100.$$

In 2004, the number of involuntary part-time workers was 922,000, the labour force was 17.18 million, and the involuntary part-time rate was 5.4 percent.

Figure 21.3 shows the involuntary part-time rate (plotted on the right-hand scale). (The break occurs because the criterion for involuntary changed in 1997.) You can see that an increasing percentage of the labour force wants full-time work but is not able to get full-time work. You can also see that the fluctuations in the involuntary part-time rate are like those in the unemployment rate.

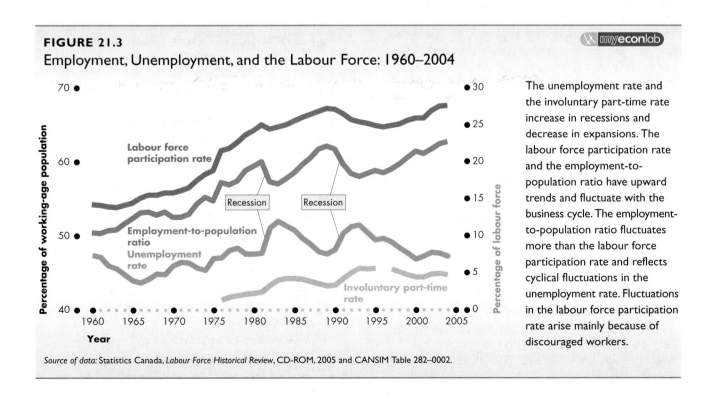

FIGURE 21.3

Employment, Unemployment, and the Labour Force: 1960–2004

The unemployment rate and the involuntary part-time rate increase in recessions and decrease in expansions. The labour force participation rate and the employment-to-population ratio have upward trends and fluctuate with the business cycle. The employment-to-population ratio fluctuates more than the labour force participation rate and reflects cyclical fluctuations in the unemployment rate. Fluctuations in the labour force participation rate arise mainly because of discouraged workers.

Source of data: Statistics Canada, *Labour Force Historical Review*, CD-ROM, 2005 and CANSIM Table 282–0002.

The Labour Force Participation Rate The number of people of working age who join the labour force is an indicator of the willingness of people to take jobs. The **labour force participation rate** is the percentage of the working-age population who are members of the labour force. That is,

$$\text{Labour force participation rate} = \frac{\text{Labour force}}{\text{Working-age population}} \times 100.$$

In 2004, the labour force was 17.18 million and the working-age population was 25.43 million. By using the above equation, you can calculate the labour force participation rate. It was 67.6 percent (17.18 million ÷ 25.43 million × 100).

Figure 21.3 shows the labour force participation rate (graphed in red and plotted on the left-hand scale). It has followed an upward trend and has increased from 54.1 percent during the early 1960s to 67.6 percent in 2004. It has also had some mild fluctuations. They result from unsuccessful job seekers becoming discouraged workers. **Discouraged workers** are people who are available and willing to work but have not made specific efforts to find a job within the previous four weeks. These workers often temporarily leave the labour force during a recession and re-enter during an expansion and become active job seekers.

The Employment-to-Population Ratio The number of people of working age who have jobs is an indicator of both the availability of jobs and the degree of match between people's skills and jobs. The **employment-to-population ratio** is the percentage of people of working age who have jobs. That is,

$$\text{Employment-to-population ratio} = \frac{\text{Number of people employed}}{\text{Working-age population}} \times 100.$$

In 2004, the number of people employed was 15.95 million and the working-age population was 25.43 million. By using the above equation, you can calculate the employment-to-population ratio. It was 62.7 percent (15.95 million ÷ 25.43 million × 100).

Figure 21.3 shows the employment-to-population ratio (graphed in blue and plotted against the left-hand scale). It increased from 50 percent during the early 1960s to 62.7 percent in 2004. The increase in the

employment-to-population ratio means that the Canadian economy has created jobs at a faster rate than the working-age population has grown. This labour market indicator also fluctuates, and its fluctuations coincide with but are opposite to those in the unemployment rate. The employment-to-population ratio falls during a recession and increases during an expansion.

Why have the labour force participation rate and the employment-to-population ratio increased? The main reason is an increase in the number of women in the labour force. Figure 21.4 shows this increase. Shorter work hours, higher productivity, and an increased emphasis on white-collar jobs have expanded the job opportunities and wages available to women. At the same time, technological advances have increased productivity in the home and freed up women's time to take jobs outside the home.

Figure 21.4 also shows another remarkable trend in the Canadian labour force: The labour force par-

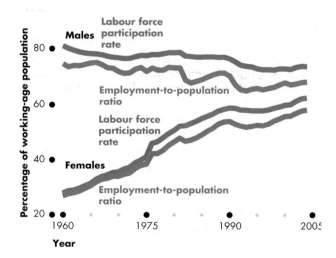

FIGURE 21.4

The Changing Face of the Labour Market

The upward trends in the labour force participation rate and the employment-to-population ratio are accounted for mainly by the increasing participation of women in the labour market. The male labour force participation rate and employment-to-population ratio have decreased.

Source of data: Statistics Canada, CANSIM Table 282–0002.

ticipation rate and the employment-to-population ratio for men have *decreased*. These indicators decreased because increasing numbers of men were remaining in school longer and because some were retiring earlier.

Aggregate Hours

The four labour market indicators that we've just examined are useful signs of the health of the economy and directly measure what matters to most people: jobs. But these four indicators don't tell us the quantity of labour used to produce real GDP, and we cannot use them to calculate the productivity of labour. The productivity of labour is significant because it influences the wages people earn.

The reason why the number of people employed does not measure the quantity of labour employed is that jobs are not all the same. People in part-time jobs might work just a few hours a week. People in full-time jobs work around 35 to 40 hours a week. And some people regularly work overtime. For example, a 7-11 store might hire six students who work for 3 hours a day each. Another 7-11 store might hire two full-time workers who work 9 hours a day each. The number of people employed in these two stores is eight, but the total hours worked by six of the eight is the same as the total hours worked by the other two. To determine the total amount of labour used to produce real GDP, we measure labour in hours rather than in jobs. **Aggregate hours** are the total number of hours worked by all the people employed, both full time and part time, during a year.

Figure 21.5(a) shows aggregate hours in the Canadian economy from 1960 to 2004. Like the employment-to-population ratio, aggregate hours have an upward trend. But aggregate hours have not grown as quickly as has the number of people employed. Between 1960 and 2004, the number of people employed in Canada increased by 163 percent. During that same period, aggregate hours increased by a bit more than 118 percent. Why the difference? Because average hours per worker decreased.

Figure 21.5(b) shows average hours per worker. After hovering at a bit more than 40 hours a week during the early 1960s, average hours per worker decreased to about 33 hours a week during the 2000s. This shortening of the average workweek arose partly because of a decrease in the average hours worked by full-time workers, but mainly because the number of

FIGURE 21.5
Aggregate Hours: 1960–2004

(a) Aggregate hours

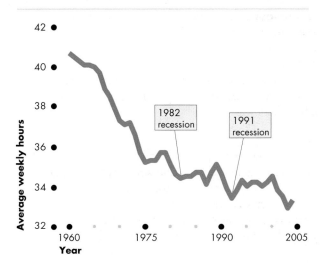

(b) Average weekly hours per person

Aggregate hours (part a) measure the total labour used to produce real GDP more accurately than does the number of people employed because an increasing proportion of jobs are part time. Between 1960 and 2004, aggregate hours increased by an average of 1.8 percent a year. Fluctuations in aggregate hours coincide with the business cycle. Aggregate hours have increased at a slower rate than the number of jobs because the average workweek has shortened (part b).

Source of data: Statistics Canada, CANSIM Tables 282–0002 and 282–0022.

part-time jobs increased faster than the number of full-time jobs.

Fluctuations in aggregate hours and average hours per worker line up with the business cycle. Figure 21.5 highlights the past two recessions, during which aggregate hours decreased and average hours per worker decreased more quickly than the trend.

Real Wage Rate

The **real wage rate** is the quantity of goods and services that an hour's work can buy. It is equal to the money wage rate (dollars per hour) divided by the price level. If we use the GDP deflator to measure the price level, the real wage rate is expressed in 1997 dollars because the GDP deflator is 100 in 1997. The real wage rate is a significant economic variable because it measures the reward for labour.

What has happened to the real wage rate in Canada? Figure 21.6 answers this question. Figure 21.6 shows the broadest measure of the average hourly real wage rate in the Canadian economy.

The money wage rate is calculated from the national income accounts and aggregate hours. We know from the income side of the national income accounts the total amount of labour income. This total includes wages and salaries and all supplementary labour income such as health and insurance benefits. It includes all labour income, not just that of people who are paid by the hour. If we divide this total by aggregate hours, we arrive at an estimate of the economy-wide average money wage rate. This average includes all types of labour in all parts of the economy.

The real wage rate follows an upward path. But the trend growth rate slowed during the 1970s and early 1980s in the *productivity growth slowdown*. This productivity growth slowdown is the main reason for this behaviour of the average real wage rate.

The average real wage rate usually increases but you can see in Fig. 21.6 that it sometimes decreases. The real wage rate decreased during the late 1970s, the 1990s, and the early 2000s.

FIGURE 21.6   myeconlab
Real Wage Rate: 1960–2004

The average hourly real wage rate follows an upward trend. But the trend growth rate of the real wage rate slowed during the 1970s and early 1980s. Occasionally, the real wage rate falls, as it did in the late 1970s, the 1990s, and the early 2000s.

Source of data: Statistics Canada, CANSIM Tables 282–0002, 282–0022, and 380–0001.

REVIEW QUIZ

1 What are the trends in the unemployment rate, the labour force participation rate, and the employment-to-population ratio?
2 How do the unemployment rate, the labour force participation rate, and the employment-to-population ratio fluctuate over the business cycle?
3 Has the female labour force participation rate been similar to or different from the male labour force participation rate?
4 How have aggregate hours changed since 1960?
5 How did the average hourly real wage rate change during the 1990s?

myeconlab   **Study Plan 21.2**

You've now seen how we measure employment, unemployment, and the real wage rate. Your next task is to study the anatomy of unemployment and see why it never disappears, even at full employment.

Unemployment and Full Employment

HOW DO PEOPLE BECOME UNEMPLOYED, AND how does a period of unemployment end? How long do people remain unemployed on the average? Who is at greatest risk of becoming unemployed? Let's answer these questions by looking at the anatomy of unemployment.

The Anatomy of Unemployment

People become unemployed if they

1. Lose their jobs and search for another job.
2. Leave their jobs and search for another job.
3. Enter or re-enter the labour force to search for a job.

People end a spell of unemployment if they

1. Are hired or recalled.
2. Withdraw from the labour force.

People who are laid off from their jobs, either permanently or temporarily, are called *job losers*. Some job losers become unemployed, but some immediately withdraw from the labour force. People who voluntarily quit their jobs are called *job leavers*. Like job losers, some job leavers become unemployed and search for a better job, while others withdraw from the labour force temporarily or permanently retire from work. People who enter or re-enter the labour force are called *entrants* and *re-entrants*. Entrants are mainly people who have just left school. Some entrants get a job right away and are never unemployed, but many spend time searching for their first job, and during this period, they are unemployed. Re-entrants are people who have previously withdrawn from the labour force. Most of these people are formerly discouraged workers. Figure 21.7 shows these labour market flows.

The Sources of Unemployment Figure 21.8 shows unemployment by reason for becoming unemployed. Job losers are the biggest source of unemployment. On the average, they account for around half of total unemployment. Also, their number fluctuates a great deal. At the trough of the recession of 1990–1991, on any given day, almost 1 million of

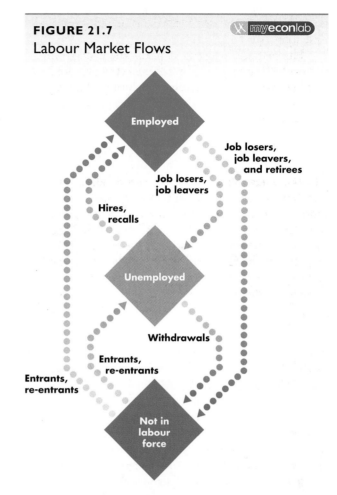

FIGURE 21.7
Labour Market Flows

Unemployment results from employed people losing or leaving their jobs (job losers and job leavers) and from people entering the labour force (entrants and re-entrants). Unemployment ends because people get hired or recalled or because they withdraw from the labour force.

the 1.6 million people unemployed were job losers. In contrast, at the business cycle peak year of 1989, fewer than 600,000 of the 1 million people unemployed were job losers.

Entrants and re-entrants also make up a large component of the unemployed, and their number fluctuates but more mildly than the fluctuations in the number of job losers.

Job leavers are the smallest and most stable source of unemployment. On any given day, less than 200,000 people are unemployed because they are job leavers. The number of job leavers is remarkably

FIGURE 21.8
Unemployment by Reason

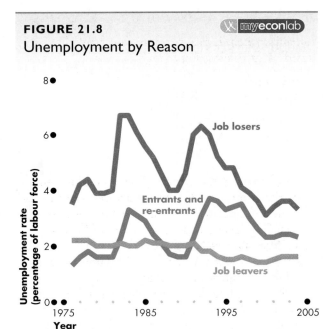

Everyone who is unemployed is a job loser, a job leaver, or an entrant or re-entrant into the labour force. Most unemployment results from job loss. The number of job losers fluctuates more closely with the business cycle than do the numbers of job leavers and entrants and re-entrants. Entrants and re-entrants are the second most common type of unemployed people. Their number fluctuates with the business cycle because of discouraged workers. Job leavers are the least common type of unemployed people.

Source of data: Statistics Canada, *Labour Force Historical Review* CD-ROM, 2005.

FIGURE 21.9
Unemployment by Duration

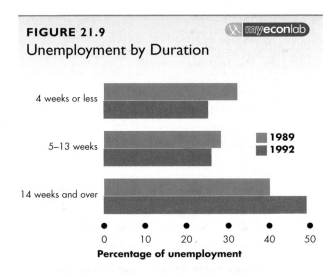

Close to a business cycle peak in 1989, when the unemployment rate was 7.5 percent, 32 percent of unemployment lasted for 4 weeks or less, 28 percent lasted for 5 to 13 weeks, and less than 40 percent lasted for 14 weeks or more. In a business cycle trough in 1992, when the unemployment rate was 11 percent, 25 percent of unemployment lasted for 4 weeks or less, 26 percent lasted for 5 to 13 weeks, and 49 percent lasted for 14 weeks or more.

Source of data: Statistics Canada, *Labour Force Historical Review* CD-ROM, 2001.

constant, although to the extent that it fluctuates, it does so in line with the business cycle: A slightly larger number of people leave their jobs in good times than in bad times.

The Duration of Unemployment   Some people are unemployed for a week or two, and others are unemployed for periods of a year or more. The longer the spell of unemployment, the greater the personal cost to the unemployed. The average duration of unemployment varies over the business cycle.

Figure 21.9 compares the duration of unemployment at a business cycle peak in 1989, when the unemployment rate was low, with that at a business cycle trough in 1992, when the unemployment rate

was high. In 1989 when the unemployment rate hit a low of 7.5 percent, 32 percent of the unemployed were in that situation for less than 4 weeks and less than 40 percent of the unemployed were jobless for longer than 13 weeks. In 1992 when the unemployment rate reached a high of 11 percent, only 25 percent of the unemployed found a new job in 4 weeks or less and 49 percent were unemployed for more than 13 weeks. At both low and high unemployment rates, about 27 percent of the unemployed take between 4 weeks and 13 weeks to find a job.

The Demographics of Unemployment   Figure 21.10 shows unemployment for different demographic groups. The figure shows that high unemployment rates occur among young workers. In the business cycle trough in 1992, the teenage unemployment rate was 20 percent. Even in 1989, when the national unemployment rate was 7.5 percent, the teenage unemployment rate was 13 percent.

FIGURE 21.10
Unemployment by Demographic Group

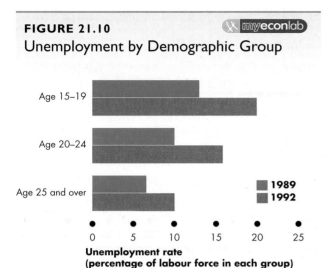

Teenagers experience the highest unemployment rates. In the 1992 business cycle trough (when unemployment was at its highest rate, 11 percent), the teenage unemployment rate was 20 percent. Even at the 1989 business cycle peak (when the unemployment rate was at its lowest, 7.5 percent), the teenage unemployment rate was 13 percent.

Source of data: Statistics Canada, CANSIM Table 282–0002.

Why is the unemployment rate of young people so high? There are three reasons. First, young people are still in the process of discovering what they are good at and trying different lines of work. So they leave their jobs more frequently than do older workers. Second, firms sometimes hire teenagers on a short-term trial basis. So the rate of job loss is higher for teenagers than for other people. Third, most young persons are not in the labour force but are in school. This fact means that the percentage of the young adult population that is unemployed is much lower than the percentage of the young labour force that is unemployed. In 2001, for example, 340,000 15-to-24 year olds were unemployed and 2.3 million were employed. So the 15-to-24 year olds' unemployment rate was 12.9 percent. But 4 million were enrolled in post-secondary education. If we considered being in school as the equivalent of having a job and measured the unemployment rate as the percentage of the labour force plus the school population, we would record a 5.1 percent unemployment rate among 15-to-24 year olds.

Types of Unemployment

Unemployment is classified into four types that are based on its origins. They are

- Frictional
- Structural
- Seasonal
- Cyclical

Frictional Unemployment The unemployment that arises from normal labour turnover—from people entering and leaving the labour force and from the ongoing creation and destruction of jobs—is called **frictional unemployment**. This type of unemployment is a permanent and healthy phenomenon in a dynamic, growing economy.

The unending flow of people into and out of the labour force and the processes of job creation and job destruction create the need for people to search for jobs and for businesses to search for workers. Always, there are businesses with unfilled jobs and people seeking jobs. Look in your local newspaper, and you will see that there are always some jobs being advertised. Businesses don't usually hire the first person who applies for a job, and unemployed people don't usually take the first job that comes their way. Instead, both firms and workers spend time searching out what they believe will be the best match available. By this search process, people can match their own skills and interests with the available jobs and find a satisfying job and income. While these unemployed people are searching, they are frictionally unemployed.

The amount of frictional unemployment depends on the rate at which people enter and re-enter the labour force and on the rate at which jobs are created and destroyed. During the 1970s, the amount of frictional unemployment increased as a consequence of the post-war baby boom that began during the 1940s. By the late 1970s, the baby boom created a bulge in the number of people leaving school. As these people entered the labour force, the amount of frictional unemployment increased.

The amount of frictional unemployment is influenced by unemployment compensation. The greater the number of unemployed people covered by employment insurance and the more generous the unemployment benefits they receive, the longer is the average time taken in job search and the greater is the amount of frictional unemployment. Canadian employment insurance is among the most comprehensive and generous in the world. It is much more comprehensive than that in the United States. This factor is one reason why the Canadian unemployment rate has exceeded the U.S. unemployment rate since the early 1980s. But there are other reasons. Canadian workers, especially young workers who make up the so-called Generation X, have shorter spells of employment and more frequent intervening spells of unemployment, supported by employment insurance, than do young U.S. workers.[4]

Structural Unemployment The unemployment that arises when changes in technology or international competition change the skills needed to perform jobs or change the locations of jobs is called **structural unemployment**. This type of unemployment usually lasts longer than frictional unemployment because workers must retrain and possibly relocate to find a job. For example, when a steel plant in Hamilton, Ontario, is automated, some jobs in that city are destroyed. Meanwhile, in the Ottawa valley and Vancouver, new jobs for security guards, life-insurance salespeople, and retail clerks are created. The unemployed former steelworkers remain unemployed for several months until they move, retrain, and get one of these jobs. Structural unemployment is painful, especially for older workers for whom the best available option might be to retire early but with a lower income than they had expected.

At some times the amount of structural unemployment is modest. At other times it is large, and at such times, structural unemployment can become a serious long-term problem. It was especially large during the late 1970s and early 1980s. During those years, oil price hikes and an increasingly competitive international environment destroyed jobs in traditional Canadian industries, such as auto and steel, and created jobs in new industries, such as electronics and bioengineering, as well as in banking and insurance. Structural unemployment was also present dur-

ing the early 1990s as many businesses and governments "downsized."

Seasonal Unemployment Many jobs are available only at certain times of the year. **Seasonal unemployment** is the unemployment that arises because the number of jobs available has decreased because of the season. Most seasonal unemployment in Canada occurs in the winter because construction and outdoor farming essentially close down for several months.

Cyclical Unemployment The unemployment that fluctuates over the business cycle is called **cyclical unemployment**. This type of unemployment increases during a recession and decreases during an expansion. An auto worker who is laid off because the economy is in a recession and who gets rehired some months later when the expansion begins has experienced cyclical unemployment.

Full Employment

There is always *some* unemployment. So what do we mean by *full employment*? **Full employment** occurs when there is no cyclical unemployment or, equivalently, when all the unemployment is frictional, structural, and seasonal. The unemployment rate at full employment is called the **natural rate of unemployment**. The divergence of the unemployment rate from the natural rate of unemployment is cyclical unemployment.

There can be a lot of unemployment at full employment, and the term "full employment" is an example of a technical economic term that does not correspond with everyday language. The term "natural rate of unemployment" is another technical economic term whose meaning does not correspond with everyday language. For most people—especially for unemployed workers—there is nothing *natural* about unemployment.

So why do economists call a situation with a lot of unemployment "full employment"? And why is the unemployment at full employment called "natural"?

The reason is that the economy is a complex mechanism that is always changing. Every day, some people retire, new workers enter the labour force, some businesses downsize or fail and others expand or start up. This process of change creates unavoidable frictions and dislocations, which create unemployment. Economists don't agree about the size of the natural rate of unemployment or the extent to which it fluctuates.

---

[4] These conclusions are based on the work of David Card and Craig W. Riddell, "A Comparative Analysis of Unemployment in Canada and the United States," *Small Differences that Matter: Labour Markets and Income Maintenance in Canada and the United States*, edited by Richard Freeman and David Card, Chicago: University of Chicago Press and NBER, 1993, pp. 149–189; and Audra J. Bowlus, "What Generation X Can Tell Us About the U.S.–Canadian Unemployment Rate Gap," University of Western Ontario, 1996.

FIGURE 21.11
Unemployment and Real GDP

(a) Real GDP

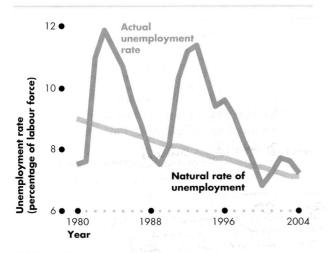

(b) Unemployment rate

As real GDP fluctuates around potential GDP (part a), the unemployment rate fluctuates around the natural rate of unemployment (part b). In the deep 1982 recession, the unemployment rate reached almost 12 percent. In the milder 1990–1991 recession, the unemployment rate peaked at about 11 percent. The natural rate of unemployment has gradually decreased since 1980.

Sources of data: Statistics Canada, CANSIM Tables 282–0002 and 380–0002, and International Monetary Fund, *World Economic Outlook*, Output gap series.

Real GDP and Unemployment Over the Cycle

The quantity of real GDP at full employment is called **potential GDP**. You will study the forces that determine potential GDP in Chapter 30 (pp. 712–713). Over the business cycle, real GDP fluctuates around potential GDP and the unemployment rate fluctuates around the natural rate of unemployment. Figure 21.11 illustrates these fluctuations in Canada between 1980 and 2004—real GDP in part (a) and the unemployment rate in part (b).

When the economy is at full employment, the unemployment rate equals the natural rate of unemployment and real GDP equals potential GDP. When the unemployment rate is less than the natural rate of unemployment, real GDP is greater than potential GDP. And when the unemployment rate is greater than the natural rate of unemployment, real GDP is less than potential GDP.

Figure 21.11(b) shows one view of the natural rate of unemployment. Keep in mind that economists do not know the magnitude of the natural rate of unemployment, so the natural rate shown in the figure is only one estimate. In Fig. 21.11(b), the natural rate of unemployment has gradually fallen from about 9 percent in 1980 to about 7 percent in 2004. This estimate of the natural rate of unemployment in Canada is one that many, but not all, economists would accept.

REVIEW QUIZ

1 What are the categories of people who become unemployed?
2 Define frictional unemployment, structural unemployment, seasonal unemployment, and cyclical unemployment and provide an example of each type of unemployment.
3 What is the natural rate of unemployment?
4 How might the natural rate of unemployment change and what factors might make it change?
5 How does the unemployment rate fluctuate over the business cycle?

myeconlab **Study Plan 21.3**

Your final task in this chapter is to learn about another vital sign that gets monitored every month: the Consumer Price Index (CPI). What is the CPI, how do we measure it, and what does it mean?

The Consumer Price Index

STATISTICS CANADA CALCULATES THE CONSUMER Price Index every month. The **Consumer Price Index (CPI)** is a measure of the average of the prices paid by urban consumers for a fixed "basket" of consumer goods and services. What you learn in this section will help you to make sense of the CPI and relate it to your own economic life. The CPI tells you what has happened to the value of the money in your pocket.

Reading the CPI Numbers

The CPI is defined to equal 100 for a period called the **base period**. Currently, the base period is 1992. That is, for the average of the 12 months of 1992, the CPI equals 100.

In August 2005, the CPI was 128. This number tells us that the average of the prices paid by urban consumers for a fixed market basket of consumer goods and services was 28 percent higher in August 2005 than it was on the average during 1992.

In August 2004, the CPI was 124.8. Comparing the August 2005 CPI with the August 2004 CPI tells us that the index of the prices paid by urban consumers for a fixed basket of consumer goods and services increased during the year ended August 2005 by 3.2—from 124.8 to 128.0—or 2.6 percent.

Constructing the CPI

Constructing the CPI is a huge operation that costs millions of dollars and involves three stages:

- Selecting the CPI basket
- Conducting the monthly price survey
- Calculating the CPI

Selecting the CPI Basket The first stage in constructing the CPI is to select what is called the CPI basket. This "basket" contains the goods and services represented in the index and the relative importance attached to each of them. The idea is to make the relative importance of the items in the CPI basket the same as that in the budget of an average urban household. For example, because people spend more on housing than on bus rides, the CPI places more weight on the price of housing than on the price of bus rides.

Statistics Canada uses several baskets and calculates several alternative CPIs. The goal of the alternatives is to omit items that are highly volatile and that mask the deeper changes in the index. Here, we'll look only at the main "All-Items" index.

To determine the spending patterns of households and to select the CPI basket, Statistics Canada conducts a survey of consumer's expenditure. This survey is costly and so is undertaken only once every few years. Today's CPI basket is based on data gathered in a Consumer Expenditure Survey of 1996.

Figure 21.12 shows the CPI basket at the end of 2001. The basket contains thousands of individual goods and services arranged in the eight large groups shown in the figure. The most important item in a household's budget is shelter, which accounts for 26.8 percent of total expenditure. Transportation comes next at 19.8 percent. Third in relative importance is food at 16.9 percent. These three groups account for almost two-thirds of the average household budget.

FIGURE 21.12
The CPI Basket

The CPI basket consists of the items that an average urban household buys. It consists mainly of shelter (26.8 percent), transportation (19.8 percent), and food (16.9 percent). All other items add up to 36.5 percent of the total.

Source of data: Statistics Canada, Catalogue 62-001-XIB.

Statistics Canada breaks down each of these categories into smaller ones. For example, the recreation, education, and reading category breaks down into textbooks and supplies, tuition, telephone services, and personal computer services.

As you look at the relative importance of the items in the CPI basket, remember that they apply to the *average* household. *Individual* households are spread around the average. Think about your own expenditure and compare the basket of goods and services you buy with the CPI basket.

Conducting the Monthly Price Survey Each month, Statistics Canada employees check the prices of the goods and services in the CPI basket in 64 urban centres. Because the CPI aims to measure price *changes*, it is important that the prices recorded each month refer to exactly the same item. For example, suppose that the price of a box of jellybeans has increased, but a box now contains more beans. Has the price of jellybeans increased? Statistics Canada employees must record the details of changes in quality or packaging so that price changes can be isolated from other changes.

Once the raw price data are in hand, the next task is to calculate the CPI.

Calculating the CPI The CPI calculation has three steps:

1. Find the cost of the CPI basket at base period prices.
2. Find the cost of the CPI basket at current period prices.
3. Calculate the CPI for the base period and the current period.

We'll work through these three steps for a simple example. Suppose the CPI basket contains only 10 oranges and 5 haircuts. We'll construct an annual CPI rather than a monthly CPI with the base period 2004 and the current period 2005.

Table 21.1 shows the quantities in the CPI basket and the prices in the base period and current period.

Part (a) contains the data for the base period. In that period, the price of an orange was $1 and the price of a haircut was $8. To find the cost of the CPI basket at base period prices, multiply the quantities in the CPI basket by the base period prices. The cost of oranges is $10 (10 at $1 each), and the cost of haircuts is $40 (5 at $8 each). So the total cost of the CPI basket at base period prices was $50 ($10 + $40).

Part (b) contains the price data for the current period. The price of an orange increased from $1 to $2, which is a 100 percent increase ($1 ÷ $1 × 100 = 100). The price of a haircut increased from $8 to $10, which is a 25 percent increase ($2 ÷ $8 × 100 = 25).

The CPI provides a way of averaging these price increases by comparing the costs of the CPI basket rather than the prices of the items. To find the cost of the CPI basket at the current period prices multiply the quantities in the CPI basket by their 2005 prices. The cost of oranges is $20 (10 at $2 each), and the cost of haircuts is $50 (5 at $10 each). So the total cost of the fixed CPI basket at current period prices is $70 ($20 + $50).

You've now taken the first two steps towards calculating the CPI: calculating the cost of the CPI basket in the base period and the cost in the current period. The third step uses the numbers you've just calculated to find the CPI for 2004 and 2005.

The formula for the CPI is

$$CPI = \frac{\text{Cost of CPI basket at current period prices}}{\text{Cost of CPI basket at base period prices}} \times 100.$$

Table 21.1   The CPI: A Simplified Calculation

(a) **The cost of the CPI basket at base period prices: 2004**

Item	Quantity	Price	Cost of CPI basket
Oranges	10	$1	$10
Haircuts	5	$8	$40
Cost of CPI basket at base period prices			$50

(b) **The cost of the CPI basket at current period prices: 2005**

Item	Quantity	Price	Cost of CPI basket
Oranges	10	$2	$20
Haircuts	5	$10	$50
Cost of CPI basket at current period prices			$70

In Table 21.1, you have established that in 2004, the cost of the CPI basket was $50 and in 2005, it was $70. You also know that the base period is 2004. So the cost of the CPI basket at base period prices is $50. If we use these numbers in the CPI formula, we can find the CPI for 2004 and 2005.

$$\text{CPI in 2004} = \frac{\$50}{\$50} \times 100 = 100.$$

$$\text{CPI in 2005} = \frac{\$70}{\$50} \times 100 = 140.$$

The principles that you've applied in this simplified CPI calculation apply to the calculations performed every month by Statistics Canada.

Measuring Inflation

A major purpose of the CPI is to measure *changes* in the cost of living and in the value of money. To measure these changes, we calculate the **inflation rate**—the percentage change in the price level from one year to the next. To calculate the inflation rate, we use the formula:

$$\text{Inflation rate} = \frac{(\text{CPI this year} - \text{CPI last year})}{\text{CPI last year}} \times 100.$$

We can use this formula to calculate the inflation rate. The CPI in August 2005 was 128.0, and the CPI in August 2004 was 124.8. So the inflation rate during the year to August 2005 was

$$\text{Inflation rate} = \frac{(128.0 - 124.8)}{124.8} \times 100 = 2.6.$$

Figure 21.13 shows the CPI and the inflation rate in Canada during the 34 years from 1970 and 2004. The two parts of the figure are related.

Figure 21.13 shows that when the price *level* in part (a) rises rapidly, the inflation rate in part (b) is high, and when the price level in part (a) rises slowly, the inflation rate in part (b) is low. Notice in part (a) that the CPI increased every year during this period. During the late 1970s and early 1980s, the CPI increased rapidly, but its rate of increase slowed after 1985 to an average of 2.9 percent a year.

The CPI is not a perfect measure of the price level, and changes in the CPI probably overstate the inflation rate. Let's look at the sources of bias.

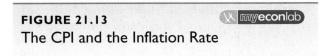

FIGURE 21.13

The CPI and the Inflation Rate

(a) CPI: 1970–2004

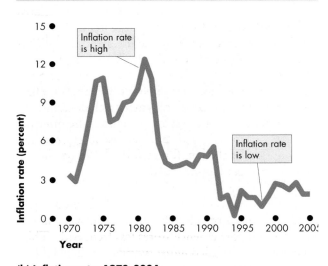

(b) Inflation rate: 1970–2004

In part (a), the CPI (the price level) has increased every year. In part (b), the inflation rate has averaged 5.25 percent a year. When the price level increased rapidly during the 1970s and early 1980s, the inflation rate was high and sometimes exceeded 10 percent a year. But after 1985, the price level increased slowly and the inflation rate fell to an average of 2.9 percent a year.

Source of data: Statistics Canada, CANSIM Table 326–0002.

The Biased CPI

The main sources of bias in the CPI are

- New goods bias
- Quality change bias
- Commodity substitution bias
- Outlet substitution bias

New Goods Bias If you want to compare the price level in 2005 with that in 1975, you must somehow compare the price of a computer today with that of a typewriter in 1975. Because a PC is more expensive than a typewriter was, the arrival of the PC puts an upward bias into the CPI and its inflation rate.

Quality Change Bias Cars, CD players, television sets and many other items get better every year. Part of the rise in the prices of these items is a payment for improved quality and is not inflation. But the CPI counts the entire price rise as inflation and so overstates inflation.

Commodity Substitution Bias Changes in relative prices lead consumers to change the items they buy. For example, if the price of beef rises and the price of chicken remains unchanged, people buy more chicken and less beef. Suppose they switch from beef to chicken on a scale that provides the same amount of protein and the same enjoyment as before and their expenditure is the same as before. The price of protein has not changed. But because it ignores the substitution of chicken for beef, the CPI says the price of protein has increased.

Outlet Substitution Bias When confronted with higher prices, people use discount stores more frequently and convenience stores less frequently. This phenomenon is called *outlet substitution*. The CPI surveys do not monitor outlet substitutions.

The Magnitude of the Bias

How big is the bias in the measurement of the CPI? The answer varies from country to country. In the United States, the bias is believed to range between 1 percent and 2 percent a year. But in Canada, it is believed to be at most 1 percent a year and probably less than this amount.

To reduce the bias problems, Statistics Canada revises the basket used for calculating the CPI about every 10 years. Also, Statistics Canada tries to estimate the quantitative effects of the various sources of bias and eliminate them by statistical adjustments. It is these adjustments that make Canada's CPI a more reliable measure of the price level than the CPI in the United States is of the U.S. price level.

Some Consequences of the Bias

The bias in the CPI has three main consequences. It

- Distorts private contracts.
- Increases government outlays.
- Biases estimates of real earnings.

Many private agreements, such as wage contracts, are linked to the CPI. For example, a firm and its workers might agree to a three-year wage deal that increases the wage rate by 2 percent a year *plus* the percentage increase in the CPI. Such a deal ends up giving the workers more *real* income than the firm intended.

Close to a third of federal government outlays are linked directly to the CPI. And while a bias of 1 percent a year seems small, accumulated over a decade, it adds up to billions of dollars of additional expenditures.

Trade unions and businesses bargain over wages based in part on changes in the CPI. If the CPI is biased upwards, businesses might agree to wage increases that are larger than they would accept if the CPI were measured accurately.

REVIEW QUIZ

1 What is the CPI and how is it calculated?
2 How do we calculate the inflation rate and what is the relationship between the CPI and the inflation rate?
3 What are the four main ways in which the CPI is an upward-biased measure of the price level?
4 What problems arise from the CPI bias?

ⓧ myeconlab **Study Plan 21.4**

◆ *Readings Between the Lines* on pp. 502–503 looks at the CPI in 2005. You've now completed your study of the measurement of macroeconomic performance. Your task in the following chapters is to learn what determines that performance and how policy actions might improve it.

The Monthly CPI Report

THE DAILY, 22 SEPTEMBER 2005

August 2005 CPI Report

... In August, consumers paid 2.6% more than in August 2004 for the goods and services included in the Consumer Price Index (CPI) basket, up strongly from the 2.0% increase recorded in July. However, the 12-month change in the All-items index excluding energy rose more moderately from 1.4% in July to 1.6% in August.

Gasoline prices were the primary reason for the jump in the 12-month change in the All-items index. After rising 12.3% between July 2004 and July 2005, gasoline prices soared 20.1% between August 2004 and August 2005. ...

The main contributors towards moderating these increases were lower prices for computer equipment and supplies and for traveller accommodation. ...

Prices for restaurant meals were up 2.9% compared with August 2004. Higher operating costs were the main reason behind the higher prices. This increase was similar to those observed in recent months. ...

All major components of the CPI posted 12-month increases with the exception of recreation, education and reading, which edged down 0.2% due to lower prices for computer equipment and supplies. Transportation (+5.8%), shelter (+2.9%), and food (+2.6%) exerted the strongest upward pressure on the All-items index.

Alcoholic beverages and tobacco products (+2.3%), health and personal care (+1.9%), household operations and furnishings (+0.7%), and clothing and footwear (+0.4%) also rose, but to a lesser extent.

The substantial increase in gasoline prices pushed up the CPI monthly index. With strong upward pressure from gasoline prices, the CPI rose by 0.4% in August to 128.0 (1992=100). To a lesser extent, prices for the purchase and leasing of automotive vehicles also contributed to the rise in the All-items index. Lower prices for fresh vegetables, natural gas and fresh fruit nonetheless moderated this increase.

Excerpt: "August 2005 CPI Report," adapted from the Statistics Canada publication *The Daily*, Catalogue 11–001, September 22, 2005, available at www.statcan.ca/Daily/English/050922/d050922a.htm.

Essence of the Story

■ Statistics Canada reported that the inflation rate between August 2004 and August 2005 was 2.6 percent.

■ Gasoline prices increased by 20.1 percent between August 2004 and August 2005, and this increase was reported as the primary reason for the jump in the inflation rate.

■ Lower prices for computer equipment and traveller accommodation moderated the overall rise in consumer prices.

Economic Analysis

■ Statistics Canada reports the nation's Consumer Price Index (CPI) numbers every month.

■ The CPI is an indicator of the changes in consumer prices experienced by Canadians.

■ The CPI is obtained by comparing the price of a fixed basket of commodities purchased by Canadians over different time periods—the CPI basket.

■ The CPI basket includes food, shelter, household operations and furnishings, clothing and footwear, transportation, health and personal care, recreation, education and reading, and alcoholic beverages and tobacco products.

■ Figure 1 shows the CPI for each month from January 2002 through August 2005.

■ In January 2002, the CPI was 116.2 and in August 2005, it was 128.

■ Figure 2 shows the annual inflation rate for each month between January 2002 and August 2005. You can see that the inflation rate was on a rising trend through 2002 and on a falling through 2003.

■ Through 2004 and 2005, the inflation rate was in the middle of its target range of 1 percent to 3 percent a year.

■ In addition to reporting the CPI, Statistics Canada also reports a monthly index for each component of the CPI basket.

■ Figure 3 shows the percentage changes in each component of the CPI basket between July and August 2005 expressed as annualized percentage changes.

■ These price changes tell us about the changes in *relative prices*. They do not tell us anything about inflation. Nor do they tell us *why* the inflation rate changed.

■ It is a common mistake in the media to say that the inflation rate increased (or decreased) *because* a particular price increased (or decreased).

■ The price of gasoline increased, which increased the relative price of transportation. But this change in relative prices provides no information about why the inflation rate changed. Lots of relative prices changed, as Fig. 3 shows.

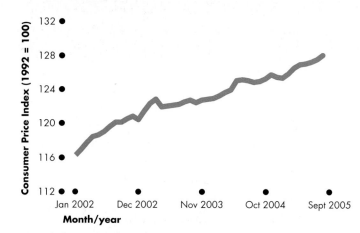

Figure 1 Consumer Price Index

Figure 2 Inflation rate

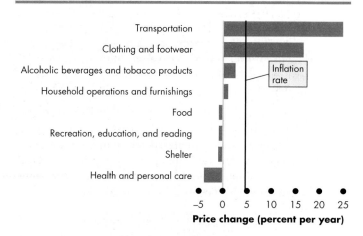

Figure 3 Relative price changes between July and August 2005

503

SUMMARY

KEY POINTS

The Business Cycle (pp. 486–487)

- A recession is a significant decline in activity spread across the economy and lasting more than a few months.
- Another definition of recession is a decrease in real GDP that lasts for at least two quarters.
- The ECRI has identified only four recessions and expansions in Canada since World War II.

Jobs and Wages (pp. 488–492)

- The unemployment rate averaged 7.8 percent between 1960 and 2004. It increases in recessions and decreases in expansions.
- The labour force participation rate and the employment-to-population ratio have an upward trend and fluctuate with the business cycle.
- The labour force participation rate has increased for females and decreased for males.
- Aggregate hours have an upward trend, and they fluctuate with the business cycle.
- Average hourly real wage rate grows but the growth rate slowed during the 1970s.

Unemployment and Full Employment (pp. 493–497)

- People are constantly entering and leaving the state of unemployment.
- The duration of unemployment fluctuates over the business cycle. But the demographic patterns of unemployment are constant.
- Unemployment can be frictional, structural, seasonal, and cyclical.
- When all unemployment is frictional, structural, and seasonal, the economy is at full employment, the unemployment rate equals the natural rate of unemployment, and real GDP equals potential GDP.
- Over the business cycle, real GDP fluctuates around potential GDP and the unemployment rate fluctuates around the natural rate of unemployment.

The Consumer Price Index (pp. 498–501)

- The Consumer Price Index (CPI) measures the average of the prices paid by urban consumers for a fixed basket of consumer goods and services.
- The CPI is defined to equal 100 for the base period—currently 1992.
- The inflation rate is the percentage change in the CPI from one year to the next.
- Changes in the CPI probably overstate the inflation rate slightly.
- The bias in the CPI distorts private contracts and increases government outlays.

KEY FIGURES

KEY TERMS

PROBLEMS

Go to ⓧ myeconlab for solutions to odd-numbered problems and additional exercises.

1. Statistics Canada reported the following data for January 2000: Labour force: 15,537,700 Employment: 14,339,200 Working-age population: 24,137,100. Calculate the
   a. Unemployment rate.
   b. Labour force participation rate.
   c. Employment-to-population ratio.

2. Statistics Canada reported the following data for January 2001: Labour force: 16,219,800 Employment: 14,990,400 Working-age population: 24,764,100. Calculate the
   a. Unemployment rate.
   b. Labour force participation rate.
   c. Employment-to-population ratio.

3. During 2000, the working-age population in Canada increased by 327,100, employment increased by 280,900, and the labour force increased by 330,400. Use these numbers and the data in problem 1 to calculate the change in unemployment and the change in the number of people not in the labour force in 2000.

4. During 2001, the working-age population in Canada increased by 299,900, employment decreased by 16,600, and the labour force increased by 329,200. Use these data and the data in problem 2 to calculate the change in unemployment and the change in the number of people not in the labour force in 2001.

5. In August 2000, the unemployment rate was 7.2 percent. In August 2001, the unemployment rate was 7.5 percent. Use this information to predict what happened between August 2000 and August 2001 to the numbers of
   a. Job losers and job leavers.
   b. Labour force entrants and re-entrants.

6. In January 2001, the unemployment rate was 7.5 percent. In January 2002, the unemployment rate was 8.6 percent. Use these data to predict what happened between January 2001 and January 2002 to the numbers of
   a. Job losers and job leavers.
   b. Labour force entrants and re-entrants.

7. In July 2005, on Sandy Island, 10,000 people were employed, 1,000 were unemployed, and 5,000 were not in the labour force. During August 2005, 80 people lost their jobs, 20 quit their jobs, 150 were hired or recalled, 50 withdrew from the labour force, and 40 entered or re-entered the labour force. Calculate for July 2005
   a. The labour force.
   b. The unemployment rate.
   c. The working-age population.
   d. The employment-to-population ratio.
   And calculate for the end of August 2005
   e. The number of people unemployed.
   f. The number of people employed.
   g. The labour force.
   h. The unemployment rate.

8. In July 2006 on Sandy Island, 11,000 people were employed, 900 were unemployed, and 5,000 were not in the labour force. During August 2006, 40 people lost their jobs, 10 quit their jobs, 180 were hired, 20 withdrew from the labour force, and 60 entered or re-entered the labour force. Calculate for July 2006
   a. The labour force.
   b. The unemployment rate.
   c. The working-age population.
   d. The employment-to-population ratio.
   And calculate for the end of August 2006
   e. The number of people unemployed.
   f. The number of people employed.
   g. The labour force.
   h. The unemployment rate.

9. A typical family on Sandy Island buys only juice and cloth. The cost of the CPI basket at base year prices was $65 ($40 for juice at $4 a bottle and $25 for cloth at $5 a length). In the current year, juice is $4 a bottle and cloth is $6 a length. Calculate
   a. The CPI basket.
   b. The CPI in the current year.
   c. The inflation rate in the current year.

10. A typical family on Lizard Island buys only mangoes and nuts. The cost of the CPI basket at base year prices was $70 ($60 on nuts at $3 a bag and $10 on mangoes at $1 each). In the current year, mangoes are $1.50 each and nuts are $4 a bag. Calculate
    a. The CPI basket.
    b. The CPI in the current year.
    c. The inflation rate in the current year.

CRITICAL THINKING

1. Study *Reading Between the Lines* on pp. 502–503 and then answer the following questions:
   a. Describe the changes in the CPI that occurred during 2005.
   b. Explain the difference between a change in a relative price and inflation. Which relative prices increased most in August 2005 and which increased least or fell?
   c. Do you think the news article did a good job reporting the August CPI numbers? Write a brief report that does a better job and explain why it is better.

2. Thinking about the economy of Sandy Island in problems 7 and 8:
   a. In what phase of its business cycle was Sandy Island during 2006?
   b. What do you predict would be happening to real GDP on Sandy Island? Why?
   c. What do you predict would be happening to real GDP per person on Sandy Island? Why?

3. Describe the main features of the labour market at the peak of the business cycle.

4. Describe the main features of the labour market at the trough of the business cycle.

5. You've seen in this chapter that the average workweek has shortened over the years. Do you think that shorter work hours are a problem or a benefit? Do you expect the average workweek to keep getting shorter? Why or why not?

6. An increasing number of jobs are part-time jobs. Can you think of some reasons for this trend? Who benefits from part-time jobs: the employer, the worker, or both? Explain with examples.

7. You've seen that the CPI is biased and over-states the true inflation rate. It would be a simple matter to adjust the CPI for the known average bias. Yet we continue to keep a flawed measure of inflation in place. Why do you think we don't adjust the CPI for the known average bias so that its measure of the inflation rate is more accurate? Explain who gains from the biased measure and who loses from it. Try to think of reasons why those who lose have not persuaded those who win to adopt a more accurate measure.

WEB EXERCISES

Use the links on myeconlab to work the following exercise.

1. Visit the Web site of the Bank of Canada and review the latest Monetary Policy Report of the Bank of Canada. In which phase of the business cycle is the economy in your region? How does your region compare to the nation as a whole?

2. Visit the Web site of Statistics Canada and find labour market data for your own province.
   a. What have been the trends in employment, unemployment, and labour force participation in your province during the past two years?
   b. On the basis of what you know about your own province, how would you set about explaining these trends?
   c. Try to identify those industries that have expanded most and those that have shrunk.
   d. What are the problems with your own provincial labour market that you think need provincial government action to resolve?
   e. What actions do you think your provincial government must take to resolve these problems? Answer this question by using the demand and supply model of the labour market and predict the effects of the actions you prescribe.
   f. Compare the labour market performance of your own province with that of Canada.
   g. If your province is performing better than the national average, to what do you attribute the success? If your province is performing worse than the national average, to what do you attribute its problems? What federal actions are needed in your provincial labour market?

3. Visit the Web site of Statistics Canada and find CPI data for your own province.
   a. What have been the trends in the CPI in your province during the past two years?
   b. Compare the CPI performance of your own province with that of Canada as a whole.
   c. On the basis of what you know about your own province, how would you set about explaining its deviation from the Canadian average?

Aggregate Supply and Aggregate Demand

CHAPTER 22

Production and Prices

During the ten years from 1995 to 2005, Canadian real GDP increased by 40 percent. Expanding at this pace, real GDP doubles every 21 years. What forces bring persistent and rapid expansion of real GDP?

Expanding real GDP brings a rising standard of living. Inflation brings a rising cost of living. Because of inflation, you need $2 today to buy what $1 bought in 1980. What causes inflation?

You saw in the previous chapter that our economy doesn't expand at a constant pace. Instead, it ebbs and flows over the business cycle. You also saw that we had a recession during 1990 and early 1991. For half a year, real GDP decreased. Since that time, our economy has expanded, but at a variable rate. Why do we have a business cycle?

Because our economy fluctuates, the government and the Bank of Canada try to smooth its path. How do the policy actions of the government and the Bank of Canada affect production and prices?

◆ To answer questions like these, we need a *model* of real GDP and the price level. Our main task in this chapter is to study such a model: the *aggregate supply–aggregate demand model*. Our second task is to use the aggregate supply–aggregate demand (or *AS–AD*) model to answer the questions we've just posed. You'll discover that this model enables us to understand the forces that make our economy expand, that bring inflation, and that cause business cycle fluctuations. At the end of the chapter, in *Reading Between the Lines*, we'll put the *AS–AD* model to work to understand the macroeconomic effects of implementing the Kyoto agreement on climate control.

After studying this chapter, you will be able to

- ■ **Define and explain what determines aggregate supply**
- ■ **Define and explain what determines aggregate demand**
- ■ **Explain macroeconomic equilibrium and the effects of fluctuations in aggregate supply and aggregate demand**
- ■ **Explain Canadian economic growth, inflation, and the business cycle by using the *AS–AD* model**

Aggregate Supply

THE AGGREGATE SUPPLY–AGGREGATE DEMAND model enables us to understand three features of macroeconomic performance:

- Growth of potential GDP
- Inflation
- Business cycle fluctuations

The model uses the concepts of *aggregate* supply and *aggregate* demand to determine *real GDP* and the *price level* (the GDP deflator). We begin by looking at the limits to production that influence aggregate supply.

Aggregate Supply Fundamentals

The *quantity of real GDP supplied* (Y) depends on

1. The quantity of labour (L)
2. The quantity of capital (K)
3. The state of technology (T)

The influence of these three factors on the quantity of real GDP supplied is described by the **aggregate production function**, which is written as the equation:

$$Y = F(L, K, T).$$

In words, the quantity of real GDP supplied is determined by (is a function F of) the quantities of labour and capital and the state of technology. The larger is L, K, or T, the greater is Y.

At any given time, the quantity of capital and the state of technology are fixed. They depend on decisions that were made in the past. The population is also fixed. But the quantity of labour is not fixed. It depends on decisions made by people and firms about the supply of and demand for labour.

The labour market can be in any one of three states: at full employment, above full employment, or below full employment.

Even at full employment, there are always some people looking for jobs and some firms looking for people to hire. The reason is that there is a constant churning of the labour market. Every day, some jobs are destroyed as businesses reorganize or fail. Some jobs are created as new businesses start up or existing ones expand. Some workers decide, for any of a thousand personal reasons, to quit their jobs. And other people decide to start looking for a job. This constant churning in the labour market prevents unemployment from ever disappearing. The unemployment rate at full employment is called the **natural rate of unemployment**.

Another way to think about full employment is as a state of the labour market in which the quantity of labour demanded equals the quantity supplied. Firms demand labour only if it is profitable to do so. And the lower the wage rate, which is the cost of labour, the greater is the quantity of labour demanded. People supply labour only if doing so is the most valuable use of their time. And the higher the wage rate, which is the return to labour, the greater is the quantity of labour supplied. The wage rate that makes the quantity of labour demanded equal to the quantity of labour supplied is the equilibrium wage rate. At this wage rate, there is full employment. (You can study the labour market at full employment in Chapter 30 on pp. 712–713.)

The quantity of real GDP at full employment is *potential GDP*, which depends on the full-employment quantity of labour, the quantity of capital, and the state of technology. Over the business cycle, employment fluctuates around full employment and real GDP fluctuates around potential GDP.

To study aggregate supply in different states of the labour market, we distinguish between

- Long-run aggregate supply
- Short-run aggregate supply

Long-Run Aggregate Supply

The economy is constantly bombarded by events that move real GDP away from potential GDP and, equivalently, that move employment away from full employment. Following such an event, forces operate to take real GDP back towards potential GDP and restore full employment. The **macroeconomic long run** is a time frame that is sufficiently long for these forces to have done their work so that real GDP equals potential GDP and full employment prevails.

The **long-run aggregate supply curve** is the relationship between the quantity of real GDP supplied and the price level in the long run when real GDP equals potential GDP. Figure 22.1 shows this relationship as the vertical line labelled *LAS*. Along the long-run aggregate supply curve, as the price level changes, real GDP remains at potential GDP, which in Fig. 22.1 is $1,000 billion. The long-run aggregate supply curve is always vertical and is located at potential GDP.

FIGURE 22.1
Long-Run Aggregate Supply

The long-run aggregate supply curve (*LAS*) shows the relationship between potential GDP and the price level. Potential GDP is independent of the price level, so the *LAS* curve is vertical at potential GDP.

The long-run aggregate supply curve is vertical because potential GDP is independent of the price level. The reason for this independence is that a movement along the *LAS* curve is accompanied by a change in *two* sets of prices: the prices of goods and services—the price level—and the prices of productive resources. A 10 percent increase in the prices of goods and services is matched by a 10 percent increase in the money wage rate and other resource prices. That is, the price level, money wage rate, and other resource prices all change by the same percentage, and *relative prices* and the *real wage rate* remain constant. When the price level changes but relative prices and the real wage rate remain constant, real GDP also remains constant.

Production at a Pepsi Plant You can see why real GDP remains constant when all prices change by the same percentage if you think about production decisions at a Pepsi bottling plant. The plant is producing the quantity of Pepsi that maximizes profit. The plant

can increase production but only by incurring a higher *marginal cost* (see Chapter 2, p. 37). So the firm has no incentive to change production.

Short-Run Aggregate Supply

The **macroeconomic short run** is a period during which real GDP has fallen below or risen above potential GDP. At the same time, the unemployment rate has risen above or fallen below the natural rate of unemployment.

The **short-run aggregate supply curve** is the relationship between the quantity of real GDP supplied and the price level in the short run when the money wage rate, the prices of other resources, and potential GDP remain constant. Figure 22.2 shows a short-run aggregate supply curve as the upward-sloping curve labelled *SAS*. This curve is based on the short-run aggregate supply schedule, and each point on the *SAS* curve corresponds to a row of the aggregate supply schedule. For example, point *A* on the *SAS* curve and row A of the schedule tell us that if the price level is 100, the quantity of real GDP supplied is $900 billion.

At point *C*, the price level is 110 and the quantity of real GDP supplied is $1,000 billion, which equals potential GDP. If the price level is higher than 110, real GDP exceeds potential GDP; if the price level is below 110, real GDP is less than potential GDP.

Back at the Pepsi Plant You can see why the short-run aggregate supply curve slopes upward by returning to the Pepsi bottling plant. The plant produces the quantity that maximizes profit. If the price of Pepsi rises and the money wage rate and other costs don't change, the *relative price* of Pepsi rises and the firm has an incentive to increase its production. The higher relative price of Pepsi covers the higher marginal cost of producing more Pepsi, so the firm increases production.

Similarly, if the price of Pepsi falls and the money wage rate and other costs don't change, the lower relative price is not sufficient to cover the marginal cost of Pepsi, so the firm decreases production.

Again, what's true for Pepsi bottlers is true for the producers of all goods and services. So when the price level rises and the money wage rate and other resource prices remain constant, the quantity of real GDP supplied increases.

FIGURE 22.2

Short-Run Aggregate Supply

	Price level	Real GDP
	(GDP deflator)	(billions of 1997 dollars)
A	100	900
B	105	950
C	110	1,000
D	115	1,050
E	120	1,100

The short-run aggregate supply curve shows the relationship between the quantity of real GDP supplied and the price level when the money wage rate, other resource prices, and potential GDP remain the same. The short-run aggregate supply curve, *SAS*, is based on the schedule in the table. This curve is upward-sloping because firms' marginal costs increase as output increases, so a higher price is needed, relative to the prices of productive resources, to bring forth an increase in the quantity produced. On the *SAS* curve, when the price level is 110, real GDP equals potential GDP. If the price level is greater than 110, real GDP exceeds potential GDP; if the price level is below 110, real GDP is less than potential GDP.

Movements Along the *LAS* and *SAS* Curves

Figure 22.3 summarizes what you've just learned about the *LAS* and *SAS* curves. When the price level, the money wage rate, and other resource prices rise by the same percentage, relative price remains constant and real GDP remains at potential GDP. There is a *movement along* the *LAS* curve.

When the price level rises but the money wage rate and other resource prices remain the same, the quantity of real GDP supplied increases and there is a *movement along* the *SAS* curve.

Let's next study the influences that bring changes in aggregate supply.

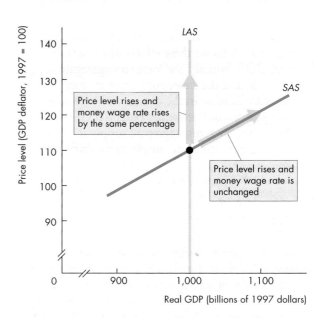

FIGURE 22.3

Movements Along the Aggregate Supply Curves

A rise in the price level with no change in the money wage rate and other resource prices brings an increase in the quantity of real GDP supplied and a movement along the short-run aggregate supply curve, *SAS*.

A rise in the price level with equal percentage increases in the money wage rate and other resource prices keeps the quantity of real GDP supplied constant at potential GDP and brings a movement along the long-run aggregate supply curve, *LAS*.

Changes in Aggregate Supply

You've just seen that a change in the price level brings a movement along the aggregate supply curves but does not change aggregate supply. Aggregate supply changes when influences on production plans other than the price level change. Let's begin by looking at factors that change potential GDP.

Changes in Potential GDP When potential GDP changes, both long-run aggregate supply and short-run aggregate supply change. Potential GDP changes for three reasons:

1. A change in the full-employment quantity of labour
2. A change in the quantity of capital
3. An advance in technology

An increase in the full-employment quantity of labour, an increase in the quantity of capital, or an advance in technology increases potential GDP. And an increase in potential GDP changes both the long-run aggregate supply and short-run aggregate supply.

Figure 22.4 shows these effects of a change in potential GDP. Initially, the long-run aggregate supply curve is LAS_0 and the short-run aggregate supply curve is SAS_0. If an increase in the quantity of capital or a technological advance increases potential GDP to $1,100 billion, long-run aggregate supply increases and the long-run aggregate supply curve shifts rightward to LAS_1. Short-run aggregate supply also increases, and the short-run aggregate supply curve shifts rightward to SAS_1.

Let's look more closely at the influences on potential GDP and the aggregate supply curves.

A Change in the Full-Employment Quantity of Labour

A Pepsi bottling plant that employs 100 workers bottles more Pepsi than an otherwise identical plant that employs ten workers. The same is true for the economy as a whole. The larger the quantity of labour employed, the greater is GDP.

Over time, potential GDP increases because the labour force increases. But (with constant capital and technology) *potential* GDP increases only if the full-employment quantity of labour increases. Fluctuations in employment over the business cycle bring fluctuations in real GDP. But these changes in real GDP are fluctuations around potential GDP. They are not changes in potential GDP and long-run aggregate supply.

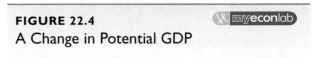

FIGURE 22.4

A Change in Potential GDP

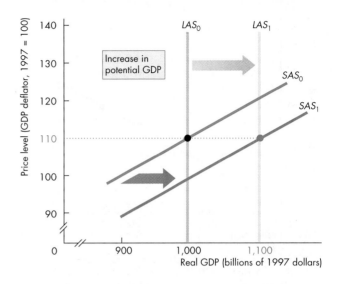

An increase in potential GDP increases both long-run aggregate supply and short-run aggregate supply and shifts both aggregate supply curves rightward, from LAS_0 to LAS_1 and from SAS_0 to SAS_1.

A Change in the Quantity of Capital

A Pepsi bottling plant with two production lines bottles more Pepsi than an otherwise identical plant that has only one production line. For the economy, the larger the quantity of capital, the more productive is the labour force and the greater is its potential GDP. Potential GDP per person in capital-rich Canada is vastly greater than that in capital-poor China and Russia.

Capital includes *human capital*. One Pepsi plant is managed by an economics major with an MBA and has a labour force with an average of ten years of experience. This plant produces a much larger output than an otherwise identical plant that is managed by someone with no business training or experience and that has a young labour force that is new to bottling. The first plant has a greater amount of human capital than the second. For the economy as a whole, the larger the quantity of *human capital*—the skills that people have acquired in school and through on-the-job training—the greater is potential GDP.

An Advance in Technology A Pepsi plant that has pre-computer age machines produces less than one that uses the latest robot technology. Technological change enables firms to produce more from any given amount of inputs. So even with fixed quantities of labour and capital, improvements in technology increase potential GDP.

Technological advances are by far the most important source of increased production over the past two centuries. Because of technological advances, one farmer in Canada today can feed 100 people and one auto worker can produce almost 14 cars and trucks in a year.

Let's now look at the effects of changes in the money wage rate.

Changes in the Money Wage Rate and Other Resource Prices When the money wage rate or the money prices of other resources (such as the price of oil) change, short-run aggregate supply changes but long-run aggregate supply does not change.

Figure 22.5 shows the effect on aggregate supply of an increase in the money wage rate. Initially, the short-run aggregate supply curve is SAS_0. A rise in the money wage rate *decreases* short-run aggregate supply and shifts the short-run aggregate supply curve leftward to SAS_2.

The money wage rate (and resource prices) affect short-run aggregate supply because they influence firms' costs. The higher the money wage rate, the higher are firms' costs and the smaller is the quantity that firms are willing to supply at each price level. So an increase in the money wage rate decreases short-run aggregate supply.

A change in the money wage rate does *not* change long-run aggregate supply because on the *LAS* curve, a change in the money wage rate is accompanied by an equal percentage change in the price level. With no change in *relative* prices, firms have no incentive to change production and real GDP remains constant at potential GDP.

In Fig. 22.5, the vertical distance between the original *SAS* curve and the new *SAS* curve is determined by the percentage change in the money wage rate. That is, the percentage increase in the price level between point *A* and point *B* equals the percentage increase in the money wage rate.

Because potential GDP does not change when the money wage rate changes, long-run aggregate supply does not change. The long-run aggregate supply curve remains at *LAS*.

FIGURE 22.5

A Change in the Money Wage Rate

A rise in the money wage rate decreases short-run aggregate supply and shifts the short-run aggregate supply curve leftward from SAS_0 to SAS_2. A rise in the money wage rate does not change potential GDP, so the long-run aggregate supply curve does not shift.

REVIEW QUIZ

1 If price level rises and if the money wage rate also rises by the same percentage, what happens to the quantity of real GDP supplied? Along which aggregate supply curve does the economy move?

2 If the price level rises and the money wage rate remains constant, what happens to the quantity of real GDP supplied? Along which aggregate supply curve does the economy move?

3 If potential GDP increases, what happens to aggregate supply? Is there a shift of or a movement along the *LAS* curve and the *SAS* curve?

4 If the money wage rate rises and potential GDP remains the same, what happens to aggregate supply? Is there a shift of or a movement along the *LAS* curve and the *SAS* curve?

myeconlab **Study Plan 22.1**

Aggregate Demand

THE QUANTITY OF REAL GDP DEMANDED IS THE sum of the real consumption expenditure (C), investment (I), government expenditures (G), and exports (X) minus imports (M). That is,

$$Y = C + I + G + X - M.$$

The *quantity of real GDP demanded* is the total amount of final goods and services produced in Canada that people, businesses, governments, and foreigners plan to buy.

These buying plans depend on many factors. Some of the main ones are

- The price level
- Expectations
- Fiscal policy and monetary policy
- The world economy

We first focus on the relationship between the quantity of real GDP demanded and the price level. To study this relationship, we keep all other influences on buying plans the same and ask: How does the quantity of real GDP demanded vary as the price level varies?

The Aggregate Demand Curve

Other things remaining the same, the higher the price level, the smaller is the quantity of real GDP demanded. This relationship between the quantity of real GDP demanded and the price level is called **aggregate demand**. Aggregate demand is described by an aggregate demand schedule and an aggregate demand curve.

Figure 22.6 shows an aggregate demand curve (*AD*) and an aggregate demand schedule. Each point on the *AD* curve corresponds to a row of the table. For example, point C' on the *AD* curve and row C' of the table tell us that if the price level is 110, the quantity of real GDP demanded is $1,000 billion.

The aggregate demand curve slopes downward for two reasons:

- Wealth effect
- Substitution effects

Wealth Effect When the price level rises but other things remain the same, *real* wealth decreases. Real

FIGURE 22.6
Aggregate Demand

	Price level (GDP deflator)	Real GDP (billions of 1997 dollars)
A'	90	1,100
B'	100	1,050
C'	110	1,000
D'	120	950
E'	130	900

The aggregate demand curve (*AD*) shows the relationship between the quantity of real GDP demanded and the price level. The aggregate demand curve is based on the aggregate demand schedule in the table. Each point A' through E' on the curve corresponds to the row in the table identified by the same letter. When the price level is 110, the quantity of real GDP demanded is $1,000 billion, shown by point C'. A change in the price level with all other influences on aggregate buying plans remaining the same brings a change in the quantity of real GDP demanded and a movement along the *AD* curve.

wealth is the amount of money in the bank, bonds, stocks, and other assets that people own, measured not in dollars but in terms of the goods and services that this money, bonds, and stocks will buy.

People save and hold money, bonds, and stocks for many reasons. One reason is to build up funds for education expenses. Another reason is to build up enough funds to meet possible medical or other big bills. But the biggest reason is to build up enough funds to provide a retirement income.

If the price level rises, real wealth decreases. People then try to restore their wealth. To do so, they must increase saving and, equivalently, decrease current consumption. Such a decrease in consumption is a decrease in the quantity of real GDP demanded.

Maria's Wealth Effect You can see how the wealth effect works by thinking about Maria's buying plans. Maria lives in Moscow, Russia. She has worked hard all summer and saved 20,000 rubles (the currency of Russia), which she plans to spend attending graduate school when she has finished her economics degree. So Maria's wealth is 20,000 rubles. Maria has a part-time job, and her income from this job pays her current expenses. The price level in Russia rises by 100 percent, and now Maria needs 40,000 rubles to buy what 20,000 rubles once bought. To try to make up some of the fall in value of her savings, Maria saves even more and cuts her current spending to the bare minimum.

Substitution Effects When the price level rises and other things remain the same, interest rates rise. The reason is related to the wealth effect that you've just studied. A rise in the price level decreases the real value of the money in people's pockets and bank accounts. With a smaller amount of real money around, banks and other lenders can get a higher interest rate on loans. But faced with higher interest rates, people and businesses delay plans to buy new capital and consumer durable goods and cut back on spending.

This substitution effect involves substituting goods in the future for goods today and is called an *intertemporal* substitution effect—a substitution across time. To increase future consumption, consumption today must decrease and saving increase.

To see this intertemporal substitution effect more clearly, think about your own plan to buy a new computer. At an interest rate of 5 percent a year, you might borrow $2,000 and buy the new machine you've been researching. But at an interest rate of 10 percent a year, you might decide that the payments would be too high. You don't abandon your plan to buy the computer, but you decide to delay your purchase.

A second substitution effect works through international prices. When the Canadian price level rises and other things remain the same, Canadian-made goods and services become more expensive relative to foreign-made goods and services. This change in *relative prices* encourages people to spend less on Canadian-made items and more on foreign-made items. For example, if the Canadian price level rises relative to the U.S. price level, Americans buy fewer Canadian-made cars (Canadian exports decrease) and Canadians buy more U.S.-made cars (Canadian imports increase). Canadian GDP decreases.

Maria's Substitution Effects In Moscow, Russia, Maria makes some substitutions. She was planning to trade in her old motor scooter and get a new one. But with a higher price level and faced with higher interest rates, she decides to make her old scooter last one more year. Also, with the prices of Russian goods sharply increasing, Maria substitutes a low-cost dress made in Malaysia for the Russian-made dress she had originally planned to buy.

Changes in the Quantity of Real GDP Demanded When the price level rises and other things remain the same, the quantity of real GDP demanded decreases—a movement up the *AD* curve as shown by the arrow in Fig. 22.6. When the price level falls and other things remain the same, the quantity of real GDP demanded increases—a movement down the *AD* curve.

We've now seen how the quantity of real GDP demanded changes when the price level changes. How do other influences on buying plans affect aggregate demand?

Changes in Aggregate Demand

A change in any factor that influences buying plans other than the price level brings a change in aggregate demand. The main factors are

- Expectations
- Fiscal policy and monetary policy
- The world economy

Expectations An increase in expected future income, other things remaining the same, increases the quantity of consumption goods (especially big-ticket items such as cars) that people plan to buy today and increases aggregate demand today.

An increase in the expected future inflation rate increases aggregate demand today because people decide to buy more goods and services at today's relatively lower prices. An increase in expected future profit increases the investment that firms plan to undertake today and increases aggregate demand today.

Fiscal Policy and Monetary Policy The government's attempt to influence the economy by setting and changing taxes, making transfer payments, and purchasing goods and services is called **fiscal policy**. A tax cut or an increase in transfer payments—for example, unemployment benefits or welfare payments—increases aggregate demand. Both of these influences operate by increasing households' disposable income. **Disposable income** is aggregate income minus taxes plus transfer payments. The greater the disposable income, the greater is the quantity of consumption goods and services that households plan to buy and the greater is aggregate demand.

Government expenditures on goods and services are one component of aggregate demand. So if the government spends more on hospitals, schools, and highways, aggregate demand increases.

Monetary policy consists of changes in interest rates and in the quantity of money in the economy. Interest rates and the quantity of money are determined by the Bank of Canada (described in Chapters 25 and 28). An increase in the quantity of money in the economy increases aggregate demand. To see why money affects aggregate demand, imagine that the Bank of Canada borrows the army's helicopters, loads them with millions of new $10 bills, and sprinkles these bills like confetti across the nation. People gather the newly available money and plan to spend some of it. So the quantity of goods and services demanded increases. But people don't plan to spend all the new money. They plan to save some of it and lend it to others through the banks. Interest rates fall, and with lower interest rates, people plan to buy more consumer durables and firms plan to increase their investment.

The World Economy Two main influences that the world economy has on aggregate demand are the foreign exchange rate and foreign income. The *foreign exchange rate* is the amount of a foreign currency that you can buy with a Canadian dollar. Other things remaining the same, a rise in the foreign exchange rate decreases aggregate demand. To see how the foreign exchange rate influences aggregate demand, suppose

FIGURE 22.7 myeconlab
Changes in Aggregate Demand

Aggregate demand

Decreases if:

- Expected future income, inflation, or profits decrease

- Fiscal policy decreases government expenditures, increases taxes, or decreases transfer payments

- Monetary policy increases interest rates and decreases the quantity of money

- The foreign exchange rate increases or foreign income decreases

Increases if:

- Expected future income, inflation, or profits increase

- Fiscal policy increases government expenditures, decreases taxes, or increases transfer payments

- Monetary policy decreases interest rates and increases the quantity of money

- The foreign exchange rate decreases or foreign income increases

that $1 exchanges for 100 Japanese yen. A Fujitsu phone (made in Japan) costs 12,500 yen, and an equivalent Nortel phone (made in Canada) costs $110. In Canadian dollars, the Fujitsu phone costs $125, so people around the world buy the cheaper

Canadian phone. Now suppose the foreign exchange rate rises to 125 yen per dollar. At 125 yen per dollar, the Fujitsu phone costs $100 and is now cheaper than the Nortel phone. People will switch from the Canadian phone to the Japanese phone. Canadian exports will decrease and Canadian imports will increase, so Canadian aggregate demand will decrease.

An increase in foreign income increases Canadian exports and increases Canadian aggregate demand. For example, an increase in income in Japan and Germany increases Japanese and German consumers' and producers' planned expenditures on Canadian-made goods and services.

Shifts of the Aggregate Demand Curve When aggregate demand changes, the aggregate demand curve shifts. Figure 22.7 shows two changes in aggregate demand and summarizes the factors that bring about such changes.

Aggregate demand increases and the aggregate demand curve shifts rightward from AD_0 to AD_1 when expected future income, inflation, or profit increases; government expenditures on goods and services increase; taxes are cut; transfer payments increase; the quantity of money increases and interest rates fall; the foreign exchange rate falls; or foreign income increases.

Aggregate demand decreases and the aggregate demand curve shifts leftward from AD_0 to AD_2 when expected future income, inflation, or profit decreases; government expenditures on goods and services decrease; taxes increase; transfer payments decrease; the quantity of money decreases and interest rates rise; the foreign exchange rate rises; or foreign income decreases.

REVIEW QUIZ

1 What does the aggregate demand curve show? What factors change and what factors remain the same when there is a movement along the aggregate demand curve?

2 Why does the aggregate demand curve slope downward?

3 How do changes in expectations, fiscal policy and monetary policy, and the world economy change aggregate demand and shift the aggregate demand curve?

 myeconlab **Study Plan 22.2**

Macroeconomic Equilibrium

THE PURPOSE OF THE AGGREGATE SUPPLY–aggregate demand model is to explain changes in real GDP and the price level. To achieve this purpose, we combine aggregate supply and aggregate demand and determine macroeconomic equilibrium. There is a macroeconomic equilibrium for each of the time frames for aggregate supply: a long-run equilibrium and a short-run equilibrium. Long-run equilibrium is the state towards which the economy is heading. Short-run equilibrium is the normal state of the economy as it fluctuates around potential GDP.

We'll begin our study of macroeconomic equilibrium by looking first at the short run.

Short-Run Macroeconomic Equilibrium

The aggregate demand curve tells us the quantity of real GDP demanded at each price level, and the short-run aggregate supply curve tells us the quantity of real GDP supplied at each price level. **Short-run macroeconomic equilibrium** occurs when the quantity of real GDP demanded equals the quantity of real GDP supplied. That is, short-run equilibrium occurs at the point of intersection of the *AD* curve and the *SAS* curve. Figure 22.8 shows such an equilibrium at a price level of 110 and real GDP of $1,000 billion (points *C* and *C'*).

To see why this position is the equilibrium, think about what happens if the price level is something other than 110. Suppose, for example, that the price level is 120 and that real GDP is $1,100 billion (at point *E* on the *SAS* curve). The quantity of real GDP demanded is less than $1,100 billion, so firms are unable to sell all their output. Unwanted inventories pile up, and firms cut both production and prices. Production and prices are cut until firms can sell all their output. This situation occurs only when real GDP is $1,000 billion and the price level is 110.

Now suppose the price level is 100 and real GDP is $900 billion (at point *A* on the *SAS* curve). The quantity of real GDP demanded exceeds $900 billion, so firms are unable to meet the demand for their output. Inventories decrease, and customers clamour for goods and services. So firms increase production and raise prices. Production and prices increase until firms can meet demand. This situation

FIGURE 22.8
Short-Run Equilibrium

Short-run macroeconomic equilibrium occurs when real
GDP demanded equals real GDP supplied—at the intersection of the aggregate demand curve (AD) and the short-
run aggregate supply curve (SAS). Here, such an equilibrium
occurs at points C and C', where the price level is 110 and
real GDP is $1,000 billion. If the price level is 120 and real
GDP is $1,100 billion (point E), firms will not be able to
sell all their output. They will decrease production and cut
prices. If the price level is 100 and real GDP is $900 billion
(point A), people will not be able to buy all the goods and
services they demand. Firms will increase production and
raise their prices. Only when the price level is 110 and real
GDP is $1,000 billion can firms sell all that they produce
and can people buy all that they demand. This is the short-
run macroeconomic equilibrium.

occurs only when real GDP is $1,000 billion and the
price level is 110.

In short-run equilibrium, the money wage rate is
fixed. It does not adjust to bring full employment. So
in the short run, real GDP can be greater than or less
than potential GDP. But in the long run, the money
wage rate does adjust and real GDP moves towards
potential GDP. We are going to study this adjustment
process. But first, let's look at the economy in long-run
equilibrium.

Long-Run Macroeconomic Equilibrium

Long-run macroeconomic equilibrium occurs when
real GDP equals potential GDP—equivalently, when
the economy is on its *long-run* aggregate supply curve.
Figure 22.9 shows *long-run* equilibrium, which occurs
at the intersection of the aggregate demand curve and
the long-run aggregate supply curve (the blue curves).
Long-run equilibrium comes about because the
money wage rate adjusts. Potential GDP and aggregate demand determine the price level, and the price
level influences the money wage rate. In long-run
equilibrium, the money wage rate has adjusted to put
the (green) short-run aggregate supply curve through
the long-run equilibrium point.

We'll look at this money wage adjustment
process later in this chapter. But first, let's see how
the *AS–AD* model helps us to understand economic
growth and inflation.

FIGURE 22.9
Long-Run Equilibrium

In long-run macroeconomic equilibrium, real GDP equals
potential GDP. So long-run equilibrium occurs where the
aggregate demand curve intersects the long-run aggregate
supply curve. In the long run, aggregate demand determines
the price level and has no effect on real GDP. The money
wage rate adjusts in the long run, so the SAS curve intersects the LAS curve at the long-run equilibrium price level.

Economic Growth and Inflation

Economic growth occurs because over time, the quantity of labour grows, capital is accumulated, and technology advances. These changes increase potential GDP and shift the long-run aggregate supply curve rightward. Figure 22.10 shows such a shift. The growth rate of potential GDP is determined by the pace at which labour grows, capital is accumulated, and technology advances.

Inflation occurs when, over time, aggregate demand increases by more than long-run aggregate supply increases. That is, inflation occurs if the aggregate demand curve shifts rightward by more than the rightward shift in the long-run aggregate supply curve. Figure 22.10 shows such shifts.

If aggregate demand increased at the same pace as long-run aggregate supply, we would experience real GDP growth with no inflation.

In the long run, the main influence on aggregate demand is the growth rate of the quantity of money. At times when the quantity of money is growing quickly, aggregate demand also grows quickly and the inflation rate is high. When the growth rate of the quantity of money slows, other things remaining the same, the inflation rate eventually decreases.

Our economy experiences growth and inflation, like that shown in Fig. 22.10. But it does not experience *steady* economic growth and *steady* inflation. Real GDP fluctuates around potential GDP in a business cycle, and inflation also fluctuates. When we study the business cycle, we ignore economic growth. By doing so, we can see the business cycle more clearly.

The Business Cycle

The business cycle occurs because aggregate demand and short-run aggregate supply fluctuate but the money wage rate does not adjust quickly enough to keep real GDP at potential GDP. Figure 22.11 shows three types of short-run equilibrium.

In part (a), there is a below full-employment equilibrium. A **below full-employment equilibrium** is a macroeconomic equilibrium in which potential GDP exceeds real GDP. When potential GDP exceeds real GDP, the *output gap* is negative[1] and is called a **recessionary gap**. This name reminds us that a gap has opened up between potential GDP and real GDP either because the economy has experienced a recession or because real GDP, while growing, has grown more slowly than potential GDP.

The below full-employment equilibrium shown in Fig. 22.11(a) occurs where the aggregate demand curve AD_0 intersects the short-run aggregate supply curve SAS_0 at a real GDP of $980 billion and a price level of 110. The recessionary gap is $20 billion. The Canadian economy was in a situation similar to that shown in Fig. 22.11(a) during the early 1980s, and again during the early 1990s. In those years, real GDP was less than potential GDP.

Figure 22.11(b) is an example of *long-run equilibrium*, in which real GDP equals potential GDP. In this example, the equilibrium occurs where the aggregate demand curve AD_1 intersects the short-run aggregate supply curve SAS_1 at an actual and potential GDP of $1,000 billion. The Canadian economy was in a situation such as that shown in Fig. 22.11(b) in 1999.

---

[1] A negative output gap is also sometimes called an Okun gap (see p. 451). An Okun gap and a recessionary gap are alternative names for the same phenomenon.

FIGURE 22.10   myeconlab
Economic Growth and Inflation

Economic growth is the persistent increase in potential GDP. Economic growth is shown as an ongoing rightward shift of the *LAS* curve. Inflation is the persistent rise in the price level. Inflation occurs when aggregate demand increases by more than the increase in long-run aggregate supply.

Figure 22.11(c) shows an above full-employment equilibrium. An **above full-employment equilibrium** is a macroeconomic equilibrium in which real GDP exceeds potential GDP. When real GDP exceeds potential GDP, the *output gap* is positive and is called an **inflationary gap**. This name reminds us that a gap has opened up between real GDP and potential GDP and that this gap creates inflationary pressure.

The above full-employment equilibrium shown in Fig. 22.11(c) occurs where the aggregate demand curve AD_2 intersects the short-run aggregate supply curve SAS_2 at a real GDP of $1,020 billion and a price

level of 110. Real GDP exceeds potential GDP and the inflationary gap is $20 billion. The Canadian economy was last in a situation similar to that depicted in Fig. 22.11(c) in 2000.

The economy moves from one type of equilibrium to another as a result of fluctuations in aggregate demand and in short-run aggregate supply. These fluctuations produce fluctuations in real GDP and the price level. Figure 22.11(d) shows how real GDP fluctuates around potential GDP.

Let's now look at some of the sources of these fluctuations around potential GDP.

FIGURE 22.11

The Business Cycle

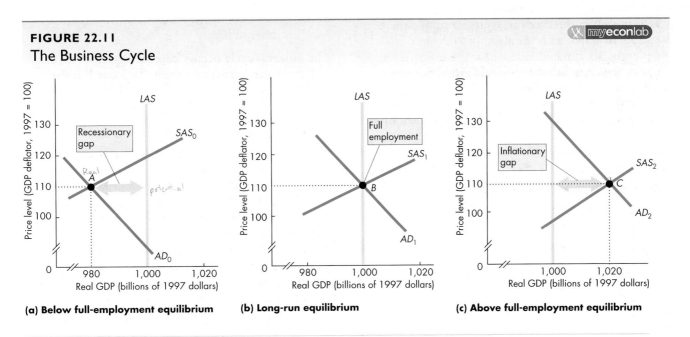

(a) Below full-employment equilibrium   **(b) Long-run equilibrium**   **(c) Above full-employment equilibrium**

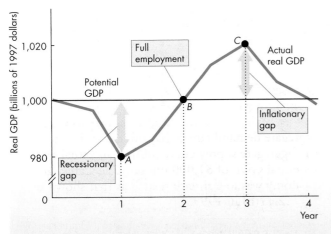

(d) Fluctuations in real GDP

Part (a) shows a below full-employment equilibrium in year 1; part (b) shows a long-run equilibrium in year 2; and part (c) shows an above full-employment equilibrium in year 3. Part (d) shows how real GDP fluctuates around potential GDP in a business cycle.

In year 1, a recessionary gap exists and the economy is at point A (in parts a and d). In year 2, the economy is in long-run equilibrium and the economy is at point B (in parts b and d). In year 3, an inflationary gap exists and the economy is at point C (in parts c and d).

Fluctuations in Aggregate Demand

One reason real GDP fluctuates around potential GDP is that aggregate demand fluctuates. Let's see what happens when aggregate demand increases.

Figure 22.12(a) shows an economy in long-run equilibrium. The aggregate demand curve is AD_0, the short-run aggregate supply curve is SAS_0, and the long-run aggregate supply curve is LAS. Real GDP equals potential GDP at $1,000 billion, and the price level is 110.

Now suppose that the world economy expands and that the demand for Canadian-made goods increases in Japan and Europe. The increase in Canadian exports increases aggregate demand, and the aggregate demand curve shifts rightward from AD_0 to AD_1 in Fig. 22.12(a).

Faced with an increase in demand, firms increase production and raise prices. Real GDP increases to $1,050 billion, and the price level rises to 115. The economy is now in an above full-employment equilibrium. Real GDP exceeds potential GDP, and there is an inflationary gap.

The increase in aggregate demand has increased the prices of all goods and services. Faced with higher prices, firms have increased their output rates. At this stage, prices of goods and services have increased but the money wage rate has not changed. (Recall that as we move along a short-run aggregate supply curve, the money wage rate is constant.)

The economy cannot produce in excess of potential GDP forever. Why not? What are the forces at work that bring real GDP back to potential GDP?

Because the price level has increased and the money wage rate is unchanged, workers have experienced a fall in the buying power of their wages and firms' profits have increased. In these circumstances, workers demand higher wages and firms, anxious to maintain their employment and output levels, meet those demands. If firms do not raise the money wage rate, they will either lose workers or have to hire less productive ones.

As the money wage rate rises, the short-run aggregate supply curve begins to shift leftward. In Fig. 22.12(b), the short-run aggregate supply curve moves

FIGURE 22.12

An Increase in Aggregate Demand

(a) Short-run effect

(b) Long-run effect

An increase in aggregate demand shifts the aggregate demand curve from AD_0 to AD_1. In short-run equilibrium, real GDP increases to $1,050 billion and the price level rises to 115. In this situation, an inflationary gap exists. In the long run, the money wage rate rises and the short-run aggregate

supply curve shifts leftward from SAS_0 to SAS_1 in part (b). As the SAS curve shifts leftward, it intersects the aggregate demand curve AD_1 at higher price levels and real GDP decreases. Eventually, the price level rises to 125 and real GDP decreases to $1,000 billion—potential GDP.

from SAS_0 towards SAS_1. The rise in the money wage rate and the shift in the *SAS* curve produce a sequence of new equilibrium positions. Along the adjustment path, real GDP decreases and the price level rises. The economy moves up along its aggregate demand curve as the arrowheads show.

Eventually, the money wage rate rises by the same percentage as the price level. At this time, the aggregate demand curve AD_1 intersects SAS_1 at a new long-run equilibrium. The price level has risen to 125, and real GDP is back where it started, at potential GDP.

A decrease in aggregate demand has similar but opposite effects to those of an increase in aggregate demand. That is, a decrease in aggregate demand shifts the aggregate demand curve leftward. Real GDP decreases to less than potential GDP, and a recessionary gap emerges. Firms cut prices. The lower price level increases the purchasing power of wages and increases firms' costs relative to their output prices because the money wage rate remains unchanged. Eventually, the money wage rate falls and the short-run aggregate supply curve shifts rightward. But the money wage rate changes slowly, so real GDP slowly returns to potential GDP and the price level falls slowly.

Let's now work out how real GDP and the price level change when aggregate supply changes.

Fluctuations in Aggregate Supply

Fluctuations in short-run aggregate supply can bring fluctuations in real GDP around potential GDP. Suppose that initially real GDP equals potential GDP. Then there is a large but temporary rise in the price of oil. What happens to real GDP and the price level?

Figure 22.13 answers this question. The aggregate demand curve is AD_0, the short-run aggregate supply curve is SAS_0, and the long-run aggregate supply curve is *LAS*. Real GDP is $1,000 billion, which equals potential GDP, and the price level is 110. Then the price of oil rises. Faced with higher energy and transportation costs, firms decrease production. Short-run aggregate supply decreases, and the short-run aggregate supply curve shifts leftward to SAS_1. The price level rises to 120, and real GDP decreases to $950 billion. Because real GDP decreases, the economy experiences recession. Because the price level increases, the economy experiences inflation. A combination of recession and inflation, called *stagflation*, actually occurred in the United States in the mid-1970s. But events like this are not common and Canada escaped the worst of that recession.

FIGURE 22.13
A Decrease in Aggregate Supply

An increase in the price of oil decreases short-run aggregate supply and shifts the short-run aggregate supply curve from SAS_0 to SAS_1. Real GDP decreases from $1,000 billion to $950 billion, and the price level increases from 110 to 120. The economy experiences both recession and inflation—a situation known as stagflation.

REVIEW QUIZ

1 Does economic growth result from increases in aggregate demand, short-run aggregate supply, or long-run aggregate supply?

2 Does inflation result from increases in aggregate demand, short-run aggregate supply, or long-run aggregate supply?

3 Describe three types of short-run macroeconomic equilibrium.

4 How do fluctuations in aggregate demand and short-run aggregate supply bring fluctuations in real GDP around potential GDP?

myeconlab **Study Plan 22.3**

Let's put our new knowledge of aggregate supply and aggregate demand to work and see how we can explain recent Canadian macroeconomic performance.

Canadian Economic Growth, Inflation, and Cycles

THE ECONOMY IS CONTINUALLY CHANGING. IF you imagine the economy as a video, then an aggregate supply–aggregate demand figure such as Fig. 22.13 is a freeze-frame. We're going to run the video—an instant replay—but keep our finger on the freeze-frame button and look at some important parts of the previous action. Let's run the video from 1961.

Figure 22.14 shows the state of the economy in 1961 at the point of intersection of its aggregate demand curve, AD_{61}, and short-run aggregate supply curve, SAS_{61}. Real GDP was $240 billion, and the GDP deflator was 17 (less than one-fifth of its 2004 level). In 1961, real GDP equalled potential GDP—the economy was on its long-run aggregate supply curve, LAS_{61}.

By 2004, the economy had reached the point marked by the intersection of aggregate demand curve AD_{04} and short-run aggregate supply curve SAS_{04}. Real

GDP was $1,124 billion, and the GDP deflator was 115. Potential GDP in 2004 was also $1,124 billion.

The path traced by the blue and red dots in Fig. 22.14 shows three key features:

- Economic growth
- Inflation
- Business cycles

Economic Growth

Over the years, real GDP grows—shown in Fig. 22.14 by the rightward movement of the points. The faster real GDP grows, the larger is the horizontal distance between successive dots in the figure. The forces that generate economic growth are those that increase potential GDP. Potential GDP grows because the quantity of labour grows, we accumulate physical capital and human capital, and our technologies advance.

These forces that bring economic growth were strongest during the 1960s and late 1990s through 2002.

FIGURE 22.14

Aggregate Supply and Aggregate Demand: 1961–2004

Each point shows the GDP deflator and real GDP in a given year. In 1961, the aggregate demand curve, AD_{61}, and the short-run aggregate supply curve, SAS_{61}, determined these variables. Each point is generated by the gradual shifting of the AD and SAS curves. By 2004, the curves were AD_{04} and SAS_{04}. Real GDP grew, and the price level increased. Real GDP grew quickly and inflation was moderate during the 1960s; real GDP growth sagged in 1974–1975 and again in 1982. Inflation was rapid during the 1970s but slowed after the 1982 recession. The period from 1982 to 1989 was one of persistent expansion. A recession began in 1990, and a further strong and sustained expansion resumed in the late 1990s and through 2002.

Source of data: Statistics Canada, CANSIM Tables 326–0002 and 380–0003.

Inflation

The price level rises over the years—shown in Fig. 22.14 by the upward movement of the points. The larger the rise in the price level, the larger is the vertical distance between successive dots in the figure. The main force generating the persistent increase in the price level is a tendency for aggregate demand to increase at a faster pace than the increase in long-run aggregate supply. All of the factors that increase aggregate demand and shift the aggregate demand curve influence the pace of inflation. But one factor—the growth of the quantity of money—is the main source of *persistent* increases in aggregate demand and persistent inflation.

Business Cycles

Over the years, the economy grows and shrinks in cycles—shown in Fig. 22.14 by the wavelike pattern made by the points, with the recessions highlighted. The cycles arise because the expansion of short-run aggregate supply and the growth of aggregate demand do not proceed at a fixed, steady pace. Although the economy has cycles, recessions do not usually follow quickly on the heels of their predecessors; "double-dip" recessions like the one in the cartoon are rare.

The Evolving Economy: 1961–2004

During the 1960s, real GDP growth was rapid and inflation was low. This was a period of rapid increases in aggregate supply and of moderate increases in aggregate demand.

The mid-1970s were years of rapid inflation and slow growth. The major source of these developments was a series of massive oil price increases that slowed the rightward shift of the aggregate supply curve and rapid increases in the quantity of money that speeded the rightward shift of the aggregate demand curve. The short-run aggregate supply curve shifted rightward at a slower pace than the aggregate demand curve shifted rightward.

The rest of the 1970s saw high inflation—the price level increased quickly—and only moderate growth in real GDP. By 1980, inflation was a major problem and the Bank of Canada decided to take strong action against it. The Bank permitted interest rates to rise to previously unknown levels. Consequently, aggregate demand decreased. By 1982, the decrease in aggregate demand put the economy into a deep recession.

"Please stand by for a series of tones. The first indicates the official end of the recession, the second indicates prosperity, and the third the return of the recession."

During the years 1983–1990, capital accumulation and steady technological advance resulted in a sustained rightward shift of the *LAS* curve. Wage growth was moderate, and the *SAS* curve shifted rightward. Aggregate demand growth kept pace with the growth of aggregate supply. Sustained but steady growth in aggregate supply and aggregate demand kept real GDP growing and inflation steady. The economy moved from a recession with real GDP less than potential GDP in 1982 to above full employment in 1990. It was in this condition when a decrease in aggregate demand led to the 1990–1991 recession. The economy stagnated for a year and then began to expand again, expanding rapidly during the late 1990s. Growth slowed in 2001 before expanding again.

◆ The *AS–AD* model explains economic growth, inflation, and the business cycle. The model is a useful one because it enables us to keep our eye on the big picture. But it lacks detail. It does not tell us as much as we need to know about the deeper forces that lie behind aggregate supply and aggregate demand. The chapters that follow begin to fill in the details on aggregate demand. But before you embark on this next stage, take a look at *Reading Between the Lines* on pp. 524–525, which looks at the effects of implementing the Kyoto agreement on climate control on aggregate supply and aggregate demand in the Canadian economy in 2010.

Kyoto in the AS–AD Model

FINANCIAL POST, OCTOBER 12, 2002

Kyoto could cost 244,000 jobs

The federal government conceded yesterday that implementing the Kyoto Protocol on climate change could cost the Canadian economy as many as a quarter of a million jobs, and $21-billion in output, by the end of the decade.

In a long awaited impact study of Kyoto, federal officials predicted the accord could mean between 61,000 and 244,000 fewer jobs by 2010. They also forecast the accord could mean gross domestic product would be between 0.4% ($5-billion) and 1.6% ($21-billion) lower than expected by the same year.

The federal document argued that the 244,000 job figure and 1.6% drop in GDP growth was a worst-case scenario. Officials said the lower figures were more likely. ...

Private-sector estimates place the cost of implementing Kyoto at 450,000 jobs by 2010, and $4.5-billion annually.

Pierre Alvarez, president of the Canadian Association of Petroleum Producers, called the federal calculations "empty numbers," adding that Ottawa's Kyoto plan remains a mystery.

"This is a model based on hypothetical assumptions, assumptions no one else has ever seen," he said.

"To extrapolate from that, they are simply empty numbers that are of little value to the current debate."

He added: "The assumptions are based on estimates we don't necessarily agree ..."

Nancy Hughes Anthony, president of the Canadian Chamber of Commerce, charged yesterday the government's economic model leaves a "false impression" about the impact of the Kyoto Protocol by presenting optimistic projections.

But she said it is even clear from the best and worst-case scenarios in the federal analysis that the prosperity of Canadians will suffer if Jean Chrétien, the Prime Minister, pushes ahead with ratification of Kyoto by the end of the year. ...

Reprinted by permission of the National Post.

Essence of the Story

■ The federal government predicts that ratifying the Kyoto accord will lower employment by between 61,000 and 244,000 jobs by 2010.

■ The government also predicts that ratifying the Kyoto accord will lower real GDP by between 0.4 percent ($5 billion) and 1.6 percent ($21 billion) by 2010.

■ The government regards the higher numbers —244,000 jobs and $21 billion real GDP—as the worst-case scenario.

■ Private-sector estimates place the cost of implementing Kyoto at 450,000 jobs by 2010 and $4.5 billion annually.

Economic Analysis

■ Implementing the Kyoto accord requires Canada to cut its emissions of "greenhouse" gases, measured as carbon dioxide equivalent, from more than 700 million tonnes a year in 2002 to 540 million tonnes a year by 2010.

■ To achieve this large cut in emissions, we must generate electricity more cleanly and use technologies that are more costly and less productive.

■ We must also increase the fuel efficiency of automobiles and trucks.

■ These activities decrease the productivity of labour, slow the accumulation of productive capital, and slow the pace of productivity-enhancing technological change.

■ The overall consequence of this slowdown in productivity growth is a slower growth rate of potential GDP.

■ By not implementing the Kyoto accord and maintaining recent trends, real GDP will grow by 3 percent a year.

■ Maintaining the recent inflation trends (and the Bank of Canada's target for inflation), the inflation rate will be 2 percent a year.

■ Figure 1 shows that if these trends persist, by 2010 real GDP will be $1,240 billion, up by 27 percent from its 2002 level; and the price level will be 125, up by 17 percent from its 2002 level.

■ Figure 2 shows the difference that implementing Kyoto will make, using the government's worst-case scenario.

■ Relative to the base line case, long-run aggregate supply will be lower at LAS_1, and real GDP will be $21 billion lower.

■ If the Bank of Canada continues to pursue an inflation target of 2 percent a year, aggregate demand growth will slow to match the growth of potential GDP. The AD curve and SAS curve will be at AD_1 and SAS_1, and the price level will be unaffected by Kyoto.

■ If aggregate demand growth does not slow to match the slower growth rate of potential GDP, Kyoto will bring increased inflation.

■ The decrease in employment that results from Kyoto will either decrease the labour force or increase the natural rate of unemployment. It will not affect cyclical unemployment.

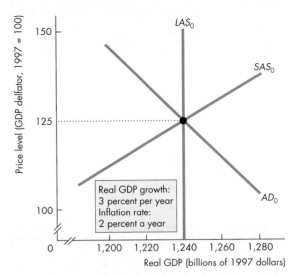

Figure 1 Base line case—no Kyoto

Figure 2 Government's Kyoto worst-case scenario

You're the Voter

■ Based just on its macroeconomic consequences, do you think that implementing Kyoto is a big deal?

■ What macroeconomic reasons would you give for supporting or opposing the implementation of Kyoto?

525

SUMMARY

KEY POINTS

Aggregate Supply (pp. 508–512)

- In the long run, the quantity of real GDP supplied is potential GDP, which is independent of the price level. The long-run aggregate supply curve is vertical.

- In the short run, the money wage rate is constant, so a rise in the price level increases the quantity of real GDP supplied. The short-run aggregate supply curve is upward sloping.

- A change in potential GDP changes both long-run and short-run aggregate supply. A change in the money wage rate or other resource prices changes only short-run aggregate supply.

Aggregate Demand (pp. 513–516)

- A rise in the price level decreases the quantity of real GDP demanded, other things remaining the same.

- The reason is that the higher price level decreases the quantity of *real* money, raises the interest rate, and raises the price of domestic goods compared with foreign-made goods.

- Changes in expected future income, inflation, and profit; changes in fiscal policy and monetary policy; and changes in world real GDP and the foreign exchange rate change aggregate demand.

Macroeconomic Equilibrium (pp. 516–521)

- In the short run, real GDP and the price level are determined by aggregate demand and short-run aggregate supply.

- In the long run, real GDP equals potential GDP and aggregate demand determines the price level and the money wage rate.

- Economic growth occurs because potential GDP increases.

- Inflation occurs because aggregate demand grows more quickly than potential GDP grows.

- Business cycles occur because aggregate demand and aggregate supply fluctuate.

Canadian Economic Growth, Inflation, and Cycles (pp. 522–523)

- Potential GDP grew fastest during the 1960s and late 1990s through 2002 and slowest during the late 1970s and early 1990s.

- Inflation persists because aggregate demand grows faster than potential GDP.

- Business cycles occur because aggregate supply and aggregate demand change at an uneven pace.

KEY FIGURES

KEY TERMS

PROBLEMS

Go to (X myeconlab) for solutions to odd-numbered problems and additional exercises.

1. The following events occur that influence the economy of Toughtimes:
   - A deep recession hits the world economy.
   - Oil prices rise sharply.
   - Businesses expect huge losses in the near future.
   a. Explain the separate effects of each of these events on real GDP and the price level, starting from a position of long-run equilibrium.
   b. Explain the combined effects of these events on real GDP and the price level, starting from a position of long-run equilibrium.
   c. Explain what the Toughtimes government and the Bank of Toughtimes can do to overcome the problems faced by the economy.

2. The following events occur that influence the economy of Coolland:
   - There is a strong expansion in the world economy.
   - Businesses expect huge profits in the near future.
   - The Coolland government cuts its expenditure.
   a. Explain the separate effects of each of these events on real GDP and the price level, starting from a position of long-run equilibrium.
   b. Explain the combined effects of these events on real GDP and the price level, starting from a position of long-run equilibrium.
   c. Explain why the Coolland government or the Bank of Coolland might want to take action to influence the Coolland economy.

3. The economy of Mainland has the following aggregate demand and supply schedules:

Price level	Real GDP demanded	Real GDP supplied in the short run
	(billions of 1997 dollars)	
90	450	350
100	400	400
110	350	450
120	300	500
130	250	550
140	200	600

a. In a figure, plot the aggregate demand curve and the short-run aggregate supply curve.
b. What are the values of real GDP and the price level in Mainland in a short-run macroeconomic equilibrium?
c. Mainland's potential GDP is $500 billion. Plot the long-run aggregate supply curve in the same figure in which you answered part (a).

4. The economy of Miniland has the following aggregate demand and supply schedules:

Price level	Real GDP demanded	Real GDP supplied in the short run
	(billions of 1997 dollars)	
90	600	150
100	500	200
110	400	250
120	300	300
130	200	350
140	100	400

a. In a figure, plot the aggregate demand curve and the short-run aggregate supply curve.
b. What are the values of real GDP and the price level in Miniland in a short-run macroeconomic equilibrium?
c. Miniland's potential GDP is $250 billion. Plot the long-run aggregate supply curve in the same figure in which you answered part (a).

5. In problem 3, aggregate demand increases by $100 billion. How do real GDP and the price level change in the short run?

6. In problem 4, aggregate demand decreases by $150 billion. How do real GDP and the price level change in the short run?

7. In problem 3, aggregate supply decreases by $100 billion. What now is the short-run macroeconomic equilibrium?

8. In problem 4, aggregate supply increases by $150 billion. What now is the short-run macroeconomic equilibrium?

9. In the economy shown in the figure on the next page, initially the short-run aggregate supply is SAS_0 and aggregate demand is AD_0. Then some events change aggregate demand, and the aggregate demand curve shifts rightward to AD_1. Later, some other events change aggregate supply, and the short-run aggregate supply curve shifts leftward to SAS_1.

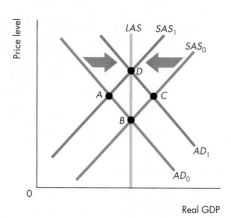

a. What is the short-run equilibrium point after the change in aggregate demand?
b. What is the equilibrium point after the change in aggregate supply?
c. What events could have changed aggregate demand from AD_0 to AD_1?
d. What events could have changed aggregate supply from SAS_0 to SAS_1?

10. In the economy shown in the figure, initially long-run aggregate supply is LAS_0, short-run aggregate supply is SAS_0, and aggregate demand is AD. Then some events change aggregate supply, and the aggregate supply curves shift rightward to LAS_1 and SAS_1.

a. What is the short-run equilibrium point after the change in aggregate supply?
b. What events could have changed long-run aggregate supply from LAS_0 to LAS_1?
c. What events could have changed short-run aggregate supply from SAS_0 to SAS_1?
d. After the increase in aggregate supply, is real GDP greater than or less than potential GDP?
e. What change in aggregate demand will make real GDP equal to potential GDP?

CRITICAL THINKING

1. After you have studied the effects of implementing the Kyoto agreement on aggregate supply and aggregate demand in the Canadian economy in *Reading Between the Lines* on pp. 524–525:
   a. List the factors that influence long-run aggregate supply and explain how Kyoto might impact each of these factors.
   b. List the factors that influence short-run aggregate supply and explain how Kyoto might impact each of these factors.
   c. List the factors that influence aggregate demand and explain how Kyoto might impact each of these factors.
   d. Use the *AS–AD* model to illustrate and to explain why Kyoto need not increase the inflation rate, even if it brings a large decrease in potential GDP.

WEB EXERCISES

Use the links on **myeconlab** to work the following exercise.

1. Find data on recent changes in and forecasts of real GDP and the price level in Canada.
   a. What is your forecast of next year's real GDP?
   b. What is your forecast of next year's price level?
   c. What is your forecast of the inflation rate?
   d. What is your forecast of the growth rate of real GDP?
   e. Do you think there will be a recessionary gap or an inflationary gap next year?

2. Find data on recent changes in and forecasts of real GDP and the price level in Japan.
   a. What is your forecast of next year's real GDP?
   b. What is your forecast of next year's price level?
   c. What is your forecast of the inflation rate?
   d. What is your forecast of the growth rate of real GDP?
   e. Compare and contrast the performance of the Canadian and Japanese economies.

The Big Picture

Macroeconomics is a large and controversial subject that is interlaced with political ideological disputes. And it is a field in which charlatans as well as serious thinkers have much to say. This page is a map that looks back at the road you've just travelled and forward at the path you will take from here.

You began your study of macroeconomics with the core questions of the subject. What are the causes of

- Economic growth?
- Business cycles?
- Unemployment?
- Inflation?

In Chapter 19, you took your first look at each of these questions. You learned some facts about economic growth, business cycles, unemployment, and inflation. In Chapter 20, you learned how we measure the economy's output and the price level. These measures are used to calculate the economic growth rate, business cycle fluctuations, and inflation. You discovered that making these measurements is not straightforward and that small measurement errors can have a big effect on our perceptions about how we are doing.

In Chapter 21, you learned how we measure the state of the labour market—the levels of employment and unemployment and wages. And in Chapter 22, you studied the macroeconomic version of supply and demand—*aggregate supply* and *aggregate demand*. You saw that the aggregate supply–aggregate demand model is the big picture model. It explains both the long-term trends in economic growth and inflation and the short-term business cycle fluctuations in production, jobs, and inflation.

The chapters that lie ahead of you look behind aggregate supply and aggregate demand, beginning on the aggregate demand side. In Chapters 23 through 29, you will study aggregate demand, inflation, and recession and learn about the macroeconomics that Keynes developed as a response to the Great Depression. And you will learn about money and the banking system and the effects of monetary policy and fiscal policy on aggregate demand.

Then, in Chapters 30 through 32, you will study aggregate supply, economic growth, and international trade. In Chapter 30, you study the economy at full employment and the forces that change potential GDP. In Chapter 31, you study the process of economic growth. Here, you learn today's answer to the question posed by Adam Smith—what are the causes of differences in the wealth of nations? In Chapter 32 you will study the globalization of economic activity and international trade.

Before continuing your study of macroeconomics, spend a few minutes with John Maynard Keynes and Jean-Baptiste Say, the leading scholars who developed this subject. And spend a few minutes with one of today's leading Canadian macroeconomists, Peter Howitt of Brown University.

Macroeconomic Revolutions

> "The ideas of economists and political philosophers, both when they are right and when they are wrong, are more powerful than is commonly understood. Indeed the world is ruled by little else."

JOHN MAYNARD KEYNES *The General Theory of Employment, Interest, and Money*

THE ECONOMIST

John Maynard Keynes, *born in England in 1883, was one of the outstanding minds of the twentieth century. He wrote on probability as well as economics, represented Britain at the Versailles peace conference at the end of World War I, was a master speculator on international financial markets (an activity he conducted from bed every morning and which made and lost him several fortunes), and played a prominent role in creating the International Monetary Fund. He was a member of the Bloomsbury Group, a circle of outstanding artists and writers that included E. M. Forster, Bertrand Russell, and Virginia Woolf. Keynes was a controversial and quick-witted figure. A critic once complained that Keynes had changed his opinion on some matters, to which Keynes retorted: "When I discover I am wrong, I change my mind. What do you do?"*

THE ISSUES

During the Industrial Revolution, as technological change created new jobs and destroyed old ones, people began to wonder whether the economy could create enough jobs and sufficient demand to buy all the things that the new industrial economy could produce.

Jean-Baptiste Say argues that production creates incomes that are sufficient to buy everything that is produced—supply creates its own demand—an idea that came to be called Say's Law.

Say and Keynes would have had a lot to disagree about. Jean-Baptiste Say, born in Lyon, France, in 1767 (he was 9 years old when Adam Smith's *Wealth of Nations* was published), suffered the wrath of Napoleon for his views on government and the economy. In today's world, Say would be leading a radical conservative charge for a smaller and leaner government. Say was the most famous economist of his era on both sides of the Atlantic. His book, *Traité d'économie politique (A Treatise in Political Economy)*, published in 1803, became a best-selling university economics textbook in both Europe and North America.

As the Great Depression of the 1930s became more severe and more prolonged, Say's Law looked less and less relevant. John Maynard Keynes revolutionized macroeconomics thinking by turning Say's Law on its head, arguing that production does not depend on supply. Instead, it depends on what people are willing to buy—on demand. Or as Keynes put it, production depends on effective demand. It is possible, argued Keynes, for people to refuse to spend all of their incomes. If businesses fail to spend on new capital the amount that people plan to save, demand might be less than supply. In this situation, resources might go unemployed and remain unemployed indefinitely.

The influence of Keynes persists even today, more than 60 years after the publication of his main work. But during the past 20 years, Nobel Laureate Robert E. Lucas, Jr., with significant contributions from a list of outstanding macroeconomists too long to name, has further revolutionized macroeconomics. Today, we know a lot about economic growth, unemployment, inflation, and business cycles. And we know how to use fiscal policy and monetary policy to improve macroeconomic performance. But we don't yet have all the answers. Macroeconomics remains a field of lively controversy and exciting research.

THEN

In 1776, James Hargreaves, an English weaver and carpenter, developed a simple hand-operated machine called a spinning jenny (pictured here). Using this machine, a person could spin 80 threads at once. Thousands of hand-wheel spinners, operators of machines that could spin only one thread, lost their jobs. They protested by wrecking spinning jennies. In the long run, the displaced hand-wheel spinners found work, often in factories that manufactured the machines that had destroyed their previous jobs. From the earliest days of the Industrial Revolution to the present day, people have lost their jobs as new technologies have automated what human effort had previously been needed to accomplish.

NOW

Advances in computer technology have made it possible for us to dial our own telephone calls to any part of the world and get connected in a flash. A task that was once performed by telephone operators, who made connections along copper wires, is now performed faster and more reliably by computers along fibre-optic cables. Just as the Industrial Revolution transformed the textile industry, so today's Information Revolution is transforming the telecommunications industry. In the process, the mix of jobs is changing. There are fewer jobs for telephone operators but more jobs for telephone systems designers, builders, managers, and marketers. In the long run, as people spend the income they earn in their changing jobs, supply creates its own demand, just as Say predicted. But does supply create its own demand in the short run, when displaced workers are unemployed?

Peter Howitt, whom you can meet on the following pages, is one of the most distinguished macroeconomists. He has contributed much to our understanding of economic growth and the business cycle and played a significant role in the contemporary macroeconomic revolution.

531

TALKING WITH

Peter Howitt is Lyn Crost Professor of Social Sciences in the Department of Economics at Brown University. Born in 1946 in Toronto, he was an undergraduate at McGill University and a graduate student at Northwestern University. He began his research and teaching career at the University of Western Ontario in 1972, where he spent many productive years before moving to the United States in 1996. Professor Howitt is a past president of the Canadian Economics Association and is one of the world's leading macroeconomists. He has done research on all aspect of macroeconomics, with a focus in recent years on economic growth.

Micheal Parkin and Robin Bade talked with Peter Howitt about his work and the major macroeconomic problems facing Canada today.

Peter Howitt

What attracted you to economics?

When I was in high school I had a part-time job as office boy with a small company that imported wool from around the world and sold it to textile mills in Ontario and Quebec. I was fascinated by the way wool prices went up and down all the time, and this curiosity led me to enroll in an honours economics course. My interests soon switched to macroeconomics, but I was always driven by curiosity to find out more about the workings of the human anthill.

You have made outstanding contributions to our understanding of all the major problems of macroeconomics, notably unemployment, economic growth, and inflation. Which of these issues do you believe is the most serious one for Canada today? Can they be separated?

Right now [near the end of 1996] growth and unemployment are the most important. Inflation has been under control for several years. We still have what was once called "creeping inflation," as the price level is rising by about 2 percent per year, but that's a less serious problem than the fact that over 10 percent of the labour force is unemployed and that the economy appears no longer to be growing at the high rates we experienced in the 1950s and 1960s.

Of course, all of these problems are interrelated. Learning about all the interrelationships is one of the things that makes economics so interesting. Take the relationship between growth and unemployment, for example. If you take a short-run perspective, then these two variables would appear to be negatively related. If the economy grows faster, there will be more jobs, and better paying jobs, which will draw people out of unemployment. But in the long run it looks quite different. You can't maintain a high growth rate indefinitely by continuing to put idle people to work, because at some point you will have everyone in the economy working. Instead, to keep the economy growing at a high rate you have to keep finding ways to make people more productive. You get this from having technological progress, from innovations that improve the efficiency of production processes and that allow people to produce new goods that contribute to our material welfare in ways that previous generations never have imagined.

Now the industrial innovations that underlie economic growth in the long run usually come at a cost. This is what Schumpeter meant by the term "creative destruction." For example, if I invent a new good this will create new jobs for people to produce the good, but it will also destroy the jobs of people who produce the goods that mine will replace. So an economy that is going through a period of rapid technological change is likely to have good growth prospects, but it may also have a high rate of unemployment. The people whose jobs are destroyed may eventually find even better jobs but it will take time, so there will be a lot of people in a temporary situation of unemployment. To make a long story short, even though a short burst of growth from one quarter to the next is likely to reduce the rate of unemployment, a sustained rise in the rate of growth from one decade to the next will create a rise in the rate of unemployment.

> " ... *industrial innovations that underlie economic growth in the long run usually come at a cost. This is what Schumpeter meant by the term "creative destruction."* "

What does your research tell us about the main sources of Canada's persistently high unemployment rate during the 1980s and 1990s?

I think a lot of what has taken place in Canada is an example of the effects of creative destruction that I talked about. A lot of technological change destroys low-skill jobs, and also destroys the value of old skills. In particular, a lot of clerical and middle management jobs have been made redundant by computers. Computers open up new jobs for people able to master the technology, but a lot of people don't have the skills or the knowledge to profit from these opportunities. This is a global phenomenon, not just limited to Canada. Computers are having a revolutionary effect on economic life all over the world. In the United States it hasn't appeared to produce much unemployment. Instead what you see is a growing gap between the wages of skilled and unskilled workers. In Canada that gap isn't as visible, largely because we have more generous minimum wages and unemployment insurance benefits, which means that a fall in the demand for low-skill workers shows up more in a rise in unemployment and less in a fall in their wages than in the United States.

Why did our economic growth rate slow during the 1980s?

The short answer is that no one knows. But I think the answer probably lies in the computer revolution that I have talked about. Ultimately I think this revolution is going to give us a higher growth rate. But we have to accumulate a lot of knowledge in order to profit from it. We have been going through a collective learning experience that has been enormously costly, and this has been a continual drag on productivity, even though in the end I expect it will greatly enhance productivity.

Also, I think we are underestimating growth rates nowadays. This is because we are investing a lot in knowledge—knowledge of how to harness the power of the computer and to exploit the opportunities that it presents. Investment in knowledge is like investment in machinery in that it entails the sacrifice of resources now in return for the promise of more income sometime in the future. But while the national income accountant measures investment in machines as part of the economy's output of final goods and services, investment in knowledge is just treated as wasted resources.

Was the pursuit of low inflation worthwhile? Have we now got too low an inflation rate?

I think the pursuit of low inflation was definitely worthwhile, although in retrospect we maybe should have been more patient. Inflation impairs one of the most useful devices in the economic system—the conventional measure of value. Now that we have almost eliminated inflation we have a much healthier economic system. I don't think we should go much further, however, because you may have to raise unemployment even higher in order to get inflation all the way down to zero, and once you have it down to 2 percent you have little more to gain by reducing it even further. Also, further reductions in inflation may impair the working of the labour market. That is, people whose real wages are falling for whatever reason may be more inclined to continue working if they can at least avoid having to submit to a nominal wage cut, but can instead take the real-wage cut through the back door of inflation. With 2 percent inflation there is still lots of room for this sort of real-wage flexibility, but with no inflation there is none at all.

> *... one of the great things about economics is that you can be paid well for spending your time satisfying your curiosity.*

Some economists say that the Bank of Canada can speed up the economic growth rate by forgetting about low inflation and keeping interest rates low. Others say the best hope for increasing the growth rate is low inflation. Who is right?

The first group is certainly not right, except perhaps in a very short-run sense. You can't sustain a high growth rate for long by printing more money. Before long you'll end up with a higher rate of inflation and even higher interest rates as lenders seek compensation for the fall in the value of money. A lot of recent econometric evidence has been produced by various writers studying the experience of different countries that shows over long periods of time that inflation and growth are negatively correlated. More inflation from one decade to the next is likely to produce a fall in the growth rate rather than a rise. The effect doesn't appear to be numerically very large, but even a small drop in the growth rate can have a significant depressing effect on the level of real income if sustained for a decade or two.

What advice would you give to a student who wants to become a professional economist today?

My first advice for anyone interested in doing economics is to give full reign to your curiosity. The greatest satisfaction that I have received as an economist has been from discovering things about how the world works, from seeing a little more clearly some of the complex interactions between the different parts of the economy. I can still remember the excitement I felt when I started to see how demand and supply work, and when I learned about the circular flow of economic activity and how it can be affected by saving and investment decisions. I am happy to say that this sense of excitement has never left me. Furthermore, one of the great things about economics is that you can be paid well for spending your time satisfying your curiosity. Satisfying your curiosity is enjoyable, but if you want to accomplish something you can't let yourself be satisfied easily. You have to keep asking questions, and trying to answer them. It's easy to think you have solved a problem when you haven't explored things deeply enough. The best way for a student to do this is to do lots of exercises, and to discuss what you are doing with others. The same applies throughout one's career.

Expenditure Multipliers

CHAPTER 23

Economic Amplifier or Shock Absorber?

Céline Dion sings into a microphone in a barely audible whisper. Increasing in volume, through the magic of electronic amplification, her voice fills Toronto's Molson Amphitheatre.

Ralph Klein, the premier of Alberta, and his secretary are being driven to a business meeting along one of Edmonton's less well-repaired streets. The car's wheels bounce and vibrate over some of the worst potholes in the nation, but its passengers are completely undisturbed and the secretary's notes are written without a ripple, thanks to the car's efficient shock absorbers.

Investment and exports fluctuate like the volume of Céline Dion's voice and the uneven surface of an Edmonton street. How does the economy react to those fluctuations? Does it react like a limousine, absorbing the shocks and providing a smooth ride for the economy's passengers? Or does it behave like an amplifier, blowing up the fluctuations and spreading them out to affect the many millions of participants in an economic rock concert?

◆ You will explore these questions in this chapter. You will learn how a recession or an expansion begins when a change in investment or exports induces an amplified change in aggregate expenditure and real GDP. And you'll learn the crucial role played by business inventories in the transition from expansion to recession and back to expansion. *Reading Between the Lines* at the end of the chapter looks at the multiplier at work during the first half of 2005, when real GDP was expanding quickly.

After studying this chapter, you will be able to

- ■ **Explain how expenditure plans and real GDP are determined when the price level is fixed**
- ■ **Explain equilibrium expenditure at a fixed price level**
- ■ **Explain the expenditure multiplier and how recessions and expansions begin**
- ■ **Explain the relationship between aggregate expenditure and aggregate demand and how the multiplier gets smaller as the price level changes**

Expenditure Plans and GDP

THE COMPONENTS OF AGGREGATE EXPENDITURE are consumption expenditure (C), investment (I), government expenditures on goods and services (G), and net exports—exports (X) minus imports (M). The sum of these components is real GDP (Y). (See Chapter 20, p. 468). That is,

$$Y = C + I + G + X - M.$$

Two of these components—consumption expenditure and imports—depend on the level of real GDP. Because real GDP influences consumption expenditure and imports, and because consumption expenditure and imports are components of aggregate expenditure, there is a two-way link between aggregate expenditure and GDP. You are going to learn how this two-way link determines real GDP at a given price level.

The starting point is to consider the first piece of the two-way link: the influence of real GDP on planned consumption expenditure and saving.

Consumption and Saving Plans

Several factors influence consumption expenditure and saving. The most direct influence, especially in the short term, is disposable income. **Disposable income** is real GDP or aggregate income (Y) minus net taxes (NT)—taxes minus transfer payments. And aggregate income equals real GDP. The equation for disposable income (YD) is

$$YD = Y - NT.$$

Disposable income is either spent on consumption goods and services—consumption expenditure (C)—or saved (S). So planned consumption expenditure plus planned saving equals disposable income. That is,

$$YD = C + S.$$

The table in Fig. 23.1 shows some examples of planned consumption expenditure and planned saving at different levels of disposable income. The greater the disposable income, the greater is consumption expenditure and the greater is saving. Also, at each amount of disposable income, consumption expenditure plus saving equals disposable income.

The relationship between consumption expenditure and disposable income, with other things remaining the same, is called the **consumption function**. The relationship between saving and disposable income, with other things remaining the same, is called the **saving function**. Let's look at the consumption function and saving function in Fig. 23.1.

Consumption Function Figure 23.1(a) shows a consumption function. The y-axis measures consumption expenditure and the x-axis measures disposable income. Along the consumption function, the points labelled A through F correspond to the rows of the table. For example, point E shows that when disposable income is $800 billion, consumption expenditure is $750 billion. Along the consumption function, as disposable income increases, consumption expenditure also increases.

At point A on the consumption function, consumption expenditure is $150 billion even though disposable income is zero. This consumption expenditure is called *autonomous consumption*, and it is the amount of consumption expenditure that would take place in the short run even if people had no current income. You can think of this amount as the expenditure on the vital necessities of life.

When consumption expenditure exceeds disposable income, past savings are used to pay for current consumption. Such a situation cannot last forever, but it can occur temporarily.

Consumption expenditure in excess of autonomous consumption is called *induced consumption*—expenditure that is induced by an increase in disposable income.

45° Line Figure 23.1(a) also contains a 45° line, the height of which measures disposable income. At each point on this line, consumption expenditure equals disposable income. In the range over which the consumption function lies above the 45° line—between A and D—consumption expenditure exceeds disposable income. In the range over which the consumption function lies below the 45° line—between D and F—consumption expenditure is less than disposable income. And at the point at which the consumption function intersects the 45° line—at point D—consumption expenditure equals disposable income.

Saving Function Figure 23.1(b) shows a saving function. The x-axis is exactly the same as that in part (a). The y-axis measures saving. Again, the points marked A through F correspond to the rows of the table. For example, point *E* shows that when disposable income is $800 billion, saving is $50 billion. Along the saving function, as disposable income increases, saving also increases. At disposable incomes less than $600 billion (point *D*), saving is negative. Negative saving is called *dissaving*. At disposable incomes greater than $600 billion, saving is positive, and at $600 billion, saving is zero.

Notice the connection between the two parts of Fig. 23.1. When consumption expenditure exceeds

disposable income in part (a), saving is negative in part (b). When consumption expenditure is less than disposable income in part (a), saving is positive in part (b). And when consumption expenditure equals disposable income in part (a), saving is zero in part (b).

When saving is negative (when consumption expenditure exceeds disposable income), past savings are used to pay for current consumption. Such a situation cannot last forever, but it can occur if disposable income falls temporarily.

FIGURE 23.1
Consumption Function and Saving Function

(a) Consumption function

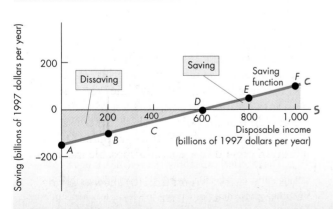

(b) Saving function

	Disposable income	Planned consumption expenditure	Planned saving
	(billions of 1997 dollars per year)		
A	0	150	−150
B	200	300	−100
C	400	450	−50
D	600	600	0
E	800	750	50
F	1,000	900	100

The table shows consumption expenditure and saving plans at various levels of disposable income. Part (a) of the figure shows the relationship between consumption expenditure and disposable income (the consumption function). The height of the consumption function measures consumption expenditure at each level of disposable income. Part (b) shows the relationship between saving and disposable income (the saving function). The height of the saving function measures saving at each level of disposable income. Points A through F on the consumption and saving functions correspond to the rows in the table. The height of the 45° line in part (a) measures disposable income. So along the 45° line, consumption expenditure equals disposable income. Consumption expenditure plus saving equals disposable income. When the consumption function is above the 45° line, saving is negative (dissaving occurs). When the consumption function is below the 45° line, saving is positive. At the point where the consumption function intersects the 45° line, all disposable income is consumed and saving is zero.

Marginal Propensity to Consume

The amount by which consumption expenditure changes when disposable income changes depends on the marginal propensity to consume. The **marginal propensity to consume** (*MPC*) is the fraction of a *change* in disposable income that is consumed. It is calculated as the *change* in consumption expenditure (ΔC) divided by the *change* in disposable income (ΔYD) that brought it about. That is,

$$MPC = \frac{\Delta C}{\Delta YD}.$$

In the table in Fig. 23.1, when disposable income increases from $600 billion to $800 billion, consumption expenditure increases from $600 billion to $750 billion. The $200 billion increase in disposable income increases consumption expenditure by $150 billion. The *MPC* is $150 billion divided by $200 billion, which equals 0.75.

The marginal propensity to consume is the slope of the consumption function. You can check this fact out in Fig. 23.2(a). Here, a $200 billion increase in disposable income from $600 billion to $800 billion is the base of the red triangle. The increase in consumption expenditure that results from this increase in disposable income is $150 billion and is the height of the triangle. The slope of the consumption function is given by the formula "slope equals rise over run" and is $150 billion divided by $200 billion, which equals 0.75—the *MPC*.

Marginal Propensity to Save

The amount by which saving changes when disposable income changes depends on the marginal propensity to save. The **marginal propensity to save** (*MPS*) is the fraction of a *change* in disposable income that is saved. It is calculated as the *change* in saving (ΔS) divided by the *change* in disposable income (ΔYD) that brought it about. That is,

$$MPS = \frac{\Delta S}{\Delta YD}.$$

In the table in Fig. 23.1, an increase in disposable income from $600 billion to $800 billion increases saving from zero to $50 billion. The $200 billion increase in disposable income increases saving by $50 billion. The *MPS* is $50 billion divided by $200 billion, which equals 0.25.

Marginal Propensities to Consume and Save

(a) Consumption function

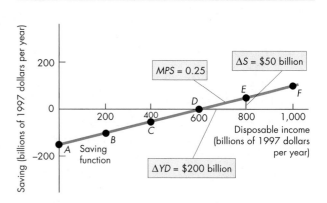

(b) Saving function

The marginal propensity to consume, *MPC*, is equal to the change in consumption expenditure divided by the change in disposable income, other things remaining the same. It is measured by the slope of the consumption function. In part (a), the *MPC* is 0.75.

The marginal propensity to save, *MPS*, is equal to the change in saving divided by the change in disposable income, other things remaining the same. It is measured by the slope of the saving function. In part (b), the *MPS* is 0.25.

The marginal propensity to save is the slope of the saving function. You can check this fact out in Fig. 23.2(b). Here, a $200 billion increase in disposable income from $600 billion to $800 billion (the base of the red triangle) increases saving by $50 billion (the height of the triangle). The slope of the saving function is $50 billion divided by $200 billion, which equals 0.25—the *MPS*.

The marginal propensity to consume plus the marginal propensity to save always equals 1. They sum to 1 because consumption expenditure and saving exhaust disposable income. Part of each dollar increase in disposable income is consumed, and the remaining part is saved. You can see that these two marginal propensities sum to 1 by using the equation:

$$\Delta C + \Delta S = \Delta YD.$$

Divide both sides of the equation by the change in disposable income to obtain

$$\frac{\Delta C}{\Delta YD} + \frac{\Delta S}{\Delta YD} = 1.$$

$\Delta C/\Delta YD$ is the marginal propensity to consume (*MPC*), and $\Delta S/\Delta YD$ is the marginal propensity to save (*MPS*), so

$$MPC + MPS = 1.$$

Other Influences on Consumption Expenditure and Saving

You've seen that a change in disposable income leads to changes in consumption expenditure and saving. A change in disposable income brings movements along the consumption function and saving function. A change in any other influence on consumption expenditure and saving shifts the consumption function and the saving function as shown in Fig. 23.3.

The main other influences are

1. Expected future disposable income
2. The real interest rate
3. Wealth

An increase in expected future disposable income makes people feel better off and leads to an increase in current consumption expenditure and a decrease in current saving. A fall in the real interest rate, other things remaining the same, encourages an increase in

FIGURE 23.3 myeconlab

Shifts in the Consumption and Saving Functions

(a) Consumption function

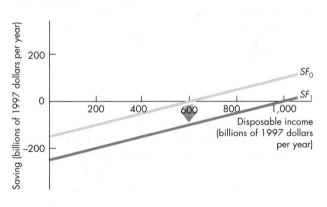

(b) Saving function

An increase in expected future disposable income, a fall in the real interest rate, or an increase in wealth shifts the consumption function upward from CF_0 to CF_1 and the saving function downward from SF_0 to SF_1.

A decrease in expected future disposable income, a rise in the real interest rate, or a decrease in wealth shifts the consumption function downward and shifts the saving function upward.

borrowing and consumption expenditure and a decrease in saving. And an increase in wealth, other things remaining the same, stimulates consumption expenditure and decreases saving.

When expected future disposable income increases, the real interest rate falls, or when wealth increases, consumption expenditure increases and saving decreases. In Fig. 23.3 the consumption function shifts upward from CF_0 to CF_1, and the saving function shifts downward from SF_0 to SF_1.

When expected future disposable income decreases, the real interest rate rises, or when wealth decreases, consumption expenditure decreases and saving increases. The consumption function shifts downward and the saving function shifts upward. Such shifts often occur when a recession begins because at such a time, expected future disposable income decreases.

We've studied the theory of the consumption function. Let's now see how that theory applies to the Canadian economy.

The Canadian Consumption Function

Figure 23.4 shows the Canadian consumption function. Each point identified by a blue dot represents consumption expenditure and disposable income for a particular year. (The dots are for the years 1961 to 2004. Five of the years are identified in the figure.) The line labelled CF_{61} is an estimate of the Canadian consumption function in 1961, and the line labelled CF_{04} is an estimate of the Canadian consumption function in 2004.

The slope of the consumption function in Fig. 23.4 is 0.85, which means that a $100 billion increase in disposable income brings a $85 billion increase in consumption expenditure. This slope, which is an estimate of the marginal propensity to consume, is an assumption that is at the middle of the range of values that economists have estimated for the marginal propensity to consume.

The consumption function shifts upward over time as other influences on consumption expenditure change. Of these other influences, expected future disposable income, the real interest rate, and wealth fluctuate and so bring upward *and* downward shifts in the consumption function. A low real interest rate and rise in wealth that came from a real estate boom brought a strong increase in autonomous consumption expenditure and an upward shift of the consumption function in 2003 and 2004.

FIGURE 23.4
The Canadian Consumption Function

The consumption function shifts upward over time as economic growth brings higher expected future income

$MPC = 0.85$

Each blue dot shows consumption expenditure and disposable income for a particular year. The lines CF_{61} and CF_{04} are estimates of the Canadian consumption function in 1961 and 2004, respectively. Here, the (assumed) marginal propensity to consume is 0.85.

Source of data: Statistics Canada, CANSIM Tables 380–0002, 384–0013, and 384–0035.

Consumption as a Function of Real GDP

You've seen that consumption expenditure changes when disposable income changes. And you've seen that disposable income is equal to real GDP minus net taxes. So consumption expenditure is a function of real GDP. An increase in real GDP increases disposable income, which increases consumption expenditure. But an increase in real GDP also increases net taxes. So when real GDP increases, consumption expenditure increases but by less than it would if net taxes were unchanged. We're going to use this link between consumption expenditure and real GDP to determine equilibrium expenditure. But before we do so, we need to look at one other component of aggregate expenditure: imports. Like consumption expenditure, imports are influenced by real GDP.

Import Function

Canadian imports are determined by many factors, but in the short run, one factor dominates: Canadian real GDP. Other things remaining the same, the greater the Canadian real GDP, the larger is the quantity of Canadian imports.

The relationship between imports and real GDP is determined by the marginal propensity to import. The **marginal propensity to import** is the fraction of an increase in real GDP that is spent on imports. It is calculated as the change in imports divided by the change in real GDP that brought it about, other things remaining the same. For example, if a $100 billion increase in real GDP increases imports by $25 billion, the marginal propensity to import is 0.25.

In recent years, since the North American Free Trade Agreement (NAFTA) was implemented, Canadian imports have surged. For example, between 1991 and 2005, real GDP increased by $398 billion and imports increased by $262 billion. If no factors other than real GDP influenced imports during this period, these numbers would imply a marginal propensity to import of 0.66 ($262 billion divided by $398 billion). But NAFTA and other factors (such as lower communication costs) increased imports. If one half of the increase in imports resulted from other factors and the other half from the increase in real GDP, the marginal propensity to import is 0.33.

REVIEW QUIZ
1 Which components of aggregate expenditure are influenced by real GDP?
2 Define the marginal propensity to consume. What is your estimate of your own marginal propensity to consume? After you graduate, will it change? Why or why not?
3 How do we calculate the effects of real GDP on consumption expenditure and imports?
myeconlab Study Plan 23.1

Real GDP influences consumption expenditure and imports. But consumption expenditure and imports—along with investment, government expenditures, and exports—influence real GDP. Your next task is to study this second piece of the two-way link between aggregate expenditure and real GDP and see how all the components of aggregate planned expenditure interact to determine real GDP.

Equilibrium Expenditure at a Fixed Price Level

MOST FIRMS ARE LIKE YOUR LOCAL SUPERMAR-KET. They set their prices, advertise their products and services, and sell the quantities their customers are willing to buy. If they persistently sell a greater quantity than they plan to and are constantly running out of inventory, they eventually raise their prices. And if they persistently sell a smaller quantity than they plan to and have inventories piling up, they eventually cut their prices. But in the very short term, their prices are fixed. They hold the prices they have set, and the quantities they sell depend on demand, not supply.

The Aggregate Implications of Fixed Prices

Fixed prices have two immediate implications for the economy as a whole:

1. Because each firm's price is fixed, the *price level* is fixed.
2. Because demand determines the quantities that each firm sells, *aggregate demand* determines the aggregate quantity of goods and services sold, which equals real GDP.

So to understand how real GDP is determined when the price level is fixed, we must understand how aggregate demand is determined. Aggregate demand is determined by aggregate expenditure plans. We define **aggregate planned expenditure** as *planned* consumption expenditure plus *planned* investment plus *planned* government expenditures plus *planned* exports minus *planned* imports.

You've just studied planned consumption expenditure and planned imports and seen that these two components of aggregate planned expenditure are influenced by real GDP. The other components of aggregate expenditure—investment, government expenditures, and exports—are not influenced by real GDP. They fluctuate for many reasons but not because real GDP fluctuates.

You are now going to study a model called the *aggregate expenditure model*, which explains how consumption expenditure, imports, and real GDP are *simultaneously* determined by a two-way link between expenditure plans and real GDP.

The Aggregate Expenditure Model

You are now going to discover how aggregate expenditure plans interact to determine real GDP when the price level is fixed. First, we will study the relationship between aggregate planned expenditure and real GDP. Second, we'll learn about the key distinction between *planned* expenditure and *actual* expenditure. And third, we'll study equilibrium expenditure, a sit-uation in which aggregate planned expenditure and actual expenditure are equal.

The relationship between aggregate planned expenditure and real GDP can be described by either an aggregate expenditure schedule or an aggregate expenditure curve. The *aggregate expenditure schedule* lists aggregate planned expenditure generated at each level of real GDP. The *aggregate expenditure curve* is a graph of the aggregate expenditure schedule.

FIGURE 23.5
Aggregate Expenditure

The aggregate expenditure schedule shows the relationship between aggregate planned expenditure and real GDP. Aggregate planned expenditure is the sum of planned consumption expenditure, investment, government expenditures, and exports minus imports. For example, in row *B* of the table, when real GDP is $800 billion, planned consumption expenditure is $560 billion, planned investment is $150 billion, planned government expenditures on goods and services are $180 billion, planned exports are $170 billion, and planned imports are $160 billion. So when real GDP is $800 billion, aggregate planned expenditure is $900 billion ($560 + $150 + $180 + $170 − $160). The schedule shows that aggregate planned expenditure increases as real GDP increases.

This relationship is graphed as the aggregate expenditure curve *AE*. The components of aggregate expenditure that increase with real GDP are consumption expenditure and imports. The other components—investment, government expenditures, and exports—do not vary with real GDP.

	Real GDP (Y)	Consumption expenditure (C)	Investment (I)	Government expenditures (G)	Exports (X)	Imports (M)	Aggregate planned expenditure (AE = C + I + G + X − M)
				(billions of 1997 dollars)			
	0	0	150	180	170	0	500
A	700	490	150	180	170	140	850
B	800	560	150	180	170	160	900
C	900	630	150	180	170	180	950
D	1,000	700	150	180	170	200	1,000
E	1,100	770	150	180	170	220	1,050
F	1,200	840	150	180	170	240	1,100

Aggregate Planned Expenditure and Real GDP

The table in Fig. 23.5 sets out an aggregate expenditure schedule together with the components of aggregate planned expenditure. To calculate aggregate planned expenditure at a given real GDP, we add the various components together. The first column of the table shows real GDP, and the second column shows the consumption expenditure generated by each level of real GDP. A $100 billion increase in real GDP generates a $70 billion increase in consumption expenditure—the *MPC* is 0.7.

The next two columns show investment and government expenditures on goods and services. Investment depends on such factors as the real interest rate and the expected future profit. But at a given point in time, these factors generate a particular level of investment. Suppose this level of investment is $150 billion. Also, suppose that government expenditures on goods and services is $180 billion.

The next two columns show exports and imports. Exports are influenced by income in the rest of the world, prices of foreign-made goods and services relative to the prices of similar Canadian-made goods and services, and foreign exchange rates. But exports are not directly affected by real GDP in Canada. Exports are a constant $170 billion no matter what real GDP in Canada is. Imports increase as real GDP increases. A $100 billion increase in real GDP generates a $20 billion increase in imports—the marginal propensity to import is 0.2.

The final column shows aggregate planned expenditure—the sum of planned consumption expenditure, investment, government expenditures on goods and services, and exports minus imports.

Figure 23.5 plots an aggregate expenditure curve. Real GDP is shown on the *x*-axis, and aggregate planned expenditure is shown on the *y*-axis. The aggregate expenditure curve is the red line *AE*. Points *A* through *F* on that curve correspond to the rows of the table. The *AE* curve is a graph of aggregate planned expenditure (the last column) plotted against real GDP (the first column).

Figure 23.5 also shows the components of aggregate expenditure. The constant components—investment (*I*), government expenditures on goods and services (*G*), and exports (*X*)—are shown by the horizontal lines in the figure. Consumption expenditure (*C*) is the vertical gap between the lines labelled $I + G + X$ and $I + G + X + C$.

To construct the *AE* curve, subtract imports (*M*) from the line labelled $I + G + X + C$. Aggregate expenditure is expenditure on Canadian-made goods and services. But the components of aggregate expenditure—*C*, *I*, and *G*—include expenditure on imported goods and services. For example, if you buy a new cell phone, your expenditure is part of consumption expenditure. But if the cell phone is a Nokia made in Finland, your expenditure on it must be subtracted from consumption expenditure to find out how much is spent on goods and services produced in Canada—on Canadian real GDP. Money paid to Nokia for cell phone imports from Finland does not add to aggregate expenditure in Canada.

Because imports are only a part of aggregate expenditure, when we subtract imports from the other components of aggregate expenditure, aggregate planned expenditure still increases as real GDP increases, as you can see in Fig. 23.5.

Consumption expenditure minus imports, which varies with real GDP, is called **induced expenditure**. The sum of investment, government expenditures, and exports, which does not vary with real GDP, is called **autonomous expenditure**. Consumption expenditure and imports can also have an autonomous component—a component that does not vary with real GDP. Another way of thinking about autonomous expenditure is that it would be the amount of aggregate planned expenditure if real GDP were zero.

In Fig. 23.5, autonomous expenditure is $500 billion—aggregate planned expenditure when real GDP is zero. For each $100 billion increase in real GDP, induced expenditure increases by $50 billion.

The aggregate expenditure curve summarizes the relationship between aggregate *planned* expenditure and real GDP. But what determines the point on the aggregate expenditure curve at which the economy operates? What determines *actual* aggregate expenditure?

Actual Expenditure, Planned Expenditure, and Real GDP

Actual aggregate expenditure is always equal to real GDP, as we saw in Chapter 20 (p. 468). But aggregate *planned* expenditure is not necessarily equal to actual aggregate expenditure and therefore is not necessarily equal to real GDP. How can actual expenditure and planned expenditure differ from each other? Why don't expenditure plans get implemented? The main reason is that firms might end up with greater inventories than planned or with smaller inventories than planned. People carry out their consumption expenditure plans, the government implements its planned purchases of goods and services, and net exports are as planned. Firms carry out their plans to purchase new buildings, plant, and equipment. But one component of investment is the change in firms' inventories. If aggregate planned expenditure is less than real GDP, firms don't sell all the goods they produce and they

end up with inventories they hadn't planned. If aggregate planned expenditure exceeds real GDP, firms sell more than they produce and inventories decrease below the level that firms had planned.

Equilibrium Expenditure

Equilibrium expenditure is the level of aggregate expenditure that occurs when aggregate *planned* expenditure equals real GDP. It is the level of aggregate

FIGURE 23.6
Equilibrium Expenditure

(a) Equilibrium expenditure

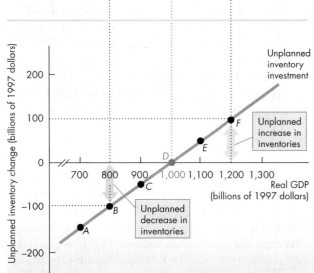

(b) Unplanned inventory changes

	Real GDP (Y)	Aggregate planned expenditure (AE)	Unplanned inventory change (Y − AE)
		(billions of 1997 dollars)	
A	700	850	−150
B	800	900	−100
C	900	950	−50
D	1,000	1,000	0
E	1,100	1,050	50
F	1,200	1,100	100

The table shows expenditure plans at different levels of real GDP. When real GDP is $1,000 billion, aggregate planned expenditure equals real GDP.

Part (a) of the figure illustrates equilibrium expenditure, which occurs when aggregate planned expenditure equals real GDP at the intersection of the 45° line and the AE curve. Part (b) of the figure shows the forces that bring about equilibrium expenditure. When aggregate planned expenditure exceeds real GDP, inventories decrease—for example, at point B in both parts of the figure. Firms increase production, and real GDP increases.

When aggregate planned expenditure is less than real GDP, inventories increase—for example, at point F in both parts of the figure. Firms decrease production, and real GDP decreases. When aggregate planned expenditure equals real GDP, there are no unplanned inventory changes and real GDP remains constant at equilibrium expenditure.

expenditure and real GDP at which everyone's spending plans are fulfilled. When the price level is fixed, equilibrium expenditure determines real GDP. When aggregate planned expenditure and actual aggregate expenditure are unequal, a process of convergence towards equilibrium expenditure occurs. And throughout this convergence process, real GDP adjusts. Let's examine equilibrium expenditure and the process that brings it about.

Figure 23.6(a) illustrates equilibrium expenditure. The table sets out aggregate planned expenditure at various levels of real GDP. These values are plotted as points A through F along the AE curve. The 45° line shows all the points at which aggregate planned expenditure equals real GDP. Thus where the AE curve lies above the 45° line, aggregate planned expenditure exceeds real GDP; where the AE curve lies below the 45° line, aggregate planned expenditure is less than real GDP; and where the AE curve intersects the 45° line, aggregate planned expenditure equals real GDP. Point D illustrates equilibrium expenditure. At this point, real GDP is $1,000 billion.

Convergence to Equilibrium

What are the forces that move aggregate expenditure towards its equilibrium level? To answer this question, we must look at a situation in which aggregate expenditure is away from its equilibrium level. Suppose that in Fig. 23.6, real GDP is $800 billion. With real GDP at $800 billion, actual aggregate expenditure is also $800 billion. But aggregate *planned* expenditure is $900 billion (point B in Fig. 23.6a). Aggregate planned expenditure exceeds real GDP. When people spend $900 billion and firms produce goods and services worth $800 billion, firms' inventories fall by $100 billion (point B in Fig. 23.6b). Recall that *investment* is the purchase of new plant, equipment and buildings and *additions to inventories*. Because the change in inventories is part of investment, *actual* investment is $100 billion less than *planned* investment.

Real GDP doesn't remain at $800 billion for very long. Firms have inventory targets based on their sales. When inventories fall below target, firms increase production to restore inventories to the target level. To increase inventories, firms hire additional labour and increase production. Suppose that they increase production in the next period by $100 billion. Real GDP increases by $100 billion to $900 billion. But again, aggregate planned expenditure

exceeds real GDP. When real GDP is $900 billion, aggregate planned expenditure is $950 billion (point C in Fig. 23.6a). Again, inventories decrease, but this time by less than before. With real GDP of $900 billion and aggregate planned expenditure of $950 billion, inventories decrease by $50 billion (point C in Fig. 23.6b). Again, firms hire additional labour, and production increases; real GDP increases yet further.

The process that we've just described—planned expenditure exceeds real GDP, inventories decrease, and production increases—ends when real GDP has reached $1,000 billion. At this real GDP, there is equilibrium. Unplanned inventory changes are zero. Firms do not change their production.

You can do an experiment similar to the one we've just done but starting with a level of real GDP greater than equilibrium expenditure. In this case, aggregate planned expenditure is less than real GDP, inventories pile up, and firms cut production. As before, real GDP keeps on changing (decreasing this time) until it reaches its equilibrium level of $1,000 billion.

REVIEW QUIZ

1   What is the relationship between aggregate planned expenditure and real GDP in expenditure equilibrium?

2   How does equilibrium expenditure come about? What adjusts to achieve equilibrium?

3   If real GDP and aggregate expenditure are less than their equilibrium levels, what happens to firms' inventories? How do firms change their production? And what happens to real GDP?

4   If real GDP and aggregate expenditure are greater than their equilibrium levels, what happens to firms' inventories? How do firms change their production? And what happens to real GDP?

 myeconlab   **Study Plan 23.2**

We've learned that when the price level is fixed, real GDP is determined by equilibrium expenditure. And you have seen how unplanned changes in inventories and the production response that they generate brings a convergence towards equilibrium expenditure. We're now going to study *changes* in equilibrium expenditure and discover an economic amplifier called the *multiplier*.

The Multiplier

INVESTMENT AND EXPORTS CAN CHANGE FOR many reasons. A fall in the real interest rate might induce firms to increase their planned investment. A wave of innovation, such as occurred with the spread of multimedia computers in the 1990s, might increase expected future profits and lead firms to increase their planned investment. An economic boom in the United States and Western Europe might lead to a large increase in their expenditure on Canadian-produced goods and services—on Canadian exports. These are all examples of increases in autonomous expenditure.

When autonomous expenditure increases, aggregate expenditure increases, and so do equilibrium expenditure and real GDP. But the increase in real GDP is *larger* than the change in autonomous expenditure. The **multiplier** is the amount by which a change in autonomous expenditure is magnified or multiplied to determine the change in equilibrium expenditure and real GDP.

To get the basic idea of the multiplier we'll work with an economy in which there are no income taxes and no imports. So we'll first assume that these factors are absent. Then, when you understand the basic idea, we'll bring these factors back into play and see what difference they make to the multiplier.

The Basic Idea of the Multiplier

Suppose that investment increases. The additional expenditure by businesses means that aggregate expenditure and real GDP increase. The increase in real GDP increases disposable income, and with no income taxes, real GDP and disposable income increase by the same amount. The increase in disposable income brings an increase in consumption expenditure, which in turn adds even more to aggregate expenditure. Real GDP and disposable income increase further, and so does consumption expenditure. The initial increase in investment brings an even bigger increase in aggregate expenditure because it induces an increase in consumption expenditure. The magnitude of the increase in aggregate expenditure that results from an increase in autonomous expenditure is determined by the *multiplier*.

The table in Fig. 23.7 sets out aggregate planned expenditure. When real GDP is $900 billion, aggregate planned expenditure is $925 billion. For each

$100 billion increase in real GDP, aggregate planned expenditure increases by $75 billion. This aggregate expenditure schedule is shown in the figure as the aggregate expenditure curve AE_0. Initially, equilibrium expenditure is $1,000 billion. You can see this equilibrium in row B of the table and in the figure where the curve AE_0 intersects the 45° line at the point marked B.

Now suppose that autonomous expenditure increases by $50 billion. What happens to equilibrium expenditure? You can see the answer in Fig. 23.7. When this increase in autonomous expenditure is added to the original aggregate planned expenditure, aggregate planned expenditure increases by $50 billion at each level of real GDP. The new aggregate expenditure curve is AE_1. The new equilibrium expenditure, highlighted in the table (row D'), occurs where AE_1 intersects the 45° line and is $1,200 billion (point D'). At this real GDP, aggregate planned expenditure equals real GDP.

The Multiplier Effect

In Fig. 23.7, the increase in autonomous expenditure of $50 billion increases equilibrium expenditure by $200 billion. That is, the change in autonomous expenditure leads, like Céline Dion's electronic equipment, to an amplified change in equilibrium expenditure. This amplified change is the *multiplier effect*—equilibrium expenditure increases by *more than* the increase in autonomous expenditure. The multiplier is greater than 1.

Initially, when autonomous expenditure increases, aggregate planned expenditure exceeds real GDP. As a result, inventories decrease. Firms respond by increasing production so as to restore their inventories to the target level. As production increases, so does real GDP. With a higher level of real GDP, *induced expenditure* increases. Thus equilibrium expenditure increases by the sum of the initial increase in autonomous expenditure and the increase in induced expenditure. In this example, induced expenditure increases by $150 billion, so equilibrium expenditure increases by $200 billion.

Although we have just analyzed the effects of an *increase* in autonomous expenditure, the same analysis applies to a decrease in autonomous expenditure. If initially the aggregate expenditure curve is AE_1, equilibrium expenditure and real GDP are $1,200 billion. A decrease in autonomous expenditure of $50 billion shifts the aggregate expenditure

FIGURE 23.7
The Multiplier

A $50 billion increase in autonomous expenditure shifts the AE curve upward by $50 billion from AE_0 to AE_1. Equilibrium expenditure increases by $200 billion from $1,000 billion to $1,200 billion. The increase in equilibrium expenditure is 4 times the increase in autonomous expenditure, so the multiplier is 4.

Real GDP	Aggregate planned expenditure			
(Y)	Original (AE_0)		New (AE_1)	
	(billions of 1997 dollars)			
900	A	925	A'	975
1,000	B	1,000	B'	1,050
1,100	C	1,075	C'	1,125
1,200	D	1,150	D'	1,200
1,300	E	1,225	E'	1,275

curve downward by $50 billion to AE_0. Equilibrium expenditure decreases from $1,200 billion to $1,000 billion. The decrease in equilibrium expenditure ($200 billion) is larger than the decrease in autonomous expenditure that brought it about ($50 billion).

Why Is the Multiplier Greater Than 1?

We've seen that equilibrium expenditure increases by more than the increase in autonomous expenditure. This makes the multiplier greater than 1.

How come? Why does equilibrium expenditure increase by more than the increase in autonomous expenditure?

The multiplier is greater than 1 because of induced expenditure—an increase in autonomous expenditure *induces* further increases in expenditure. If Rogers Cablesystems spends $10 million on a new pay-per-view system, aggregate expenditure and real GDP immediately increase by $10 million. But that is not the end of the story. Video system designers and computer producers now have more income, and they spend part of the extra income on cars, microwave ovens, vacations, and a host of other goods and services. Real GDP now increases by the initial $10 million plus the extra consumption expenditure induced by the $10 million increase in income. The producers of cars, microwave ovens, vacations, and other goods and services now have increased incomes, and they, in turn, spend part of the increase in their incomes on consumption goods and services. Additional income induces additional expenditure, which creates additional income.

We have seen that a change in autonomous expenditure has a multiplier effect on real GDP. But how big is the multiplier effect?

The Size of the Multiplier

The *multiplier* is the amount by which a change in autonomous expenditure is multiplied to determine the change in equilibrium expenditure that it generates. To calculate the multiplier, we divide the change in equilibrium expenditure by the change in autonomous expenditure. Let's calculate the multiplier for the example in Fig. 23.7. Initially, equilibrium expenditure is $1,000 billion. Then autonomous expenditure increases by $50 billion, and equilibrium expenditure increases by $200 billion, to $1,200 billion. So

$$\text{Multiplier} = \frac{\text{Change in equilibrium expenditure}}{\text{Change in autonomous expenditure}}$$

$$= \frac{\$200 \text{ billion}}{\$50 \text{ billion}} = 4.$$

The Multiplier and the Slope of the *AE* Curve

What determines the magnitude of the multiplier? The answer is the slope of the *AE* curve. The steeper the slope of the *AE* curve, the larger is the multiplier. To see why, think about what the slope of the *AE* curve tells you. It tells you by how much induced expenditure increases when real GDP increases. The steeper the *AE* curve, the greater is the increase in induced expenditure that results from a given increase in real GDP. Let's do a calculation to show the relationship between the slope of the *AE* curve and the multiplier.

The change in real GDP (ΔY) equals the change in induced expenditure (ΔN) plus the change in autonomous expenditure (ΔA). That is,

$$\Delta Y = \Delta N + \Delta A.$$

The slope of the *AE* curve equals the "rise," ΔN, divided by the "run," ΔY. That is,

$$\text{Slope of } AE \text{ curve} = \Delta N \div \Delta Y.$$

So

$$\Delta N = \text{Slope of } AE \text{ curve} \times \Delta Y.$$

Now use this equation to replace ΔN in the first equation above to give

$$\Delta Y = (\text{Slope of } AE \text{ curve} \times \Delta Y) + \Delta A.$$

Now, solve for ΔY as

$$(1 - \text{Slope of } AE \text{ curve}) \times \Delta Y = \Delta A$$

and rearrange to give

$$\Delta Y = \frac{\Delta A}{1 - \text{Slope of the } AE \text{ curve}}.$$

Finally, divide both sides of the previous equation by ΔA to give

$$\text{Multiplier} = \frac{\Delta Y}{\Delta A} = \frac{1}{1 - \text{Slope of } AE \text{ curve}}.$$

Using the numbers for Fig. 23.7, the slope of the *AE* curve is 0.75, so the multiplier is

$$\text{Multiplier} = \frac{1}{1 - 0.75} = \frac{1}{0.25} = 4.$$

When there are no income taxes and no imports, the slope of the *AE* curve equals the marginal propensity to consume (*MPC*). So the multiplier is

$$\text{Multiplier} = \frac{1}{1 - MPC}.$$

There is another formula for the multiplier in this special case. Because the marginal propensity to consume (*MPC*) plus the marginal propensity to save (*MPS*) sum to 1, the term $(1 - MPC)$ equals *MPS*. Therefore, another formula for the multiplier is

$$\text{Multiplier} = \frac{1}{MPS}.$$

Because the marginal propensity to save (*MPS*) is a number between 0 and 1, the multiplier is greater than 1.

Figure 23.8 illustrates the multiplier process. In round 1, autonomous expenditure increases by $50 billion (shown by the green bar). At this time, induced expenditure does not change, so aggregate expenditure and real GDP increase by $50 billion. In round 2, the larger real GDP induces more consumption expenditure. Induced expenditure increases by 0.75 times the increase in real GDP, so the increase in real GDP of $50 billion induces a further increase in expenditure of $37.5 billion. This change in induced expenditure (the green bar in round 2), when added to the previous increase in expenditure (the blue bar in round 2), increases aggregate expenditure and real GDP by $87.5 billion. The round 2 increase in real GDP induces a round 3 increase in expenditure. The process repeats through successive rounds. Each increase in real GDP is 0.75 times the previous increase. The cumulative increase in real GDP gradually approaches $200 billion.

So far, we've ignored imports and income taxes. Let's now see how these two factors influence the multiplier.

Imports and Income Taxes

The multiplier is determined, in general, not only by the marginal propensity to consume but also by the marginal propensity to import and by the marginal tax rate.

Imports make the multiplier smaller than it otherwise would be. To see why, think about what happens following an increase in investment. An increase in

FIGURE 23.8
The Multiplier Process

Autonomous expenditure increases in round 1 by $50 billion. As a result, real GDP increases by the same amount. With a marginal propensity to consume of 0.75, each additional dollar of real GDP induces an additional 0.75 of a dollar of aggregate expenditure. The round 1 increase in real GDP induces an increase in consumption expenditure of $37.5 billion in round 2. At the end of round 2, real GDP has increased by $87.5 billion. The extra $37.5 billion of real GDP in round 2 induces a further increase in consumption expenditure of $28.1 billion in round 3. Real GDP increases yet further to $115.6 billion. This process continues with real GDP increasing by ever-smaller amounts. When the process comes to an end, real GDP has increased by a total of $200 billion.

investment increases real GDP, which in turn increases consumption expenditure. But part of the increase in consumption expenditure is expenditure on imported goods and services, not Canadian-produced goods and services. Only expenditure on Canadian-produced goods and services increases Canadian real GDP. The larger is the marginal propensity to import, the smaller is the change in Canadian real GDP.

Income taxes also make the multiplier smaller than it otherwise would be. Again, think about what happens following an increase in investment. Real GDP increases. But because income taxes increase, disposable income increases by less than the increase in real GDP. Consequently, consumption expenditure increases by less than it would if taxes had not changed. The larger the marginal tax rate, the smaller is the change in disposable income and real GDP.

The marginal propensity to import and the marginal tax rate together with the marginal propensity to consume determine the multiplier. And their combined influence determines the slope of the *AE* curve. The multiplier is equal to 1 divided by (1 minus the slope of the *AE* curve).

Figure 23.9 compares two situations. In Fig. 23.9(a), there are no imports and no taxes. The slope of the *AE* curve equals the marginal propensity to consume, which is 0.75, and the multiplier is 4. In Fig. 23.9(b), imports and income taxes decrease the slope of the *AE* curve to 0.5. In this case, the multiplier is 2.

Over time, the value of the multiplier changes as tax rates change and as the marginal propensity to consume and the marginal propensity to import change. These ongoing changes make the multiplier hard to predict. But they do not change the fundamental fact that an initial change in autonomous expenditure leads to a magnified change in aggregate expenditure and real GDP.

The math note on pp. 558–559 shows the effects of taxes, imports, and the *MPC* on the multiplier.

Now that we've studied the multiplier and the factors that influence its magnitude, let's use what we've learned to gain some insights into business cycle turning points.

Business Cycle Turning Points

At business cycle turning points, the economy moves from expansion to recession or from recession to expansion. Economists understand these turning points as seismologists understand earthquakes. They know quite a lot about the forces and mechanisms that produce them, but they can't predict them. The forces that bring business cycle turning points are the swings in autonomous expenditure such as investment and exports. The mechanism that gives momentum to the economy's new direction is the multiplier. Let's use what we've now learned to examine these turning points.

FIGURE 23.9
The Multiplier and the Slope of the *AE* Curve

(a) Multiplier is 4

Imports and income taxes make the *AE* curve less steep and reduce the value of the multiplier. In part (a), with no imports and income taxes, the slope of the *AE* curve is 0.75 (the marginal propensity to consume) and the multiplier is 4.

(b) Multiplier is 2

But with imports and income taxes, the slope of the *AE* curve is less than the marginal propensity to consume. In part (b), the slope of the *AE* curve is 0.5. In this case, the multiplier is 2.

An Expansion Begins An expansion is triggered by an increase in autonomous expenditure that increases aggregate planned expenditure. At the moment the economy turns the corner into expansion, aggregate planned expenditure exceeds real GDP. In this situation, firms see their inventories taking an unplanned dive. The expansion now begins. To meet their inventory targets, firms increase production, and real GDP begins to increase. This initial increase in real GDP brings higher incomes that increase disposable income and stimulate consumption expenditure. The multiplier process kicks in, and the expansion picks up speed.

A Recession Begins The process we've just described works in reverse at a business cycle peak. A recession is triggered by a decrease in autonomous expenditure that decreases aggregate planned expenditure. At the moment the economy turns the corner into recession, real GDP exceeds aggregate planned

expenditure. In this situation, firms see unplanned inventories piling up. The recession now begins. To lower their inventories, firms cut production, and real GDP begins to decrease. This initial decrease in real GDP brings lower incomes that cut consumption expenditure. The multiplier process reinforces the initial cut in autonomous expenditure, and the recession takes hold.

The Next Canadian Recession? Since 1991, the Canadian economy has been in a business cycle expansion. The last real GDP trough was in the first quarter of 1991. The science of macroeconomics cannot predict when the next recession will begin. A recession seemed possible in 1998 following a rapid buildup of inventories during 1997. But firms had planned that inventory buildup. In late 2005, there was still no immediate prospect of the next recession. But it will surely come. And when it does, the mechanism you've just studied will operate.

inventories exceed planned consumption

The economy's potholes are changes in investment and exports. The economy does not operate like the shock absorbers on Ralph Klein's car. While the price level is fixed, the effects of the economic potholes are not smoothed out. Instead, they are amplified like Céline Dion's voice. But we've considered only the adjustments in spending that occur when the price level is fixed. What happens after a long enough time lapse for the price level to change? Let's answer this question.

The Multiplier and the Price Level

WHEN FIRMS CAN'T KEEP UP WITH SALES AND THEIR inventories fall below target, they increase production, but at some point, they raise their prices. Similarly, when firms find unwanted inventories piling up, they decrease production, but eventually they cut their prices. So far, we've studied the macroeconomic consequences of firms changing their production levels when their sales change, but we haven't looked at the effects of price changes. When individual firms change their prices, the economy's price level changes.

To study the simultaneous determination of real GDP and the price level, we use the *aggregate supply–aggregate demand model*, which is explained in Chapter 22. But to understand how aggregate demand adjusts, we need to work out the connection between the aggregate supply–aggregate demand model and the equilibrium expenditure model that we've used in this chapter. The key to understanding the relationship between these two models is the distinction between the aggregate *expenditure* and aggregate *demand* and the related distinction between the aggregate *expenditure curve* and the aggregate *demand curve*.

Aggregate Expenditure and Aggregate Demand

The aggregate expenditure curve is the relationship between aggregate planned expenditure and real GDP when all other influences on aggregate planned expenditure remain the same. The aggregate demand curve is the relationship between the aggregate quantity of goods and services demanded and the price level when all other influences on aggregate demand remain the same. Let's explore the links between these two relationships.

Aggregate Expenditure and the Price Level

When the price level changes, aggregate planned expenditure changes and the quantity of real GDP demanded changes. The aggregate demand curve slopes downward. Why? There are two main reasons:

■ Wealth effect
■ Substitution effects

Wealth Effect Other things remaining the same, the higher the price level, the smaller is the purchasing power of people's real wealth. For example suppose you have $100 in the bank and the price level is 110. If the price level rises to 130, your $100 buys fewer goods and services. You are less wealthy. With less wealth, you will probably want to try to spend a bit less and save a bit more. The higher the price level, other things remaining the same, the lower is aggregate planned expenditure.

Substitution Effects A rise in the price level today, other things remaining the same, makes current goods and services more costly relative to future goods and services and people delay making their purchases—an *intertemporal substitution*. A rise in the price level, other things remaining the same, makes Canadian-produced goods more expensive relative to foreign-produced goods and services and increases imports and decreases exports—an *international substitution*.

When the price level rises, each of these effects reduces aggregate planned expenditure at each level of real GDP. As a result, when the price level *rises*, the *AE* curve shifts *downward*. A fall in the price level has the opposite effect. When the price level *falls*, the *AE* curve shifts *upward*.

Figure 23.10(a) shows the shifts of the *AE* curve. When the price level is 110, the aggregate expenditure curve is *AE*$_0$, which intersects the 45° line at point *B*. Equilibrium expenditure is $1,000 billion. If the price level increases to 130, the aggregate expenditure curve shifts downward to *AE*$_1$, which intersects the 45° line at point *A*. Equilibrium expenditure is $900 billion. If the price level decreases to 90, the aggregate expenditure curve shifts upward to *AE*$_2$, which intersects the 45° line at point *C*. Equilibrium expenditure is $1,100 billion.

We've just seen that when the price level changes, other things remaining the same, the *AE* curve shifts and the equilibrium expenditure changes. And when the price level changes, other things remaining the same, there is a movement along the *AD* curve. Figure 23.10(b) shows these movements along the *AD* curve. At a price level of 110, the aggregate quantity of goods and services demanded is $1,000 billion—point *B* on the *AD* curve. If the price level rises to 130, the aggregate quantity of goods and services demanded decreases to $900 billion. There is a movement along the *AD* curve to point *A*. If the price level falls to 90, the aggregate quantity of goods and services demanded increases to $1,100 billion. There is a movement along the *AD* curve to point *C*.

Each point on the *AD* curve corresponds to a point of equilibrium expenditure. The equilibrium expenditure points *A, B*, and *C* in Fig. 23.10(a) correspond to the points *A, B*, and *C* on the *AD* curve in Fig. 23.10(b).

A change in the price level, other things remaining the same, shifts the *AE* curve and brings a movement along the *AD* curve. A change in any other influence on aggregate planned expenditure shifts *both* the *AE* curve and the *AD* curve. For example, an increase in investment or in exports increases both aggregate planned expenditure and aggregate demand and shifts both the *AE* curve and the *AD* curve. Figure 23.11 illustrates the effect of such an increase.

Initially, the aggregate expenditure curve is *AE*$_0$ in part (a) and the aggregate demand curve is *AD*$_0$ in part (b). The price level is 110, real GDP is $1,000 billion, and the economy is at point *A* in both parts of the figure. Now suppose that investment increases by $100 billion. At a constant price level of 110, the aggregate expenditure curve shifts upward by $100 billion to *AE*$_1$. This curve intersects the 45° line at an equilibrium expenditure of $1,200 billion (point *B*).

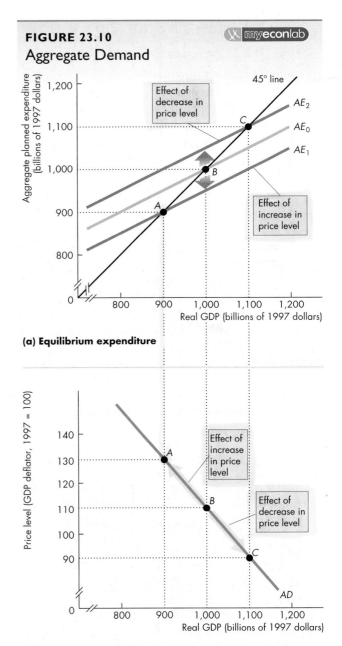

FIGURE 23.10
Aggregate Demand

(a) Equilibrium expenditure

(b) Aggregate demand

A change in the price level *shifts* the *AE* curve and results in a *movement along* the *AD* curve. When the price level is 110, the *AE* curve is *AE*$_0$ and equilibrium expenditure is $1,000 billion at point *B*. When the price level rises to 130, the *AE* curve is *AE*$_1$ and equilibrium expenditure is $900 billion at point *A*. When the price level falls to 90, the *AE* curve is *AE*$_2$ and equilibrium expenditure is $1,100 billion at point *C*. Points *A, B*, and *C* on the *AD* curve in part (b) correspond to the equilibrium expenditure points *A, B*, and *C* in part (a).

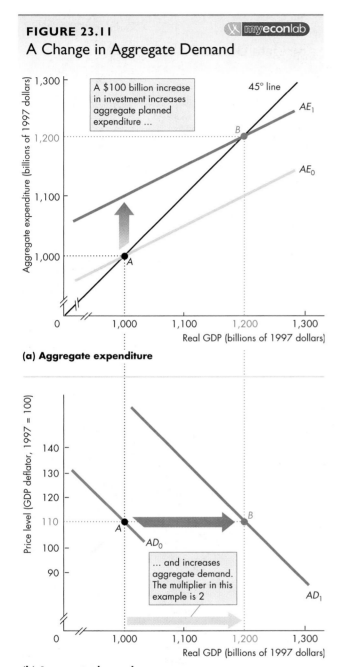

FIGURE 23.11   ⓧ myeconlab

A Change in Aggregate Demand

(a) **Aggregate expenditure**

(b) **Aggregate demand**

The price level is 110. When the aggregate expenditure curve is AE_0 (part a), the aggregate demand curve is AD_0 (part b). An increase in autonomous expenditure shifts the AE curve upward to AE_1. In the new equilibrium, real GDP is $1,200 billion (at point B). Because the quantity of real GDP demanded at a price level of 110 increases to $1,200 billion, the AD curve shifts rightward to AD_1.

This equilibrium expenditure of $1,200 billion is the aggregate quantity of goods and services demanded at a price level of 110, as shown by point B in part (b). Point B lies on a new aggregate demand curve. The aggregate demand curve has shifted rightward to AD_1.

But how do we know by how much the AD curve shifts? The multiplier determines the answer. The larger the multiplier, the larger is the shift in the AD curve that results from a given change in autonomous expenditure. In this example, the multiplier is 2. A $100 billion increase in investment produces a $200 billion increase in the aggregate quantity of goods and services demanded at each price level. That is, a $100 billion increase in autonomous expenditure shifts the AD curve rightward by $200 billion.

A decrease in autonomous expenditure shifts the AE curve downward and shifts the AD curve leftward. You can see these effects by reversing the change that we've just described. If the economy is initially at point B on the aggregate expenditure curve AE_1, the aggregate demand curve is AD_1. A decrease in autonomous expenditure shifts the aggregate planned expenditure curve downward to AE_0. The aggregate quantity of goods and services demanded decreases from $1,200 billion to $1,000 billion, and the aggregate demand curve shifts leftward to AD_0.

Let's summarize what we have just discovered:

If some factor other than a change in the price level increases autonomous expenditure, the AE curve shifts upward and the AD curve shifts rightward.

The size of the AD curve shift depends on the change in autonomous expenditure and the multiplier.

Equilibrium GDP and the Price Level

In Chapter 22, we learned that aggregate demand and short-run aggregate supply determine equilibrium real GDP and the price level. We've now put aggregate demand under a more powerful microscope and have discovered that a change in investment (or in any component of autonomous expenditure) changes aggregate demand and shifts the aggregate demand curve. The magnitude of the shift depends on the multiplier. But whether a change in autonomous expenditure results ultimately in a change in real GDP, a change in the price level, or a combination of the two depends on aggregate supply. There are two time frames to consider: the short run and the long run. First we'll see what happens in the short run.

An Increase in Aggregate Demand in the Short Run Figure 23.12 describes the economy. In part (a), the aggregate expenditure curve is AE_0 and equilibrium expenditure is $1,000 billion—point A. In part (b), aggregate demand is AD_0 and the short-run aggregate supply curve is SAS. (Chapter 22, pp. 509–510 explains the SAS curve.) Equilibrium is at point A, where the aggregate demand and short-run aggregate supply curves intersect. The price level is 110, and real GDP is $1,000 billion.

Now suppose that investment increases by $100 billion. With the price level fixed at 110, the aggregate expenditure curve shifts upward to AE_1. Equilibrium expenditure increases to $1,200 billion—point B in part (a). In part (b), the aggregate demand curve shifts rightward by $200 billion, from AD_0 to AD_1. How far the aggregate demand curve shifts is determined by the multiplier when the price level is fixed.

But with this new aggregate demand curve, the price level does not remain fixed. The price level rises, and as it does so, the aggregate expenditure curve shifts downward. The short-run equilibrium occurs when the aggregate expenditure curve has shifted downward to AE_2 and the new aggregate demand curve, AD_1, intersects the short-run aggregate supply curve. Real GDP is $1,130 billion, and the price level is 123 (at point C).

When price level effects are taken into account, the increase in investment still has a multiplier effect on real GDP, but the multiplier effect is smaller than it would be if the price level were fixed. The steeper the slope of the SAS curve, the larger is the increase in the price level and the smaller is the multiplier effect on real GDP.

An Increase in Aggregate Demand in the Long Run Figure 23.13 illustrates the long-run effect of an increase in aggregate demand. In the long run, real GDP equals potential GDP and the economy is at full employment. Potential GDP is $1,000 billion, and the long-run aggregate supply curve is LAS. Initially, the economy is at point A (parts a and b).

Investment increases by $100 billion. The aggregate expenditure curve shifts to AE_1, and the aggregate demand curve shifts to AD_1. With no change in the price level, the economy would move to point B and real GDP would increase to $1,200 billion. But in the short run, the price level rises to 123 and real GDP increases to only $1,130 billion. With the higher price level, the AE curve shifts from AE_1 to AE_2. The econ-

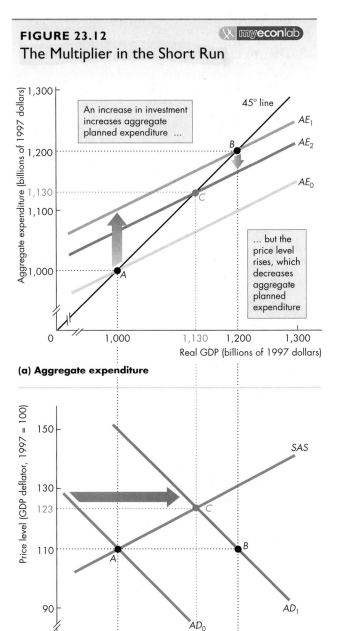

FIGURE 23.12

The Multiplier in the Short Run

(a) Aggregate expenditure

(b) Aggregate demand

An increase in investment shifts the AE curve from AE_0 to AE_1 (part a) and shifts the AD curve from AD_0 to AD_1 (part b). The price level does not remain at 110 but rises, and the higher price level shifts the AE curve downward from AE_1 to AE_2. The economy moves to point C in both parts. In the short run, when prices are flexible, the multiplier effect is smaller than when the price level is fixed.

FIGURE 23.13

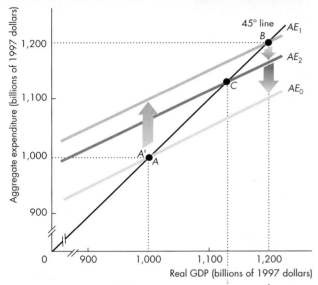

The Multiplier in the Long Run

(a) Aggregate expenditure

(b) Aggregate demand

Starting from point A, an increase in investment shifts the AE curve to AE_1 and shifts the AD curve to AD_1. In the short run, the economy moves to point C. In the long run, the money wage rate rises, which shifts the SAS curve to SAS_1. The price level rises, the AE curve shifts back to AE_0, and real GDP decreases. The economy moves to point A'. In the long run, the multiplier is zero.

omy is now in a short-run equilibrium at point C.

Real GDP is now above potential GDP. The labour force is more than fully employed, and shortages of labour increase the money wage rate. The higher money wage rate increases costs, which decreases short-run aggregate supply and shifts the SAS curve leftward to SAS_1. The price level rises further, and real GDP decreases. There is a movement along AD_1, and the AE curve shifts downward from AE_2 towards AE_0. When the money wage rate and the price level have increased by the same percentage, real GDP is again equal to potential GDP and the economy is at point A'. In the long run, the multiplier is zero.

REVIEW QUIZ

1 How does a change in the price level influence the AE curve and the AD curve?

2 If autonomous expenditure increases with no change in the price level, what happens to the AE curve and the AD curve? Which curve shifts by an amount that is determined by the multiplier and why?

3 How does real GDP change in the short run when there is an increase in autonomous expenditure? Does real GDP change by the same amount as the change in aggregate demand? Why or why not?

4 How does real GDP change in the long run when there is an increase in autonomous expenditure? Does real GDP change by the same amount as the change in aggregate demand? Why or why not?

myeconlab Study Plan 23.4

◆ You are now ready to apply what you've learned about aggregate expenditure fluctuations and study the role of fiscal policy in smoothing the business cycle. That is the topic of Chapter 24, in which we study the effects of government expenditures, taxes, and the government deficit.

But before you leave the current topic, look at *Reading Between the Lines* on pp. 556–557, which looks at the rapid expansion of real GDP that occurred in Canada during the first half of 2005.

The Aggregate Expenditure Multiplier in Action

CALGARY HERALD, 1 JULY 2005

Spring economic rebound stronger than expected: Increased oilsand production boosts activity

The Canadian economy was off to a hot start this spring, with a stronger than expected rebound in growth in April and a record surge in homes sales in May. Economic activity bounced back 0.4 per cent in April after declining 0.1 per cent in March, boosted by increased oilsands production, an end to a student strike in Quebec, and strong auto sales, Statistics Canada reported Thursday.

... Meanwhile, in its report on economic growth, Statistics Canada noted milder than usual weather in April in most parts of the country and in the northern U.S. lowered the demand for natural gas and reduced the output of related activities. Mining activity increased on the strength of higher output by copper, nickel, lead and zinc ore mines, while a strike brought iron ore mining. Retail and wholesale sales, meanwhile, were boosted by new car sales, although the gain in retail sales gains was widespread. Manufacturing output increased slightly, regaining some of the ground lost in February and March although auto production continued to decline. While sales of existing homes were strong in May, residential construction in April fell for the fourth straight month. "Since the beginning of the year, residential construction activity has decreased 3.3 percent," Statistics Canada noted. Non-residential building construction also dipped by 0.1 percent.

Material reprinted with the express permission of CANWEST NEWS SERVICE, a CanWest Partnership.

Essence of the Story

■ In 2005, Canada had record household spending, a 30-year low in its unemployment rate, and the highest ever company profits.

■ Real GDP was expected to grow by 3 percent—up from 2.6 percent a year earlier.

■ Canada had the second-best performing economy in the G7.

■ Oil production has brought a burst of investment.

■ A government budget surplus, low inflation, and low interest rates are boosting confidence and stimulating growth.

Economic Analysis

■ During the first half of 2005, real GDP increased by $15 billion.

■ The table shows the amounts by which the components of aggregate expenditure increased.

■ On the average, an additional dollar of real GDP brings about 66 cents of additional consumption expenditure and about 33 cents of additional imports.

■ Using these two values, the slope of the *AE* curve is 0.33 and we can calculate the multiplier: $1/(1 - \text{Slope of } AE \text{ curve})$ $= 1/(1 - 0.33)$ $= 1/0.67 = 1.5$.

■ The increase in consumption expenditure was $14 billion. Of this, $10 billion was induced by the increase in real GDP. The rest was an increase in autonomous consumption—the consumption function shifted upward during the first half of 2005 by $4 billion.

■ The increase in autonomous consumption most likely resulted from low real interest rates that made consumers willing to borrow to finance large purchases of durable goods.

■ The increase in imports was $8 billion and about $5 billion was in-duced by the $15 billion increase in real GDP and the rest came from an increase in autonomous imports—an upward shift in the import function of $3 billion.

■ The increases in fixed investment, government expenditures, exports, and investment in inventories sum to $9 billion.

■ Adding the increase in autonomous consumption, $4 billion, and subtracting the increase in autonomous imports, $3 billion, gives an increase in autonomous expenditure of $10 billion.

■ Based on the assumptions just described, Fig. 1 shows the *AE* curve in the fourth quarter of 2004, AE_0, and in the second quarter of 2005, AE_1.

■ The *AE* curve shifted upward by $10 billion (the assumed increase in autonomous expenditure), and real GDP increased from $1,037 billion to $1,052 billion, an increase of $15 billion.

■ Check that the increase in real GDP equals the increase in autonomous expenditure, $10 billion, multiplied by 1.5, the multiplier.

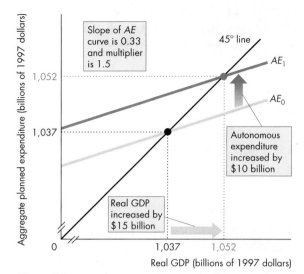

Figure 1 Increase in autonomous expenditure and multiplier

Item	Increase (billions of 1997 dollars)
Consumption expenditure	+14
Fixed investment	+8
Government expenditure	+4
Exports	+7
minus Imports	−8
Investment in inventories	−10
Real GDP	+15

Mathematical Note
The Algebra of the Multiplier

THIS NOTE EXPLAINS THE MULTIPLIER IN GREATER detail than that presented on p. 548. We begin by defining the symbols we need:

- Aggregate planned expenditure, AE
- Real GDP, Y
- Consumption expenditure, C
- Investment, I
- Government expenditures, G
- Exports, X
- Imports, M
- Net taxes, NT
- Disposable income, YD
- Autonomous consumption expenditure, a
- Marginal propensity to consume, b
- Marginal propensity to import, m
- Marginal tax rate, t
- Autonomous expenditure, A

Aggregate Expenditure

Aggregate planned expenditure (AE) is the sum of the planned amounts of consumption expenditure (C), investment (I), government expenditures (G), and exports (X) minus the planned amount of imports (M). That is,

$$AE = C + I + G + X - M.$$

Consumption Function Consumption expenditure (C) depends on disposable income (YD), and we write the consumption function as

$$C = a + bYD.$$

Disposable income (YD) equals real GDP minus net taxes ($Y - NT$). So if we replace YD with ($Y - NT$), the consumption function becomes

$$C = a + b(Y - NT).$$

Net taxes equal real GDP (Y) multiplied by the marginal tax rate (t). That is,

$$NT = tY.$$

Use this equation in the previous one to obtain

$$C = a + b(1 - t)Y.$$

This equation describes consumption expenditure as a function of real GDP.

Import Function Imports depend on real GDP, and the import function is

$$M = mY.$$

Aggregate Expenditure Curve Use the consumption function and the import function to replace C and M in the aggregate planned expenditure equation. That is,

$$AE = a + b(1 - t)Y + I + G + X - mY.$$

Collect the terms on the right side of the equation that involve Y to obtain

$$AE = (a + I + G + X) + [b(1 - t) - m]Y.$$

Autonomous expenditure (A) is ($a + I + G + X$), and the slope of the AE curve is $[b(1 - t) - m]$. So the equation for the AE curve, which is shown in Fig. 1, is

$$AE = A + [b(1 - t) - m]Y.$$

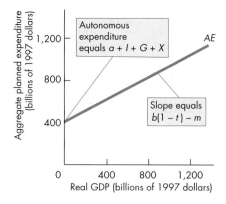

Figure 1 The *AE* curve

Equilibrium Expenditure

Equilibrium expenditure occurs when aggregate planned expenditure (AE) equals real GDP (Y). That is,

$$AE = Y.$$

In Fig. 2, the scales of the x-axis (real GDP) and the y-axis (aggregate planned expenditure) are identical, so the 45° line shows the points at which aggregate planned expenditure equals real GDP.

Figure 2 shows the point of equilibrium expenditure at the intersection of the AE curve and the 45° line.

To calculate equilibrium expenditure and real GDP, we solve the equations for the AE curve and the 45° line for the quantity Y. So starting with

$$AE = A + [b(1 - t) - m]Y$$

$$AE = Y,$$

replace AE with Y in the AE equation to obtain

$$Y = A + [b(1 - t) - m]Y.$$

The solution for Y is

$$Y = \frac{1}{1 - [b(1 - t) - m]}A.$$

The Multiplier

The multiplier equals the change in equilibrium expenditure and real GDP (Y) that results from a change in autonomous expenditure (A) divided by the change in autonomous expenditure.

A change in autonomous expenditure (ΔA) changes equilibrium expenditure and real GDP (ΔY) by

$$\Delta Y = \frac{1}{1 - [b(1 - t) - m]}\Delta A.$$

So

$$\text{Multiplier} = \frac{1}{1 - [b(1 - t) - m]}.$$

The size of the multiplier depends on the slope of the AE curve, $b(1 - t) - m$. The larger the slope, the larger is the multiplier. So the multiplier is larger,

- The greater the marginal propensity to consume (b)
- The smaller the marginal tax rate (t)
- The smaller the marginal propensity to import (m)

An economy with no imports and no marginal taxes has $m = 0$ and $t = 0$. In this special case, the multiplier equals $1/(1 - b)$. If b is 0.75, then the multiplier is 4, as shown in Fig. 3.

In an economy with taxes and imports, if $t = 0.2$, $m = 0.1$, and $b = 0.75$, the multiplier is $1 \div [1 - 0.75(1 - 0.2) - 0.1]$, which equals 2.

Make up some more examples to show the effects of b, t, and m on the multiplier.

Figure 2 Equilibrium expenditure

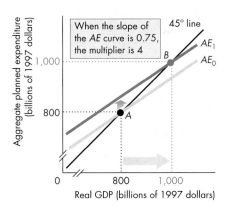

Figure 3 The multiplier

SUMMARY

KEY POINTS

Expenditure Plans and GDP (pp. 536–541)

- When the price level is fixed, expenditure plans determine real GDP.
- Consumption expenditure is determined by disposable income, and the marginal propensity to consume (*MPC*) determines the change in consumption expenditure brought about by a change in disposable income. Real GDP is the main influence on disposable income.
- Imports are determined by real GDP, and the marginal propensity to import determines the change in imports brought about by a change in real GDP.

Equilibrium Expenditure at a Fixed Price Level (pp. 541–545)

- Aggregate *planned* expenditure depends on real GDP.
- Equilibrium expenditure occurs when aggregate planned expenditure equals actual expenditure and real GDP.

The Multiplier (pp. 546–551)

- The multiplier is the magnified effect of a change in autonomous expenditure on real GDP.
- The multiplier equals 1 divided by (1 minus the slope of the *AE* curve).
- The multiplier is influenced by the marginal propensity to consume, the marginal propensity to import, and the marginal tax rate.

The Multiplier and the Price Level (pp. 551–555)

- The *AD* curve is the relationship between the quantity of real GDP demanded and the price level, other things remaining the same.
- The *AE* curve is the relationship between aggregate planned expenditure and real GDP, other things remaining the same.

- At a given price level, there is a given *AE* curve. A change in the price level changes aggregate planned expenditure and shifts the *AE* curve. A change in the price level also creates a movement along the *AD* curve.
- A change in autonomous expenditure that is not caused by a change in the price level shifts the *AE* curve and shifts the *AD* curve. The magnitude of the shift of the *AD* curve depends on the multiplier and on the change in autonomous expenditure.
- The multiplier decreases as the price level changes and the multiplier in the long run is zero.

KEY FIGURES

KEY TERMS

PROBLEMS

Go to **myeconlab** for solutions to odd-
numbered problems and additional exercises.

1. You are given the following information about
   the economy of Heron Island:

Disposable income (millions of dollars per year)	Consumption expenditure (millions of dollars per year)
0	5
10	10
20	15
30	20

   Calculate Heron Island's

   a. Marginal propensity to consume.
   b. Saving at each level of disposable income.
   c. Marginal propensity to save.

2. You are given the following information about
   the economy of Spendthrift Island:

Disposable income (millions of dollars per year)	Saving (millions of dollars per year)
0	−10
50	−5
100	0
150	5
200	10

   a. Calculate the marginal propensity to save.
   b. Calculate consumption at each level of dis-
      posable income.
   c. Calculate the marginal propensity to consume.
   d. Why is the island called "Spendthrift"?

3. Turtle Island has no imports, exports, or taxes,
   and the price level is fixed. The figure shows the
   components of aggregate planned expenditure.

   a. What is autonomous expenditure?
   b. What is the marginal propensity to consume?
   c. What is aggregate planned expenditure when
      real GDP is $6 billion?
   d. If real GDP is $2 billion, what is happening
      to inventories?
   e. If real GDP is $6 billion, what is happening
      to inventories?
   f. What is the multiplier?

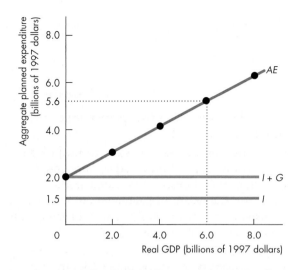

4. The spreadsheet lists the components of aggregate planned expenditure in Spice Bay. The
   numbers are in billions of cloves, the currency
   of Spice Bay.

	A	B	C	D	E	F	G
1		Y	C	I	G	X	M
2	A	100	110	50	60	60	15
3	B	200	170	50	60	60	30
4	C	300	230	50	60	60	45
5	D	400	290	50	60	60	60
6	E	500	350	50	60	60	75
7	F	600	410	50	60	60	90

   In Spice Bay,

   a. What is autonomous expenditure?
   b. What is the marginal propensity to con-
      sume?
   c. What is aggregate planned expenditure when
      real GDP is 200 billion cloves?
   d. If real GDP is 200 billion cloves, what is
      happening to inventories?
   e. If real GDP is 500 billion cloves, what is
      happening to inventories?
   f. What is the multiplier in Spice Bay?

5. You are given the following information about
   the economy of Zeeland: Autonomous consumption expenditure is $100 billion, and the
   marginal propensity to consume is 0.9.
   Investment is $460 billion, government expen-
   ditures on goods and services are $400 billion,
   and net taxes are a constant $400 billion—they
   do not vary with income.

a. What is the consumption function?

b. What is the equation that describes the *AE* curve?

c. Calculate equilibrium expenditure.

d. If investment falls to $360 billion, what is the change in equilibrium expenditure and what is the size of the multiplier?

6. You are given the following information about the economy of Antarctica: Autonomous consumption expenditure is $1 billion, and the marginal propensity to consume is 0.8. Investment is $5 billion, government expenditures on goods and services are $4 billion, and net taxes are a constant $4 billion—they do not vary with income.

a. What is the consumption function?

b. What is the equation that describes the *AE* curve?

c. Calculate equilibrium expenditure.

d. If investment falls to $3 billion, what is the change in equilibrium expenditure and what is the size of the multiplier?

7. Suppose that in problem 5, the price level is 100 and real GDP equals potential GDP.

a. If investment increases by $100 billion, what happens to the quantity of real GDP demanded?

b. In the short run, does equilibrium real GDP increase by more than, less than, or the same amount as the increase in the quantity of real GDP demanded?

c. In the long run, does equilibrium real GDP increase by more than, less than, or the same amount as the increase in the quantity of real GDP demanded?

d. In the short run, does the price level in Zeeland rise, fall, or remain unchanged?

e. In the long run, does the price level in Zeeland rise, fall, or remain unchanged?

8. Suppose that in problem 6, the price level is 100 and real GDP equals potential GDP.

a. If investment increases by $1 billion, what happens to the quantity of real GDP demanded?

b. In the long run, does equilibrium real GDP increase by more than, less than, or the same amount as the increase in the quantity of real GDP demanded?

c. In the short run, does the price level in Antarctica rise, fall, or remain unchanged?

CRITICAL THINKING

1. Study *Reading Between the Lines* on pp. 556–557 and then:

a. Describe the changes in the components of aggregate expenditure during the first half of 2005.

b. Suppose that the assumptions about the extent to which a change in real GDP induces a change in consumption expenditure and imports on p. 557 are incorrect and that the slope of the *AE* curve is 0.3, not 0.33. What does this imply about the change in autonomous expenditure during the first half of 2005? What does it imply about the magnitude of the multiplier?

c. Draw the *AE* curves for the fourth quarter of 2004 and second quarter of 2005 on the assumption that the slope of the *AE* curve is 0.3.

WEB EXERCISES

Use the links on myeconlab **to work the following exercise.**

1. Obtain data on real GDP per person and consumption as a percentage of real GDP for Canada, China, South Africa, and Mexico since 1960.

a. In a spreadsheet, multiply your real GDP data by the consumption percentage and divide by 100 to obtain data on real consumption expenditure per person.

b. Make graphs like Fig. 23.4 that show the relationship between consumption and real GDP for these four countries.

c. On the basis of the numbers you've obtained, in which country do you expect the multiplier to be largest (other things being equal)?

d. What other data would you need to be able to calculate the multipliers for these countries?

2. You are a research assistant in the office of the Prime Minister. Draft a note for the Prime Minister that explains the power and limitations of the multiplier. The Prime Minister wants only 250 words of crisp, clear, jargon-free explanation together with a lively example.

Fiscal Policy

CHAPTER 24

Balancing Acts on Parliament Hill

In 2004, the federal government spent 15.5 cents of every dollar that Canadians earned and collected 16 cents of every dollar earned in taxes. What are the effects of government spending and taxes on the economy? Does a dollar spent by the government have the same effect as a dollar spent by someone else? Does it create jobs, or does it destroy them?

Do taxes harm employment and economic growth?

For many years during the 1980s and 1990s, the government had a large budget deficit and ran up a debt. During the late 1990s, spending cuts brought the deficit under control and created a surplus. But in 2004, your share of government debt stood at $16,500. Does it matter if the government doesn't balance its books? What are the effects of an ongoing government deficit and accumulating debt? Do they slow economic growth? Do they impose a burden on future generations—on you and your children? Was the deficit-cutting exercise of the late 1990s beneficial to our economy?

◆ These are the fiscal policy issues that you will study in this chapter. We'll begin by describing the federal budget and the process of creating it. We'll also look at the recent history of the budget. We'll then use the multiplier analysis of Chapter 23 and the *AS–AD* model of Chapter 22 to study the effects of the budget on the economy. At the end of the chapter, in *Reading Between the Lines*, we'll look at the federal government's winter heating budget measures.

After studying this chapter, you will be able to

- Describe how federal and provincial budgets are created and describe their recent history
- Distinguish between automatic and discretionary fiscal policy and define and explain the fiscal policy multipliers
- Explain the effects of fiscal policy in both the short run and the long run
- Distinguish between and explain the demand-side and supply-side effects of fiscal policy

Government Budgets

THE ANNUAL STATEMENT OF THE OUTLAYS AND revenues of the government of Canada, together with the laws and regulations that approve and support those outlays and revenues, make up the **federal budget**. Similarly, a **provincial budget** is an annual statement of the revenues and outlays of a provincial government, together with the laws and regulations that approve or support those revenues and outlays.

Before World War II, the federal budget had no purpose other than to finance the business of government. But since the late 1940s, the federal budget has assumed a second purpose, which is to pursue the government's fiscal policy. **Fiscal policy** is the use of the federal budget to achieve macroeconomic objectives such as full employment, sustained long-term economic growth, and price level stability. Our focus is this second purpose.

Budget Making

The federal government and Parliament make fiscal policy. The process begins with long drawn-out consultations between the Minister of Finance and Department of Finance officials and their counterparts in the provincial governments. These discussions deal with programs that are funded and operated jointly by the two levels of government. The Minister also consults with business and consumer groups on a wide range of issues.

After all these consultations, and using economic projections made by Department of Finance economists, the Minister develops a set of proposals, which are discussed in Cabinet and which become government policy. The Minister finally presents a budget plan to Parliament, which debates the plan and enacts the laws necessary to implement it.

Highlights of the 2005 Budget

Table 24.1 shows the main items in the federal budget. The numbers are projected amounts for the fiscal year beginning on April 1, 2005. The three main items shown are

- Revenues
- Outlays
- Budget balance

TABLE 24.1   The Federal Budget in 2005–06

Item	Projections (billions of dollars)	
Revenues	**200**	
Personal income taxes		94
Corporate income taxes		29
Indirect taxes		66
Investment income		11
Outlays	**196**	
Transfer payments		119
Expenditures on goods and services		42
Debt interest		35
Budget balance	**+4**	

Sources of data: Department of Finance *Budget Plan* 2005 and Statistics Canada, CANSIM Table 183–0004.

Revenues Revenues are the federal government's receipts, which in the 2005–06 budget were projected at $200 billion. These revenues come from four sources:

1. Personal income taxes
2. Corporate income taxes
3. Indirect taxes
4. Investment income

The largest revenue source is *personal income taxes*, which in 2005–06 were projected to be $94 billion. These are the taxes paid by individuals on their incomes. The second largest source of revenue is *indirect taxes*, which in 2005–06 were projected to be $66 billion. These taxes include the Goods and Services Tax (the GST) and taxes on the sale of gasoline, alcoholic drinks, and a few other items. The smallest revenue sources are *corporate income taxes*, which are the taxes paid by companies on their profits, and *investment income*, which is the income from government enterprises and investments.

In 2005–06, corporate income taxes were projected to raise $29 billion and investment income was projected at $11 billion. Total federal government revenue in 2005–06 was projected at $200 billion.

Outlays Outlays are classified in three categories:

1. Transfer payments
2. Expenditures on goods and services
3. Debt interest

The largest outlay, and by a big margin, is *transfer payments*. Transfer payments are payments to individuals, businesses, other levels of government, and the rest of the world. In 2005–06, this item was $119 billion. It includes unemployment cheques and welfare payments to individuals, farm subsidies, grants to provincial and local governments, aid to developing countries, and dues to international organizations such as the United Nations.

Expenditures on goods and services are expenditures on final goods and services, and in 2005–06 this item totalled $42 billion. These expenditures include those on national defence, computers for Canada Revenue Agency, government cars, and highways. This component of the federal budget is *government expenditures on goods and services* that appears in the circular flow of expenditure and income and in the national income and product accounts (see Chapter 20, pp. 467–468).

Debt interest is the interest on the government debt. In 2005–06, this item was $35 billion—almost as much as government expenditures on goods and services. This interest payment is large because the government has a large debt—$524 billion. This large debt has arisen because, until recently, the federal government has had a large and persistent budget deficit.

Budget Balance The government's budget balance is equal to its revenues minus its outlays. That is,

$$\text{Budget balance} = \text{Revenues} - \text{Outlays}.$$

If revenues exceed outlays, the government has a **budget surplus**. If outlays exceed revenues, the government has a **budget deficit**. If revenues equal outlays, the government has a **balanced budget**. In 2005–06, with projected outlays of $196 billion and revenues of $200 billion, the government projected a budget surplus of $4 billion.

How typical is the federal budget of 2005–06? Let's look at its recent history.

The Budget in Historical Perspective

Figure 24.1 shows the government's revenues, outlays, and budget balance since 1961. To get a better sense of the magnitudes of these items, they are shown as percentages of GDP. Expressing them in this way lets us see how large the government is

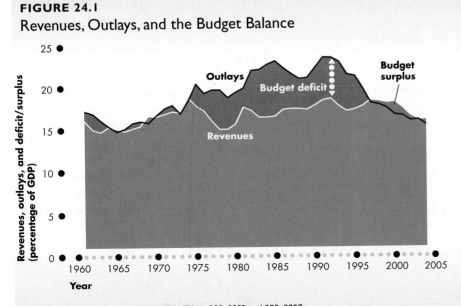

FIGURE 24.1

Revenues, Outlays, and the Budget Balance

The figure records the federal government's revenues, outlays, and budget balance as percentages of GDP from 1961 to 2004. During the 1960s, outlays and revenues increased. During the late 1970s and through the 1980s, outlays continued to rise but revenues fell, so a budget deficit arose. During the 1990s, spending cuts eliminated the budget deficit and after 1997, the federal government had a budget surplus.

Source of data: Statistics Canada, CANSIM Tables 380–0002 and 380–0007.

relative to the size of the economy, and also helps us to study *changes* in the scale of government over time. You can think of the percentages of GDP as telling you how many cents of each dollar that Canadians earn get paid to and spent by the government.

During the 1960s, government expanded but outlays and revenues kept pace with each other. But from 1971 through 1996, the federal budget was in deficit, and the average deficit over these years was 4.2 percent of GDP. The deficit climbed to a peak of 6.6 percent of GDP in 1985. It then decreased through the rest of the 1980s. During the recession of 1990–1991, the deficit increased again. The deficit remained above 4 percent of GDP for most of the 1980s and early 1990s.

Only in 1997 did the federal government finally eradicate its deficit. And it did so by cutting outlays, especially transfer payments to provincial governments.

Why did the government deficit grow during the early 1980s and remain high through the early 1990s? The immediate answer is that outlays increased while revenues remained relatively constant. But which components of outlays increased? And did all the sources of revenues remain constant?

To answer these questions, we need to examine each of the sources of revenues and outlays in detail. We'll begin by looking at the sources of revenues.

Revenues Figure 24.2 shows the components of government revenues since 1961. Total revenues have no strong trend. They increased through the 1960s and again through the 1980s. But they decreased during the 1970s and the first-half of the 2000s. The main source of the fluctuations in revenues was personal income taxes. Indirect taxes also fluctuated but corporate income taxes and investment income were more stable than the other two revenue components.

The increase in personal income taxes during the 1980s resulted from increases in tax rates in successive budgets.

Indirect taxes decreased during the 1990s mainly because an old Federal Sales Tax was replaced by the Goods and Services Tax or GST. Initially, this switch maintained revenues at a constant level, but gradually, the revenue from indirect taxes (as a percentage of GDP) fell.

Outlays Figure 24.3 shows the components of government outlays since 1961. Total outlays increased steadily from 1971 through 1985, were relatively flat through 1993, and then decreased sharply after 1993. The main source of the changing trend in outlays is transfer payments to provincial governments. These payments swelled during the 1980s and were cut drastically during the late 1990s.

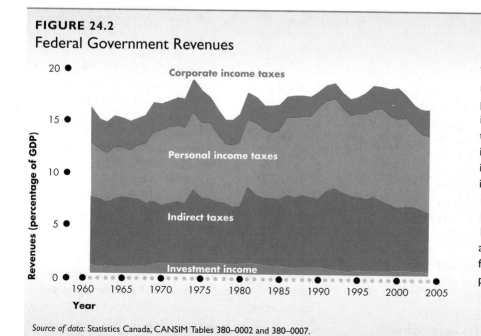

FIGURE 24.2
Federal Government Revenues

The figure shows four main components of government revenues (as percentages of GDP): personal income taxes, corporate income taxes, indirect taxes, and investment income. Revenues from personal income taxes fluctuated most. They increased during the 1960s and early 1970s, decreased during the late 1970s, increased again during the 1980s and 1990s, and then decreased again during the 2000s. Indirect taxes fell after 1990. The other two components of revenues remained steady.

Source of data: Statistics Canada, CANSIM Tables 380–0002 and 380–0007.

FIGURE 24.3
Federal Government Outlays

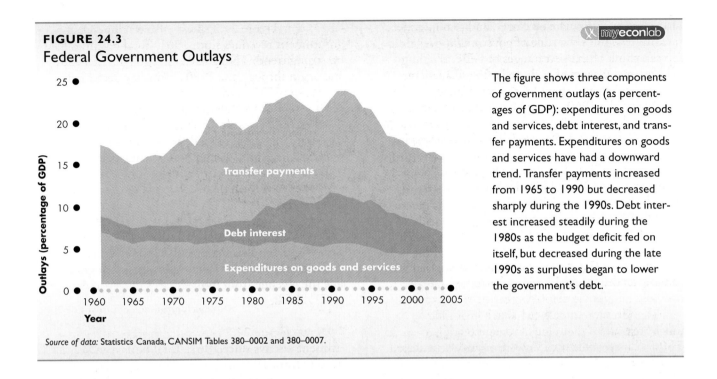

The figure shows three components of government outlays (as percentages of GDP): expenditures on goods and services, debt interest, and transfer payments. Expenditures on goods and services have had a downward trend. Transfer payments increased from 1965 to 1990 but decreased sharply during the 1990s. Debt interest increased steadily during the 1980s as the budget deficit fed on itself, but decreased during the late 1990s as surpluses began to lower the government's debt.

Source of data: Statistics Canada, CANSIM Tables 380–0002 and 380–0007.

To understand the changes in debt interest, we need to see the connection between the budget deficit and government debt.

Deficit and Debt The government borrows to finance its deficit. And **government debt** is the total amount of government borrowing. It is the sum of past deficits minus the sum of past surpluses. When the government has a deficit, its debt increases. Once a persistent deficit emerged during the 1980s, the deficit began to feed on itself. The deficit led to increased borrowing; increased borrowing led to larger debt and larger interest payments; and larger interest payments led to a larger deficit and yet larger debt. That is the story of the increasing deficit of the 1980s.

Figure 24.4 shows the history of government debt since 1940. By the end of World War II, debt (as a percentage of GDP) was at an all-time high of 113 percent. Huge wartime deficits had increased debt to the point that it exceeded GDP. Post-war budget surpluses lowered the debt to GDP ratio through 1974, by which time it stood at 18 percent, its lowest point since World War II. Small deficits increased the debt to GDP ratio slightly through the 1970s, and large deficits increased it dramatically between 1981 and 1986. During the late 1980s, the

FIGURE 24.4
Federal Government Debt

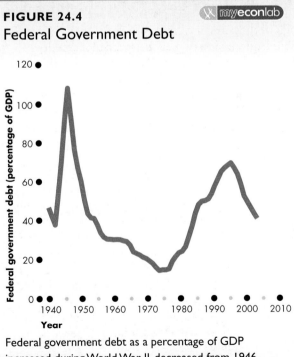

Federal government debt as a percentage of GDP increased during World War II, decreased from 1946 through 1974, increased through 1997, and then began to decrease again.

Source of data: Statistics Canada, CANSIM Tables 380–0002 and 385–0010.

ratio continued to increase but at a more moderate rate. It grew quickly again during the 1990–1991 recession, but its growth rate slowed after 1995 and debt interest decreased as a percentage of GDP.

Debt and Capital When individuals and businesses incur debts, they usually do so to buy capital—assets that yield a return. In fact, the main point of debt is to enable people to buy assets that will earn a return that exceeds the interest paid on the debt. The government is similar to individuals and businesses in this regard. Some government expenditure is investment—the purchase of public capital that yields a return. Highways, major irrigation schemes, public schools and universities, public libraries, and the stock of national defence capital all yield a social rate of return that probably far exceeds the interest rate the government pays on its debt.

But government debt, which is $524 billion, is much larger than the value of the public capital stock. This fact means that some government debt has been incurred to finance public consumption expenditure.

Provincial and Local Government Budgets

The *total government* sector of Canada includes provincial and local governments as well as the federal government. In 2004, when federal government outlays were $196 billion, provincial and local government outlays were $246 billion and total government outlays were $442 billion. Most provincial and local government outlays are on public hospitals and public schools, colleges, and universities.

Provincial government outlays and revenue sources vary a great deal across the provinces. Figure 24.5 shows the range of variation. Part (a) shows outlays as a percentage of provincial GDP. You can see that outlays of Northern and Atlantic governments are greatest, and government outlays of Ontario, Alberta, British Columbia, and Saskatchewan are the least. Part (b) shows the sources of provincial revenues as a percentage of total outlays. The Northern and Atlantic provinces receive the largest transfers from the federal government, while Alberta, Ontario, Quebec, and British Columbia receive the least.

Figure 24.6 shows the revenues, outlays, and deficits of the federal government and of total government between 1961 and 2004.

You can see that federal government outlays and revenues and total government outlays and revenues

FIGURE 24.5
Provincial Government Budgets

(a) Outlays

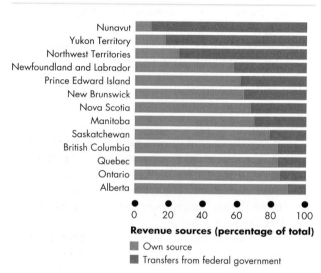

■ Own source
■ Transfers from federal government

(b) Revenues

Provincial government budgets vary a lot across the provinces. As a percentage of provincial GDP, outlays (part a) are highest in Northern and Atlantic Canada and lowest in Ontario, Alberta, British Columbia, and Saskatchewan. The Northern and Atlantic regions receive the largest share of revenues from the federal government (part b) while Alberta, Ontario, Quebec, and British Columbia receive the least.

Source of data: Statistics Canada, CANSIM Tables 384–0002 and 385–0002.

FIGURE 24.6
Total Government Budgets

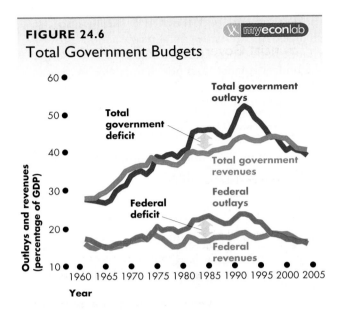

Total government is the sum of the federal, provincial, and local governments. Total government expanded from 1961 through the early 1990s and then shrank rapidly. Both the federal government and the provincial governments had large deficits during the 1980s but these deficits decreased after 1995 and then turned to surpluses.

Source of data: Statistics Canada, CANSIM Tables 380–0002 and 380–0007.

FIGURE 24.7
Government Deficits Around the World in 2005

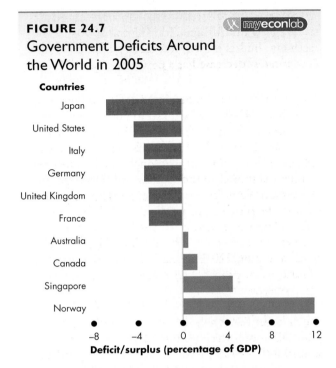

Governments in most countries had budget deficits in 2005. The largest ones were in Japan, the United States, Italy, and Germany. Australia, Canada, Singapore, and Norway had budget surpluses. As a percentage of GDP, Norways' surplus is huge.

Source of data: International Monetary Fund, *World Economic Outlook*, April 2005.

fluctuate in similar ways, but the total government is much larger than the federal government. In other words, the provincial and local governments are a large component of total government. You can also see that total government outlays fluctuate more than federal government outlays.

How does the Canadian government budget balance compare with budgets in other countries?

The Canadian Government Budget in Global Perspective

Is Canada unusual in having eliminated its budget deficit and now to be running a budget surplus? Do other countries have budget surpluses, or do they have budget deficits? Figure 24.7 answers these questions. In today's world, most countries have budget deficits. To compare countries, we measure the budget surplus or deficit as a percentage of GDP. The biggest deficit relative to GDP is found in Japan, where the deficit is almost 7 percent of GDP. The United States along with France, Italy, Germany, and

the United Kingdom also have budget deficits. Only a handful of countries, with Canada, have budget surpluses. But Norway has a huge surplus.

REVIEW QUIZ

1 What are the main items of government revenues and outlays?
2 Under what circumstances does the government have a budget surplus?
3 Explain the connection between a government budget deficit and a government debt.

 Study Plan 24.1

Your next task is to study the effects of the government's budget on the economy and learn about fiscal policy multipliers.

Fiscal Policy Multipliers

FISCAL POLICY ACTIONS CAN BE EITHER AUTO-matic or discretionary. **Automatic fiscal policy** is a change in fiscal policy that is triggered by the state of the economy. For example, an increase in unemployment triggers an automatic increase in payments to the unemployed. A fall in incomes triggers an automatic decrease in tax revenues. That is, this type of fiscal policy adjusts automatically. **Discretionary fiscal policy** is a policy action that is initiated by an act of Parliament. It requires a change in tax laws or in some spending program. For example, a cut in income tax rates and an increase in defence spending are discretionary fiscal policy actions. That is, discretionary fiscal policy is a deliberate policy action.

We begin by studying the effects of *discretionary* changes in government expenditures and taxes. To focus on the essentials, we'll initially study a model economy that is simpler than the one in which we live. In our model economy, there is no international trade and the taxes are autonomous. **Autonomous taxes** are taxes that do not vary with real GDP. The government fixes them, and they change when the government changes them. But they do not vary automatically with the state of the economy.

The main example of an autonomous tax is the *property tax*. This tax varies across individuals and depends on the value of the property a person occupies. But unlike the income tax, it does not change simply because a person's income changes.

We use autonomous taxes in our model economy because they make the principles we are studying easier to understand. Once we've grasped the principles, we'll explore our real economy with its international trade and income taxes—taxes that *do* vary with real GDP.

Like our real economy, the model economy we study is bombarded by spending fluctuations. Business investment in new buildings, plant and equipment, and inventories fluctuates because of swings in profit expectations and interest rates. These fluctuations set up multiplier effects that begin a recession or an expansion. If a recession takes hold, unemployment increases and incomes fall. If an expansion becomes too strong, inflationary pressures build up. To minimize the effects of these swings in spending, the government might change either its expenditures on goods and services or taxes. By changing either of these items, the government can influence aggregate expenditure and real GDP, but

the government's budget deficit or surplus also changes. An alternative fiscal policy action is to change both expenditures and taxes together so that the budget balance does not change. We are going to study the initial effects of these discretionary fiscal policy actions in the very short run when the price level is fixed. Each of these actions creates a multiplier effect on real GDP. These multipliers are the

- Government expenditures multiplier
- Autonomous tax multiplier

Government Expenditures Multiplier

The **government expenditures multiplier** is the magnification effect of a change in government expenditures on goods and services on equilibrium expenditure and real GDP.

Government expenditures are a component of aggregate expenditure. So when government expenditures on goods and services change, aggregate expenditure and real GDP change. The change in real GDP induces a change in consumption expenditure, which brings a further change in aggregate expenditure. A multiplier process ensues. This multiplier process is like the one described in Chapter 23 (pp. 546–549). Let's look at an example.

A Mackenzie Valley Pipeline Multiplier Canada's Arctic region is rich in natural gas. But to get that gas to Canadian and U.S. markets, a huge $6 billion pipeline would have to be built. Although it is a controversial project because of its potential impact on the environment, building a pipeline in this region would have a large multiplier effect. Construction workers would be hired who would spend much of their income in the Arctic region. Retail stores, schools, health-care centres, hotels and motels, and recreational facilities would open and hire yet more people. Some of the income earned by this second wave of workers would also be spent in the region. The Arctic economy would expand until aggregate planned expenditure again equalled aggregate income.

The Size of the Multiplier Our task is to find equilibrium expenditure and the change in real GDP when government expenditures change. Table 24.2 illustrates the government expenditures multiplier with a numerical example. The first data column lists various possible levels of real GDP. The second column shows *induced expenditures*—induced consump-

TABLE 24.2 The Government Expenditures Multiplier

	Real GDP (Y)	Induced expenditure (N)	Initial autonomous expenditure (A)	Initial aggregate planned expenditure (AE = N + A)	New autonomous expenditures (A')	New aggregate planned expenditure (AE' = N + A')
				(billions of dollars)		
A	900	525	400	925	450	975
B	1,000	600	400	1,000	450	1,050
C	1,100	675	400	1,075	450	1,125
D	1,200	750	400	1,150	450	1,200
E	1,300	825	400	1,225	450	1,275

tion expenditure minus imports. In this example, a $100 billion increase in real GDP induces a $75 billion increase in aggregate planned expenditure. For example when real GDP increases from $900 billion (row *A*) to $1,000 billion, (row *B*), induced expenditure increases from $525 billion to $600 billion. This relationship between real GDP and induced expenditure means that the *slope of the aggregate expenditure (AE) curve* is 0.75.

The third column shows the initial level of autonomous expenditure—investment plus government expenditures plus exports plus the autonomous component of consumption expenditure. In this example, autonomous expenditure is initially equal to $400 billion.

The next column shows the initial level of aggregate planned expenditure, which is the sum of induced expenditure and the initial level of autonomous expenditure.

Equilibrium expenditure and real GDP occur when aggregate planned expenditure equals actual expenditure. In this example, equilibrium expenditure is $1,000 billion (highlighted in row *B* of the table.)

The final two columns of the table show what happens when government expenditures increase by $50 billion. The new level of autonomous expenditure is $450 billion. And at each level of real GDP the new level of aggregate planned expenditure is $50 billion higher than the initial level. For example, at the initial real GDP of $1,000 billion (row *B*), aggregate planned expenditure increases to $1,050 billion.

Because at the initial equilibrium real GDP, aggregate planned expenditure exceeds real GDP, inventories decrease. So firms increase production. Output, incomes, and expenditure increase. Increased incomes bring a further increase in induced expenditure, which is less than the increase in income. Aggregate planned expenditure increases and eventually, a new equilibrium is reached. The new equilibrium is at a real GDP of $1,200 billion (highlighted in row *D*).

A $50 billion increase in government expenditures has increased equilibrium expenditure and real GDP by $200 billion. So the government expenditures multiplier is 4.

Just as in the case of the investment multiplier, the size of the multiplier depends on the slope of the *AE* curve and is

$$\text{Government expenditures multiplier} = \frac{1}{1 - \text{Slope of } AE \text{ curve}}.$$

Let's use this formula with the numbers in the above example and confirm that the multiplier is 4. You've seen that the slope of the *AE* curve is 0.75. So the government expenditures multiplier is

$$\text{Government expenditures multiplier} = \frac{1}{1 - 0.75} = \frac{1}{0.25} = 4.$$

Figure 24.8 illustrates the government expenditures multiplier. Initially, aggregate planned expenditure is shown by the curve labelled AE_0. The points on this curve, labelled *A* through *E,* correspond with

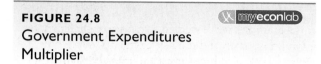

FIGURE 24.8

Government Expenditures Multiplier

myeconlab

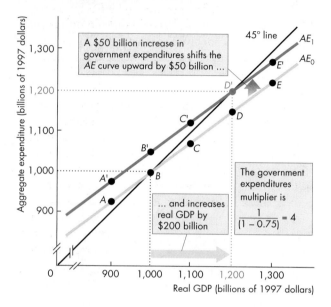

A $50 billion increase in government expenditures shifts the *AE* curve upward by $50 billion ...

... and increases real GDP by $200 billion

The government expenditures multiplier is

$$\frac{1}{(1 - 0.75)} = 4$$

Initially, the aggregate expenditure curve is AE_0, and real GDP is $1,000 billion (at point *B*). An increase in government expenditures of $50 billion increases aggregate planned expenditure at each level of real GDP by $50 billion. The aggregate expenditure curve shifts upward from AE_0 to AE_1—a parallel shift.

At the initial real GDP of $1,000 billion, aggregate planned expenditure is now $1,050 billion. Because aggregate planned expenditure is greater than real GDP, real GDP increases. The new equilibrium is reached when real GDP is $1,200 billion—the point at which the AE_1 curve intersects the 45° line (at point *D'*). In this example, the government expenditures multiplier is 4.

the rows of Table 24.2. This *AE* curve intersects the 45° line at point *B*. Equilibrium expenditure and real GDP are $1,000 billion.

When government expenditures increase by $50 billion, the *AE* curve shifts upward by that amount to AE_1. With this new *AE* curve, equilibrium expenditure and real GDP increase by $200 billion to $1,200 billion. The increase in real GDP is 4 times the increase in government expenditures. The government expenditures multiplier is 4.

You've seen that in the very short term, when the price level is fixed, an increase in government expenditures increases real GDP. But to produce more output, more people must be employed, so in the short term, an increase in government expenditures can create jobs.

A second way in which the government might act to increase real GDP in the very short run is by cutting taxes or increasing transfer payments. And the government might change autonomous taxes (or transfer payments) or induced taxes (or transfer payments.) Let's see how these actions work.

Autonomous Tax Multiplier

The **autonomous tax multiplier** is the magnification effect of a change in autonomous taxes on equilibrium aggregate expenditure and real GDP. An *increase* in taxes *decreases* disposable income, which *decreases* consumption expenditure. The amount by which consumption expenditure initially changes is determined by the marginal propensity to consume. Suppose that the marginal propensity to consume is 0.9, so a $1 tax cut increases disposable income by $1 and increases aggregate expenditure initially by 90¢.

This initial change in aggregate expenditure has a multiplier just like the government expenditures multiplier. We've seen that the government expenditures multiplier is 1/(1− Slope of the *AE* curve). Because a tax *increase* leads to a *decrease* in expenditure, the autonomous tax multiplier is *negative*. And because a change in autonomous taxes changes aggregate expenditure initially by only *MPC* multiplied by the tax change, the autonomous tax multiplier is

$$\frac{\text{Autonomous}}{\text{tax multiplier}} = \frac{-MPC}{1 - \text{Slope of } AE \text{ curve}}.$$

Figure 24.9 illustrates the autonomous tax multiplier. Initially, the aggregate expenditure curve is AE_0 and equilibrium expenditure is $1,000 billion. Taxes increase by $50 billion, and disposable income falls by that amount. With a marginal propensity to consume of 0.9, aggregate expenditure decreases initially by $45 billion and the *AE* curve shifts downward by that amount to AE_1. Equilibrium expenditure and real GDP decrease by $180 billion, to $820 billion. The autonomous tax multiplier is

$$\frac{\text{Autonomous}}{\text{tax multiplier}} = \frac{-0.9}{1 - 0.75} = -3.6.$$

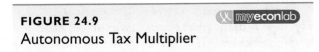

FIGURE 24.9
Autonomous Tax Multiplier

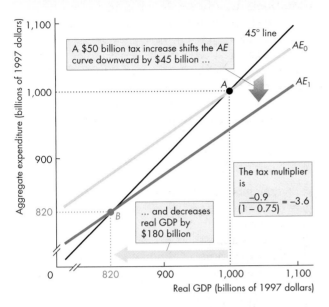

Initially, the aggregate expenditure curve is AE_0 and equilibrium expenditure is $1,000 billion. The marginal propensity to consume is 0.9. Autonomous taxes increase by $50 billion, so disposable income falls by $50 billion. The decrease in aggregate expenditure is found by multiplying this change in disposable income by the marginal propensity to consume and is $50 billion × 0.9 = $45 billion. The aggregate expenditure curve shifts *downward* by this amount to AE_1. Equilibrium expenditure decreases by $180 billion, from $1,000 billion to $820 billion. The autonomous tax multiplier is –3.6.

Autonomous Transfer Payments The autonomous tax multiplier also tells us the effects of a change in autonomous transfer payments. Transfer payments are like negative taxes, so an increase in transfer payments works like a decrease in taxes. Because the tax multiplier is negative, a decrease in taxes increases expenditure. An increase in transfer payments also increases expenditure. So the autonomous transfer payments multiplier is positive. It is

$$\frac{\text{Autonomous transfer}}{\text{payments multiplier}} = \frac{MPC}{1 - \text{Slope of } AE \text{ curve}}.$$

Induced Taxes and Transfer Payments

In the examples we've studied so far, we've changed only autonomous taxes and transfer payments. We're now going to look at induced taxes and transfer payments.

The tax laws define tax *rates* to be paid, not tax *dollars* to be paid. Tax *dollars* paid depend on tax *rates* and incomes. But incomes vary with real GDP, so tax *revenues* depend on real GDP. When the economy expands, tax revenues increase because real GDP increases. When the economy is in a recession, tax revenues decrease because real GDP decreases.

On the outlay side of the budget, the government creates programs that entitle suitably qualified people and businesses to receive benefits. The spending on such programs is not fixed in dollars and it results in transfer payments that depend on the economic state of individual citizens and businesses. When the economy is in a recession, unemployment is high, the number of people experiencing economic hardship increases, and a larger number of firms and farms experience hard times. Transfer payments increase. When the economy expands, transfer payments decrease.

Net taxes (taxes minus transfer payments) that vary with real GDP are called **induced taxes**. And the change in induced taxes equals the change in real GDP multiplied by the marginal tax rate. The *marginal tax rate* is the proportion of an additional dollar of real GDP that flows to the government in net taxes. The higher the marginal tax rate, the larger is the proportion of an additional dollar of real GDP that is paid to the government and the smaller is the induced change in aggregate expenditure.

An increase in the marginal tax rate decreases disposable income, decreases consumption expenditure, and has a multiplier effect on real GDP.

But an increase in the marginal tax rate also decreases the magnitude of the autonomous expenditure multipliers (the investment, government expenditures, autonomous tax and autonomous transfer payments multipliers). It does so by decreasing the slope of the AE curve. With a high marginal tax rate, when real GDP increases, induced taxes increase by more and disposable income and consumption expenditure by less than they do with a low marginal tax rate. So aggregate expenditure increases by less than it otherwise would have. The AE curve is flatter, its slope is smaller, and the multipliers are smaller.

International Trade and Fiscal Policy Multipliers

Not all expenditure in Canada is on Canadian-produced goods and services. Some of it is on imports—on foreign-produced goods and services. Imports affect the fiscal policy multipliers in the same way that they influence the investment multiplier, as explained in Chapter 23 (see pp. 548–549). The extent to which an additional dollar of real GDP is spent on imports is determined by the *marginal propensity to import*. Expenditure on imports does not generate Canadian real GDP and does not lead to an increase in Canadian consumption expenditure. The larger the marginal propensity to import, the smaller are the government expenditures and autonomous tax and transfer payments multipliers.

The math note on pp. 584–585 explains the details of the effects of induced taxes and transfer payments and imports on the fiscal policy multipliers.

So far, we've studied *discretionary* fiscal policy. Let's now look at *automatic* stabilizers.

Automatic Stabilizers

Automatic stabilizers are mechanisms that stabilize real GDP without explicit action by the government. Their name is borrowed from engineering and conjures up images of shock absorbers, thermostats, and sophisticated devices that keep airplanes and ships steady in turbulent air and seas. But automatic fiscal stabilizers do not actually stabilize. They just make the fluctuations less severe. These stabilizers operate because income taxes and transfer payments fluctuate with real GDP. If real GDP begins to decrease, tax revenues fall and transfer payments rise and the government's budget deficit increases. Let's look at the budget deficit over the business cycle.

Budget Deficit Over the Business Cycle Figure 24.10 shows the business cycle and fluctuations in the budget deficit between 1980 and 2004. Part (a) shows the fluctuations of real GDP around potential GDP. Part (b) shows the federal budget deficit (as a percentage of GDP). Both parts highlight recessions by shading those periods. By comparing the two parts of the figure, you can see the relationship between the business cycle and the budget deficit. As a rule, when the economy is in an expansion, the budget deficit declines. (In the figure, a declining deficit means a deficit that is getting closer to zero.) As the expansion slows before the recession begins, the

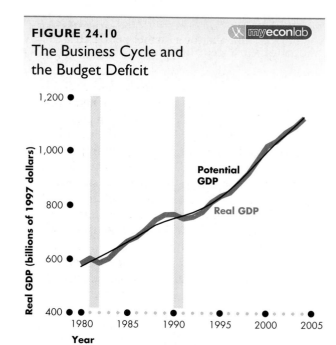

FIGURE 24.10

The Business Cycle and the Budget Deficit

(a) Growth and recessions

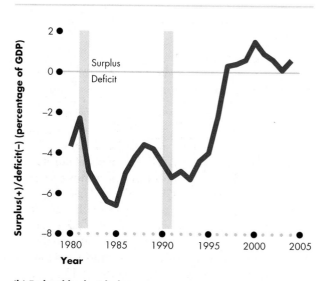

(b) Federal budget balance

As real GDP fluctuates around potential GDP (part a), the budget deficit fluctuates (part b). During a recession (shaded years), tax revenues decrease, transfer payments increase, and the budget deficit increases. The deficit also increases *before* a recession as real GDP growth slows and *after* a recession before real GDP growth speeds up.

Source of data: Statistics Canada, CANSIM Tables 380–0002 and 380–0007.

budget deficit increases. It continues to increase during the recession and for a further period after the recession is over. Then, when the expansion is well underway, the budget deficit declines again.

The budget deficit fluctuates with the business cycle because tax revenues and transfer payments fluctuate with real GDP. As real GDP increases in an expansion, tax revenues increase and transfer payments decrease, so the budget deficit automatically decreases. As real GDP decreases in a recession, tax revenues decrease and transfer payments increase, so the budget deficit automatically increases.

Fluctuations in investment and exports have a multiplier effect on real GDP. But fluctuations in tax revenues (and the budget deficit) act as an automatic stabilizer. They decrease the swings in disposable income and make the multiplier effect smaller. They dampen both expansions and recessions.

Cyclical and Structural Balances Because the government budget balance fluctuates with the business cycle, we need a method of measuring the budget surplus or deficit as a temporary cyclical phenomenon or a persistent structural phenomenon. A temporary cyclical surplus or deficit vanishes when full employment returns. A persistent structural surplus or deficit requires government action to remove it.

To determine whether the budget balance is persistent or temporary, economists have developed the concepts of the structural budget balance and the cyclical budget balance. The **structural surplus or deficit** is the budget balance that would occur if the economy were at full employment and real GDP were equal to potential GDP. The **cyclical surplus or deficit** is the actual surplus or deficit minus the structural surplus or deficit. That is, the cyclical surplus or deficit is the part of the budget balance that arises purely because real GDP does not equal potential GDP. For example, suppose that the budget deficit is $10 billion. And suppose that economists have determined that there is a structural deficit of $2.5 billion. Then there is a cyclical deficit of $7.5 billion.

Figure 24.11 illustrates the concepts of the cyclical surplus or deficit and the structural surplus or deficit. The blue curve shows government outlays. The outlays curve slopes downward because transfer payments, a component of government outlays, decrease as real GDP increases. The green curve shows revenues. The revenues curve slopes upward because most components of tax revenues increase as incomes and real GDP increase.

FIGURE 24.11 ✕ myeconlab

Cyclical and Structural Deficits and Surpluses

(a) Cyclical deficit and cyclical surplus

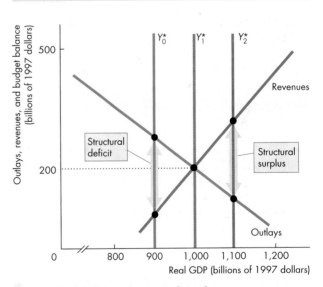

(b) Structural deficit and structural surplus

In part (a), potential GDP is $1,000 billion. If real GDP equals potential GDP, the government has a *balanced budget.* There is no *structural deficit.* If real GDP is less than potential GDP, the budget deficit is in a *cyclical deficit.* If real GDP exceeds potential GDP, the budget surplus is in a *cyclical surplus.* In part (b), if real GDP and potential GDP are $900 billion, there is a *structural deficit.* But if real GDP and potential GDP are $1,100 billion, there is a *structural surplus.*

In Fig. 24.11(a), potential GDP is $1,000 billion. If real GDP is $1,000 billion, outlays and revenues each equal $200 billion. Real GDP equals potential GDP, so the government has a *balanced budget*. If real GDP is $900 billion (below potential GDP), the government has a budget deficit and this deficit is a *cyclical deficit*. If real GDP is $1,100 billion (above potential GDP) the government has a budget surplus and this surplus is a *cyclical surplus*.

In Fig. 24.11(b), if both real GDP and potential GDP are $900 billion, the budget deficit is a structural deficit. If both real GDP and potential GDP are $1,000 billion, the budget is balanced—a structural balance of zero. When both real GDP and potential GDP are $1,100 billion, the budget surplus is a structural surplus.

The Canadian federal government had a structural budget deficit starting in the mid-1970s and continuing through the mid-1990s. That is, even if the economy had been at full employment with real GDP equal to potential GDP, the budget would have been in deficit. Worse, the structural deficit was so large that even at the peak of a business cycle, the budget was in deficit. At the end of the 1990s, a budget surplus emerged. It is probable that this surplus was a structural surplus because the economy was close to full employment.

REVIEW QUIZ

1 What are the government expenditures multiplier and the autonomous tax multiplier? How do these multiplier effects work?

2 Which has the larger multiplier effect: a change in government expenditures or a change in autonomous taxes? Why is one larger than the other?

3 How do income taxes and imports influence the size of the fiscal policy multipliers?

4 How do income taxes and transfer payments work as automatic stabilizers to dampen the business cycle?

5 How do we tell whether a budget deficit needs government action to remove it?

myeconlab Study Plan 24.2

Your next task is to see how, with the passage of more time and with some price level adjustments, these multiplier effects change.

Fiscal Policy Multipliers and the Price Level

WE'VE SEEN HOW REAL GDP RESPONDS TO changes in fiscal policy when the price level is fixed and all the adjustments that take place are in spending, income, and production. The period over which this response occurs is very short. Once production starts to change, regardless of whether it increases or decreases, prices also start to change. The price level and real GDP change together, and the economy moves to a new short-run equilibrium.

To study the simultaneous changes in real GDP and the price level, we use the *AS–AD* model of Chapter 22. In the long run, both the price level and the money wage rate respond to fiscal policy. As these further changes take place, the economy gradually moves towards a new long-run equilibrium. We also use the *AS–AD* model to study these adjustments.

We begin by looking at the effects of fiscal policy on aggregate demand and the aggregate demand curve.

Fiscal Policy and Aggregate Demand

You learned about the relationship between aggregate demand, aggregate expenditure, and equilibrium expenditure in Chapter 23 (pp. 551–553). You are now going to use what you learned there to work out what happens to aggregate demand, the price level, and real GDP when fiscal policy changes. We'll start by looking at the effects of a change in fiscal policy on aggregate demand.

Figure 24.12 shows the effects of an increase in government expenditures on aggregate demand. Initially, the aggregate expenditure curve is AE_0 in part (a), and the aggregate demand curve is AD_0 in part (b). The price level is 110, real GDP is $1,000 billion, and the economy is at point A in both parts of the figure. Now suppose that the government increases its expenditures by $50 billion. At a constant price level of 110, the aggregate expenditure curve shifts upward to AE_1. This curve intersects the 45° line at an equilibrium expenditure of $1,200 billion at point B. This amount is the aggregate quantity of goods and services demanded at a price level of 110, as shown by point B in part (b). Point B lies on a new aggregate demand curve. The aggregate demand curve has shifted rightward to AD_1.

The government expenditures multiplier determines the distance by which the aggregate demand

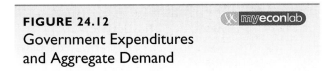

FIGURE 24.12

Government Expenditures and Aggregate Demand

(a) Aggregate expenditure

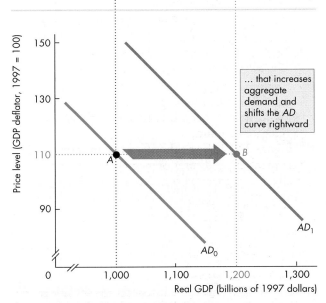

(b) Aggregate demand

The price level is 110, the aggregate planned expenditure curve is AE_0 (part a), and the aggregate demand curve is AD_0 (part b). An increase in government expenditures shifts the AE curve to AE_1 and increases equilibrium real GDP to $1,200 billion. The AD curve shifts rightward to AD_1.

curve shifts rightward. The larger the multiplier, the larger is the shift in the aggregate demand curve resulting from a given change in government expenditures. In this example, a $50 billion increase in government expenditures produces a $200 billion increase in the aggregate quantity of goods and services demanded at each price level. The multiplier is 4. So the $50 billion increase in government expenditures shifts the aggregate demand curve rightward by $200 billion.

Figure 24.12 shows the effects of an increase in government expenditures. But a similar effect occurs for *any* expansionary fiscal policy. An **expansionary fiscal policy** is an increase in government expenditures or a decrease in taxes. But the distance that the aggregate demand curve shifts is smaller for a decrease in taxes than for an increase in government expenditures of the same size.

Figure 24.12 can also be used to illustrate the effects of a **contractionary fiscal policy**—a decrease in government expenditures or an increase in taxes. In this case, start at point *B* in each part of the figure and decrease government expenditures or increase taxes. Aggregate demand decreases and the aggregate demand curve shifts leftward from AD_1 to AD_0.

Equilibrium GDP and the Price Level in the Short Run We've seen how an increase in government expenditures increases aggregate demand. Let's now see how it changes real GDP and the price level. Figure 24.13(a) describes the economy. Aggregate demand is AD_0, and the short-run aggregate supply curve is *SAS*. (Check back to Chapter 22, pp. 509–510, to refresh your understanding of the *SAS* curve.) Equilibrium is at point *A*, where the aggregate demand and short-run aggregate supply curves intersect. The price level is 110, and real GDP is $1,000 billion.

An increase in government expenditures of $50 billion shifts the aggregate demand curve rightward from AD_0 to AD_1. While the price level is fixed at 110, the economy moves towards point *B* and real GDP increases towards $1,200 billion. But during the adjustment process, the price level does not remain constant. It gradually rises, and the economy moves along the short-run aggregate supply curve to the point of intersection of the short-run aggregate supply curve and the new aggregate demand curve—point *C*. The price level rises to 123, and real GDP increases to only $1,130 billion.

FIGURE 24.13

Fiscal Policy, Real GDP, and the Price Level

(a) Fiscal policy with unemployment

(b) Fiscal policy at full employment

An increase in government expenditures shifts the AD curve from AD_0 to AD_1 (part a). With a fixed price level, the economy would have moved to point B. But the price level rises, and in the short run, the economy moves along the SAS curve to point C. The price level increases to 123, and real GDP increases to $1,130 billion.

At point C, real GDP exceeds potential GDP and unemployment is below the natural rate (part b). The money wage rate rises, and short-run aggregate supply decreases. The SAS curve shifts leftward to SAS_1, and in the long run, the economy moves to point A'. The price level rises to 150, and real GDP returns to $1,000 billion.

When we take the price level effect into account, the increase in government expenditures still has a multiplier effect on real GDP, but the effect is smaller than it would be if the price level remained constant. Also, the steeper the slope of the SAS curve, the larger is the increase in the price level, the smaller is the increase in real GDP, and the smaller is the government expenditures multiplier. But the multiplier is not zero.

In the long run, real GDP equals potential GDP—the economy is at full-employment equilibrium. When real GDP equals potential GDP, an increase in aggregate demand has the same short-run effect as we've just worked out, but its long-run effect is different. The increase in aggregate demand raises the price level but leaves real GDP unchanged at potential GDP.

To study this case, let's see what happens if the government embarks on an expansionary fiscal policy when real GDP equals potential GDP.

Fiscal Expansion at Potential GDP

Suppose that real GDP is equal to potential GDP, which means that unemployment is equal to the natural rate of unemployment. But suppose also that the unemployment rate is high and that most people, including the government, mistakenly think that unemployment must be above the natural rate. In this situation, the government tries to lower the unemployment rate by using an expansionary fiscal policy.

Figure 24.13(b) shows the effect of an expansionary fiscal policy when real GDP equals potential GDP. In this example, potential GDP is $1,000 billion. Aggregate demand increases, and the aggregate demand curve shifts rightward from AD_0 to AD_1. The short-run equilibrium, point C, is an above full-employment equilibrium. Now the money wage rate begins to increase and short-run aggregate supply decreases. The SAS curve shifts leftward from SAS_0 to

SAS_1. The economy moves up the aggregate demand curve AD_1 towards point A'.

When all the wage and price adjustments have occurred, the price level is 150 and real GDP is again at potential GDP of $1,000 billion. The multiplier is zero. There has been only a temporary increase in real GDP but a permanent rise in the price level.

Limitations of Fiscal Policy

Because the short-run fiscal policy multipliers are not zero, expansionary fiscal policy can be used to increase real GDP and decrease the unemployment rate in a recession. Contractionary fiscal policy can also be used, if the economy is overheating, to decrease real GDP and help to keep inflation in check. But two factors limit the use of fiscal policy.

First, the legislative process is slow, which means that it is difficult to take fiscal policy actions in a timely way. The economy might be able to benefit from fiscal stimulation right now, but it will take Parliament many months, perhaps more than a year, to act. By the time the action is taken, the economy might need an entirely different fiscal medicine.

Second, it is not always easy to tell whether real GDP is below (or above) potential GDP. A change in aggregate demand can move real GDP away from potential GDP, or a change in aggregate supply can change real GDP and change potential GDP. This difficulty is a serious one because, as you've seen, fiscal stimulation might occur too close to full employment, in which case it will increase the price level and have no long-run effect on real GDP.

REVIEW QUIZ

1 How do changes in the price level influence the multiplier effects of fiscal policy on real GDP?

2 What are the long-run effects of fiscal policy on real GDP and the price level when real GDP equals potential GDP?

myeconlab Study Plan 24.3

So far, we've ignored any potential effects of fiscal policy on aggregate supply. Yet many economists believe that the supply-side effects of fiscal policy are the biggest. Let's now look at these effects.

Supply-Side Effects of Fiscal Policy

TAX CUTS INCREASE DISPOSABLE INCOME AND increase aggregate demand. But tax cuts also strengthen incentives to work and save, which increase aggregate supply. The strength of the supply-side effects of tax cuts is not known with certainty. Some economists believe that the supply-side effects are large and exceed the demand-side effects. Other economists, while agreeing that supply-side effects are present, believe that they are relatively small.

The controversy over the magnitude of the effects of taxes on aggregate supply is a political controversy. Generally speaking, people on the conservative or right wing of the political spectrum believe that supply-side effects are powerful, and people on the liberal or left wing of the political spectrum view supply-side effects as being small.

Regardless of which view is correct, we can study the supply-side effects of tax cuts by using the AS–AD model. Let's study the effects of taxes on potential GDP and then see how the supply-side effects and demand-side effects together influence real GDP and the price level.

Fiscal Policy and Potential GDP

Potential GDP depends on the full-employment quantity of labour, the quantity of capital, and the state of technology. Taxes can influence all three of these factors. The main tax to consider is the income tax. By taxing the incomes people earn when they work or save, the government weakens the incentives to work and save. The result is a smaller quantity of labour and capital and a smaller potential GDP. Also, the income tax weakens the incentive to develop new technologies that increase income. So the pace of technological change might be slowed, which slows the growth rate of potential GDP. Let's look at the effect of the income tax on both the quantity of labour and the quantity of capital.

Labour Market Taxes The quantity of labour is determined by demand and supply in the labour market. Figure 24.14(a) shows a labour market. The demand for labour is LD and the supply is LS. The equilibrium real wage rate is $15 an hour and 30 billion hours of labour per year are employed.

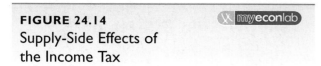

FIGURE 24.14

Supply-Side Effects of
the Income Tax

(a) The labour market

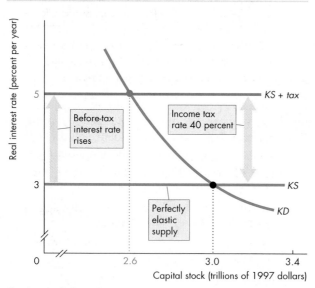

(b) The capital market

In part (a), an income tax decreases the supply of labour
and shifts the supply curve from *LS* to *LS + tax*. The quantity of labour decreases. In part (b), the income tax
decreases the supply of capital and shifts the supply curve
from *KS* to *KS + tax*. The quantity of capital decreases.
With less labour and less capital, potential GDP decreases.

Now suppose that an income tax is introduced.
An income tax weakens the incentive to work and
decreases the supply of labour. With a 20 percent
income tax, the labor supply curve shifts to *LS + tax*.
If workers are willing to supply the 30 billionth hour
a year for $15.00 with no tax, then with a 20 percent
tax, they are willing to supply the 30 billionth hour
only if the wage rate is $18.75 an hour. The quantity
of labour employed decreases to 25 billion hours a
year. The *before-tax* real wage rate rises to $16 an
hour and the *after-tax* real wage rate falls to $12.80
an hour.

Capital and the Income Tax The quantity of capital is determined by demand and supply in the capital market. Figure 24.14(b) shows the capital market.
The demand for capital is *KD* and the supply is *KS*.
Because capital is internationally mobile, its supply is
highly elastic. In this example, with no income tax,
quantity of capital is $3 trillion and the interest rate
is 3 percent a year.

A tax on the income from capital weakens the
incentive to save and decreases the supply of capital.
The supply curve shifts to *KS + tax*. With the new
supply of capital curve, the quantity of capital decreases
to $2.6 trillion. With a 40 percent income tax, the
before-tax interest rate rises to 5 percent a year and the
after-tax interest rate remains at 3 percent a year.

Potential GDP and *LAS* Because the income tax
decreases the equilibrium quantities of labour and
capital, it also decreases potential GDP. But potential
GDP determines long-run aggregate supply. So the
income tax decreases long-run aggregate supply and
shifts the *LAS* curve leftward.

Supply Effects and Demand Effects

Let's now bring the supply-side effects and demand-
side effects of fiscal policy together. Figure 24.15(a)
shows the most likely effects of a tax cut. The tax cut
increases aggregate demand and shifts the *AD* curve
rightward, just as before. But a tax cut that increases
the incentive to work and save also increases aggregate supply. It shifts the long-run and short-run
aggregate supply curves rightward. Here we focus on
the short run and show the effect on the *SAS* curve,
which shifts rightward to *SAS₁*. In this example, the
tax cut has a large effect on aggregate demand and a
small effect on aggregate supply. The *AD* curve shifts
rightward by a larger amount than the rightward shift

FIGURE 24.15

Two Views of the Supply-Side Effects of Fiscal Policy

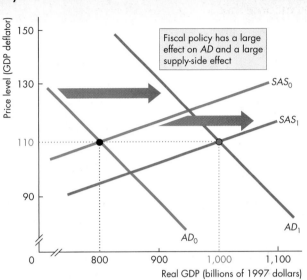

(a) The traditional view

A tax cut increases aggregate demand and shifts the *AD* curve rightward from AD_0 to AD_1 (both parts). Such a policy change also has a supply-side effect. If the supply-side effect is small, the *SAS* curve shifts rightward from SAS_0 to SAS_1 in part (a). The demand-side effect dominates the supply-side effect, real GDP increases, and the price level rises.

(b) The supply-side view

If the supply-side effect of a tax cut is large, the *SAS* curve shifts to SAS_1 in part (b). Here, the supply-side effect is the same as the demand-side effect—an increase of $200 billion. Real GDP increases, and the price level remains constant. But if the supply-side effect were larger than the demand-side effect, the price level would actually fall.

in the *SAS* curve. The outcome is a rise in the price level and an increase in real GDP. But notice that the price level rises by *less* and real GDP increases by *more* than would occur if there were no supply-side effects.

Figure 24.15(b) shows the effects that supply-siders believe occur. A tax cut still has a large effect on aggregate demand, but it has a similarly large effect on aggregate supply. Both the *AD* curve and the *SAS* curve shift rightward by $200 billion. In this particular case, the price level remains constant and real GDP increases by $200 billion. A slightly larger increase in aggregate supply would have brought a fall in the price level, a possibility that some supply-siders believe could occur.

The general point, with which everyone agrees, is that a tax cut that strengthens the incentives to work and save increases real GDP by more and is less inflationary than an equal-size expansionary fiscal policy that does not change or that weakens incentives.

REVIEW QUIZ

1 How do income taxes and payroll taxes influence the labour market, and how would a cut in these taxes influence real GDP?

2 How would an income tax cut influence aggregate supply and aggregate demand?

3 How would an income tax cut influence real GDP and the price level?

Study Plan 24.4

◆ You've seen how fiscal policy influences real GDP and potential GDP. *Reading Between the Lines* on pp. 582–583 looks at Finance Minister Goodale's plan to spend $2 billion helping low-income families cope with the high cost of winter heating.

Your next task is to study the other main arm of macroeconomic policy: monetary policy.

A Winter Heating Multiplier

NATIONAL POST, OCTOBER 5, 2005

Ottawa to announce $2-billion program to help poor with high heating bills

The federal government is set to commit more than $2 billion to a five-year plan that will help Canadians cope with high heating costs, The Canadian Press has learned.

Most of the money will be used to make low-income housing more energy efficient, a federal official said on condition of anonymity.

But some will be distributed to low-income families directly in rebate cheques, the source said.

The cheques will go to recipients of Guaranteed Income Supplement and the National Child Benefit Tax Supplement. ...

Earlier Tuesday, Finance Minister Ralph Goodale said legislation will be introduced Friday to provide assistance to "the most vulnerable in society."

It was not clear how much of the $2 billion will be "new" money. The sum might include funds from the

Finance minister Ralph Goodale.
(CP PHOTO/Tom Hanson)

Kyoto implementation plan. It could also include $100 million for energy efficiency that was added to the budget last year. ...

Reprinted by permission of The Canadian Press.

Essence of the Story

■ The federal government plans to spend $2 billion to help low-income families cope with high heating costs.

■ Most of this money will be spent on high-efficiency furnaces for low-income housing.

■ Some of this money will be spent by sending cheques to families who receive income support and child benefits from the government.

■ Some (but a small part) of the money might come from funds already committed to implementing the Kyoto agreement.

Economic Analysis

■ In mid-2005, real GDP was $1,152 billion (1997 dollars) and the GDP deflator was 115.

■ The economy was close to full employment with an estimated output gap of 0.1 percent of real GDP or a bit more than $1 billion.

■ The government planned to increase expenditures on home heating for low-income families by $2 billion over a 5-year period.

■ You can see why the government needed to be cautious about how quickly it injected these expenditures into the economy. If the entire $2 billion were spent in a single year, real GDP would go above potential GDP and inflationary pressure would arise.

■ Figure 1 shows the aggregate expenditure curve in mid-2005 as AE_0. Equilibrium expenditure was $1,152 billion.

■ If the government increased expenditure by $2 billion, the AE curve would shift upward by that amount. The reason is that although some of the expenditure is a transfer payment, because it is a transfer to the poor, it is likely that all of it would be spent

(and none saved)—the marginal propensity to consume of poor people is 1.

■ Assuming a slope for the AE curve of 0.33, the multiplier is 1.5 (see p. 557) and an increase in autonomous expenditure of $2 billion increases equilibrium expenditure by $3 billion.

■ So, in Figure 1, when the AE curve shifts upward to AE_1, equilibrium expenditure increases to $1,155 billion.

■ In Figure 2, the aggregate demand curve shifts rightward by $3 billion from AD_0 to AD_1.

■ The increase in aggregate demand turns a recessionary gap into an inflationary gap and the price level rises.

■ The inflationary gap brings a rise in the money wage rate and a decrease in short-run aggregate supply. The SAS curve shifts from SAS_0 to SAS_1 and the price level rises further.

■ By spreading its help to low-income families over a number of years, the government will avoid the inflationary consequences illustrated here.

Figure 1 Aggregate expenditure

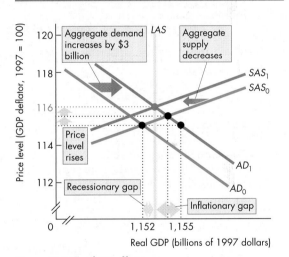

Figure 2 AD and AS effects

You're the Voter

■ Do you think the federal government's method of helping low-income families is sound?

■ Do you think the federal government should finance its help to low-income families with a tax increase? Explain why or why not.

Mathematical Note
The Algebra of the Fiscal Policy Multipliers

THIS MATHEMATICAL NOTE DERIVES FORMULAS FOR the fiscal policy multipliers. We begin by defining the symbols we need:

- Aggregate planned expenditure, AE
- Real GDP, Y
- Consumption expenditure, C
- Investment, I
- Government expenditures, G
- Exports, X
- Imports, M
- Net taxes, NT
- Autonomous consumption expenditure, a
- Autonomous taxes, T_a
- Autonomous transfer payments, T_r
- Marginal propensity to consume, b
- Marginal propensity to import, m
- Marginal tax rate, t
- Autonomous expenditure, A

Equilibrium Expenditure

Aggregate planned expenditure is
$$AE = C + I + G + X - M.$$

The consumption function is
$$C = a + b(Y - NT).$$

Net taxes equals autonomous taxes minus autonomous transfer payments plus induced taxes, which is
$$NT = T_a - T_r + tY.$$

Use the last equation in the consumption function to give consumption expenditure as a function of GDP:
$$C = a - bT_a + bT_r + b(1 - t)Y.$$

The import function is
$$M = mY.$$

Use the consumption function and the import function to replace C and M in the aggregate planned expenditure equation to obtain
$$AE = a - bT_a + bT_r + b(1 - t)Y + I + G + X - mY.$$

Collect the terms that involve Y on the right side of the equation to obtain
$$AE = (a - bT_a + bT_r + I + G + X) + [b(1 - t) - m]Y.$$

Autonomous expenditure (A) is given by
$$A = a - bT_a + bT_r + I + G + X$$

and the slope of the AE curve is $[b(1 - t) - m]$, so
$$AE = A + [b(1 - t) - m]Y.$$

Equilibrium expenditure occurs when aggregate planned expenditure (AE) equals real GDP (Y). That is,
$$AE = Y.$$

To calculate equilibrium expenditure, we solve the equation:
$$Y = A + [b(1 - t) - m]Y$$

to obtain
$$Y = \frac{1}{1 - [b(1 - t) - m]}A.$$

Government Expenditures Multiplier

The government expenditures multiplier equals the change in equilibrium expenditure (Y) that results from a change in government expenditures (G) divided by the change in government expenditures. Because autonomous expenditure is equal to
$$A = a - bT_a + bT_r + I + G + X,$$

the change in autonomous expenditure equals the change in government expenditures. That is,
$$\Delta A = \Delta G.$$

The government expenditures multiplier is found by working out the change in Y that results from the change in A. You can see from the solution for Y that
$$\Delta Y = \frac{1}{1 - [b(1 - t) - m]}\Delta G.$$

The government expenditures multiplier equals
$$\frac{1}{1 - [b(1 - t) - m]}.$$

In an economy in which $t = 0$ and $m = 0$, the government expenditures multiplier is $1/(1 - b)$. With $b = 0.75$, the government expenditures multiplier equals 4, as part (a) of the figure below shows. Make up some examples and use the above formula to show how b, m, and t influence the government expenditures multiplier.

Autonomous Tax Multiplier

The autonomous tax multiplier equals the change in equilibrium expenditure (Y) that results from a change in autonomous taxes (T_a) divided by the change in autonomous taxes. Because autonomous expenditure is equal to

$$A = a - bT_a + bT_r + I + G + X,$$

the change in autonomous expenditure equals *minus* b multiplied by the change in autonomous taxes. That is,

$$\Delta A = -b\Delta T_a.$$

You can see from the solution for equilibrium expenditure Y that

$$\Delta Y = \frac{-b}{1 - [b(1 - t) - m]}\Delta T_a.$$

The autonomous tax multiplier equals

$$\frac{-b}{1 - [b(1 - t) - m]}.$$

In an economy in which $t = 0$ and $m = 0$, the autonomous tax multiplier is $-b/(1 - b)$. With $b = 0.75$, the autonomous tax multiplier equals -3, as part (b) of the figure shows. Make up some examples and use the above formula to show how b, m, and t influence the autonomous tax multiplier.

Autonomous Transfer Payments Multiplier

The autonomous transfer payments multiplier equals the change in equilibrium expenditure (Y) that results from a change in autonomous transfer payments (T_r) divided by the change in autonomous transfer payments. Because autonomous expenditure is equal to

$$A = a - bT_a + bT_r + I + G + X,$$

the change in autonomous transfer payments changes autonomous expenditure such that

$$\Delta A = b\Delta T_r.$$

Because transfer payments are like negative taxes, the autonomous transfer payments multiplier equals minus the autonomous tax multiplier. The autonomous transfer payments multiplier equals

$$\frac{b}{1 - [b(1 - t) - m]}.$$

In an economy in which $t = 0$ and $m = 0$, the autonomous transfer payments multiplier is $b/(1 - b)$. With $b = 0.75$, the autonomous transfer payments multiplier equals 3, as part (c) of the figure shows. Make up some examples and use the above formula to show how b, m, and t influence the autonomous transfer payments multiplier.

(a) Government expenditures multiplier

(b) Autonomous tax multiplier

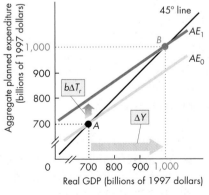

(c) Autonomous transfer payments multiplier

SUMMARY

KEY POINTS

Government Budgets (pp. 564–569)

- The federal budget finances the activities of the government and is used to stabilize real GDP.
- Federal revenues come from personal income taxes, corporate income taxes, indirect taxes, and investment income. Federal outlays include transfer payments, expenditures on goods and services, and debt interest.
- When government revenues exceed outlays, the government has a budget surplus.

Fiscal Policy Multipliers (pp. 570–576)

- Fiscal policy actions are discretionary or automatic.
- Government expenditures, taxes, and transfer payments have multiplier effects on real GDP.
- The government expenditures multiplier equals (1 − Slope of AE curve). The autonomous tax multiplier equals $-MPC / (1 - \text{Slope of } AE \text{ curve})$.
- The transfer payments multiplier is equal to the magnitude of autonomous tax multiplier but is positive.
- Induced taxes and transfer payments and imports make the fiscal policy multipliers smaller.
- Income taxes and transfer payments act as automatic stabilizers.

Fiscal Policy Multipliers and the Price Level (pp. 576–579)

- An expansionary fiscal policy increases aggregate demand and shifts the aggregate demand curve rightward. It increases real GDP and raises the price level. (A contractionary fiscal policy has the opposite effects.)
- Price level changes dampen fiscal policy multiplier effects.
- At potential GDP, an expansionary fiscal policy raises the price level but leaves real GDP unchanged. The fiscal policy multipliers are zero.

Supply-Side Effects of Fiscal Policy (pp. 579–581)

- Fiscal policy has supply-side effects because increases in taxes weaken the incentives to work and save.
- A tax cut increases both aggregate demand and aggregate supply and increases real GDP, but the tax cut has an ambiguous effect on the price level.

KEY FIGURES

Figure 24.8   Government Expenditures Multiplier, 572
Figure 24.9   Autonomous Tax Multiplier, 573
Figure 24.10   The Business Cycle and the Budget Deficit, 574
Figure 24.11   Cyclical and Structural Deficits and Surpluses, 575
Figure 24.12   Government Expenditures and Aggregate Demand, 577
Figure 24.13   Fiscal Policy, Real GDP, and the Price Level, 578
Figure 24.15   Two Views of the Supply-Side Effects of Fiscal Policy, 581

KEY TERMS

Automatic fiscal policy, 570
Automatic stabilizers, 574
Autonomous taxes, 570
Autonomous tax multiplier, 572
Balanced budget, 565
Budget deficit, 565
Budget surplus, 565
Contractionary fiscal policy, 577
Cyclical surplus or deficit, 575
Discretionary fiscal policy, 570
Expansionary fiscal policy, 577
Federal budget, 564
Fiscal policy, 564
Government debt, 567
Government expenditures multiplier, 570
Induced taxes, 573
Provincial budget, 564
Structural surplus or deficit, 575

PROBLEMS

Go to **myeconlab** for solutions to odd-numbered problems and additional exercises.

1. In the economy of Zap, the marginal propensity to consume is 0.9. Investment is $50 billion, government expenditures on goods and services are $40 billion, and autonomous taxes are $40 billion. Zap has no exports and no imports.
   a. The government cuts its expenditures on goods and services to $30 billion. What is the change in equilibrium expenditure?
   b. What is the value of the government expenditures multiplier?
   c. The government continues to buy $40 billion worth of goods and services and cuts autonomous taxes to $30 billion. What is the change in equilibrium expenditure?
   d. What is the value of the autonomous tax multiplier?
   e. The government simultaneously cuts both its expenditures on goods and services and taxes to $30 billion. What is the change in equilibrium expenditure? Why does equilibrium expenditure decrease?

2. In the economy of Zip, the marginal propensity to consume is 0.8. Investment is $60 billion, government expenditures on goods and services are $50 billion, and autonomous taxes are $60 billion. Zip has no exports and no imports.
   a. The government increases its expenditures on goods and services to $60 billion. What is the change in equilibrium expenditure?
   b. What is the value of the government expenditures multiplier?
   c. The government continues to buy $60 billion worth of goods and services and increases autonomous taxes to $70 billion. What is the change in equilibrium expenditure?
   d. What is the value of the autonomous tax multiplier?
   e. The government simultaneously increases both its expenditures on goods and services and taxes by $10 billion. What is the change in equilibrium expenditure? Why does equilibrium expenditure increase?

3. Suppose that the price level in the economy of Zap as described in problem 1 is 100. The economy is also at full employment.
   a. If the government of Zap increases its expenditures on goods and services by $10 billion, what happens to the quantity of real GDP demanded?
   b. How does Zap's aggregate demand curve change? Draw a two-part figure that is similar to Fig. 24.12 to illustrate the change in both the *AE* curve and the *AD* curve.
   c. In the short run, does equilibrium real GDP increase by more than, less than, or the same amount as the increase in the quantity of real GDP demanded?
   d. In the long run, does equilibrium real GDP increase by more than, less than, or the same amount as the increase in the quantity of real GDP demanded?
   e. In the short run, does the price level in Zap rise, fall, or remain unchanged?
   f. In the long run, does the price level in Zap rise, fall, or remain unchanged?

4. Suppose that the price level in the economy of Zip as described in problem 2 is 100. The economy is also at full employment.
   a. If the government of Zip decreases its expenditures on goods and services by $5 billion, what happens to the quantity of real GDP demanded?
   b. How does Zip's aggregate demand curve change? Draw a two-part figure that is similar to Fig. 24.12 to illustrate the change in both the *AE* curve and the *AD* curve.
   c. In the short run, does equilibrium real GDP decrease by more than, less than, or the same amount as the increase in the quantity of real GDP demanded?
   d. In the short run, does the price level in Zip rise, fall, or remain unchanged?
   e. Why does real GDP decrease by a smaller amount than the decrease in aggregate demand?

5. The figure shows outlays and revenues of the government of Dreamland. Potential GDP is $40 million.

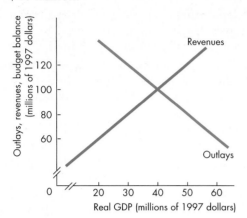

a. What is the government's budget balance if real GDP equals potential GDP?
b. Does Dreamland have a structural surplus or deficit if its real GDP is $40 million? What is the size of the structural surplus or deficit? Explain why.
c. What is the government's budget balance if real GDP is $30 million?
d. If Dreamland's real GDP is $30 million, does Dreamland have a structural surplus or deficit? What is its size? Explain why.
e. If Dreamland's real GDP is $50 million, does Dreamland have a structural surplus or deficit? What is its size? Explain why.

6. In problem 5, if Dreamland's real GDP is $50 million,
a. What is the government's budget balance?
b. Does Dreamland have a structural surplus? What is its size? Explain why.
c. What is the government's budget balance if potential GDP is $30 million?
d. If Dreamland's potential GDP is $30 million, does Dreamland have a structural surplus or deficit? What is its size? Explain why.
e. What would Dreamland's real GDP have to be for it to have neither a structural deficit or surplus nor a cyclical deficit or surplus if its potential GDP is $40 million?

CRITICAL THINKING

1. Study *Reading Between the Lines* on pp. 582–583 and then
a. Describe the federal government's plan to help low-income Canadians with the high cost of winter heating.
b. Do you think the government is planning to finance this expenditure in an appropriate manner?
c. What do you predict would happen to aggregate demand if instead of spreading this expenditure over five years, the government spent the money in a single year?
d. Suppose the economy went into a recession in 2006. Would such an event change your answer to parts b and c? If so, how? If not, why not?

2. Thinking about the supply-side effects of the 2006 budget,
a. What would be the main effects of lower income tax rates on the level of potential GDP?
b. How would lower income taxes influence the real wage rate and the real interest rate?
c. What are the main costs of lower income taxes?

WEB EXERCISES

Use the links on (myeconlab) **to work the following exercises.**

1. Visit the Department of Finance and obtain data on the current federal budget. Use the information that you find, together with the fiscal policy multiplier analysis that you've learned about in this chapter, to predict the effects of the Canadian budget on real GDP and the price level. Explain reasons for your predictions.
2. Visit Statistics Canada and obtain the most recent data you can find on the revenues, outlays, and budget surplus or deficit for Canada and for the province in which you live.
a. What are the main features of the two sets of budget data?
b. What are the main trends in the budget data?
c. Predict the effects of your province's budget on provincial GDP.

Money, Banking, and Interest Rates

Money Makes the World Go Around

Money, like fire and the wheel, has been around for a long time. Wampum (beads made from shells) was used as money by the First Nations of North America, and tobacco was used by early American colonists. Today, we use coins, bank notes, cheques, debit cards, and credit cards. Tomorrow, we'll use "smart cards" that keep track of spending. Are all these things money?

When we deposit some coins or notes into a bank, are they still money?

There are enough coins and Bank of Canada notes circulating today for every Canadian to have a wallet stuffed with more than $1,300. In addition, there is enough money deposited in banks and other financial institutions for every Canadian to have a deposit of more than $27,000. Why do we hold all this money?

During 2004, interest rates fell to historically low levels and then, in 2005, they began to edge upward. What determines interest rates and what makes them fall or rise?

◆ In this chapter, you'll study the functions of money, the functions of banks and other financial institutions, and the Bank of Canada. You will learn how banks create money, and how interest rates are determined. At the end of the chapter, in *Reading Between the Lines*, we look at the growth in the use of debit cards and credit cards and the surprisingly small effect these electronic payment methods are having on the amount of cash we use.

After studying this chapter, you will be able to

- **Define money and describe its functions**
- **Describe the banking system and explain the economic functions of banks, the Bank of Canada, and the payments system**
- **Explain how banks create money**
- **Explain what determines the demand for money**
- **Explain what determines the supply of money and the interest rate**

What Is Money?

WHAT DO WAMPUM, TOBACCO, AND NICKELS AND dimes have in common? Why are they all examples of money? To answer these questions, we need a definition of money. **Money** is any commodity or token that is generally acceptable as the means of payment. A **means of payment** is a method of paying for goods and services or of settling a debt. When a payment has been made, there is no remaining obligation between the parties to a transaction. So what wampum, tobacco, and nickels and dimes have in common is that they have served (or still do serve) as the means of payment. But money performs three other functions:

■ Medium of exchange
■ Unit of account
■ Store of value

Medium of Exchange

A *medium of exchange* is an object that is generally accepted in exchange for goods and services. Money acts as such a medium. Without a medium of exchange, we would exchange one good or service directly for another in an exchange called **barter**. For example, if you want to buy a hamburger, you offer the paperback novel you've just finished reading in exchange for it. Barter requires a *double coincidence* of wants, a situation that occurs when Joe wants to buy what Ann wants to sell and Ann wants to buy what Joe wants to sell. To get your hamburger, you must find someone who's selling hamburgers and who wants your paperback novel. Money ensures that there is a double coincidence of wants because people with something to sell will always accept money in exchange for it.

Unit of Account

A *unit of account* is an agreed measure for stating the prices of goods and services. To get the most out of your budget, you have to figure out whether seeing one more movie is worth its opportunity cost. But that cost is not dollars and cents. It is the number of ice-cream cones, cans of pop, or phone calls that you must give up. It's easy to do such calculations when all these goods have prices in terms of dollars and cents (see Table 25.1). If the price of a movie is $6 and the price of a six-pack of pop is $3, you know right away that seeing one movie costs you 2 six-packs of pop. If

TABLE 25.1	**A Unit of Account Simplifies Price Comparisons**	
Good	Price in money units	Price in units of another good
Movie	$6.00 each	2 six-packs of pop
Pop	$3.00 per six-pack	2 ice-cream cones
Ice cream	$1.50 per cone	3 packs of jelly beans
Jelly beans	50¢ per pack	2 local phone calls
Phone call	25¢ per call	1/2 pack of jelly beans

Money as a unit of account: The price of a movie is $6 and the price of a local phone call is 25¢, so the opportunity cost of a movie is 24 local phone calls ($6.00 ÷ 25¢ = 24).

No unit of account: You go to a movie theatre and learn that the price of a movie is 2 six-packs of pop. You go to a candy store and learn that a pack of jelly beans costs 2 local phone calls. But how many phone calls does seeing a movie cost you? To answer that question, you go to the convenience store and find that a six-pack of pop costs 2 ice-cream cones. Now you head for the ice-cream shop, where an ice-cream cone costs 3 packs of jelly beans. Now you get out your pocket calculator: 1 movie costs 2 six-packs of pop, or 4 ice-cream cones, or 12 packs of jelly beans, or 24 phone calls!

jelly beans are 50¢ a pack, one movie costs 12 packs of jelly beans. You need only one calculation to figure out the opportunity cost of any pair of goods and services.

But imagine how troublesome it would be if your local movie theatre posted its price as 2 six-packs of pop, and if the convenience store posted the price of a six-pack of pop as 2 ice-cream cones, and if the ice-cream shop posted the price of a cone as 3 packs of jelly beans, and if the candy store priced a pack of jelly beans as 2 local phone calls! Now how much running around and calculating would you have to do to figure out how much that movie is going to cost you in terms of the pop, ice cream, jelly beans, or phone calls that you must give up to see it?

You get the answer for pop right away from the sign posted at the movie theatre. But for all the other goods you'd have to visit many different stores to establish the price of each commodity in terms of another and then calculate prices in units that are relevant for your own decision. Cover up the column labelled "price in money units" in Table 25.1 and see how hard it is to figure out the number of local phone calls it costs to see one movie. It's enough to make a person swear off movies! How much simpler it is if all the prices are expressed in dollars and cents.

Store of Value

Anything that can be held and exchanged later for goods and services is a *store of value*. Money acts as a store of value. If it did not, it would not be acceptable in exchange for goods and services.

No store of value is completely safe. The value of a physical object—such as a house, a car, or a work of art—fluctuates over time. The value of money fluctuates, and when there is inflation, its value persistently falls. The more stable the value of money, the better it can act as a store of value and the more useful it is as a means of payment.

Money in Canada Today

In Canada today, money consists of

- Currency
- Deposits at banks and other financial institutions

Currency The coins and Bank of Canada notes that we use today are known as **currency**. Currency is money because the government declares it to be so. Look at a Bank of Canada note and notice the words

> "CE BILLET A COURS LÉGAL—THIS NOTE IS LEGAL TENDER."

Currency is the most convenient type of money for settling small debts and buying low-priced items.

Deposits Deposits at banks and other financial institutions are also money. Deposits are money because they can be converted into currency and because they are used to settle debts. When you write a cheque or use a debit card, you are telling your bank to transfer money from your account to the account of the person from whom you are buying. Bank deposits are the most convenient type of money for settling large debts and buying big-ticket items.

Official Measures of Money There is no unique measure of money. The two main measures used in Canada today are M1 and M2+. Figure 25.1 shows the items that make up these two measures.

M1 consists of currency held outside the banks plus demand deposits at chartered banks that are owned by individuals and businesses. M1 does *not* include currency held by banks, and it does not include currency and bank deposits owned by the government of Canada. **M2+** consists of M1 plus personal savings deposits and nonpersonal notice deposits at chartered banks plus all types of deposits at trust and mortgage loan companies, credit unions, caisses populaires, and other financial institutions.

FIGURE 25.1
Two Measures of Money

	$ billions in June 2005
M2+	**911**
Comprises all in M1, plus...	
Deposits at other financial institutions	99
Deposits at credit unions and caisses populaires	148
Deposits at trust and mortgage loan companies	11
Nonpersonal notice deposits at chartered banks	65
Personal savings deposits at chartered banks	410
M1	**178**
Demand deposits	134
Currency outside banks	44

M1
- Currency held outside banks
- Demand deposits at chartered banks that are owned by individuals and businesses

M2+
- M1
- Personal savings deposits at chartered banks
- Nonpersonal notice deposits at chartered banks
- Deposits at trust and mortgage loan companies
- Deposits at credit unions and caisses populaires
- Deposits at other financial institutions

Source of data: Bank of Canada, *Banking and Financial Statistics,* Table E1.

Are M1 and M2+ Really Money? The test of whether something is money is whether it serves as a means of payment. Currency passes the test. But what about deposits? Deposit accounts on which cheques can be written are money because they can be transferred directly from one person to another in a transaction that is equivalent to handing over currency. Because M1 consists of currency plus demand deposits and each of these is a means of payment, M1 *is money.*

But what about M2+? Some of the savings deposits in M2+ are just as much a means of payment as the demand deposits in M1. You can use the automated teller machine (ATM) at the grocery store checkout or gas station and transfer funds directly from your savings account to pay for your purchase. But other savings deposits are not means of payment. They are known as *liquid assets*. **Liquidity** is the property of being instantly convertible into a means of payment with little loss in value. Because most of the deposits in M2+ are quickly and easily converted into currency or demand deposits, they are operationally similar to M1, but they are not means of payment.

Deposits Are Money but Cheques Are Not In defining money, we include, along with currency, deposits at banks and other financial institutions. But we do not count the cheques that people write as money. Why are deposits money and cheques not?

To see why deposits are money but cheques are not, think about what happens when Colleen buys some roller blades for $200 from Rocky's Rollers. When Colleen goes to Rocky's shop, she has $500 in her deposit account at the Laser Bank. Rocky has $1,000 in his deposit account—at the same bank, as it happens. The total deposits of these two people are $1,500. Colleen writes a cheque for $200. Rocky takes the cheque to the bank and deposits it. Rocky's bank balance rises from $1,000 to $1,200 and Colleen's balance falls from $500 to $300. The total deposits of Colleen and Rocky are still the same as before: $1,500. Rocky now has $200 more and Colleen has $200 less.

This transaction has transferred money from Colleen to Rocky. The cheque itself was never money. There wasn't an extra $200 worth of money while the cheque was in circulation. The cheque instructs the bank to transfer money from Colleen to Rocky.

If Colleen and Rocky use different banks, there is an extra transaction. Rocky's bank needs to collect the $200 that it has put in Rocky's account from Colleen's bank. So when Colleen's bank takes the

$200 from her account, it pays that amount to Rocky's bank.

We describe this process of interbank payments in the next section (see pp. 595–596).

Debit Cards Are Not Money So cheques are not money. But what about debit cards? Isn't presenting a debit card to pay for your roller blades the same thing as using money? Why aren't debit cards counted as part of the quantity of money?

A debit card enables you to pay with an electronic cheque. When you use a debit card, money leaves your bank account and is deposited into the account of the person from whom you are buying at the instant of the transaction.

Credit Cards Are Not Money Sometimes you need ID and you pull out your driver's licence. Your credit card is another type of ID card—a special ID card that enables you to take a loan at the instant you buy something. When you sign a credit card sales slip, you are saying: "I agree to pay for these goods when the credit card company bills me." Once you get your statement from the credit card company, you must make the minimum payment due (or clear your balance). To make that payment you need money—you need to have currency or a bank deposit to pay the credit card company. So although you use a credit card when you buy something, the credit card is not the *means of payment* and it is not money.

REVIEW QUIZ

1 What makes something money? What functions does money perform? Why do you think packs of chewing gum don't serve as money?
2 What problems arise when a commodity is used as money?
3 What are the main components of money in Canada today?
4 What are two official measures of money in Canada? Are all the measures really money?
5 Why are cheques, debit cards, and credit cards not money?

myeconlab Study Plan 25.1

We've seen that the main component of money in Canada is deposits at banks and other financial firms. Let's take a closer look at the banking system.

The Banking System

THE BANKING SYSTEM CONSISTS OF PRIVATE AND public institutions that create money and manage the nation's monetary and payments systems. These institutions play a crucial role in financial markets and have profound effects on overall economic performance. We're going to describe these institutions and explain their economic funtions. To so so, we'll divide the institutions into three groups:

- Depository institutions
- The Bank of Canada
- The payments system

Depository Institutions

A **depository institution** is a private firm that takes deposits from households and firms and makes loans to other households and firms. The deposits of three types of depository institution are included in the nation's money. They are

- Chartered banks
- Credit unions and caisses populaires
- Trust and mortgage loan companies

Chartered Banks A **chartered bank** is a private firm, chartered under the Bank Act of 1992 to receive deposits and make loans. The chartered banks are by far the largest institutions in the banking system and conduct all types of banking and financial business. In 2005, 14 Canadian-owned banks (including the Royal Bank of Canada, CIBC, Bank of Montreal, Bank of Nova Scotia, National Bank of Canada, and TD Canada Trust) and 33 foreign-owned banks had deposits that are included in M2+ of $609 billion.

Credit Unions and Caisses Populaires A **credit union** is a cooperative organization that operates under the Co-operative Credit Association Act of 1992 and that receives deposits from and makes loans to its members. A caisse populaire is a similar type of institution that operates in Quebec. In 2005, the deposits in these institutions were $148 billion.

Trust and Mortgage Loan Companies A **trust and mortgage loan company** is a privately owned depository institution that operates under the Trust and Loan Companies Act of 1992. These institutions receive deposits, make loans, and act as trustee for pension funds and for estates. In 2005, they had deposits that are included in M2+ of $11 billion.

All Banks Now Historically, Canada made a sharp legal distinction between banks and other depository institutions. But the economic functions of all depository institutions have grown increasingly similar. This fact is recognized in laws governing these institutions that became effective in 1992. Because they all perform the same essential economic functions, we'll call all these institutions banks unless we need to distinguish among them.

Profit and Prudence: A Balancing Act The aim of any bank is to maximize the wealth of its owners. To achieve this objective, the interest rate at which a bank lends exceeds the interest rate at which it borrows. But a bank must perform a delicate balancing act. Lending is risky, and the more a bank ties up its deposits in high-risk, high-interest-rate loans, the bigger is its chance of not being able to repay its depositors. And if depositors perceive a high risk of not being repaid, they withdraw their funds and create a crisis for the bank. So a bank must be prudent in the way it uses its deposits, balancing security against profit.

Reserves and Loans To achieve security for its depositors, a bank divides its funds into two parts: reserves and loans. **Reserves** are currency in a bank's vault plus its deposit at the Bank of Canada. The currency in a bank's vaults is a reserve to meet depositors' demand for cash. The bank replenishes the ATM every time you and your friends raid it for cash for a midnight pizza. The account of a bank at the Bank of Canada is similar to your own bank account. Banks use these accounts to receive and make payments. A bank deposits cash into or draws cash out of its account at the Bank of Canada and writes cheques on that account to settle debts with other banks.

If a bank kept all its deposits as reserves, it wouldn't make any profit. In fact, it keeps only a small fraction of its funds in reserves and lends the rest. A bank has four types of assets:

1. *Overnight loans* are loans that one bank makes to another for one night only. The loan is repaid at

the start of the next business day. A bank that has surplus reserves makes overnight loans to banks that have a shortage of reserves.

2. *Liquid assets* are Canadian government Treasury bills and commercial bills. These assets are the banks' first line of defence if they need cash. They can be sold and instantly converted into cash with virtually no risk of loss. Because liquid assets are virtually risk-free, they have a low interest rate.

3. *Investment securities* are longer-term Canadian government bonds and other bonds. These assets can be sold quickly and converted into cash but at prices that fluctuate. Because their prices fluctuate, these assets are riskier than liquid assets but they have a higher interest rate.

4. *Loans* are commitments of fixed amounts of money for agreed-upon periods of time. Most banks' loans are made to corporations to finance the purchase of capital equipment and inventories and to households—personal loans—to finance purchases of consumer durable goods, such as cars or boats. The outstanding balances on credit card accounts are also bank loans. Loans are the riskiest assets of a bank because they cannot be converted into cash until they are due to be repaid. And some borrowers default and never repay. Because they are the riskiest of a bank's assets, loans also carry the highest interest rate.

The Economic Functions of Banks Banks make a profit from the spread between the interest rate they pay on deposits and the interest rate at which they lend. What services do banks perform that make depositors willing to accept a low interest rate and borrowers willing to pay a higher one? Banks provide four services for which people are willing to pay:

1. *Create liquidity*. Most of the liabilities of banks are money; others are highly liquid assets that are easily convertible into money.

    Banks create liquidity by borrowing short and lending long. Borrowing short means taking deposits but standing ready to repay them on short notice (and even on no notice in the case of demand deposits). Lending long means making loan commitments for a prearranged, and often long period. For example, when a person makes a deposit with a trust company, that deposit can be withdrawn at any time. But the trust company

makes a lending commitment to a homebuyer for 5 years.

2. *Minimize the cost of borrowing* by bringing borrowers and lenders together. Imagine how troublesome it would be if there were no banks. A firm that was looking for $1 million to buy a new production plant would probably have to hunt around for several dozen people from whom to borrow in order to acquire enough funds for its capital project. Banks lower those costs. The firm that needs $1 million can go to a single bank to obtain those funds. The bank has to borrow from a large number of people, but it's not doing that just for this one firm and the $1 million that it wants to borrow. The bank can establish an organization that is capable of raising funds from a large number of depositors and can spread the cost of this activity over a large number of borrowers.

3. *Minimize the cost of monitoring borrowers*. Lending money is a risky business. There is always a danger that the borrower may not repay. Firms are the biggest borrowers. They borrow to invest in projects that they hope will return a profit but sometimes those hopes are not fulfilled. Monitoring the activities of a borrower and ensuring that the best possible decisions are being taken to make a profit and to avoid a loss are costly and specialized activities. Imagine how costly it would be if each household that lent money to a firm had to incur the costs of monitoring that firm directly. By depositing funds with a bank, households avoid those costs. The bank performs the monitoring activity by using specialized resources that have a much lower cost than what each household would incur if it had to undertake the activity individually.

4. *Pool risk*. There is always a chance of a loan not being repaid—of default. Lending to a large number of individuals reduces the risk of default—if one person defaults on a loan, it is a nuisance but not a disaster. But if only one person borrows and that person defaults on the loan, the entire loan is a write-off. Banks enable people to pool risk in an efficient way. Thousands of people lend money to any one bank, and, in turn, the bank re-lends the money to hundreds, perhaps thousands, of individuals and firms. If any one firm defaults on its loan, that default is spread across all the depositors and no individual depositor is left exposed to a high degree of risk.

The Bank of Canada

The Bank of Canada is Canada's **central bank**, a public authority that supervises other banks and financial institutions, financial markets, and the payments system and conducts monetary policy.

You will learn much more about the Bank of Canada when we study monetary policy in Chapter 27. For now, all we need to understand is the bare outlines of what the Bank of Canada does and its place in the banking system.

The Bank of Canada is a bank. And like all banks, it accepts deposits, make loans, and holds investment securities. But the Bank of Canada is special in three important ways. It is the

- Banker to banks and government
- Lender of last resort
- Sole issuer of bank notes

Banker to Banks and Government The Bank of Canada has a restricted list of customers. They are the chartered banks, credit unions and caisses populaires, and trust and morgage loan companies that make up the banking system; the government of Canada; and the central banks of other countries. The Bank of Canada accepts deposits from these customers. And the deposits of the banks are part of their reserves.

Lender of Last Resort The Bank of Canada makes loans to banks. But it is the **lender of last resort**, which means that it stands ready to make loans when the banking system as a whole is short of reserves. If some banks are short of reserves while others have surplus reserves, the overnight loan market moves the funds from one bank to another.

Sole Issuer of Bank Notes The Bank of Canada is the only bank that is permitted to issues bank notes. You might think that such a monopoly is natural, but it isn't. In some banking systems—those of Ireland and Scotland are examples—private banks also issue bank notes. But in Canada and most other countries, the central bank has a monopoly on this activity.

The Bank of Canada's Balance Sheet The balance sheet of the Bank of Canada summarizes the activities that we've just described. The Bank of Canada's assets are government of Canada securities and last-resort loans to banks. Much of the time, there are no last-

resort loans outstanding, so the Bank's only assets are its government of Canada securities.

The Bank of Canada's liabilities are Bank of Canada notes and deposits of banks and the government. The bank notes are what we use in our daily transactions. Some of these bank notes are held by households and firms and others are in the tills and vaults of banks and in ATM machines. The total value of Bank of Canada notes in 2005 was $44 billion.

The deposits of banks at the Bank of Canada are small in magnitude but large in importance. On any given day these deposits are around $50 million. To see how tiny this amount is, compare it to the total deposits in M2+. Those deposits were $867 billion in 2005. So the $50 million of reserves on deposit at the Bank of Canada represents about one penny for every $2,000 of deposits in M2+.

How can the banks manage with such a small amount of reserves at the Bank of Canada? The answer is that Canada has an amazingly efficient payments system—one of the most efficient in the world.

The Payments System

The **payments system** is the system through which banks make payments to each other to settle transactions by their customers. You saw why we need such a system when you thought about Colleen buying some new roller blades from Rocky. If Colleen banks at TD Canada Trust and Rocky's bank is CIBC, when Colleen writes her cheque to buy the blades, TD Canada Trust must take $200 from Colleen and pay that amount to CIBC; and CIBC must put the $200 into Rocky's account.

Most transactions between two parties involve two banks and so require one bank to pay another. Think about what happens when Jack, who banks at CIBC, gets $50 cash from an Interac Automated Banking Machine. Interac gives Jack the $50 in cash and his CIBC deposit balance goes down by $50. But now, CIBC owes Interac $50.

The payments system enables banks to make payments to each other. This system in Canada is operated by the Canadian Payments Association or CPA, a not-for-profit organization created by parliament in 2000. The CPA owns and operates the two national payments systems:

- Large Value Transfer System
- Automated Clearing Settlement System

Large Value Transfer System The **Large Value Transfer System (LVTS)** is an electronic payments system that enables financial institutions and their customers to make large payments instantly and with the sure knowledge that the payment has been made. It was launched in 1999. The Bank of Canada along with 14 of the largest banks have access to the LVTS, and on an average day, it handles more than 18,000 payments worth an astonishing $140 billion.

Throughout any given day, the LVTS members send payments back and forth to each other. When the transactions are added up at the end of the day, some of these financial institutions may end up needing money, while others may have funds left over.

Every day, LVTS members borrow and lend money to each other on a one-day basis, to cover their net LVTS positions. The interest rate paid on these and other overnight loans is called the *overnight rate*. This interest rate plays a central role in the Bank of Canada's monetary policy, as you will learn in Chapter 28.

Automated Clearing Settlement System The **Automated Clearing Settlement System (ACSS)** is the system through which all payments not processed by the LVTS are handled. These payments include cheques and small-value electronic payments, such as point-of-sale debit card or ABM transactions. Unlike the LVTS, which operates continuously through the day, the ACSS settles the net amounts owed just once a day. On an average day, the ACSS handles more than 20 million payments worth around $17 billion.

REVIEW QUIZ

1 What are Canada's main depository institutions?
2 Why don't banks keep all the money that people place on deposit in their vaults?
3 What are the economic functions of banks?
4 How do banks create liquidity and pool risk?
5 How does the Bank of Canada differ from all other banks?
6 What is the payments sytem?

myeconlab Study Plan 25.2

We've described the functions of banks and other depository institutions. We're now going to see how these firms have the ability to create money.

How Banks Create Money

BANKS CREATE MONEY. BUT THIS DOESN'T MEAN that they have smoke-filled back rooms in which counterfeiters are busily working. Remember, most money is deposits, not currency. What banks create is deposits, and they do so by making loans.

Creating Deposits by Making Loans

The easiest way to see that banks create deposits is to think about what happens when Jack, who has a Visa card issued by CIBC, uses his card to buy a tank of gas from PetroCan. When Jack signs the card pay slip, he takes a loan from CIBC and obligates himself to repay the loan at a later date. At the end of the business day, a PetroCan clerk takes a pile of signed credit card sales slips, including Jack's, to PetroCan's bank. For now, let's assume that PetroCan also banks at CIBC. The bank immediately credits PetroCan's account with the value of the slips (minus the bank's commission).

You can see that these transactions have created a bank deposit and a loan. Jack has increased the size of his loan (his credit card balance) and PetroCan has increased the size of its bank deposit. And because deposits are money, CIBC has created money.

If as we've just assumed, Jack and PetroCan use the same bank, no further transactions take place. CIBC has an increase in deposits and loans. But the outcome is essentially the same when two banks are involved in the transactions. If PetroCan's bank is the Royal Bank, then CIBC pays the Royal Bank using its reserves. CIBC has an increase in loans and a decrease in reserves; the Royal Bank has an increase in reserves and an increase in deposits. And the banking system as a whole has an increase in deposits and loans and no change in reserves.

If Jack had swiped his card at an automatic payment pump, all these transactions would have occurred at the time he filled his tank, and the quantity of money would have increased by the amount of his purchase (minus the bank's commission for conducting the transactions).

The quantity of deposits that banks can create is limited by three factors:

■ The monetary base
■ Desired reserves
■ Desired currency holding

The Monetary Base The liabilities of the Bank of Canada (plus coins issued by the Canadian Mint) form the **monetary base**—the sum of Bank of Canada notes outside the Bank of Canada, banks' deposits at the Bank of Canada, and coins held by households, firms, and banks. The size of the monetary base limits the total quantity of money that the banking system can create because banks have a desired level of reserves and households and firms have a desired level of currency holding and both of these desired holdings of the monetary base depend on the quantity of money.

Desired Reserves A bank's *actual reserves* consist of the currency in its vaults and its deposit at the Bank of Canada. A bank uses its reserves to meet depositors' demand for currency and to make payments to other banks.

You've also seen that banks don't have $100 of reserves for every $100 that people have deposited with them. If the banks did behave that way, they wouldn't earn any profit.

Banks today have reserves of $3 for every $100 of M1 deposits and 40¢ for every $100 of M2+ deposits. Most of these reserves are currency. You saw in the previous section that reserves in the form of deposits at the Bank of Canada are tiny. No need for panic. These reserve levels are adequate for ordinary business needs.

The fraction of a bank's total deposits that are held in reserves is called the **reserve ratio**. So, with reserves of $3 for every $100 of M1 deposits, that reserve ratio is 0.3 or 3 pecent, and with reserves of 40¢ for every $100 of M2+ deposits, that reserve ratio is 0.004 or 0.4 percent.

A bank's *desired reserves* are the reserves that it wishes to hold. In most banking systems, banks are *required* to hold a level of reserves that does not fall below some specifed percentage of total deposits. This percentage is called the *required reserve ratio*. In Canada, the required reserve ratio was lowered during the 1990s and by the mid-1990s it was lowered to zero.

The **desired reserve ratio** is the ratio of reserves to deposits that a bank wants to hold. Because there are no required reserves, banks in Canada are free to determine the prudent level of reserves—and the desired reserve ratio—based on their daily business requirments.

A bank's reserve ratio changes when its customers make a deposit or a withdrawal. If a bank's customer makes a deposit, reserves and deposits increase by the same amount, so the bank's reserve ratio increases. Similarly, if a bank's customer makes a withdrawal, reserves and deposits decrease by the same amount, so the bank's reserve ratio decreases.

A bank's **excess reserves** are its actual reserves minus its desired reserves. Whenever the banking system as a whole has excess reserves, the banks are able to create money. Banks increase their loans and deposits when they have excess reserves and they decrease their loans and deposits when they are short of reserves—when desired reserves exceed actual reserves.

But the greater the desired reserve ratio, the smaller is the quantity of deposits and money that the banking system can create from a given amount of monetary base.

Desired Currency Holding We hold our money in the form of currency and bank deposits. The proportion of money held as currency isn't constant but at any given time, people have a definite view as to how much they want to hold in each form of money.

In 2004, for every dollar of M1 deposits held, we held 35¢ of currency and for every dollar of M2+ deposits, we held 5¢ of currency.

Because people want to hold some proportion of their money in the form of currency, when the total quantity of bank deposits increases, so does the quantity of currency that people want to hold. Because desired currency holding increases when deposits increase, currency leaves the banks when loans are made and deposits increase. We call the leakage of currency from the banking system the *currency drain*. And we call the ratio of currency to deposits the **currency drain ratio**.

The greater the currency drain ratio, the smaller is the quantity of deposits and the smaller is the quantity of money that the banking system can create from a given amount of monetary base.

The Money Creation Process

The money creation process begins when the banks have excess reserves. A sequence of events then plays out. The sequence, which keeps repeating until all the reserves are desired and no excess reserves are being held, has nine steps. They are

1. Banks have excess reserves.
2. Banks lend excess reserves.
3. Bank deposits increase.

4. The quantity of money increases.

5. New money is used to make payments.

6. Some of the new money remains on deposit.

7. Some of the new money is a *currency drain*.

8. Desired reserves increase because deposits have increased.

9. Excess reserves decrease, but remain positive.

Figure 25.2 illustrates this process.

To make the process of money creation more concrete, let's work through an example for a banking system in which each bank has a desired reserve ratio of 10 percent and the currency drain ratio is 50 percent. (Although these ratios are larger than the ones in the Canadian economy, they make the process end more quickly and enable you to see more clearly the principles at work.)

Figure 25.3 will keep track of the numbers. The process begins when all the banks have zero excess reserves except one bank, and it has excess reserves of $100,000. You can see these numbers in the first row of the "running tally" in Fig. 25.3.

The bank lends the $100,000 to Amy, who writes a cheque for $66,667 to buy a copy-shop franchise from Barb and withdraws $33,333 in currency to make some cash transactions. At this point, currency has increased by $33,333, bank deposits have increased by $66,667, and the quantity of money has increased by $100,000. You can see these numbers in Fig. 25.3 as the second row of the running tally.

For Amy's bank, that is the end of the story. But Barb's bank has now got some excess reserves. Barb's deposit has increased by $66,667 and so have the reserves of Barb's bank. With a 10 percent desired reserve ratio, Barb's bank now wants to hold an additional $6,667 in reserves and to loan the other $60,000. The bank loans $60,000 to Bob, who writes a cheque for $40,000 to buy a luxury car from Carl and withdraws $20,000 in currency.

Now currency has increased by $53,333, bank deposits have increased by $106,667, and the quantity of money has increased by $160,000. You can see these numbers in the running tally in Fig. 25.3.

FIGURE 25.2
How the Banking System Creates Money by Making Loans

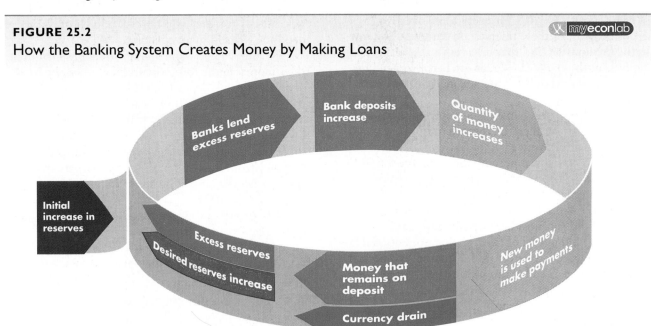

Initially, the banking system has excess reserves. Banks lend the excess reserves, new bank deposits are created, and the quantity of money increases. New money is used to make payments. Households and firms receiving payments keep some of the receipts as currency—a currency drain—and place the rest on deposit in banks. The increase in bank deposits increases banks' reserves but also increases banks' desired reserves. Desired reserves increase by less than the increase in actual reserves, so the banks still have some excess reserves, though less than before. The process repeats until excess reserves have been eliminated.

Barb's bank now has no excess reserves. But Carl's bank has now got some excess reserves. Carl's deposit has increased by $40,000 and so have the reserves of Carl's bank. With a 10 percent desired reserve ratio, Carl's bank now wants to hold an additional $4,000 in reserves and to loan the other $36,000. The bank loans $36,000 to Chuck, who writes a cheque for $24,000 to buy a boat and withdraws $12,000 in currency.

By now, currency has increased by $65,333, bank deposits have increased by $130,667, and the quantity of money has increased by $196,000. You can see these numbers in the running tally in Fig. 25.3.

Figure 25.3 shows one additional round in the process and also shows the final tallies. When the process ends, reserves have increased by $16,667, currency has increased by $83,333, deposits have increased by $166,667, and the quantity of money has increased by $250,000.

The Money Multiplier

The sequence in Fig. 25.3 is the first four stages of the process that finally reaches the totals shown in the final row of the running tally. To figure out the entire process, look closely at the numbers in the figure. The initial increase in reserves is $100,000 (call it A). At each stage, the loan is 60 percent (0.6) of the previous loan and the quantity of money increases by 0.6 of the previous increase. Call that proportion L ($L = 0.6$). We can write down the complete sequence as an

FIGURE 25.3
The Money Creation Process: An Example

A bank has excess reserves of $100,000. It loans those reserves. Of the amount loaned, $33,333 (50 percent of deposits) leaves the banks in a currency drain and $66,667 remains on deposit. Desired reserves increase by $6,667 (10 percent of the deposit) and the banks loan $60,000.

Of this amount, $20,000 leaves the banks in a currency drain and $40,000 remains on deposit. The process repeats until the banks have created enough deposits to eliminate their excess reserves. $100,000 of excess reserves creates $250,000 of money.

equation as follows:

$$A + AL + AL^2 + AL^3 + AL^4 + AL^5 \dots$$

Remember, L is a fraction, so at each stage in this sequence the amount of new loans and new money gets smaller. The total value of loans made and money created at the end of the process is the above sum, which is[1]

$$A/(1 - L).$$

If we use the numbers from the example, the total increase in the quantity of money is

$$\$100,000 + 60,000 + 36,000 + 21,600 + \dots$$

$$= \$100,000 \,(1 + 0.6 + 0.36 + 0.216 + \dots)$$

$$= \$100,000 \,(1 + 0.6 + 0.6^2 + 0.6^3 + \dots)$$

$$= \$100,000 \times 1/(1 - 0.6)$$

$$= \$100,000 \times 1/(0.4)$$

$$= \$100,000 \times 2.5$$

$$= \$250,000.$$

The **money multiplier** is the ratio of the change in the quantity of money to the change in monetary base. Here, the monetary base increased by $100,000 and the quantity of money increased by $250,000 so the money multiplier is 2.5.

The magnitude of the money multiplier depends on the desired reserve ratio and the currency drain ratio. Call the monetary base MB and the quantity of money M. When there are no excess reserves,

$$MB = \text{Desired currency holding} + \text{Desired reserves}$$

---

[1] Both here and in the expenditure multiplier process in Chapter 23, the sequence of values is called a convergent geometric series. To find the sum of a series such as this, begin by calling the sum S. Then write the sum as

$$S = A + AL + AL^2 + AL^3 + AL^4 + AL^5 + \dots.$$

Multiply by L to get,

$$LS = AL + AL^2 + AL^3 + AL^4 + AL^5 + \dots$$

and then subtract the second equation from the first to get

$$S(1 - L) = A$$

or

$$S = A/(1 - L).$$

Also,

$$M = \text{Deposits} + \text{Desired currency holding}$$

Call the currency drain ratio a and the desired reserve ratio b. Then,

$$\text{Desired currency holding} = a \times \text{Deposits}$$

$$\text{Desired reserves} = b \times \text{Deposits}$$

We can now rewrite the equations for MB and M as

$$MB = (a + b) \times \text{Deposits}$$

$$M = (1 + a) \times \text{Deposits}.$$

Divide the above equation for M by the one for MB and you see that

$$M = (1 + a)/(a + b) \times MB.$$

Use the values $a = 0.5$ and $b = 0.1$ and you will see that $(1 + a)/(a + b) = 1.5/0.6 = 2.5$.

The Money Multiplier in Canada   The money multiplier in Canada can be found by using this formula and the values of a and b in the Canadian economy.

Because we have two definitions of money, M1 and M2+, we have two money multipliers. Using the numbers for 2004: For M1, a is 0.35 and b is 0.03 so the M1 multiplier is 3.55. For M2+, a is 0.004 and b is 0.05 so the M2+ multiplier is 18.6.

REVIEW QUIZ

1 How do banks create money by making loans, and what are the factors that limit the amount of money and loans that banks can create?

2 A bank manager tells you that she doesn't create money. She just lends the money that people deposit in the bank. How do you explain to her that she's wrong and that she does create money?

3 If people decided to hold less currency and more deposits, how would the quantity of money change?

 Study Plan 25.3

You now know how money gets created. Your next task is to study the demand for money.

The Demand for Money

THE AMOUNT OF MONEY WE RECEIVE EACH WEEK in payment for our labour is income—a *flow*. The amount of money that we hold in our wallet or in a deposit account at the bank is an inventory—a *stock*. There is no limit to how much income we would like to *receive* each week. But there is a limit to how big an inventory of money each of us would like to *hold* and not spend.

The Influences on Money Holding

The quantity of money that people choose to hold depends on four main factors:

- The price level
- The interest rate
- Real GDP
- Financial innovation

The Price Level The quantity of money measured in dollars is *nominal money*. The quantity of nominal money demanded is proportional to the price level, other things remaining the same. That is, if the price level rises by 10 percent, people hold 10 percent more nominal money than before, other things remaining the same. If you hold $20 to buy your weekly movies and pop, you will increase your money holding to $22 if the prices of movies and pop—and your wage rate—increase by 10 percent.

The quantity of money measured in constant dollars (for example, in 1997 dollars) is called *real money*. Real money is equal to nominal money divided by the price level. It is the quantity of money measured in terms of what it will buy. In the above example, when the price level rises by 10 percent and you increase the amount of money that you hold by 10 percent, you keep your *real* money constant. Your $22 at the new price level buys the same quantity of goods and is the same quantity of *real money* as your $20 at the original price level. The quantity of real money held does not depend on the price level.

The Interest Rate A fundamental principle of economics is that as the opportunity cost of something increases, people try to find substitutes for it. Money is no exception. The higher the opportunity cost of holding money, other things remaining the same, the smaller is the quantity of real money demanded. But what is the opportunity cost of holding money? It is the interest rate that you must forgo on other assets that you could hold instead of money minus the interest rate that you can earn by holding money.

The interest rate that you earn on currency and demand deposits is zero. So the opportunity cost of holding these items is the interest rate on other assets such as a savings bond or Treasury bill. By holding money instead, you forgo the interest that you otherwise would have received. This forgone interest is the opportunity cost of holding money.

Money loses value because of inflation. So why isn't the inflation rate part of the cost of holding money? It is: Other things remaining the same, the higher the expected inflation rate, the higher are all interest rates and the higher, therefore, is the opportunity cost of holding money. The forces that make the interest rate change to reflect changes in the expected inflation rate are described in Chapter 27, pp. 648–649.)

Real GDP The quantity of money that households and firms plan to hold depends on the amount they are spending, and the quantity of money demanded in the economy as a whole depends on aggregate expenditure—real GDP.

Again, suppose that you hold an average of $20 to finance your weekly purchases of movies and pop. Now imagine that the prices of these goods and of all other goods remain constant but that your income increases. As a consequence you now spend more, and you keep a larger amount of money on hand to finance your higher volume of expenditure.

Financial Innovation Technological change and the arrival of new financial products—called **financial innovation**—change the quantity of money held. The major financial innovations are the widespread use of

1. Daily interest deposits
2. Automatic transfers between demand deposits and savings deposits
3. Automatic teller machines
4. Credit cards and debit cards

These innovations have occurred because the development of computing power has lowered the cost of calculations and record keeping.

We summarize the effects of the influences on money holding by using a demand for money curve.

The Demand for Money Curve

The **demand for money curve** is the relationship between the quantity of real money demanded and the interest rate when all other influences on the amount of money that people wish to hold remain the same.

Figure 25.4 shows a demand for money curve, *MD*. When the interest rate rises, other things remaining the same, the opportunity cost of holding money rises and the quantity of real money demanded decreases—there is a movement along the demand for money curve. Similarly, when the interest rate falls, the opportunity cost of holding money falls, and the quantity of real money demanded increases—there is a movement down along the demand for money curve.

When any other influence on the amount of money that people plan to hold changes, there is a change in the demand for money and the demand for money curve shifts. Let's study these shifts.

Shifts in the Demand for Money Curve

A change in real GDP or financial innovation changes the demand for money and shifts the demand for money curve.

Figure 25.5 illustrates the change in the demand for money. A decrease in real GDP decreases the demand for money and shifts the demand curve leftward from MD_0 to MD_1. An increase in real GDP has the opposite effect. It increases the demand for money and shifts the demand curve rightward from MD_0 to MD_2.

The influence of financial innovation on the demand for money curve is more complicated. It might increase the demand for some types of deposits, decrease the demand for others, and decrease the demand for currency.

We'll look at the effects of changes in real GDP and financial innovation by studying the demand for money in Canada.

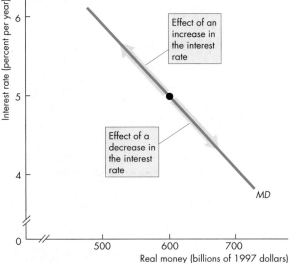

FIGURE 25.4
The Demand for Money

The demand for money curve, *MD*, shows the relationship between the quantity of real money that people plan to hold and the interest rate, other things remaining the same. The interest rate is the opportunity cost of holding money. A change in the interest rate brings a movement along the demand curve.

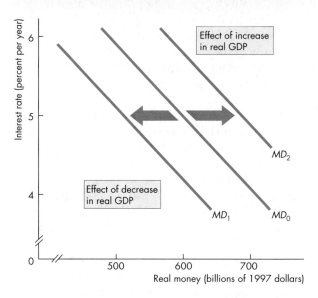

FIGURE 25.5
Changes in the Demand for Money

A decrease in real GDP decreases the demand for money and shifts the demand curve leftward from MD_0 to MD_1. An increase in real GDP increases the demand for money and shifts the demand curve rightward from MD_0 to MD_2. Financial innovation decreases the demand for some forms of money and increases the demand for other forms.

The Demand for Money in Canada

Figure 25.6 shows the relationship between the interest rate and the quantity of real money demanded in Canada between 1968 and 2004. Each dot shows the interest rate and the quantity of money held as a percentage of GDP in a given year. We've measured money as a percentage of GDP to remove the effects of rising incomes and a rising price level in order to reveal the relationship between money holding and the interest rate. In part (a), the measure of money is M1 and in part (b), it is M2+.

In 1968, the demand for M1 (in part a) was MD_0. During the 1980s, the demand for M1 decreased and the demand curve for M1 shifted leftward and by 1991, it had become MD_1. During the late 1990s and early 2000s, the demand for M1 increased and the demand curve for M1 shifted rightward. By 2004, the demand curve for M1 has shifted to MD_2.

In 1968, the demand curve for M2+ (in part b) was MD_0. During the 1970s, the demand for M2+ increased and the demand curve for M2+ shifted rightward. By 1981, it had shifted to MD_1. During the 1990s, the demand for M2+ decreased and by 2004, the demand curve for M2+ had shifted leftward to MD_2.

Why did the demand curves shift? Financial innovation is the main reason. During the 1970s, the arrival of automatic transfers between demand deposits and savings deposits made M2+ deposits increasingly attractive, so the demand for these

---

FIGURE 25.6

The Demand for Money in Canada

(a) Demand for M1

(b) Demand for M2+

The dots show the quantity of real money and the interest rate in each year between 1968 and 2004. Between 1968 and 1981, the demand for M1 was MD_0 in part (a). The demand for M1 decreased during the 1980s and the demand curve shifted leftward to MD_1. The demand for M1 increased during the late 1990s and early 2000s and the demand curve shifted rightward to MD_2.

In 1968, the demand curve for M2+ was MD_0 in part (b). During the 1970s, the demand for M2+ increased and by 1981 the demand curve had shifted rightward to MD_1. During the 1990s, the demand for M2+ decreased and the demand curve shifted leftward to MD_2. Financial innovation is the main reason for the shifts in the demand for money curves.

Source of data: Bank of Canada, *Banking and Financial Statistics*, tables E1 and F1.

deposits increased. Later, daily interest on chequing accounts increased the demand for M1 deposits.

You can see by comparing the two parts of Fig. 25.6 that the financial innovation that increased the demand for M2+ during the 1970s did not decrease the demand for M1. But rising interest rates during the 1970s decreased the quantity of M1 demanded—shown by a movement along the demand for M1 curve, MD_0, in part (a).

The opportunity cost of holding money is the interest forgone by not holding some other type of asset. But what is forgone depends partly on the interest rate that is paid on money itself. The interest rate on currency and demand deposits is zero. So for these components of money, the opportunity cost of holding money is the interest rate on non-money assets. But savings deposits and other types of deposits that are included in M2+ earn interest. So the opportunity cost of holding these forms of money is the interest rate on non-money assets minus the interest rate on these deposits.

At one time, economists believed that the quantity of money was a good indicator of the state of aggregate demand and that too rapid a growth in the quantity of money indicated that aggregate demand was growing too quickly. But the shifts in the demand for money curve have changed that belief.

REVIEW QUIZ

1 What are the main influences on the quantity of real money that people and businesses plan to hold?
2 What does the demand for money curve show?
3 How does an increase in the interest rate change the quantity of money demanded, and how would you use the demand for money curve to show the effects?
4 How does an increase in real GDP change the demand for money, and how would you use the demand for money curve to show the effects?
5 How have financial innovations changed the demand for M1 and the demand for M2+?

(X) myeconlab   **Study Plan 25.4**

Your final task in this chapter is to see how the interest rate is determined by demand and supply in the market for money.

Interest Rate Determination

AN INTEREST RATE IS THE PERCENTAGE YIELD ON a financial security such as a *bond* or a *stock*. The **interest rate** is the amount received by a lender and paid by a borrower expressed as a percentage of the amount of the loan.

A bond is a promise to make a sequence of future payments. There are many different possible sequences but the simplest one is the case of a bond called a perpetuity. A *perpetuity* is a bond that promises to pay a specified fixed amount of money each year forever. The issuer of such a bond will never buy the bond back (redeem it); the bond will remain outstanding forever and will earn a fixed dollar payment each year. Because the payment each year is a fixed dollar amount, the interest rate on a bond varies as the price of the bond varies. In the case of a perpetuity, the formula that links the interest rate to the price of the bond is a particularly simple one. That formula is

$$\text{Interest rate} = \frac{\text{Dollar payment per year}}{\text{Price of bond}} \times 100.$$

This formula states that the higher the price of a bond, other things remaining the same, the lower is the interest rate. An example will make this relationship clear. Suppose the government of Canada sells a bond that promises to pay $10 a year. If the price of the bond is $100, the interest rate is 10 percent a year—$10 is 10 percent of $100. If the price of the bond is $50, the interest rate is 20 percent a year—$10 is 20 percent of $50. If the price of the bond is $200, the interest rate is 5 percent a year—$10 is 5 percent of $200.

You've just seen the link between the price of a bond and the interest rate. Because of this link, fluctuations in the interest rate bring fluctuations in the price of a bond. People try to anticipate these fluctuations and avoid holding bonds when they expect the price of a bond to fall. But they spread their risks. To do so, they divide their wealth between bonds (and other interest-bearing financial assets) and money, and the amount they hold as money depends on the interest rate. We can study the forces that determine the interest rate either in the market for bonds or the market for money. Because the Bank of Canada can influence the supply of *money* (which we study in Chapter 27), we focus on the market for money.

Money Market Equilibrium

The supply of and the demand for money determine the interest rate. The actions of the Bank of Canada and the banking system determine the supply of money. The Bank of Canada is the sole supplier of monetary base and it can choose the terms on which currency and reserves for the banks are supplied. Two extreme cases span the range of possibilities. The Bank of Canada can either:

- Target the quantity of money
- Target the interest rate

Quantity of Money Target If the Bank of Canada targets the quantity of money, then the quantity of money supplied is fixed and the money supply curve is the vertical *MS* in Fig. 25.7.

On any given day, all the influences on the demand for money except for the interest rate are constant. But the lower the interest rate, the greater is the quantity of money demanded along the demand for money curve, *MD*.

When the quantity of money supplied equals the quantity of money demanded, the money market is in equilibrium. Equilibrium is achieved by changes in the interest rate. If the interest rate is above equilibrium, people demand a smaller quantity of money than the quantity supplied. They are holding too much money so they buy bonds. This action raises the price of a bond and lowers the interest rate. Conversely, if the interest rate is below equilibrium, people are holding too little money so they sell bonds. This action lowers the price of a bond and raises the interest rate. Only when the interest rate is at the level at which people are holding the quantity of money supplied do they willingly hold the money and take no actions that change the interest rate.

Interest Rate Target If the Bank of Canada targets the interest rate, then the quantity of monetary base supplied and the quantity of money supplied is the quantity demanded at the Bank's chosen interest rate.

In Fig. 25.7, if the Bank wants to set the interest rate at 5 percent a year, then the quantity of money demanded will equal $600 billion, so that will be the quantity of money in the economy. But if the Bank of Canada wants an interest rate of 4 percent a year, it must allow the monetary base and quantity of money to increase to equal the larger quantity demanded at 4 percent a year.

FIGURE 25.7
Money Market Equilibrium

If the Bank of Canada targets the quantity of money, equilibrium occurs when the interest rate has adjusted to make the quantity of money demanded equal to the quantity supplied. If the Bank of Canada targets the interest rate, the quantity of money adjusts to equal the quantity demanded.

REVIEW QUIZ

1. What is the relationship between the price of a bond and the interest rate?
2. How is the interest rate determined if the Bank of Canada targets the quantity of money?
3. How is the quantity of money determined if the Bank of Canada targets the interest rate?

myeconlab **Study Plan 25.5**

◆ You now know what money is, how the banking system creates it, and how its quantity influences or might be influenced by the interest rate. The next three chapters build on this one and explain how the Bank of Canada conducts its monetary policy. In the next chapter, you will see how the exchange rate is determined and how Canada's flexible exchange rate enables the Bank of Canada to target the inflation rate. In Chapter 27, you will study the inflation process. And then, in Chapter 28, you will study monetary policy.

Canada's Changing Demand for Money

FINANCIAL POST, DECEMBER 3, 2002

Odds stacked against cash

From consumer demands for speed and convenience to banks' hunger for fatter returns, a collusion of forces is ensuring that the use of paper money is sliding into decline.

"Cash is a very inefficient system, physical bills don't last very long before they need replacing, if you lose it there is no recourse and it costs a lot to count and process," says Joseph D'Cruz a professor of strategy at the Rotman School of Management at the University of Toronto. "Couple that with the very high level of trust Canadians place in their national banks and the rise of electronic banking is sure to drive down the use of cash."

If Canadians have trust in their banks, they seem to have less trust in their national currency. Retailers from Dominion to Tim Hortons and Shoppers Drug Mart have refused to accept bills in $50 or $100 denominations out of counterfeiting fears. Some stores, including Loblaws, have even started to put lowly $5 bills through a security scan. It's just one more reason that cash and other paper transactions, including cheques, are giving way to debit and credit charges. ...

... Interac Direct Payment—which polls Canadians annually to establish their preferred mode of payment for goods and services—says the use of electronic payment outstripped cash transactions in 1999. ... In 1995 well over half of all transactions were made in cash, by last year cash accounted for roughly 30% of transactions, according to Interac. ...

One of the last industries to resist accepting credit and debit has been fast food—because consumers spend roughly $5 each and the merchant pays a fee for customers to pay electronically. In Canada, however, fast food joints including McDonald's, Burger King, and Wendy's introduced debit payment several years ago.

Reprinted by permission of the *National Post*.

Essence of the Story

■ The use of paper money is decreasing, and the use of electronic credit and debit charges is increasing.

■ Joseph D'Cruz, a professor of strategy at the Rotman School of Management at the University of Toronto, says that cash is an inefficient system and because Canadians trust their banks, electronic systems will continue to decrease the use of cash.

■ Some retailers refuse to accept $50 bills or $100 bills because they fear counterfeiting, and some even put $5 bills through a security scan.

■ A survey shows that cash payments decreased from more than 50 percent of transactions in 1995 to 30 percent in 2001.

■ Because each transaction is small, the fast-food sector has been the most resistant to electronic transactions—but even in this sector, the use of cash is decreasing.

Economic Analysis

■ Figure 1 shows the amount of currency in Canada as a percentage of GDP since 1970. This percentage decreased during the 1970s and 1980s but increased during the early 1990s and was steady after 1994.

■ The news article emphasizes reasons why the amount of currency might have *decreased*. But why did currency increase during the 1990s?

■ Currency is one component of money, and the demand for money increases when real GDP increases.

■ In Fig. 1, we graph currency *as a percentage of GDP* to remove the influence of GDP on the amount of currency held.

■ So Fig. 1 tells us that even holding real GDP constant, currency increased during the early 1990s and did not decrease in the early 2000s.

■ The reason for the increase in currency is that the interest rate, which is the opportunity cost of holding currency, decreased during the 1990s.

■ Figure 2 shows the relationship between the amount of currency (as a percentage of GDP) against the interest rate on savings accounts at chartered banks.

■ You can see that, just as predicted by the theory of the demand for money, the lower the interest rate, the greater is the quantity of currency held.

■ As the opportunity cost of holding currency increased during the 1970s, the amount of currency held (as a percentage of GDP) decreased.

■ And as the opportunity cost of holding currency decreased during the 1990s, the amount of currency held (as a percentage of GDP) increased.

■ A change in the interest rate changes the quantity of currency demanded, but it does not change the demand for currency.

■ The demand for currency changes when some other influence on payment methods changes.

■ So what is left of the message in the news article? As we increasingly use debit cards, are we using less currency?

■ Figure 2 provides part of the answer. The demand for currency has decreased. The demand curve of the 1990s is to the left of the demand curve of the 1970s.

■ But the demand for currency decreased during the early 1980s, not during the late 1990s when electronic payments technologies spread.

Figure 1 Trends in currency holding

Figure 2 Currency holding and the interest rate

■ Most likely, the very high interest rate of 1981 made people think harder about how to be more economical in their use of currency, and the lesson was a permanent one.

■ Debit cards, which enable us to pay for purchases directly from our bank accounts, and credit cards, which enable us to buy on credit through the month and pay when we receive our own pay cheques, decrease our demand for currency.

■ As more and more businesses accept debit cards and credit cards and as more and more transactions are done by debit cards and credit cards, people will hold less cash.

■ But these changes are not visible in the aggregate data. Some other changes are working in the opposite direction to maintain the overall popularity of currency.

SUMMARY

KEY POINTS

What Is Money? (pp. 590–592)

- Money is the means of payment, a medium of exchange, a unit of account, and a store of value.
- M1 consists of currency and households' and businesses' demand deposits at chartered banks; M2+ consists of M1 plus savings deposits and other deposits at all types of depository institutions.

The Banking System (pp. 593–596)

- The banking system consists of depository institutions (the chartered banks, credit unions and caisses populaires, and trust and mortgage loan companies), the Bank of Canada, and the payments system.
- Banks provide four main economic services: They create liquidity, minimize the cost of obtaining funds, minimize the cost of monitoring borrowers, and pool risks.

How Banks Create Money (pp. 596–600)

- Banks create money by making loans.
- The total quantity of money that can be created depends on the monetary base, the desired reserves ratio, and the currency drain ratio.

The Demand for Money (pp. 601–604)

- The quantity of money demanded is the amount of money that people plan to hold.
- The quantity of real money equals the quantity of nominal money divided by the price level.
- The quantity of real money demanded depends on the interest rate, real GDP, and financial innovation. As the interest rate rises, the quantity of real money demanded decreases.

Interest Rate Determination (pp. 604–605)

- The Bank of Canada can set the quantity of money or the interest rate.
- If the quantity of money is fixed, the interest rate (and an asset price) adjusts to make the quantity of money demanded equal the quantity supplied.

- If the Bank of Canada wants to achieve a given interest rate, it must permit the monetary base and the quantity of money to adjust to equal the quantity of money demanded at that interest rate.

KEY FIGURES

KEY TERMS

PROBLEMS

Go to **myeconlab** for solutions to odd-numbered problems and additional exercises.

1. In Canada today, money includes which of the following items?
   a. Bank of Canada notes in the Bank of Montreal's cash machines
   b. Your Visa card
   c. The quarters inside public phones
   d. Canadian dollar coins in your pocket
   e. The cheque you have just written to pay for your rent
   f. The loan you took out last August to pay for your school fees

2. Which of the following items are money? Explain why.
   a. Demand deposits at CIBC
   b. Bell Canada stock held by individuals
   c. A "loonie"
   d. Canadian government securities

3. Sara withdraws $1,000 from her savings account at the Lucky Trust and Mortgage Company, keeps $50 in cash, and deposits the balance in her demand deposit account at the Bank of Montreal. What is the immediate change in M1 and M2+?

4. Monica takes $10,000 from her savings account at Happy Credit Union and puts the funds into her demand deposit account at the Royal Bank. What is the immediate change in M1 and M2+?

5. The banks in Zap have:

Reserves	$250 million
Loans	$1,000 million
Deposits	$2,000 million
Total assets	$2,500 million

   a. Construct the banks' balance sheet. If you are missing any assets, call them "other assets"; if you are missing any liabilities, call them "other liabilities."
   b. Calculate the banks' reserve ratio.
   c. If banks hold no excess reserves and the currency drain ratio is 10 percent, calculate the money multiplier.

6. The banks in Zip have:

Reserves	$205 million
Loans	$3,750 million
Deposits	$4,000 million
Total assets	$4,200 million

   a. Construct the banks' balance sheet. If you are missing any assets, call them "other assets"; if you are missing any liabilities, call them "other liabilities."
   b. Calculate the banks' reserve ratio.
   c. If banks hold no excess reserves and the currency drain ratio is 20 percent, calculate the money multiplier.

7. The spreadsheet provides information about the demand for money in Minland. Column A is the interest rate, R. Columns B, C, and D show the quantity of money demanded at three different levels of real GDP: Y_0 is $10 billion, Y_1 is $20 billion, and Y_2 is $30 billion. The quantity of money supplied by the Minland central bank is $3.0 billion. Initially, real GDP is $20 billion.

	A	B	C	D
1	R	Y_0	Y_1	Y_2
2	7	1.0	1.5	2.0
3	6	1.5	2.0	2.5
4	5	2.0	2.5	3.0
5	4	2.5	3.0	3.5
6	3	3.0	3.5	4.0
7	2	3.5	4.0	4.5
8	1	4.0	4.5	5.0

   What happens in Minland if
   a. The interest rate exceeds 4 percent a year?
   b. The interest rate is less than 4 percent a year?
   c. The interest rate equals 4 percent a year?

8. The Minland economy in problem 7 experiences a severe recession. Real GDP falls to $10 billion. The Minland central bank takes no action to change the quantity of money.
   a. What happens in Minland if the interest rate is 4 percent a year?
   b. What is the equilibrium interest rate?
   c. Compared with the situation in problem 7, does the interest rate in Minland rise or fall? Why?

9. The Minland economy in problem 7 experiences a severe business cycle. Real GDP rises to $30 billion and then falls to $10 billion. The Minland central bank takes no action to change the quantity of money. What happens to the interest rate in Minland
   a. During the expansion phase of the cycle?
   b. During the recession phase of the cycle?

10. Financial innovation in Minland changes the demand for money. People plan to hold $0.5 billion less than the numbers in the spreadsheet.
    a. What happens to the interest rate if the Minland central bank takes no actions?
    b. What happens to the interest rate if the Minland central bank decreases the quantity of money by $0.5 billion? Explain.

11. The figure shows the demand for real money curve in Upland.

   a. In the figure, draw the supply of money curve if the interest rate is 3 percent a year.
   b. If the Upland central bank wants to lower the interest rate by 1 percentage point, by how much must it change the quantity of real money?

12. In problem 11, a new smart card replaces currency and the demand for money changes. Also, the new smart card causes business to boom and real GDP increases.
    a. Use the figure for problem 11 and draw a new demand for real money curve.
    b. If the Upland central bank wants to prevent the interest rate from changing, what must it do to the quantity of money?

CRITICAL THINKING

1. Study *Reading Between the Lines* on pp. 606–607 and then answer the following questions.
   a. What changes in the payments technology are described in the news article?
   b. What does the news article imply has happened to the amount of currency held?
   c. What are the trends in currency use?
   d. Why did the use of currency increase during the 1990s?
   e. Does the increased use of currency during the 1990s contradict the news article?
   f. What do you expect the future trends in the use of currency to be and why?

2. Rapid inflation in Brazil during the early 1990s caused the cruzeiro, the currency of Brazil, to lose its ability to function as money. People were unwilling to accept it because it lost value too fast. Which of the following items do you think would be most likely to take the place of the cruzeiro and act as money in the Brazilian economy? Why?
   a. Tractor parts
   b. Packs of cigarettes
   c. Loaves of bread
   d. Impressionist paintings
   e. Baseball trading cards

WEB EXERCISES

Use the links on **myeconlab** to work the following exercises.

1. Visit Mark Bernkopf's Central Banking Resource Centre and read the article on Electronic Cash. Also read "The End of Cash" by James Gleick (first published in the *New York Times Magazine* on June 16, 1996). Then answer the following questions.
   a. What is e-cash?
   b. Mark Bernkopf asks: "Will 'e-cash' enable private currencies to overturn the ability of governments to make monetary policy?" Will it?
   c. When you buy an item on the Internet and pay by using a form of e-cash, are you using money? Explain why or why not.
   c. In your opinion, is the concern about e-cash a real concern or hype?

The Exchange Rate

CHAPTER 26

Many Monies!

The Canadian dollar—or loonie—is just one of more than a hundred kinds of money that circulate in the global economy. The loonie is an important money, but it isn't in the truly big league. The world's four big monies are the U.S dollar (the money of the United States), the yen (of Japan), the pound (of the United Kingdom), and the euro (of the European Union). The first three have been around for a long time, and the euro is new. But although it was launched in 1999, the euro is already an international currency. Most of the world's international trade and finance is conducted using these four currencies.

In 1976, the Canadian dollar was worth a bit more than a U.S. dollar. But in 2002, the Canadian dollar fell to 63 U.S. cents before climbing back to 85 U.S. cents in 2005.

Why does the Canadian dollar fluctuate against the U.S. dollar? Is there anything we can do or should do to stabilize the value of the dollar? And why do we have a Canadian dollar? Why doesn't North America do what Europe has done and have just one money?

◆ In this chapter, you're going to learn what determines the exchange rate and why the Canadian dollar fluctuates against other currencies. You're going to see that the Bank of Canada could intervene in the foreign exchange market to peg the value of the dollar. But you're also going to see why the Bank of Canada choses to *not* intervene in this market. You will also see why we don't scrap the Canadian dollar and use the same money as the Americans. At the end of the chapter, in *Reading Between the Lines*, we'll look at the day-to-day and longer term fluctuations in the Canadian dollar.

After studying this chapter, you will be able to

- **Describe the foreign exchange market and define the exchange rate**

- **Explain how the exchange rate is determined**

- **Explain why the exchange rate fluctuates and explain interest rate parity and purchasing power parity**

- **Describe and assess the benefits and costs of a flexible exchange rate, managed exchange rate, fixed exchange rate, and monetary union**

Currencies and Exchange Rates

WHEN WE BUY FOREIGN GOODS OR INVEST IN another country, we have to obtain some of that country's money to make the transaction. When foreigners buy Canadian-produced goods or invest in Canada, they have to obtain some Canadian dollars. We get foreign money and foreigners get Canadian dollars in the foreign exchange market.

Foreign money, like Canadian money, consists of notes and coins plus bank deposits. When we described Canadian money in Chapter 25, we distinguished between currency (notes and coins) and bank deposits. But when we talk about foreign money, we usually refer to it as foreign currency and don't make the distinction between notes, coins, and bank deposits—foreign notes, coins, and bank deposits are called **foreign currency**.

Figure 26.1 shows the magnitudes of our use of the Canadian dollar and foreign currency in our international trading activities in markets for goods and services. Beyond these markets, we also use foreign currency extensively in asset markets when we borrow and lend internationally.

The figure shows the not very surprising fact that the most important foreign currency for Canada is the U.S. dollar. The European euro comes second, followed by the Japanese yen and the U.K. pound. Dozens of other currencies make up the "others" category.

The Foreign Exchange Market

We get foreign currency in the **foreign exchange market**, which is the market in which the currency of one country is exchanged for the currency of another.

The foreign exchange market is not a place like a downtown flea market or produce market. The market is made up of thousands of people—importers and exporters, banks, and specialists in the buying and selling of foreign currency—called foreign exchange brokers.

The foreign exchange market opens on Monday morning in Hong Kong, which is still Sunday evening in Montreal and Toronto. As the day advances, markets open in Singapore, Tokyo, Bahrain, Frankfurt, London, New York, Montreal, Toronto, and Vancouver. As the West Coast markets

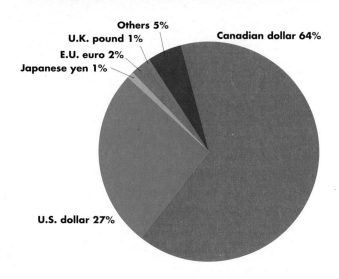

FIGURE 26.1   myeconlab

The Currencies We Use in Our Trade

Our trade in goods and services is paid for using the Canadian dollar, the U.S. dollar, the U.K. pound, the E.U. euro, the Japanese yen, and dozens of other currencies.

Source of data: Statistics Canada, CANSIM Table 376–001 and authors' assumptions.

close, Hong Kong is only an hour away from opening for the next day of business. The sun barely sets on the foreign exchange market. Dealers around the world are in continual contact by telephone, and on a typical day in 2005, 50 billion Canadian dollars changed hands on the foreign exchange market and more than $2 trillion of all currencies were traded.

Foreign Exchange Rates

The price at which one currency exchanges for another is called a **foreign exchange rate**. For example, in October 2005, one Canadian dollar bought 85 U.S. cents. The exchange rate was 85 U.S. cents per Canadian dollar.

Figure 26.2 shows the annual average exchange rate of the Canadian dollar in terms of the U.S. dollar between 1951 and 2005. You can see that the exchange rate fluctuates. Sometimes it rises, but in most years the Canadian dollar has fallen in value against the U.S. dollar.

FIGURE 26.2

The Canadian Dollar–U.S. Dollar Exchange Rate

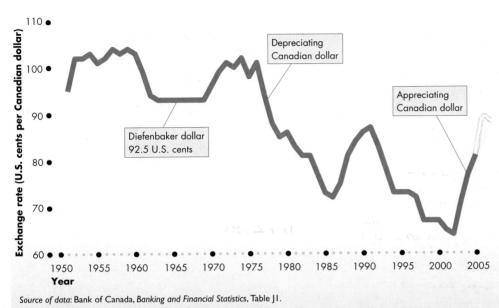

Diefenbaker dollar
92.5 U.S. cents

Depreciating
Canadian dollar

Appreciating
Canadian dollar

Source of data: Bank of Canada, *Banking and Financial Statistics*, Table J1.

The Canadian dollar exchange rate, expressed as U.S. cents per Canadian dollar, was fixed at 92.5 U.S. cents in May 1962 (when John G. Diefenbaker was Prime Minister) until June 1970. But most of the time, the Canadian dollar fluctuates against the U.S. dollar. The Canadian dollar depreciated against the U.S. dollar from 1976 through 1986 and from 1991 through 2001. It appreciated from 1986 through 1991 and from 2002 through 2005.

When a currency falls in value, we say that it depreciates. **Currency depreciation** is a fall in the value of one currency in terms of another currency. For example, when the Canadian dollar fell from 101 U.S. cents in 1976 to 94 U.S. cents in 1977, the Canadian dollar depreciated by 7 percent. When a currency rises in value, we say that it appreciates. **Currency appreciation** is the rise in the value of one currency in terms of another currency. From 1986 to 1991, the Canadian dollar appreciated against the U.S. dollar.

In some periods, the value of the dollar remains steady. From May 1962 to June 1970, the value of the Canadian dollar was pegged by the Bank of Canada at 92.5 U.S. cents. When the decision to peg the dollar was made, John G. Diefenbaker was the Prime Minister and the 92.5 cent dollar came to be known as the Diefenbaker dollar.

Cross Exchange Rates

We've just expressed the value of the Canadian dollar in terms of the U.S. dollar. But we can express the value of the Canadian dollar in terms of any currency—called cross exchange rates. Figure 26.3 shows some cross exchange rates in October 2005. These numbers tell us that when one Canadian dollar

FIGURE 26.3

The Cross Exchange Rates in 2005

	USD	EUR	GBP	JPY*	CAD
USD		1.20	1.76	0.87	0.85
EUR	0.83		1.47	0.72	0.71
GBP	0.57	0.68		0.49	0.48
JPY*	1.15	1.38	2.04		0.98
CAD	1.18	1.41	2.08	1.02	

The table shows cross exchange rates on October 19, 2005. USD is the U.S. dollar; EUR is the European Union euro; GBP is the U.K. pound; JPY* is 100 Japanese yen; CAD is the Canadian dollar.

Read the table vertically to see how much each currency buys. The CAD column shows how many USD, EUR, GBP, and 100s of JPY you get for 1 CAD.

Read the table horizontally to find the prices of the other currencies. The CAD row shows how many CADs you must pay for 1 USD, 1 EUR, 1 GBP or 100 JPY.

Source of data: Sauder School of Business, University of British Columbia, PACIFIC Exchange Rate Services (http://fx.sauder.ubc.ca/).

FIGURE 26.4

The Canadian Dollar Exchange Rate Against the U.K. Pound, E.U. Euro, and Japanese Yen

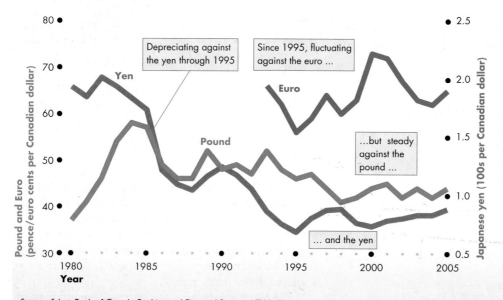

Depreciating against the yen through 1995

Since 1995, fluctuating against the euro ...

Yen

Euro

Pound

...but steady against the pound ...

... and the yen

The Canadian dollar exchange rate, expressed as Japanese yen per Canadian dollar, depreciated during the 1980s and first half of the 1990s. But since the mid-1990s, although the Canadian dollar has fluctuated against the yen, pound, and euro, it has neither depreciated nor appreciated on the average.

Source of data: Bank of Canada, Banking and Financial Statistics, Table J1.
Note: The euro was launched on January 1, 1999. It was preceded by the ECU (European Currency Unit). The exchange rate shown before 1999 is for the ECU.

bought 85 U.S. cents, it also bought 71 euro cents, 98 Japanese yen, or 48 U.K pence.

In the table in Fig. 26.3, we use the standard 3-letter names for the major currencies: CAD for the Canadian dollar, USD for the U.S. dollar, EUR for the euro, GBP for the U.K. (or Great Britain) pound, and JPY for the Japanese yen. Because the yen has a tiny value relative to the other currencies, it is common to measure the yen in 100s.

Figure 26.4 shows the longer history of the Canadian dollar against the other three major currencies—the pound, the euro and the yen—since 1980. You can see that the Canadian dollar depreciated against the yen through the 1980s and early 1990s. But since 1995, the Canadian dollar–yen exchange rate has seen only slight fluctuations and no tendency to either depreciate or appreciate.

Similarly, there has been no trend either up or down in the exchange rates between the Canadian dollar and the pound or the euro.

The performance of the Canadian dollar in the foreign exchange market raises a number of questions that we address in the rest of this chapter. First, how is the exchange rate determined? Second, why has the

Canadian dollar depreciated against the U.S. dollar and the yen? Third, how does a central bank control the exchange rate, as the Bank of Canada did during the 1960s? Fourth, how does the Bank of Canada operate in the foreign exchange market today? And fifth, why do we have our own currency? Why don't we just use the U.S. dollar and avoid currency fluctuations altogether?

REVIEW QUIZ

1 What is the foreign exchange market and what prices get determined in this market?
2 Distinguish between currency appreciation and currency depreciation.
3 When was the value of the Canadian dollar last pegged against the U.S. dollar?
4 What are the world's major currencies?
5 Against which major currencies has the Canadian dollar depreciated on the average over the past 25 years?

myeconlab **Study Plan 26.1**

The Foreign Exchange Market

AN EXCHANGE RATE IS A PRICE—THE PRICE OF one currency in terms of another. And like all prices, an exchange rate is determined in a market—the foreign exchange market.

The Canadian dollar trades in the foreign exchange market and is supplied and demanded by tens of thousands of traders every hour of every business day. Because it has many traders and no restrictions on who may trade, the foreign exchange market is a competitive market.

In a competitive market, demand and supply determine the price. So to understand the forces that determine the exchange rate, we need to study the factors that influence demand and supply in the foreign exchange market. But there is a feature of the foreign exchange market that makes it special.

The Demand for One Money Is the Supply of Another Money

When people who are holding the money of some other country want to exchange it for Canadian dollars, they demand Canadian dollars and supply that other country's money. And when people who are holding Canadian dollars want to exchange them for

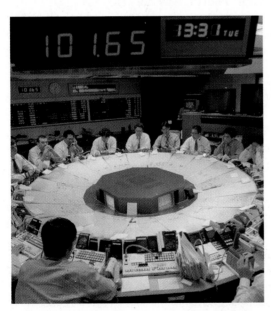

Dealers in the foreign exchange market

the money of some other country, they supply Canadian dollars and demand that other country's money.

So the factors that influence the demand for Canadian dollars also influence the supply of U.S. dollars, E.U. euros, U.K. pounds, and Japanese yen. And the factors that influence the demand for those other country's money also influence the supply of Canadian dollars.

We'll first look at the influences on the demand for Canadian dollars in the foreign exchange market.

Demand in the Foreign Exchange Market

People buy Canadian dollars in the foreign exchange market so that they can buy Canadian-made goods and services—Canadian exports. They also buy Canadian dollars so they can buy Canadian assets such as bonds, stocks, businesses, and real estate, or so that they can keep part of their money holding in a Canadian dollar bank account.

The quantity of Canadian dollars demanded in the foreign exchange market is the amount that traders plan to buy during a given time period at a given exchange rate. This quantity depends on many factors but the main ones are

1. The exchange rate
2. World demand for Canadian exports
3. Interest rates in Canada and other countries
4. The expected future exchange rate

So that we can first isolate the exchange rate and see how it is determined, we'll look first at the relationship between the quantity of Canadian dollars demanded in the foreign exchange market and the exchange rate when the other three influences remain the same—the law of demand in the foreign exchange market. In the next section, we'll consider what happens when these other influences change.

The Law of Demand for Foreign Exchange

The law of demand applies to dollars just as it does to anything else that people value. Other things remaining the same, the higher the exchange rate, the smaller is the quantity of Canadian dollars demanded in the foreign exchange market. For example, if the price of the Canadian dollar rose from 80 U.S. cents to 90 U.S. cents but nothing else changed, the quantity of Canadian dollars that people plan to buy in the foreign exchange market would decrease. The exchange rate influences the quantity of dollars demanded for two reasons:

- Exports effect
- Expected profit effect

Exports Effect The larger the value of Canadian exports, the larger is the quantity of Canadian dollars demanded on the foreign exchange market. But the value of Canadian exports depends on the prices of Canadian-made goods and services *expressed in the currency of the foreign buyer*. But these prices depend on the exchange rate. The lower the exchange rate, with other things remaining the same, the lower are the prices of Canadian-produced goods and services to foreigners and the greater is the volume of Canadian exports. So if the exchange rate falls (and other influences remain the same), the quantity of Canadian dollars demanded on the foreign exchange market increases.

To see this effect at work, think about Bombardier, a Montreal firm, that produces a popular airplane called the Canada Regional Jet or CRJ. If the price of a CRJ is $C1 million and the exchange rate is 90 U.S. cents per dollar, the price of this airplane to American Airlines is $US900,000. American Airlines decides that this price is too high, so it doesn't by a CRJ. If the exchange rate falls to 80 U.S. cents per Canadian dollar and nothing else changes, the price of a CRJ now falls to $US800,000. American Airlines now decides to buy a CRJ and buys Canadian dollars on the foreign exchange market.

Expected Profit Effect The larger the expected profit from holding Canadian dollars, the greater is the quantity of Canadian dollars demanded today. But expected profit depends on the exchange rate. The lower today's exchange rate, other things remaining the same, the larger is the expected profit from buying Canadian dollars and the greater is the quantity of Canadian dollars demanded today.

To see this effect at work, suppose that American Express expects the Canadian dollar exchange rate to be 90 U.S. cents at the end of the year. If today's exchange rate is also 90 U.S. cents, there is no gain from buying Canadian dollars now and selling them

at the end of the year. But if the Canadian dollar falls to 80 U.S. cents, and other things remain the same, there is now a 10 cents per dollar profit to be earned.

The lower today's exchange rate, other things remaining the same, the greater is the expected profit from holding Canadian dollars and the greater is the quantity of Canadian dollars demanded today on the foreign exchange market.

Demand Curve for Canadian Dollars

Figure 26.5 shows the demand curve for Canadian dollars in the foreign exchange market. A change in the exchange rate, other things remaining the same, brings a change in the quantity of Canadian dollars demanded and a movement along the demand curve as shown by the arrows.

We will look at the factors that change demand in the next section of this chapter. But first, let's see what determines the supply of Canadian dollars.

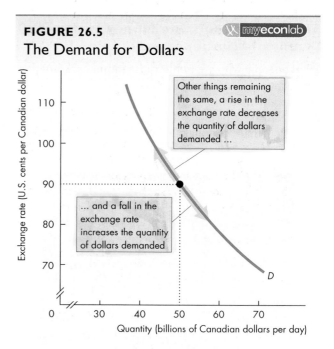

FIGURE 26.5   ⓧ myeconlab
The Demand for Dollars

Other things remaining the same, a rise in the exchange rate decreases the quantity of dollars demanded ...

... and a fall in the exchange rate increases the quantity of dollars demanded

The quantity of Canadian dollars that people plan to buy depends on the exchange rate. Other things remaining the same, if the exchange rate rises, the quantity of dollars demanded decreases and there is a movement up along the demand curve for dollars. If the exchange rate falls, the quantity of dollars demanded increases and there is a movement down along the demand curve for dollars.

Supply in the Foreign Exchange Market

People sell Canadian dollars and buy other currencies so that they can buy foreign-made goods and services—Canadian imports. People also sell Canadian dollars and buy foreign currencies so that they can buy foreign assets such as bonds, stocks, businesses, and real estate, or so that they can hold part of their money in bank deposits denominated in a foreign currency.

The quantity of Canadian dollars supplied in the foreign exchange market is the amount that traders plan to sell during a given time period at a given exchange rate. This quantity depends on many factors but the main ones are

1. The exchange rate
2. Canadian demand for imports
3. Interest rates in Canada and other countries
4. The expected future exchange rate

Let's look at the relationship between the quantity of Canadian dollars supplied in the foreign exchange market and the exchange rate when the other three influences remain the same—the law of supply in the foreign exchange market.

The Law of Supply of Foreign Exchange

Other things remaining the same, the higher the exchange rate, the greater is the quantity of dollars supplied in the foreign exchange market. For example, if the price of the Canadian dollar rose from 80 U.S. cents to 90 U.S. cents but nothing else changed, the quantity of Canadian dollars that people plan to sell in the foreign exchange market would increase.

The exchange rate influences the quantity of dollars supplied for two reasons:

- Imports effect
- Expected profit effect

Imports Effect The larger the value of Canadian imports, the larger is the quantity of Canadian dollars supplied on the foreign exchange market. But the value of Canadian imports depends on the prices of foreign-made goods and services *expressed in Canadian dollars*. So these prices depend on the exchange rate. The higher the exchange rate, with other things remaining the same, the lower are the prices of foreign-produced goods and services to Canadians and the greater is the volume of Canadian imports. So if the exchange rate rises (and other

influences remain the same), the quantity of Canadian dollars supplied on the foreign exchange market increases.

Expected Profit Effect This effect works just like that on the demand for the Canadian dollar but in the opposite direction. The higher the exchange rate, other things remaining the same, the larger is the expected profit from selling Canadian dollars and the greater is the quantity of Canadian dollars supplied.

Supply Curve for Canadian Dollars

Figure 26.6 shows the supply curve of Canadian dollars in the foreign exchange market. A change in the exchange rate, other things remaining the same, brings a change in the quantity of Canadian dollars supplied and a movement along the supply curve as shown by the arrows.

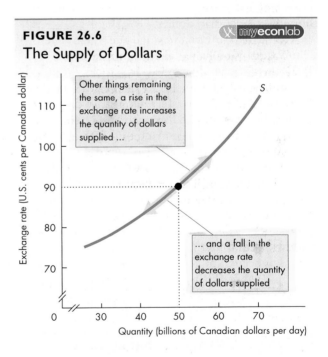

FIGURE 26.6
The Supply of Dollars

Other things remaining the same, a rise in the exchange rate increases the quantity of dollars supplied ...

... and a fall in the exchange rate decreases the quantity of dollars supplied

The quantity of Canadian dollars that people plan to sell depends on the exchange rate. Other things remaining the same, if the exchange rate rises, the quantity of Canadian dollars supplied increases and there is a movement up along the supply curve of dollars. If the exchange rate falls, the quantity of Canadian dollars supplied decreases and there is a movement down along the supply curve of dollars.

Market Equilibrium

Equilibrium in the foreign exchange market depends on how the Bank of Canada operates. Here, we will study equilibrium when the Bank keeps out of this market. In a later section (on pp. 623–625), we examine the effects of alternative actions that the Bank of Canada might take in the foreign exchange market.

Figure 26.7 shows the demand curve for Candian dollars, *D*, from Fig. 26.5 and the supply curve of Canadian dollars, *S*, from Fig. 26.6, and the equilibrium exchange rate.

The exchange rate acts as a regulator of the quantities demanded and supplied. If the exchange rate is too high, there is a surplus—the quantity supplied exceeds the quantity demanded. For example, in Fig. 26.7, if the exchange rate is 100 U.S. cents per Canadian dollar, there is a surplus of Canadian dollars. If the exchange rate is too low, there is a shortage—the quantity supplied is less than the quantity demanded. For example, in Fig. 26.7, if the exchange rate is 80 U.S. cents per Canadian dollar, there is a shortage of Canadian dollars.

At the equilibrium exchange rate, there is neither a shortage nor a surplus. The quantity supplied equals the quantity demanded. In Fig. 26.7, the equilibrium exchange rate is 90 U.S. cents per Canadian dollar. At this exchange rate, the quantity demanded and the quantity supplied are each $50 billion a day.

The foreign exchange market is constantly pulled to its equilibrium by the forces of supply and demand. Foreign exchange dealers are constantly looking for the best price they can get. If they are selling, they want the highest price available. If they are buying, they want the lowest price available. Information flows from dealer to dealer through the worldwide computer network and the price adjusts second by second to keep buying plans and selling plans in balance. That is, price adjusts minute by minute to keep the market at its equilibrium.

Equilibrium Cross Exchange Rates

In Fig. 26.7, we look only at the exchange rate between the Canadian dollar and the U.S. dollar. The exchange rates between the Canadian dollar and all other currencies are determined in a similar way. But all the cross exchange rates (see Fig 26.3, p. 613) line up so that no profit can be made by buying one currency, selling it for a second one, and then buying back the first one.

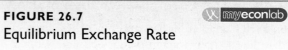

FIGURE 26.7
Equilibrium Exchange Rate

The demand curve for dollars is *D* and the supply curve is *S*. If the exchange rate is 100 U.S. cents per dollar, there is a surplus of dollars and the exchange rate falls. If the exchange rate is 80 U.S. cents per dollar, there is a shortage of dollars and the exchange rate rises. If the exchange rate is 90 U.S. cents per dollar, there is neither a shortage nor a surplus of dollars and the exchange rate remains constant. The foreign exchange market is in equilibrium.

REVIEW QUIZ

1 What are the influences on the demand for Canadian dollars in the foreign exchange market?
2 Provide an example of the exports effect on the demand for Canadian dollars.
3 What are the influences on the supply of Canadian dollars in the foreign exchange market?
4 Provide an example of the imports effect on the supply of Canadian dollars.
5 How is the equilibrium exchange rate determined?

myeconlab Study Plan 26.2

Changes in Demand and Supply: Exchange Rate Fluctuations

WHEN THE DEMAND FOR DOLLARS OR THE SUPPLY of dollars changes, the exchange rate changes. We'll now look at the factors that make demand and supply change, starting with the demand side of the market.

Changes in the Demand for Dollars

The demand for dollars on the foreign exchange market changes when any of the following influences change:

- World demand for Canadian exports
- Interest rates in Canada and other countries
- The expected future exchange rate

World Demand for Canadian Exports An increase in world demand for Canadian exports increases the demand for Canadian dollars. To see this effect, think further about Bombardier's sales of CRJ aircraft. An increase in demand for air travel in the United States sends U.S. airlines on a global shopping spree. They decide that the CRJ is the ideal product for them so they order 50 airplanes from Bombardier. The demand for Canadian dollars now increases.

Interest Rates in Canada and Other Countries The higher the interest rate that people can make on Canadian assets compared with foreign assets, the more Canadian assets they buy and the more Canadian dollars they demand on the foreign exchange market.

What matters is not the *level* of Canadian interest rates, but the Canadian interest rate minus the foreign interest rate—a gap called the **Canadian interest rate differential.**

If the Canadian interest rate differential increases by 1 percentage point and other things remain the same, people can earn an extra 1 percent by borrowing in the United States and lending in Canada. As people take advantage of this profit opportunity, the demand for Canadian dollars increases.

The Expected Future Exchange Rate For a given current exchange rate, and all other things remaining the same, a rise in the expected future exchange rate increases the profit that people expect to earn by

holding Canadian dollars and increases the demand for Canadian dollars today.

Figure 26.8 summarizes the influences on the demand for dollars. If the demand for Canadian dollars increases, the demand curve shifts rightward from D_0 to D_1. And if the demand for Canadian dollars decreases, the demand curve shifts leftward from D_0 to D_2.

FIGURE 26.8

Changes in the Demand for Dollars

A change in any influence on the quantity of Canadian dollars that people plan to buy, other than today's exchange rate, brings a change in the demand for Canadian dollars.

The demand for Canadian dollars

Increases if:	*Decreases if:*
■ World demand for Canadian exports increases	■ World demand for Canadian exports decreases
■ The Canadian interest rate differential increases	■ The Canadian interest rate differential decreases
■ The expected future exchange rate rises	■ The expected future exchange rate falls

Changes in the Supply of Dollars

The supply of dollars in the foreign exchange market changes when any of the following influences change:

- Canadian demand for imports
- Interest rates in Canada and other countries
- The expected future exchange rate

Canadian Demand for Imports An increase in Canadian demand for imports increases the supply of the Canadian dollar on the foreign exchange market. To see why, think about Bell Canada's purchase of database systems. An increase in demand for telecommunication services sends Bell Canada out shopping for more equipment and services. Bell decides that Oracle's database system produced in the United States is just what it needs, so it increases its purchases from Oracle. The supply of Canadian dollars now increases as Bell goes to the foreign exchange market to get more U.S. dollars.

Interest Rates in Canada and Other Countries The effect of the Canadian interest rate differential on the supply of Canadian dollars is the opposite of its effect on the demand for Canadian dollars. The larger the Canadian interest rate differential, the *smaller* is the supply of Canadian dollars on the foreign exchange market. The supply is smaller because the demand for *foreign* assets is smaller. If people spend less on foreign assets, they supply a smaller quantity of Canadian dollars on the foreign exchange market. So, a rise in the Canadian interest rate, other things remaining the same, decreases the supply of Canadian dollars.

The Expected Future Exchange Rate For a given current exchange rate, and all other things remaining the same, a fall in the expected future exchange rate decreases the profit that people expect to earn by holding Canadian dollars and decreases the quantity of Canadian dollars that people want to hold. To lower their holdings of Canadian dollar assets, people must sell dollars. When they do so, the supply of Canadian dollars on the foreign exchange market increases.

Figure 26.9 summarizes the influences on the supply of dollars. If the supply of Canadian dollars decreases, the supply curve shifts leftward from S_0 to S_1. And if the supply of Canadian dollars increases, the supply curve shifts rightward from S_0 to S_2.

Changes in the Exchange Rate

If the demand for dollars increases and the supply of dollars does not change, the exchange rate rises. If the demand for dollars decreases and the supply of dollars does not change, the exchange rate falls. Similarly, if the supply of dollars decreases and the demand for dollars does not change, the exchange rate rises. If the supply of dollars increases and the demand for dollars does not change, the exchange rate falls. Let's look at two episodes in the life of the Canadian dollar.

FIGURE 26.9
Changes in the Supply of Dollars

A change in any influence on the quantity of Canadian dollars that people plan to sell, other than today's exchange rate, brings a change in the supply of Canadian dollars.

The supply of Canadian dollars

Increases if:

- Canadian import demand increases
- The Canadian interest rate differential decreases
- The expected future exchange rate falls

Decreases if:

- Canadian import demand decreases
- The Canadian interest rate differential increases
- The expected future exchange rate rises

A Depreciating Dollar: 1991–2002 Between 1991 and 2002, the Canadian dollar fell from 87 U.S. cents to 64 U.S. cents per dollar. Figure 26.10(a) provides a possible explanation for this fall.

In 1991, the demand and supply curves were those labelled D and S_{91}. The exchange rate was 87 U.S. cents per dollar and $30 billion a day were traded.

During the 1990s, the North American Free Trade Agreement (NAFTA) came into effect and the volume of trade between Canada and the United States increased. The supply of Canadian dollars increased. The demand for Canadian dollars would have increased but traders expected the Canadian dollar to depreciate, which offset the factors leading to an increase in demand. Figure 26.10 assumes no change in demand and an increase in supply to S_{02}. The increase in supply with no change in demand lowered the exchange rate and increased the quantity of dollars traded.

An Appreciating Dollar: 2002–2005 Between 2002 and 2005 the Canadian dollar appreciated. It rose from 64 U.S. cents in 2002 to 81 U.S. cents per dollar in 2005. Figure 26.10(b) provides a possible explanation for this rise.

In 2002, the demand and supply curves were those labelled D_{02} and S_{02}—the same curves that Fig. 26.10(a) ends with.

During 2004 and 2005, the world demand for resources increased, driven mainly by rapid economic growth in China and India. The result was a large increase in the world demand for Canadian exports and an increase in the demand for the Canadian dollar. The demand curve shifted from D_{02} to D_{05}. This increase in demand and rise in the Canadian dollar was expected and, as a result, the supply of dollars decreased. The supply curve shifted from S_{02} to S_{05}. The increase in demand and decrease in supply raised the exchange rate from 64 U.S. cents to 81 U.S. cents but left the quantity traded unchanged.

FIGURE 26.10

Exchange Rate Fluctuations

(a) 1991 to 2002

(b) 2002 to 2005

Between 1991 and 2002 in part (a), the Canadian dollar fell from 87 U.S. cents to 64 U.S. cents per dollar. This depreciation occurred because as NAFTA came into effect, the volume of trade increased, which increased both the supply and demand for dollars. But traders expected this depreciation, which offset the increase in demand.

Between 2001 and 2005 in part (b), the exchange rate rose from 64 U.S. cents to 81 U.S. cents per dollar. This appreciation occurred because the world demand for resources increased Canadian exports and increased the demand for dollars. Traders' expected this appreciation, which decreased the supply of dollars.

Exchange Rate Expectations

The changes in the exchange rate that we've just examined occurred in part because the exchange rate was *expected to change*. Explaining a change as arising because it was expected sounds a bit like a self-fulfilling forecast. What makes expectations change? The answer is new information about the deeper forces that influence the value of money. Two such forces are

- Purchasing power parity
- Interest rate parity

Purchasing Power Parity Money is worth what it will buy. But two kinds of money, Canadian dollars and U.S. dollars, for example, might buy different amounts of goods and services. Suppose a Big Mac costs $C4 in Toronto and $US3 in New York. If the Canadian dollar exchange rate is 75 U.S. cents per Canadian dollar, the two monies have the same value. You can buy a Big Mac in either Toronto or New York for either $C4 or $US3.

The situation we've just described is called **purchasing power parity**, which means *equal value of money*. If purchasing power parity does not prevail, some powerful forces go to work. To understand these forces, let's suppose that the price of a Big Mac in New York rises to $US4 but in Toronto it remains at $C4. Suppose the exchange rate remains at 75 U.S. cents per Canadian dollar. In this case, a Big Mac in Toronto still costs $C4 or $US3. But in New York, it costs $US4 or $C5.33. Money buys more in Canada than in the United States. Money is not of equal value in the two countries.

If all (or most) prices have increased in the United States and have not increased in Canada, then people will generally expect that the value of the Canadian dollar on the foreign exchange market must rise. In this situation, the exchange rate is expected to rise. The demand for Canadian dollars increases and the supply of Canadian dollars decreases. The exchange rate rises, as expected. If the exchange rate rises to $US1.00 per Canadian dollar and there are no further price changes, purchasing power parity is restored. A Big Mac now costs $4 in either Canadian or U.S. dollars in New York and in Toronto.

If prices increase in Canada but remain constant in other countries, then people will generally expect that the value of the Canadian dollar on the foreign exchange market is too high and that it is going to

fall. In this situation, the exchange rate is expected to fall. The demand for Canadian dollars decreases and the supply of Canadian dollars increases. The exchange rate falls, as expected.

Ultimately, the value of money is determined by the price level, which in turn is determined by aggregate supply and aggregate demand (see Chapter 22). So the deeper forces that influence the exchange rate have tentacles that spread throughout the economy. If the price level rises more quickly in Canada than in other countries, the exchange rate falls. And if the price level rises more slowly in Canada than in other countries, the exchange rate rises.

Interest Rate Parity Money is worth what it can earn. Again two kinds of money, Canadian dollars and U.S. dollars, might earn different amounts. For example, suppose a Canadian dollar bank deposit in Toronto earns 4 percent a year and a U.S. dollar bank deposit in New York earns 5 percent a year. In this situation, why does anyone deposit money in Toronto? Why doesn't all the money flow to New York? The answer is: because of exchange rate expectations. Suppose people expect the Canadian dollar to appreciate by 1 percent a year. This 1 percent appreciation must be added to the 4 percent interest to obtain a return of 5 percent a year that an American can earn by depositing funds in a Toronto bank. The two returns are equal. This situation is one of **interest rate parity**, which means *equal interest rates* when exchange rate changes are taken into account.

Adjusted for risk, interest rate parity always prevails. Funds move to get the highest return available. If for a few seconds a higher return is available in Toronto than in New York, the demand for Canadian dollars rises and the exchange rate rises until the expected returns are equal.

REVIEW QUIZ

1 Why does the demand for dollars change?
2 Why does the supply of dollars change?
3 What makes the dollar fluctuate?
4 What is purchasing power parity and what happens when this condition doesn't hold?
5 What is interest rate parity and what happens if this condition doesn't hold?

 myeconlab   **Study Plan 26.3**

Exchange Rate Policy

BECAUSE THE EXCHANGE RATE IS THE PRICE OF A country's money in terms of another country's money, governments and central banks must have a policy towards the exchange rate. Four distinctly different exchange rate policies are

- Flexible exchange rate
- Fixed exchange rate
- Crawling peg
- Currency union

Flexible Exchange Rate

A **flexible exchange rate** policy is one that permits the exchange rate to be determined by demand and supply with no direct intervention in the foreign exchange market by the central bank. The Bank of Canada operates a flexible exchange rate.

But even a flexible exchange rate is influenced by central bank actions. If the Bank of Canada raises the Canadian interest rate and other countries keep their interest rates unchanged, the demand for Canadian dollars increases, the supply of Canadian dollars decreases, and the exchange rate rises. (Similarly, if the Bank of Canada lowers the Canadian interest rate, the demand for Canadian dollars decreases, the supply increases, and the exchange rate falls.)

In a flexible exchange rate regime, when the central bank changes the interest rate, its purpose is *not* to influence the exchange rate. Its purpose is to achieve some other monetary policy objective. (We return to this topic at length in Chapter 28.)

Fixed Exchange Rate

A **fixed exchange rate** policy is one that pegs the exchange rate at a value decided by the government or central bank and that blocks the unregulated forces of demand and supply by direct intervention in the foreign exchange market. The Bank of Canada operated a fixed exchange rate during the 1960s when the dollar was pegged at 92.5 U.S. cents.

To maintain a fixed exchange rate, the Bank of Canada would buy dollars to prevent the exchange rate from falling below the target value and sell dollars to prevent the exchange rate from rising above the target value. There is no limit to the quantity of dollars that the Bank of Canada can sell. But there is a

limit to the quantity of dollars the Bank of Canada can buy. That limit is set by the Bank's and the government of Canada's holdings of foreign currency reserves.

Let's look at the foreign exchange interventions that the Bank of Canada can make.

Suppose the Bank of Canada wants the exchange rate to be steady at 90 U.S. cents per dollar. If the exchange rate rises above 90 U.S. cents, the Bank sells dollars. If the exchange rate falls below 90 U.S. cents, the Bank buys dollars. By these actions, it changes the supply of dollars and keeps the exchange rate close to its target rate of 90 U.S. cents per Canadian dollar.

Figure 26.11 shows the Bank of Canada's intervention in the foreign exchange market. The supply of dollars is S and initially the demand for dollars is D_0. The equilibrium exchange rate is 90 U.S. cents

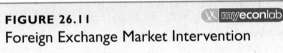

FIGURE 26.11

Foreign Exchange Market Intervention

Initially, the demand for dollars is D_0, the supply of dollars is S, and the exchange rate is 90 U.S. cents per dollar. The Bank of Canada can intervene in the foreign exchange market to keep the exchange rate close to its target rate (90 U.S. cents per dollar in this example). If demand increases from D_0 to D_1, the Bank sells dollars to increase supply. If demand decreases from D_0 to D_2, the Bank buys dollars to decrease supply. Persistent intervention on one side of the foreign exchange market cannot be sustained.

per dollar. This exchange rate is the Bank's target rate, shown by the horizontal red line.

When the demand for dollars increases and the demand curve shifts rightward to D_1, the Bank of Canada sells $10 billion. This action increases the supply of dollars by $10 billion and prevents the exchange rate from rising. When the demand for dollars decreases and the demand curve shifts leftward to D_2, the Bank buys $10 billion. This action decreases the supply of dollars by $10 billion and prevents the exchange rate from falling.

If the demand for dollars fluctuates between D_1 and D_2 and on the average is D_0, the Bank of Canada can repeatedly intervene in the way we've just seen. Sometimes the Bank buys and sometimes it sells but, on the average, it neither buys nor sells.

But suppose the demand for dollars increases permanently from D_0 to D_1. The Bank cannot now maintain the exchange rate at 90 U.S. cents indefinitely. For to do so, the Bank would have to sell dollars every day. When the Bank sells dollars in the foreign exchange market, it buys foreign currency. So the Bank would be piling up foreign currency.

Now suppose the demand for dollars decreases permanently from D_0 to D_2. Again the Bank cannot maintain the exchange rate at 90 U.S. cents indefinitely. In this situation, to hold the exchange rate at 90 U.S. cents per dollar the Bank would have to buy dollars every day. When the Bank buys dollars in the foreign exchange market, it uses its holdings of foreign currency. So the Bank would be losing foreign currency. Eventually, it would run out of foreign currency and would then have to abandon its attempt to fix the exchange rate.

Crawling Peg

A **crawling peg** exchange rate policy is one that selects a target path for the exchange rate with intervention in the foreign exchange market to achieve that path. The Bank of Canada has never operated a crawling peg. But some prominent countries do use this system. China is one of the most recent to do so.

A crawling peg works like a fixed exchange rate except that the target value changes. Sometimes the target changes once a month and sometimes it changes every day.

The idea behind a crawling peg is to avoid wild swings in the exchange rate that might happen if expectations became volatile and to avoid the prob-

lem of running out of reserves, which can happen with a fixed exchange rate.

Currency Union

A **currency union** is a merger of the currencies of a number of countries to form a single money and avoid foreign exchange transactions. The most recently formed currency union is that of the European Union, which has replaced the national monies of France, Germany, Italy, and several other countries with the euro.

Although a currency union is not on the Canadian political agenda, two well-respected Canadian economists, Thomas J. Courchene of Queen's University and Richard Harris of Simon Fraser University, have advocated a currency union between Canada and the United States. What are the benefits and costs of a currency union?

The benefits of a currency union are

- Transparency and competition improve
- Transactions costs fall
- Foreign exchange risk is eliminated
- The real interest rate falls

Transparency and Competition Improve A single currency provides a single unit of account, so prices are easily compared across all the members of the currency union. A country might gain a competitive advantage by becoming more efficient, but it cannot gain an advantage by artificially lowering the prices of its exports through currency depreciation.

Transactions Costs Fall A single currency eliminates foreign exchange transactions costs—the costs of converting Canadian dollars to U.S. dollars or the reverse conversion. To see how big these costs are, take a look at the price you would pay for some U.S. dollars and then look at the price you could get in Canadian dollars if you had some U.S. dollars to sell. You will be shocked at the size of the margin that the banks take when they do a foreign exchange transaction for an ordinary person or small business.

For the European Union, it has been estimated that eliminating foreign exchange transactions has saved 0.4 percent of GDP each year. If Canada saved 0.4 percent of its GDP, it would gain more than $4 billion a year.

Foreign Exchange Risk Eliminated With a single currency, exporters and importers no longer face foreign exchange risk. For example, Focus, a Canadian firm that makes snowboards, sells a consignment of boards to Big5, a U.S. sporting goods retailer. The boards are sold for \$US400,000, which, on the day they are shipped is \$C500,000. When Big5 gets around to paying for the boards six weeks later, Focus will get \$C500,000 only if the exchange rate hasn't changed. But the exchange rate might increase or decrease, exposing Focus to unwanted risk. Focus can avoid this risk by buying Canadian dollars for U.S. dollars in the forward exchange market but only by paying a commission.

The elimination of this exchange risk greatly simplifies the life of Focus and thousands of firms like it.

Real Interest Rates Fall The real interest rate is the cost of capital and the return to saving. It includes a premium for risk. One type of risk is that of default: a borrower not repaying a lender. This type of risk is not affected by currency arrangements. But another type of risk arises from currency fluctuations and inflation fluctuations. If a single currency can eliminate or at least lower these risks, it can lower the real interest rate and stimulate saving and investment.

A currency union also has costs. The two major ones are:

- Shocks that need national monetary policy
- Loss of sovereignty

Shocks that Need National Monetary Policy A single currency means a single monetary policy—in the North American context, one monetary policy for the United States and Canada. But many economic shocks call for a monetary policy response that is specific to the economy receiving the shock. For example, a global energy boom increases aggregate demand in Canada by a bigger percentage than in the United States. So if Canada wants to avoid inflation, it needs to take greater offsetting actions when such a shock occurs than the United States needs to take. Similarly, faster productivity growth in the United States means that aggregate demand can grow faster there than in Canada while avoiding inflation. So to allow for this difference, Canada would want aggregate demand to grow more slowly.

A single common monetary policy is inadequate to deal with differences of these types.

Loss of Sovereignty If a country joins with another or group of other countries to form a currency union, each country surrenders some sovereignty. No longer can each government decide what its monetary policy will be. In principle, national fiscal policy might be used to pursue national economic policy goals where monetary policy is not available. But usually, before a currency union can be agreed upon, some limits must also be agreed for the use of fiscal policy. In Europe, for example, the nations that use the euro have entered into a *Stability and Growth Pact* that places limits on the use of fiscal policy and replaces national freedom of action with a common regional policy.

It is very unlikely that Canada will abandon the Canadian dollar in favour of the U.S. dollar and equally unlikely that the Americans would want to abandon their dollar and join with Canada (and Mexico) in creating a North American dollar equivalent to the euro. In fact, many people are holding their breath waiting for the euro to vanish!

It is also unlikely that Canada will want to abandon its flexible exchange rate policy in favour of a fixed rate or a sliding peg. We'll see in Chapter 28 how Canada takes advantage of the freedom and flexibility that its foreign exchange market policy permits.

REVIEW QUIZ

1 What is a flexible exchange rate and how does it work?
2 What is a fixed exchange rate and how does it get fixed?
3 What is a crawling peg and how does it work?
4 What is a currency union and what are its benefits and costs?

 Study Plan 26.4

◆ *Reading Between the Lines* on pages 626–627 looks at the strengthening of the Canadian dollar in 2005. In the next chapter, we look at the constraint on monetary policy imposed by the short-run output inflation tradeoff. Then in Chapter 28, we see how the Bank of Canada conducts its monetary policy.

The Strengthening Canadian Dolar

RESOURCE NEWS INTERNATIONAL, NOVEMBER 23, 2005

Canadian Dollar and Business Outlook

The Canadian dollar continued to show some strength Wednesday morning as favorable domestic data and a generally weaker tone for the US dollar supported the Canadian currency. Strong natural gas and crude oil prices also helped support the Canadian dollar.

Canada's leading indicator was up 0.5% in October compared to the previous month, reported Statistics Canada. The increase came in above analyst expectations for a 0.3% rise, and provided some support for the Canadian dollar.

In addition, recent news out of the US suggests that the US Fed may slow down their pace of interest rate hikes. Meanwhile, the Bank of Canada is still expected to continue raising rates into the new year.

Currently the Bank of Canada's overnight rate of 3.00% compares with the US rate of 4.00%.

Activity was light in the currency markets, as some participants start to back away ahead of the US Thanksgiving holiday on Thursday.

The Canadian dollar was trading at 85.27 US cents (C$1.1728) early in the day, up from Tuesday's North American closing level of 85.13 US cents (C$1.1747). ...

Reprinted by permission of Resource News International.

Essence of the Story

■ The Canadian dollar exchange rate rose slightly on November 23, 2005.

■ The identified sources of the rise were rising energy prices, a stronger than expected economy, and the prospect of rising Canadian interest rates and constant U.S. interest rates.

■ The volume of activity on the foreign exchange market was light as traders began to head for the U.S. Thanksgiving holiday.

■ The exchange rate was 85.27 U.S. cents, up from 85.13 U.S. cents during the day.

Economic Analysis

■ This news article is an example of a similar article that appears every business day.

■ Notice how small movements in the exchange rate (down to 100ths of a cent) are regarded as significant and in need of explanation.

■ Much of the daily movement in the exchange rate is random noise.

■ Figure 1 shows the daily, weekly, and monthly changes in the Canadian dollar exchange rate (all expressed at monthly percentage rates.)

■ The grey line is the daily change, the blue line is the weekly change, and the red line is the monthly change.

■ You can see that most of the daily changes reverse themselves a day or two later.

■ The weekly changes are also noisy and tend to reverse themselves.

■ The monthly changes reveal the more permanent movements and the general direction of change in the exchange rate.

■ Figure 2 shows the monthly changes since 2000, this time expressed as annual rates of change.

■ You can see that the dollar appreciated strongly during 2003 and again, more slowly but persistently during 2005.

■ Changes in world prices of energy and other commodity resources of which Canada has a comparative abundance, are one of the major influences on these broader trends in the exchange rate.

■ The Canadian-U.S. inflation difference and interest rate differential are two other factors.

Figure 1 Daily, weekly, and monthly changes in the exchange rate

Figure 2 The dollar since 2000

627

SUMMARY

KEY POINTS

Currencies and Exchange Rates (pp. 612–614)

- Foreign currency is obtained in exchange for domestic currency in the foreign exchange market.
- The exchange rate is the price of one currency in terms of another.
- Exchange rates fluctuate and a currency might depreciate or appreciate against other currencies.

The Foreign Exchange Market (pp. 615–618)

- Demand and supply in the foreign exchange market determine the exchange rate.
- The higher the exchange rate, the smaller is the quantity of dollars demanded and the greater is the quantity of dollars supplied.
- The equilibrium exchange rate makes the quantity of dollars demanded equal the quantity of dollars supplied.

Changes in Demand and Supply: Exchange Rate Fluctuations (pp. 619–622)

- Changes in the world demand for Canadian exports, the expected future exchange rate, or the Canadian interest rate differential change the demand for Canadian dollars and shift the demand curve.
- Changes in Canadian demand for imports, the expected future exchange rate, or the Canadian interest rate differential change the supply of Canadian dollars and shift the supply curve.
- Fluctuations in the demand for and supply of dollars bring fluctuations in the exchange rate.
- Exchange rate expectations are influenced by interest rate parity and purchasing power parity.

Exchange Rate Policy (pp. 623–625)

- The government of Canada and the Bank of Canada can adopt any of four alternative exchange rate policies: a flexible exchange rate, a fixed exchange rate, a crawling peg, or a currency union.

- Canada had a fixed exchange rate during the 1960s but now has a flexible exchange rate.
- Some economists advocate a currency union between Canada and the United States, but such a union is not on the political agenda.

KEY FIGURES

KEY TERMS

PROBLEMS

Go to **myeconlab** for solutions to odd-numbered problems and additional exercises.

1. The Canadian dollar exchange rate increased from 80 U.S. cents in 2004 to 85 U.S. cents in 2005.
   a. Did the Canadian dollar appreciate or depreciate against the U.S. dollar?
   b. What was the value of the U.S. dollar in terms of Canadian dollars in 2004?
   c. What was the value of the U.S. dollar in terms of Canadian dollars in 2005?
   d. Did the U.S. dollar appreciate or depreciate in terms of the Canadian dollar?

2. The Canadian dollar exchange rate decreased from 73 euro cents in 2000 to 65 euro cents in 2005.
   a. Did the Canadian dollar appreciate or depreciate in terms of the euro?
   b. What was the value of the euro in terms of Canadian dollars in 2000?
   c. What was the value of the euro in terms of Canadian dollars in 2005?
   d. Did the euro appreciate or depreciate against the Canadian dollar?

3. The table sets out some cross exchange rates. Use the table to answer the following questions.

	USD	EUR	GBP	JPY*	CAD
USD					
EUR	0.80				
GBP	0.60				
JPY*	1.18				
CAD	1.22				

   a. What do the numbers in the first column tell you?
   b. What are the numbers that go in the first row of the table and what do those numbers tell you?
   c. What are the numbers that go in the second row of the table and what do those numbers tell you?
   d. What are the numbers that go in the third row of the table and what do those numbers tell you?
   e. What are the numbers that go in the fourth row of the table and what do those numbers tell you?

   f. What are the numbers that go in the last row of the table and what do those numbers tell you?
   g. What do the numbers in the second through last columns of the table tell you?

4. The table sets out some cross exchange rates. Use the table to answer the following questions.

	USD	EUR	GBP	JPY*	CAD
USD		1.25	1.80	0.95	0.90
EUR					
GBP					
JPY*					
CAD					

   a. What do the numbers in the first row tell you?
   b. What are the numbers that go in the first column of the table and what do those numbers tell you?
   c. What are the numbers that go in the second column of the table and what do those numbers tell you?
   d. What are the numbers that go in the third column of the table and what do those numbers tell you?
   e. What are the numbers that go in the fourth column of the table and what do those numbers tell you?
   f. What are the numbers that go in the last column of the table and what do those numbers tell you?
   g. What do the numbers in the second through last rows of the table tell you?

5. There is a large increase in the global demand for roses and Colombia is the biggest producer of roses. At the same time, the central bank of Colombia increases the interest rate. What happens in the foreign exchange market for Colombian pesos to:
   a. The demand for pesos?
   b. The supply of pesos?
   c. The quantity of pesos demanded?
   d. The quantity of pesos supplied?
   e. The exchange rate of the pesos against the U.S. dollar?

6. There is a large increase in the global demand for diamonds and South Africa is the biggest producer of diamonds. At the same time, the central bank of South Africa cuts the interest

rate. What happens in the foreign exchange market for South African rand to:

a. The demand for rand?
b. The supply of rand?
c. The quantity of rand demanded?
d. The quantity of rand supplied?
f. The exchange rate of the rand against the U.S. dollar?

7. The Canadian dollar appreciates, and Canada's official reserves increase. What can you say about

a. Intervention in the foreign exchange market by the Bank of Canada?
b. The possible Bank of Canada sources of the currency appreciation?
c. The possible private actions behind the appreciation?

8. Canada has a lower inflation rate than the United States. Canada also has more rapid economic growth. The Bank of Canada does not intervene in the foreign exchange market. What can you say about each of the following (and why)?

a. The exchange rate
b. The expected exchange rate
c. The interest rate differential
d. Interest rate parity
d. Purchasing power parity

9. The Canadian dollar is trading at 85 U.S. cents per Canadian dollar. There is purchasing power parity at this exchange rate. The interest rate in Canada is 5 percent a year and the interest rate in the United States is 4 percent a year.

a. Calculate the Canadian interest rate differential?
b. What is the Canadian dollar expected to be worth one year from now?
c. Which country most likely has the lower inflation rate? How can you tell?

10. The Canadian dollar is trading at 90 U.S. cents per Canadian dollar and it is overvalued relative to purchasing power parity. The interest rate in Canada is 5 percent a year and the interest rate in the United States is 4 percent a year.

a. Calculate the Canadian interest rate differential?
b. Is the Canadian dollar expected to appreciate or depreciate?
c. Which country most likely has the lower inflation rate? How can you tell?

CRITICAL THINKING

1. Study *Reading Between the Lines* on pp. 626–627 and then answer the following questions:

a. What do the daily, weekly, and monthly changes in the exchange rate tell us?
b. What, according to the news article, caused the change in the exchange rate on November 22, 2005?
c. Is the explanation given in the news article consistent with interest rate parity?
d. If Canada has an inflation rate persistently below that of the United States, what will happen to the Canadian dollar over the longer term (other things remaining the same)?

2. Why do some economists think we should have a currency union with the United States? What do you think about this idea? Prepare an executive summary of your ideas for the governor of the Bank of Canada.

WEB EXERCISES

Use the links on (X myeconlab) to work the following exercises.

1. Visit Statistics Canada and find data on the exchange rate.

a. When did the Canadian dollar appreciate most recently?
b. When did the Canadian dollar depreciate most recently?
c. When was the last time the Canadian dollar had a fixed exchange rate?

2. Visit PACIFIC (an exchange rate service) and read the page on purchasing power parity.

a. What is purchasing power parity?
b. Which currencies are the most overvalued relative to the U.S. dollar today?
c. Which currencies are the most undervalued relative to the U.S. dollar today?
d. Can you offer some suggestions as to why some currencies are overvalued and some are undervalued?
d. Do you think that the information on overvaluation and undervaluation is useful to currency speculators? Why or why not?

Inflation

CHAPTER 27

From Rome to Rio de Janeiro

At the end of the third century, Roman Emperor Diocletian struggled to contain an inflation that raised prices by more than 300 percent a year. At the end of the twentieth century, Brazil's president, Fernando Henrique Cardoso, struggled to contain an inflation that hit a rate of 40 percent per month—or 5,600 percent a year.

Today, the Bank of Canada targets the inflation rate and Canada has remarkable price stability. But during the 1970s, the Canadian price level more than doubled—an inflation of more than 100 percent over the decade. Why do inflation rates vary? And why do serious inflations break out from time to time?

Can we be confident that the Bank of Canada will keep inflation in check? Or might inflation increase so our savings buy less? Or might inflation decrease so our debts are harder to repay? To make good decisions, we need good forecasts of inflation, and not for just next year but for many years into the future. How do people try to forecast inflation? And how do expectations of inflation influence the economy?

In targeting inflation, does the Bank of Canada face a tradeoff between inflation and unemployment? And does a low unemployment rate signal a rising inflation rate? How does inflation affect the interest rate?

◆ We'll answer these questions in this chapter and in doing so, we'll set the stage for the next chapter in which we study the Bank of Canada's inflation-targeting monetary policy. We'll begin by reviewing what inflation is and how it is measured. And we'll end, in *Reading Between the Lines*, by looking at the views of Nobel Laureate George Akerlof on the links between inflation and unemployment in Canada.

After studying this chapter, you will be able to

- **Distinguish between inflation and a change in the price level and between demand-pull inflation and cost-push inflation**
- **Explain the quantity theory of money**
- **Describe the effects of inflation**
- **Explain the short-run and long-run relationships between inflation and unemployment**
- **Explain the short-run and long-run relationships between inflation and interest rates**

Inflation: Demand-Pull and Cost-Push

THE MAIN TASK OF THE BANK OF CANADA IS TO keep inflation under control. You will learn about the tools and strategies that the Bank uses in the next chapter. Here, we explain what causes inflation and explore the short-run tradeoffs between inflation and output and between inflation and unemployment. We begin by distinguishing between inflation and a change in the price level.

Inflation and a Change in the Price Level

Inflation is a process in which the *price level is rising* and *money is losing value.*

A change in *one price* is not inflation. For example, if the price of a hot dog jumps to $25 and all other money prices fall slightly so that the price level remains constant, there is no inflation. Instead, the relative price of a hot dog has increased. But if the price of a hot dog and all other prices rise by a similar percentage, then there is inflation.

Inflation is an *ongoing process*, so a one-time jump in the price level is not inflation. Figure 27.1 illustrates this distinction. The red line shows the price level rising continuously. That is inflation. The blue line shows a one-time jump in the price level. That is not inflation.

To measure the inflation *rate,* we calculate the annual percentage change in the price level. For

"Three hundred dollars' of regular."

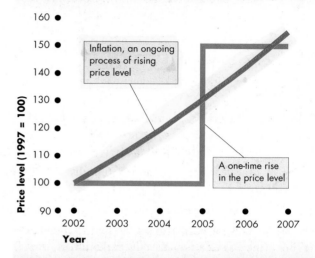

FIGURE 27.1   myeconlab

Inflation Versus a One-Time Rise in the Price Level

Inflation, an ongoing process of rising price level

A one-time rise in the price level

Along the red line, an economy experiences inflation because the price level is rising persistently. Along the blue line, an economy experiences a one-time rise in the price level.

example, if this year's price level is 126 and last year's price level was 120, the inflation rate is 5 percent per year. That is,

$$\text{Inflation rate} = \frac{126 - 120}{120} \times 100$$
$$= 5 \text{ percent per year.}$$

This equation shows the connection between the *inflation rate* and the *price level.* A high price level isn't the same as a high inflation rate. For a *given price level last year,* the higher the price level in the current year, the higher is the inflation rate.

If the price level is *rising,* the inflation rate is *positive.* And if the price level is *falling,* the inflation rate is *negative.* If the price level rises at a *faster* rate, the inflation rate *increases.* And if the price level rises at a *slower* rate, the inflation rate *decreases.*

Inflation can result from either an aggregate demand shock or an aggregate supply shock. These two sources of impulses are called

- Demand-pull inflation
- Cost-push inflation

We'll first study demand-pull inflation.

Demand-Pull Inflation

An inflation that results from an initial increase in aggregate demand is called **demand-pull inflation**. Demand-pull inflation can arise from *any* factor that increases aggregate demand, such as an

1. Increase in the quantity of money
2. Increase in government expenditures
3. Increase in exports

Initial Effect of an Increase in Aggregate Demand
Suppose that last year the price level was 110 and real GDP was $1,000 billion. Potential GDP was also $1,000 billion. Figure 27.2(a) illustrates this situation. The aggregate demand curve is AD_0, the short-run aggregate supply curve is SAS_0, and the long-run aggregate supply curve is LAS.

In the current year, aggregate demand increases to AD_1. Such a situation arises if, for example, the Bank of Canada loosens its grip on the quantity of money, or the government increases its expenditures on goods and services, or exports increase.

With no change in potential GDP, and with no change in the money wage rate, the long-run aggregate supply curve and the short-run aggregate supply curve remain at LAS and SAS_0, respectively.

The price level and real GDP are determined at the point where the aggregate demand curve AD_1 intersects the short-run aggregate supply curve. The price level rises to 113, and real GDP increases above potential GDP to $1,050 billion. The economy experiences a 2.7 percent rise in the price level (a price level of 113 compared with 110 in the previous year) and a rapid expansion of real GDP. Unemployment falls below its natural rate. The next step in the unfolding story is a rise in the money wage rate.

Money Wage Rate Response Real GDP cannot remain above potential GDP forever. With unemployment below its natural rate, there is a shortage of labour. In this situation, the money wage rate begins

---

FIGURE 27.2
A Demand-Pull Rise in the Price Level

(a) Initial effect

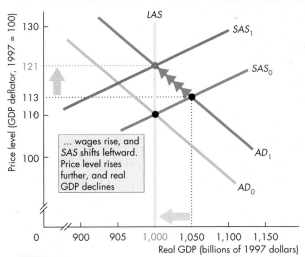

(b) Wages adjust

In part (a), the aggregate demand curve is AD_0, the short-run aggregate supply curve is SAS_0, and the long-run aggregate supply curve is LAS. The price level is 110, and real GDP is $1,000 billion, which equals potential GDP. Aggregate demand increases to AD_1. The price level rises to

113, and real GDP increases to $1,050 billion. In part (b), starting from above full employment, the money wage rate begins to rise and the short-run aggregate supply curve shifts leftward towards SAS_1. The price level rises further, and real GDP returns to potential GDP.

to rise. As it does so, short-run aggregate supply decreases and the *SAS* curve starts to shift leftward. The price level rises further, and real GDP begins to decrease.

With no further change in aggregate demand—that is, the aggregate demand curve remains at AD_1—this process ends when the short-run aggregate supply curve has shifted to SAS_1 in Fig. 27.2(b). At this time, the price level has increased to 121 and real GDP has returned to potential GDP of $1,000 billion, the level from which it started.

A Demand-Pull Inflation Process The process we've just studied eventually ends when, for a given increase in aggregate demand, the money wage rate has adjusted enough to restore the real wage rate to its full-employment level. We've studied a one-time rise in the price level like that described in Fig. 27.1. For inflation to proceed, aggregate demand must persistently increase.

The only way in which aggregate demand can persistently increase is if the quantity of money persistently increases. Suppose the government has a budget deficit that it finances by selling bonds. Also suppose that the Bank of Canada buys some of these bonds. When the Bank of Canada buys bonds, it creates more money. In this situation, aggregate demand increases year after year. The aggregate demand curve keeps shifting rightward. This persistent increase in aggregate demand puts continual upward pressure on the price level. The economy now experiences demand-pull inflation.

Figure 27.3 illustrates the process of demand-pull inflation. The starting point is the same as that shown in Fig. 27.2. The aggregate demand curve is AD_0, the short-run aggregate supply curve is SAS_0, and the long-run aggregate supply curve is *LAS*. Real GDP is $1,000 billion, and the price level is 110. Aggregate demand increases, shifting the aggregate demand curve to AD_1. Real GDP increases to $1,050 billion, and the price level rises to 113. The economy is at an above full-employment equilibrium. There is a shortage of labour, and the money wage rate rises. The short-run aggregate supply curve shifts to SAS_1. The price level rises to 121, and real GDP returns to potential GDP.

But the Bank of Canada increases the quantity of money again, and aggregate demand continues to increase. The aggregate demand curve shifts rightward to AD_2. The price level rises further to 125, and real GDP again exceeds potential GDP at $1,050 bil-

FIGURE 27.3   myeconlab
A Demand-Pull Inflation Spiral

Each time the quantity of money increases, aggregate demand increases, and the aggregate demand curve shifts rightward from AD_0 to AD_1 to AD_2, and so on. Each time real GDP goes above potential GDP, the money wage rate rises and the short-run aggregate supply curve shifts leftward from SAS_0 to SAS_1 to SAS_2, and so on. The price level rises from 110 to 113, 121, 125, 133, and so on. There is a perpetual demand-pull inflation. Real GDP fluctuates between $1,000 billion and $1,050 billion.

lion. Yet again, the money wage rate rises and decreases short-run aggregate supply. The *SAS* curve shifts to SAS_2, and the price level rises further, to 133. As the quantity of money continues to grow, aggregate demand increases and the price level rises in an ongoing demand-pull inflation process.

The process you have just studied generates inflation—an ongoing process of a rising price level.

Demand-Pull Inflation in Chatham You may better understand the inflation process that we've just described by considering what is going on in an individual part of the economy, such as a Chatham ketchup-bottling plant. Initially, when aggregate demand increases, the demand for ketchup increases and the price of ketchup rises. Faced with a higher price, the ketchup plant works overtime and increases production. Conditions are good for workers in Chatham, and the ketchup factory finds it hard to hang onto its best people. To do so, it has to offer a higher money wage rate. As the wage rate rises, so do the ketchup factory's costs.

What happens next depends on what happens to aggregate demand. If aggregate demand remains constant (as in Fig. 27.2b), the firm's costs are increasing, but the price of ketchup is not increasing as quickly as its costs. Production is scaled back. Eventually, the money wage rate and costs increase by the same percentage as the rise in the price of ketchup. In real terms, the ketchup factory is in the same situation as it was initially—before the increase in aggregate demand. The plant produces the same amount of ketchup and employs the same amount of labour as before the increase in demand for ketchup.

But if aggregate demand continues to increase, so does the demand for ketchup and the price of ketchup rises at the same rate as wages. The ketchup factory continues to operate above full employment, and there is a persistent shortage of labour. Prices and wages chase each other upward in an unending spiral.

Demand-Pull Inflation in Canada A demand-pull inflation like the one you've just studied occurred in Canada during the late 1960s and early 1970s. In 1960, inflation was a moderate 2 percent a year, but its rate increased slowly through the mid-1960s. Then, between 1966 and 1969, the inflation rate surged upward. Inflation then decreased slightly during 1970 and 1971, but it took off again in 1972. By 1973, the inflation rate was approaching 10 percent a year.

These increases in inflation resulted from increases in aggregate demand that had two main sources. The first was from the United States, where large increases in government expenditures and in the quantity of money increased aggregate demand in the entire world economy. The second source was an increase in Canadian government expenditures and an increase in the quantity of money.

With the economy above full employment, the money wage rate started to rise more quickly and the SAS curve shifted leftward. The Bank of Canada responded with a further increase in the money growth rate, and a demand-pull inflation spiral unfolded. By 1974, the inflation rate had reached double digits.

Next, let's see how shocks to aggregate supply can create cost-push inflation.

Cost-Push Inflation

An inflation that results from an initial increase in costs is called **cost-push inflation**. The two main sources of increases in costs are

1. An increase in money wage rates
2. An increase in the money prices of raw materials

At a given price level, the higher the cost of production, the smaller is the amount that firms are willing to produce. So if money wage rates rise or if the prices of raw materials (for example, oil) rise, firms decrease their supply of goods and services. Aggregate supply decreases, and the short-run aggregate supply curve shifts leftward.[1] Let's trace the effects of such a decrease in short-run aggregate supply on the price level and real GDP.

Initial Effect of a Decrease in Aggregate Supply Suppose that last year the price level was 110 and real GDP was $1,000 billion. Potential real GDP was also $1,000 billion. Figure 27.4 illustrates this situation. The aggregate demand curve was AD_0, the short-run aggregate supply curve was SAS_0, and the long-run aggregate supply curve was LAS. In the current year, the world's oil producers form a price-fixing organization that strengthens their market power and increases the relative price of oil. They raise the price of oil, and this action decreases short-run aggregate supply. The short-run aggregate supply curve shifts leftward to SAS_1. The price level rises to 117, and real GDP decreases to $950 billion. The combination of a rise in the price level and a fall in real GDP is called *stagflation*.

This event is a one-time rise in the price level, like that in Fig. 27.1. It is not inflation. In fact, a supply shock on its own cannot cause inflation. Something more must happen to enable a one-time supply shock, which causes a one-time rise in the price level, to be converted into a process of money growth and ongoing inflation. The quantity of money must persistently increase. And it often does increase, as you will now see.

---

[1] Some cost-push forces, such as an increase in the price of oil accompanied by a decrease in the availability of oil, can also decrease long-run aggregate supply. We'll ignore such effects here and examine cost-push factors that change only short-run aggregate supply.

FIGURE 27.4
A Cost-Push Rise in the Price Level

Initially, the aggregate demand curve is AD_0, the short-run aggregate supply curve is SAS_0, and the long-run aggregate supply curve is LAS. A decrease in aggregate supply (for example, resulting from a rise in the world price of oil) shifts the short-run aggregate supply curve to SAS_1. The economy moves to the point where the short-run aggregate supply curve SAS_1 intersects the aggregate demand curve AD_0. The price level rises to 117, and real GDP decreases to $950 billion.

Aggregate Demand Response When real GDP falls, the unemployment rate rises above its natural rate. In such a situation, there is usually an outcry of concern and a call for action to restore full employment. Suppose that the Bank of Canada increases the quantity of money. Aggregate demand increases. In Fig. 27.5, the aggregate demand curve shifts rightward to AD_1. The increase in aggregate demand has restored full employment. But the price level rises to 121, a 10 percent increase over the initial price level.

A Cost-Push Inflation Process The oil producers now see the prices of everything that they buy increase by 10 percent. So they increase the price of oil again to restore its new high relative price. Figure 27.6 continues the story.

The short-run aggregate supply curve now shifts to SAS_2, and another bout of stagflation ensues. The price level rises further, to 129, and real GDP falls to $950 billion. Unemployment increases above its natural rate. If the Bank of Canada responds yet again with an increase in the quantity of money, aggregate demand increases and the aggregate demand curve shifts to AD_2. The price level rises even higher—to 133—and full employment is again restored. A cost-push inflation spiral results. But if the Bank of Canada does not respond, the economy remains below full employment until the price of oil falls.

You can see that the Bank of Canada has a dilemma. If it increases the quantity of money to restore full employment, the Bank invites another oil price hike that will call forth yet a further increase in the quantity of money. Inflation will rage along at a rate decided by the oil-exporting nations. If the Bank of Canada keeps the lid on money growth, the economy operates with a high level of unemployment.

FIGURE 27.5
Aggregate Demand Response to Cost Push

Following a cost-push increase in the price level, real GDP is below potential GDP and unemployment is above its natural rate. If the Bank of Canada responds by increasing aggregate demand to restore full employment, the aggregate demand curve shifts rightward to AD_1. The economy returns to full employment but the price level rises to 121.

Cost-Push Inflation in Chatham What is going on in the Chatham ketchup-bottling plant when the economy is experiencing cost-push inflation? When the oil price increases, so do the costs of bottling ketchup. These higher costs decrease the supply of ketchup, increasing its price and decreasing the quantity produced. The ketchup plant lays off some workers. This situation will persist until either the Bank of Canada increases aggregate demand or the price of oil falls. If the Bank of Canada increases aggregate demand, as it did in the mid-1970s, the demand for ketchup increases and so does its price. The higher price of ketchup brings higher profits, and the bottling plant increases its production. The ketchup factory rehires the laid-off workers.

Cost-Push Inflation in Canada A cost-push inflation like the one you've just studied occurred in Canada during the 1970s. It began in 1974 when the Organization of the Petroleum Exporting Countries (OPEC) raised the price of oil fourfold. The higher oil price decreased aggregate supply, which caused the price level to rise more quickly and real GDP to shrink. The Bank of Canada then faced a dilemma: Would it increase the quantity of money and accommodate the cost-push forces, or would it keep aggregate demand growth in check by limiting money growth? In 1975, 1976, and 1977, the Bank of Canada repeatedly allowed the quantity of money to grow quickly and inflation proceeded at a rapid rate. In 1979 and 1980, OPEC was again able to push oil prices higher. On that occasion, the Bank of Canada decided not to respond to the oil price hike with an increase in the quantity of money. The result was a recession but also, eventually, a fall in inflation.

FIGURE 27.6

A Cost-Push Inflation Spiral

When a cost increase decreases short-run aggregate supply from SAS_0 to SAS_1, the price level rises to 117 and real GDP decreases to $950 billion. The Bank of Canada responds with an increase in the quantity of money. The aggregate demand curve shifts from AD_0 to AD_1, the price level rises to 121, and real GDP returns to $1,000 billion. A further cost increase occurs, which shifts the short-run aggregate supply curve again, this time to SAS_2. Stagflation is repeated, and the price level rises to 129. The Bank of Canada responds again, and the cost-price inflation spiral continues.

REVIEW QUIZ

1 How does demand-pull inflation begin? What are the initial effects of demand-pull inflation on real GDP?

2 When real GDP moves above potential GDP, what happens to the money wage rate and short-run aggregate supply? How do real GDP and the price level respond?

3 What must happen to create a demand-pull inflation spiral?

4 How does cost-push inflation begin? What are the initial effects of a cost-push rise in the price level?

5 What is *stagflation* and why does cost-push inflation cause stagflation?

6 What must the Bank of Canada do to convert a one-time rise in the price level into a freewheeling cost-push inflation?

myeconlab **Study Plan 27.1**

Inflation requires an ongoing increase in the quantity of money. The quantity theory of money explains the link between money growth and inflation.

The Quantity Theory of Money

YOU'VE SEEN THAT REGARDLESS OF WHETHER inflation originates in a demand-pull or a cost-push, to convert a one-time rise in the price level into an ongoing inflation, aggregate demand must increase. And although many factors can and do influence aggregate demand, only one factor can persistently increase in the long run: the quantity of money. This special place of money gives rise to a special long-run theory of inflation: the quantity theory of money.

The **quantity theory of money** is the proposition that in the long run, an increase in the quantity of money brings an equal percentage increase in the price level. To explain the quantity theory of money, we first need to define *the velocity of circulation* and *the equation of exchange*.

The **velocity of circulation** is the average number of times a dollar of money is used annually to buy GDP. But GDP equals the price level (P) multiplied by *real* GDP (Y). That is,

$$GDP = PY.$$

Call the quantity of money M. The velocity of circulation, V, is determined by the equation

$$V = PY/M.$$

For example, if GDP is $1,000 billion ($PY$ = $1,000 billion) and the quantity of money is $250 billion, the velocity of circulation is 4. ($1,000 billion divided by $250 billion equals 4.)

The **equation of exchange** states that the quantity of money (M) multiplied by the velocity of circulation (V) equals GDP, or

$$MV = PY.$$

Given the definition of the velocity of circulation, this equation is always true—it is true by definition. With M equal to $250 billion and V equal to 4, MV is equal to $1,000 billion, the value of GDP.

The equation of exchange becomes the quantity theory of money if the quantity of money does not influence

1. The velocity of circulation
2. Potential GDP

In this case, the equation of exchange tells us that a change in the quantity of money brings about an equal proportional change in the price level. You can

see why by solving the equation of exchange for the price level. Divide both sides of the equation by real GDP (Y) to give

$$P = (V/Y) \times M.$$

In the long run, real GDP equals potential GDP, so if potential GDP and velocity are not influenced by the quantity of money, then the relationship between the change in the price level (ΔP) and the change in the quantity of money (ΔM) is

$$\Delta P = (V/Y) \times \Delta M.$$

Divide this equation by $P = (V/Y) \times M$, and multiply by 100 to get

$$(\Delta P/P) \times 100 = (\Delta M/M) \times 100.$$

$(\Delta P/P) \times 100$ is the inflation rate and $(\Delta M/M) \times 100$ is the growth rate of the quantity of money. So this equation is the quantity theory of money: The percentage increase in the price level and the percentage increase in the quantity of money are equal.

Evidence on the Quantity Theory

Figure 27.7 summarizes some Canadian evidence on the quantity theory of money. The figure reveals that

1. On the average, the money growth rate exceeds the inflation rate.
2. The money growth rate is correlated with the inflation rate.

Money growth exceeds inflation because real GDP grows. Money growth that matches real GDP growth does not create inflation. But money growth in excess of real GDP growth does create inflation.

Money growth and inflation are correlated—move up and down together. For example, the rise in the inflation rate during the 1970s was accompanied by a rise in the money growth rate. And the decrease in the inflation rate during the 1980s and 1990s was accompanied by a decrease in the money growth rate. But the correlation is not perfect. Nor does a correlation tell us that money growth *causes* inflation.

Money growth might cause inflation; inflation might cause money growth; or some third variable might simultaneously cause inflation and money growth.

Figure 27.8 shows two scatter diagrams of the inflation rate and the money growth rate for 134 countries in part(a) and for those countries with inflation rates below 20 percent a year in part (b).

FIGURE 27.7 myeconlab
Money Growth and Inflation in Canada

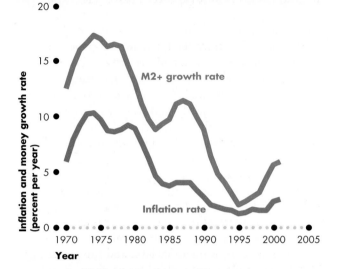

On the average, the money growth rate exceeds the inflation rate because real GDP grows. Money growth and inflation are correlated—they rise and fall together.

Source of data: Statistics Canada, CANSIM Tables 176–0020, 380–0056.

You can see a general tendency for money growth and inflation to be correlated but the quantity theory (shown by the red lines) does not enable us to predict inflation very precisely from the money growth rate.

REVIEW QUIZ

1 What is the quantity theory of money?
2 What is the velocity of circulation of money and how is it calculated?
3 What is the equation of exchange? Can the equation of exchange be wrong?
4 What does the long-run historical evidence and international evidence on the relationship between money growth and inflation tell us about the quantity theory of money?

myeconlab **Study Plan 27.2**

We next turn to an examination of the effects of inflation.

FIGURE 27.8 myeconlab
Money Growth and Inflation in the World

(a) 134 Countries: 1990–2004

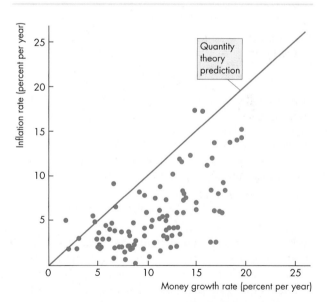

(b) 104 Lower-inflation countries: 1990–2004

Inflation and money growth in 134 countries in part (a) and 104 low-inflation countries in part (b) show a positive relationship between money growth and inflation.

Sources of data: International Financial Statistics Yearbook, 2004 and International Monetary Fund, World Economic Outlook Database, September 2005.

Effects of Inflation

REGARDLESS OF WHETHER INFLATION IS DEMAND pull or cost push, the failure to correctly *anticipate* it results in unintended consequences. These unintended consequences impose costs in both labour markets and capital markets. Let's examine these costs.

Unanticipated Inflation in the Labour Market

Unanticipated inflation has two main consequences for the operation of the labour market:

- Redistribution of income
- Departure from full employment

Redistribution of Income Unanticipated inflation redistributes income between employers and workers. Sometimes employers gain at the expense of workers, and sometimes they lose. If an unexpected increase in aggregate demand increases the inflation rate, then the money wage rate will not have been set high enough. Profits will be higher than expected, and real wages will buy fewer goods than expected. In this case, employers gain at the expense of workers. But if aggregate demand is expected to increase at a rapid rate and it fails to do so, workers gain at the expense of employers. With a high inflation rate anticipated, the money wage rate is set too high and profits are squeezed. Redistribution between employers and workers creates an incentive for both firms and workers to try to forecast inflation correctly.

Departure from Full Employment Redistribution brings gains to some and losses to others. But a departure from full employment imposes costs on everyone. To see why, let's return to the ketchup-bottling plant in Chatham.

If the bottling plant and its workers do not anticipate inflation but inflation occurs, the money wage rate does not rise to keep up with inflation. The real wage rate falls, and the firm tries to hire more labour and increase production. But because the real wage rate has fallen, the firm has a hard time attracting the labour it wants to employ. It pays overtime rates to its existing work force, and because it runs its plant at a faster pace, it incurs higher plant maintenance and parts replacement costs. But also, because the real

wage rate has fallen, workers begin to quit the bottling plant to find jobs that pay a real wage rate that is closer to one that prevailed before the outbreak of inflation. This labour turnover imposes additional costs on the firm. So even though its production increases, the firm incurs additional costs and its profits do not increase as much as they otherwise would. The workers incur additional costs of job search, and those who remain at the bottling plant wind up feeling cheated. They've worked overtime to produce the extra output, and when they come to spend their wages, they discover that prices have increased so their wages buy a smaller quantity of goods and services than expected.

If the bottling plant and its workers anticipate a high inflation rate but it does not occur, the money wage rate increases by too much and the real wage rate rises. At the higher real wage rate, the firm lays off some workers and the unemployment rate increases. The workers who keep their jobs gain, but those who become unemployed lose. Also, the bottling plant loses because its output and profits fall.

Unanticipated Inflation in the Market for Financial Capital

Unanticipated inflation has two consequences for the operation of the market for financial capital:

- Redistribution of income
- Too much or too little lending and borrowing

Redistribution of Income Unanticipated inflation redistributes income between borrowers and lenders. Sometimes borrowers gain at the expense of lenders, and sometimes they lose. When inflation is unexpected, interest rates are not set high enough to compensate lenders for the falling value of money. In this case, borrowers gain at the expense of lenders. But if inflation is expected and then fails to occur, interest rates are set too high. In this case, lenders gain at the expense of borrowers. Redistributions of income between borrowers and lenders create an incentive for both groups to try to forecast inflation correctly.

Too Much or Too Little Lending and Borrowing If the inflation rate turns out to be either higher or lower than expected, the interest rate does not incorporate a correct allowance for the falling value of money and the real interest rate is either lower or higher than it otherwise would be. When the real interest rate turns out to be too low, which occurs when inflation is *higher* than expected, borrowers wish they had borrowed more and lenders wish they had lent less. Both groups would have made different lending and borrowing decisions with greater foresight about the inflation rate. When the real interest rate turns out to be too high, which occurs when inflation is lower than expected, borrowers wish they had borrowed less and lenders wish they had lent more. Again, both groups would have made different lending and borrowing decisions with greater foresight about the inflation rate.

So unanticipated inflation imposes costs regardless of whether the inflation turns out to be higher or lower than anticipated. The presence of these costs gives everyone an incentive to forecast inflation correctly. Let's see how people go about this task.

Forecasting Inflation

Inflation is difficult to forecast for two reasons. First, there are several sources of inflation—the demand-pull and cost-push sources you've just studied. Second, the speed with which a change in either aggregate demand or aggregate supply translates into a change in the price level varies. This speed of response also depends, as you will see below, on the extent to which the inflation is anticipated.

Because inflation is costly and difficult to forecast, people devote considerable resources to improving inflation forecasts. Some people specialize in forecasting, and others buy forecasts from specialists. The specialist forecasters are economists who work for public and private macroeconomic forecasting agencies and for banks, insurance companies, labour unions, and large corporations. The returns these specialists make depend on the quality of their forecasts, so they have a strong incentive to forecast as accurately as possible. The most accurate forecast possible is the one that is based on all the relevant information available and is called a **rational expectation.**

A rational expectation is not necessarily a correct forecast. It is simply the best forecast available. It will often turn out to be wrong, but it was the best forecast that could have been made with the information available.

You've seen the effects of inflation when people fail to anticipate it. And you've seen why it pays to try to anticipate inflation. Let's now see what happens if inflation is correctly anticipated.

Anticipated Inflation

In the demand-pull and cost-push inflations that we studied in this chapter, the money wage rate is sticky. When aggregate demand increases, either to set off a demand-pull inflation or to accommodate a cost-push inflation, the money wage rate does not change immediately. But if people correctly anticipate increases in aggregate demand, they will adjust the money wage rate so that it keeps up with anticipated inflation.

In this case, inflation proceeds with real GDP equal to potential GDP and unemployment equal to its natural rate. Figure 27.9 explains why. Suppose that last year the price level was 110 and real GDP was $1,000 billion, which is also potential GDP. The aggregate demand curve was AD_0, the aggregate supply curve was SAS_0, and the long-run aggregate supply curve was LAS.

Suppose that potential GDP does not change, so the LAS curve does not shift. Also suppose that aggregate demand is expected to increase and that the expected aggregate demand curve for this year is AD_1. In anticipation of this increase in aggregate demand, the money wage rate rises and the short-run aggregate supply curve shifts leftward. If the money wage rate rises by the same percentage as the price level rises, the short-run aggregate supply curve for next year is SAS_1.

If aggregate demand turns out to be the same as expected, the aggregate demand curve is AD_1. The short-run aggregate supply curve SAS_1 and AD_1 determine the actual price level at 121. Between last year and this year, the price level increased from 110 to 121 and the economy experienced an inflation rate of 10 percent, the same as the inflation rate that was anticipated. If this anticipated inflation is ongoing, in the following year aggregate demand increases (as anticipated) and the aggregate demand curve shifts to AD_2. The money wage rate rises to reflect the anticipated inflation, and the short-run aggregate supply curve shifts to SAS_2. The price level rises by a further 10 percent to 133.

What has caused this inflation? The immediate answer is that because people expected inflation, the money wage rate increased and the price level increased. But the expectation was correct. Aggregate demand was expected to increase, and it did increase. Because aggregate demand was *expected* to increase from AD_0 to AD_1, the short-run aggregate supply curve shifted from SAS_0 to SAS_1. Because aggregate demand actually did increase by the amount that was expected, the actual aggregate demand curve shifted from AD_0 to AD_1. The combination of the anticipated and actual shifts of the aggregate demand curve rightward produced an increase in the price level that was anticipated.

Only if aggregate demand growth is correctly forecasted does the economy follow the course described in Fig. 27.9. If the expected growth rate of aggregate demand is different from its actual growth rate, the expected aggregate demand curve shifts by an amount that is different from the actual aggregate demand curve. The inflation rate departs from its expected level, and to some extent, there is unanticipated inflation.

FIGURE 27.9
Anticipated Inflation

Potential real GDP is $1,000 billion. Last year, the aggregate demand curve was AD_0, and the short-run aggregate supply curve was SAS_0. The actual price level was the same as the expected price level—110. This year, aggregate demand is expected to increase to AD_1. The rational expectation of the price level changes from 110 to 121. As a result, the money wage rate rises and the short-run aggregate supply curve shifts to SAS_1. If aggregate demand actually increases as expected, the actual aggregate demand curve AD_1 is the same as the expected aggregate demand curve. Real GDP is $1,000 billion and the actual price level is 121. The inflation is correctly anticipated. Next year, the process continues with aggregate demand increasing as expected to AD_2 and the money wage rate rising to shift the short-run aggregate supply curve to SAS_2. Again, real GDP remains at $1,000 billion, and the price level rises, as anticipated, to 133.

Unanticipated Inflation

When aggregate demand increases by *more* than expected, there is some unanticipated inflation that looks just like the demand-pull inflation that you studied earlier. Some inflation is expected, and the money wage rate is set to reflect that expectation. The *SAS* curve intersects the *LAS* curve at the expected price level. Aggregate demand then increases but by more than expected. So the *AD* curve intersects the *SAS* curve at a level of real GDP that exceeds potential GDP. With real GDP above potential GDP and unemployment below its natural rate, the money wage rate rises. So the price level rises further. If aggregate demand increases again, a demand-pull inflation spiral unwinds.

When aggregate demand increases by *less* than expected, there is some unanticipated inflation that looks like the cost-push inflation that you studied earlier. Again, some inflation is expected, and the money wage rate is set to reflect that expectation. The *SAS* curve intersects the *LAS* curve at the expected price level. Aggregate demand then increases but by less than expected. So the *AD* curve intersects the *SAS* curve at a level of real GDP below potential GDP. Aggregate demand increases to restore full employment. But if aggregate demand is expected to increase by more than it actually does, the money wage rate again rises, short-run aggregate supply again decreases, and a cost-push spiral unwinds.

We've seen that only when inflation is unanticipated does real GDP depart from potential GDP. When inflation is anticipated, real GDP remains at potential GDP. Does this mean that an anticipated inflation has no costs?

The Costs of Anticipated Inflation

The costs of an anticipated inflation depend on its rate. At a moderate rate of 2 or 3 percent a year, the cost is probably small. But as the anticipated inflation rate rises, so does its cost, and an anticipated inflation at a rapid rate can be extremely costly.

Anticipated inflation decreases potential GDP and slows economic growth. These adverse consequences arise for three major reasons:

■ Transactions costs
■ Tax effects
■ Increased uncertainty

Transactions Costs The first transactions costs are known as the "boot leather costs." These are costs that arise from an increase in the velocity of circulation of money and an increase in the amount of running around that people do to try to avoid incurring losses from the falling value of money.

When money loses value at a rapid anticipated rate, it does not function well as a store of value and people try to avoid holding money. They spend their incomes as soon as they receive them, and firms pay out incomes—wages and dividends—as soon as they receive revenue from their sales. The velocity of circulation increases. During the 1920s in Germany, when inflation reached *hyperinflation* levels (rates more than 50 percent a month), wages were paid and spent twice in a single day!

The range of estimates of the boot leather costs is large. Some economists put them at close to zero. Others estimate them to be as much as 2 percent of GDP for a 10 percent inflation. For a rapid inflation, these costs are much more.

The boot leather costs of inflation are just one of several transactions costs that are influenced by the inflation rate. At high anticipated inflation rates, people seek alternatives to money as means of payment and use tokens and commodities or even barter, all of which are less efficient than money as a means of payment. For example, in Russia during the 1990s, when inflation reached 1,000 percent a year, the U.S. dollar started to replace the increasingly worthless Russian ruble. Consequently, people had to keep track of the exchange rate between the ruble and the dollar hour by hour and had to engage in many additional and costly transactions in the foreign exchange market.

Because anticipated inflation increases transactions costs, it diverts resources from producing goods and services and it decreases potential GDP. The faster the anticipated inflation rate, the greater is the decrease in potential GDP and the farther leftward does the *LAS* curve shift.

Tax Effects Anticipated inflation interacts with the tax system and creates serious distortions in incentives. Its major effect is on real interest rates.

Anticipated inflation swells the dollar returns on investments. But dollar returns are taxed, so the effective tax rate rises. This effect becomes serious at even modest inflation rates. Let's consider an example.

Suppose the real interest rate is 4 percent a year and the tax rate is 50 percent. With no inflation, the nominal interest rate is also 4 percent a year and 50 percent of this rate is taxable. The real *after-tax* interest rate is 2 percent a year (50 percent of 4 percent). Now suppose the inflation rate is 4 percent a year, and the nominal interest rate is 8 percent a year. The *after-tax* nominal rate is 4 percent a year (50 percent of 8 percent). Now subtract the 4 percent inflation rate from this amount, and you see that the *after-tax real interest rate* is zero! The true tax rate on interest income is 100 percent.

The higher the inflation rate, the higher is the effective tax rate on income from capital. And the higher the tax rate, the higher is the interest rate paid by borrowers and the lower is the after-tax interest rate received by lenders.

With a low after-tax real interest rate, the incentive to save is weakened and the saving rate falls. With a high cost of borrowing, the amount of investment decreases. And with a fall in saving and investment, the pace of capital accumulation slows and so does the long-term growth rate of real GDP.

Increased Uncertainty When the inflation rate is high, there is increased uncertainty about the long-term inflation rate. Will inflation remain high for a long time, or will price stability be restored? This increased uncertainty makes long-term planning difficult and gives people a shorter-term focus. Investment falls, and the economic growth rate slows.

But this increased uncertainty also misallocates resources. Instead of concentrating on the activities at which they have a comparative advantage, people find it more profitable to search for ways of avoiding the losses that inflation inflicts. As a result, inventive talent that might otherwise work on productive innovations works on finding ways of profiting from the inflation instead.

The implications of inflation for economic growth have been estimated to be enormous. Peter Howitt of Brown University, building on work by Robert Barro of Harvard University, has estimated that if inflation is lowered from 3 percent a year to zero, the growth rate of real GDP will rise by between 0.06 and 0.09 percentage points a year. These numbers might seem small, but they are growth rates. After 30 years, real GDP would be 2.3 percent higher and the present value of all the future output would be 85 percent of current GDP—$850 billion! In the rapid anticipated inflations of Brazil and Russia, the costs are much greater than the numbers given here.

You've seen that an increase in aggregate demand that is not fully anticipated increases both the price level and real GDP. It also decreases unemployment. Similarly, a decrease in aggregate demand that is not fully anticipated decreases the price level and real GDP. It also increases unemployment. Do these relationships mean that there is a tradeoff between inflation and unemployment? Does low unemployment always bring inflation and does low inflation bring high unemployment? We explore these questions.

Inflation and Unemployment: The Phillips Curve

THE *AS–AD* MODEL FOCUSES ON THE PRICE LEVEL and real GDP. Knowing how these two variables change, we can work out what happens to the inflation rate and the unemployment rate. But the *AS–AD* model does not place inflation and unemployment at the centre of the stage.

A more direct way of studying inflation and unemployment uses a relationship called the Phillips curve. The Phillips curve approach uses the same basic ideas as the *AS–AD* model, but it focuses directly on inflation and unemployment. The Phillips curve is so named because New Zealand economist A.W. Phillips popularized it. A **Phillips curve** is a curve that shows a relationship between inflation and unemployment. There are two time frames for Phillips curves:

■ The short-run Phillips curve
■ The long-run Phillips curve

The Short-Run Phillips Curve

The **short-run Phillips curve** is a curve that shows the tradeoff between inflation and unemployment, holding constant

1. The expected inflation rate
2. The natural rate of unemployment

You've just seen what determines the expected inflation rate. The natural rate of unemployment and the factors that influence it are explained in Chapter 21, pp. 496–497 and Chapter 30, pp. 719–721.

Figure 27.10 shows a short-run Phillips curve, *SRPC*. Suppose that the expected inflation rate is 10 percent a year and the natural rate of unemployment is 6 percent, point *A* in the figure. A short-run Phillips curve passes through this point. If inflation

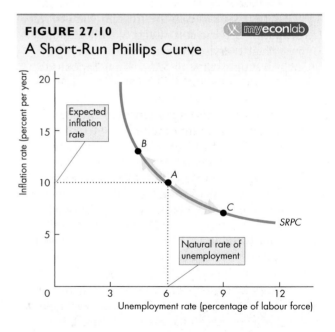

FIGURE 27.10   **myeconlab**
A Short-Run Phillips Curve

The short-run Phillips curve (*SRPC*) shows the relationship between inflation and unemployment at a given expected inflation rate and a given natural rate of unemployment. With an expected inflation rate of 10 percent a year and a natural rate of unemployment of 6 percent, the short-run Phillips curve passes through point A. An unanticipated increase in aggregate demand lowers unemployment and increases inflation—a movement up along the short-run Phillips curve. An unanticipated decrease in aggregate demand increases unemployment and lowers inflation—a movement down along the short-run Phillips curve.

rises above its expected rate, unemployment falls below its natural rate. This joint movement in the inflation rate and the unemployment rate is illustrated as a movement up along the short-run Phillips curve from point *A* to point *B* in the figure. Similarly, if inflation falls below its expected rate, unemployment rises above its natural rate. In this case, there is movement down along the short-run Phillips curve from point *A* to point *C*.

This negative relationship between inflation and unemployment along the short-run Phillips curve is explained by the *AS–AD* model. Figure 27.11 shows the connection between the two approaches. Initially, the aggregate demand curve is AD_0, the short-run aggregate supply curve is SAS_0, and the long-run aggregate supply curve is *LAS*. Real GDP is $1,000 billion, and the price level is 100. Aggregate demand is expected to increase, and the aggregate demand curve is expected to shift rightward to AD_1. Anticipating this increase in aggregate demand, the money wage rate rises, which shifts the short-run aggregate supply curve to SAS_1. What happens to actual inflation and real GDP depends on the *actual* change in aggregate demand.

First, suppose that aggregate demand actually increases by the amount expected, so the aggregate demand curve shifts to AD_1. The price level rises from 100 to 110, and the inflation rate is an anticipated 10 percent a year. Real GDP remains at potential GDP, and unemployment remains at its natural rate—6 percent. The economy moves to point *A* in Fig. 27.11, and it can equivalently be described as being at point *A* on the short-run Phillips curve in Fig. 27.10.

Alternatively, suppose that aggregate demand is expected to increase to AD_1 but actually increases by more than expected, to AD_2. The price level now rises to 113, a 13 percent inflation rate. Real GDP increases above potential GDP, and unemployment falls below its natural rate. We can now describe the economy as moving to point *B* in Fig. 27.11 or as being at point *B* on the short-run Phillips curve in Fig. 27.10.

Finally, suppose that aggregate demand is expected to increase to AD_1 but actually remains at AD_0. The price level now rises to 107, a 7 percent inflation rate. Real GDP falls below potential GDP, and unemployment rises above its natural rate. We can now describe the economy as moving to point *C* in Fig. 27.11 or as being at point *C* on the short-run Phillips curve in Fig. 27.10.

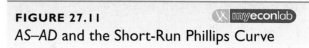

FIGURE 27.11

AS–AD and the Short-Run Phillips Curve

If aggregate demand is expected to increase and shift the aggregate demand curve from AD_0 to AD_1, then the money wage rate rises by an amount that shifts the short-run aggregate supply curve from SAS_0 to SAS_1. If aggregate demand increases as expected, the price level rises to 110, a 10 percent rise, and the economy is at point A in this figure and at point A on the short-run Phillips curve in Fig. 27.10. If, with the same expectations, aggregate demand increases and shifts the aggregate demand curve from AD_0 to AD_2, the price level rises to 113, a 13 percent rise, and the economy is at point B in this figure and at point B on the short-run Phillips curve in Fig. 27.10. If, with the same expectations, aggregate demand does not change, the price level rises to 107, a 7 percent rise, and the economy is at point C in this figure and at point C on the short-run Phillips curve in Fig. 27.10.

The short-run Phillips curve is like the short-run aggregate supply curve. A movement along the *SAS* curve that brings a price level above that expected and an increase in real GDP is equivalent to a movement along the short-run Phillips curve that brings an increase in the inflation rate and a decrease in the unemployment rate. (Similarly, a movement along the *SAS* curve that brings a price level below that expected and a decrease in real GDP is equivalent to a movement along the short-run Phillips curve that brings a decrease in the inflation rate and an increase in the unemployment rate.)

The Long-Run Phillips Curve

The **long-run Phillips curve** shows the relationship between inflation and unemployment when the actual inflation rate equals the expected inflation rate. The long-run Phillips curve is vertical at the natural rate of unemployment. In Fig. 27.12, it is the vertical line *LRPC*. The long-run Phillips curve tells us that any anticipated inflation rate is possible at the natural rate of unemployment. This proposition is consistent with the *AS–AD* model, which predicts that when inflation is anticipated, real GDP equals potential GDP and unemployment is at its natural rate.

When the expected inflation rate changes, the short-run Phillips curve shifts but the long-run Phillips curve does not shift. If the expected inflation rate is 10 percent a year, the short-run Phillips curve is $SRPC_0$. If the expected inflation rate falls to 7 per-cent a year, the short-run Phillips curve shifts down-ward to $SRPC_1$. The distance by which the short-run Phillips curve shifts downward when the expected inflation rate falls is equal to the change in the expected inflation rate.

To see why the short-run Phillips curve shifts when the expected inflation rate changes, let's do a thought experiment. There is full employment, and a 10 percent a year anticipated inflation is raging. The Bank of Canada now begins an attack on inflation by slowing money growth. Aggregate demand growth slows, and the inflation rate falls to 7 percent a year. At first, this decrease in inflation is *un*anticipated, so the money wage rate continues to rise at its original rate. The short-run aggregate supply curve shifts left-ward at the same pace as before. Real GDP decreases, and unemployment increases. In Fig. 27.12, the economy moves from point *A* to point *C* on $SRPC_0$.

If the actual inflation rate remains steady at 7 per-cent a year, this rate eventually comes to be expected. As this happens, wage growth slows and the short-run aggregate supply curve shifts leftward less quickly. Eventually, it shifts leftward at the same pace at which the aggregate demand curve is shifting rightward. The actual inflation rate equals the expected inflation rate, and full employment is restored. Unemployment is back at its natural rate. In Fig. 27.12, the short-run Phillips curve has shifted from $SRPC_0$ to $SRPC_1$ and the economy is at point *D*.

An increase in the expected inflation rate has the opposite effect to that shown in Fig. 27.12. Another important source of shifts in the Phillips curve is a change in the natural rate of unemployment.

Changes in the Natural Rate of Unemployment

The natural rate of unemployment changes for many reasons (see Chapter 30, pp. 719–721). A change in the natural rate of unemployment shifts both the short-run and long-run Phillips curves. Figure 27.13 illustrates such shifts. If the natural rate of unemploy-ment increases from 6 percent to 9 percent, the long-run Phillips curve shifts from $LRPC_0$ to $LRPC_1$, and if expected inflation is constant at 10 percent a year, the short-run Phillips curve shifts from $SRPC_0$ to $SRPC_1$. Because the expected inflation rate is constant, the short-run Phillips curve $SRPC_1$ intersects the long-run curve $LRPC_1$ (point *E*) at the same inflation rate at which the short-run Phillips curve $SRPC_0$ intersects the long-run curve $LRPC_0$ (point *A*).

FIGURE 27.12   ⓧ **myeconlab**

Short-Run and Long-Run Phillips Curves

The long-run Phillips curve is *LRPC*. A fall in the expected inflation rate from 10 percent a year to 7 percent a year shifts the short-run Phillips curve downward from $SRPC_0$ to $SRPC_1$. The new short-run Phillips curve intersects the long-run Phillips curve at the new expected inflation rate—point *D*. With the original expected inflation rate (of 10 per-cent), a fall in the actual inflation rate to 7 percent a year increases the unemployment rate from 6 percent to 9 per-cent, at point *C*.

FIGURE 27.13

A Change in the Natural Rate of Unemployment

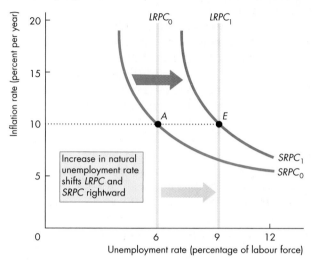

A change in the natural rate of unemployment shifts both the short-run and long-run Phillips curves. Here, the natural rate of unemployment increases from 6 percent to 9 percent, and the two Phillips curves shift right to $SRPC_1$ and $LRPC_1$. The new long-run Phillips curve intersects the new short-run Phillips curve at the expected inflation rate—point E.

The Canadian Phillips Curve

Figure 27.14(a) is a scatter diagram of inflation and unemployment since 1962. The data follow a course like a Formula 1 race track with 2004 almost at the same spot as 1962. Figure 27.14(b) interprets the data in terms of the Phillips curve. In 1962, the natural rate of unemployment was 5 percent so the long-run Phillips curve was $LRPC_1$. The expected inflation rate was 3 percent a year so the short-run Phillips curve, $SRPC_1$, intersects $LRPC_1$ at point A. During the 1970s and through 1982, the expected inflation rate and the natural rate of unemployment increased. The long-run curve shifted to $LRPC_2$ and the short-run curve shifted to $SRPC_2$. During the 1980s and 1990s, the expected inflation rate and the natural rate of unemployment decreased. The long-run curve shifted to $LRPC_3$ and the short-run curve shifted back to $SRPC_1$. The $SRPC$ of 2004 is the same as that of 1962, but in 2004, the natural rate of unemployment is higher and the expected inflation rate is lower than in 1962.

FIGURE 27.14

Phillips Curves in Canada

(a) The time sequence

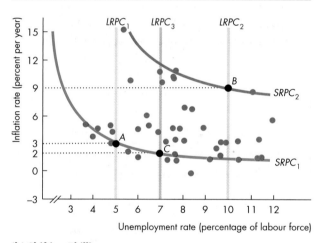

(b) Shifting Phillips curves

In part (a), each dot represents the combination of inflation and unemployment for a particular year in Canada. Part (b) interprets the data with a shifting short-run Phillips curve. The black dots A, B, and C show the combination of the natural rate of unemployment and the expected inflation rate in different periods. The short-run Phillips curve was $SRPC_1$ during the 1960s and the late 1990s and early 2000s. It was $SRPC_2$ during the early 1970s and early 1980s. The long-run Phillips curve was $LRPC_1$ during the 1960s, $LRPC_2$ during the 1970s and early 1980s, and $LRPC_3$ during the 1990s.

Source of data: Statistics Canada, CANSIM Tables 380–0002 and 380–0056.

1 How would you use the Phillips curve to illustrate an unanticipated change in the inflation rate?

2 What are the effects of an unanticipated increase in the inflation rate on the unemployment rate?

3 If the expected inflation rate increases by 10 percentage points, how do the short-run Phillips curve and the long-run Phillips curve change?

4 If the natural rate of unemployment increases, what happens to the short-run Phillips curve and the long-run Phillips curve?

5 Does Canada have a stable short-run Phillips curve? Explain why or why not.

6 Does Canada have a stable long-run Phillips curve? Explain why or why not.

myeconlab   Study Plan 27.4

So far, we've studied the effects of inflation on real GDP, real wages, employment, and unemployment. But inflation lowers the value of money and changes the real value of the amounts borrowed and repaid. As a result, interest rates are influenced by inflation. Let's see how.

Interest Rates and Inflation

TODAY, BUSINESSES IN CANADA CAN BORROW AT interest rates of around 6 percent a year. Businesses in Russia pay interest rates of 13 percent a year, those in Turkey pay 16 percent a year, and those in Brazil pay 20 percent a year. Canadian businesses also faced interest rates of 20 percent during the early 1980s. Why do interest rates vary so much both across countries and over time? Part of the answer is because risk differences make *real interest rates* vary across countries. Borrowers in high-risk countries pay higher interest rates than do those in low-risk countries. But another part of the answer is that the inflation rate varies.

Figure 27.15 shows that the higher the inflation rate, the higher is the nominal interest rate. This proposition is true for Canada over time in part (a) and the world in 2005 in part (b).

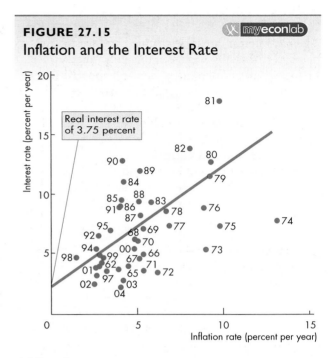

FIGURE 27.15   **myeconlab**
Inflation and the Interest Rate

(a) Canada

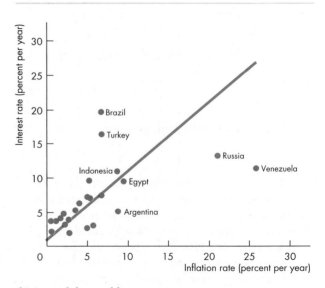

(b) Around the world

Other things remaining the same, the higher the inflation rate, the higher is the nominal interest rate. Part (a) shows this relationship between nominal interest rates and the inflation rate in Canada, and part (b) shows the relationship across a number of countries in 2005.

Sources of data: Statistics Canada, Tables 176–0043 and 380–0056, World Economic Outlook Database, International Monetary Fund, and *The Economist*, Sep. 2005

How Interest Rates Are Determined

The *real* interest rate is determined by investment demand and saving supply in the global market for financial capital. Investment demand and saving supply depend on the real interest rate. And the real interest rate adjusts to make investment plans and saving plans equal. You can think of the forces that determine the equilibrium real interest rate by using the standard demand and supply model. National real interest rates vary around the world-average real interest rate because of national differences in risk.

A *nominal* interest rate is determined by the demand for money and the quantity of money in each nation's money market. The demand for money depends on the nominal interest rate, and the quantity of money is determined by the central bank's monetary policy—the Bank of Canada's monetary policy in Canada. The nominal interest rate adjusts to make the quantity of money demanded equal to the quantity supplied. (Chapter 25, p. 604–605, explains the forces that determine the equilibrium nominal interest rate.)

Why Inflation Influences the Nominal Interest Rate

Because the real interest rate is determined in the global capital market and nominal interest rates are determined in each nation's money market, there is no tight and mechanical link between the two interest rates. But on the average, and other things remaining the same, a 1 percentage point rise in the inflation rate leads to a 1 percentage point rise in the nominal interest rate. Why? The answer is that the financial capital market and the money market are closely interconnected. The investment, saving, and demand for money decisions that people make are connected and the result is that the equilibrium nominal interest rate approximately equals the real interest rate plus the expected inflation rate.

To see why this relationship between the real interest rate and the nominal interest rate arises, think about the investment, saving, and demand for money decisions that people make. Imagine first that there is no inflation. Investment equals saving at a real interest rate of 6 percent a year. The demand for money equals the supply of money at a nominal interest rate of 6 percent a year. Teleglobe Canada is willing to pay an interest rate of 6 percent a year to get the funds it needs to pay for its global investment in new satellites. Sue and thousands of people like her are willing to save and lend Teleglobe Canada the amount it needs for its satellites if

they can get a *real* return of 6 percent a year. (Sue is saving to buy a new car.) And Teleglobe Canada, Sue, and everyone else are willingly holding the quantity of (real) money supplied by the Bank of Canada.

Now imagine that the inflation rate is steady at 4 percent a year and is expected to remain at 4 percent a year. All dollar amounts, including satellite service profits and car prices, are rising by 4 percent a year. If Teleglobe Canada was willing to pay a 6 percent interest rate when there was no inflation, it is now willing to pay 10 percent interest. Its profits are rising by 4 percent a year, so it is *really* paying only 6 percent. Similarly, if Sue was willing to lend at a 6 percent interest rate when there was no inflation, she is now willing to lend only if she gets 10 percent interest. The price of the car Sue is planning to buy is rising by 4 percent a year, so she is *really* getting only a 6 percent interest rate.

Because borrowers are willing to pay the higher rate and lenders are willing to lend only if they get the higher rate when inflation is anticipated, the *nominal interest rate* increases by an amount equal to the expected inflation rate. The *real interest rate* remains constant.

At a nominal interest rate of 10 percent a year, people are willingly holding the quantity of (real) money supplied by the Bank of Canada. This quantity is less than that with zero inflation.

REVIEW QUIZ

1 What is the relationship between the real interest rate, the nominal interest rate, and the expected inflation rate?
2 Why does inflation change the nominal interest rate?

myeconlab **Study Plan 27.5**

◆ *Reading Between the Lines* on pp. 650–651 looks at the views of an economist who believes there is a long-run tradeoff between inflation and unemployment.

Your task in the next chapter is to see how the Bank of Canada uses the tools of monetary policy to influence the inflation rate and to try to keep its rate inside a target range.

Inflation–Unemployment Tradeoff

THE VANCOUVER SUN, JUNE 18, 2002

High jobless rate avoidable

Canada could have done more to stimulate employment through the 1990s without risking inflation, the winner of the 2001 Nobel Prize in Economics said Monday.

Dr. George Akerlof said during a meeting of the Canadian Institute for Advanced Research that the chairman of the U.S. Federal Reserve Board, Alan Greenspan, went against the advice of his staff and traditional economic theory and kept stimulating the economy with low interest rates as unemployment hit historic lows.

Canada took a more conservative and ideological approach.

The result was Canada had an unemployment rate much higher than that in the United States, where inflation stayed low even when unemployment fell below five per cent as a result of the investment generated by the economic stimulus program.

"The Canadian economy serves up a sober lesson," said Akerlof, who is a professor of economics at the University of California at Berkeley.

As the economy stalled in the past couple of years, the Bank of Canada lowered interest rates, but unemployment rates have been held high by the global recession, Akerlof said.

"You can't expect that Canada wouldn't have the same repercussions that are happening in the rest of the world," he said.

Akerlof recommended that in future, Canada adopt a policy similar to that employed in the U.S.

"I sincerely hope the Canadian unemployment of the 1990s is not going to repeat itself," he said.

...

Akerlof won the Nobel Prize for work he did more than 30 years ago, describing how markets break down when buyers and sellers have conflicting needs and expectations.

Craig McInnes/*The Vancouver Sun.*

Essence of the Story

■ George Akerlof, a professor of economics at the University of California at Berkeley and a Nobel Laureate, says that Canada could have had higher employment (lower unemployment) with no higher inflation rate during the 1990s.

■ He contrasted Canada with the United States and said that as the unemployment rate hit historic lows, the U.S. kept stimulating the economy with low interest rates.

■ U.S. inflation stayed low even when unemployment fell below 5 percent because of the investment generated by the economic stimulus program.

■ Canada took a more conservative and ideological approach and had an unemployment rate much higher than that in the United States.

Economic Analysis

■ It is difficult to recognize the Canada portrayed by George Akerlof.

■ Canada's unemployment rate was indeed higher than the U.S. unemployment rate.

■ But the gap between the Canadian and U.S. unemployment rates, which opened up during the early 1980s (not the 1990s), was persistent and not cyclical. And the gap narrowed during the early 2000s.

■ Figure 1 shows the unemployment rates in the two countries.

■ Because the unemployment gap was persistent, it is likely that it represents an increase in the natural rate of unemployment in Canada.

■ If Canada's natural rate of unemployment is higher than the U.S. rate, stimulating aggregate demand will bring no improvement in the unemployment situation, but will bring greater inflation.

■ Canada had a more severe inflation problem than the United States during the early 1980s.

■ But Canada brought its inflation under control and had lower inflation than the United States during the 1990s and the early 2000s.

■ Figure 2 shows the inflation records in the two countries.

■ George Akerlof says that U.S. unemployment fell because of a high investment rate.

■ He implies that Canada's investment rate was too low and could have been boosted.

■ Figure 3 shows that generally Canada has invested a larger percentage of its GDP than the United States has invested.

■ It is true that U.S. investment increased during the 1990s. But it increased from a very low level and began to catch up to Canada's higher investment rate.

■ Canada chose to fight inflation and accept a temporarily higher unemployment rate. But the persistently higher unemployment rate in Canada is a natural phenomenon that cannot be changed with demand stimulation.

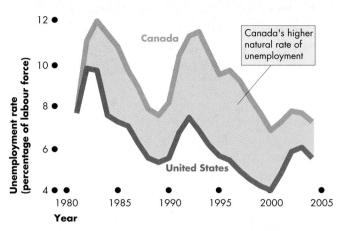

Figure 1 Unemployment in Canada and the United States

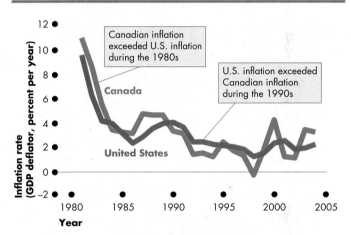

Figure 2 Inflation in Canada and the United States

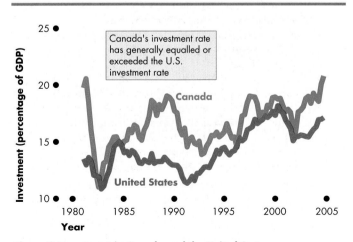

Figure 3 Investment in Canada and the United States

651

SUMMARY

KEY POINTS

Inflation: Demand-Pull and Cost-Push
(p. 632–637)

- Inflation is a process of persistently rising prices and falling value of money
- Demand-pull inflation arises from increasing aggregate demand.
- The main sources of increases in aggregate demand are increases in the quantity of money, government expenditures, or exports.
- Cost-push inflation can result from any factor that decreases aggregate supply.
- The main sources of decreases in aggregate supply are increasing money wage rates and increasing prices of key raw materials.

The Quantity Theory of Money (pp. 638–639)

- The quantity theory of money is the proposition that money growth and inflation move up and down together in the long run.
- The Canadian and international evidence is consistent with the quantity theory on the average.

Effects of Inflation (pp. 640–644)

- Inflation is costly when it is unanticipated because it creates inefficiencies and redistributes income and wealth.
- People try to anticipate inflation to avoid its costs.
- Forecasts of inflation based on all the available relevant information are called rational expectations.
- A moderate anticipated inflation has a small cost. A rapid anticipated inflation is costly because it decreases potential GDP and slows economic growth.

Inflation and Unemployment: The Phillips Curve (pp. 644–648)

- The short-run Phillips curve shows the tradeoff between inflation and unemployment when the expected inflation rate and the natural rate of unemployment are constant.

- The long-run Phillips curve, which is vertical, shows that when the actual inflation rate equals the expected inflation rate, the unemployment rate equals the natural rate of unemployment.
- Unexpected changes in the inflation rate bring movements along the short-run Phillips curve.
- Changes in expected inflation shift the short-run Phillips curve.
- Changes in the natural rate of unemployment shift both the short-run and long-run Phillips curves.

Interest Rates and Inflation (pp. 648–649)

- The higher the expected inflation rate, the higher is the nominal interest rate.
- As the expected inflation rate rises, borrowers willingly pay a higher interest rate and lenders successfully demand a higher interest rate.
- The nominal interest rate adjusts to equal the real interest rate plus the expected inflation rate.

KEY FIGURES

KEY TERMS

PROBLEMS

Go to ⓧ myeconlab for solutions to odd-numbered problems and additional exercises.

1. The figure shows an economy's long-run aggregate supply curve *LAS*; three aggregate demand curves AD_0, AD_1, and AD_2; and three short-run aggregate supply curves SAS_0, SAS_1, and SAS_2. The economy starts out on the curves AD_0 and SAS_0.

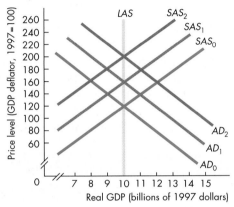

Some events occur that generate a demand-pull inflation.

a. List the events that might cause a demand-pull inflation.

b. Using the figure, describe the initial effects of a demand-pull inflation.

c. Using the figure, describe what happens as a demand-pull inflation spiral unwinds.

2. In the economy described in problem 1, some events then occur that generate a cost-push inflation.

a. List the events that might cause a cost-push inflation.

b. Using the figure, describe the initial effects of a cost-push inflation.

c. Using the figure, describe what happens as a cost-push inflation spiral unwinds.

3. Quantecon is a country in which the quantity theory of money operates. The country has a constant population, capital stock, and technology. In year 1, real GDP was $400 million, the price level was 200, and the velocity of circulation of money was 20. In year 2, the quantity of money was 20 percent higher than in year 1.

a. What was the quantity of money in year 1?

b. What was the quantity of money in year 2?

c. What was the price level in year 2?

d. What was the level of real GDP in year 2?

e. What was the velocity of circulation in year 2?

4. In Quantecon described in problem 3, in year 3, the quantity of money falls to one-fifth of its year 2 level.

a. What is the quantity of money in year 3?

b. What is the price level in year 3?

c. What is the level of real GDP in year 3?

d. What is the velocity of circulation in year 3?

e. If it takes more than one year for the full quantity theory effect to occur, what do you predict happens to real GDP in Quantecon in year 3? Why?

5. The economy described in problem 1 starts out on the curves AD_0 and SAS_0. Some events now occur that generate a perfectly anticipated inflation.

a. List the events that might cause a perfectly anticipated inflation.

b. Using the figure, describe the initial effects of an anticipated inflation.

c. Using the figure, describe what happens as an anticipated inflation proceeds.

6. In the economy described in problem 1, suppose that people anticipate deflation (a falling price level) but aggregate demand turns out not to change.

a. What happens to the short-run and long-run aggregate supply curves? (Draw some new curves if you need to.)

b. Using the figure, describe the initial effects of an anticipated deflation.

c. Using the figure, describe what happens as it becomes obvious to everyone that the anticipated deflation is not going to occur.

7. An economy has an unemployment rate of 4 percent and an inflation rate of 5 percent at point *A* in the figure. Some events then occur that move the economy to point *D*.

a. Describe the events that could move the economy from point *A* to point *D*.

b. Draw in the figure the economy's short-run and long-run Phillips curves when the economy is at point *A*.

c. Draw in the figure the economy's short-run and long-run Phillips curves when the economy is at point *D*.

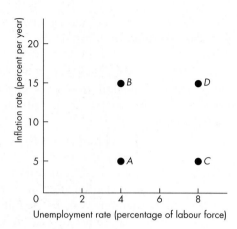

8. In the economy described in problem 7, some events occur that move the economy from point *B* to point *C*.
   a. Describe the events that could move the economy from point *B* to point *C*.
   b. Draw in the diagram the economy's short-run and long-run Phillips curves when the economy is at point *B*.
   c. Draw in the diagram the economy's short-run and long-run Phillips curves when the economy is at point *C*.

9. An economy with a natural rate of unemployment of 4 percent and an expected inflation rate of 6 percent a year has the following inflation and unemployment history:

Year	Inflation rate (percent per year)	Unemployment rate (percentage of labour force)
2001	10	2
2002	8	3
2003	6	4
2004	4	5
2005	2	6

   a. Draw a graph of the economy's short-run and long-run Phillips curves.
   b. If the actual inflation rate rises from 6 percent a year to 8 percent a year, what is the change in the unemployment rate? Explain why it occurs.

10. For the economy described in problem 9, the natural rate of unemployment increases to 5 percent and the expected inflation rate falls to 5 percent a year. Draw the new short-run and long-run Phillips curves in the graph.

CRITICAL THINKING

1. Study *Reading Between the Lines* on pp. 650–651 and then answer the following questions:
   a. What does George Akerlof believe about the tradeoff between inflation and unemployment?
   b. Why, according to Akerlof, did the United States have a better unemployment performance than Canada?
   c. Do you think the data on inflation and unemployment are consistent with the view that the natural rate of unemployment is 7 percent? Explain why or why not.

WEB EXERCISES

Use the links on myeconlab **to work the following exercises.**

1. Obtain data on the growth rate of the quantity of money and the inflation rate in Canada since 2000.
   a. Calculate the average growth rate of the quantity of money since 2000.
   b. Calculate the average inflation rate since 2000.
   c. Make a graph of the growth rate of the quantity of money and the inflation rate since 2000.
   d. Interpret your graph and explain what it tells you about the forces that generate inflation and the relationship between money growth and inflation.

2. Obtain data on the inflation rate and the unemployment rate in the United States during the 1990s and 2000s.
   a. Make a graph using the data you've obtained that is similar to Fig. 27.14.
   b. Describe the similarities and the differences in relationship between inflation and unemployment found in the United States and in Canada.

Monetary Policy

Fiddling with the Knobs

On eight pre-set dates a year, the Bank of Canada announces whether the interest rate will rise, fall, or remain constant until the next decision date. Financial market traders and economic journalists watch the economy for clues about what the Bank will decide. Then, every business day, the Bank of Canada operates in financial markets to implement its decision and ensure that its target interest rate is achieved.

How does the Bank of Canada make its interest rate decision? What exactly does the Bank do every day to keep interest rates where it wants them? And do the Bank's interest rate changes influence the economy in the way the Bank wants and with enough precision? Can the Bank speed up economic growth and reduce unemployment by lowering interest rates and keep inflation in check by raising interest rates?

The Bank of Canada's current monetary policy strategy is relatively new. And it is not the only strategy that might be used. Is the current monetary policy strategy the best one? What are the benefits and what are the risks associated with the strategy?

◆ You learned about the functions of the Bank of Canada and its role in the payments system in Chapter 25. In this chapter, you will learn about the Bank of Canada's monetary policy. You will learn how the Bank influences interest rates and how interest rates influence the economy. You will also review the alternative ways in which monetary policy might be conducted. In *Reading Between the Lines* at the end of the chapter, you will see the dilemma that the Bank of Canada sometimes faces as it tries to steer a steady course between inflation and recession.

After studying this chapter, you will be able to

- **Describe Canada's monetary policy objectives and the framework for setting and achieving them**

- **Explain how the Bank of Canada makes its interest rate decision and achieves it interest rate target**

- **Explain the transmission channels through which the Bank of Canada influences the inflation rate**

- **Explain and compare alternative monetary policy strategies**

Monetary Policy Objective and Framework

CANADA'S MONETARY POLICY OBJECTIVE AND the framework for setting and achieving that objective stem from the relationship between the Bank of Canada and the government of Canada.

We'll first discuss the objective of monetary policy and then describe the framework and assignment of responsibility for achieving the objective.

Monetary Policy Objective

The objective of monetary policy is ultimately political, and it stems from the mandate of the Bank that is set out in the Bank of Canada Act.

Bank of Canada Act The objective of monetary policy as set out in the preamble to the Bank of Canada Act of 1935 is to

regulate credit and currency in the best interests of the economic life of the nation ... and to mitigate by its influence fluctuations in the general level of production, trade, prices and employment, so far as may be possible within the scope of monetary action ...

In simple language, these words have come to mean that the Bank's job is to control the quantity of money and interest rates in order to avoid inflation and, when possible, prevent excessive swings in real GDP growth and unemployment.

This emphasis on inflation has been made concrete by an agreement between the Bank and government.

Joint Statement of the Government of Canada and the Bank of Canada In a joint statement (the most recent of which was made in 2001), the government of Canada and the Bank of Canada have agreed that

- The inflation control target range will be 1 to 3 percent a year.
- Policy will aim at keeping the trend of inflation at the 2 percent target midpoint.
- The agreement will run for five years and be reviewed before the end of 2006.

Interpretation of the Agreement The inflation-control target uses the Consumer Price Index (or CPI) as the measure of inflation. So it is the CPI inflation rate that the Bank has agreed to keep on a 2 percent target trend.

But the Bank also pays close attention to **core inflation**, which is the CPI excluding the eight most volatile prices—the prices of fruit, vegetables, gasoline, fuel oil, natural gas, mortgage interest, intercity transportation, and tobacco—and also excluding changes in indirect taxes—taxes such as GST, HST, and provincial sales taxes.

The Bank believes that the core inflation rate provides a better measure of the underlying inflation trend and a better prediction of future CPI inflation.

Although the Bank watches the core inflation rate closely, it must take into account the possibility that the eight volatile elements that it excludes have a different *trend* inflation rate from the remaining items. As it turns out, between 1995 and 2000, the core and overall CPI trends were the same. But between 2000 and 2005, the core inflation rate ran at about 0.5 percent a year below the overall CPI inflation rate.

Actual Inflation The performance of Canada's inflation since the mid-1990s, when the current target was set, has been close to target. Figure 28.1 shows just how close.

In Fig. 28.1(a), you can see the target range of 1 to 3 percent a year. And you can see that the actual inflation rate has only rarely gone outside the target range. You can also see that the inflation rate has been both above target and below target on occasion, so there is no bias or tendency for inflation to be persistently above or below target.

In Fig. 28.1(b), you can see the trend of inflation at the 2 percent target midpoint. The actual path of the CPI was on trend from 1995 through 1998 and again from 2001 into 2005. But between 1999 and 2001, the CPI moved *below* the 2 percent trend line.

The general message of Fig. 28.1 is that the Bank of Canada has done a remarkable job of holding inflation to its 2 percent target with only small and temporary deviations from that goal.

Rationale for an Inflation-Control Target Two main benefits flow from adopting an inflation-control target. The first benefit is that the purpose of the Bank of Canada's policy actions is more clearly

FIGURE 28.1

Inflation-Control Targets and Outcome

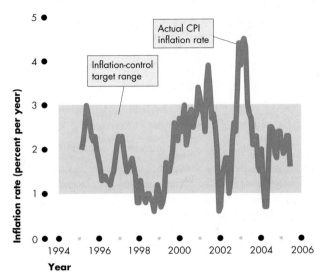

(a) Inflation target and outcome

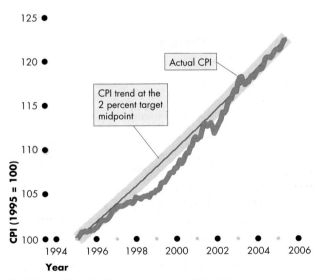

(b) CPI trend at the 2 percent target midpoint

The Bank of Canada and the government of Canada agreed that the inflation-control target range will be 1 percent to 3 percent (part a) and that policy will aim at keeping the trend of inflation at the 2 percent target midpoint (part b).

Sources of data: Statistics Canada, Table 326–0016 and Bank of Canada, Joint Statement of the Government of Canada and the Bank of Canada on the Renewal of the Inflation-Control Target, 17 May, 2001.

understood by financial market traders. A clearer understanding leads to fewer surprises and mistakes on the part of savers and investors.

The second benefit is that the target provides an anchor for expectations about future inflation. Firmly held expectations of low inflation make the short-run output-inflation (or unemployment-inflation) trade-off as favourable as possible. (see Chapter 27, pp. 644–648). Firmly held (and correct) inflation expectations help people make better economic decisions, which in turn helps to achieve a more efficient allocation of resources and a more stable economic growth.

Controversy About the Inflation-Control Target

Not everyone agrees that the adoption of an infla-tion-control target brings benefits. Critics argue that by focusing on inflation, the Bank of Canada some-times permits the unemployment rate or real GDP growth rate to suffer.

The fear of these critics is that if the inflation rate begins to edge upward towards and perhaps beyond the upper limit of the target range, the Bank of Canada might reign in aggregate demand and push the economy into recession. The Bank might also end up permitting the dollar to appreciate on the foreign exchange market and making exports suffer.

One response of supporters of inflation targeting is that by keeping inflation low and stable, monetary policy makes its maximum possible contribution towards achieving full employment and sustained economic growth.

Another response is, "look at the record." The last time the Bank of Canada created a recession was at the beginning of the 1990s when it was faced with the threat of ongoing double-digit inflation. Since that time, monetary policy has been sensitive to the state of employment while maintaining its focus on achieving its inflation target.

Responsibility for Monetary Policy

The government of Canada and the Bank of Canada jointly agree on the monetary policy target but the Bank of Canada Act places responsibility for the con-duct of monetary policy on the Bank's Governing Council.

Governing Council of the Bank of Canada The members of the Bank's Governing Council are the Governor, Senior Deputy Governor, and four Deputy

Governors. All the members of the Governing Council are experts in monetary economics and monetary policymaking and, normally, they are people who have been promoted from withing the ranks of economists working in the Bank's research and policy departments.

The current Governor (appointed in 2001) is David Dodge, an economist who has had wide experience both in government departments and the Bank.

Bank of Canada Economists The Bank of Canada employs research economists who write papers on monetary policy and the state of the Canadian and international economies. These economists provide the Governing Council with extensive briefings that guide monetary policy.

Consultations with the Government The Bank of Canada Act requires regular consultations on monetary policy between the Governor and the Minister of Finance. The Act also lays out what must happen if the Governor and the Minister disagree in a profound way.

In such an event, the Minister would direct the Bank in writing to follow a specified course and the Bank would be obliged to accept the directive. The Governor would most likely resign in such a situation. While in the past there have been disagreements between the government and the Bank, no formal directive has ever been issued.

You now know the objective of monetary policy and can describe the framework and assignment of responsibility for achieving that objective. Your next task is to see how the Bank of Canada conducts its monetary policy.

REVIEW QUIZ

1 What is the objective of monetary policy?
2 What are the two parts of the inflation-control target?
3 What is core inflation and how does it differ from overall CPI inflation?
4 What is the Bank of Canada's record in achieving its inflation-control target?

Ⓧ myeconlab   **Study Plan 28.1**

The Conduct of Monetary Policy

IN THIS SECTION, WE DESCRIBE THE WAY IN which the Bank of Canada conducts its monetary policy. We follow this description in the next section with an account of alternative approaches to monetary policy and an evaluation of the Bank's approach.

Choosing a Policy Instrument

As the sole issuer of Canadian money, the Bank of Canada can decide to control the quantity of money (the monetary base), the price of Canadian money on the foreign exchange market (the exchange rate), or the opportunity cost of holding money (the short-term interest rate). If you need a quick refresher, check back to Chapter 25, pp 604–605 to see how the quantity of money affects the interest rate and to Chapter 26, pp. 623–624 to see how the interest rate or direct intervention in the foreign exchange market affects the exchange rate.

While the Bank of Canada can set any *one* of these three variables, it cannot set all three. The values of two of them are the consequence of the value at which the third one is set. If the Bank decided to decrease the quantity of money, both the interest rate and the exchange rate would rise. If the Bank decided to raise the interest rate, the quantity of money would decrease and the exchange rate would rise. And if the Bank decided to lower the exchange rate, the quantity of money would increase and the interest rate would fall.

So the Bank must decide which of these three instruments to use. It might decide to select one and stick with it. Or it might switch among them.

The Overnight Rate

The Bank of Canada's choice of policy instrument (which is the same choice as that made by most other major central banks) is a short-term interest rate. Given this choice, the Bank permits the exchange rate and the quantity of money to find their own equilibrium values and has no preset views about what those values should be.

The specific interest rate that the Bank of Canada targets is the **overnight loans rate**, which is the interest rate on overnight loans that members of the Large Value Transfer System or LVTS (the big banks) make to each other. (For a refresher about the LVTS, see p. 596.)

Figure 28.2 shows the overnight loans rate since 1995. You can see that the overnight loans rate was a bit more than 8 percent a year in 1995 and it was increased to around 6 percent a year on two occasions. All of these periods of a high overnight loans rate are ones in which inflation was a concern.

In recent years, the overnight rate has been at historically low levels. The reason is that with inflation well anchored inside its target range, the Bank wanted to lean in the direction of avoiding recession.

Since late 2000, the Bank has established eight fixed dates on which it announces its overnight rate target for the coming period of approximately six weeks. Before 2000, the Bank announced changes in the overnight rate whenever it thought a change was required.

Although the Bank can change the overnight rate by any (reasonable) amount that it chooses, it normally changes the rate by only a quarter of a percentage point.[2]

How does the Bank decide the appropriate level for the overnight rate? And how, having made that decision, does the Bank get the overnight rate to move to the target level? We'll now answer these two questions.

The Bank's Decision-Making Process

Two alternative decision-making processes might be used. They are summarized by the terms:

- Instrument rule
- Targeting rule

Instrument Rule An **instrument rule** is a decision rule for monetary policy that sets the policy instrument at a level that is based on the current state of the economy. The best known instrument rule is the *Taylor rule*, which sets the interest rate at a level that depends on the deviation of the inflation rate from target and the size and direction of the output gap. For each percentage point by which inflation is above target the interest rate is set one percentage point higher. And for each percentage point by which real GDP exceeds potential GDP (the percentage size of the output gap), the interest rate is set another percentage point higher. (We examine the Taylor rule later in this chapter—see p. 670.)

Targeting Rule A **targeting rule** is a decision rule for monetary policy that sets the policy instrument at a level that makes the forecast of the ultimate policy target equal to the target. Where the ultimate policy target is the inflation rate and the instrument is the overnight rate, the targeting rule sets the overnight rate at a level that makes the forecast of the inflation rate equal to the inflation target.

To implement such a targeting rule, a central bank must gather and process a large amount of information about the economy, the way it responds to shocks, and the way it responds to policy. It must then process all this data and come to a judgement about the best setting for the policy instrument.

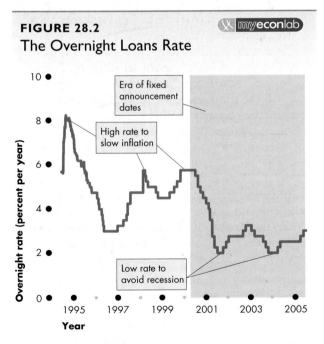

FIGURE 28.2

The Overnight Loans Rate

Era of fixed announcement dates

High rate to slow inflation

Low rate to avoid recession

The Bank of Canada sets a target range for the overnight loans rate and then takes actions to keep the rate inside its target range. When the Bank wants to slow inflation, it takes actions that raise the overnight loans rate. When the Bank wants to avoid recession and inflation is low, it takes actions that lower the overnight loans rate.

Source of data: Bank of Canada, *Banking and Financial Statistics*, Table F1.

_____

[2] A quarter of a percentage point is also called 25 *basis points*. A basis point is one-hundredth of one percentage point.

The Bank of Canada (along with most other central banks) follows a process that uses a targeting rule. For the Bank of Canada, the process begins with an exercise that uses a model of the Canadian economy that you can think of as a sophisticated version of the *AS–AD* model (see Chapter 22). The Bank's economists provide the Governor and Governing Council with a base line forecast that has the overnight rate set at a level that hits the inflation target two years in the future.

All the available regional, national, and international data on macroeconomic performance, financial markets, and inflation expectations are reviewed, discussed, and weighed in a careful deliberative process that ends with the Governing Council finding a consensus on the interest rate level to set.

After announcing an interest rate decision, the Bank engages in a public communication to explain the reasons for the Bank's decision.

Hitting the Overnight Rate Target

Once an interest rate decision is made, the Bank of Canada achieves its target by using two tools:

- Operating band
- Open market operations

Operating Band   The **operating band** is the target overnight rate plus or minus 0.25 percentage points. So the operating band is 0.5 percentage points wide. The Bank of Canada creates the operating band by setting two other interest rates: bank rate and the interest rate on reserves.

Bank rate is the interest rate that the Bank of Canada charges big (LVTS participating) banks on loans. If a bank is short of reserves, it can always obtain reserves from the Bank of Canada but it must pay bank rate on the amount of borrowed reserves.

The Bank of Canada sets bank rate at the target overnight rate plus 0.25 percentage points. So, for example, when the target overnight rate is 4 percent a year, bank rate is 4.25 percent a year.

Because the Bank of Canada is willing to lend funds to banks at this interest rate, bank rate acts as a cap on the overnight loans rate. If a bank can borrow from the Bank of Canada at bank rate, it will not borrow from another bank unless the overnight loans rate is lower than or equal to bank rate.

The Bank of Canada pays banks interest on their reserves at the Bank of Canada. The Bank calls these

reserves "settlement balances" and the interest rate that they earn is the **settlement balances rate**. The Bank of Canada sets the settlement balances rate at the target overnight rate minus 0.25 percentage point, which also equals the low end of the Bank's target range for the overnight loans rate. If banks can earn the settlement balances rate from the Bank of Canada, they will not make overnight loans to other banks unless they earn a higher interest rate than what the Bank of Canada is paying.

You can see now that the Bank of Canada can always make the overnight loans rate remain within 0.25 percentage points of its target. But the Bank wants to do better than that. It wants to keep the overnight loans rate at its target and not at one end of the range or the other. The second policy tool is used to move the overnight loans rate to its target.

Open Market Operations   An **open market operation** is the purchase or sale of government of Canada securities—Treasury bills and government bonds—by the Bank of Canada from or to a chartered bank or the public. When the Bank of Canada buys securities, it pays for them with newly created reserves that are held by banks. When the Bank of Canada sells securities, it is paid for them with reserves held by banks. So open market operations directly influence the reserves of banks.

During the morning of each business day, banks trade loans with each other. And just before noon, the Bank of Canada conducts open market operations if they are needed.

If the overnight rate is <u>above</u> target, the Bank <u>buys</u> securities to increase the reserves of the banking system and increase the supply of overnight funds. If the overnight rate is <u>below</u> target, the Bank <u>sells</u> securities to decrease the reserves of the banking system and decrease the supply of overnight funds. If the overnight rate is at the target level, the Bank neither buys nor sells securities.

How an Open Market Operation Works

When the Bank of Canada conducts an open market operation, the reserves of the banking system change. To see why this outcome occurs, we'll trace the effects of an open market operation in which the Bank of Canada *buys* $100 million of government securities in the open market from CIBC.

When the Bank of Canada makes this transaction:

1. CIBC has $100 million less securities, and the Bank of Canada has $100 million more securities.
2. The Bank of Canada pays for the securities by placing $100 million in CIBC's deposit account at the Bank of Canada.

Figure 28.3 shows the effects of these actions on the balance sheets of the Bank of Canada and the CIBC. Ownership of the securities passes from CIBC to the Bank of Canada, so CIBC's assets decrease by $100 million and the Bank of Canada's assets increase by $100 million, as shown by the blue arrow running from CIBC to the Bank of Canada.

The Bank of Canada pays for the securities by placing $100 million in CIBC's deposit account at the Bank of Canada, as shown by the green arrow running from the Bank of Canada to CIBC.

The Bank of Canada's assets increase by $100 million, and its liabilities also increase by $100 million. CIBC's total assets are unchanged. It has sold securities in exchange for reserves.

If the Bank of Canada *sells* $100 million of government securities in the open market, the events that you've just seen occur in reverse.

When the Bank of Canada sells securities:

1. CIBC has $100 million more securities, and the Bank of Canada has $100 million less securities.
2. CIBC pays for the securities by using $100 million of its deposit account at the Bank of Canada. CIBC's reserves decrease by $100 million.

Figure 28.4 shows the effects of these actions on the balance sheets of the Bank of Canada and CIBC. Ownership of the securities passes from the Bank of Canada to CIBC, so CIBC's assets increase by $100 million and the Bank of Canada's assets decrease by $100 million, as shown by the blue arrow running from the Bank of Canada to CIBC.

CIBC uses $100 million of its deposit account at the Bank of Canada to pay for the securities, as the green arrow running from CIBC to the Bank of Canada shows.

The Bank of Canada's assets decrease by $100 million, and its liabilities also decrease by $100 million. CIBC's total assets are unchanged. It has used reserves to buy securities.

An increase or a decrease in reserves changes the overnight loans rate by changing the demand for and supply of overnight loans.

FIGURE 28.3   myeconlab

The Bank of Canada Buys Securities in the Open Market

The Bank of Canada

Assets		Liabilities	
Securities	+$100	Reserves of CIBC	+$100

The Bank of Canada buys securities from a bank ... | ... and pays for the securities by increasing the reserves of the bank

CIBC

Assets		Liabilities
Securities	−$100	
Reserves	+$100	

When the Bank of Canada buys securities in the open market, it creates reserves. Bank of Canada assets and liabilities increase and the selling bank exchanges securities for reserves.

FIGURE 28.4   myeconlab

The Bank of Canada Sells Securities in the Open Market

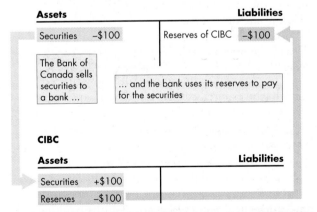

The Bank of Canada

Assets		Liabilities	
Securities	−$100	Reserves of CIBC	−$100

The Bank of Canada sells securities to a bank ... | ... and the bank uses its reserves to pay for the securities

CIBC

Assets		Liabilities
Securities	+$100	
Reserves	−$100	

When the Bank of Canada sells securities in the open market, it reduces reserves. Bank of Canada assets and liabilities decrease and the buying bank exchanges reserves for securities.

Equilibrium in the Market for Reserves

To see how an open market operation changes the overnight loans rate, we must see what happens in the market for the reserves of the banks.

Banks hold reserves so they can make payments. The amount that a bank will be called on to pay at any given moment fluctuates and cannot be forecast accurately. If a bank runs out of reserves and is obliged to make a payment, reserves must be borrowed from the Bank of Canada. So bank rate is the opportunity cost of borrowed reserves.

The more reserves a bank holds, the less likely it will need to borrow at bank rate. But reserves are costly to hold. The alternative to holding reserves is to lend them to someone else. The higher the interest rate at which reserves can be loaned, the higher is the opportunity cost of holding reserves. And the higher the opportunity cost, the greater is the incentive to economize on the quantity of reserves.

So the quantity of reserves demanded by banks depends on the overnight loans rate. The higher the overnight rate, other things remaining the same, the smaller is the quantity of reserves demanded.

Figure 28.5 shows the demand curve for reserves as the curve labelled *RD*. The *x*-axis measures the quantity of reserves held. If the entire banking system is borrowing from the Bank of Canada, reserves are negative. The *y*-axis measures the overnight rate. You can see that the overnight rate always lies inside the operating band. Why?

The overnight rate cannot exceed bank rate because, if it did, a bank could earn a profit by borrowing from the Bank of Canada and lending to another bank. But all banks can borrow from the Bank of Canada at bank rate, so no bank is willing to pay more than bank rate to borrow reserves.

The overnight rate cannot fall below the settlement balances rate because, if it did, a bank could earn a profit by borrowing from another bank and increasing its reserves at the Bank of Canada. But all banks can earn the settlement balances rate at the Bank of Canada, so no bank is willing to lend reserves at a rate below the settlements balances rate.

The Bank of Canada's open market operations determine the quantity of reserves in the banking system. Equilibrium in the market for reserves—where the quantity of reserves demanded equals the quantity supplied—determines the overnight rate. So by using the open market operations, the Bank of Canada can keep the overnight rate on target.

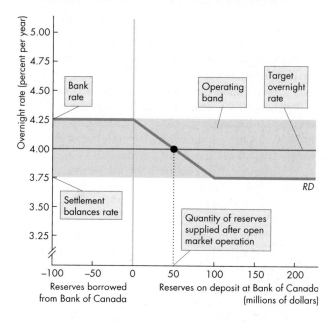

FIGURE 28.5

The Market for Reserves of LVTS Participating Banks

The demand curve for reserves is *RD*. If the overnight rate equals bank rate, banks are indifferent between borrowing reserves and lending reserves. The demand curve is horizontal at bank rate. If the overnight rate equals the settlement balances rate, banks are indifferent between holding reserves and lending reserves. The demand curve is horizontal at the settlement balances rate. Equilibrium, where the quantity of reserves demanded equals the quantity supplied, determines the overnight rate.

REVIEW QUIZ

1 What is the Bank of Canada's monetary policy instrument?

2 Summarize the Bank of Canada's monetary policy decision-making process.

3 What is the operating band? What does it do?

4 What happens when the Bank of Canada buys or sells securities in the open market?

5 How is the overnight rate determined in the market for reserves?

myeconlab **Study Plan 28.2**

Monetary Policy Transmission

YOU'VE SEEN THAT THE BANK OF CANADA'S GOAL is to keep the inflation rate as close as possible to 2 percent a year. And you've seen how the Bank of Canada can use its power in the market for bank reserves to set the overnight rate at its desired level. We're now going to trace the events that follow a change in the overnight rate and see how those events lead to the ultimate goal of keeping inflation in check. We'll begin with a quick overview of the transmission process and then look at each step a bit more closely.

Quick Overview

When the Bank of Canada lowers the overnight rate, other interest rates and the exchange rate also decrease. The quantity of money increases, and the amount of credit and loans that people and businesses take increases. The lower interest rate increases consumption expenditure and investment. And the lower exchange rate makes Canadian exports cheaper and imports more costly. So net exports increase. Easier bank credit brings an expansion of loans, which reinforces the effects of lower interest rates on consumption expenditure and investment. Aggregate demand increases, which increases real GDP and the price level relative to what they would have been. So real GDP growth and inflation increase.

Similarly, when the Bank of Canada raises the overnight rate, other interest rates and the exchange rate also increase. The quantity of money decreases, and the amount of credit and loans that people and businesses take decreases. The higher interest rate decreases consumption expenditure and investment. And the higher exchange rate makes Canadian exports more expensive and imports cheaper. So net exports decrease. Tighter bank credit brings a contraction of loans, which reinforces the effects of higher interest rates on consumption expenditure and investment. Aggregate demand decreases, which decreases real GDP and the price level relative to what they would have been. So real GDP growth and inflation decrease.

Figure 28.6 provides a schematic summary of these ripple effects, which stretch out over a period of between one and two years. The interest rate and

FIGURE 28.6 myeconlab
The Channels for the Ripple Effects of a Change in the Overnight Rate

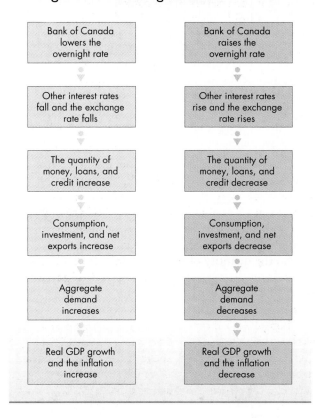

exchange rate effects are immediate. The effects on money, loans, and credit follow in a few weeks and run for a few months. Spending plans change and real GDP growth changes after about one year. And the inflation rate changes between one year and two years after the change in the overnight rate.

We're going to look at each stage in the transmission process, starting with the interest rate effects.

Interest Rate Fluctuations

The first effect of monetary policy is a change in the interest rate. This effect occurs quickly and relatively predictably. Figure 28.7 shows the fluctuations in four interest rates: the overnight loans rate, the 3-month Treasury bill rate, the 10-year government bond rate, and the long-term corporate bond rate. We've run this graph back to the mid-1970s so that you can see the relationships among the interest rates through turbulent as well as calmer periods.

You know that the Bank of Canada sets the target for the overnight rate and hits that target directly with its open market operations. So there is no doubt about where these interest rate changes are generated. They are driven by monetary policy.

The Treasury Bill Rate The 3-month Treasury bill rate is the rate paid by the government of Canada on short-term debt. It is also similar to the interest rate paid by Canadian businesses on short-term funds. Notice how closely the 3-month Treasury bill rate follows the overnight loans rate. Figure 28.7 shows that these two rates are almost identical.

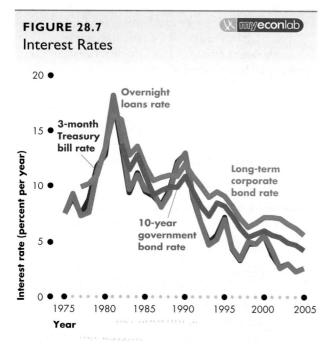

FIGURE 28.7
Interest Rates

The short-term interest rates—the overnight loans rate and the 3-month Treasury bill rate—move closely together. The long-term interest rates—the 10-year government bond rate and the long-term corporate bond rate—also move closely together. But the short-term rates fluctuate more than the long-term rates, although both move in the same general direction. The overnight loans rate peaked at 18 percent a year in 1981. It fell during the 1980s but increased again to 13 percent a year in 1990. It fell again through the 1990s and remained low during the early 2000s.

Source of data: Bank of Canada, *Banking and Financial Statistics*, Table F1.

A powerful substitution effect keep these two interest rates close. The big banks have a choice about how to hold their short-term liquid assets. And an overnight loan to another big bank is a close substitute for short-term securities such as Treasury bills. If the interest rate on Treasury bills is higher than the overnight loans rate, the supply of overnight loans decreases and the demand for Treasury bills increases. The price of Treasury bills rises and their interest rate falls.

Similarly, if the interest rate on Treasury bills is lower than the overnight loans rate, the supply of overnight loans increases and the demand for Treasury bills decreases. The price of Treasury bills falls and their interest rate rises.

When the interest rate on Treasury bill is close to the overnight loans rate, there is no incentive for banks to switch between overnight loans and Treasury bills and the two markets are in equilibrium.

The Long-Term Rates The 10-year government bond rate is the interest rate paid by the government of Canada on longer term loans and the long-term corporate bond rate is the interest rate that large businesses pay to finance investment.

Notice that the fluctuations in the two long-term interest rates are similar but the corporate rate is a bit higher than the government rate. The reason is that corporations are riskier than the government. Notice also how the long-term rates move with the short-term rates. The long-term rates don't fluctuate as much as the short-term rates but they move in similar general directions.

Substitution effects are again responsible for these interest rate movements. Long-term government bonds and long-term corporate bonds are close substitutes, so the interest rates on these bonds move up and down in close harmony.

Short-term loans and long-term loans are substitutes but not close substitutes. So when the Bank of Canada changes the overnight loans rate, its action has a powerful and immediate effect on the other short-term interest rates but a less powerful and less predictable effect on the long-term interest rates.

You can see, for example, that when the Bank of Canada raised the overnight loans rate in 1995, the long-term rates kept falling. A similar thing happened in 1998.

But generally, the long-term rates do move in the same direction as the overnight loans rate.

Exchange Rate Fluctuations

The exchange rate responds to changes in the interest rate in Canada relative to the interest rates in other countries. But other factors are also at work, which make the exchange rate hard to predict. The red line in Fig. 28.8 shows the gap between the Canadian and U.S. overnight loans rates—the Canadian-U.S. interest rate differential. And the blue line shows the exchange rate of the Canadian dollar against the U.S. dollar. You can see that sometimes when the interest rate differential widens (when the Canadian interest rate rises relative to the U.S. rate), the Canadian dollar appreciates. Also, sometimes, when the interest rate differential narrows (when the Canadian interest rate falls relative to the U.S. rate), the Canadian dollar

FIGURE 28.8   myeconlab

The Interest Rate and the Exchange Rate

Other things remaining the same, when the gap between Canadian and U.S. short-term interest rates widens, the Canadian dollar rises in value or its value falls less quickly, and when the gap between Canadian and U.S. short-term interest rates narrows, the Canadian dollar falls in value or its value rises less quickly. Most of the time, other things do not remain the same, so the relationship between the interest rate differential and the exchange rate is weak.

Sources of data: Bank of Canada, *Banking and Financial Statistics,* Tables FI and II.

depreciates. But the relationship between the interest rate gap and the exchange rate is weak. The exchange rate often changes independently of the interest rate differential.

So, while monetary policy influences the exchange rate, many other factors also make the exchange rate change.

Money and Loans

You saw in Chapter 25 that the quantity of money demanded depends on the interest rate. The lower the interest rate, the greater is the quantity of money demanded, other things remaining the same. Because most money is in the form of bank deposits, a lower interest rate increases the volume of bank deposits and bank loans. And a higher interest rate decreases the volume of bank deposits and bank loans.

So, when the Bank of Canada lowers the overnight loans rate, the quantity of money and the quantity of loans increase.

The Interest Rate and Expenditure Plans

The interest rate influences people's spending decisions. But the interest rate that is relevant for a spending decision is the real interest rate.

Nominal Interest and Real Interest The **nominal interest rate** is the percentage return on an asset such as a bond expressed in terms of money. It is the interest rate that is quoted in everyday transactions and news reports. The **real interest rate** is the percentage return on an asset expressed in terms of what money will buy. It is the nominal interest rate adjusted for inflation and is approximately equal to the nominal interest rate minus the inflation rate.

Suppose that the nominal interest rate is 10 percent a year and the inflation rate is 4 percent a year. The real interest rate is 6 percent a year—10 percent minus 4 percent.[3]

To see why the real interest rate is 6 percent, think about the following example. Jackie lends Joe $1,000 for one year. At the end of the year, Joe repays Jackie

---

[3] The exact calculation allows for the change in the purchasing power of the interest as well as the amount of the loan. To calculate the *exact* real interest rate, use the formula: *real interest rate = (nominal interest rate − inflation rate)* divided by $(1 + inflation\ rate/100)$. If the nominal interest rate is 10 percent and the inflation rate is 4 percent, the real interest rate is $(10 − 4) ÷ (1 + 0.04) = 5.77$ percent.

the $1,000 plus interest. At 10 percent a year, the interest is $100, so Jackie receives $1,100 from Joe.

Because of inflation, the money that Joe uses to repay Jackie is worth less than the money that Jackie originally lent to Joe. At an inflation rate of 4 percent a year, Jackie needs an extra $40 a year to compensate her for the fall in the value of money. So when Joe repays the loan, Jackie needs $1,040 to buy the same items that she could have bought for $1,000 when she made the loan. Because Joe pays Jackie $1,100, the interest that she *really* earns is $60, which is 6 percent of the $1,000 that she lent to Joe.

Interest Rate and Opportunity Cost Now that you understand the distinction between the nominal interest rate and the real interest rate, let's think about the effects of interest rates on decisions.

The interest rate influences decisions because it is an opportunity cost. *The nominal interest rate is the opportunity cost of holding money.* And it is the nominal interest rate that is determined by the demand for real money and the supply of real money in the money market. To see why the nominal interest rate is the opportunity cost of holding money, think about the *real* interest rate on money compared with the real interest rate on other financial assets. Money loses value at the inflation rate. So the real interest rate on money equals *minus* the inflation rate. The real interest rate on other financial assets equals the nominal interest rate minus the inflation rate. So the difference between the real interest rate on money and the real interest rate on other financial assets is the nominal interest rate. By holding money rather than some other financial asset, we incur a *real* opportunity cost equal to the nominal interest rate.

The real interest rate is the opportunity cost of spending. Spending more today means spending less in the future. But spending one additional dollar today means cutting future spending by more than a dollar. And the real amount by which future spending must be cut is determined by the *real* interest rate.

A change in the real interest rate changes the opportunity cost of two components of aggregate expenditure:

- Consumption expenditure
- Investment

Consumption Expenditure Other things remaining the same, the lower the real interest rate, the greater is the amount of consumption expenditure and the smaller is the amount of saving.

You can see why the real interest rate influences consumption expenditure and saving by thinking about the effect of the interest rate on a student loan. If the real interest rate on a student loan fell to 1 percent a year, students would be happy to take larger loans and spend more. But if the real interest rate on a student loan jumped to 20 percent a year, students would cut their expenditure—buy cheaper food and find lower-rent accommodation, for example—to pay off their loans as quickly as possible.

The effect of the real interest rate on consumption expenditure is probably not large. It is certainly not as powerful as the effect of disposable income that we studied in Chapter 23 (pp. 536–540). You can think of the real interest rate as influencing *autonomous consumption expenditure* (p. 536). The lower the real interest rate, the greater is autonomous consumption expenditure.

Investment Other things remaining the same, the lower the real interest rate, the greater is the amount of investment.

The funds used to finance investment might be borrowed, or they might be the financial resources of the firm's owners (the firm's retained earnings). But regardless of the source of the funds, the opportunity cost of the funds is the real interest rate. The real interest paid on borrowed funds is an obvious cost. The real interest rate is also the cost of using retained earnings because these funds could be lent to another firm. The real interest rate forgone is the opportunity cost of using retained earnings to finance an investment project.

To decide whether to invest in new capital, firms compare the real interest rate with the expected profit rate from the investment. For example, suppose that Ford expects to earn 20 percent a year from a new car assembly plant. It is profitable for Ford to invest in this new plant as long as the real interest rate is less than 20 percent a year. That is, at a real interest rate below 20 percent a year, Ford will build this assembly plant; at a real interest rate in excess of 20 percent a year, Ford will not. Some projects are profitable at a high real interest rate, but other projects are profitable only at a low real interest rate. So the higher the real interest rate, the smaller is the number of projects that are worth undertaking and the smaller is the amount of investment.

The interest rate has another effect on expenditure plans—it changes net exports.

Net Exports and the Interest Rate A change in the interest rate changes the exchange rate. And a change in the exchange rate changes exports and imports. (See Chapter 26, pp. 616–617).

Interest-Sensitive Expenditure Curve Figure 28.9 illustrates the effects of the real interest rate on aggregate expenditure plans and summarizes those effects in the interest-sensitive expenditure curve. The **interest-sensitive expenditure curve** (the *IE* curve) shows the relationship between interest-sensitive expenditure and the real interest rate when all other influences on expenditure plans remain the same.

Figure 28.9(a) shows the components of interest-sensitive expenditure, autonomous consumption expenditure, investment, and net exports (*NX*). When the real interest rate is 5 percent a year, autonomous consumption expenditure is $20 billion on the curve *CD*. Investment is $50 billion, so when we add investment and autonomous consumption expenditure together, we get $70 billion on the curve

CD + *ID*. Net exports are $30 billion, so when we add this amount to $70 billion, we obtain the sum of all the interest-sensitive components of aggregate expenditure, which is $100 billion on the *IE* curve.

In Fig. 28.9(b), as the real interest rate changes, interest-sensitive expenditure changes along the *IE* curve. Other things remaining the same, when the real interest rate falls to 3 percent a year, interest-sensitive expenditure increases to $150 billion. And when the real interest rate rises to 7 percent a year, interest-sensitive expenditure decreases to $50 billion.

Loose Link from Overnight Rate to Spending You've seen that long-term interest rates that influence spending plans are linked only loosely to the overnight rate. Also, the response of the *real* long-term interest rate to a change in the nominal rate depends on how inflation expectations change. And the response of expenditure plans to changes in the real interest rate depend on many factors that make the response hard to predict.

FIGURE 28.9
The Interest Rate and Expenditure Plans

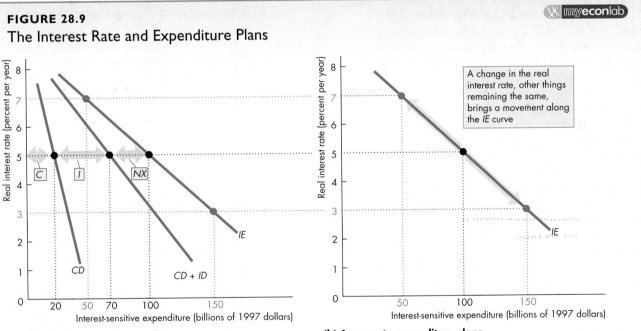

(a) The components of expenditure

(b) Aggregate expenditure plans

In part (a), when the interest rate is 5 percent a year, autonomous consumption expenditure is $20 billion, investment is $50 billion, net exports are $30 billion, and interest-sensitive expenditure is $100 billion. In part (b), when the real interest rate is 5 percent a year, interest-sensitive expendi-

ture is $100 billion a year on the *IE* curve. Other things remaining the same, when the interest rate falls to 3 percent a year, interest-sensitive expenditure increases to $150 billion a year and when the interest rate rises to 7 percent a year, interest-sensitive expenditure decreases to $50 billion a year.

The Change in Aggregate Demand, Real GDP, and the Price Level

The final link in the transmission chain is a change in aggregate demand and a resulting change in real GDP and the price level. By changing real GDP and the price level relative to what they would have been without a change in the overnight rate, the Bank of Canada influences its ultimate goal, the inflation rate.

If the Bank believes that inflation is at (or heading below) the bottom of the target range because real GDP is below potential GDP, it believes that the economy is in the state shown in Fig. 28.10 at the intersection of aggregate demand curve AD_0 and short-run aggregate supply curve SAS. Real GDP is only $950 billion and the price level is 105.

The Bank of Canada lowers the overnight rate and the transmission process that we've just described unfolds. Eventually, aggregate demand increases and the aggregate demand curve shifts rightward to AD_1.

In the new equilibrium, full employment is restored and the price level rises by more than it would have done in the absence of the overnight rate cut. If the Bank of Canada got everything right, the inflation rate associated with the new price level will be in the middle of the target range.

If the Bank believes that inflation is at (or heading above) the top of the target range because real GDP is above potential GDP, it believes that the economy is in the state shown in Fig. 28.11 at the intersection of aggregate demand curve AD_0 and short-run aggregate supply curve SAS. Real GDP is $1,050 billion and the price level is 115.

The Bank of Canada raises the overnight rate and the transmission process that we've just described unfolds. Eventually, aggregate demand decreases and the aggregate demand curve shifts leftward to AD_1.

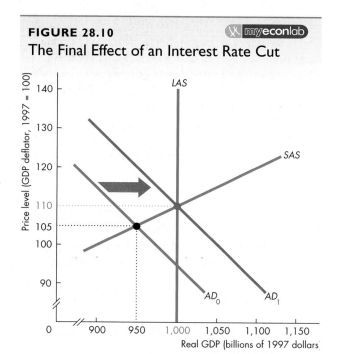

FIGURE 28.10   ⓧ myeconlab

The Final Effect of an Interest Rate Cut

With real GDP at $950 billion, below potential GDP of $1,000, inflation is low, unemployment is high, and the overnight rate is decreased. Eventually, aggregate demand increases and the AD curve shifts rightward from AD_0 to AD_1. Real GDP increases to potential GDP. The price level rises above what it would otherwise have been but not by so much that it sends the inflation rate above its target.

FIGURE 28.11   ⓧ myeconlab

The Final Effect of an Interest Rate Rise

With real GDP at $1,050 billion, above potential GDP of $1,000, inflation is rising, unemployment is low, and the overnight rate is increased. Eventually, aggregate demand decreases and the AD curve shifts leftward from AD_0 to AD_1. Real GDP decreases to potential GDP and the price level falls below what it would otherwise have been. The inflation rate is held inside its target range.

In the new equilibrium, the inflation threat is eliminated, full employment is restored, and the price level rises by less than it would have done in the absence of the overnight rate rise. Again, if the Bank of Canada got everything right, the inflation rate associated with the new price level will be in the middle of the target range.

Time Lags in the Adjustment Process To achieve its goal of 2 percent inflation, the Bank of Canada needs a combination of good judgment and good luck. Too large a cut in the overnight rate in an underemployed economy can bring inflation, as it did during the 1970s. And too large an increase in the overnight rate in an inflationary economy can create unemployment, as it did in 1981 and again in 1991.

The Bank is especially handicapped by the fact that the monetary policy transmission process is long drawn out. Also, the economy does not always respond in exactly the same way to policy. Further, many factors other than policy are constantly changing and bringing a new situation for policy to respond to.

But monetary policy actions do have a powerful influence. We can see this influence on real GDP growth in Fig. 28.12. A change in the overnight rate feeds through to change real GDP after about a year.

In Fig.28.12, the blue line shows the overnight rate that the Bank of Canada targets minus the long-term bond rate. Changes in the overnight rate have some effect on the long-term bond rate, but this effect is small. The long-term bond rate is also influenced by saving and investment plans and by inflation expectations.

The red line in Fig. 28.12 is the real GDP growth rate *one year later*. You can see that when the overnight rate rises or the long-term bond rate falls, the real GDP growth rate slows down in the following year. The long-term bond rate fluctuates less than the overnight rate, so when the overnight rate rises above the long-term bond rate, it is because the Bank of Canada has pushed the overnight rate up. And when the overnight rate falls below the long-term bond rate, it is because the Bank of Canada has pushed the overnight rate down. So when the Bank of Canada stimulates aggregate demand (pushes the overnight rate down), the real GDP growth rate speeds up, and when the Bank of Canada lowers aggregate demand (pushes the overnight rate up), the real GDP growth rate slows. The inflation rate increases and decreases in sympathy with these fluctuations in the real GDP growth rate. But the effects on the inflation rate take even longer.

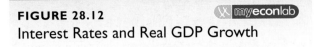

FIGURE 28.12
Interest Rates and Real GDP Growth

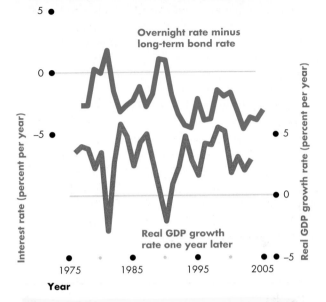

When the overnight interest rate rises relative to the long-term bond rate, the real GDP growth rate usually slows about one year later. Similarly, when the overnight rate falls relative to the long-term bond rate, the real GDP growth rate speeds up about one year later.

Sources of data: Interest Rates, see Fig. 28.7; Real GDP Growth, Statistics Canada, CANSIM Table 380–0002.

REVIEW QUIZ

1 Describe the channels by which monetary policy ripples through the economy and explain why each channel operates.

2 Do interest rates fluctuate in response to the Bank of Canada's actions?

3 How do the Bank of Canada's actions influence the exchange rate?

4 How do the Bank of Canada's actions influence real GDP and how long does it take for real GDP to respond to the Bank's policy actions?

5 How do the Bank of Canada's actions influence inflation and how long does it take for inflation to respond to the Bank's policy actions?

myeconlab **Study Plan 28.3**

Alternative Monetary Policy Strategies

SO FAR IN THIS CHAPTER, WE'VE DESCRIBED AND analyzed the Bank of Canada's method of conducting monetary policy. But the Bank does have choices among alternative monetary policy strategies. We're going to end our discussion of monetary policy by examining the alternatives and explains why the Bank of Canada has rejected them in favour of the interest rate strategy that we've described.

You've seen that we can summarize monetary policy strategies in two broad categories, *instrument rules* and *targeting rules*. And you've seen that the Bank of Canada uses a *targeting rule* approach. So the Bank has rejected instrument rules. It has also rejected other possible targeting rules.

The Bank of Canada might have chosen any of four alternative monetary policy strategies: Two of them are instrument rules and two are alternative targeting rules. The four alternatives are

- Overnight rate instrument rule
- Monetary base instrument rule
- Exchange rate targeting rule
- Money targeting rule

Overnight Rate Instrument Rule

The idea of setting the overnight rate based on a rule was suggested by Stanford University economist John B. Taylor, and the rule bears his name.

The **Taylor rule** sets the overnight rate in response to only the current inflation rate and the current estimate of the output gap. Calling the overnight rate R, the neutral real overnight rate R^*, the inflation rate π, the target inflation rate $\pi*$, and the output gap (as a percentage of potential GDP), G, the Taylor rule says, set the overnight rate to equal

$$R = R^* + \pi + 0.5(\pi - \pi^*) + 0.5G.$$

Taylor suggests that the neutral real overnight rate is 2 percent a year. So if inflation was on target and the output gap was zero (full employment) and with a 2 percent inflation target, the overnight rate would be 4 percent. It would be less than 4 percent if the economy were below full employment and above 4 percent if the economy were above full employment.

If the Bank of Canada had followed the Taylor rule, the overnight rate would have fluctuated much more than it did. And on some occasions, it would have been much higher than the Bank wanted. For example, during 2005 when the overnight rate was 2.5 percent, the Taylor rule would have put it at 4.5 percent. And in 2003, when the inflation rate temporarily increased to more than 4 percent, the Taylor rule would have raised the overnight rate to more than 8 percent. The overnight rate was actually raised to only 3.25 percent.

The Bank believes that because it uses much more information than just the current inflation rate and the output gap, it is able to set the overnight rate more intelligently than any simple rule can set.

Monetary Base Instrument Rule

Although the Bank of Canada uses open market operations to hit its overnight loans rate target, it could, instead, shoot for a monetary base target.

The idea of setting the monetary base using a rule has been suggested by Carnegie-Mellon University economist Bennet T. McCallum, and a monetary base rule bears his name.

The **McCallum rule** makes the growth rate of the monetary base respond to the long-term average growth rate of real GDP and medium-term changes in the velocity of circulation of the monetary base. The rule is based on the *quantity theory of money* (see Chapter 27, pp 638–639). McCallum's idea is that by making the monetary base grow at a rate equal to the target inflation rate plus the long-term real GDP growth rate minus the medium-term velocity growth rate, inflation will be kept close to target.

An advantage of the McCallum rule over the Taylor rule is that the Bank does not need to estimate either the neutral real overnight rate or the output gap. Both of these inputs to the Taylor rule are impossible to know exactly and are subject to estimation errors that could send the inflation rate badly off course.

A disadvantage of the McCallum rule compared to the Taylor rule is that it relies on the velocity of circulation being reasonably stable.

The Bank of Canada believes that the velocity of circulation is in fact too unstable and that the Bank does better than it would by following the McCallum rule because the Bank isolates the inflation rate from volatile changes in the velocity of circulation.

Exchange Rate Targeting Rule

The Bank of Canada could, if it wished to do so, intervene in the foreign exchange market to target the exchange rate. A fixed exchange rate is one possible exchange rate target.

But with a fixed exchange rate, a country has no control over its inflation rate. The reason is that for internationally traded goods, *purchasing power parity* (see p. 622) moves domestic prices in line with foreign prices. If a computer chip costs $US100 in Detroit, and if the exchange rate is $C1.20 per $US1.00, then the computer chip will sell for $120 (ignoring local taxes) in Windsor, Ontario. If this purchasing power parity didn't prevail, it would be possible to earn a profit by buying at the lower price and selling at the higher price. This trading would compete away the profit and price difference.

So under a fixed exchange rate, prices of traded goods (and in the long-run the prices of all goods and services) must rise at the same rate in Canada as they do in the United States.

But the Bank of Canada could use a *crawling peg* (see p. 624) as a means of achieving an inflation target. To do so, the Bank would make the exchange rate change at a rate equal to the U.S. inflation rate minus the target inflation rate. If the U.S. inflation rate is 3 percent a year and Canada wants an inflation rate of 2 percent a year, the Bank of Canada would make the Canadian dollar appreciate at a rate of 1 percent a year.

Some developing countries that have an inflation problem use this monetary policy strategy to lower the inflation rate. The main reason for choosing this method is that these countries don't have well-functioning markets for bonds and overnight loans, so they cannot use the policy approach that relies on these features of a banking system.

A major disadvantage of a crawling peg to target the inflation rate is that the real exchange rate often changes in unpredictable ways. Canada's **real exchange rate** with the United States is the relative price of the GDP baskets of goods and services in the two countries. Canadian GDP contains a larger proportion of natural resource products (minerals, oil, and natural gas) than U.S. GDP contains. So when the prices of natural resources change, our real exchange rate changes. To use a crawling peg to target the inflation rate, we would need to be able to identify changes in the real exchange rate and offset them. This task is difficult to accomplish.

Money Targeting Rule

As long ago as 1948, Nobel Laureate Milton Friedman proposed a targeting rule for the quantity of money. Friedman's **k-percent rule** makes the quantity of money grow at a rate of k percent a year, where k equals the growth rate of potential GDP.

Friedman's idea remained just that until the 1970s, when inflation increased to more than 10 percent a year in Canada and several other major countries. In 1976, in a bid to end the inflation, the Bank of Canada adopted the *k*-percent rule for the growth rate of M1. The inflation rate fell, but the policy was abandoned in 1982. (The period from 1982 to 1991 when the first inflation target was adopted were years of evolution towards the policy approach of today).

Money targeting works when the demand for money curve is stable and predictable. But in the world of the 1980s, and of today, technological change in the banking system leads to large and unpredictable shifts in the demand for money curve, which make the use of monetary targeting unreliable.

Why Rules?

You might be wondering why all monetary policy strategies involve *rules*. Why doesn't the Bank of Canada just do what seems best every day, month, and year, at its *discretion*? The answer is that monetary policy is about managing inflation expectations. In both financial markets and labour markets, people must make long-term commitments. So these markets work best when plans are based on correctly anticipated inflation outcomes. A well-understood monetary policy rule helps to create an environment in which inflation is easier to forecast and manage.

REVIEW QUIZ

1 What are the four main alternative rules for conducting monetary policy (other than the one used by the Bank of Canada)?

2 Explain, briefly, why does the Bank of Canada reject each of these alternatives?

myeconlab **Study Plan 28.4**

◆ As you complete your study of monetary policy, take a look at *Reading Between the Lines* on pages 672–673 and see the Bank of Canada's challenge in 2005.

Monetary Policy in Action

GLOBE AND MAIL, NOVEMBER 9, 2005

The great Canadian interest rate paradox

The Bank of Canada is at risk of making a serious error in monetary policy because research shows Ontario and Quebec are extra-sensitive to the effects of rising interest rates, while Alberta is almost immune.

It's well-known that the Bank of Canada already faces a conundrum in setting interest rates as oil and gas power Alberta's economy while the struggling manufacturing sector drags down Central Canada.

But the issues facing bank Governor David Dodge are not just cyclical. They're structural too, argues Benjamin Tal, economist at CIBC World Markets.

Ontario and Quebec are sensitive to rate hikes because their economies are dominated by interest-sensitive sectors, such as construction, manufacturing and utilities, he said. Alberta, on the other hand, is dominated by oil and gas —not very sensitive to interest rates and far more sensitive to global supply and demand.

...

Central bank officials have also argued that they can only base monetary policy decisions on national eco-

nomic trends, and can't focus on regional diversions.

That's obviously true, Mr. Tal responded, but he warns that the bank needs to take into account that, in Central Canada, "the Bank of Canada is probably more powerful than at any time," while in Alberta, "I'm not sure how much higher interest rates will change the momentum.

"The cost of making a mistake here can be significant," he said. For him, raising rates another 50 basis points (or half a percentage point) over the next year would be fine, but 150 points (or 1.5 percentage points) would be too much.

But economist Carl Gomez sees little chance of a major mistake by the central bank. Numerous indicators point to the need to raise rates, and yet the Bank of Canada has been very cautious and moved slowly, he said in an interview.

If higher rates have an adverse effect on Ontario and Quebec, their weakness will show up in the national numbers that the bank uses to make its decisions on monetary policy, said Mr. Gomez, an economist at Toronto-Dominion Bank.

Essence of the Story

■ The Bank of Canada risks a serious monetary policy error.

■ Strong demand points to the need for a higher interest rate. But the strongest demand is in Alberta and a higher interest rate will have a limited effect there and a big effect in Ontario and Quebec.

■ An interest rate increase of half a percentage point will not do any harm, but an increase of 1.5 percentage points will be too much, according to a CIBC economist.

■ The Bank of Canada says that it must respond to national trends, not regional ones.

Economic Analysis

■ In the fall of 2005, the Canadian economy was operating at or perhaps a bit above full employment.

■ The CPI inflation rate for September 2005 was 3.4 percent, a rate that exceeded the upper limit of the inflation-control target range.

■ In line with this underlying economic condition, the Bank of Canada was slowly but surely increasing the overnight rate.

■ The rate was increased in October and was set for a further increase in December (a week before these words were written).

■ This news article is concerned about an issue that is often raised: the difficulty of addressing regional variation with monetary policy.

■ The figures illustrate the regional problem by showing a key part of the monetary transmission mechanism broken into two parts: one for Alberta (in Fig. 1) and one for the rest of Canada (in Fig. 2). Figure 3 shows Canada as a whole.

■ Suppose that initially there is full employment and no inflationary pressure. Then, world demand for oil and gas exports increases and in Alberta, the interest-sensitive expenditure curve shifts rightward from IE_0 to IE_1.

■ In Fig. 3 the Canadian interest-sensitive expenditure curve shifts rightward.

■ But expenditure plans in the rest of Canada (Fig. 2) do not change.

■ The Bank of Canada now sees inflationary pressure and raises the interest rate to 4 percent a year to bring total spending back to the level from which it increased.

■ Expenditure decreases by a small amount in Alberta. Even in Alberta, contrary to the news article, spending plans are sensitive to the interest rate.

■ But the decrease in Alberta spending from the higher interest rate is not as great as the initial increase. So Alberta continues to run at a hot pace.

■ The higher interest rate decreases spending in the rest of Canada, and for Canada as a whole (Fig. 3) expenditure returns to its initial level.

■ Monetary policy has removed the threat of inflation, but it has not addressed the regional imbalance. Market forces (and perhaps fiscal actions) will do that.

You're the Voter

■ Do you think the Bank of Canada can influence regional differences in economic performance?

Figure 1 Alberta

Figure 2 Rest of Canada

Figure 3 Canada

SUMMARY

KEY POINTS

Monetary Policy Objective and Framework
(pp. 656–658)

- The Bank of Canada Act requires the Bank to use monetary policy to avoid inflation and moderate cycles in real GDP and employment.
- The government of Canada and the Bank of Canada have jointly agreed that the Bank will seek to keep CPI inflation between 1 percent and 3 percent a year and will aim for the 2 percent midpoint.
- The Bank has successfully achieved its inflation-control targets.
- The Bank's Governing Council has the responsibility for the conduct of monetary policy, but the Bank and government must consult regularly.

The Conduct of Monetary Policy (pp. 658–662)

- The Bank of Canada's monetary policy instrument is the overnight loans rate.
- The Bank sets the overnight rate target and announces changes on eight fixed dates each year.
- An *instrument rule* for monetary policy makes the instrument respond predictably to the state of the economy. The Bank does *not* use such a rule.
- A *targeting rule* for monetary policy sets the instrument to make the forecast of the inflation rate equal to the target inflation rate. The Bank *does* use such a rule.
- The Bank hits its overnight rate target by setting an operating band and using open market operations.
- By buying or selling government securities in the open market, the Bank of Canada is able to change the reserves of the banking system and change the overnight rate.

Monetary Policy Transmission (pp. 663–669)

- A change in the overnight rate changes other interest rates, the exchange rate, the quantity of money, credit, and loans, aggregate demand, and eventually real GDP and the price level.
- A change in the overnight rate changes real GDP about one year later and changes the inflation rate with an even longer time lag.

Alternative Monetary Policy Strategies
(pp. 670–671)

- The main alternatives are the rule for setting the overnight rate, a monetary base rule, exchange rate targeting, or money targeting.
- Rules dominate discretion in monetary policy because they better enable the central bank to manage inflation expectations.

KEY FIGURES

Figure 28.1   Inflation-Control Targets and Outcome, 657
Figure 28.2   The Overnight Loans Rate, 659
Figure 28.5   The Market for Reserves of LVTS Participating Banks, 662
Figure 28.6   The Channels for the Ripple Effects of a Change in the Overnight Rate, 663
Figure 28.9   The Interest Rate and Expenditure Plans, 667
Figure 28.10 The Final Effect of an Interest Rate Cut, 668
Figure 28.11 The Final Effect of an Interest Rate Rise, 668

KEY TERMS

Bank rate, 660
Core inflation, 656
Instrument rule, 659
Interest-sensitive expenditure curve, 667
k-percent rule, 671
McCallum rule, 670
Nominal interest rate, 665
Open market operation, 660
Operating band, 660
Overnight loans rate, 658
Real exchange rate, 671
Real interest rate, 665
Settlement balances rate, 660
Targeting rule, 659
Taylor rule, 670

PROBLEMS

Go to myeconlab for solutions to odd-numbered problems and additional exercises.

1. Suppose that the Bank of Canada had an inflation-control target expressed as keeping inflation between 1 percent and 3 percent a year but with no requirement to keep trend inflation at the midpoint of the range.
   a. Starting from a price level of 100 and the Bank achieves its target,
      i   Calculate the highest price level that might occur after 10 years.
      ii. Calculate the lowest price level that might occur after 10 years.
      iii. What is the range of uncertainty about the price level after 10 years?
   b. Would this type of inflation-control target serve the financial markets well and provide an anchor for inflation expectations?

2. Suppose the Bank of Canada had an inflation-control target expressed as keeping inflation between 0 percent and 4 percent a year but was also required to keep trend inflation at the midpoint of the range.
   a. Starting from a price level of 100, what is the likely price level after 10 years if the bank achieves its target?
   b. Comparing this economy with the one in problem 1. Which economy has the greater certainty about inflation over the longer term? Which has the greater short-term certainty?

3. The overnight rate target is 4 percent and the Bank of Canada wants to increase it by 0.25 percentage points.
   a. What bank rate does the Bank of Canada set?
   b. What settlement balances rate does the Bank of Canada set?
   c. Does the Bank buy or sell securities in the open market to raise the overnight rate?
   d. Describe the changes in the balance sheets of the Bank of Canada and a chartered bank following the open market operation in part (c).
   e. Draw a graph like Fig. 28.5 to illustrate the effects of the Bank of Canada's actions in the market for reserves of LVTS participating banks.

4. The target for the overnight rate is 4 percent a year and the Bank of Canada wants to decrease it by 0.25 percentage points.
   a. What bank rate does the Bank of Canada set?
   b. What settlement balances rate does the Bank of Canada set?
   c. Does the Bank of Canada buy or sell securities in the open market to lower the overnight rate?
   d. Describe the changes in the balance sheets of the Bank of Canada and a chartered bank following the open market operation in part (c).
   e. Draw a graph like Fig. 28.5 to illustrate the effects of the Bank of Canada's actions in the market for reserves of LVTS participating banks.

5. The figure shows the economy of Freezone. The aggregate demand curve is AD and the short-run aggregate supply curve is SAS_A. Potential GDP is $300 billion.

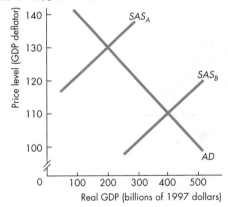

   a. What is the price level and real GDP?
   b. Does Freezone have an unemployment problem or an inflation problem? Why?
   c. What do you predict will happen in Freezone if the central bank takes no monetary policy actions?
   d. What monetary policy action would you advise the central bank to take, and what do you predict will be the effect of that action?

6. Suppose that in Freezone, shown in problem 5, the aggregate demand curve is AD and potential GDP is $300 billion, but the short-run aggregate supply curve is SAS_B.
   a. What is the price level and real GDP?
   b. Does Freezone have an unemployment problem or an inflation problem? Why?

c. What do you predict will happen in Freezone if the central bank takes no monetary policy actions?

d. What monetary policy action would you advise the central bank to take and what do you predict the effect of that action will be?

7. Suppose that in Freezone, shown in problem 5, the short-run aggregate supply curve is SAS_B and potential GDP increases to $350 billion.

a. What happens in Freezone if the central bank lowers the overnight interest rate and buys securities on the open market?

b. What happens in Freezone if the central bank increases the overnight interest rate and sells securities on the open market?

c. Do you recommend that the central bank lower the interest rate and buy securities or increase the interest rate and sell securities? Why?

8. Suppose that in Freezone, shown in problem 5, the short-run aggregate supply curve is SAS_A and a drought decreases potential GDP to $250 billion.

a. What happens in Freezone if the central bank lowers the overnight interest rate and buys securities on the open market?

b. What happens in Freezone if the central bank increases the overnight interest rate and sells securities on the open market?

c. Do you recommend that the central bank lower the interest rate and buy securities or increase the interest rate and sell securities?

CRITICAL THINKING

1. Study *Reading Between the Lines* on pp. 672–673 and then answer the following questions:

a. Why does the CIBC economist say the Bank of Canada risks increasing the overnight rate by too much?

b. What does the Bank of Canada say in response?

c. With which view do you agree and why?

d. Do you think the Bank of Canada went on to get its monetary policy right during 2006, or would you have raised or lowered the interest rate relative to what the Bank set? Provide reasons.

2. When the Bank of Canada brought inflation under control during the early 1990s, it created a recession. Do you think a recession could have been avoided while still lowering the inflation rate? Explain why or why not.

WEB EXERCISES

Use the links on ⓧ myeconlab to work the following exercises.

1. Visit the Bank of Canada and obtain the latest data on the core inflation rate and the overall CPI inflation rate as well as the overnight interest rate. Then answer the following questions.

a. Is the Bank of Canada trying to slow the economy or speed it up? How can you tell?

b. What open market operations do you think the Bank of Canada has undertaken during the past few months?

c. In the light of the Bank of Canada's recent actions, what ripple effects do you expect over the coming months?

d. What do you think the effects of the Bank of Canada's recent actions will be on bond prices, stock prices, and the exchange rate?

2. Visit Statistics Canada and look at the current economic conditions.

a. On the basis of the current state of the Canadian economy, do you predict that the Bank of Canada will raise interest rates, lower interest rates, or hold interest rates steady?

b. Write a brief summary of your predictions and reasons.

Fiscal and Monetary Interactions

CHAPTER 29

Sparks Fly in Ottawa

In 2005, the Parliament of Canada approved a federal government budget that showed a large surplus. Not far from Parliament Hill, on Sparks Street, the Bank of Canada pulls the nation's monetary policy levers that directly target the overnight interest rate and indirectly influence other interest rates, the exchange rate, and the quantity of money and loans. How does the government's fiscal policy interact with the Bank of Canada's monetary policy to influence real GDP, the price level, and the inflation rate?

Does it matter if fiscal and monetary policy come into conflict—creating sparks on Sparks Street?

If a recession is looming on the horizon, is an interest rate cut by the Bank of Canada just as good as a tax cut by Parliament? If the economy is overheating, is an interest rate hike by the Bank of Canada just as good as a tax increase by Parliament?

◆ You already know a lot about the effects of fiscal policy and monetary policy. And you know that their ultimate effects work through their influences on both aggregate demand and aggregate supply. This chapter gives you a deeper understanding of the aggregate demand side of the economy and how the combined actions of the federal government and the Bank of Canada affect aggregate demand. In *Reading Between the Lines* at the end of the chapter, we look at what David Dodge, governor of the Bank of Canada, thinks about the appropriate roles for monetary policy and fiscal policy.

After studying this chapter, you will be able to

- Explain macroeconomic equilibrium
- Explain how fiscal policy influences real GDP and the price level
- Explain how monetary policy influences real GDP and the price level
- Explain the Keynesian–monetarist debate
- Explain the effects of fiscal and monetary policies at full employment
- Explain how fiscal and monetary policies might be coordinated or in conflict

Macroeconomic Equilibrium

YOUR GOAL IN THIS CHAPTER IS TO LEARN HOW fiscal policy and monetary policy interact to influence real GDP, the price level, and the inflation rate. You studied fiscal policy in Chapter 24 and monetary policy in Chapter 28. But these two accounts of the effects of policy didn't explain how fiscal and monetary policy interact. We need to know how they interact because we want to know whether we can use either on its own to achieve the same goals or whether they must be used in the correct combination.

You know that the Bank of Canada targets the inflation rate by influencing the overnight interest rate. The quantity of money is a consequence of the Bank's interest rate decision. Despite the Bank of Canada's approach, we will explore fiscal and monetary policy interactions when the central bank targets the quantity of money. By doing so, we are able to review a long-running debate about policy between Keynesians and monetarists. And we are able to see the potential benefits and risks of the interest rate targeting approach favoured by the Bank of Canada.

To study policy effects, we ask how a given policy action changes the equilibrium. So we begin by describing macroeconomic equilibrium with a fixed target for the quantity of money.

Two Markets in Short-Run Equilibrium

In a short-run equilibrium, the interest rate adjusts to make the quantity of money demanded equal to the quantity of money supplied (Chapter 25, p. 605). And the price level adjusts to make the quantity of real GDP demanded equal to the quantity of real GDP supplied (Chapter 22, pp. 516–517).

But real GDP and the price level influence the demand for money. And the interest rate influences aggregate demand. So the money market and the market for goods and services (for real GDP) are linked together.

Other things remaining the same, the greater the level of aggregate demand, the higher are real GDP and the price level. A higher real GDP means a greater demand for money; a higher price level means a smaller supply of real money; so a greater level of aggregate demand means a higher interest rate.

Aggregate demand depends on the interest rate because consumption expenditure, investment, and net exports are influenced by the interest rate (see Chapter 28, pp. 666–667). So, other things remaining the same, the lower the interest rate, the greater is aggregate demand.

Only one level of aggregate demand and one interest rate are consistent with each other in macroeconomic equilibrium. Figure 29.1 describes this unique equilibrium.

In Fig. 29.1(a), the intersection of the aggregate demand curve, AD, and the short-run aggregate supply curve, SAS, determines real GDP at $1,000 billion and the price level at 110. In Fig. 29.1(b), the intersection of the demand for money curve, MD, and the supply of money curve, MS, determines the interest rate at 5 percent a year. In Fig. 29.1(c) at an interest rate of 5 percent a year, the interest-sensitive expenditure curve, IE, determines the amount of interest-sensitive expenditure at $100 billion.

The position of the AD curve depends on the quantity of money, and the demand for and supply of real money depend on the AD and SAS curves.

Simultaneous Equilibrium

The AS–AD equilibrium in Fig. 29.1(a), the money market equilibrium in Fig. 29.1(b), and interest-sensitive expenditure in Fig. 29.1(c) are consistent with each other. There is no other equilibrium.

To check this claim, assume that aggregate demand is less than AD in Fig. 29.1(a) so that real GDP is less than $1,000 billion. If this assumption is correct, the demand for money curve lies to the left of MD in Fig. 29.1(b) and the equilibrium interest rate is less than 5 percent a year. With an interest rate less than 5 percent a year, interest-sensitive expenditure exceeds the $100 billion in Fig. 29.1(c). If interest-sensitive expenditure exceeds $100 billion, the AD curve lies to the right of the one we assumed and equilibrium real GDP exceeds $1,000 billion. So if we assume a real GDP of less than $1,000 billion, equilibrium real GDP is greater than $1,000 billion. There is an inconsistency. The assumed equilibrium real GDP is too small.

Now assume that aggregate demand is greater than AD in Fig. 29.1(a) so that real GDP exceeds $1,000 billion. If this assumption is correct, the demand for money curve lies to the right of MD in Fig. 29.1(b) and the equilibrium interest rate exceeds 5 percent a year. With an interest rate above 5 percent a year, interest-sensitive expenditure is less than the $100 billion in Fig. 29.1(c), in which case the

FIGURE 29.1

Equilibrium Real GDP, Price Level, Interest Rate, and Expenditure

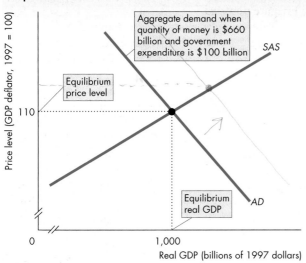

(a) Aggregate supply and aggregate demand

In part (a), the intersection of the aggregate demand curve, AD, and the short-run aggregate supply curve, SAS, determines real GDP at $1,000 billion and the price level at 110. Behind the AD curve, interest-sensitive expenditure is $100 billion, government expenditure is $100 billion, and the rest of real GDP is $800 billion. In part (b), when real GDP is $1,000 billion, the demand for money curve is MD and when the price level is 110, the supply of real money curve is MS. The intersection of the demand for money curve, MD, and the supply of money curve, MS, determines the interest rate at 5 percent a year. In part (c), on the IE curve, interest-sensitive expenditure is $100 billion at the equilibrium interest rate of 5 percent a year.

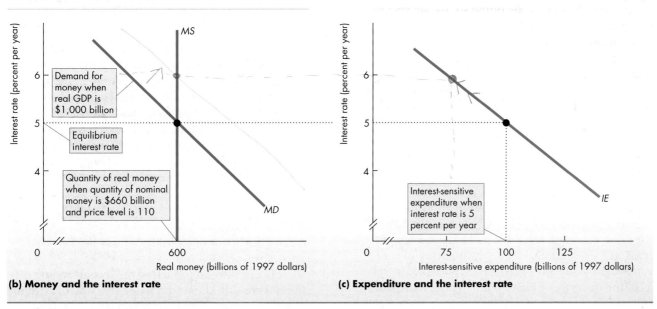

(b) Money and the interest rate

(c) Expenditure and the interest rate

AD curve must lie to the left of the one we assumed and equilibrium real GDP must be smaller than $1,000 billion. So if we assume that real GDP exceeds $1,000 billion, equilibrium real GDP is less than $1,000 billion. There is another inconsistency. The assumed equilibrium real GDP is too large.

Only one level of aggregate demand delivers the same money market equilibrium and AS–AD equilibrium. In this example, it is the aggregate demand curve AD in Fig. 29.1(a). Assuming this level of

aggregate demand implies this level of aggregate demand. Assuming a lower level of aggregate demand implies a higher level. And assuming a higher level of aggregate demand implies a lower level.

Now that you understand how aggregate demand and the interest rate are simultaneously determined, let's study the effects of a change in government expenditures.

Study Plan 29.1

Fiscal Policy in the Short Run

REAL GDP GROWTH IS SLOWING, AND THE finance minister is concerned that a recession is likely. So the government decides to try to head off the recession by using fiscal policy to stimulate aggregate demand. A fiscal policy that increases aggregate demand is called an *expansionary fiscal policy*.

The effects of an expansionary fiscal policy are similar to those of throwing a pebble into a pond. There's an initial splash followed by a series of ripples that become ever smaller. The initial splash is the "first round effect" of the fiscal policy action. The ripples are the "second round effects." You've already met the first round effects in Chapter 24, so here is a refresher.

First Round Effects of Fiscal Policy

The economy starts out in the position shown in Fig. 29.1. Real GDP is $1,000 billion, the price level is 110, the interest rate is 5 percent a year, and interest-sensitive expenditure is $100 billion. The government now increases its expenditures on goods and services by $100 billion.

Figure 29.2 shows the first round effects of this action. The increase in government expenditures has a multiplier effect because it brings an increase in induced expenditure. (You can refresh your memory about the government expenditures multiplier on pp. 570–572.) Let's assume that the multiplier is 2, so a $100 billion increase in government expenditures increases aggregate demand at a given price level by $200 billion. The aggregate demand curve shifts rightward from AD_0 to AD_1. At a price level of 110, the quantity of real GDP demanded increases from $1,000 billion to $1,200 billion.

Real GDP now starts to increase and the price level starts to rise. These are the first round effects of expansionary fiscal policy.

Second Round Effects of Fiscal Policy

Through the second round, real GDP increases and the price level rises until a new macroeconomic equilibrium is reached. But to find that equilibrium and to describe the changes that result from the initial increase in government expenditures, we must keep

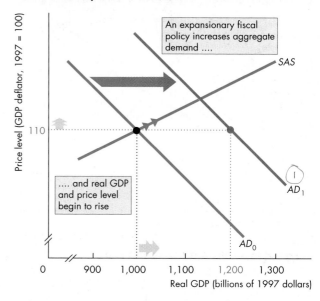

FIGURE 29.2

First Round Effects of an Expansionary Fiscal Policy

Initially, the aggregate demand curve is AD_0, real GDP is $1,000 billion, and the price level is 110. A $100 billion increase in government expenditures on goods and services has a multiplier effect and increases aggregate demand by $200 billion. The aggregate demand curve shifts rightward to AD_1. Real GDP begins to increase and the price level begins to rise. These are the first round effects of an expansionary fiscal policy.

track of further changes in the money market and in expenditure plans.

It is easier to keep track of the second round effects if we split them into two parts: one that results from the increasing real GDP, and the other that results from the rising price level. We follow these effects in Fig. 29.3.

First, the increasing real GDP increases the demand for money. In Fig. 29.3(b), the demand for money curve shifts rightward. Eventually, it shifts to MD_1 and the interest rate rises to 6 percent a year. At this interest rate, interest-sensitive expenditure decreases to $75 billion in Fig. 29.3(c). The decrease in planned expenditure decreases aggregate demand and the aggregate demand curve shifts leftward to AD_2 in Fig. 29.3(a).

FIGURE 29.3

Second Round Effects of an Expansionary Fiscal Policy

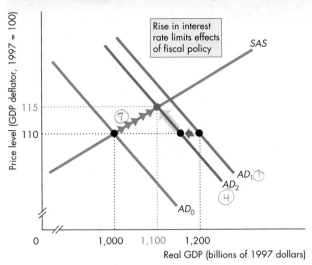

(a) Aggregate supply and aggregate demand

Initially in part (b), the money demand curve is MD_0, the real money supply curve is MS_0, and the interest rate is 5 percent a year. With an interest rate of 5 percent a year, interest-sensitive expenditure is $100 billion on the curve IE (part c). With increased government expenditures, the aggregate demand curve is AD_1 in part (a). Real GDP is increasing, and the price level is rising. The increasing real GDP increases the demand for money and the money demand curve shifts rightward to MD_1. The higher interest rate decreases interest-sensitive expenditure, which decreases aggregate demand to AD_2. The rising price level brings a movement along the new AD curve. It does so because it decreases the quantity of real money. The money supply curve shifts leftward to MS_1, which in turn raises the interest rate further and decreases expenditure. The new equilibrium occurs when real GDP has increased to $1,100 billion and the price level has risen to 115.

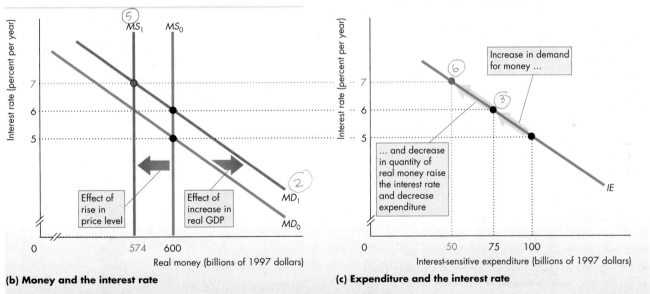

(b) Money and the interest rate

(c) Expenditure and the interest rate

Second, with a given quantity of nominal money, the rising price level decreases the quantity of real money. In Fig. 29.3(b), the money supply curve shifts leftward to MS_1. The decrease in the quantity of real money raises the interest rate further to 7 percent a year. In Fig. 29.3(c), the higher interest rate decreases interest-sensitive expenditure to $50 billion. Because this decrease in spending plans is induced by a rise in the price level, it decreases the quantity of real GDP

demanded and is shown as a movement up along the aggregate demand curve AD_2 in Fig. 29.3(a).

During this second round process, real GDP is increasing and the price level is rising in a gradual movement up along the short-run aggregate supply curve as indicated by the arrows. In the new equilibrium, real GDP is $1,100 billion, the price level is 115, the interest rate is 7 percent a year, and interest-sensitive expenditure is $50 billion.

FIGURE 29.4

How the Economy Adjusts to an Expansionary Fiscal Policy

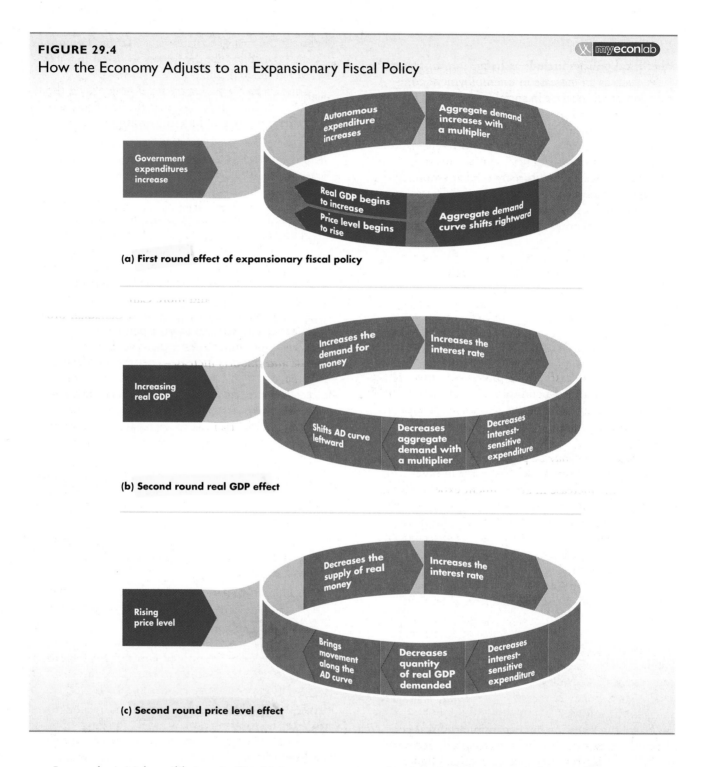

(a) First round effect of expansionary fiscal policy

(b) Second round real GDP effect

(c) Second round price level effect

Just as the initial equilibrium in Fig. 29.1 was consistent, so the new equilibrium is consistent. The *AS–AD* equilibrium in Fig. 29.3(a), the money market equilibrium in Fig. 29.3(b), and interest-sensitive expenditure in Fig. 29.3(c) are all consistent with each other. And there is no other equilibrium.

Figure 29.4(a) summarizes the first round effect of an expansionary fiscal policy action. Figures 29.4(b) and 29.4(c) summarize the two parts of the second round adjustment as the economy responds.

Other Fiscal Policies

Other fiscal policies include a change in transfer payments, such as an increase in unemployment compensation or an increase in social benefits and a change in taxes. All fiscal policy actions work by changing expenditure. But the magnitude of the initial change in expenditure differs for different fiscal actions. For example, changes in taxes and transfer payments change expenditure by smaller amounts than does a change in government expenditures on goods and services. But fiscal policies that change autonomous expenditure by a given amount and in a given direction have similar effects on equilibrium real GDP, the price level, and the interest rate regardless of the initial fiscal action. Let's take a closer look at the effect of the rise in the interest rate.

Crowding Out and Crowding In

Because an expansionary fiscal policy increases the interest rate, it decreases all the interest-sensitive components of aggregate expenditure. One of these components is investment, and the decrease in investment that results from an expansionary fiscal action is called **crowding out.**

Crowding out may be partial or complete. Partial crowding out occurs when the decrease in investment is less than the increase in government expenditures. This is the normal case—and the case we've just seen.

Complete crowding out occurs if the decrease in investment equals the initial increase in government expenditures. For complete crowding out to occur, a small change in the demand for real money must lead to a large change in the interest rate, and the change in the interest rate must lead to a large change in investment.

But another potential influence of government expenditures on investment works in the opposite direction to the crowding-out effect and is called "crowding in." **Crowding in** is the tendency for expansionary fiscal policy to *increase* investment. This effect works in three ways.

First, in a recession, an expansionary fiscal policy might create expectations of a more speedy recovery and bring an increase in expected profits. Higher expected profits might increase investment despite a higher interest rate.

Second, government expenditures might be productive and lead to more profitable business opportunities. For example, a new government-built highway

might cut the cost of transporting a farmer's produce to a market and induce the farmer to invest in a new fleet of refrigerated trucks.

Third, if an expansionary fiscal policy takes the form of a cut in taxes on business profits, firms' after-tax profits increase and investment might increase.

The Exchange Rate and International Crowding Out

We've seen that an expansionary fiscal policy leads to higher interest rates. But a change in interest rates also affects the exchange rate. Higher interest rates make the dollar appreciate against other currencies. With interest rates higher in Canada than in the rest of the world, funds flow into Canada and people around the world demand more Canadian dollars. As the dollar appreciates, foreigners find Canadian-produced goods and services more expensive and Canadians find imports less expensive. Exports decrease and imports increase—net exports decrease. The tendency for an expansionary fiscal policy to decrease net exports is called **international crowding out.** The decrease in net exports offsets, to some degree, the initial increase in aggregate expenditure brought about by an expansionary fiscal policy.

REVIEW QUIZ

1. Describe macroeconomic equilibrium. What conditions are met in such an equilibrium? What are the links between aggregate demand, the money market, and interest-sensitive expenditure?
2. What is an expansionary fiscal policy and what are its first round effects? What is happening at the end of the first round?
3. What are the second round effects of an expansionary fiscal policy action? Describe the forces at work and the changes that occur in the interest rate, interest-sensitive expenditure, real GDP, and the price level.
4. What is crowding out? What is crowding in? How do they influence the outcome of a fiscal policy action?
5. How does an expansionary fiscal policy affect the exchange rate? What happens to imports and exports?

 Study Plan 29.2

Monetary Policy in the Short Run

TO STUDY THE EFFECTS OF AN EXPANSIONARY monetary policy, we look at the first round effects and the second round effects, just as we did for fiscal policy. Figure 29.5 describes the economy. The quantity of real money is $600 billion, the interest rate is 5 percent a year, interest-sensitive expenditure is $100 billion, real GDP is $1,000 billion, and the price level is 110. With a price level of 110, the quantity of money is $660 billion.

The Bank of Canada now increases the quantity of money to $1,155 billion. With a price level of 110, the quantity of real money increases to $1,050 billion. Figure 29.5(a) shows the immediate effect. The real money supply curve shifts rightward from MS_0 to MS_1, and the interest rate falls from 5 percent to 1 percent a year. The lower interest rate increases

FIGURE 29.5
First Round Effects of an Expansionary Monetary Policy

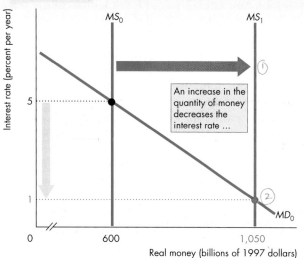

(a) Change in quantity of money

(b) Change in expenditure

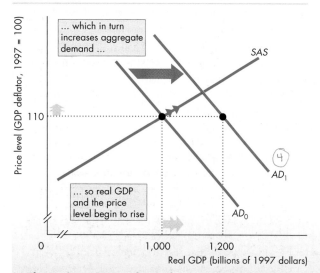

(c) Change in aggregate demand

Initially, the real money demand curve is MD_0, the real money supply curve is MS_0, and the interest rate is 5 percent a year (part a). With an interest rate of 5 percent a year, interest-sensitive expenditure is $100 billion on the IE curve (part b). The aggregate demand curve is AD_0. Equilibrium real GDP is $1,000 billion, and the price level is 110 (part c).

An increase in the quantity of money shifts the money supply curve rightward to MS_1 (part a). The interest rate falls to 1 percent a year and interest-sensitive expenditure increases to $200 billion (part b). The increase in expenditure increases aggregate demand and shifts the aggregate demand curve to AD_1 (in part c). Real GDP begins to increase and the price level begins to rise.

interest-sensitive expenditure to $200 billion in part (b). The increase in interest-sensitive expenditure increases aggregate demand and shifts the *AD* curve rightward from AD_0 to AD_1 (part c). The increase in aggregate demand sets off a multiplier process in which real GDP and the price level begin to increase.

These are the first round effects of an expansionary monetary policy. An increase in the quantity of money lowers the interest rate and increases aggregate demand. Real GDP and the price level begin to increase.

Let's now look at the second round effects.

Second Round Effects

The increasing real GDP and rising price level set off the second round, which Fig. 29.6 illustrates. And as in the case of fiscal policy, it is best to break the second round into two parts: the consequence of increasing real GDP, and the consequence of the rising price level.

The increasing real GDP increases the demand for money from MD_0 to MD_1 in Fig. 29.6(a). The increased demand for money raises the interest rate

---

FIGURE 29.6
Second Round Effects of an Expansionary Monetary Policy

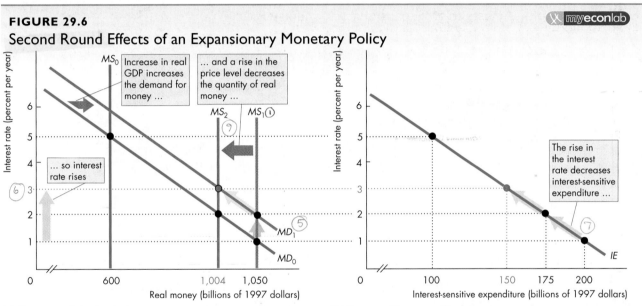

(a) Money and the interest rate

(b) Decrease in expenditure

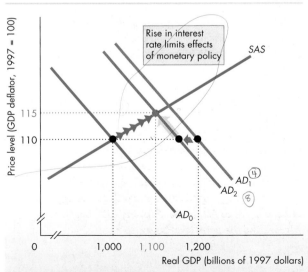

(c) Aggregate demand and aggregate supply

At the start of the second round, the money demand curve is still MD_0 in part (a), the real money supply curve is MS_1, and the interest rate is 1 percent a year. With an interest rate of 1 percent a year, interest-sensitive expenditure is $200 billion on the curve *IE* in part (b). With the increased quantity of money and interest-sensitive expenditure, the aggregate demand curve is AD_1 in part (c). Real GDP is increasing, and the price level is rising. The increasing real GDP increases the demand for money and the money demand curve shifts rightward to MD_1. The higher interest rate decreases interest-sensitive expenditure, which decreases aggregate demand to AD_2. The rising price level brings a movement along the new *AD* curve. It does so because the rising price level decreases the quantity of real money and the money supply curve shifts to MS_2. The interest rate rises further and expenditure decreases. The new equilibrium occurs when real GDP has increased to $1,100 billion and the price level has risen to 115.

from 1 percent a year to 2 percent a year. The higher interest rate brings a decrease in interest-sensitive expenditure from $200 billion to $175 billion in Fig. 29.6(b). And the lower level of expenditure decreases aggregate demand and shifts the aggregate demand curve leftward from AD_1 to AD_2 in Fig. 29.6(c).

The rising price level brings a movement along the new aggregate demand curve in Fig. 29.6(c). This movement occurs because the rising price level decreases the quantity of real money. As the price level rises, the quantity of real money decreases to $1,004 billion and the money supply curve shifts leftward from MS_1 to MS_2 (part a). The interest rate rises further to 3 percent a year. And interest-sensitive expenditure decreases to $150 billion (part b).

In the new short-run equilibrium, real GDP has increased to $1,100 billion, and the price level has risen to 115, where aggregate demand curve AD_2 intersects the short-run aggregate supply curve SAS.

FIGURE 29.7

How the Economy Adjusts to an Expansionary Monetary Policy

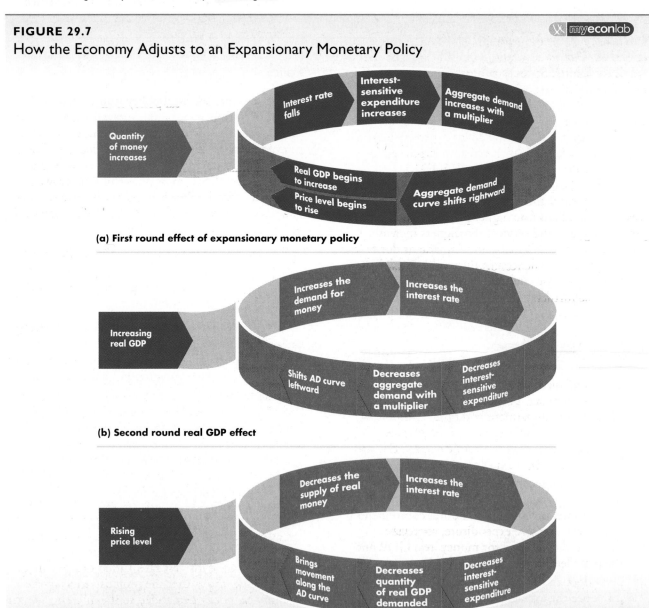

(a) First round effect of expansionary monetary policy

(b) Second round real GDP effect

(c) Second round price level effect

The money demand curve is MD_1, the money supply curve is MS_2, and the interest rate is 3 percent a year in part (a). With an interest rate of 3 percent a year, interest-sensitive expenditure is $150 billion in part (b).

The new equilibrium is the only consistent one and is like that of Fig. 29.1. Figure 29.7 summarizes the adjustments that occur to bring the economy to this new equilibrium.

Money and the Exchange Rate

An increase in the money supply lowers the interest rate. If the interest rate falls in Canada but does not fall in the United States, Japan, and Western Europe, international investors buy the now higher-yielding foreign assets and sell the relatively lower-yielding Canadian assets. As they make these transactions, they sell Canadian dollars. So the dollar depreciates against other currencies. (This mechanism is explained in greater detail in Chapter 26, pp. 615–621.)

With a cheaper Canadian dollar, foreigners face lower prices for Canadian-produced goods and services and Canadians face higher prices for foreign-produced goods and services. Foreigners increase their imports from Canada, and Canadians decrease their imports from the rest of the world. Canadian net exports increase, and real GDP and the price level increase further.

REVIEW QUIZ

1 What are the first round effects of an expansionary monetary policy? What happens to the interest rate, investment and other components of interest-sensitive expenditure, aggregate demand, the demand for money, real GDP, and the price level in the first round?

2 What are the second round effects of an expansionary monetary policy? What happens to the interest rate, investment and other components of interest-sensitive expenditure, aggregate demand, the demand for money, real GDP, and the price level in the second round?

3 How does an expansionary monetary policy influence the exchange rate, imports, and exports?

myeconlab Study Plan 29.3

Relative Effectiveness of Policies

WE'VE SEEN THAT AGGREGATE DEMAND AND REAL GDP are influenced by both fiscal policy and monetary policy. But which policy is the more potent? This question was once at the centre of a controversy among macroeconomists. Later in this section we'll look at that controversy and see how it was settled. But we begin by discovering what determines the effectiveness of fiscal policy.

Effectiveness of Fiscal Policy

The effectiveness of fiscal policy is measured by the magnitude of the increase in aggregate demand that results from a given increase in government expenditures (or decrease in taxes). The effectiveness of fiscal policy depends on the strength of the crowding-out effect. Fiscal policy is most powerful if no crowding out occurs. Fiscal policy is impotent if there is complete crowding out. And the strength of the crowding-out effect depends on two things:

1. The responsiveness of expenditure to the interest rate
2. The responsiveness of the quantity of money demanded to the interest rate

If expenditure is not very responsive to a change in the interest rate, the crowding-out effect is small. But if expenditure is highly responsive to a change in the interest rate, the crowding-out effect is large. Other things remaining the same, the smaller the responsiveness of expenditure to the interest rate, the smaller is the crowding-out effect and the more effective is fiscal policy.

The responsiveness of the quantity of money demanded to the interest rate also affects the size of the crowding-out effect. An increase in real GDP increases the demand for money and with no change in the quantity of money, the interest rate rises. But the extent to which the interest rate rises depends on the responsiveness of the quantity of money demanded to the interest rate. Other things remaining the same, the greater the responsiveness of the quantity of money demanded to the interest rate, the smaller is the rise in the interest rate, the smaller is the crowding-out effect, and the more effective is fiscal policy.

Effectiveness of Monetary Policy

The effectiveness of monetary policy is measured by the magnitude of the increase in aggregate demand that results from a given increase in the quantity of money. Like fiscal policy, the effectiveness of monetary policy depends on two things:

1. The responsiveness of the quantity of money demanded to the interest rate
2. The responsiveness of expenditure to the interest rate

The starting point for monetary policy is a change in the quantity of money that changes the interest rate. A given change in the quantity of money might bring a small change or a large change in the interest rate. The less responsive the quantity of money demanded to the interest rate, the greater is the change in the interest rate. So other things remaining the same, the larger the initial change in the interest rate, the more effective is monetary policy.

But effectiveness of monetary policy also depends on how much expenditure changes. If expenditure is not very responsive to a change in the interest rate, monetary actions do not have much effect on expenditure. But if expenditure is highly responsive to a change in the interest rate, monetary actions have a large effect on aggregate expenditure. The greater the responsiveness of expenditure to the interest rate, the more effective is monetary policy.

The effectiveness of fiscal policy and monetary policy that you've just studied was once controversial. During the 1950s and 1960s, this issue lay at the heart of what was called the Keynesian–monetarist controversy. Let's look at the dispute and see how it was resolved.

Keynesian–Monetarist Controversy

The Keynesian–monetarist controversy was an ongoing dispute in macroeconomics between two broad groups of economists. A **Keynesian** is a macroeconomist who regards the economy as being inherently unstable and as requiring active government intervention to achieve stability. Keynesian views about the functioning of the economy are based on the theories of John Maynard Keynes, published in Keynes' *General Theory* (see pp. 530–531). Traditionally, Keynesians assigned a low degree of importance to monetary policy and a high degree of importance to fiscal policy. Modern Keynesians

assign a high degree of importance to both types of policy. A **monetarist** is a macroeconomist who believes that most macroeconomic fluctuations are caused by fluctuations in the quantity of money and that the economy is inherently stable and requires no active government intervention. Monetarist views about the functioning of the economy are based on theories most forcefully set forth by Milton Friedman (see pp. 700–701). Traditionally monetarists assigned a low degree of importance to fiscal policy. But modern monetarists, like modern Keynesians, assign a high degree of importance to both types of policy.

The nature of the Keynesian–monetarist debate has changed over the years. During the 1950s and 1960s, it was a debate about the relative effectiveness of fiscal policy and monetary policy in changing aggregate demand. We can see the essence of that debate by distinguishing three views:

- Extreme Keynesianism
- Extreme monetarism
- The intermediate position

Extreme Keynesianism The extreme Keynesian hypothesis is that a change in the quantity of money has no effect on aggregate demand and a change in government expenditures on goods and services or in taxes has a large effect on aggregate demand. The two circumstances in which a change in the quantity of money has no effect on aggregate demand are when

1. Expenditure is completely insensitive to the interest rate
2. The quantity of money demanded is highly sensitive to the interest rate

If expenditure is completely insensitive to the interest rate (if the *IE* curve is vertical), a change in the quantity of money changes the interest rate, but the change does not affect aggregate expenditure. Monetary policy is impotent.

If the quantity of money demanded is highly sensitive to the interest rate (if the *MD* curve is horizontal), people are willing to hold any amount of money at a given interest rate—a situation called a *liquidity trap*. With a liquidity trap, a change in the quantity of money affects only the amount of money held. It does not affect the interest rate. With an unchanged interest rate, expenditure remains constant. Monetary policy is impotent. Some people believe that Japan was in a liquidity trap during the late 1990s.

Extreme Monetarism The extreme monetarist hypothesis is that a change in government expenditures on goods and services or in taxes has no effect on aggregate demand and that a change in the quantity of money has a large effect on aggregate demand. Two circumstances give rise to these predictions:

1. Expenditure is highly sensitive to the interest rate
2. The quantity of money demanded is completely insensitive to the interest rate

If an increase in government expenditures on goods and services induces an increase in the interest rate that is sufficiently large to reduce expenditure by the same amount as the initial increase in government expenditures, then fiscal policy has no effect on aggregate demand. This outcome is complete crowding out. For this result to occur, either the quantity of money demanded must be insensitive to the interest rate—a fixed amount of money is held regardless of the interest rate—or expenditure must be highly sensitive to the interest rate—any amount of expenditure will be undertaken at a given interest rate.

The Intermediate Position The intermediate position is that both fiscal policy and monetary policy affect aggregate demand. Crowding out is not complete, so fiscal policy does have an effect. There is no liquidity trap and expenditure responds to the interest rate, so monetary policy does indeed affect aggregate demand. This position is the one that now appears to be correct and is the one that we've explored in most of this chapter. Let's see how economists came to this conclusion.

Sorting Out the Competing Claims

The dispute between monetarists, Keynesians, and those taking an intermediate position was essentially a disagreement about the magnitudes of two economic parameters:

1. The responsiveness of expenditure to the interest rate
2. The responsiveness of the demand for real money to the interest rate

If expenditure is highly sensitive to the interest rate or the demand for real money is barely sensitive to the interest rate, then monetary policy is powerful and fiscal policy relatively ineffective. In this case, the world looks similar to the claims of extreme monetarists. If expenditure is very insensitive to the interest rate, or the demand for real money is highly sensitive, then fiscal policy is powerful and monetary policy is relatively ineffective. In this case, the world looks similar to the claims of the extreme Keynesians.

By using statistical methods to study the demand for real money and expenditure and by using data from a wide variety of historical and national experiences, economists were able to settle this dispute. Neither extreme position turned out to be supported by the evidence, and the intermediate position won. The demand curve for real money slopes downward. And expenditure *is* interest sensitive. Neither the money demand curve nor the interest-sensitive expenditure curve is vertical or horizontal, so the extreme Keynesian and extreme monetarist hypotheses are rejected.

Interest Rate and Exchange Rate Effectiveness

Although fiscal policy and monetary policy are alternative ways of changing aggregate demand, they have opposing effects on the interest rate and the exchange rate. A fiscal policy action that increases aggregate demand raises the interest rate and increases the exchange rate. A monetary policy action that increases aggregate demand lowers the interest rate and decreases the exchange rate. Because of these opposing effects on interest rates and the exchange rate, if the two policies are combined to increase aggregate demand, their separate effects on the interest rate and the exchange rate can be minimized.

REVIEW QUIZ

1 What two macroeconomic parameters influence the relative effectiveness of fiscal policy and monetary policy?
2 Under what circumstances is the Keynesian view correct and under what circumstances is the monetarist view correct?
3 How can fiscal policy and monetary policy be combined to increase aggregate demand yet at the same time keep the interest rate constant?

myeconlab Study Plan 29.4

We're now going to look at expansionary fiscal and monetary policy at full employment.

Policy Actions at Full Employment

AN EXPANSIONARY FISCAL POLICY OR MONETARY policy can bring the economy to full employment. But it is often difficult to determine whether the economy is below full employment. So an expansionary fiscal policy or monetary policy might be undertaken when the economy is at full employment. What happens then? Let's answer this question starting with an expansionary fiscal policy.

Expansionary Fiscal Policy at Full Employment

Suppose the economy is at full employment and the government increases its expenditures. All the effects that we worked out earlier in this chapter occur. But these effects determine only a *short-run equilibrium*. That is, the first round and second round effects of policy both occur in the short run. There is a third round, which is the long-run adjustment.

Starting out at full employment, an expansionary fiscal policy will create an above full-employment equilibrium in which there is an *inflationary gap*. The money wage rate begins to rise, short-run aggregate supply decreases, and a long-run adjustment occurs in which real GDP decreases to potential GDP and the price level rises.

Figure 29.8 illustrates the combined first and second round short-run effects and the third round long-run adjustment.

In Fig. 29.8, potential GDP is $1,000 billion. Real GDP equals potential GDP on aggregate demand curve AD_0 and short-run aggregate supply curve SAS_0. An expansionary fiscal action increases aggregate demand. The combined first round and second round effect increases aggregate demand to AD_1. Real GDP increases to $1,100 billion and the price level rises to 115. There is an inflationary gap of $100 billion.

With the economy above full employment, a shortage of labour puts upward pressure on the money wage rate, which now begins to rise. And a third round of adjustment begins. The rising money wage rate decreases short-run aggregate supply and the SAS curve starts moving leftward towards SAS_1.

As short-run aggregate supply decreases, real GDP decreases and the price level rises. This process

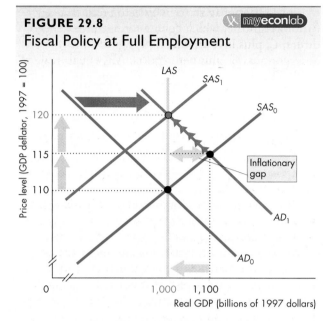

FIGURE 29.8
Fiscal Policy at Full Employment

The long-run aggregate supply curve is *LAS* and initially the aggregate demand curve is AD_0 and the short-run aggregate supply curve is SAS_0. Real GDP is $1,000 billion and the GDP deflator is 110. Fiscal policy and monetary policy changes shift the aggregate demand curve to AD_1. At the new short-run equilibrium, real GDP is $1,100 billion and the GDP deflator is 115. Because real GDP exceeds potential GDP, the money wage rate begins to rise and the short-run aggregate supply curve begins to shift leftward to SAS_1. At the new long-run equilibrium, the GDP deflator is 120 and real GDP is back at its original level.

continues until the inflationary gap has been eliminated and the economy returns to full employment. At long-run equilibrium, real GDP is $1,000, which is potential GDP, and the price level is 120.

Crowding Out at Full Employment

You've just seen that when government expenditures increase at full employment, the long-run change in real GDP is zero. The entire effect of the increase in aggregate demand is to increase the price level. This outcome implies that at full employment, an increase in government expenditures *completely crowds out private expenditure* or *creates an international (net exports) deficit*, or results in a combination of the two.

The easiest way to see why is to recall that aggregate expenditure, which equals consumption expenditure, C, plus investment, I, plus government expenditures, G, plus net exports, NX, equals real GDP. That is,

$$Y = C + I + G + NX.$$

Comparing the initial situation with the final outcome, real GDP has not changed. So aggregate expenditure, $C + I + G + NX$, is constant between the two situations.

But government expenditures have increased, so the sum of consumption, investment, and net exports must have decreased. If net exports don't change, consumption plus investment decreases by the full amount of the increase in government expenditures. If consumption and investment don't change, net exports decrease by an amount equal to the increase in government expenditures. A decrease in net exports is an increase in our international deficit.

You've now seen that the effects of expansionary fiscal policy are extremely sensitive to the state of the economy when the policy action is taken. At less than full employment, an expansionary fiscal policy can move the economy towards full employment. At full employment, an expansionary fiscal policy raises the price level and crowds out private expenditure or creates an international deficit.

Expansionary Monetary Policy at Full Employment

Now suppose the economy is at full employment and the Bank of Canada increases the quantity of money. Again, all the effects that we worked out earlier in this chapter occur. But again, these effects determine only a *short-run equilibrium*. That is, the first round and second round effects of monetary policy both occur in the short run. And again, there is a third round, which is the long-run adjustment.

Starting out at full employment, an expansionary monetary policy will create an above full-employment equilibrium in which there is an *inflationary gap*. The money wage rate begins to rise, short-run aggregate supply decreases, and a long-run adjustment occurs in which real GDP decreases to potential GDP and the price level rises.

To illustrate the effects of monetary policy at full employment, look back at Fig. 29.8 but now think of the increase in aggregate demand as resulting from an increase in the quantity of money. You can see that in the short run, an expansionary monetary policy increases real GDP and the price level. But in the long run, expansionary monetary policy increases only the price level and leaves real GDP unchanged at potential GDP.

Long-Run Neutrality

In the long run, a change in the quantity of money changes only the price level and leaves real GDP unchanged. The independence of real GDP from the quantity of money is an example of the long-run neutrality of money.

But long-run neutrality applies not only to real GDP but also to all real variables. The so-called **long-run neutrality** proposition is that in the long run, a change in the quantity of money changes the price level and leaves all real variables unchanged.

You can see this outcome in the case of real GDP in Fig. 29.8. With no change in real GDP, the demand for money does not change. The price level rises by the same percentage as the increase in the quantity of money, so the quantity of real money does not change. With no change in the demand for money and no change in the quantity of real money, the interest rate does not change. And with no change in the interest rate, expenditure remains the same.

Finally, with no change in real GDP or the real interest rate, consumption expenditure, investment, government expenditures, and net exports are unchanged.

REVIEW QUIZ

1 Contrast the short-run effects of an expansionary fiscal policy on real GDP and the price level with its long-run effects when the policy action occurs at full employment.
2 Contrast the short-run effects of an expansionary monetary policy on real GDP and the price level with its long-run effects when the policy action occurs at full employment.
3 Explain crowding out at full employment.
4 Explain the long-run neutrality of money.

Ⓧ myeconlab **Study Plan 29.5**

Policy Coordination, Conflict, and Risk

SO FAR, WE'VE STUDIED THE INTERACTION OF fiscal policy and monetary policy with each conducted in isolation from the other. We are now going to consider what happens if the two branches of policy are coordinated and if they come into conflict.

Policy coordination occurs when the government and the Bank of Canada work together to achieve a common set of goals.

Policy conflict occurs when the government and the Bank of Canada pursue different goals and the actions of one make it harder (perhaps impossible) for the other to achieve its goals.

Policy Coordination

The basis for policy coordination is the fact that either fiscal policy or monetary policy can be used to influence aggregate demand. Starting from a *below full-employment equilibrium*, an increase in aggregate demand increases real GDP and decreases unemployment. If the size and timing of the policy action is well judged, it can restore full employment. Similarly, starting from an *above full-employment equilibrium*, a decrease in aggregate demand decreases real GDP and can, again if the timing and size of the action is well judged, eliminate an *inflationary gap*. Because either a fiscal policy or a monetary policy action can achieve these objectives, the two policies can (in principle) be combined to also achieve the same outcome.

If either or both policies can restore full employment and eliminate inflation, why does it matter which policy is used? It matters because the two policies have different side effects—different effects on other variables about which people care. These side effects arise because policy influences two key variables:

- The interest rate
- The exchange rate

Interest Rate Effects An expansionary fiscal policy *raises* the interest rate, while an expansionary monetary policy *lowers* the interest rate. When the interest rate changes, investment changes, so an expansionary fiscal policy lowers investment (crowding out) while an expansionary monetary policy increases investment. So if an expansionary fiscal policy increases

aggregate demand, consumption expenditure increases and investment decreases. But if an expansionary monetary policy increases aggregate demand, consumption expenditure and investment increase.

By coordinating fiscal policy and monetary policy and increasing aggregate demand with an appropriate combination of the two, it is possible to increase real GDP and lower unemployment with either no change in the interest rate or any desired change in the interest rate. A big dose of fiscal expansion and a small dose of monetary expansion raises the interest rate and decreases investment, while a small dose of fiscal expansion and a big dose of monetary expansion lowers the interest rate and increases investment.

The interest rate affects our long-term growth prospects because the growth rate of potential GDP depends on the level of investment. The connection between investment, capital, and economic growth is explained in Chapter 31.

Exchange Rate Effects An expansionary fiscal policy raises not only the interest rate but also the exchange rate. In contrast, an expansionary monetary policy *lowers* the exchange rate. When the exchange rate changes, net exports change. An expansionary fiscal policy lowers net exports (international crowding out) while an expansionary monetary policy increases net exports. So if full employment is restored by expansionary policy, net exports decrease with fiscal expansion and increase with monetary expansion.

Policy Conflict

Policy conflicts are not planned. But they sometimes happen. When they arise, it is usually because there is a divergence of the political priorities of the government and the objectives of the Bank of Canada.

Governments (both federal and provincial) pay a lot of attention to employment and production over a short time horizon. They look for policies that make their re-election chances high. The Bank of Canada pays a lot of attention to price level stability and has a long time horizon. It doesn't have an election to worry about.

So a situation might arise in which the government wants the Bank to pursue an expansionary monetary policy but the Bank wants to keep its foot on the monetary brake. The government says that an increase in the quantity of money is essential to lower interest rates and the exchange rate and to boost investment and exports. The Bank says that the problem is with fiscal policy. Spending is too high and revenues too low. With fiscal policy too expansionary, interest rates and the exchange rate are high and they cannot be lowered permanently by monetary policy. To lower interest rates and give investment and exports a boost, fiscal policy must become contractionary. Only then can an expansionary monetary policy be pursued.

A Policy Interaction Risk

In the standard analysis of policy interaction that we've studied in this chapter, the central bank targets the quantity of money and money market equilibrium determines the interest rate. But as you learned in Chapter 28, the Bank of Canada conducts monetary policy by targeting the overnight interest rate and money market equilibrium determines the quantity of money.

When a central bank targets the quantity of money, an expansionary fiscal policy action automatically raises the interest rate. It does so by increasing the demand for money. The higher interest rate moderates the effects of the expansionary fiscal policy. Aggregate demand increases and real GDP and the price level rise, but by less than they would if the interest rate were unchanged.

So when a central bank targets the interest rate rather than the quantity of money, an expansionary fiscal policy raises the interest rate only if the central bank takes an explicit action. If the central bank raises the interest rate by the amount that the market would have raised it with a given quantity of money, the outcome will be identical under the two alternative monetary policies.

But if the central bank is slow to change the interest rate, an expansionary fiscal policy might increase aggregate demand by too much. And if the central bank reacts to expansionary fiscal policy with a more aggressive increase in the interest rate, aggregate demand might increase by too little.

The key problem for monetary policy is to make a correct determination of the appropriate interest rate to accompany a change in fiscal policy. The problem is more acute at full employment than in a recession but it is a problem in either situation.

In a recession, if the central bank raises the interest rate too little and too late, an expansionary fiscal policy could overshoot full employment and create an inflationary gap. If the central bank raises the interest rate too much and too soon, an expansionary fiscal policy could undershoot full employment and leave an unwanted recessionary gap.

At full employment, if the central bank raises the interest rate too little and too late, an expansionary fiscal policy would create an inflationary gap that would bring faster inflation, a fall in the real interest rate and a further increase in the inflationary gap. A cumulative inflation would take hold until the central bank moved the interest rate high enough to eliminate the inflationary gap. And if at full employment the central bank raises the interest rate too much and too soon in response to an expansionary fiscal policy, real GDP would fall below full employment and a recessionary gap would emerge. The gap would persist until the central bank lowered the interest rate.

REVIEW QUIZ

1 What are the main things that can be achieved by coordinating fiscal policy and monetary policy?

2 What are the main sources of conflict in policy between the Bank of Canada and the government of Canada?

3 What are the main consequences of the government and the Bank of Canada pursuing conflicting policies? Are all the consequences bad?

myeconlab Study Plan 29.6

◆ You have now studied the interaction of fiscal policy and monetary policy. *Reading Between the Lines* on pp. 694–695 examines the views of David Dodge, governor of the Bank of Canada, on the appropriate roles for monetary policy and fiscal policy today.

You've seen that monetary and fiscal policies are alternative ways of changing aggregate demand and real GDP. But they have different effects on the interest rate and the exchange rate. You've seen what determines the relative effectiveness of fiscal and monetary policies and how the mix of these policies can influence the composition of aggregate expenditure. But you've also seen that the ultimate effects of these policies on real GDP and the price level depend not only on the behaviour of aggregate demand but also on aggregate supply and the state of the labour market.

We next turn to the aggregate supply side of the economy and learn about the factors that determine potential GDP and the economic growth rate.

READING BETWEEN THE LINES

Monetary and Fiscal Tensions

CALGARY HERALD, SEPTEMBER 4, 2002

Central bank boss warns against big spending

The head of the Bank of Canada has warned the Chrétien government against eroding the country's hard-earned anti-inflation credibility.

The not-so-veiled warning by governor David Dodge came amid rising speculation that the prime minister is about to go on a social policy spending spree in advance of his retirement in 18 months.

It also came on the eve of what many analysts expect will be another interest rate increase aimed at reducing the stimulus that is already in the economy. Earlier this year, the bank rate was the lowest in more than four decades.

In a speech to other central bankers in Jackson Hole, Wyo., last weekend Dodge stressed the importance of the credibility that the bank and government have earned with "joint agreements on inflation-control targets" and "a framework that greatly reduces the probability of running a fiscal deficit and thus puts the debt-to-GDP ratio on a clear downward track."

"Fiscal and monetary credibility is high," Dodge said, noting that markets, businesses and individuals "trust" that the central bank will meet its inflation target and that the government will not start spending more than it takes in.

"Initially, the credibility of these policies was not high," Dodge noted. "So it was essential to demonstrate clearly our resolve to achieve greater fiscal prudence and lower inflation until credibility was gained."

To do that, he said, it meant that the bank at times had to keep interest rates higher, and that the government had to keep a tighter rein on spending than otherwise necessary.

Dodge also said it was fortunate the government in its last budget did not inject a lot of new spending into the economy.

"I say fortunately because ... there was more underlying strength in the economy than we expected," Dodge explained.

He went on to note that the bank had already injected a lot of stimulus into the economy by cutting interest rates.

"Therefore, added fiscal stimulus was not necessary to get the economy going and the monetary stimulus provided is proving much easier to turn around."

Essence of the Story

■ In a speech at a conference of central bankers, Bank of Canada governor David Dodge said that the joint agreements on inflation-control targets between the Bank and government have created a high degree of trust that inflation targets will be met.

■ He warned against increasing government spending and said it was fortunate that in its last budget, the government did not inject a lot of new spending into the economy because the economy was already expanding strongly.

■ He noted that the Bank of Canada had injected a lot of stimulus into the economy by cutting interest rates and that added fiscal stimulus was neither necessary nor as easy to reverse as monetary policy actions.

Economic Analysis

■ Today, Canada's fiscal policy is not in conflict with monetary policy goals. But David Dodge's 2002 speech makes a timeless point.

■ The Governor of the Bank of Canada wants to maintain the Bank's credibility and keep the inflation rate close to 2 percent a year.

■ He thinks that macroeconomic stability —low inflation *and* full employment—is best achieved by using monetary policy alone and fears that if fiscal policy were to become expansionary, inflation would take off.

■ Figure 1 illustrates David Dodge's concern.

■ In Fig. 1, potential GDP is $1,084, but aggregate demand, AD_0, and short-run aggregate supply, SAS_0, intersect at a below full-employment equilibrium so there is a recessionary gap.

■ If to stimulate aggregate demand the Bank of Canada cuts the interest rate and at the same time the government increases its expenditure, the AD curve shifts rightward to AD_1.

■ These expansionary fiscal and monetary policies bring an inflationary gap.

■ With an inflationary gap, the money wage rate begins to rise and the SAS curve starts to shift leftward towards SAS_1.

■ Real GDP decreases towards potential GDP, but inflation takes off as the price level rises to 127.

■ Figure 2 shows what David Dodge would like to achieve.

■ With the same initial recessionary gap, the Bank of Canada takes action to stimulate aggregate demand by cutting the interest rate.

■ The government holds expenditure steady so that fiscal policy does not increase aggregate demand.

■ The AD curve shifts rightward to AD_2 and full employment is achieved while the inflation rate remains low.

■ If the Bank of Canada sees an inflationary gap, it can take quick action in the opposite direction—raise the interest rate—to decrease aggregate demand.

■ In contrast, if increased government spending brings an inflationary gap, it is difficult to cut spending.

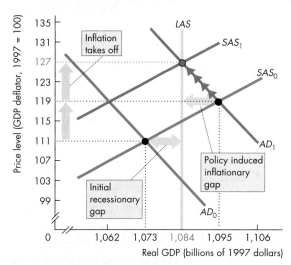

Figure 1 Fiscal and monetary stimulus

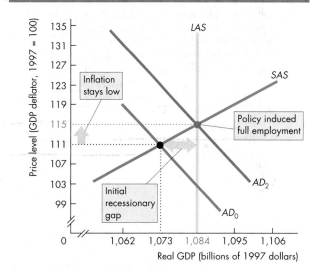

Figure 2 Monetary stimulus alone

You're the Voter

■ Do you agree with David Dodge that monetary policy alone is the appropriate tool for achieving low inflation and full employment?

■ Do you think there is ever a role for fiscal policy?

■ Would you vote for an expansionary fiscal policy today? Explain why or why not.

SUMMARY

KEY POINTS

Macroeconomic Equilibrium (pp. 678–679)

- Equilibrium real GDP, the price level, and the interest rate are determined simultaneously by money market equilibrium and *AS–AD* equilibrium.

Fiscal Policy in the Short Run (pp. 680–683)

- The first round effects of an expansionary fiscal policy are an increase in aggregate demand, an increasing real GDP, and a rising price level.
- The second round effects are an increasing demand for money and a decreasing quantity of real money that increase the interest rate and limit the increase in real GDP and the rise in the price level.
- Interest-sensitive expenditure, which includes investment and net exports, decreases.

Monetary Policy in the Short Run (pp. 684–687)

- The first round effects of an expansionary monetary policy are a fall in the interest rate, an increase in aggregate demand, an increasing real GDP, and a rising price level.
- The second round effects are an increasing demand for money and a decreasing quantity of real money that increase the interest rate and limit the increase in real GDP and the rise in the price level.
- Interest-sensitive expenditure, which includes investment and net exports, increases.

Relative Effectiveness of Policies (pp. 687–689)

- The relative effectiveness of fiscal and monetary policy depends on the interest-sensitivity of both expenditure and the quantity of money demanded.
- The extreme Keynesian position is that only fiscal policy affects aggregate demand. The extreme monetarist position is that only monetary policy affects aggregate demand. Neither extreme is correct.
- The mix of fiscal policy and monetary policy influences the composition of aggregate demand.

Policy Actions at Full Employment (pp. 690–691)

- An expansionary fiscal policy at full employment increases real GDP and the price level in the short run but increases only the price level in the long run. Complete crowding out of investment occurs or the international deficit increases.
- An expansionary monetary policy at full employment increases real GDP and the price level in the short run but increases only the price level in the long run. Money is neutral—has no real effects—in the long run.

Policy Coordination, Conflict, and Risk (pp. 692–693)

- Policy coordination can make changes in the interest rate and the exchange rate small.
- Policy conflict can avoid inflation in the face of a government deficit.

KEY FIGURES

KEY TERMS

PROBLEMS

Go to myeconlab for solutions to odd-numbered problems and additional exercises.

1. In the economy described in Fig. 29.1, suppose the government decreases its expenditures on goods and services.
   a. Work out the first round effects.
   b. Explain how real GDP and the interest rate change.
   c. Explain the second round effects that take the economy to a new equilibrium.

2. In the economy described in Fig. 29.1, suppose the government increases its expenditures on goods and services by $25 billion.
   a. Work out the first round effects.
   b. Explain how real GDP and the interest rate change.
   c. Explain the second round effects that take the economy to a new equilibrium.
   d. Compare the equilibrium in part (c) with the one described on pp. 680–682. In which case is the change in real GDP larger? In which case is the change in the interest rate larger? Why?

3. In the economy described in Fig. 29.1, suppose the Bank of Canada decreases the quantity of money.
   a. Work out the first round effects.
   b. Explain how real GDP and the interest rate change.
   c. Explain the second round effects that take the economy to a new equilibrium.

4. In the economy described in Fig. 29.1, suppose the Bank of Canada increases the quantity of money by $250 billion.
   a. Work out the first round effects.
   b. Explain how real GDP and the interest rate change.
   c. Explain the second round effects that take the economy to a new equilibrium.
   d. Compare the equilibrium in part (c) with the one described on pp. 684–686. In which case is the change in real GDP larger? In which case is the change in the interest rate larger? Why?

5. The economies of two countries, Alpha and Beta, are identical in every way except the following: in Alpha, a change in the interest rate of 1 percentage point (for example, from 5 percent to 6 percent) results in a $1 billion change in the quantity of real money demanded. In Beta, a change in the interest rate of 1 percentage point results in a $0.1 billion change in the quantity of real money demanded.
   a. In which economy does an increase in government expenditures on goods and services have a larger effect on real GDP?
   b. In which economy is the crowding-out effect weaker?
   c. In which economy does a change in the quantity of money have a larger effect on equilibrium real GDP?
   d. Which economy, if either, is closer to the Keynesian extreme and which is closer to the monetarist extreme?

6. The economies of two countries, Gamma and Delta, are identical except: In Gamma, a change in the interest rate of 1 percentage point (for example, from 5 percent to 6 percent) results in a $0.1 billion change in interest-sensitive expenditure. In Delta, a change in the interest rate of 1 percentage point results in a $10 billion change in interest-sensitive expenditure.
   a. In which economy does an increase in government expenditures on goods and services have a larger effect on real GDP?
   b. In which economy is the crowding-out effect weaker?
   c. In which economy does a change in the quantity of money have a larger effect on equilibrium real GDP?
   d. Which economy, if either, is closer to the Keynesian extreme and which is closer to the monetarist extreme?

7. The economy is in a recession and the government wants to increase aggregate demand, stimulate exports, and increase investment. It has three policy options: increase government expenditures on goods and services, decrease taxes, and increase the quantity of money.
   a. Explain the mechanisms at work under each alternative policy.
   b. What is the effect of each policy on the composition of aggregate demand?
   c. What are the short-run effects of each policy on real GDP and the price level?
   d. Which policy would you recommend that the government adopt? Why?

8. The economy has an inflationary gap and the government wants to decrease aggregate demand, cut exports, and decrease investment. It has three policy options: decrease government expenditures on goods and services, increase taxes, and decrease the quantity of money.

   a. Explain the mechanisms at work under each alternative policy.
   b. What is the effect of each policy on the composition of aggregate demand?
   c. What are the short-run effects of each policy on real GDP and the price level?
   d. Which policy would you recommend that the government adopt? Why?

9. The economy is at full employment, but the government is disappointed with the growth rate of real GDP. It wants to increase real GDP growth by stimulating investment. At the same time, it wants to avoid an increase in the price level.

   a. Suggest a combination of fiscal and monetary policies that will achieve the government's objective.
   b. Which policy would you recommend that the government adopt?
   c. Explain the mechanisms at work under your recommended policy.
   d. What is the effect of your recommended policy on the composition of aggregate demand?
   e. What are the short-run and long-run effects of your recommended policy on real GDP and the price level?

10. The economy is at full employment, and the government is worried that the growth rate of real GDP is too high because it is depleting the country's natural resources. The government wants to lower real GDP growth by lowering investment. At the same time it wants to avoid a fall in the price level.

    a. Suggest a combination of fiscal and monetary policies that will achieve the government's objective.
    b. Which policy would you recommend that the government adopt?
    c. Explain the mechanisms at work under your recommended policy.
    d. What is the effect of your recommended policy on the composition of aggregate demand?
    e. What are the short-run and long-run effects of your recommended policy on real GDP and the price level?

CRITICAL THINKING

1. Study *Reading Between the Lines* on pp. 694–695 and then answer the following questions:

   a. What does David Dodge think the government's fiscal policy should be?
   b. What are your predictions about the effects of a large increase in government expenditure on real GDP, the price level, interest rates, investment, the exchange rate, and net exports?
   c. What actions do you think that the Bank of Canada would need to take to ensure that an increase in government expenditure doesn't bring an increase in the inflation rate?
   d. What would happen if the Bank of Canada decided to raise interest rates at the same time that the government increased its expenditure? Explain the likely effects on real GDP, the price level, investment, the exchange rate, and net exports.

WEB EXERCISES

Use the links on myeconlab to work the following exercises.

1. Visit the Web sites of the Department of Finance, the Bank of Canada, and Statistics Canada to find information on the current condition of the Canadian economy and current fiscal and monetary policy. On the basis of the current state of the Canadian economy, and in light of what you now know about fiscal and monetary policy interaction, what do you predict would happen to real GDP and the price level

   a. If the Bank of Canada conducted an expansionary monetary policy?
   b. If the Bank of Canada conducted a contractionary monetary policy?
   c. If the government of Canada conducted an expansionary fiscal policy?
   d. If the government of Canada conducted a contractionary fiscal policy?
   e. If the Bank of Canada conducted an expansionary monetary policy and the government of Canada conducted a contractionary fiscal policy?
   f. If the Bank of Canada conducted a contractionary monetary policy and the government of Canada conducted an expansionary fiscal policy?

Money Chasing Goods

Aggregate demand fluctuations bring recessions and expansions. If aggregate demand expands more rapidly than long-run aggregate supply, we get inflation. So understanding the forces that determine aggregate demand helps us to understand both the business cycle and inflation.

It took economists a long time to achieve this knowledge, and we still don't know enough about aggregate demand to be able to forecast it more than a few months ahead. But we do know the basic factors that influence aggregate demand. And we know a lot about how those factors interact to send shock waves rippling through the economy.

Fundamentally, aggregate demand is a monetary phenomenon. The quantity of money is the single most significant influence on aggregate demand. This insight was first outlined more than 200 years ago by David Hume, a Scottish philosopher and close friend of Adam Smith. Said Hume, "In every Kingdom into which money begins to flow in greater abundance than formerly, everything takes a new face: labour and industry gain life; the merchant becomes more enterprising, the manufacturer more diligent and skilful, and even the farmer follows his plough with greater alacrity and attention." Milton Friedman and other economists known as monetarists also emphasize the central role of money. Money lies at the centre of Keynes' theory of aggregate demand as well. But Keynes also called attention to the power of independent changes in government expenditures, taxes, and business investment to influence aggregate demand.

In the modern world, we also recognize the effect of changes in exports on aggregate demand.

The chapters in this part explain the factors that influence aggregate demand and help you to understand how they interact to bring multiplier effects on aggregate expenditure. Chapter 23 explained the effects of changes in business investment and the multiplier effect they have on consumption expenditure and aggregate expenditure. Chapter 24 looked at fiscal policy and applied the model of Chapter 23 to study the effects of changes in government expenditures and taxes. Chapter 25 brought money into the picture and explained what money is, how banks create it, and how the interest rate is determined. Chapter 26 examined the foreign exchange market and the determination of the exchange rate between currencies. Chapter 27 explained inflation and showed how the trend in money growth determines the trend in inflation and how fluctuations in aggregate demand bring fluctuations in inflation, employment, and unemployment. Chapter 28 returned to the Bank of Canada and studied the way the Bank seeks to control inflation by targeting the overnight loans rate. Then, Chapter 29 examined the interactions of fiscal policy and monetary policy.

Many economists have developed the insights you've learned in these chapters. One of the truly outstanding ones is Milton Friedman, whom you can meet on the next page. You can also meet one of today's leading monetary economists, Michael Woodford of Princeton University.

Understanding Inflation

THE ECONOMIST

Milton Friedman *was born into a poor immigrant family in New York City in 1912. He was an undergraduate at Rutgers and graduate student at Columbia University during the Great Depression. Today, Professor Friedman is a Senior Fellow at the Hoover Institution at Stanford University. But his reputation was built between 1946 and 1983, when he was a leading member of the "Chicago School," an approach to economics developed at the University of Chicago and based on the views that free markets allocate resources efficiently and that stable and low money supply growth delivers macroeconomic stability.*

Friedman has advanced our understanding of the forces that determine aggregate demand and clarified the effects of the quantity of money. And for this work, he was awarded the (much overdue, in the opinion of his many admirers) 1977 Nobel Prize for Economic Science.

By reasoning from basic economic principles, Friedman predicted that persistent demand stimulation would not increase output but would cause inflation. When output growth slowed and inflation broke out in the 1970s, Friedman seemed like a prophet, and for a time, his policy prescription, known as monetarism, was embraced around the world.

700

THE ISSUES

The combination of history and economics has taught us a lot about the causes of inflation. Severe inflation—hyperinflation—arises from a breakdown of the normal fiscal policy processes at times of war or political upheaval. Tax revenues fall short of government spending, and newly printed money fills the gap between them. As inflation increases, the quantity of money that is needed to make payments increases, and a shortage of money can even result. So the rate of money growth increases yet further, and prices rise yet faster. Eventually, the monetary system collapses. Such was the experience of Germany during the 1920s and Brazil during the 1990s.

In earlier times, when commodities were used as money, inflation resulted from the discovery of new sources of money. The most recent occurrence of this type of inflation was at the end of the nineteenth century when gold, then used as money, was discovered in Australia, the Klondike, and South Africa.

In modern times, inflation has resulted from keeping the interest rate low so that increases in aggregate demand accommodate increases in costs. The most dramatic such inflations occurred during the 1970s when the Bank of Canada, the Federal Reserve, and other central banks around the world accommodated oil price increases.

To avoid inflation, the interest rate must be set high enough to keep the growth rate of money and aggregate demand in check. But at times of severe cost pressure, central banks feel a strong tug in the direction of avoiding recession and accommodating the cost pressure.

Yet in recent years, the central banks of most of the advanced economies have avoided inflation. They have done so by establishing inflation-control targets, a clearly explained and understood policy process, and a careful public reporting system. The Bank of Canada (along with the Bank of England, the European Central Bank, and the Reserve Banks of Australia and New Zealand) has been a leader in this move towards greater stablity, clarity, and accountability.

But there are risks in the monetary policy strategy favoured by central banks today. The inflation rate that they target is only loosely under their control. And when tested with a large enough shock, inflation could again break loose.

THEN

When inflation is especially rapid, as it was in Germany in 1923, money becomes almost worthless. In Germany at that time, bank notes were more valuable as fire kindling than as money, and the sight of people burning Reichmarks was a common one. To avoid having to hold money for too long, wages were paid and spent twice a day. Banks took deposits and made loans, but at interest rates that compensated both depositors and the bank for the falling value of money—interest rates that could exceed 100 percent a month. The price of a dinner would increase during the course of an evening, making lingering over coffee a very expensive pastime.

NOW

In 1994, Brazil had a computer-age hyperinflation, an inflation rate that was close to 50 percent a month. Banks installed ATMs on almost every street corner and refilled them several times an hour. Brazilians tried to avoid holding currency. As soon as they were paid, they went shopping and bought enough food to get them through to the next payday. Some shoppers filled as many as six carts on a single monthly trip to the supermarket. Also, instead of using currency, Brazilians used credit cards whenever possible. But they paid their card balances off quickly because the interest rate on unpaid balances was 50 percent a month. Only at such a high interest rate did it pay banks to lend to cardholders, because banks themselves were paying interest rates of 40 percent a month to induce depositors to keep their money in the bank.

Many economists today are working on aggregate demand and inflation. One distinguished contributor, whom you can meet on the following pages, is Michael Woodford of Princeton University.

701

Michael Woodford *is Harold H. Helm '20 Professor of Economics and Banking at Princeton University. Born in 1955 in Chicopee, Massachusetts, he was an undergraduate at the University of Chicago and a doctoral student at the Yale Law School before pursuing his doctorate in economics at the Massachusetts Institute of Technology. Professor Woodford's research on money and monetary policy has challenged much traditional thinking, and his ideas about a (future) world without money are attracting a great deal of interest. His advanced text,* Interest and Prices: Foundations of a Theory of Monetary Policy, *is published by Princeton University Press.*

Michael Parkin and Robin Bade talked with Michael Woodford about his work and the progress that economists have made in designing effective monetary policy rules.

Michael Woodford

Why, after completing law school, did you decide to become an economist?

Almost every class in law school was full of economic reasoning. I became fascinated by economic analysis, and thought that I would have to get a better foundation in economics in order to think clearly about legal issues. In the end I found that I liked economics enough to become an economist.

I am able to address questions of public policy, which is what had originally drawn me to law, but in a way that also allows me to indulge a taste for thinking about what the world might be like or should be like, and not simply the way that it already is.

In a world as rapidly changing as ours is, I think that the perspective provided by economics is essential for understanding which kinds of laws and rules make sense.

You are a supporter of rules for monetary policy. Why are rules so important?

In my view, rules are important not because central bankers can't be relied upon to take the public interest to heart, or because they don't know what they're doing, but because the effects of monetary policy depend critically upon what the private sector expects about future policy, and hence about the future course of the economy. Thus effective monetary policy depends more on the successful *management of expectations* than on any direct consequences of the current level of interest rates.

In order to steer people's expectations about future monetary policy in the way that it would like, a central bank needs to communicate details about how policy will be conducted in the future. The best way to do this is by being explicit about the rule that guides its decision making. The central bank also needs to establish a reputation for actually following the rule.

Following the rule means *not* always doing what might seem best in given current conditions. What is best for the economy now will be independent of what people may have expected in the past. But if the central bank doesn't feel bound to follow through on its prior commitments, people will learn that they don't mean anything. Then those commitments will not shape people's expectations in the desired way.

There is actually a strong parallel between monetary policy rules and the law, and the desirability of rules is an example of the perspective that I gained from the study of law. A judge doesn't simply seek to determine, in each individual case, what outcomes would do the most good, given the individual circumstances. Instead, the judge makes a decision based on rules established either by precedent or by statute. Because the law is rule-based, people are able to forecast more accurately the consequences of their contemplated actions.

A central banker is often portrayed as the captain of the economic ship, steering it skillfully between the rocks of inflation and unemployment in a choppy sea. But a ship's captain doesn't need to care about how the ocean will interpret his actions. So the parallel isn't a good one. In my view, the role of a central banker is more similar to that of a judge than to that of a ship's captain. Both central bankers and judges care enormously about the effects of their decisions on the expectations of people whose behaviour depends on expected future decisions.

> " *Following the rule means not always doing what might seem best in given current conditions.* "

The rule that you favour is different from that suggested by Milton Friedman. What is wrong with the Friedman rule?

Friedman's rule involves a target for the growth rate of some definition of the quantity of money. I don't think that the best monetary rule involves a target of any kind for the growth rate of a monetary aggregate. Friedman's rule is not the worst sort of rule, as simple rules go, but we can do better.

Just a century ago, no one had any idea how to establish a reasonably predictable monetary standard except by guaranteeing the convertibility of money into a precious metal such as gold. We didn't have the surprisingly modern concept of index numbers and today's routinely calculated price indexes like the CPI that enable us to measure, to a decent approximation, the purchasing power of the dollar.

We now understand that pegging the value of money to something like gold is a cruder solution to the problem than is necessary. We don't need to leave

the value of money hostage to the vagaries of the gold market simply in order to maintain confidence that a dollar means *something*.

Friedman recognizes the value of a well-managed fiat currency, but supposes that there is unlikely to be much predictability to the value of money unless the central bank is committed to a fixed target growth path for the quantity of money. But that again is a more indirect solution to the problem of maintaining a stable and predictable value for money than is necessary.

And there is a potentially large cost of such a crude approach when the relation between one's favourite monetary aggregate and the value of money shifts over time. A focus on stabilizing a monetary aggregate means less stability than would otherwise have been possible in the purchasing power of money.

So what would be a good monetary rule?

First, there should be a clearly defined target in terms of variables that policymakers actually care about, such as the inflation rate, rather than an "intermediate target" such as a monetary aggregate. Second, the central bank should be as clear as possible about the decision making process through which it determines the level of interest rates that is believed to be consistent with achieving the target.

"Inflation targeting," as currently practised in the United Kingdom, Canada, and New Zealand, is an example of the general approach that I would advocate. But I think that central banks of the inflation-targeting countries could do a better job of explaining the procedures used to determine the interest rate that is judged to be consistent with the inflation target—they could be more transparent.

And all of these countries could better explain to the public the ways in which variables other than inflation are also taken into consideration. I'm not sure that inflation targeting needs to be *stricter*, in the sense that considerations other than inflation should be more scrupulously ruled out. But I think that it is desirable to make it more of a *rule*.

One of the most intriguing issues that you've worked on is the question of what determines the price level in a "cashless economy." How would we control inflation in such a world?

One advantage of the approach to monetary policy that I've just mentioned is that the form of the policy rule that is appropriate need not change much at all if we were to progress to a "cashless economy." As long as the central bank can still control the overnight interest rate—the overnight loans rate in Canada—the *rule* for adjusting the interest rate need not change. Yet there might no longer be any meaning to a target path for a monetary aggregate in such a world.

The critical question is whether a central bank would still be able to control the overnight interest rate in such a world. Some argue that central banks only control interest rates in the interbank market for reserves because the private sector cannot supply a good substitute for reserves and the central bank is therefore a monopoly supplier. They then worry that if private substitutes for reserves were available, central banks would lose control of the interest rate.

But this line of reasoning assumes, as do most textbooks (even the good ones!), that central banks can change the interest rate *only* by changing the *opportunity cost* of holding reserves, which should only be possible in the presence of market power. But central banks can change the overnight interest rate *without* changing the opportunity cost of holding reserves. Indeed, the Bank of Canada already does so. It pays interest on reserves and maintains a fixed difference between the interest rate on reserves and the discount rate—the rate at which it stands willing to lend reserves to the banks. The overnight rate fluctuates inside the range of these two rates, so by changing the interest rate on reserves, the Bank of Canada controls the overnight rate but doesn't change the opportunity cost of holding reserves.

Every central bank, including the Federal Reserve, would have to adjust the interest rate in a way similar to this in a "cashless economy."

Where do you stand on the sources of aggregate fluctuations? Are they primarily an efficient response to the uneven pace of technical change, or are they primarily the consequence of market failure and demand fluctuations?

I don't think that they are primarily an *efficient* response to variations in technical progress or to other real disturbances of that kind. I think that there are important distortions that often result in *inefficient* responses of the economy to real disturbances, and this is why monetary policy matters. But I do think

that real disturbances are important—for example, I don't think that exogenous variations in monetary policy have been responsible for too much of the economic instability in the U.S. economy in recent decades—and I think that their supply-side effects are important, too.

The important issue, to my mind, is not whether the disturbances are thought to have more to do with supply or demand factors; it is whether the economy can be relied upon to respond efficiently to them, regardless of the nature of monetary policy. I don't think that that occurs automatically. The goal of good monetary policy is to bring about such a world: one in which monetary policy is not itself a source of disturbances, and in which the responses to real disturbances are efficient ones. The first part simply requires that monetary policy be systematic, but the second part depends upon the choice of a monetary policy rule of the right sort.

What advice do you have for a student who is just starting to study economics? Is it a good subject in which to major? What other subjects would you urge students to study alongside economics?

I think economics is an excellent major for students with many different interests. Most people who study economics are probably looking for an edge in the business world, and economics is valuable for that. But it's also all extremely valuable background for people interested in careers in law, government, or public policy. And of course, to some of us, the subject is interesting in its own right. I find that the challenges just get deeper the farther I get into the subject.

Probably the most important other subject for someone thinking of actually becoming an economist is mathematics. This is often the determining factor as to how well a student will do in graduate study, because the research literature is a good deal more mathematical than many people suspect from their undergraduate economics courses. But economics is not a branch of mathematics. It's a subject that seeks to understand people and social institutions, and so all sorts of other subjects—history, politics, sociology, psychology, moral and political philosophy—are useful background for an economist, too. I don't at all regret the amount of time I spent in liberal arts courses as an undergraduate.

The Economy at Full Employment

Production and Jobs

Over time, we become more productive and our incomes grow. For each hour we worked in 2004, we earned twice what we earned in 1964. What makes production and incomes grow? Why did productivity grow during a recession?

Our population also grows every year. How does population size influence employment, wage rates, and potential GDP?

We hear a lot about the need to increase our national saving to invest in new capital, the importance of education, and the need to support science and technology. How do capital accumulation, education, and advances in technology influence employment, wage rates, and potential GDP?

You know that when we talk about full employment, we don't mean there is no unemployment. But what determines the amount of unemployment when the economy is at full employment?

◆ We'll answer these questions in this chapter. We'll discover how changes in population, capital, and technology influence production, jobs, and incomes over long periods of time. We'll learn about the forces that create unemployment when the economy is at full employment. And in *Reading Between the Lines* at the end of this chapter, we'll compare productivity in Canada with that in the United States.

After studying this chapter, you will be able to

- ■ **Describe the relationship between the quantity of labour employed and real GDP**

- ■ **Explain what determines the demand for labour and the supply of labour and how labour market equilibrium determines employment, the real wage rate, and potential GDP**

- ■ **Explain how an increase in the population, an increase in capital, and an advance in technology change employment, the real wage rate, and potential GDP**

- ■ **Explain what determines unemployment when the economy is at full employment**

Real GDP and Employment

TO PRODUCE MORE OUTPUT, WE MUST USE MORE inputs. We can increase real GDP by employing more labour, increasing the quantity of capital, or developing technologies that are more productive. In the short term, the quantity of capital and the state of technology are fixed. So to increase real GDP in the short term, we must increase the quantity of labour employed. Let's look at the relationship between real GDP and the quantity of labour employed.

Production Possibilities

When you studied the limits to production in Chapter 2 (see p. 34), you learned about the *production possibilities frontier*, which is the boundary between those combinations of goods and services that can be produced and those that cannot. We can think about the production possibilities frontier for any pair of goods or services when we hold the quantities of all other goods and services constant. Let's think about the production possibilities frontier for two special items: real GDP and leisure time.

Real GDP is a measure of the final goods and services produced in the economy in a given time period valued at constant prices. We measure real GDP as a number of 1997 dollars, but the measure is a *real* one. Real GDP is not a pile of dollars. It is a pile of goods and services. Think of it as a number of big shopping carts filled with goods and services. Each cart contains some of each kind of different goods and services produced, and one cartload of items costs $100 billion. To say that real GDP is $1,000 billion means that real GDP is 10 very big shopping carts of goods and services.

The quantity of leisure time is the number of hours we spend not working. It is the time we spend playing or watching sports, seeing movies, and hanging out with friends. Leisure time is a special type of good or service.

Each hour that we spent pursuing fun could have been an hour that we spent working. So when the quantity of leisure time increases by one hour, the quantity of labour employed decreases by one hour. If we spent all our time having fun rather than working, we would not produce anything. Real GDP would be zero. The more leisure time we forgo to work, the greater is the quantity of labour employed and the greater is real GDP.

The relationship between leisure time and real GDP is a *production possibilities frontier* (*PPF*). Figure 30.1(a) shows an example of this frontier. The economy has 45 billion hours of leisure time available. If people use all these hours to pursue leisure, no labour is employed and real GDP is zero. As people forgo leisure and work more, real GDP increases. If people spent 20 billion hours working and took 25 billion hours in leisure, real GDP would be $1,000 billion at point *A*. If people spent all the available hours working, real GDP would be $1,500 billion.

The bowed-out *PPF* displays increasing opportunity cost. The opportunity cost of a given amount of real GDP is the amount of leisure time forgone to produce it. As real GDP increases, each additional unit of real GDP costs an increasing amount of forgone leisure. The reason is that we use the most productive labour first, and as we use more labour, we use increasingly less productive labour.

The Production Function

The **production function** is the relationship between real GDP and the quantity of labour employed when all other influences on production remain the same: It shows how real GDP varies as the quantity of labour employed varies.

Because one more hour of labour employed means one less hour of leisure, the production function is like a mirror image of the leisure time–real GDP *PPF*. Figure 30.1(b) shows the production function (*PF*) for the economy whose *PPF* is shown in Fig. 30.1(a). You can see that when the quantity of labour employed is zero, real GDP is also zero. And as the quantity of labour employed increases, so does real GDP. When 20 billion labour hours are employed, real GDP is $1,000 billion (at point *A*).

A decrease in leisure hours and the corresponding increases in the quantity of labour employed and real GDP bring a movement along the production possibilities frontier and along the production function. The arrows along the *PPF* and the *PF* in Fig. 30.1 show these movements. Such movements occurred when employment and real GDP surged during World War II.

But the increase in real GDP during World War II changed for an additional reason. Labour became more productive. Let's study the influences on the productivity of labour.

FIGURE 30.1

myeconlab

Production Possibilities and the Production Function

(a) Production possibility frontier

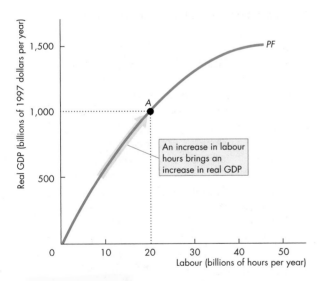

(b) Production function

On the production possibilities frontier in part (a), if we enjoy 45 billion hours of leisure, we produce no real GDP. If we forgo 20 billion hours of leisure time to work and spend 25 billion hours of leisure time, we produce a real GDP of $1,000 billion, at point A. At point A on the production function in part (b), we use 20 billion hours of labour to produce $1,000 billion of real GDP.

Changes in Productivity

When we talk about *productivity*, we usually mean labour productivity. **Labour productivity** is real GDP per hour of labour. Three factors influence labour productivity:

- Physical capital
- Human capital
- Technology

Physical Capital A farm worker equipped with only a stick and primitive tools can cultivate almost no land and grow barely enough food to feed a single family. A farmer equipped with a steel plow pulled by an animal can cultivate more land and produce enough food to feed a small village. A farmer equipped with a modern tractor, plow, and harvester can cultivate thousands of hectares and produce enough food to feed hundreds of people.

By using physical capital on our farms and in our factories, shops, and offices, we get an enormous increase labour productivity. And the more physical capital we use, the greater is labour productivity, other things remaining the same.

Human Capital An economy's **human capital** is the knowledge and skill that people have obtained from education and on-the-job training.

The average university graduate has a greater amount of human capital than the average high school graduate possesses. Consequently, the university graduate is able to perform some tasks that are beyond the ability of the high school graduate. The university graduate is more productive. For the nation as a whole, the greater the amount of schooling its citizens complete, the greater is its real GDP, other things remaining the same.

Regardless of how much schooling a person has completed, not much production is accomplished on the first day at work. Learning about the new work environment consumes the newly hired worker. But as time passes and experience accumulates, the worker becomes more productive. We call this on-the-job education activity **learning-by-doing**.

Learning-by-doing increases labour productivity. The more experienced the labour force, the greater is its labour productivity, and other things remaining the same, the greater is real GDP.

World War II provides a carefully documented example of the importance of this source of increase in labour productivity. In the shipyards that produced the transport vessels called Liberty ships, labour productivity increased by an astonishing 30 percent purely as a result of learning-by-doing.

Technology A student equipped with a pen can complete a readable page of writing in perhaps 10 minutes. This same task takes 5 minutes with a typewriter and 2 minutes with a computer. Travelling on foot from Toronto to Vancouver takes a person (a fit person!) more than 100 days. In a car, the trip takes a comfortable 5 days. And in an airplane, the trip takes 5 hours. These are examples of the impact of technology on productivity. Imagine the profound effect of these advances in technology on the productivity of a movie director who works in Toronto and Vancouver!

Shifts in the Production Function

Any influence on production that increases labour productivity shifts the production function upward. Real GDP increases at each level of labour hours. In Fig. 30.2(a), the production function is initially PF_0. Then an increase in physical capital and human capital or an advance in technology occurs. The production function shifts upward to PF_1.

At each quantity of labour employed, real GDP is greater on the new production function than it was on the original one. For example, at 20 billion hours, real GDP increases from $1,000 billion (point A) to $1,100 billion (point B).

Figure 30.2(b) shows how the production function in Canada shifted upward between 1980 and 2004. Along the production function PF_{04}, labour productivity is 60 percent greater than that on PF_{80}—an increase of 1.9 percent a year.

FIGURE 30.2
An Increase in Labour Productivity

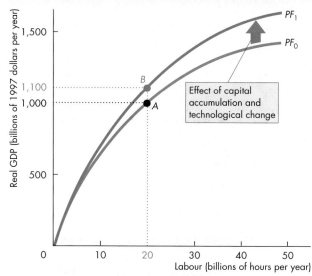

(a) An increase in labour productivity

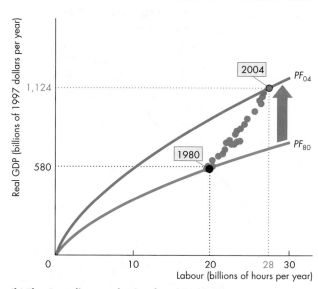

(b) The Canadian production function

On PF_0 in part (a), 20 billion labour hours produce a real GDP of $1,000 billion (point A). An increase in capital or an advance in technology shifts the production function upward to PF_1. Now, 20 billion labour hours produce a real GDP of $1,100 billion (point B). Canadian real GDP has increased (part b) because labour has become more productive and the quantity of labour has increased.

REVIEW QUIZ

1 What is the relationship between the leisure hours–real GDP *PPF* and the production function?

2 What does the outward-bowed shape of the leisure hours–real GDP *PPF* imply about the opportunity cost of real GDP and why is the *PPF* bowed outward?

3 Why does the production function shift upward when capital increases and/or technology advances?

myeconlab **Study Plan 30.1**

The Labour Market and Aggregate Supply

YOU'VE SEEN THAT IN A GIVEN YEAR, WITH A given amount of physical and human capital and given technology, real GDP depends on the quantity of labour hours employed. To produce more real GDP, we must employ more labour hours. The labour market determines the quantity of labour hours employed. We'll learn how by studying

- The demand for labour
- The supply of labour
- Labour market equilibrium

The Demand for Labour

The **quantity of labour demanded** is the number of labour hours hired by all the firms in the economy. The **demand for labour** is the relationship between the quantity of labour demanded and the real wage rate when all other influences on firms' hiring plans remain the same. The **real wage rate** is the quantity of goods and services that an hour of labour earns. In contrast, the **money wage rate** is the number of dollars that an hour of labour earns. A real wage rate is equal to a money wage rate divided by the price of a good. For the economy as a whole, the average real wage rate equals the average money wage rate divided by the price level. So we express the real wage rate in constant dollars. (Today, we express this real wage rate in 1997 dollars.)

The *real* wage rate influences the quantity of labour demanded because what matters to firms is how much output they must sell to earn the number of dollars they pay for labour (the money wage rate).

We can represent the demand for labour as either a demand schedule or a demand curve. The table in Fig. 30.3 shows part of a demand for labour schedule. It tells us the quantity of labour demanded at three different real wage rates. For example, if the real wage rate falls from $40 an hour to $35 an hour, the quantity of labour demanded increases from 15 billion hours a year to 20 billion hours a year. (You can find these numbers in rows *A* and *B* of the table.) The demand for labour curve is *LD*. Points *A*, *B*, and *C* on the curve correspond to rows *A*, *B*, and *C* of the demand schedule.

Why does the quantity of labour demanded *increase* as the real wage rate *decreases*? That is, why

does the demand for labour curve slope downward? To answer these questions, we must learn about the marginal product of labour.

The Marginal Product of Labour The **marginal product of labour** is the additional real GDP produced by an additional hour of labour when all other influences on production remain the same. The marginal product of labour is governed by the **law of diminishing returns**, which states that as the quantity of labour increases, other things remaining the same, the marginal product of labour decreases.

FIGURE 30.3
The Demand for Labour

	Real wage rate (1997 dollars per hour)	Quantity of labour demanded (billions of hours per year)
A	40	15
B	35	20
C	30	25

The table shows part of a demand for labour schedule. Points A, B, and C on the demand for labour curve correspond to the rows of the table. The lower the real wage rate, the greater is the quantity of labour demanded.

The Law of Diminishing Returns Diminishing returns arise because the amount of capital is fixed. Two people operating one machine are not twice as productive as one person operating one machine. Eventually, as more labour hours are hired, workers get in each other's way and output barely increases.

Marginal Product Calculation We calculate the marginal product of labour as the change in real GDP divided by the change in the quantity of labour employed. Figure 30.4(a) shows some calculations, and Fig. 30.4(b) shows the marginal product curve.

In Fig. 30.4(a), when the quantity of labour employed increases from 10 billion hours to 20 billion hours, an increase of 10 billion hours, real GDP increases from $600 billion to $1,000 billion, an increase of $400 billion. The marginal product of labour equals the increase in real GDP ($400 billion) divided by the increase in the quantity of labour employed (10 billion hours), which is $40 an hour.

When the quantity of labour employed increases from 20 billion hours to 30 billion hours, an increase of 10 billion hours, real GDP increases from $1,000 billion to $1,300 billion, an increase of $300 billion. The marginal product of labour equals $300 billion divided by 10 billion hours, which is $30 an hour.

In Fig. 30.4(b), as the quantity of labour employed increases, the marginal product of labour diminishes. Between 10 billion and 20 billion hours (at 15 billion hours), marginal product is $40 an hour. And between 20 billion and 30 billion hours (at 25 billion hours), marginal product is $30 an hour.

Diminishing Marginal Product and the Demand for Labour Firms are in business to maximize profits. Each hour of labour that a firm hires increases output and adds to costs. Initially, an extra hour of labour produces more output than the real wage that the labour costs. Marginal product exceeds the real wage rate. But each additional hour of labour produces less additional output than the previous hour—the marginal product of labour diminishes.

As a firm hires more labour, eventually the extra output from an extra hour of labour is exactly what that hour of labour costs. At this point, marginal product equals the real wage rate. Hire one less hour and marginal product exceeds the real wage rate. Hire one more hour and the real wage rate exceeds marginal product. In either case, profit is less.

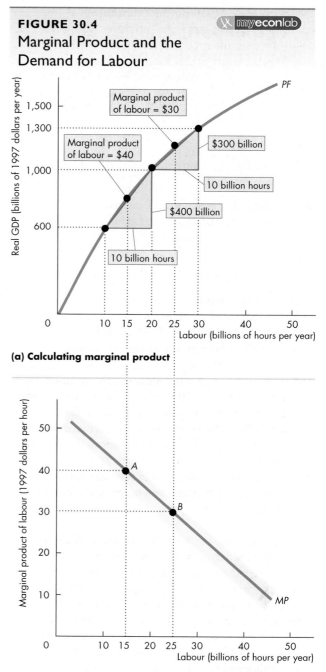

FIGURE 30.4

Marginal Product and the Demand for Labour

(a) Calculating marginal product

(b) The marginal product curve

In part (a), between 10 billion and 20 billion hours, the marginal product of labour is $40 an hour. Between 20 billion and 30 billion hours, the marginal product of labour is $30 an hour. In part (b), at 15 billion hours (midway between 10 billion and 20 billion), the marginal product of labour is $40 an hour at point A on the MP curve. The MP curve is the demand for labour curve.

Because marginal product diminishes as the quantity of labour employed increases, the lower the real wage rate, the greater is the quantity of labour that a firm can profitably hire. The marginal product curve is the same as the demand for labour curve.

You might gain a clearer understanding of the demand for labour by looking at an example.

Demand for Labour in a Ketchup Factory

Suppose that when a ketchup factory employs one additional hour of labour, output increases by 11 bottles. Marginal product is 11 bottles an hour. If the money wage rate is $5.50 an hour and ketchup sells for 50¢ a bottle, the real wage rate is 11 bottles an hour. (We calculate the factory's real wage rate as the money wage rate of $5.50 an hour divided by a price of 50¢ a bottle, which equals a real wage rate of 11 bottles an hour.) Because marginal product diminishes, we know that if the firm did not hire this hour of labour, marginal product would exceed 11 bottles. Because the firm can hire the hour of labour for a real wage rate of 11 bottles, it just pays it to do so.

If the price of ketchup remains at 50¢ a bottle and the money wage rate falls to $5.00 an hour, the real wage rate falls to 10 bottles an hour and the firm increases the quantity of labour demanded.

Similarly, if the money wage rate remains at $5.50 an hour and the price of ketchup rises to 55¢ a bottle, the real wage rate falls to 10 bottles an hour and the firm increases the quantity of labour demanded.

When the firm pays a real wage rate equal to the marginal product of labour, it is maximizing profit.

Changes in the Demand for Labour When the marginal product of labour changes, the demand for labour changes and the demand for labour curve shifts. You've seen that an increase in capital (both physical and human) and an advance in technology that increases labour productivity shift the production function upward. These same forces increase the demand for labour and shift the demand for labour curve rightward.

The Supply of Labour

The **quantity of labour supplied** is the number of labour hours that all the households in the economy plan to work. The **supply of labour** is the relationship between the quantity of labour supplied and the real wage rate when all other influences on work plans remain the same.

We can represent the supply of labour as either a supply schedule or a supply curve. The table in Fig. 30.5 shows a supply of labour schedule. It tells us the quantity of labour supplied at three different real wage rates. For example, if the real wage rate rises from $15 an hour (row *A*) to $35 an hour (row *B*), the quantity of labour supplied increases from 15 billion hours a year to 20 billion hours a year. The curve *LS* is a supply of labour curve. Points *A*, *B*, and *C* on the curve correspond to rows *A*, *B*, and *C* of the supply schedule.

The *real* wage rate influences the quantity of labour supplied because what matters to people is not the number of dollars they earn (the money wage rate) but what those dollars will buy.

FIGURE 30.5
The Supply of Labour

	Real wage rate (1997 dollars per hour)	Quantity of labour supplied (billions of hours per year)
A	15	15
B	35	20
C	55	25

The table shows part of a supply of labour schedule. Points A, B, and C on the supply of labour curve correspond to the rows of the table. The higher the real wage rate, the greater is the quantity of labour supplied.

The quantity of labour supplied increases as the real wage rate increases for two reasons:

- Hours per person increase
- Labour force participation increases

Hours per Person In choosing how many hours to work, a household considers the opportunity cost of not working. This opportunity cost is the real wage rate. The higher the real wage rate, the greater is the opportunity cost of taking leisure and not working. And as the opportunity cost of taking leisure rises, the more the household chooses to work, other things remaining the same.

But other things don't remain the same. The higher the real wage rate, the greater is the household's income. And the higher the household's income, the more it wants to consume. One item that it wants to consume more of is leisure.

So a rise in the real wage rate has two opposing effects. By increasing the opportunity cost of leisure, it makes the household want to consume less leisure and to work more. And by increasing the household's income, it makes the household want to consume more leisure and to work fewer hours. For most households, the opportunity cost effect is stronger than the income effect. So the higher the real wage rate, the greater is the amount of work that the household chooses to do.

Labour Force Participation Some people have productive opportunities outside the labour force. These people choose to work only if the real wage rate exceeds the value of these other productive activities. For example, a parent might spend time caring for her or his child. The alternative is day care. The parent will choose to work only if he or she can earn enough per hour to pay the cost of child care and have enough left to make the work effort worthwhile. The higher the real wage rate, the more likely it is that a parent will choose to work and so the greater is the labour force participation rate.

Labour Supply Response The quantity of labour supplied increases as the real wage rate rises. But the quantity of labour supplied is not highly responsive to the real wage rate. A large percentage change in the real wage rate brings a small percentage change in the quantity of labour supplied.

Let's now see how the labour market determines employment and the real wage rate.

Labour Market Equilibrium

The forces of supply and demand operate in labour markets just as they do in the markets for goods and services. The price of labour is the real wage rate. A rise in the real wage rate eliminates a shortage of labour by decreasing the quantity demanded and increasing the quantity supplied. A fall in the real wage rate eliminates a surplus of labour by increasing the quantity demanded and decreasing the quantity supplied. If there is neither a shortage nor a surplus, the labour market is in equilibrium.

In macroeconomics, we study the economy-wide labour market to determine the total quantity of labour employed and the average real wage rate.

Figure 30.6(a) shows a labour market in equilibrium. The demand curve *LD* and the supply curve *LS* are the same as those in Fig. 30.3 and Fig. 30.5, respectively.

If the real wage rate exceeds $35 an hour, the quantity of labour supplied exceeds the quantity demanded and there is a surplus of labour. In this situation, the real wage rate falls.

If the real wage rate is less than $35 an hour, the quantity of labour demanded exceeds the quantity supplied and there is a shortage of labour. In this situation, the real wage rate rises.

If the real wage rate is $35 an hour, the quantity of labour demanded equals the quantity supplied and there is neither a shortage nor a surplus of labour. The labour market is in equilibrium, the real wage rate remains constant, and the equilibrium quantity of labour is 20 billion hours a year. This labour market equilibrium is a *full-employment equilibrium*. The full-employment real wage rate is $35 an hour and the full-employment quantity of labour is 20 billion hours a year.

Potential GDP

You've seen that the production function tells us how much real GDP a given amount of employment can produce. When the economy is at full employment, real GDP produced is potential GDP. So the full-employment quantity of labour produces potential GDP.

Figure 30.6(b) shows potential GDP. The full-employment quantity of labour in Fig. 30.6(a) is 20 billion hours. The production function in Fig. 30.6(b) tells us that 20 billion hours of labour can produce a real GDP of $1,000 billion. This amount is potential GDP.

FIGURE 30.6

The Labour Market and Potential GDP

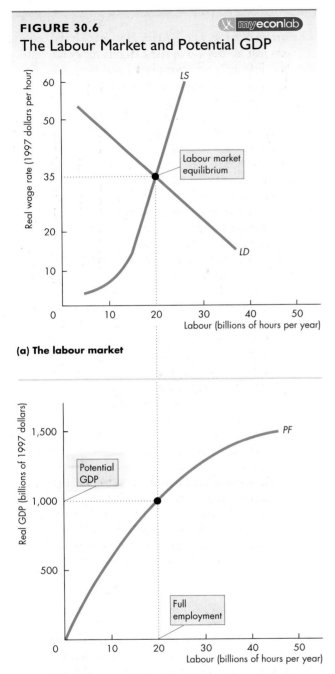

(a) The labour market

(b) Potential GDP

The economy is at full employment in part (a) when the quantity of labour demanded equals the quantity of labour supplied. The real wage rate is $35 an hour, and 20 billion labour hours are employed. In part (b), potential GDP is the quantity of real GDP determined by the production function and the full-employment quantity of labour.

Aggregate Supply

The **long-run aggregate supply curve** is the relationship between the quantity of real GDP supplied and the price level when real GDP equals potential GDP. Figure 30.7 shows this relationship as the vertical *LAS* curve. Along the long-run aggregate supply curve, as the price level changes, the money wage rate also changes to keep the real wage rate at the full-employment equilibrium level in Fig. 30.6(a). With no change in the real wage rate and no change in employment, real GDP remains at potential GDP.

The **short-run aggregate supply curve** is the relationship between the quantity of real GDP supplied and the price level when the money wage rate and potential GDP remain constant. Figure 30.7 shows a short-run aggregate supply curve as the upward-sloping *SAS* curve. Along the short-run aggregate supply curve, as the price level rises, the money wage rate remains fixed, so the real wage rate *falls*. In Fig. 30.6,

FIGURE 30.7

The Aggregate Supply Curves

When the price level and the money wage rate change by the same percentage, the real wage rate and the quantity of real GDP supplied are constant. There is a movement along the *LAS* curve. When the price level changes with no change in the money wage rate, the real wage rate changes and employment and the quantity of real GDP supplied change. There is a movement along the *SAS* curve.

when the real wage rate falls, the quantity of labour demanded increases and real GDP increases.

When the economy is at a point on the *SAS* curve and real GDP is above potential GDP, the real wage rate is below the full-employment equilibrium level. And when the economy is at a point on the *SAS* curve and real GDP is below potential GDP, the real wage rate is above the full-employment equilibrium level. In both cases, the quantity of labour that firms employ departs from the quantity that households would like to supply.

Production is efficient in the sense that the economy operates on its production possibilities frontier. But production is inefficient in the sense that the economy operates at the wrong point on the frontier. When the real wage rate is below the full-employment equilibrium, people do too much work and produce too much real GDP. When the real wage rate is above the full-employment equilibrium, people do too little work and produce too little real GDP.

When the real wage rate departs from its full-employment equilibrium level, the resulting shortage or surplus of labour brings market forces into play that move the real wage rate and quantity of labour employed back towards their full-employment levels.

The appendix on pp. 724–729 explains in detail how to derive the *LAS* and *SAS* curves.

REVIEW QUIZ

1 Why does a rise in the real wage rate bring a decrease in the quantity of labour demanded, other things remaining the same?

2 Why does a rise in the real wage rate bring an increase in the quantity of labour supplied, other things remaining the same?

3 What happens in the labour market if the real wage rate is above or below the full-employment level?

4 How is potential GDP determined?

5 What is the relationship between full-employment equilibrium in the labour market and long-run aggregate supply?

6 What is the relationship between the labour market and short-run aggregate supply?

myeconlab   **Study Plan 30.2**

Let's now look at *changes* in full-employment equilibrium and potential GDP.

Changes in Potential GDP

REAL GDP WILL INCREASE IF

1. The economy recovers from recession.
2. Potential GDP increases.

Recovery from recession means that the economy moves along the real GDP–leisure *PPF* from a point at which real GDP and employment are too low relative to the full-employment equilibrium point. Equivalently, the economy moves along the short-run aggregate supply curve. Economists have a lot to say about such a move and Chapter 22 explains this type of short-term change in real GDP.

Increasing *potential* GDP means expanding production possibilities. We're going to study the expansion of production possibilities in two steps. First, we look at the factors that change potential GDP. Then, in Chapter 31, we study the process and pace of economic growth.

Potential GDP increases following:

■ An increase in population
■ An increase in labour productivity

An Increase in Population

As the population increases and the additional people reach working age, the supply of labour increases. With more labour available, the economy's production possibilities expand. But does the expansion of production possibilities mean that potential GDP increases? And does it mean that potential GDP *per person* increases?

The answers to these questions have intrigued economists for many years. And they cause heated political debate today. In China, for example, families are under enormous pressure to limit the number of children they have. In some other countries, such as France, the government encourages large families.

We can study the effects of an increase in population by using the model of the full-employment economy in Fig. 30.8. In Fig. 30.8(a), the demand for labour is *LD* and initially the supply of labour is *LS*$_0$. At full employment, the real wage rate is $35 an hour and the level of employment is 20 billion hours a year. In Fig. 30.8(b), the production function (*PF*) shows that with 20 billion hours of labour employed, potential GDP is $1,000 billion.

FIGURE 30.8 myeconlab

The Effects of an Increase in Population

(a) The labour market

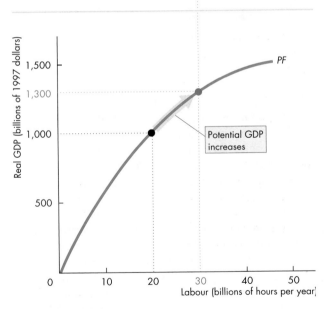

(b) Potential GDP

An increase in population increases the supply of labour. In part (a), the real wage rate falls, and the full-employment quantity of labour increases. In part (b), the increase in full employment increases potential GDP. Because the marginal product of labour diminishes, the increased population increases potential GDP but potential GDP per hour of work decreases.

An increase in the population increases the number of people of working age, and the supply of labour increases. The labour supply curve shifts rightward to LS_1. At a real wage rate of $35 an hour, there is now a surplus of labour. So the real wage rate falls. In this example, it falls until it reaches $25 an hour. At $25 an hour, the quantity of labour demanded equals the quantity of labour supplied. Equilibrium employment increases to 30 billion hours a year.

Figure 30.8(b) shows the effect of the increase in equilibrium employment on real GDP. As the full-employment quantity of labour increases from 20 billion hours to 30 billion hours, potential GDP increases from $1,000 billion to $1,300 billion.

So at full employment, an increase in population increases full employment, increases potential GDP, and lowers the real wage rate.

An increase in population also decreases potential GDP per hour of work. You can see this decrease by dividing potential GDP by total labour hours. Initially, with potential GDP at $1,000 billion and labour hours at 20 billion, potential GDP per hour of work was $50. With the increase in population, potential GDP is $1,300 billion and labour hours are 30 billion. Potential GDP per hour of work is $43.33. Diminishing returns are the source of the decrease in potential GDP per hour of work.

You've seen that an increase in population increases potential GDP and decreases potential GDP per work hour. Some people challenge this conclusion and argue that people are the ultimate economic resource. They claim that a larger population brings forth a greater amount of scientific discovery and technological advance. Consequently, they argue that an increase in population never takes place in isolation. It is always accompanied by an increase in labour productivity. Let's now look at the effects of this influence on potential GDP.

An Increase in Labour Productivity

We've seen that three factors increase labour productivity:

■ An increase in physical capital
■ An increase in human capital
■ An advance in technology

Saving and investment increase the quantity of physical capital over time. Education and on-the-job training and experience increase human capital.

Research and development efforts bring advances in technology. In Chapter 31, we study how all these forces interact to determine the growth rate of potential GDP.

Here, we study the *effects* of an increase in physical capital, an increase in human capital, or an advance in technology on the labour market and potential GDP. We'll see how potential GDP, employment, and the real wage rate change when any of these three influences on labour productivity changes.

An Increase in Physical Capital If the quantity of physical capital increases, labour productivity increases. With labour being more productive, the economy's production possibilities expand. How does such an expansion of production possibilities change the real wage rate, employment, and potential GDP?

The additional capital increases the real GDP that each quantity of labour can produce. It also increases the marginal product of labour and so increases the demand for labour. Some physical capital replaces some types of labour, so the demand for those types of labour decreases when capital increases. But an increase in physical capital creates a demand for the types of labour that build, sell, and maintain the additional capital. The increases in demand for labour are always larger than the decreases in demand, and the economy-wide demand for labour increases.

With an increase in the economy-wide demand for labour, the real wage rate rises and the quantity of labour supplied increases. Equilibrium employment increases.

Potential GDP now increases for two reasons. First, a given level of employment produces more real GDP. Second, full employment increases.

An Increase in Human Capital If the quantity of human capital increases, labour productivity increases. Again, with labour being more productive, the economy's production possibilities expand. And this expansion of production possibilities changes the equilibrium real wage rate, full employment, and potential GDP in a similar manner to the effects of a change in physical capital.

An Advance in Technology As technology advances, labour productivity increases. And exactly as in the case of an increase in capital, the economy's production possibilities expand. Again, just as in the case of

an increase in capital, the new technology increases the real GDP that each quantity of labour can produce and increases the marginal product of labour and the demand for labour.

With an increase in the demand for labour, the real wage rate rises, the quantity of labour supplied increases, and equilibrium employment increases. And again, potential GDP increases because a given level of employment produces more real GDP and because full employment increases.

Illustrating the Effects of an Increase in Labour Productivity Figure 30.9 shows the effects of an increase in labour productivity that results from an increase in capital or an advance in technology. In part (a), the demand for labour initially is LD_0 and the supply of labour is LS. The real wage rate is $35 an hour, and full employment is 20 billion hours a year.

In part (b), the production function initially is PF_0. With 20 billion hours of labour employed, potential GDP is $1,000 billion.

Now an increase in capital or an advance in technology increases labour productivity. In Fig. 30.9(a), the demand for labour increases and the demand curve shifts rightward to LD_1. In Fig. 30.9(b), labour productivity increases and the production function shifts upward to PF_1.

In Fig. 30.9(a), at the original real wage rate of $35 an hour, there is now a shortage of labour. So the real wage rate rises. In this example, it keeps rising until it reaches $45 an hour. At $45 an hour, the quantity of labour demanded equals the quantity of labour supplied and full employment increases to 22.5 billion hours a year.

Figure 30.9(b) shows the effects of the increase in full employment combined with the new production function on potential GDP. As full employment increases from 20 billion hours to 22.5 billion hours, potential GDP increases from $1,000 billion to $1,500 billion.

Potential GDP per hour of work also increases. You can see this increase by dividing potential GDP by total labour hours. Initially, with potential GDP at $1,000 billion and labour hours at 20 billion, potential GDP per hour of work was $50. With the increase in labour productivity, potential GDP is $1,500 billion and labour hours are 22.5 billion, so potential GDP per hour of work is $66.67.

Let's use what you've just learned to examine an episode in the life of the Canadian economy.

FIGURE 30.9

The Effects of an Increase in Labour Productivity

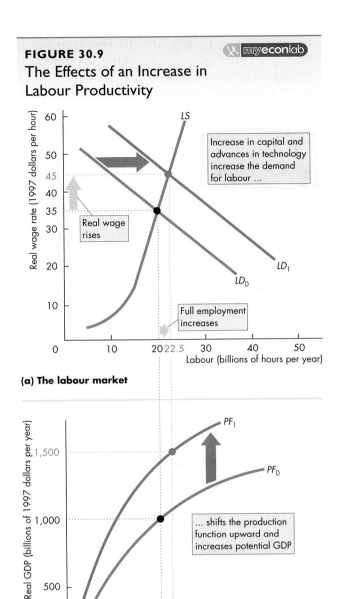

(a) The labour market

(b) Potential GDP

An increase in labour productivity shifts the demand for labour curve rightward from LD_0 to LD_1 in part (a) and the production function upward from PF_0 to PF_1 in part (b). The real wage rate rises from \$35 to \$45 an hour, and full employment increases from 20 billion to 22.5 billion hours. Potential GDP increases from \$1,000 billion to \$1,500 billion. Potential GDP increases because labour becomes more productive and full employment increases.

Population and Productivity in Canada

The Canadian economy was close to full employment in 2004. It was also close to full employment in 1980. We're going to compare these two years and look at the forces that moved the economy from one full-employment equilibrium to another.

In 1980, real GDP in Canada was \$580 billion, employment was 20 billion hours, and the real wage rate was \$15.77 an hour. (We are using 1997 dollars.)

By 2004, real GDP had increased to \$1,124 billion, labour hours had increased to 28 billion, and the real wage rate had risen to \$20.35 an hour. (Again, we are using 1997 dollars.)

The factors that you've just studied—an increase in population, increases in physical and human capital, and advances in technology—brought these changes.

Population Increase In 1980, the working-age population of Canada was 18.7 million. By 2004, this number had increased to 25.4 million. The 2004 working-age population was 36 percent larger than the 1980 working-age population. Recall that labour hours were 20 billion in 1980. A 36 percent increase would take labour hours in 2004 to 27.2 billion. But labour hours actually increased to 28 billion. Why? The increased labour productivity increased the real wage rate, which increased the quantity of labour supplied by increasing the labour force participation rate.

Capital Increase In 1980, the capital stock in Canada was estimated to be \$2.5 trillion (in 1997 dollars). By 2004, the capital stock had increased to \$4.9 trillion. This increase in capital increased labour productivity. But the increase in capital was not the only influence on labour productivity. Technological advances also occurred.

Technological Advances In 1980, we were just getting into the information revolution. Personal computers had just arrived. They were slow, had little memory, and had no hard drive, much less the CD-ROM and DVD drives of today. The Internet existed as a tool used by academic researchers for e-mail and file transfers, but no one had imagined the World Wide Web. Telephones couldn't remember numbers or record messages. Communication was slower and more costly than it was to become by 2004.

Production processes were beginning to be computerized but on a limited scale. Banks equipped with ATMs were in the future. Supermarkets with

FIGURE 30.10

Full Employment in Canada: 1980 and 2004

(a) The Canadian labour market in 1980 and 2004

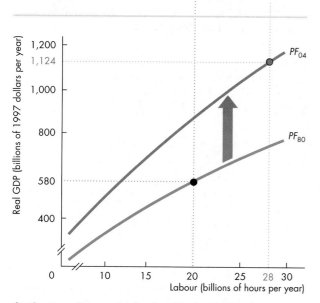

(b) The Canadian production function in 1980 and 2004

In 1980, the real wage rate was $15.77 an hour and the quantity of labour employed was 20 billion hours at the intersection of LD_{80} and LS_{80} in part (a). Potential GDP was $580 billion on PF_{80} in part (b). By 2004, the real wage rate had increased to $20.35 an hour and the quantity of labour employed had increased to 28 billion hours at the intersection of LD_{04} and LS_{04} in part (a). Potential GDP had increased to $1,124 billion on PF_{04} in part (b).

laser scanners were only a dream. Robots in car factories and coal mines were still unknown. The biotechnology sector had yet to be developed. The combined effects of capital accumulation and technological advance have made the workers on our farms and in our factories, shops and offices more productive.

Figure 30.10 shows these effects along with the effects of the increase in population that occurred. In 1980, the demand for labour curve was LD_{80}, the supply of labour curve was LS_{80}, the full-employment real wage rate was $15.77 an hour, and 20 billion hours of labour were employed. The production function in 1980 was PF_{80}. With 20 billion hours of labour employed, real GDP (and potential GDP) was $580 billion.

By 2004, the increase in population had increased the working-age population by 36 percent. This increase in population increased the supply of labour and shifted the labour supply curve rightward to LS_{04}.

The accumulation of capital and advances in technology increased labour productivity. The demand for labour increased, and the demand for labour curve shifted rightward to LD_{04}. And the production function shifted upward to PF_{04}.

The real wage rate increased to $20.35 an hour, and employment increased to 28 billion hours. At this quantity of labour, real GDP (and potential GDP) increased to $1,124 billion.

So in Canada, the effects of an increase in capital and advances in technology have been larger than the effects of increases in population. The forces that increase labour productivity have been strong enough to overcome the effects of an increase in population.

REVIEW QUIZ

1 When the population increases but nothing else changes, why does real GDP per hour of work decrease?

2 How does an increase in capital change the real wage rate, full employment, and potential GDP?

3 How do advances in technology change the real wage rate, full employment, and potential GDP?

4 If, as some people suggest, capital accumulation and technological change always accompany an increase in population, is it possible for potential GDP per hour of work to decrease?

myeconlab   Study Plan 30.3

Unemployment at Full Employment

SO FAR, WE'VE FOCUSED ON THE FORCES THAT determine the real wage rate, the quantity of labour employed, and potential GDP. And we've studied the effects of changes in population, capital, and technology on these variables. We're now going to bring unemployment into the picture.

In Chapter 21, we learned how unemployment is measured. We described how people become unemployed—they lose jobs, leave jobs, and enter or re-enter the labour force—and we classified unemployment—it can be frictional, structural, seasonal, and cyclical. We also learned that we call the unemployment rate at full employment the *natural rate of unemployment*.

But measuring, describing, and classifying unemployment do not *explain* it. Why is there always some unemployment? Why does the unemployment rate fluctuate? Why was the unemployment rate lower during the 1960s and the early 2000s than during the 1980s and early 1990s?

We studied the forces that make the unemployment rate fluctuate around the natural rate in Chapter 22. Here, we look at the churning economy and the reasons why we have unemployment, even when the economy is at full employment.

Unemployment is ever present for two broad reasons:

- Job search
- Job rationing

Job Search

Job search is the activity of looking for an acceptable vacant job. There are always some people who have not yet found a suitable job and who are actively searching for one. The reason is that the labour market is in a constant state of change. The failure of existing businesses destroys jobs. The expansion of existing businesses and the startup of new businesses that use new technologies and develop new markets create jobs. As people pass through different stages of life, some enter or re-enter the labour market. Others leave their jobs to look for better ones, and still others retire. This constant churning in the labour market means that there are always some people looking for jobs, and these people are the unemployed.

The amount of job search depends on a number of factors, one of which is the real wage rate. In Fig. 30.11, when the real wage rate is $35 an hour, the economy is at a full-employment equilibrium. The amount of job search that takes place at this wage rate generates unemployment at the natural rate. If the real wage rate is above the full-employment equilibrium—for example, at $45 an hour—there is a surplus of labour. At this higher real wage rate, more job search takes place and the unemployment rate rises above the natural rate. If the real wage rate is below the full-employment equilibrium—for example, at $25 an hour—there is a shortage of labour. At this real wage rate, less job search takes place and the unemployment rate falls below the natural rate.

The market forces of supply and demand move the real wage rate towards the full-employment

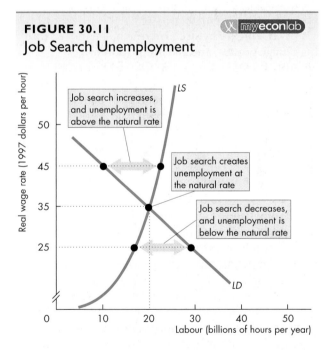

FIGURE 30.11
Job Search Unemployment

Job search increases, and unemployment is above the natural rate

Job search creates unemployment at the natural rate

Job search decreases, and unemployment is below the natural rate

When the real wage rate is at its full-employment level— $35 an hour in this example—job search puts unemployment at the natural rate. If the real wage rate is above the full-employment level, there is a surplus of labour. Job search increases, and unemployment rises above the natural rate. If the real wage rate is below the full-employment level, there is a shortage of labour. Job search decreases, and unemployment falls below the natural rate.

equilibrium. And these same forces move the amount of job search towards the level that creates unemployment at the natural rate.

But other influences on the amount of job search bring changes, over time, in the natural rate of unemployment. The main sources of these changes are

■ Demographic change
■ Unemployment compensation
■ Structural change

Demographic Change An increase in the proportion of the population that is of working age brings an increase in the entry rate into the labour force and an increase in the unemployment rate. This factor has been important in the Canadian labour market in recent years. The bulge in the birth rate that occurred from the late 1940s through the late 1950s increased the proportion of new entrants into the labour force during the 1970s and brought an increase in the natural rate of unemployment.

As the birth rate declined, the bulge moved into higher age groups, and the proportion of new entrants declined during the 1980s. During this period, the natural rate of unemployment decreased.

Another demographic trend is an increase in the number of households with two paid workers. When one of these workers becomes unemployed, it is possible, with income still flowing in, to take longer to find a new job. This factor might have increased frictional unemployment.

Unemployment Compensation The length of time that an unemployed person spends searching for a job depends, in part, on the opportunity cost of job search. An unemployed person who receives no unemployment compensation faces a high opportunity cost of job search. In this situation, search is likely to be short and the person is likely to accept a less attractive job rather than continue a costly search process. An unemployed person who receives generous unemployment compensation faces a low opportunity cost of job search. In this situation, search is likely to be prolonged. The unemployed worker will continue to search for an ideal job.

The extension of unemployment compensation to larger groups of workers during the late 1960s and 1970s lowered the opportunity cost of job search. Consequently, the amount of job search and the natural rate of unemployment increased during those years.

Structural Change Labour market flows and unemployment are influenced by the pace and direction of technological change. Sometimes, technological change brings a *structural slump*, a condition in which some industries die and some regions suffer while other industries are born and other regions flourish. When these events occur, labour turnover is high—the flows between employment and unemployment increase and the number of unemployed people increases. The decline of industries in the Maritimes and the rapid expansion of industries in the Ottawa Valley illustrate the effects of technological change and were a source of the increase in unemployment during the 1970s and early 1980s. While these changes were taking place, the natural rate of unemployment increased.

Job Rationing

You've learned that markets *allocate* scarce resources by adjusting the market price to make buying plans and selling plans agree. Another word that has a meaning similar to "allocate" is "ration." Markets *ration* scarce resources by adjusting prices. In the labour market, the real wage rate rations employment and therefore rations jobs. Changes in the real wage rate keep the number of people seeking work and the number of jobs available in balance.

But the real wage rate is not the only possible instrument for rationing jobs. And in some industries, the real wage rate is set above the market equilibrium level. **Job rationing** is the practice of paying a real wage rate above the equilibrium level and then rationing jobs by some method.

Two reasons why the real wage rate might be set above the equilibrium level are

■ Efficiency wage
■ Minimum wage

Efficiency Wage It is costly for a firm to pay its workers more than the market wage rate. But doing so also brings benefits. An **efficiency wage** is a real wage rate that is set above the full-employment equilibrium wage rate that balances the costs and benefits of this higher wage rate to maximize the firm's profit.

The cost of paying a higher wage is direct. It is the addition to the firm's wage bill. The benefits of paying a higher wage rate are indirect.

First, a firm that pays a high wage rate can attract the most productive workers. Second, the firm can get greater productivity from its work force if it threatens to fire those who do not perform at the desired standard. The threat of losing a well-paid job stimulates greater work effort. Third, workers are less likely to quit their jobs, so the firm faces a lower rate of labour turnover and lower training costs. Fourth, the firm's recruiting costs are lower. The firm always faces a steady stream of available new workers.

Faced with benefits and costs, a firm offers a wage rate that balances productivity gains from the higher wage rate against its additional cost. This wage rate maximizes the firm's profit and is the efficiency wage.

Minimum Wage

A **minimum wage** law determines the lowest wage rate at which a firm may legally hire labour. If the minimum wage is set *below* the equilibrium wage, the minimum wage has no effect. The minimum wage law and market forces are not in conflict. But if a minimum wage is set *above* the equilibrium wage, the minimum wage is in conflict with the market forces and does have some effects on the labour market.

In Canada, provincial governments set the minimum wages. In 2005, the minimum wage ranged from a low of $6.25 an hour in Newfoundland to highs of $7.25 an hour in Manitoba, $7.45 an hour in Ontario, and $8.00 an hour in British Columbia. The minimum wage increases from time to time and has fluctuated relative to the average wage of all workers.

Job Rationing and Unemployment

Regardless of the reason, if the real wage rate is set above the equilibrium level, the natural rate of unemployment increases. The above-equilibrium real wage rate decreases the quantity of labour demanded and increases the quantity of labour supplied. So even at full employment, the quantity of labour supplied exceeds the quantity of labour demanded.

The surplus of labour is an addition to the amount of unemployment. The unemployment that results from a non-market wage rate and job rationing increases the natural rate of unemployment because it is added to the job search that takes place at full-employment equilibrium.

Economists broadly agree that efficiency wages can create persistent unemployment. And most economists believe that the minimum wage contributes to unemployment, especially among low-skilled young

workers. But David Card of the University of California at Berkeley and Alan Krueger of Princeton University have challenged this view. And the challenge has been rebutted.

Card and Krueger say that an increase in the minimum wage works like an efficiency wage. It makes workers more productive and less likely to quit. Most economists remain skeptical about this suggestion. If higher wages make workers more productive and reduce labour turnover, why don't firms freely pay the wage rates that encourage the correct work habits? Daniel Hamermesh of the University of Texas at Austin says that firms anticipate increases in the minimum wage and cut employment before they occur. Looking for the effects of an increase in the minimum wage after it has occurred misses its effects. Finis Welch of Texas A&M University and Kevin Murphy of the University of Chicago say that regional differences in economic growth and not changes in the minimum wage explain the facts that Card and Krueger found.

REVIEW QUIZ

1 Why does the economy experience unemployment at full employment?

2 Why does the natural rate of unemployment fluctuate?

3 What is job rationing and why does it occur?

4 How does an efficiency wage influence the real wage rate, employment, and unemployment?

5 How does the minimum wage create unemployment?

 Study Plan 30.4

◆ In this chapter, you've seen how the economy operates at full employment. *Reading Between the Lines* on pp. 722–723 uses what you have learned to compare labour productivity in Canada with that in the United States.

In this chapter, we've studied the real factors that influence potential GDP in a given year. And we've compared potential GDP in different times and places. Your next task is the study the process of economic growth—the interaction of capital accumulation, technological change, and population growth—that brings ever expanding potential GDP.

Canada–U.S. Productivity Gap

WINNIPEG FREE PRESS, OCTOBER 25, 2005

Taxes blamed for lagging Canadian productivity

Over-taxed Canadians are less productive than Americans and, as a result earn more than $9,000 a year less, says a group of accountants which yesterday joined the chorus of business and taxpayer groups calling for more tax relief in the next budget.

Canadian productivity has fallen off dramatically this decade leaving Canadians earning nearly 20 per cent less than Americans, an annual income gap of $9,242 per Canadian, the Certified Management Accountants of Canada told the House of Commons finance committee's pre-budget hearings.

Bank of Canada governor David Dodge, who also appeared before the committee, warned Canadians' living standards can't rise without an improvement in their productivity, commonly measured as output per hour worked.

"Over the longer haul, unless we can get higher productivity growth ... the standard of living can't rise," Dodge told the committee. ...

The accountants, as well as the Canadian Taxpayers Federation, argued in the briefs to the committee lower taxes would also boost productivity and in turn prosperity. ...

But not all groups are calling for tax cuts.

A major public-sector union today will tell the committee a better way to boost productivity is to invest more in public services. "Public services, along with full employment and fairer taxation policies, will increase productivity, improve our quality of life and lead to greater social inclusion," the Canadian Union of Public Employees says in a summary of its brief to the committee.

Essence of the Story

■ A group of accountants believes that the widening gap between Canadian and U.S. productivity is the result of high Canadian taxes.

■ The accountants say that Canadians earn almost 20 percent less than Americans and the annual income gap is $9,242 per person.

■ The accountants call for tax cuts, which they say will boost Canadian productivity.

■ A labour union disagrees with the accountants and says that greater investment in public services and other measures, not tax cuts, will boost Canadian productivity.

Economic Analysis

■ Comparisons of Canada and the United States reveal a widening gap in production per person and incomes.

■ Different methods of making the comparison lead to slightly different numbers, but the picture that Fig. 1 presents is reasonably accurate.

■ Figure 1 shows the ratio of real GDP per person in Canada to real GDP per person in the United States, with the values converted to a common currency using the purchasing power parity (*PPP*) exchange rate between the Canadian and U.S. dollars.

■ Figure 1 illustrates the accountant's concerns. The productivity gap widened between 1984 and 2004 when relative productivity fell from 90 percent to 80 percent.

■ Because income per person equals the value of production per person, the income gap between Canada and the United States has widened in the same way as the productivity gap has widened.

■ Figure 2 illustrates the production functions in Canada and the United States. With more productive capital and technologies, the U.S. production function, PF_{US}, is above the Canadian production function, PF_C.

■ Figure 3 illustrates the implications of the greater productivity for the labour market.

■ The U.S. demand for labour curve, LD_{US}, is above the Canadian demand for labour curve, LD_C.

■ The supply of labour (per person) is LS_{US} in the United States and LS_C in Canada.

■ The equilibrium real wage rate is higher in the United States than in Canada.

■ The accountants base their argument for tax cuts on a comparison of taxes in Canada and the United States.

■ There is no evidence that the labour union's idea of spending more on social services and other government programs would increase Canadian productivity.

You're the Voter

■ Do you agree with the accountants that Canada's low productivity is caused by high taxes? How might you test this view?

■ Do you agree with the labour union that Canada's low productivity is caused low social spending? How might you test this view?

■ Would you vote for lower taxes or more spending on social programs? Why?

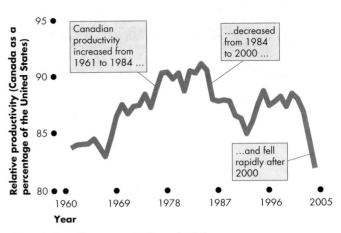

Figure 1 Canadian versus U.S. productivity

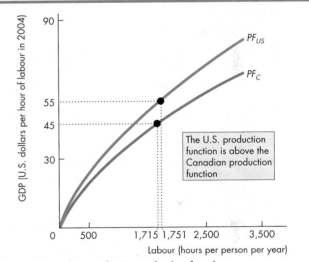

Figure 2 Canadian and U.S. production functions

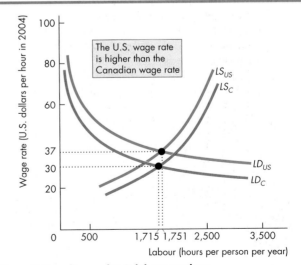

Figure 3 Canadian and U.S. labour markets

723

APPENDIX

Deriving the Long-Run and Short-Run Aggregate Supply Curves

After studying this appendix, you will be able to

- **Derive the long-run aggregate supply curve, explain why it is vertical, and explain the factors that make it shift**
- **Describe and explain short-run equilibrium in the labour market**
- **Derive the short-run aggregate supply curve, explain the factors that make it shift, and explain what determines its shape**

The Aggregate Supply Curves

THIS APPENDIX EXPLAINS HOW TO DERIVE THE long-run aggregate supply curve and the short-run aggregate supply curve. It shows the link between the labour market, the production function, and the long-run aggregate supply curve when prices and the money wage rate are fully adjusted. And it shows the link between the labour market, the production function, and the short-run aggregate supply curve when the money wage rate is sticky. You can think of this appendix as filling in the steps between Fig. 30.6 and Fig. 30.7 on p. 713 of this chapter.

This appendix also explains the factors that change aggregate supply and shift the aggregate supply curves. Finally, the appendix explains why the long-run aggregate supply curve is vertical and why the short-run aggregate supply curve slopes upward.

For many years, economists neglected aggregate supply and placed almost all their attention on aggregate demand. This neglect of aggregate supply was unfortunate because even in the short run, aggregate supply plays a role in determining real GDP. And in the long run, aggregate supply alone determines real GDP.

Deriving the Long-Run Aggregate Supply Curve

FIGURE A30.1 SHOWS HOW TO DERIVE THE LONG-run aggregate supply curve. Part (a) shows the labour market. The demand and supply curves shown are similar to those in Fig. 30.6(a) on p. 713. The equilibrium, a real wage of $35 an hour and employment of 20 billion hours, is exactly the same equilibrium that was determined in that figure.

Figure A30.1(b) shows the production function. This production function is similar to that in Fig. 30.1(b) on p. 707. We know from the labour market (part a) that 20 billion hours of labour are employed. Part (b) tells us that when 20 million hours of labour are employed, real GDP is $1,000 billion.

Figure A30.1(c) shows the long-run aggregate supply curve. That curve tells us that real GDP is $1,000 billion regardless of the price level. To see why, look at what happens when the price level changes.

Start with the economy is at point *J* in part (c) of the figure. The GDP deflator is 100 and real GDP is $1,000 billion. We've determined, in part (a), that the real wage rate is $35 an hour. With a GDP deflator of 100, the money wage rate (the wage rate in current dollars) is also $35 an hour.

What happens to real GDP if the GDP deflator falls from 100 to 80 (a 20 percent decrease in the price level)? If the money wage rate remains at $35 an hour, the real wage rate rises and the quantity of labour supplied exceeds the quantity demanded. In the long run, the money wage rate will fall. It falls to $28 an hour. With a money wage rate of $28 an hour and a GDP deflator of 80, the real wage rate is still $35 an hour ($28 divided by 80 and multiplied by 100 equals $35). With the lower money wage rate but a constant real wage rate, employment remains at 20 billion hours and real GDP remains at $1,000 billion. The economy is at point *K* in Fig. A30.1(c).

What happens to real GDP if the GDP deflator rises from 100 to 120 (a 20 percent increase in the price level)? If the money wage rate stays at $35 an hour, the real wage rate falls and the quantity of labour demanded exceeds the quantity supplied. In the long run, the money wage rate rises. It keeps rising until it reaches $42 an hour. At that money wage rate, the real wage rate is $35 an hour ($42 divided by 120 and multiplied by 100 equals $35) and the quantity of labour demanded equals the quantity supplied. Employment remains at 20 billion hours and real GDP remains at $1,000 billion. The economy is at point *I* in Fig. A30.1(c).

Points *J*, *K*, and *I* in part (c) all lie on the long-run aggregate supply curve. We have considered only three price levels. We can consider any price level and we will reach the same conclusion: A change in the price level generates a proportionate change in the money

wage rate and leaves the real wage rate unchanged. Employment and real GDP are also unchanged.

Because in the long run the price level *and the money wage rate* adjust to achieve full employment, the real wage rate, employment, and real GDP remain constant as the price level changes. In the long run, one level of real GDP—potential GDP—occurs at any price level and the *LAS* curve is vertical.

FIGURE A30.1

The Labour Market and Long-Run Aggregate Supply

(a) The labour market

(c) Long-run aggregate supply curve

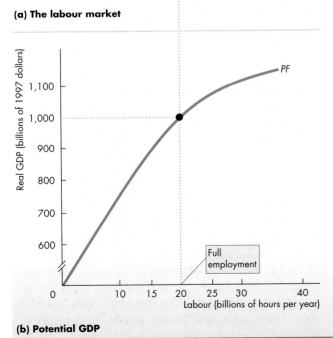

(b) Potential GDP

Equilibrium in the labour market determines the real wage rate and employment. The demand for labour curve (*LD*) intersects the supply of labour curve (*LS*) at a real wage rate of $35 an hour and 20 billion hours of employment (part a). The production function (*PF*) and employment of 20 billion hours determine real GDP at $1,000 billion (part b). Potential GDP is $1,000 billion and in the long run, real GDP supplied is $1,000 billion regardless of the price level. The long-run aggregate supply curve (*LAS*) is the vertical line in part (c). If the GDP deflator is 100, the economy is at point *J*. If the GDP deflator is 120, the money wage rate rises to keep the real wage rate constant at $35 an hour, employment remains at 20 billion hours, and real GDP is $1,000 billion. The economy is at point *I*. If the GDP deflator is 80, the money wage rate falls to keep the real wage rate constant at $35 an hour, employment remains at 20 billion hours, and real GDP is $1,000 billion. The economy is at point *K*.

Changes in Long-Run Aggregate Supply

Long-run aggregate supply can change for two reasons:

■ Change in labour supply
■ Change in labour productivity

Change in Labour Supply The supply of labour can change for many reasons, but the biggest one is a change in the population. Over time, the population grows and the supply of labour increases.

We study and illustrate the effects of an increase in the supply of labour on potential GDP on pp. 714–715. An increase in the supply of labour means the supply of labour curve shifts rightward. The real wage rate falls and full employment increases. Potential GDP increases.

Now that we've derived the long-run aggregate supply curve, you can see that when potential GDP changes, long-run aggregate supply also changes and the long-run aggregate supply curve shifts. Because an increase in the supply of labour increases potential GDP, it also increases long-run aggregate supply and shifts the long-run aggregate supply curve rightward. The new (vertical) long-run aggregate supply curve is located at the increased level of potential GDP.

Change in Labour Productivity An increase in labour productivity means that a given amount of labour can produce a larger quantity of real GDP. The production function shifts upward and the demand for labour curve shifts rightward. The real wage rate rises, full employment increases. Potential GDP increases.

We study and illustrate the effects of an increase in productivity on the quantity of labour, the real wage rate, and potential GDP on pp. 715–717.

Again, because an increase in labour productivity increases potential GDP, it also increases long-run aggregate supply and shifts the long-run aggregate supply curve rightward. The new (vertical) long-run aggregate supply curve is located at the increased level of potential GDP.

Whether the real wage rate increases when long-run aggregate supply increases depends on the source of the increase in potential GDP. If the source is an increase in the supply of labour, the real wage rate falls. If the source is an increase in labour productivity, the real wage rate rises.

Short-Run Aggregate Supply

SHORT-RUN AGGREGATE SUPPLY IS THE RELATIONship between the quantity of real GDP supplied and the price level when the money wage rate and all other influences on production plans remain the same. We are now going to learn about the connection between short-run aggregate supply and the labour market. But before we can derive the short-run aggregate supply curve, we must understand how the labour market works when the money wage rate is fixed.

Short-Run Equilibrium in the Labour Market

When the money wage rate is fixed, a change in the price level changes the real wage rate. Suppose the money wage rate is $35 an hour and the GDP deflator is 100. Then the real wage rate is also $35 an hour.

Now suppose that the money wage rate remains at $35 an hour but the GDP deflator rises to 116.7. In this case, the real wage rate falls to $30 an hour. A money wage rate of $35 an hour and a GDP deflator of 116.3 enables people to buy the same goods and services that a money wage rate of $30 an hour buys when the GDP deflator is 100.

Alternatively, suppose that the GDP deflator falls to 87.5. In this case, the real wage rate rises to $40 an hour. A money wage rate of $35 an hour with a GDP deflator of 87.5 buys the same quantity of goods and services that a money wage rate of $40 an hour buys when the GDP deflator is 100.

Figure A30.2 shows the labour market in the short run at the three price levels we've just considered. As before, the demand for labour is LD and the supply of labour is LS. The money wage rate is constant at $35 an hour and the higher the price level, the lower is the real wage rate. The three points B, C, and D tell us the quantities of labour demanded at the three real wage rates. If the price level is 87.5, the real wage rate is $40 an hour and the quantity of labour demanded is 15 billion hours a year (point B). If the price level is 100, the real wage rate is $35 an hour and the quantity of labour demanded is 20 billion hours a year (point C). If the price level is 116.7, the real wage rate is $30 an hour and the quantity of labour demanded is 25 billion hours a year (point D).

FIGURE A30.2   myeconlab
The Labour Market in the Short Run

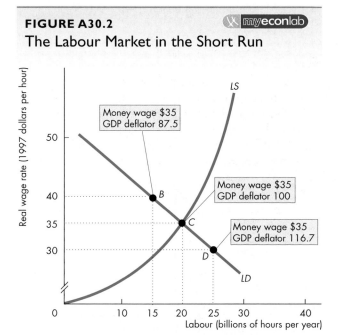

The labour demand curve is LD and the labour supply curve is LS. The money wage rate is fixed at $35 an hour. If the GDP deflator is 100, the *real* wage rate is $35 an hour and 20 billion hours of labour are employed. The economy operates at point C. If the GDP deflator is 87.5, the real wage rate is $40 an hour and 15 billion hours of labour are employed. The economy operates at point B. If the GDP deflator is 116.7, the real wage rate is $30 an hour and 25 billion hours of labour are employed. The economy operates at point D.

You can see that when the money wage rate is fixed and the price level rises, the real wage rate falls, and the quantity of labour *demanded* increases. But what determines the quantity of labour *employed*?

Employment with Sticky Wages When the real wage rate is not at its full-employment equilibrium level, there are many possible ways in which employment could be determined. It is assumed that when the labour market is not at full employment, firms decide the level of employment and provided that firms pay the agreed money wage rate, households supply whatever quantity of labour firms demand. In the short run, households are willing to be "off" their labour supply curves.

In Fig. A30.2, with a money wage rate of $35 an hour and a price level of 87.5 (point B) employment is 15 billion hours. The real wage rate is $40 an hour and in this situation, people supply less labour than they would like to. If the GDP deflator is 116.7, the real wage rate is $30 an hour and employment is 25 billion hours (point D). The real wage rate is $30 an hour and in this case, people supply more labour than they would like to.

It is easy to understand why people might supply less labour than they would like to. But why would people supply *more* labour than they would like to? In the long run, they would not. But in the short run, during the life of an existing wage contract, it is quite likely that people will agree to supply whatever quantity of labour their employer demands. The employer gives the employee an "all-or-nothing" choice. The employee must either work the hours requested or find another job.

Deriving the Short-Run Aggregate Supply Curve

The short-run aggregate supply curve is the relationship between the quantity of real GDP supplied and the price level when the money wage rate and all other influences on production plans remain the same. Along the short-run aggregate supply curve, the money wage rate is fixed, so when the price level changes, the *real wage rate changes*. With a change in the real wage rate, employment and real GDP change. The short-run aggregate supply curve is upward sloping.

Figure A30.3 shows the derivation of the short-run aggregate supply curve. Part (a) shows the aggregate labour market. The demand and supply curves are the same as those in Fig. A30.2. The long-run equilibrium, a real wage of $35 an hour and employment of 20 billion hours, is exactly the same equilibrium that was determined in that figure.

Focus first on part (a). It shows the three short-run equilibrium levels of the real wage rate and employment that we discovered in Fig. A30.2. The money wage rate is fixed at $35 an hour. If the price level is 100, the real wage rate is also $35 an hour and 20 billion hours of labour are employed—point C. If the price level is 87.5, the real wage rate is $40 an hour and employment is 15 billion hours—point B. If the price level is 116.7, the real wage rate is $30 an hour and employment is 25 billion hours—point D.

FIGURE A30.3
The Labour Market and Short-Run Aggregate Supply

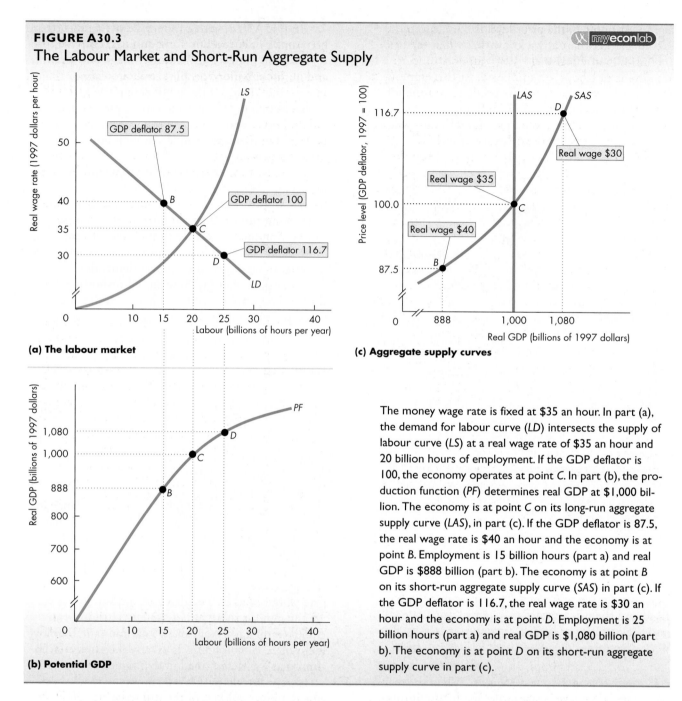

(a) The labour market

(b) Potential GDP

(c) Aggregate supply curves

The money wage rate is fixed at $35 an hour. In part (a), the demand for labour curve (*LD*) intersects the supply of labour curve (*LS*) at a real wage rate of $35 an hour and 20 billion hours of employment. If the GDP deflator is 100, the economy operates at point *C*. In part (b), the production function (*PF*) determines real GDP at $1,000 billion. The economy is at point *C* on its long-run aggregate supply curve (*LAS*), in part (c). If the GDP deflator is 87.5, the real wage rate is $40 an hour and the economy is at point *B*. Employment is 15 billion hours (part a) and real GDP is $888 billion (part b). The economy is at point *B* on its short-run aggregate supply curve (*SAS*) in part (c). If the GDP deflator is 116.7, the real wage rate is $30 an hour and the economy is at point *D*. Employment is 25 billion hours (part a) and real GDP is $1,080 billion (part b). The economy is at point *D* on its short-run aggregate supply curve in part (c).

Figure A30.3(b) shows the production function. We know from the labour market (part a) that at different price levels, different quantities of labour are employed. Part (b) shows the real GDP produced by these employment levels. For example, when employment is 15 billion hours, real GDP is $888 billion—point *B*. When employment is 20 billion hours, real GDP is $1,000 billion—point *C*. And when employ-

ment is 25 billion hours, real GDP is $1,080 billion—point *D*.

Figure A30.3(c) shows the short-run aggregate supply curve. It also shows the long-run aggregate supply curve, *LAS*, that we derived in Fig. A30.1. The short-run aggregate supply curve, *SAS*, is derived from the labour market and production function. To see how, first focus on point *B* in all three parts of the figure. At point *B*, the price level is 87.5. From the labour market (part a) we know that when the price level is 87.5, the real wage is $40 an hour, and 15 billion hours of labour are employed. At this employment level, we know from the production function (part b) that real GDP is $888 billion. That's what point *B* on the *SAS* curve in part (c) tells us—when the price level is 87.5, the quantity of real GDP supplied is $888 billion. The other two points on the *SAS* curve, *C* and *D*, are derived in the same way. At point *D*, the price level is 116.7 so the real wage rate is $30 an hour and 25 billion hours of labour are employed (part a). This employment level produces a real GDP of $1,080 billion (part b).

The short-run aggregate supply curve intersects the long-run aggregate supply curve at the price level that delivers the equilibrium real wage rate in the labour market. In this example, that price level is 100. At labour market equilibrium, the economy is at full employment and real GDP equals potential GDP. At price levels above 100, the quantity of real GDP supplied in the short run exceeds potential GDP; at price levels below 100, the quantity of real GDP supplied in the short run falls short of potential GDP.

Changes in Short-Run Aggregate Supply

Short-run aggregate supply can change for two reasons:

- Change in long-run aggregate supply
- Change in money wage rate

Change in Long-Run Aggregate Supply

Anything that changes long-run aggregate supply also changes short-run aggregate supply. That is, anything that increases potential GDP increases the quantity of real GDP supplied at each and every price level. Both long-run aggregate supply and short-run aggregate supply increase and both curves shift rightward.

A key feature of the *SAS* curve is that it intersects the *LAS* curve at the price level that puts the real wage rate at its full-employment level—that is, the real wage rate at which the labour market is in equilibrium. So if long-run aggregate supply changes and the *LAS* curve shifts, the short-run aggregate supply curve also shifts. And the new *SAS* curve intersects the new *LAS* curve at the price level that makes the real wage rate equal to its *new* full-employment level.

Change in Money Wage Rate

Short-run aggregate supply changes and long-run aggregate supply remains unchanged if the money wage rate changes and all other influences on production plans remain the same. A rise in the money wage rate with a given price level means that the real wage rate has increased. Faced with a higher real wage rate, firms decrease the quantity of labour demanded. Employment decreases and firms produce less output, so the quantity of real GDP supplied decreases.

But the changes that we've just described would occur at any given price level. So short-run aggregate supply decreases. The *SAS* curve shifts leftward.

Short-Run Changes in the Quantity of Real GDP Supplied

Even if short-run aggregate supply does not change, real GDP can change in the short run. The reason is that there can be a *change in the quantity of real GDP supplied*, which appears as a *movement along the SAS curve*. These changes in real GDP are brought about by changes in aggregate demand. All the factors that can change aggregate demand result in a shift of the aggregate demand curve and movement along the *SAS* curve. Real GDP changes and so does the price level. They both change in the same direction. An increase in aggregate demand brings an increase in real GDP and a rise in the price level; a decrease in aggregate demand brings a decrease in real GDP and a fall in the price level.

The Shape of the Short-Run Aggregate Supply Curve

The short-run aggregate supply curve that we've derived in Fig. A30.3(c) is *curved*. Along this *SAS* curve, as the price level rises, real GDP increases. But for given increments in the price level, the increments in real GDP become successively smaller. In contrast, the *SAS* curve in Fig. 30.7 on p. 713, like that in Chapter 22, is linear—a curve that graphs as a straight line. Along a linear *SAS* curve, as the price level rises, real GDP increases. You can regard the linear *SAS* curve as an approximation over a small range of real GDP in the neighbourhood of potential GDP. The farther the economy moves away from potential GDP, the less close is the approximation.

SUMMARY

KEY POINTS

Real GDP and Employment (pp. 706–708)

- To produce real GDP, we must forgo leisure time.
- As the quantity of labour increases, real GDP increases.
- Labour productivity increases if the amount of physical capital or human capital increases or if technology advances.

The Labour Market and Aggregate Supply (pp. 709–714)

- The quantity of labour demanded increases as the real wage rate falls, other things remaining the same.
- The diminishing marginal product of labour is the reason the quantity of labour demanded increases as the real wage rate falls.
- The quantity of labour supplied increases as the real wage rate rises, other things remaining the same.
- At full-employment equilibrium, the quantity of labour demanded equals the quantity of labour supplied.
- Potential GDP is real GDP produced by the full-employment quantity of labour.
- Along the *LAS* curve, the real wage rate is constant at its full-employment level. Along the *SAS* curve, the real wage rate, employment, and real GDP change.

Changes in Potential GDP (pp. 714–718)

- An increase in population increases the supply of labour, lowers the real wage rate, increases the full-employment quantity of labour, and increases potential GDP. It decreases potential GDP per hour of work.
- An increase in capital or an advance in technology increases labour productivity. It shifts the production function upward and the demand for labour curve rightward. The real wage rate rises, the full-employment quantity of labour increases, and potential GDP increases.

Unemployment at Full Employment (pp. 719–721)

- The unemployment rate at full employment is the natural rate of unemployment.
- Unemployment is ever present because of job search and job rationing.
- Job-search unemployment is influenced by demographic change, unemployment compensation, and structural change.
- Job-rationing unemployment arises from efficiency wages and the minimum wage.

KEY FIGURES

KEY TERMS

PROBLEMS

Go to (X myeconlab) for solutions to odd-numbered problems and additional exercises.

1. Robinson Crusoe lives on a desert island on the equator. He has 12 hours of daylight every day to allocate between leisure and work. The table shows seven alternative combinations of leisure and real GDP in Crusoe's economy:

Possibility	Leisure (hours per day)	Real GDP (dollars per day)
A	12	0
B	10	10
C	8	18
D	6	24
E	4	28
F	2	30
G	0	30

a. Make a table and a graph of Crusoe's production function.
b. Find the marginal product of labour for Crusoe at different quantities of labour.

2. The people of Nautica have a total of 100 hours every day to allocate between leisure and work. The table shows the combinations of real GDP and leisure in the economy of Nautica:

Possibility	Leisure (hours per day)	Real GDP (dollars per hour)
A	0	75
B	20	70
C	40	60
D	60	45
E	80	25
F	100	0

a. Make a table and a graph of Nautica's production function.
b. Find the marginal product of labour for Nautica at different quantities of labour.

3. Use the information provided in problem 1 about Robinson Crusoe's economy. Also, use the information that at a real wage rate of $4.50 an hour, Crusoe is willing to work any number of hours between zero and the total available to him.

a. Make a table that shows Crusoe's demand for labour schedule and draw Crusoe's demand for labour curve.
b. Make a table that shows Crusoe's supply of labour schedule and draw Crusoe's supply of labour curve.
c. What are the full-employment equilibrium real wage rate and quantity of labour in Crusoe's economy?
d. Find Crusoe's potential GDP.

4. Use the information provided in problem 2 about the economy of Nautica. Also, use the information that the people of Nautica are willing to work 20 hours a day for a real wage rate of $10 an hour. And for each 50¢ an hour *increase* in the real wage, they are willing to work an *additional* hour a day.

a. Make a table that shows Nautica's demand for labour schedule and draw Nautica's demand for labour curve.
b. Make a table that shows Nautica's supply of labour schedule and draw Nautica's supply of labour curve.
c. Find the full-employment equilibrium real wage rate and quantity of labour in Nautica's economy.
d. Find Nautica's potential GDP.

5. Robinson Crusoe, whose economy is described in problems 1 and 3, gets a bright idea. He diverts a stream and increases his food production by 50 percent. That is, each hour that he works produces 50 percent more real GDP than before.

a. Make a table that shows Crusoe's new production function and new demand for labour schedule.
b. Find the new full-employment equilibrium real wage rate and quantity of labour in Crusoe's economy.
c. Find Crusoe's new potential GDP.
d. Explain and interpret the results you obtained in parts (a), (b), and (c).

6. Nautica's economy, described in problems 2 and 4, experiences a surge in its population. The supply of labour increases, and 50 percent more hours are supplied at each real wage rate.

a. Make a table that shows Nautica's new supply of labour schedule.
b. Find the new full-employment equilibrium real wage rate and quantity of labour in Nautica's economy.

c. Find Nautica's new potential GDP.
d. Explain and interpret the results you obtained parts in (a), (b), and (c).

7. The figure describes the labour market on Cocoa Island. In addition (not shown in the figure), a survey tells us that when Cocoa Island is at full employment, people spend 1,000 hours a day in job search.

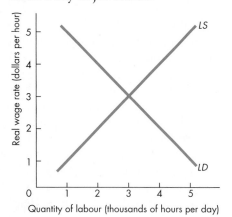

a. Find the full-employment equilibrium real wage rate and quantity of labour employed.
b. Find potential GDP on Cocoa Island. (*Hint*: The demand for labour curve tells you the *marginal* product of labour. How do we calculate the marginal product of labour?)
c. Calculate the natural rate of unemployment on Cocoa Island.

8. On Cocoa Island described in the figure and in problem 7, the government introduces a minimum wage of $4 an hour.
a. Find the new equilibrium real wage rate and quantity of labour employed.
b. What now is potential GDP on Cocoa Island?
c. Calculate the new natural rate of unemployment on Cocoa Island.
d. How much of the unemployment results from the minimum wage?

CRITICAL THINKING

1. Study *Reading Between the Lines* on pp. 722–723 and then answer the following questions:
a. Describe the labour productivity difference between Canada and the United States.
b. List the factors that influence a nation's production function that might explain why there is a gap between U.S. and Canadian labour productivity.
c. List the factors that influence a nation's supply of labour that might explain why the gap between U.S. and Canadian labour productivity has widened.
d. List the factors that influence a nation's production function that might be manipulated by Canadian economic policy to narrow the gap between U.S. and Canadian labour productivity.

2. You are working for the Finance Minister and must write a memo for the minister that provides a checklist of policy initiatives that will increase potential GDP. Be as imaginative as possible, but justify each of your suggestions with reference to the concepts and tools that you have learned about in this chapter.

WEB EXERCISES

Use the links on ⓧ myeconlab **to work the following exercises.**

1. Obtain information about the economy of Russia during the 1990s. Try to figure out what happened to the production possibilities frontier and production function and to the demand for labour and supply of labour in Russia during the 1990s. Tell a story about the Russian economy during those years using only the concepts and tools that you have learned about in this chapter.

2. Obtain information about the economy of China during the period since 2000. Try to figure out what happened to the production possibilities frontier and production function and to the demand for labour and supply of labour in China since 2000. Tell a story about the Chinese economy during those years using only the concepts and tools that you have learned in this chapter.

Economic Growth

Transforming People's Lives

Real GDP per person in Canada more than doubled between 1961 and 2005. If you live in a dorm that was built during the 1960s it is equipped with two electrical outlets: one for a desk lamp and one for a bedside lamp. Today, with the help of a power bar (or two), your room bulges with a personal computer, television and DVD player, stereo system, microwave, refrigerator, coffee maker, and toaster—the list goes on. What has brought about this growth in living standards?

We see even greater change if we look at modern Asia. On the banks of the Li River in Southern China, Songman Yang breeds cormorants, amazing birds that he trains to fish and deliver their catch to a basket on his simple bamboo raft. Songman's work, the capital equipment and technology he uses, and the income he earns are similar to those of his ancestors going back some 2,000 years. Yet all around Songman, in China's bustling cities, people are participating in an economic miracle. They are creating businesses, investing in new technologies, developing local and global markets, and transforming their lives. Why are incomes in China growing so rapidly?

◆ In this chapter, we study the forces that make real GDP grow, that make some countries grow faster than others, and that make our own growth rate sometimes slow down and sometimes speed up. And at the end of the chapter, in *Reading Between the Lines*, we examine Canada's recent productivity growth and find that it has been falling further behind that of the United States.

After studying this chapter, you will be able to

- **Describe the long-term growth trends in Canada and other countries and regions**
- **Identify the main sources of long-term real GDP growth**
- **Explain the productivity growth slowdown in Canada during the 1970s and the speedup during the 1990s**
- **Explain the theories of economic growth**

Long-Term Growth Trends

THE LONG-TERM GROWTH TRENDS THAT WE study in this chapter are the trends in *potential GDP*. We are interested in long-term growth primarily because it brings rising incomes *per person*. So we begin by looking at some facts about the level and the growth rate of real GDP per person in Canada and around the world. Let's look first at real GDP per person in Canada over the past 75 years.

Growth in the Canadian Economy

Figure 31.1 shows real GDP *per person* in Canada for the 78 years from 1926 to 2004. The average growth rate over this period is 2.2 percent a year.

The earliest years in the graph are dominated by two extraordinary events: the Great Depression of the 1930s and World War II of the 1940s. The fall in real GDP during the depression and the bulge during the war obscure the changes in the long-term growth trend that occurred within these years. Averaging out the depression and the war, the long-term growth rate was close to its 75-year average of 2.2 percent a year.

The 1950s had slow growth but then, during the 1960s, the growth rate speeded up and averaged 3.6 percent a year. The 1970s growth slowed to 2.8 percent a year and in the 1980s the growth rate slowed to a crawl of 1.0 percent a year. After 1996, the growth rate increased again and for the eight years between 1996 and 2004, the growth rate was back at its 75-year average.

A major goal of this chapter is to explain why our economy grows and why the long-term growth rate varies. Why did growth speed up during the 1960s, slow through the 1970s and 1980s, and then speed up again during the late 1990s and early 2000s? Another goal is to explain variations in the growth rate across countries. Let's look at some facts about the growth rates of other nations and compare them with Canada's growth rate.

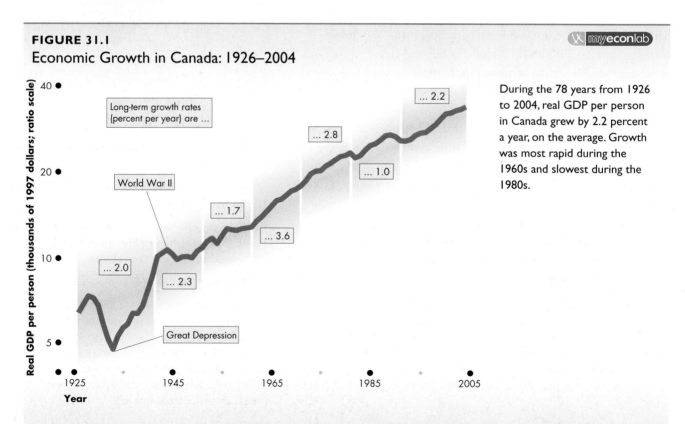

FIGURE 31.1
Economic Growth in Canada: 1926–2004

During the 78 years from 1926 to 2004, real GDP per person in Canada grew by 2.2 percent a year, on the average. Growth was most rapid during the 1960s and slowest during the 1980s.

Sources of data: F.H. Leacy (ed.), *Historical Statistics of Canada*, 2nd ed., catalogue 11–516, series A1, F32, F55, Statistics Canada, Ottawa, 1983; Statistics Canada, Tables 380–0002 and 051–0005.

Real GDP Growth in the World Economy

Figure 31.2 shows real GDP per person in Canada and in other countries between 1960 and 2005. (The data shown in this figure are in 2000 U.S. dollars.) Part (a) looks at the seven richest countries—known as the G7 nations. Among these nations, the United States has the highest real GDP per person.

In 2005, Canada had the second-highest real GDP per person and Japan the third. Before the 1990s, Japan grew faster than the United States and was catching up. Japan also grew faster than the Europe Big 4 (France, Germany, Italy, and the United Kingdom) and overtook Europe in the mid-1980s. But during the 1990s, the Japanese economy stagnated while Europe's continued to expand, so by 2005, these nations had similar levels of real GDP per person.

Across a broader group of poorer countries, economic growth has been slower than in Canada and income gaps have widened.

In Fig. 31.2(b), you can see that Africa and Central and South America have grown more slowly than Canada. Real GDP per person in Central and South America slipped from 33 percent of the Canadian level of real GDP per person in 1960 to 28 percent in 2005. Africa slipped from 14 percent of the Canadian level of real GDP per person in 1960 to 9 percent in 2005.

Figure 31.2(b) also shows that after growing during the 1970s and 1980s, the former communist countries of Central Europe stagnated and fell increasingly behind Canada. But by the late 1990s,

---

FIGURE 31.2
Economic Growth Around the World

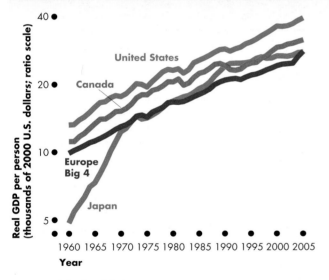

(a) Growth in the rich G7

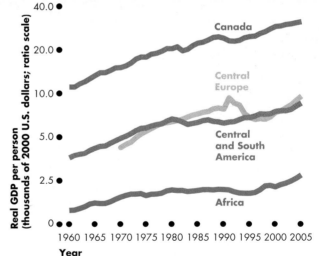

(b) Persistent gaps between rich and poor

Real GDP per person has grown throughout the world economy. Among the rich industrial countries (part a), real GDP growth has been similar in Canada, the Europe Big 4 (France, Germany, Italy, and the United Kingdom), and the United States. Growth in Japan was very rapid during the 1960s, slower during the 1980s, and even slower during the 1990s.

Part (b) shows income per person in a wider range of groups of countries. Central Europe was growing more quickly than Canada during the 1970s and 1980s, but slumped during the 1990s transition to a market economy. Growth in Central and South America and in Africa has been slower than in Canada, so the income gaps between Canada and these countries have widened.

Sources of data: 1960–2000: Alan Heston, Robert Summers and Bettina Aten, Penn World Table Version 6.1, Center for International Comparisons at the University of Pennsylvania (CICUP), October 2002. 2001–2005: *World Economic Outlook,* Washington, DC: International Monetary Fund, October 2005.

these countries were expanding more quickly again. But they remain a long way behind Canada.

The persistent gaps both among the G7 and the richer and poorer groups of countries in Fig. 31.2 is not a universal global phenomenon. Some economies have grown spectacularly and closed the income gap.

Figure 31.3 shows these economies. They are Hong Kong, Korea, Singapore, and Taiwan. During the 1960s, real GDP per person in these economies ranged from 10 to 25 percent of that in Canada. But by 2005, two of them, Hong Kong and Singapore, had overtaken Canada and the other two were close behind.

Figure 31.3 also shows China catching up, but more slowly and from a very long way behind. China's

real GDP per person increased from 7 percent of Canada's level in 1960 to 19 percent in 2005.

The four small Asian economies shown in Fig. 31.3 are like fast trains running on the same track at similar speeds and with a roughly constant gap between them. Hong Kong is the lead train and runs about 17 years in front of Korea, which is the last train. Real GDP per person in Korea in 2005 was similar to that of Hong Kong in 1988, 17 years earlier. Between 1960 and 2005, Hong Kong transformed itself from a poor developing economy into one of the world's richest economies.

China is now doing what Hong Kong has done. If China continues its rapid growth, the world economy will become a dramatically different place, because China is equivalent to more than 200 countries of the size of Hong Kong. Whether China will continue on its current path of rapid growth is impossible to predict.

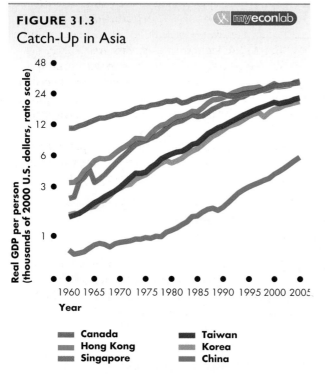

FIGURE 31.3   myeconlab

Catch-Up in Asia

Legend:
- Canada
- Hong Kong
- Singapore
- Taiwan
- Korea
- China

Catch-up has occurred in five economies in Asia. After starting out in 1960 with real GDP per person as low as 10 percent of that in Canada, Hong Kong, Korea, Singapore, and Taiwan have substantially narrowed the gap between them and Canada. And from being a very poor developing country in 1960, China now has a real GDP per person that equals that of Hong Kong in 1960. China is growing at a rate that is enabling it to continue to catch up with Canada.

Sources of data: See Fig. 31.2.

REVIEW QUIZ

1 What has been the average economic growth rate in Canada over the past 75 years? In which periods was growth most rapid and in which periods was it the slowest?

2 Describe the gaps between the levels of real GDP per person in Canada and other countries. For which countries are the gaps narrowing? For which countries are the gaps widening? And for which countries are the gaps remaining unchanged?

3 Compare the growth rates and levels of real GDP per person in Hong Kong, Korea, Singapore, Taiwan, China, and Canada. How far is China behind the other Asian economies?

myeconlab   **Study Plan 31.1**

The facts about economic growth in Canada and around the world raise some big questions that we're now going to answer. We'll study the causes of economic growth in three stages. First, we'll look at the preconditions for growth and the activities that sustain it. Second, we'll learn how economists measure the relative contributions of the sources of growth—an activity called *growth accounting*. And third, we'll study three theories of economic growth that seek to explain how the influences on growth interact to determine the growth rate. Let's take our first look at the causes of economic growth.

The Causes of Economic Growth: A First Look

MOST HUMAN SOCIETIES HAVE LIVED FOR centuries and even thousands of years, like Songman Yang and his ancestors, with no economic growth. The key reason is that they have lacked some fundamental social institutions and arrangements that are essential preconditions for economic growth. Let's see what these preconditions are.

Preconditions for Economic Growth

The most basic precondition for economic growth is an appropriate *incentive* system. Three institutions are crucial to the creation of incentives:

1. Markets
2. Property rights
3. Monetary exchange

Markets enable buyers and sellers to get information and to do business with each other, and market prices send signals to buyers and sellers that create incentives to increase or decrease the quantities demanded and supplied. Markets enable people to specialize and trade and to save and invest. But markets need property rights and monetary exchange.

Property rights are the social arrangements that govern the ownership, use, and disposal of factors of production and goods and services. They include the rights to physical property (land, buildings, and capital equipment), to financial property (claims by one person against another), and to intellectual property (such as inventions). Clearly established and enforced property rights give people an assurance that a capricious government will not confiscate their income or savings.

Monetary exchange facilitates transactions of all kinds, including the orderly transfer of private property from one person to another. Property rights and monetary exchange create incentives for people to specialize and trade, to save and invest, and to discover new technologies.

No unique political system is necessary to deliver the preconditions for economic growth. Liberal democracy, founded on the fundamental principle of the rule of law, is the system that does the best job. It provides a solid base on which property rights can be established and enforced. But authoritarian political systems have sometimes provided an environment in which economic growth has occurred.

Early human societies, based on hunting and gathering, did not experience economic growth because they lacked these preconditions. Economic growth began when societies evolved the three key institutions that create incentives. But the presence of an incentive system and the institutions that create it does not guarantee that economic growth will occur. It permits economic growth but does not make that growth inevitable.

The simplest way in which growth happens when the appropriate incentive system exists is that people begin to specialize in the activities at which they have a comparative advantage and trade with each other. You saw in Chapter 2 how everyone can gain from such activity. By specializing and trading, everyone can acquire goods and services at the lowest possible cost. Equivalently, people can obtain a greater volume of goods and services from their labour.

As an economy moves from one with little specialization to one that reaps the gains from specialization and exchange, its production and consumption grow. Real GDP per person increases, and the standard of living rises.

But for growth to be persistent, people must face incentives that encourage them to pursue three activities that generate ongoing economic growth:

- Saving and investment in new capital
- Investment in human capital
- Discovery of new technologies

These three sources of growth, which interact with each other, are the primary sources of the extraordinary growth in productivity during the past 200 years. Let's look at each in turn.

Saving and Investment in New Capital

Saving and investment in new capital increase the amount of capital per worker and increase real GDP per hour of labour—labour productivity. Labour productivity took the most dramatic upturn when the amount of capital per worker increased during the Industrial Revolution. Production processes that use hand tools can create beautiful objects, but production methods that use large amounts of capital per worker, such as auto plant assembly lines, are much more productive. The accumulation of capital on farms, in textile factories, in iron foundries and steel mills, in coal mines, on building sites, in chemical plants, in auto plants, in banks and insurance companies, and in shopping malls has added incredibly to the productivity of our economy. The next time you see a movie set in the Old West or colonial times, look carefully at the small amount of capital around. Try to imagine how productive you would be in such circumstances compared with your productivity today.

Investment in Human Capital

Human capital—the accumulated skill and knowledge of human beings—is the most fundamental source of economic growth. It is a source of both increased productivity and technological advance.

The development of one of the most basic human skills—writing—was the source of some of the earliest major gains in productivity. The ability to keep written records made it possible to reap ever-larger gains from specialization and exchange. Imagine how hard it would be to do any kind of business if all the accounts, invoices, and agreements existed only in people's memories.

Later, the development of mathematics laid the foundation for the eventual extension of knowledge about physical forces and chemical and biological processes. This base of scientific knowledge was the foundation for the technological advances of the Industrial Revolution 200 years ago and of today's information revolution.

But much human capital that is extremely productive is more humble. It takes the form of millions of individuals learning and repetitively doing simple production tasks and becoming remarkably more productive in the tasks.

One carefully studied example illustrates the importance of this kind of human capital. Between 1941 and 1944 (during World War II), U.S. shipyards produced some 2,500 units of a cargo ship, called the Liberty Ship, to a standardized design. In 1941, it took 1.2 million person-hours to build one ship. By 1942, it took 600,000 person-hours, and by 1943, it took only 500,000. Not much change occurred in the capital employed during these years. But an enormous amount of human capital was accumulated. Thousands of workers and managers learned from experience and accumulated human capital that more than doubled their productivity in two years.

Discovery of New Technologies

Saving and investment in new capital and the accumulation of human capital have made a large contribution to economic growth. But technological change—the discovery and the application of new technologies and new goods—has made an even greater contribution.

People are many times more productive today than they were a hundred years ago. We are not more productive because we have more steam engines per person and more horse-drawn carriages per person. Rather, it is because we have engines and transportation equipment that use technologies that were unknown a hundred years ago and that are more productive than the old technologies were. Technological change makes an enormous contribution to our increased productivity. It arises from formal research and development programs and from informal trial and error, and it involves discovering new ways of getting more out of our resources.

To reap the benefits of technological change, capital must increase. Some of the most powerful and far-reaching fundamental technologies are embodied in human capital—for example, language, writing, and mathematics. But most technologies are embodied in physical capital. For example, to reap the benefits of the internal combustion engine, millions of horse-drawn carriages and horses had to be replaced by automobiles; more recently, to reap the benefits of computerized word processing, millions of typewriters had to be replaced by PCs and printers.

REVIEW QUIZ

1 What economic activities that lead to economic growth do markets, property rights, and monetary exchange facilitate?
2 What are the roles of saving and investment in new capital, the growth of human capital, and the discovery of new technologies in economic growth?
3 Provide some examples of how human capital has created new technologies that are embodied in both human and physical capital.

⦻ myeconlab Study Plan 31.2

What is the quantitative contribution of the sources of economic growth? To answer this question, economists use growth accounting.

Growth Accounting

THE QUANTITY OF REAL GDP SUPPLIED (Y) depends on three factors:

1. The quantity of labour (L)
2. The quantity of capital (K)
3. The state of technology (T)

The purpose of **growth accounting** is to calculate how much real GDP growth results from growth of labour and capital and how much is attributable to technological change. The key tool of growth accounting is the **aggregate production function**, which we write as

$$Y = F(L, K, T).$$

In words, the quantity of real GDP supplied is determined by (is a function F of) the quantities of labour and capital and of the state of technology. The larger is L, K, or T, the greater is Y. And the faster L and K grow and T advances, the faster Y grows.

So understanding what makes labour and capital grow and technology advance is the key to understanding economic growth. Labour growth depends primarily on population growth. And the growth rate of capital and the pace of technological advance determine the growth rate of labour productivity.

Labour Productivity

Labour productivity is real GDP per hour of labour. Labour productivity is calculated by dividing real GDP, Y, by aggregate labour hours, L.

Labour productivity determines how much income an hour of labour generates. Figure 31.4 shows labour productivity for the period 1960–2005. Productivity growth was most rapid during the 1960s. It slowed down in 1973 to only one half of its 1960s rate, where it remained for 10 years. Productivity growth slowed even more during the late 1980s. It then speeded up in the new economy of the 1990s. But productivity growth ground to a near halt after 2002.

Growth accounting explains fluctuations in productivity growth by measuring separately the contribution of two components of productivity growth:

■ Growth in capital per hour of labour
■ Technological change

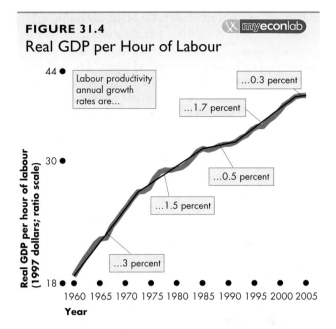

FIGURE 31.4
Real GDP per Hour of Labour

Real GDP divided by aggregate hours equals real GDP per hour of labour, which is a broad measure of productivity. During the 1960s the productivity growth rate was high. It slowed after 1973 and has fluctuated but been low since then.

Source of data: Centre for the Study of Living Standards, Aggregate Income and Productivity Trends: Canada vs United States, 1961–2004. (Updated June 14, 2005) www.csls.ca.

Capital is physical capital. Technological change includes everything that contributes to labour productivity growth that is not included in the growth in capital per hour. In particular, it includes human capital growth. Human capital growth and technological change are intimately related. Technology advances because knowledge advances. And knowledge is part of human capital. So "technological change" is a broad catchall concept.

The analytical engine of growth accounting is a relationship called the productivity curve. Let's learn about this relationship and see how it is used.

The Productivity Curve

The **productivity curve** is a relationship that shows how real GDP per hour of labour changes as the amount of capital per hour of labour changes with a given state of technology. Figure 31.5 illustrates the productivity curve. Capital per hour of labour is measured on the *x*-axis, and real GDP per hour of labour is measured on the *y*-axis. The figure shows two productivity curves. One is the curve labelled PC_0, and the other is the curve labelled PC_1.

An increase in the quantity of capital per hour of labour increases real GDP per hour of labour, which is shown by a movement along a productivity curve. For example, on PC_0, when capital per hour of labour is $30, real GDP per hour of labour is $20. If capital per hour of labour increases to $60, real GDP per hour of labour increases to $25.

Technological change increases the amount of GDP per hour of labour that can be produced by a given amount of capital per hour of labour. Technological change shifts the productivity curve upward. For example, if capital per hour of labour is $30 and a technological change increases real GDP per hour of labour from $20 to $25, the productivity curve shifts upward from PC_0 to PC_1 in Fig. 31.5. Similarly, if capital per hour of labour is $60, the same technological change increases real GDP per hour of labour from $25 to $32 and shifts the productivity curve upward from PC_0 to PC_1.

To calculate the contributions of capital growth and technological change to productivity growth, we need to know the shape of the productivity curve. The shape of the productivity curve reflects a fundamental economic law—the law of diminishing returns. The **law of diminishing returns** states that as the quantity of one input increases with the quantities of all other inputs remaining the same, output increases but by ever smaller increments. For example, in a factory that has a given amount of capital, as more labour is hired, production increases. But each *additional* hour of labour produces less *additional* output than the previous hour produced. For example, two typists working with one computer type fewer than twice as many pages per day as one typist working with one computer.

Applied to capital, the law of diminishing returns states that if a given number of hours of labour use more capital (with the same technology), the *additional* output that results from the *additional* capital gets smaller as the amount of capital increases. For example, one typist working with two computers types fewer than twice as many pages per day as one typist working with one computer. More generally, one hour of labour working with $40 of capital produces less than twice the output of one hour of labour working with $20 of capital. But how much less? The answer is given by the *one-third rule*.

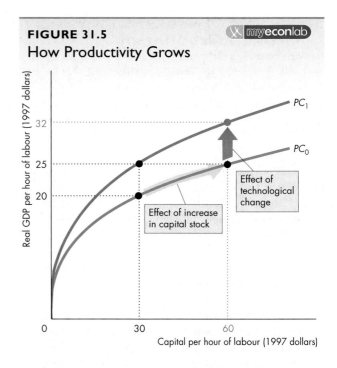

FIGURE 31.5
How Productivity Grows

Productivity is measured by real GDP per hour of labour, and it can grow for two reasons: (1) Capital per hour of labour increases, and (2) technological advances occur. The productivity curve, PC_0, shows the effects of an increase in capital per hour of labour on productivity. Here, when capital per hour of labour increases from $30 to $60, real GDP per hour of labour increases from $20 to $25 along the productivity curve PC_0. Technological advance shifts the productivity curve upward. Here, an advance in technology shifts the productivity curve from PC_0 to PC_1. When capital per hour of labour is $60, real GDP per hour of labour increases from $25 to $32.

The One-Third Rule   Robert Solow of MIT estimated a U.S. productivity curve and discovered the **one-third rule** that, on the average, with no change in technology, a 1 percent increase in capital per hour of labour brings a *one-third of 1 percent* increase in real GDP per hour of labour. This one-third rule is used to calculate the contributions of an increase in capital per hour of labour and technological change to the growth of real GDP. Let's do such a calculation.

Suppose that capital per hour of labour grows by 3 percent a year and real GDP per hour of labour grows by 2.5 percent a year. The one-third rule tells us that capital growth has contributed one-third of

3 percent, which is 1 percent, to the growth of real GDP per hour of labour. The rest of the 2.5 percent growth of real GDP per hour of labour comes from technological change. That is, technological change has contributed 1.5 percent, which is the 2.5 percent growth of real GDP per hour of labour minus the estimated 1 percent contribution of capital growth.

Accounting for the Productivity Growth Slowdown and Speedup

We can use the one-third rule to study Canadian productivity growth and the productivity growth slowdown. Figure 31.6 tells the story, starting in 1961.

Booming Sixties and Early Seventies In 1961, capital per hour of labour was $29 and real GDP per hour of labour was $18 on PC_{61} in Fig. 31.6. By 1973, capital per hour of labour had increased by 34 percent, to $39. With no change in technology, the economy would have moved to point A on PC_{61}, where real GDP per hour of labour has increased by 11.3 percent (1/3 of 34 percent). But rapid technological change shifted the productivity curve upward to PC_{73}.

Slowdown: 1973–1985 From 1973 to 1985, capital per hour of labour increased by 36 percent, to $53. With no change in technology, the economy would have moved to point B on PC_{73} in Fig. 31.6, where real GDP per hour of labour has increased by 12 percent (1/3 of 36 percent). But a small amount of technological change shifted the productivity curve upward to PC_{85}. So the productivity growth slowdown occurred because the contribution of technological change to real GDP growth slowed.

Stagnation: 1985–1991 From 1985 to 1991, capital per hour of labour increased by 9 percent and real GDP per hour of labour expanded by 3 percent (1/3 of 9 percent). The productivity curve remained stuck at its 1985 level.

The New Economy: 1991–2004 From 1991 to 2002, capital per hour of labour increased by 10 percent so with no change in technology, the economy would have moved to point C on PC_{85} in Fig. 31.6, where real GDP per hour of labour has increased by 3.3 percent (1/3 of 10 percent). But a speedup in the pace of technological change shifted the productivity curve upward to PC_{02}. But from 2002 to 2004, the

FIGURE 31.6 myeconlab

Growth Accounting and the Productivity Growth Slowdown

Between 1961 and 1973, capital per hour of labour increased from $29 to $39 and rapid technological change shifted the productivity curve upward from PC_{61} to PC_{73}. Between 1973 and 1985, capital per hour of labour increased from $39 to $53 and slower technological change shifted the productivity curve upward from PC_{73} to PC_{85}. Between 1985 and 1991, capital per hour of labour increased but with no technological change the economy moved along PC_{85}. From 1991 to 2002, capital per hour of labour increased to $64 and a speedup in technological change shifted the productivity curve upward from PC_{85} to PC_{02}. From 2002 and 2004, capital per hour of labour and productivity remained constant.

Sources of data: Centre for the Study of Living Standards, Aggregate Income and Productivity Trends: Canada vs United States, 1961–2004. (Updated June 14, 2005), www.csls.ca.

economy had no change in either capital or real GDP per hour of labour.

The growth accounting exercise that we've just worked through shows that although technological change speeded during the 1990s, its pace was slower than that during the 1960s and the so-called new economy was not such a spectacular or unusual growth phenomenon.

Technological Change During the Productivity Growth Slowdown

Technological change did not stop during the productivity growth slowdown. But its focus changed from increasing productivity to coping with

■ Energy price shocks
■ The environment

Energy Price Shocks Energy price increases that occurred in 1973–1974 and in 1979–1980 diverted research efforts towards saving energy rather than increasing productivity. Airplanes became more fuel efficient, but they didn't operate with smaller crews. Real GDP per litre of fuel increased faster, but real GDP per hour of labour increased more slowly.

The Environment The 1970s saw an expansion of laws and resources devoted to protecting the environment and improving the quality of the workplace. The benefits of these actions—cleaner air and water and safer factories—are not counted as part of real GDP. So the growth of these benefits is not measured as part of productivity growth.

Achieving Faster Growth

Growth accounting tells us that to achieve faster economic growth, we must either increase the growth rate of capital per hour of labour or increase the pace of technological advance (which includes improving human capital). The main suggestions for achieving these objectives are

■ Stimulate saving
■ Stimulate research and development
■ Target high-technology industries
■ Encourage international trade
■ Improve the quality of education

Stimulate Saving Saving finances investment, which brings capital accumulation. So stimulating saving can stimulate economic growth. The East Asian economies have the highest growth rates and the highest saving rates. Some African economies have the lowest growth rates and the lowest saving rates.

Tax incentives can increase saving. Registered Retirement Savings Plans (RRSPs) are a tax incentive to save. Economists claim that a tax on consumption rather than income provides the best saving incentive.

Stimulate Research and Development Everyone can use the fruits of *basic* research and development efforts. For example, all biotechnology firms can use advances in gene-splicing technology. Because basic inventions can be copied, the inventor's profit is limited, and the market allocates too few resources to this activity.

Governments can use public funds to finance basic research, but this solution is not foolproof. It requires a mechanism for allocating the public funds to their highest-valued use. The National Science and Engineering Research Council of Canada is one possibly efficient channel for allocating public funds to universities to finance and stimulate basic research.

Target High-Technology Industries Some people say that by providing public funds to firms in high-technology industries, a country can become the first to exploit a new technology and can earn above-average profits for a period while others are busy catching up. This strategy is risky and just as likely to use resources inefficiently as to speed growth.

Encourage International Trade Free international trade stimulates growth by extracting all the available gains from specialization and exchange. The fastest-growing nations today are those with the fastest-growing exports and imports.

Improve the Quality of Education A free market in education would produce too few educated people because education brings benefits beyond those valued by the people who receive the education. By funding basic education and by ensuring high standards in basic skills such as language, mathematics, and science, governments can contribute to a nation's growth potential. Education can also be stimulated and improved by using tax incentives to encourage improved private provision.

REVIEW QUIZ

1 Explain how the one-third rule isolates the contributions of capital growth and technological change to productivity growth.
2 Explain how growth accounting gives us information about the factors that contributed to the productivity growth slowdown of the 1970s. Why did the slowdown occur?

myeconlab Study Plan 31.3

Growth Theories

WE'VE SEEN THAT REAL GDP GROWS WHEN THE quantities of labour and capital (which includes human capital) grow and when technology advances. Does this mean that the growth of labour and capital and technological advances *cause* economic growth? It might mean that. But there are other possibilities: *One of these factors might be the cause of real GDP growth, and the others might be the effect.* We must try to discover how the influences on economic growth interact with each other to make some economies grow quickly and others grow slowly. And we must probe the reasons why a country's long-term growth rate sometimes speeds up and sometimes slows down.

Growth theories are designed to study the inter-actions among the several factors that contribute to growth and to disentangle cause and effect. They are also designed to enable us to study the way the different factors influence each other.

Growth theories are also designed to be universal. They are not theories about the growth of poor countries only or rich countries only. They are theories about why and how poor countries become rich and rich countries continue to get richer.

We're going to study three theories of economic growth, each one of which gives some insights into the process of economic growth. But none provides a definite answer to the basic questions: What causes economic growth and why do growth rates vary? Economics has some way to go before it can provide a definite answer to these most important of questions. The three growth theories we study are

- Classical growth theory
- Neoclassical growth theory
- New growth theory

Classical Growth Theory

Classical growth theory is the view that real GDP growth is temporary and that when real GDP per person rises above the subsistence level, a population explosion eventually brings real GDP per person back to the subsistence level. Adam Smith, Thomas Robert Malthus, and David Ricardo, the leading economists of the late eighteenth century and early nineteenth century, proposed this theory, but the view is most closely associated with the name of Malthus and is sometimes called the *Malthusian theory*.

Many people today are Malthusians! They say that if today's global population of 6.2 billion explodes to 11 billion by 2200, we will run out of resources and return to a primitive standard of living. We must act, say the Malthusians, to contain the population growth.

The Basic Classical Idea To understand classical growth theory, let's transport ourselves back to the world of 1776, when Adam Smith is first explaining the idea. Most of the 2.5 million people who live in the newly emerging nations of North America work on farms or on their own land and perform their tasks using simple tools and animal power. They earn an average of 2 shillings (a bit less than $12 in today's money) for working a 10-hour day.

Then advances in farming technology bring new types of plows and seeds that increase farm productivity. As farm productivity increases, farm production increases and some farm workers move from the land to the cities, where they get work producing and selling the expanding range of farm equipment. Incomes rise, and the people seem to be prospering. But will the prosperity last? Classical growth theory says it will not.

Advances in technology—in both agriculture and industry—lead to an investment in new capital, which makes labour more productive. More and more businesses start up and hire the now more productive labour. The greater demand for labour raises the real wage rate and increases employment. At this stage, economic growth has occurred and everyone has benefited from it. Real GDP has increased, and the real wage rate has increased. But the classical economists believe that this new situation can't last because it will induce a population explosion.

Classical Theory of Population Growth When the classical economists were developing their ideas about population growth, an unprecedented population explosion was underway. In Britain and other Western European countries, improvements in diet and hygiene had lowered the death rate while the birth rate remained high. For several decades, population growth was extremely rapid. For example, after being relatively stable for several centuries, the population of Britain increased by 40 percent between 1750 and 1800 and by a further 50 percent between 1800 and 1830. Meanwhile, an estimated 1 million people (about 20 percent of the 1750 population) left Britain for North

America and Australia before 1800, and outward migration continued on a similar scale through the nineteenth century. These facts are the empirical basis for the classical theory of population growth.

To explain the high rate of population growth, the classical economists used the idea of a **subsistence real wage rate**, which is the minimum real wage rate needed to maintain life. If the actual real wage rate is less than the subsistence real wage rate, some people cannot survive and the population decreases. In classical theory, when the real wage rate exceeds the subsistence real wage rate, the population grows. But a rising population brings diminishing returns to labour. So labour productivity eventually decreases. This implication led to economics being called the *dismal science*. The dismal implication is that no matter how much technological change occurs, real wage rates are always pushed back towards the subsistence level.

Classical Theory and the Productivity Curve

Figure 31.7 illustrates the classical growth theory using the productivity curve. Initially, the productivity curve is PC_0. Subsistence real GDP per hour of labour (real wage rate) is $20, shown by the horizontal line. The economy starts out at point A, with $60 of capital per hour of labour and $20 of real GDP per hour of labour, the subsistence level. Because the real wage rate is at the subsistence level, the population is constant.

Then a technological advance occurs, which shifts the productivity curve upward to PC_1. The economy now moves to point B on PC_1, and real GDP per hour of labour rises to $30. Now earning more than the subsistence real wage rate, people have more children and live longer. The population grows.

A growing population means that labour hours grow, so capital per hour of labour falls. As capital per hour of labour falls, there is a movement down along the productivity curve PC_1. Capital per hour of labour and real GDP per hour of labour fall and keep falling as long as the population grows.

This process ends when real GDP per hour of labour is back at the subsistence level at point C on productivity curve PC_1. The population stops growing and capital per hour of labour stops falling.

Repeated advances in technology play out in the same way as the advance that we've just studied. No matter how productive our economy becomes, population growth lowers capital per hour of labour and drives real GDP per hour of labour towards the sub-

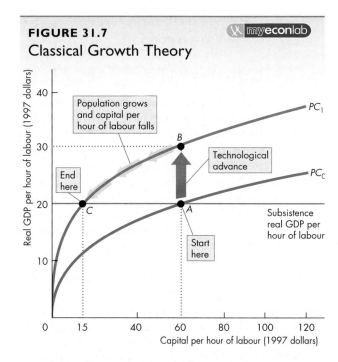

FIGURE 31.7
Classical Growth Theory

The economy starts out at point *A* with capital per hour of labour of $60 and real GDP per hour of labour of $20—the subsistence level—on productivity curve PC_0. A technological advance shifts the productivity curve upward to PC_1 and the economy moves to point *B*. The population grows, and both capital and real GDP per hour of labour decrease. The process ends at point *C* when real GDP per hour of labour is back at its subsistence level.

sistence level. Living standards temporarily improve while the population is expanding, but when the population expansion ends, the standard of living is back at the subsistence level.

Classical Theory and Capital Accumulation

In the story you've just worked through, the total quantity of capital didn't change. Suppose that people save and invest, so capital grows. Doesn't a growing quantity of capital prevent the dismal conclusion of classical theory? It does not. *Anything* that raises real GDP per hour of labour above the subsistence level triggers a population explosion that eventually wipes out the gains from greater productivity.

The dismal conclusion of classical growth theory is a direct consequence of the assumption that the population explodes if real GDP per hour of labour exceeds the subsistence level. To avoid this conclusion, we need a different view of population growth.

The neoclassical growth theory that we'll now study provides a different view.

Neoclassical Growth Theory

Neoclassical growth theory is the proposition that real GDP per person grows because technological change induces a level of saving and investment that makes capital per hour of labour grow. Growth ends only if technological change stops.

Robert Solow of MIT suggested the most popular version of neoclassical growth theory in the 1950s. But Frank Ramsey of Cambridge University in England first developed this theory in the 1920s.

Neoclassical theory's big break with its classical predecessor is its view about population growth. So we'll begin our account of neoclassical theory by examining its views about population growth.

The Neoclassical Economics of Population Growth The population explosion of eighteenth-century Europe that created the classical theory of population eventually ended. The birth rate fell, and while the population continued to increase, its rate of increase became moderate. This slowdown in population growth seemed to make the classical theory less relevant. It also eventually led to the development of a modern economic theory of population growth.

The modern view is that although the population growth rate is influenced by economic factors, the influence is not a simple and mechanical one like that proposed by the classical economists. Key among the economic influences on population growth is the opportunity cost of a woman's time. As women's wage rates increase and their job opportunities expand, the opportunity cost of having children increases. Faced with a higher opportunity cost, families choose to have fewer children and the birth rate falls.

A second economic influence works on the death rate. The technological advance that brings increased productivity and increased incomes brings advances in health care that extend lives.

These two opposing economic forces influence the population growth rate. As incomes increase, both the birth rate and the death rate decrease. It turns out that these opposing forces almost offset each other, so the rate of population growth is independent of the rate of economic growth.

This modern view of population growth and the historical trends that support it contradict the views of the classical economists and call into question the modern doomsday conclusion that the planet will one day be swamped with too many people to feed.

Neoclassical growth theory adopts this modern view of population growth. Forces other than real GDP and its growth rate determine population growth.

Technological Change In the neoclassical theory, the rate of technological change influences the rate of economic growth but economic growth does not influence the pace of technological change. It is assumed that technological change results from chance. When we get lucky, we have rapid technological change, and when bad luck strikes, the pace of technological advance slows.

Target Rate of Return and Saving The key assumption in the neoclassical growth theory concerns saving. Other things remaining the same, the higher the real interest rate, the greater is the amount that people save. To decide how much to save, people compare the real interest rate with a *target rate of return*. If the real interest rate exceeds the target rate of return, saving is sufficient to make capital per hour of labour grow. If the target rate of return exceeds the real interest rate, saving is not sufficient to maintain the current level of capital per hour of labour, so capital per hour of labour shrinks. And if the real interest rate equals a target rate of return, saving is just sufficient to maintain the quantity of capital per hour of labour at its current level.

The Basic Neoclassical Idea To understand neoclassical growth theory, imagine the world of the mid-1950s, when Robert Solow is explaining his idea. Canadians are enjoying post–World War II prosperity. Income per person is around $12,000 a year in today's money. The population is growing at about 1 percent a year. People are saving and investing about 20 percent of their incomes, enough to keep the quantity of capital per hour of labour constant. Income per person is growing, but not by much.

Then technology begins to advance at a more rapid pace across a range of activities. The transistor revolutionizes an emerging electronics industry. New plastics revolutionize the manufacture of household appliances. The national highway system revolutionizes road transportation. Jet airliners start to replace piston-engine airplanes and speed air transportation.

These technological advances bring new profit opportunities. Businesses expand, and new businesses are created to exploit the newly available profitable technologies. Investment and saving increase. The economy enjoys new levels of prosperity and growth. But will the prosperity last? And will the growth last? Neoclassical growth theory says that the *prosperity* will last but the *growth* will not last unless technology keeps advancing.

According to the neoclassical growth theory, the prosperity will persist because there is no classical population growth to induce lower wages.

But growth will stop if technology stops advancing, for two related reasons. First, high profit rates that result from technological change bring increased saving and capital accumulation. But second, capital accumulation eventually results in diminishing returns that lower the rate of return, and that eventually decrease saving and slow the rate of capital accumulation.

Neoclassical Theory and the Productivity Curve

Figure 31.8 illustrates the neoclassical growth theory using the productivity curve. Initially, the productivity curve is PC_0 and the economy is at point A, with $60 of capital per hour of labour and real GDP per hour of labour of $20.

The slope of the productivity curve measures the additional output that results from an additional unit of capital—the marginal product of capital or real interest rate. People have a target rate of return that can be illustrated by a straight line with a slope equal to the target rate of return.

At point A on productivity curve PC_0, the slope of the PC curve equals the slope of the target rate of return line. If the quantity of capital per hour of labour were less than $60, the real interest rate would exceed the target rate of return and capital per hour of labour would grow. If the quantity of capital per hour of labour were greater than $60, the real interest rate would be less than the target rate of return and capital per hour of labour would shrink. But when the quantity of capital per hour of labour is $60, the real interest rate equals the target rate of return and capital per hour of labour is constant.

Now a technological advance occurs that shifts the productivity curve upward to PC_1. The economy now moves to point B on PC_1, and real GDP per hour of labour rises to $30. It is at this point in the classical theory that forces kick in to drive real GDP per hour of labour back to the subsistence level. But in the neoclassical theory, no such forces operate. Instead, at point B, the real interest rate exceeds the target rate of return. (You can see why by comparing

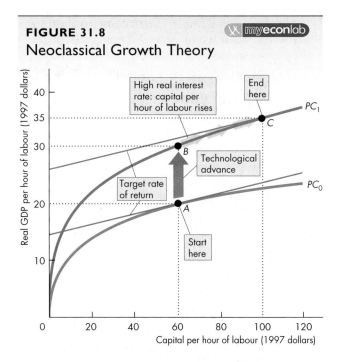

FIGURE 31.8
Neoclassical Growth Theory

The economy starts on productivity curve PC_0 at point A. The slope of the productivity curve measures the rate of return, so at point A the rate of return equals the target rate of return. A technological advance shifts the productivity curve upward to PC_1 and the economy moves to point B. The rate of return exceeds the target rate of return, and the quantity of capital per hour of labour increases—a movement up along the productivity curve PC_1. Growth ends when the rate of return again equals the target rate of return at point C.

the slopes of PC_1 at point B and the target rate of return line.)

With a high real interest rate available, saving and investment increase and the quantity of capital per hour of labour increases. There is a movement up along the productivity curve PC_1, and real GDP per hour of labour increases.

This growth process eventually ends because, as the quantity of capital per hour of labour increases, the real interest rate falls. At point C, where the process ends, the real interest rate again equals the target rate of return.

Throughout the process you've just studied, real GDP per hour of labour grows but the growth rate gradually decreases and eventually growth ends.

But if another advance in technology occurs, the process you've just seen repeats. Ongoing advances in technology constantly increase the rate of return, inducing the saving that increases capital per hour of labour. The growth process persists as long as technology advances. And the growth rate fluctuates because technological progress occurs at a variable rate.

A Problem with Neoclassical Growth Theory All economies have access to the same technologies, and capital is free to roam the globe seeking the highest available rate of return. Given these facts, neoclassical growth theory implies that growth rates and income levels per person around the globe will converge. While there is some sign of convergence among the rich countries, as Fig. 31.2(a) shows, convergence is slow, and it does not appear to be imminent for all countries, as Fig. 31.2(b) shows.

New growth theory attempts to overcome this shortcoming of neoclassical growth theory. It also attempts to explain how the rate of technological change is determined.

New Growth Theory

New growth theory holds that real GDP per person grows because of the choices people make in the pursuit of profit and that growth can persist indefinitely. Paul Romer of Stanford University developed this theory during the 1980s, but the ideas go back to the work by Joseph Schumpeter during the 1930s and 1940s.

The theory begins with two facts about market economies:

■ Discoveries result from choices.
■ Discoveries bring profit and competition destroys profit.

Discoveries and Choices When people discover a new product or technique, they think of themselves as being lucky. They are right. But the pace at which new discoveries are made—and at which technology advances—is not determined by chance. It depends on how many people are looking for a new technology and how intensively they are looking.

Discoveries and Profits Profit is the spur to technological change. The forces of competition squeeze profits, so to increase profit, people constantly seek either lower-cost methods of production or new and better

products for which people are willing to pay a higher price. Inventors can maintain a profit for several years by taking out a patent or copyright. But eventually, a new discovery is copied, and profits disappear.

Two further facts play a key role in the new growth theory:

■ Discoveries are a public capital good.
■ Knowledge is capital that is not subject to the law of diminishing returns.

Discoveries Are a Public Capital Good Economists call a good a *public good* when no one can be excluded from using it and when one person's use does not prevent others from using it. National defence is one example of a public good. Knowledge is another.

When in 1992, Marc Andreesen and his friend Eric Bina developed a browser they called Mosaic, they laid the foundation for Netscape Navigator and Internet Explorer, two pieces of capital that have increased productivity unimaginably.

While patents and copyrights protect the inventors or creators of new products and production processes and enable them to reap the returns from their innovative ideas, once a new discovery has been made, everyone can benefit from its use. And one person's use of a new discovery does not prevent others from using it. Your use of a Web browser doesn't prevent someone else from using that same browser simultaneously.

Because knowledge is a public good, as the benefits of a new discovery spread, free resources become available. These resources are free because nothing is given up when they are used. They have a zero opportunity cost. Knowledge is even more special because it is not subject to diminishing returns.

Knowledge Capital Is Not Subject to Diminishing Returns Production is subject to diminishing returns when one resource is fixed and the quantity of another resource changes. Adding labour to a fixed amount of equipment or adding equipment to a fixed amount of labour both bring diminishing marginal product—diminishing returns.

But increasing the stock of knowledge makes labour and machines more productive. Knowledge capital does not bring diminishing returns.

The fact that knowledge capital does *not* experience diminishing returns is the central novel proposition of the new growth theory. And the implication of this simple and appealing idea is astonishing. The new growth theory has no growth-stopping mechanism like those of the other two theories. As physical capital accumulates, the rate of return falls. But the incentive to innovate and earn a higher profit becomes stronger. So innovation occurs, which increases the rate of return. Real GDP per hour of labour grows indefinitely as people find new technologies that yield a higher rate of return.

The growth rate depends on people's ability to innovate and the rate of return. Over the years, the ability to innovate has changed. The invention of language and writing (the two most basic human capital tools) and later the development of the scientific method and the establishment of universities and research institutions brought huge increases in the rate of return. Today, a deeper understanding of genes is bringing profit in a growing biotechnology industry. And astonishing advances in computer technology are creating an explosion of profit opportunities in a wide range of information-age industries.

New Growth Theory and the Productivity Curve
Figure 31.9 illustrates new growth theory. Like Fig. 31.8, which illustrates neoclassical growth theory, Fig. 31.9 contains a productivity curve and a target rate of return line.

But unlike in neoclassical theory, the productivity curve in the new growth theory never stands still. The pursuit of profit means that technology is always advancing and human capital is always growing. The result is an ever upward-shifting PC curve. As physical capital is accumulated, diminishing returns lower its rate of return. But ever-advancing productivity counteracts this tendency and keeps the rate of return above the target rate of return curve.

Advancing technology and human capital growth keep the PC curve shifting upward in Fig. 31.9 from PC_0 to PC_1 to PC_2 and beyond. As the productivity curve shifts upward, capital per hour of labour and real GDP per hour of labour increase together along the line labelled "Ak line."

The new growth theory implies that although the productivity curve shows diminishing returns, if capital is interpreted more broadly as physical capital, human capital, and the technologies they embody, then real GDP per hour of labour grows at the same rate as the growth in capital per hour of labour. Real GDP per hour of labour is proportional to capital per hour of labour.

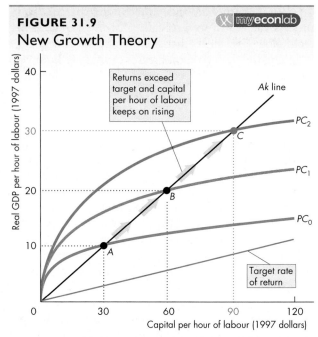

FIGURE 31.9
New Growth Theory

In new growth theory, economic growth results from incentives to innovate and from capital that does not experience diminishing returns. The productivity curve, PC, keeps shifting upward, and real GDP per hour of labour and capital per hour of labour grow along the Ak line.

Real GDP per hour of labour y is related to capital per hour of labour k by the equation:

$$y = Ak.$$

In Fig 31.9, $A = (1/3)$. When capital per hour of labour is $30, real GDP per hour of labour is $10 at point A. People look for yet more profit and accumulate yet more capital. The economy expands to point B, with capital per hour of labour of $60 and real GDP per hour of labour of $20. In pursuit of further profit, technology keeps advancing and capital per hour of labour rises to $90 with real GDP per hour of labour of $30, at point C. Real GDP per hour of labour and capital per hour of labour increase without limit.

A Perpetual Motion Economy The new growth theory sees the economy as a perpetual motion machine, which Fig. 31.10 illustrates. Insatiable wants lead us to pursue profit, innovate, and create new and better products. New firms start up and old firms go out of business. As firms start up and die, jobs are created and destroyed. New and better jobs

FIGURE 31.10

A Perpetual Motion Machine

myeconlab

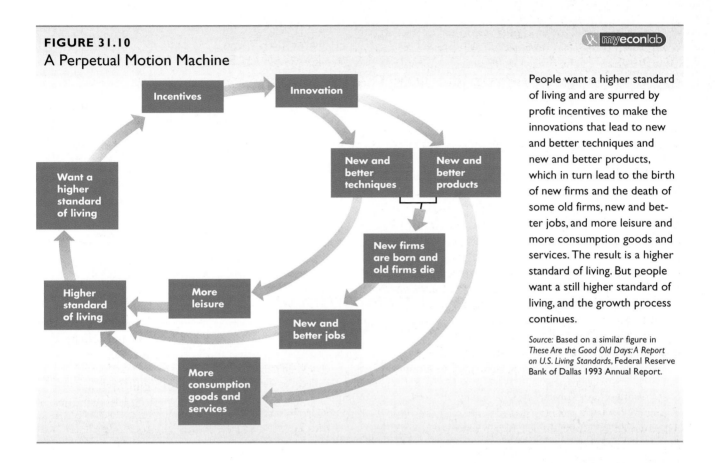

People want a higher standard of living and are spurred by profit incentives to make the innovations that lead to new and better techniques and new and better products, which in turn lead to the birth of new firms and the death of some old firms, new and better jobs, and more leisure and more consumption goods and services. The result is a higher standard of living. But people want a still higher standard of living, and the growth process continues.

Source: Based on a similar figure in *These Are the Good Old Days: A Report on U.S. Living Standards*, Federal Reserve Bank of Dallas 1993 Annual Report.

lead to more leisure and more consumption. But our insatiable wants are still there, so the process continues, going around and around a circle of wants, profits, innovation, and new products.

Sorting Out the Theories

Which theory is correct? Probably none, but they all teach us something of value. The classical theory reminds us that our physical resources are limited and that with no advances in technology, we must eventually hit diminishing returns. Neoclassical theory reaches essentially the same conclusion, but not because of a population explosion. Instead, it emphasizes diminishing returns to capital and reminds us that we cannot keep growth going just by accumulating physical capital. We must also advance technology and accumulate human capital. We must become more creative in our use of scarce resources. New growth theory emphasizes the possible capacity of human resources to innovate at a pace that offsets diminishing returns.

REVIEW QUIZ

1 What is the key idea of classical growth theory that leads to the dismal outcome?

2 What, according to the neoclassical growth theory, is the fundamental cause of economic growth?

3 What is the key proposition of the new growth theory that makes growth persist?

 Study Plan 31.4

◆ Economic growth is the single most decisive factor influencing a country's living standard. Another is the extent to which the country exploits its comparative advantage in international trade. We study this topic in the next chapter. Before embarking on this topic, take a look at *Reading Between the Lines* on pp. 750–751 and compare Canada's recent productivity growth with that of the United States.

Forecasting Economic Growth

THE GLOBE AND MAIL, NOVEMBER 14, 2005

Not everyone's pessimistic about productivity

Ottawa economist Stephen Poloz lives in a city where people are tearing their hair out over Canada's abysmal productivity record.

The country's prosperity is at stake, they argue, because for years, companies and workers have found few new ways to improve their efficiency, while the rest of the world — notably, the United States — zooms ahead.

Canada's standard of living will deteriorate, they say, unless the government cuts taxes and invests millions in new investment incentives, and unless the private sector becomes much more imaginative. They will be watching Finance Minister Ralph Goodale closely today when he delivers his mini-budget, to see whether he can give business what it needs to reverse the trend.

But Mr. Poloz, chief economist at Export Development Canada, isn't the least bit worried. He believes Canada's productivity is on the verge of a recovery, with or without the federal government's help.

"We believe it's happening," Mr. Poloz said in a recent interview.

Mr. Poloz is in a small but growing camp of experts who believe a turn-around in productivity is at hand, as Canadian companies discover the benefits of cheap imports, new technology, and low wages on the other side of the world.

But their arguments are met with skepticism from others who are as pessimistic as ever about Canada's prospects.

"I don't think we're about to see 3-per-cent productivity growth," said Andrew Sharpe, executive director of the Centre for the Study of Living Standards.

No one would disagree that Canada's productivity, defined as output as a percentage of hours, has been embarrassing these past few years. On average, Canada's productivity growth has hovered just above zero since 2000. The U.S., on the other hand, has seen productivity grow by an average of 3.8 per cent since the start of the decade.

But according to Mr. Poloz, this is about to change. ... he says, Canadian companies of all sizes are discovering how to cut costs and increase output by doing more business offshore.

Reprinted with permission of *The Globe and Mail*.

Essence of the Story

■ Canadian productivity has barely changed since 2000.

■ During that same period, U.S. productivity has grown by 3.8 percent a year.

■ Economist Stephen Poloz believes that things are about to change and that Canadian productivity growth is starting to increase.

■ Economist Andrew Sharp doesn't think we'll see 3 percent a year productivity growth.

Economic Analysis

■ Canadian real GDP per person has never been as high as that of the United States.

■ During the last 45 years (since 1961), Canadian real GDP per person has fluctuated between a low of 81 percent and a high of 92 percent of U.S. real GDP per person.

■ Figure 1 shows the data. Relative to U.S. real GDP per person, Canadian real GDP per person was steady at 85 percent during the 1960s, climbed through the 1970s, fell during the 1980s to a low in 1993, increased through 2002, and fell through 2004.

■ What explains these changes in Canadian real GDP per person relative to the U.S. level?

■ Three broad possible answers are:
(1) Canadians work fewer hours than Americans.
(2) Canadians have less capital per unit of output than Americans.
(3) Canadians have lower overall productivity—total factor productivity —than Americans.

■ Figure 2 shows that the first two possibilities do not explain the trends.

■ Hour worked per Canadian have fluctuat-ed relative to U.S. labour hours per person, and Canadian work hours did fall during the late 1980s and much of the 1990s. But Canadian work hours increased after 1997 and by 2004 exceeded U.S. hours.

■ Capital per unit of output (the capital output ratio) increased in Canada from 80 percent of the U.S. level in 1961 to 100 percent during the 2000s.

■ Figure 2 shows growth during the decade 1992–2002. Over this period, Canada tops the table and the United States places second. But the United States was top until 2000.

■ Figure 3 shows the source of Canada's problem. Total factor productivity in Canada collapsed from 99 percent of the U.S. level in 1974 to 88 percent in 1992. It increased somewhat through 2000 but then decreased again.

■ The reasons for Canada's poor growth of total factor productivity are complex and contro-versial.

■ If Stephen Poloz is to be proved correct, it is Canada's total factor productivity that must improve.

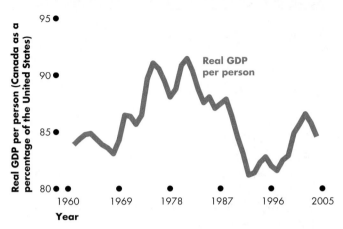

Figure 1 Real GDP compared

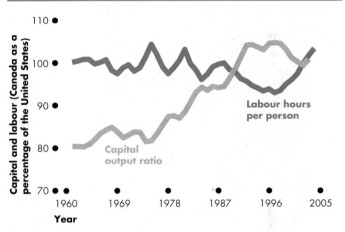

Figure 2 Factor inputs compared

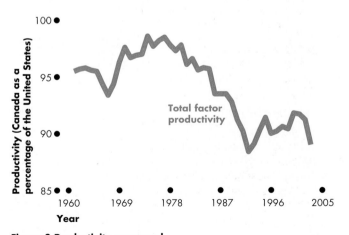

Figure 3 Productivity compared

751

SUMMARY

KEY POINTS

Long-Term Growth Trends (pp. 734–736)

- Between 1926 and 2004, real GDP per person in Canada grew at an average rate of 2.2 percent a year. Growth was most rapid during the 1960s and slowest during the 1980s.
- The real GDP per person gaps between Canada and Hong Kong, Korea, Taiwan, and China have narrowed. The gaps between Canada and Central and South America, Africa, and Central Europe have widened.

The Causes of Economic Growth: A First Look (pp. 737–738)

- Economic growth requires an *incentive* system created by markets, property rights, and monetary exchange.
- Economic growth occurs when people save, invest in physical and human capital, and discover new technologies.

Growth Accounting (pp. 739–742)

- Growth accounting measures the contributions of capital accumulation and technological change to productivity growth.
- Growth accounting uses the productivity curve and the one-third rule: A 1 percent increase in capital per hour of labour brings an increase in real GDP per hour of labour of one-third of 1 percent.
- During the productivity growth slowdown of the 1970s, technological change made no contribution to real GDP growth.
- It might be possible to achieve faster growth by stimulating saving, stimulating research and development, targeting high-technology industries, encouraging more international trade, and improving the quality of education.

Growth Theories (pp. 743–749)

- In classical theory, when technological advances increase real GDP per person above the *subsistence* level, a population explosion brings diminishing returns to labour and real GDP per person returns to the subsistence level.
- In neoclassical growth theory, when technological advances increase saving and investment, an increase in the capital stock brings diminishing returns to capital and eventually, without further technological change, the capital stock and real GDP per person stop growing.
- In new growth theory, when technological advances increase saving and investment, an increase in the capital stock *does not* bring diminishing returns to capital and growth persists indefinitely.

KEY FIGURES

KEY TERMS

PROBLEMS

Go to (X myeconlab) for solutions to odd-numbered problems and additional exercises.

1. The following information has been discovered about the economy of Longland. The economy's productivity curve is

Capital per hour of labour (1997 dollars per hour)	Real GDP per hour of labour (1997 dollars per hour)
10	3.80
20	5.70
30	7.13
40	8.31
50	9.35
60	10.29
70	11.14
80	11.94

Does this economy conform to the one-third rule? If so, explain why. If not, explain why not and explain what rule, if any, it does conform to. Explain how you would do the growth accounting for this economy.

2. The following information has been discovered about the economy of Flatland. The economy's productivity curve is

Capital per hour of labour (1997 dollars per hour)	Real GDP per hour of labour (1997 dollars per hour)
20	6.00
40	7.50
60	8.44
80	9.14
100	9.72
120	10.20
140	10.62
160	11.00

Does this economy conform to the one-third rule? If so, explain why. If not, explain why not and explain what rule, if any, it does conform to. Explain how you would do the growth accounting for this economy.

3. In Longland, described in problem 1, capital per hour of labour in 2003 was $40 and real GDP per hour of labour was $8.31. In 2005, capital per hour of labour was $50 and real GDP per hour of labour was $10.29 an hour.

a. Does Longland experience diminishing returns? Explain why or why not.
b. Use growth accounting to find the contribution of the change in capital between 2003 and 2005 to the growth of productivity in Longland.
c. Use growth accounting to find the contribution of technological change between 2003 and 2005 to the growth of productivity in Longland.

4. In Flatland, described in problem 2, capital per hour of labour in 2003 was $60 and real GDP per hour of labour was $8.44. In 2005, capital per hour of labour was $120 and real GDP per hour of labour was $12.74 an hour.

a. Does Flatland experience diminishing returns? Explain why or why not.
b. Use growth accounting to find the contribution of the change in capital between 2003 and 2005 to the growth of productivity in Flatland.
c. Use growth accounting to find the contribution of technological change between 2003 and 2005 to the growth of productivity in Flatland.

5. The following information has been discovered about the economy of Cape Despair. Subsistence real GDP per hour of labour is $15. Whenever real GDP per hour rises above this level, the population grows, and when real GDP per hour of labour falls below this level, the population falls. The productivity curve in Cape Despair is as follows:

Capital per hour of labour (1997 dollars per hour)	Real GDP per hour of labour (1997 dollars per hour)
20	8
40	15
60	21
80	26
100	30
120	33
140	35
160	36

Initially, the population of Cape Despair is constant, and real GDP per hour of labour is at its subsistence level. Then a technological advance shifts the productivity curve upward by $7 at each level of capital per hour of labour.

a. What are the initial capital per hour of labour and real GDP per hour of labour?

b. What happens to real GDP per hour of labour immediately following the technological advance?

c. What happens to the population growth rate following the technological advance?

d. What is the eventual quantity of capital per hour of labour in Cape Despair?

6. Martha's Island is an economy that behaves according to the neoclassical growth model. The economy has no growth, a target rate of return of 10 percent a year, and the following productivity curve:

Capital per hour of labour (1997 dollars per hour)	Real GDP per hour of labour (1997 dollars per hour)
40	16
80	30
120	42
160	52
200	60
240	66
280	70
320	72

A technological advance shifts the productivity curve upward.

a. What is the initial capital per hour of labour on Martha's Island?

b. What is the initial real GDP per hour of labour?

c. What happens to the real interest rate immediately following the technological advance?

d. What happens to the return on capital and the quantity of capital per hour of labour?

7. Romeria is a country that behaves according to the predictions of new growth theory. The target rate is 3 percent a year. A technological advance increases the demand for capital and raises the rate of return to 5 percent a year. Describe the events that happen in Romeria and contrast them with the events in Martha's Island in problem 6.

8. Suppose that in Romeria, described in problem 7, technological advance slows and the rate of return falls to 3 percent a year. Describe what happens in Romeria.

CRITICAL THINKING

1. Study *Reading Between the Lines* on pp. 750–751 and then answer the following questions:

a. How does the growth rate of real GDP per person in Canada compare with that of the United States?

b. What is the source of Canada's slower growth of real GDP per person. Distinguish among the contrubutions of labour, capital, and total factor productivity.

c. Suppose someone argued that Canada's growth of real GDP per person appears to be slower than that of the United States because Canada has moved from above full employment to below full employment. Explain why that argument is wrong.

2. Is faster economic growth always a good thing? Argue the case for faster growth and the case for slower growth and then reach a conclusion on whether Canadian growth should be increased or decreased.

WEB EXERCISES

Use the links on (X myeconlab) **to work the following exercises.**

1. Go to the Penn World Table Web site and obtain data on real GDP per person for Canada, China, South Africa, and Mexico since 1960.

a. Draw a graph of the data.

b. Which country has the lowest real GDP per person and which has the highest?

c. Which country has experienced the fastest growth rate since 1960 and which the slowest?

d. Explain why the growth rates in these four countries are ranked in the order you have discovered.

e. Obtain data for any four other countries that interest you. Describe and explain the patterns that you find for these countries.

2. Write a memo to your member of Parliament in which you set out the policies you believe the Canadian government must follow to speed up the growth rate of real GDP in Canada.

Trading with the World

Silk Routes and Sucking Sounds

Since ancient times, people have expanded their trading as far as technology allowed. Marco Polo opened up the silk route between Europe and China in the thirteenth century. Today, container ships laden with cars and electronics and Boeing 747s stuffed with farm-fresh foods ply sea and air routes, carrying billions of dollars' worth of goods. Why do people go to such great lengths to trade with those in other nations?

In 1994, Canada entered into a free trade agreement with the United States and Mexico—the North American Free Trade Agreement, or NAFTA. Some people predicted a "giant sucking sound" as jobs were transferred from high-wage Michigan and Ontario to low-wage Mexico. Can we compete with a country that pays its workers a fraction of Canadian wages? Are there any industries, besides perhaps the software and movie industries, in which we have an advantage?

Canada exports lumber to the United States for home building. But U.S. lumber producers say that Canadian producers receive an unfair subsidy from their government, so the United States has imposed a tariff on Canadian lumber imports. Do tariffs benefit the importing country? We examine this question in *Reading Between the Lines*.

◆ In this chapter, we're going to learn about international trade and discover how *all* nations can gain from trading with other nations. We'll discover that all nations can compete, no matter how high their wages. We'll also explain why, despite the fact that international trade brings benefits to all, governments restrict trade.

After studying this chapter, you will be able to

- ■ **Describe the trends and patterns in international trade**

- ■ **Explain comparative advantage and explain why all countries can gain from international trade**

- ■ **Explain the effects of international trade restrictions**

- ■ **Explain the arguments for trade restrictions and why they are flawed**

- ■ **Describe a country's balance of payments accounts and explain what determines the current account balance**

- ■ **Describe the North American Free Trade Agreement**

Patterns and Trends in International Trade

THE GOODS AND SERVICES THAT WE BUY FROM people in other countries are called **imports**. The goods and services that we sell to people in other countries are called **exports**. What are the most important things that we import and export? Most people would probably guess that a rich nation such as Canada imports raw materials and exports manufactured goods. Although that is one feature of Canadian international trade, it is not its most important feature. The vast bulk of our exports *and* imports is manufactured goods. We sell foreigners earth-moving equipment, airplanes, telecommunications equipment, and scientific equipment. We buy televisions, DVDs, blue jeans, and T-shirts from foreigners. Also, we are a major exporter of agricultural products and raw materials. We also import and export a huge volume of services.

Trade in Goods

Of the goods that we trade, manufactured goods account for 74 percent of our exports and 84 percent of our imports. Industrial materials (raw materials and semimanufactured items) account for 44 percent of our exports and 28 percent of our imports, and agricultural products account for only 7 percent of our exports and 5 percent of our imports. Our largest individual export and import items are capital goods and automobiles.

But goods account for only 87 percent of our exports and 83 percent of our imports. The rest of our international trade is in services.

Trade in Services

You may be wondering how a country can "export" and "import" services. Here are some examples.

If you take a vacation in France and travel there on an Air France flight from Montreal, you import transportation services from France. The money you spend in France on hotel bills and restaurant meals is also classified as the import of services. Similarly, the money spent by a French student on vacation in Canada is a Canadian export of services to France.

When we import TV sets from South Korea, the owner of the ship that transports them might be Greek and the company that insures them might be British. The payments that we make for the transportation and insurance are Canadian imports of services. Similarly, when a Canadian shipping company transports timber from British Columbia to Tokyo, the transportation cost is a Canadian export of a service to Japan. Our international trade in these types of services is large and growing.

Geographical Patterns of International Trade

Canada has trading links with every part of the world, but the United States is our biggest trading partner. In 2004, 82 percent of our exports went to the United States and 69 percent of our imports came from the United States. Our trade with the European Union is also large—6 percent of our exports and 10 percent of our imports in 2004. Other trading partners include the countries of Latin America and Japan. But our trade with Japan is only 2 percent of exports and 3 percent of imports.

Trends in the Volume of Trade

In 1978, we exported 25 percent of total output and imported 25 percent of the goods and services that we bought. In 2004, we exported 44 percent of total output and imported 39 percent of the goods and services that we bought.

On the export side, capital goods, automobiles, food, and raw materials have remained large items and held a roughly constant share of total exports. But the composition of imports has changed. Food and raw material imports have fallen steadily. Imports of fuel increased during the 1970s but decreased during the 1980s. Imports of machinery have grown and today approach 30 percent of total imports.

Net Exports and International Borrowing

The value of exports minus the value of imports is called **net exports**. In 2004, Canadian net exports were $54 billion. Our exports were $54 billion more than our imports. When we export more than we import, as we did in 2004, we lend to foreigners or buy some of their assets. When we import more than we export, we borrow from foreigners or sell some of our assets to them.

myeconlab   **Study Plan 32.1**

The Gains from International Trade

THE FUNDAMENTAL FORCE THAT GENERATES international trade is *comparative advantage*. And the basis of comparative advantage is divergent *opportunity costs*. You met these ideas in Chapter 2, when we learned about comparative advantages and the gains from specialization and trade between Liz and Joe.

Joe specializes in producing just one good, but most nations, like Liz, do not go to the extreme of specializing in a single good and importing everything else. Like Liz and Joe, nations can increase the consumption of all goods if they redirect their scarce resources towards the production of those goods and services in which they have a comparative advantage.

To see how this outcome occurs, we'll apply the same basic ideas that we learned in the case of Liz and Joe to trade among nations. We'll begin by recalling how we can use the production possibilities frontier to measure opportunity cost. Then we'll see how divergent opportunity costs bring comparative advantage and how by moving resources to increase production of the good in which each country has a comparative advantage countries can gain from international trade, just as Liz and Joe did.

Opportunity Cost in Farmland

Farmland (a fictitious country) can produce grain and cars at any point inside or along its production possibilities frontier, *PPF*, shown in Fig. 32.1. (We're holding constant the output of all the other goods that Farmland produces.) The Farmers (the people of Farmland) are consuming all the grain and cars that they produce, and they are operating at point *A* in the figure. That is, Farmland is producing and consuming 15 million tonnes of grain and 8 million cars each year. What is the opportunity cost of a car in Farmland?

We can answer that question by calculating the slope of the production possibilities frontier at point *A*. The magnitude of the slope of the frontier measures the opportunity cost of one good in terms of the other. To measure the slope of the frontier at point *A*, place a straight line tangential to the frontier at point *A* and calculate the slope of that straight line. Recall that the formula for the slope of a line is the change in the value of the variable measured on the *y*-axis divided by the change in the value of the variable

measured on the *x*-axis as we move along the line. Here, the variable measured on the *y*-axis is millions of tonnes of grain, and the variable measured on the *x*-axis is millions of cars. So the slope is the change in the number of tonnes of grain divided by the change in the number of cars.

As you can see from the red triangle at point *A* in the figure, if the number of cars produced increases by 2 million, grain production decreases by 18 million tonnes. So the magnitude of the slope is 18 million divided by 2 million, which equals 9. That is, to get 1 more car, the people of Farmland must give up 9 tonnes of grain. So the opportunity cost of 1 car is 9 tonnes of grain. Equivalently, 9 tonnes of grain cost 1 car. For the people of Farmland, these opportunity costs are the prices they face. The price of a car is 9 tonnes of grain, and the price of 9 tonnes of grain is 1 car.

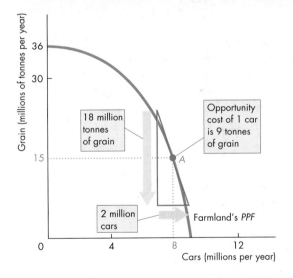

Farmland produces and consumes 15 million tonnes of grain and 8 million cars a year. That is, it produces and consumes at point A on its production possibilities frontier. Opportunity cost is equal to the magnitude of the slope of the production possibilities frontier. The red triangle tells us that at point A, 18 million tonnes of grain must be forgone to get 2 million cars. That is, at point A, 2 million cars cost 18 million tonnes of grain. Equivalently, 1 car costs 9 tonnes of grain or 9 tonnes of grain cost 1 car.

Opportunity Cost in Mobilia

Figure 32.2 shows the production possibilities frontier of Mobilia (another fictitious country). Like the Farmers, the Mobilians consume all the grain and cars that they produce. Mobilia consumes 18 million tonnes of grain a year and 4 million cars, at point A'.

Let's calculate the opportunity costs in Mobilia. At point A', the opportunity cost of a car is equal to the magnitude of the slope of the red line tangential to the production possibilities frontier, *PPF*. You can see from the red triangle that the magnitude of the slope of Mobilia's production possibilities frontier is 6 million tonnes of grain divided by 6 million cars, which equals 1 tonne of grain per car. To get 1 more car, the Mobilians must give up 1 tonne of grain. So the opportunity cost of 1 car is 1 tonne of grain, or equivalently, the opportunity cost of 1 tonne of grain is 1 car. These are the prices faced in Mobilia.

Comparative Advantage

Cars are cheaper in Mobilia than in Farmland. One car costs 9 tonnes of grain in Farmland but only

FIGURE 32.2   ⊗ myeconlab

Opportunity Cost in Mobilia

Mobilia produces and consumes 18 million tonnes of grain and 4 million cars a year. That is, it produces and consumes at point A' on its production possibilities frontier. Opportunity cost is equal to the magnitude of the slope of the production possibilities frontier. The red triangle tells us that at point A', 6 million tonnes of grain must be forgone to get 6 million cars. That is, at point A', 6 million cars cost 6 million tonnes of grain. Equivalently, 1 car costs 1 tonne of grain or 1 tonne of grain costs 1 car.

1 tonne of grain in Mobilia. But grain is cheaper in Farmland than in Mobilia—9 tonnes of grain cost only 1 car in Farmland, while that same amount of grain costs 9 cars in Mobilia.

Mobilia has a comparative advantage in car production. Farmland has a comparative advantage in grain production. A country has a comparative advantage in producing a good if it can produce that good at a lower opportunity cost than any other country. Let's see how opportunity cost differences and comparative advantage generate gains from international trade.

The Gains from Trade: Cheaper to Buy Than to Produce

If Mobilia bought grain for what it costs Farmland to produce it, then Mobilia could buy 9 tonnes of grain for 1 car. That is much lower than the cost of growing grain in Mobilia, for there it costs 9 cars to produce 9 tonnes of grain. If the Mobilians can buy grain at the low Farmland price, they will reap some gains.

If the Farmers can buy cars for what it costs Mobilia to produce them, they will be able to obtain a car for 1 tonne of grain. Because it costs 9 tonnes of grain to produce a car in Farmland, the Farmers would gain from such an opportunity.

In this situation, it makes sense for Mobilians to buy their grain from Farmers and for Farmers to buy their cars from Mobilians. But at what price will Farmland and Mobilia engage in mutually beneficial international trade?

The Terms of Trade

The quantity of grain that Farmland must pay Mobilia for a car is Farmland's **terms of trade** with Mobilia. Because Canada exports and imports many different goods and services, we measure the terms of trade in the real world as an index number that averages the terms of trade over all the items we trade.

The forces of international supply and demand determine the terms of trade. Figure 32.3 illustrates these forces in the Farmland–Mobilia international car market. The quantity of cars *traded internationally* is measured on the *x*-axis. On the *y*-axis, we measure the price of a car. This price is expressed as the *terms of trade*: tonnes of grain per car. If no international trade takes place, the price of a car in Farmland is 9 tonnes of grain, its opportunity cost, indicated by

FIGURE 32.3

myeconlab

International Trade in Cars

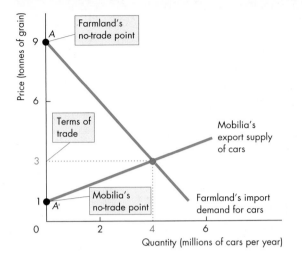

Farmland's import demand curve for cars is downward sloping, and Mobilia's export supply curve of cars is upward sloping. Without international trade, the price of a car is 9 tonnes of grain in Farmland (point A) and 1 tonne of grain in Mobilia (point A').

With free international trade, the price (terms of trade) is determined where the export supply curve intersects the import demand curve: 3 tonnes of grain per car. At that price, 4 million cars a year are imported by Farmland and exported by Mobilia. The value of grain exported by Farmland and imported by Mobilia is 12 million tonnes a year, the quantity required to pay for the cars imported.

point *A* in the figure. Again, if no trade takes place, the price of a car in Mobilia is 1 tonne of grain, its opportunity cost, indicated by point *A'* in the figure. The no-trade points *A* and *A'* in Fig. 32.3 correspond to the points identified by those same letters in Figs. 32.1 and 32.2. The lower the price of a car (terms of trade), the greater is the quantity of cars that the Farmers are willing to import from the Mobilians. This fact is illustrated by the downward-sloping curve, which shows Farmland's import demand for cars.

The Mobilians respond in the opposite direction. The higher the price of a car (terms of trade), the greater is the quantity of cars that Mobilians are willing to export to Farmers. This fact is reflected in Mobilia's export supply of cars—the upward-sloping line in Fig. 32.3.

The international market in cars determines the equilibrium terms of trade (price) and quantity traded. This equilibrium occurs where the import demand curve intersects the export supply curve. In this case, the equilibrium terms of trade are 3 tonnes of grain per car. Mobilia exports and Farmland imports 4 million cars a year. Notice that the terms of trade are lower than the initial price in Farmland but higher than the initial price in Mobilia.

Balanced Trade

The number of cars exported by Mobilia—4 million a year—is exactly equal to the number of cars imported by Farmland. How does Farmland pay for its cars? The answer is by exporting grain. How much grain does Farmland export? You can find the answer by noticing that for 1 car, Farmland must pay 3 tonnes of grain. So for 4 million cars, Farmland pays 12 million tonnes of grain. Farmland's exports of grain are 12 million tonnes a year, and Mobilia imports this same quantity of grain.

Mobilia is exchanging 4 million cars for 12 million tonnes of grain each year, and Farmland is doing the opposite: exchanging 12 million tonnes of grain for 4 million cars. Trade is balanced between these two countries. The value received from exports equals the value paid out for imports.

Changes in Production and Consumption

We've seen that international trade makes it possible for Farmers to buy cars at a lower price than they can produce them and sell their grain for a higher price. International trade also enables Mobilians to sell their cars for a higher price and buy grain for a lower price. Both countries gain. How is it possible for *both* countries to gain? What are the changes in production and consumption that accompany these gains?

An economy that does not trade with other economies has identical production and consumption possibilities. Without trade, the economy can consume only what it produces. But with international trade, an economy can consume different quantities of goods from those that it produces. The production possibilities frontier describes the limit of what a country can produce, but it does not describe the limits to what it can consume. Figure 32.4 will help you to see the distinction between production possibilities and consumption possibilities when a country trades with other countries.

FIGURE 32.4

Expanding Consumption Possibilities

(a) Farmland

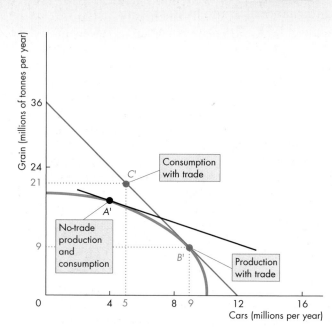

(b) Mobilia

With no international trade, the Farmers produce and consume at point *A* and the opportunity cost of a car is 9 tonnes of grain (the slope of the black line in part a). Also, with no international trade, the Mobilians produce and consume at point *A'* and the opportunity cost of 1 tonne of grain is 1 car (the slope of the black line in part b).

    Goods can be exchanged internationally at a price of 3 tonnes of grain for 1 car along the red line in each part of the figure. In part (a), Farmland decreases its production of cars and increases its production of grain, moving from

A to *B*. It exports grain and imports cars, and it consumes at point *C*. The Farmers have more of both cars and grain than they would if they produced all their own consumption goods—at point *A*. In part (b), Mobilia increases car production and decreases grain production, moving from *A'* to *B'*. Mobilia exports cars and imports grain, and it consumes at point *C'*. The Mobilians have more of both cars and grain than they would if they produced all their own consumption goods—at point *A'*.

First of all, notice that the figure has two parts: part (a) for Farmland and part (b) for Mobilia. The production possibilities frontiers that you saw in Figs. 32.1 and 32.2 are reproduced here. The slopes of the two black lines in the figure represent the opportunity costs in the two countries when there is no international trade. Farmland produces and consumes at point *A*, and Mobilia produces and consumes at *A'*. Cars cost 9 tonnes of grain in Farmland and 1 tonne of grain in Mobilia.

Consumption Possibilities The red line in each part of Fig. 32.4 shows the country's consumption possibilities with international trade. These two red

lines have the same slope, and the magnitude of that slope is the opportunity cost of a car in terms of grain on the world market: 3 tonnes per car. The *slope* of the consumption possibilities line is common to both countries because its magnitude equals the *world* price. But the position of a country's consumption possibilities line depends on the country's production possibilities. A country cannot produce outside its production possibilities curve, so its consumption possibilities curve touches its production possibilities curve. Farmland could choose to consume at point *B* with no international trade or, with international trade, at any point on its red consumption possibilities line.

Free Trade Equilibrium With international trade, the producers of cars in Mobilia can get a higher price for their output. As a result, they increase car production. At the same time, grain producers in Mobilia get a lower price for their grain, and so they reduce grain production. Producers in Mobilia adjust their output by moving along their production possibilities frontier until the opportunity cost in Mobilia equals the world price (the opportunity cost in the world market). This situation arises when Mobilia is producing at point B' in Fig. 32.4(b).

But the Mobilians do not consume at point B'. That is, they do not increase their consumption of cars and decrease their consumption of grain. Instead, they sell some of their car production to Farmland in exchange for some of Farmland's grain. They trade internationally. But to see how that works out, we first need to check in with Farmland to see what's happening there.

In Farmland, producers of cars now get a lower price and producers of grain get a higher price. As a consequence, producers in Farmland decrease car production and increase grain production. They adjust their outputs by moving along the production possibilities frontier until the opportunity cost of a car in terms of grain equals the world price (the opportunity cost on the world market). They move to point B in part (a). But the Farmers do not consume at point B. Instead, they trade some of their additional grain production for the now cheaper cars from Mobilia.

The figure shows us the quantities consumed in the two countries. We saw in Fig. 32.3 that Mobilia exports 4 million cars a year and Farmland imports those cars. We also saw that Farmland exports 12 million tonnes of grain a year and Mobilia imports that grain. So Farmland's consumption of grain is 12 million tonnes a year less than it produces, and its consumption of cars is 4 million a year more than it produces. Farmland consumes at point C in Fig. 32.4(a).

Similarly, we know that Mobilia consumes 12 million tonnes of grain more than it produces and 4 million cars fewer than it produces. Mobilia consumes at point C' in Fig. 32.4(b).

Calculating the Gains from Trade

You can now literally see the gains from trade in Fig. 32.4. Without trade, Farmers produce and consume at A (part a)—a point on Farmland's production possibilities frontier. With international trade, Farmers

consume at point C in part (a)—a point *outside* the production possibilities frontier. At point C, Farmers are consuming 3 million tonnes of grain a year and 1 million cars a year more than before. These increases in consumption of both cars and grain, beyond the limits of the production possibilities frontier, are the Farmers' gains from international trade.

Mobilians also gain. Without trade, they consume at point A' in part (b)—a point on Mobilia's production possibilities frontier. With international trade, they consume at point C'—a point outside their production possibilities frontier. With international trade, Mobilia consumes 3 million tonnes of grain a year and 1 million cars a year more than it would without trade. These are the gains from international trade for Mobilia.

Gains for Both Countries

Trade between the Farmers and the Mobilians does not create a winner and a loser. Both countries gain. Farmers selling grain and Mobilians selling cars face an increased demand for their products because the net demand by foreigners is added to domestic demand. With an increase in demand, the price rises.

Farmers buying cars and Mobilians buying grain face an increased supply of these products because the net foreign supply is added to domestic supply. With an increase in supply, the price falls.

Gains from Trade in Reality

The gains from trade that we have just studied between Farmland and Mobilia in grain and cars occur in a model economy—in a world economy that we have imagined. But these same phenomena occur every day in the real global economy.

Comparative Advantage in the Global Economy We buy TVs and DVD players from Korea, machinery from Europe, and fashion goods from Hong Kong. In exchange, we sell machinery, grain and lumber, airplanes, computers, and financial services. All this international trade is generated by comparative advantage, just like the international trade between Farmland and Mobilia in our model economy. All international trade arises from comparative advantage, even when trade is in similar goods such as tools and machines. At first thought, it seems puzzling that countries exchange manufactured goods. Why doesn't each developed country produce all the manufactured goods its citizens want to buy?

Trade in Similar Goods Why does Canada produce airplanes for export at the same time that Air Canada and our other airlines buy airplanes from the United States and Europe? Wouldn't it make more sense to produce all the airplanes that Air Canada and other Canadian airlines want to buy here in Canada? After all, we have access to the best technology available for producing planes. Aerospace workers in Canada are surely as productive as their fellow workers in the United States and Europe. So why does Canada have a comparative advantage in some types of airplanes and the United States and Europe in others?

Diversity of Taste and Economies of Scale The first part of the answer is that buyers have a large diversity of wants. Let's stick with the example of airplanes. Some airline operators sell time-share services in small executive jets, some airlines fly short routes in sparsely populated areas, some fly short routes in densely populated areas, some serve long-haul intercontinental routes that have heavy traffic, some serve long-haul intercontinental routes that have light traffic, some carry people and some specialize in cargo.

Because they face such highly varied markets, the airlines and other firms that offer air transportation services look for the types of airplanes that most closely match their wants. The large diversity in the characteristics of air transportation services means that airlines are willing to pay more for an airplane that matches their needs than they would be willing to pay for a single one-type-all-purpose airplane.

The second part of the answer to the puzzle is economies of scale—the tendency for the average cost to be lower, the larger the scale of production. In such situations, larger and larger production runs lead to ever lower average costs. Production of many goods, including airplanes, involves economies of scale. For example, if Bombardier makes only a handful of planes of a particular type and design, it must use production techniques that are much more labour-intensive and much less automated than those employed to make a hundred planes of a particular model. With short production runs and labour-intensive production techniques, costs are high. With very large production runs and automated assembly lines, production costs are much lower. But to obtain lower costs, the automated assembly lines have to produce a large number of planes.

It is the combination of diversity of wants and economies of scale that determines opportunity cost, produces comparative advantages, and generates such a large amount of international trade in similar commodities. With international trade, each airplane maker has the whole world market to serve. Each producer can specialize in a limited range of products and then sell its output to the entire world market.

This arrangement enables large production runs on the most popular planes to achieve economies of scale and low production costs.

The situation in the market for airplanes is also present in many other industries, especially those producing specialized equipment and parts. For example, Canada exports illustration software but imports database software, exports telecommunications systems but imports PCs, exports specialized video equipment but imports DVD players. International trade in similar but slightly different manufactured products is profitable.

REVIEW QUIZ

1 What is the fundamental source of the gains from international trade?
2 In what circumstances can countries gain from international trade?
3 What determines the goods and services that a country will export?
4 What determines the goods and services that a country will import?
5 What is comparative advantage and what role does it play in determining the amount and type of international trade that occurs?
6 How can it be that all countries gain from international trade and that there are no losers?
7 Provide some examples of comparative advantage in today's world.
8 Why does Canada both export and import automobiles?

myeconlab Study Plan 32.2

You've now seen how free trade brings gains for all countries. But trade is not free in our world. We'll now take a brief look at the history of trade restrictions and work out their effects. We'll see that free trade brings the greatest possible benefits and that international trade restrictions are costly.

International Trade Restrictions

GOVERNMENTS RESTRICT INTERNATIONAL TRADE to protect domestic industries from foreign competition by using two main tools:

1. Tariffs
2. Nontariff barriers

A **tariff** is a tax that is imposed by the importing country when an imported good crosses its international boundary. A **nontariff barrier** is any action other than a tariff that restricts international trade. Examples of nontariff barriers are quantitative restrictions and licensing regulations limiting imports. First, let's look at tariffs.

The History of Tariffs

The Canadian economy has always been protected by a tariff. Figure 32.5 shows the history of that tariff, from Confederation through 2004. The figure shows tariffs as a percentage of total imports—the average tariff rate. As you can see, the average tariff rate climbed from the early 1870s to exceed 20 percent by the late 1880s. The rate fluctuated but gradually decreased through the early 1920s. It increased again during the Great Depression years of the early 1930s. During these years, most countries increased their tariff rates in what became a "beggar-thy-neighbour" policy. The average tariff then decreased through the late 1930s and continued its decrease throughout the years after World War II. Today, the average tariff rate is less than 1 percent.

The reduction in tariffs after World War II followed the signing in 1947 of the **General Agreement on Tariffs and Trade** (GATT). From its formation, GATT organized a series of "rounds" of negotiations that resulted in a steady process of tariff reduction. One of these, the Kennedy Round that began in the early 1960s, resulted in large tariff cuts starting in 1967. Another, the Tokyo Round, resulted in further tariff cuts in 1979. The final round, the Uruguay Round, started in 1986 and was completed in 1994.

The Uruguay Round was the most ambitious and comprehensive of the rounds and led to the creation of the **World Trade Organization** (WTO). Membership of the WTO brings greater obligations for countries to observe the GATT rules. Canada signed the Uruguay Round agreements, and Parliament ratified them in 1994.

In 2005, the WTO embarked on the Doha Round, which aimed to further liberalize world trade. But at the end of 2005, this round was stalled by disagreement on U.S. and E.U. agricultural subsidies.

FIGURE 32.5

Canadian Tariffs: 1867–2004

Canadian tariffs were in place before Confederation. Tariffs increased sharply in the 1870s and remained high until the 1930s. Since the establishment of the GATT in 1947, tariffs have steadily declined in a series of negotiating rounds, the most significant of which are identified in the figure. Tariffs are now as low as they have ever been.

Sources of data: Statistics Canada, *Historical Statistics of Canada*, Series G485, CANSIM Tables 380–0002 and 380–0034.

In addition to the agreements under the GATT and the WTO, Canada is a party to the **North American Free Trade Agreement** (NAFTA), which became effective on January 1, 1994, and under which barriers to international trade among the United States, Canada, and Mexico will be virtually eliminated after a 15-year phasing-in period.

In other parts of the world, trade barriers have virtually been eliminated among the member countries of the European Union, which has created the largest unified tariff-free market in the world. In 1994, discussions among the Asia-Pacific Economic Cooperation (APEC) led to an agreement in principle to work towards a free-trade area that embraces China, all the economies of East Asia and the South Pacific, and the United States and Canada. These countries include the fastest-growing economies and hold the promise of heralding a global free-trade area.

The effort to achieve freer trade underlines the fact that trade in some goods is still subject to a high tariff. Textiles and footwear are among the goods that face the highest tariffs, and rates on these items average more than 10 percent. Some individual items face a tariff much higher than the average. For example, when you buy a pair of blue jeans for $20, you pay about $5 more than you would if there were no tariffs on textiles. Other goods that are protected by tariffs are agricultural products, energy and chemicals, minerals, and metals. The meat, cheese, milk, and eggs that you consume cost significantly more because of protection than they would with free international trade.

The temptation for governments to impose tariffs is a strong one. First, tariffs provide revenue to the government. Second, they enable the government to satisfy special interest groups in import-competing industries. But, as we'll see, free international trade brings enormous benefits that are reduced when tariffs are imposed. Let's see how.

How Tariffs Work

To see how tariffs work, let's return to the example of trade between Farmland and Mobilia. Figure 32.6 shows the international market for cars in which these two countries are the only traders. The volume of trade and the price of a car are determined at the point of intersection of Mobilia's export supply curve of cars and Farmland's import demand curve for cars.

In Fig. 32.6, these two countries trade cars and grain in exactly the same way that we saw in Fig. 32.3.

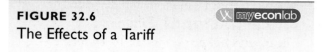

FIGURE 32.6
The Effects of a Tariff

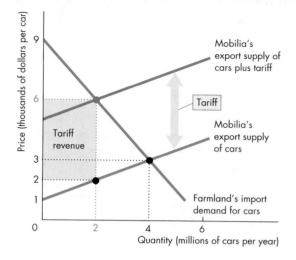

Farmland imposes a tariff on car imports from Mobilia. The tariff increases the price that Farmers have to pay for cars. It shifts the supply curve of cars in Farmland leftward. The vertical distance between the original supply curve and the new one is the amount of the tariff, $4,000 per car. The price of a car in Farmland increases, and the quantity of cars imported decreases. The government of Farmland collects a tariff revenue of $4,000 per car—a total of $8 billion on the 2 million cars imported. Farmland's exports of grain decrease because Mobilia now has a lower income from its exports of cars.

Mobilia exports cars, and Farmland exports grain. The volume of car imports into Farmland is 4 million a year, and the world market price of a car is 3 tonnes of grain. Figure 32.6 expresses prices in dollars rather than in units of grain and is based on a money price of grain of $1,000 a tonne. With grain costing $1,000 a tonne, the money price of a car is $3,000.

Now suppose that the government of Farmland, perhaps under pressure from car producers, decides to impose a tariff on imported cars. In particular, suppose that a tariff of $4,000 per car is imposed. (This is a huge tariff, but the car producers of Farmland are pretty fed up with competition from Mobilia.) What happens?

- The supply of cars in Farmland decreases.
- The price of a car in Farmland rises.
- The quantity of cars imported by Farmland decreases.
- The government of Farmland collects the tariff revenue.
- Resource use is inefficient.
- The *value* of exports changes by the same amount as the *value* of imports, and trade remains balanced.

Change in the Supply of Cars Farmland cannot buy cars at Mobilia's export supply price. It must pay that price plus the $4,000 tariff. So the supply curve in Farmland shifts leftward. The new supply curve is that labelled "Mobilia's export supply of cars plus tariff." The vertical distance between Mobilia's original export supply curve and the new supply curve is the tariff of $4,000 a car.

Rise in Price of a Car A new equilibrium occurs where the new supply curve intersects Farmland's import demand curve for cars. That equilibrium is at a price of $6,000 a car, up from $3,000 with free trade.

Fall in Imports Car imports fall from 4 million to 2 million cars a year. At the higher price of $6,000 a car, domestic car producers increase their production. Domestic grain production decreases as resources are moved into the expanding car industry.

Tariff Revenue Total expenditure on imported cars by the Farmers is $6,000 a car multiplied by the 2 million cars imported ($12 billion). But not all of that money goes to the Mobilians. They receive $2,000 a car, or $4 billion for the 2 million cars. The difference—$4,000 a car, or a total of $8 billion for the 2 million cars—is collected by the government of Farmland as tariff revenue.

Inefficiency The people of Farmland are willing to pay $6,000 for the marginal car imported. But the opportunity cost of that car is $2,000. So there is a gain from trading an extra car. In fact, there are gains—willingness to pay exceeds opportunity cost— all the way up to 4 million cars a year. Only when 4 million cars are being traded is the maximum price that a Farmer is willing to pay equal to the minimum price that is acceptable to a Mobilian. Restricting trade reduces the gains from trade.

Trade Remains Balanced With free trade, Farmland was paying $3,000 a car and buying 4 million cars a year from Mobilia. The total amount paid to Mobilia for imports was $12 billion a year. With a tariff, Farmland's imports have been cut to 2 million cars a year and the price paid to Mobilia has also been cut to only $2,000 a car. The total amount paid to Mobilia for imports has been cut to $4 billion a year. Doesn't this fact mean that Farmland now has a balance of trade surplus? It does not.

The price of a car in Mobilia has fallen. But the price of grain remains at $1 a tonne. So the relative price of a car has fallen, and the relative price of grain has increased. With free trade, the Mobilians could buy 3,000 tonnes of grain for the price of one car. Now they can buy only 2,000 tonnes for the price of a car. With a higher relative price of grain, the quantity demanded by the Mobilians decreases and Mobilia imports less grain. But because Mobilia imports less grain, Farmland exports less grain. In fact, Farmland's grain industry suffers from two sources. First, there is a decrease in the quantity of grain sold to Mobilia. Second, there is increased competition for inputs from the now-expanded car industry. The tariff leads to a contraction in the scale of the grain industry in Farmland.

It seems paradoxical at first that a country imposing a tariff on cars hurts its own export industry, lowering its exports of grain. It may help to think of it this way: Mobilians buy grain with the money they make from exporting cars to Farmland. If they export fewer cars, they cannot afford to buy as much grain. In fact, in the absence of any international borrowing and lending, Mobilia must cut its imports of grain by exactly the same amount as the loss in revenue from its export of cars. Grain imports into Mobilia are cut back to a value of $4 billion, the amount that can be paid for by the new lower revenue from Mobilia's car exports. Trade is still balanced. The tariff cuts imports and exports by the same amount. The tariff has no effect on the *balance* of trade, but it reduces the *volume* of trade.

The result that we have just derived is perhaps one of the most misunderstood aspects of international economics. On countless occasions, politicians and others call for tariffs to lower a balance of trade deficit or argue that lowering tariffs will create a balance of trade deficit. The balance of international trade is not caused by a lack of competitiveness. Its cause lies in a nation's saving as you'll see later in this chapter (on pp. 774–775).

Nontariff Barriers

The two main forms of nontariff barriers are

1. Quotas
2. Voluntary export restraints

A **quota** is a quantitative restriction on the import of a particular good, which specifies the maximum amount of the good that may be imported in a given period of time. A **voluntary export restraint** (VER) is an agreement between two governments in which the government of the exporting country agrees to restrain the volume of its own exports.

Quotas are especially prominent in agriculture. Voluntary export restraints are used to regulate trade between Japan and Canada.

How Quotas and VERs Work

To see how a quota works, suppose that Farmland imposes a quota that restricts its car imports to 2 million cars a year. Figure 32.7 shows the effects of this action. The quota is shown by the vertical red line at 2 million cars a year. Because it is illegal to exceed the quota, car importers buy only that quantity from Mobilia, for which they pay $2,000 a car. But because the import supply of cars is restricted to 2 million cars a year, people are willing to pay $6,000 per car. This is the price of a car in Farmland.

The value of imports falls to $4 billion, exactly the same as in the case of the tariff in Fig. 32.6. So with lower incomes from car exports and with a higher relative price of grain, Mobilians cut back on their imports of grain in exactly the same way that they did under a tariff.

The key difference between a quota and a tariff lies in who collects the gap between the import supply price and the domestic price. In the case of a tariff, it is the government of the importing country. In the case of a quota, it goes to the person who has the right to import under the import quota regulations.

A VER is like a quota arrangement in which quotas are allocated to each exporting country. The effects of a VER are similar to those of a quota but differ from them in that the gap between the domestic price and the export price is captured not by domestic importers but by the foreign exporter. The government of the exporting country has to establish procedures for allocating the restricted volume of exports among its producers.

FIGURE 32.7   ⓧ myeconlab
The Effects of a Quota

Farmland imposes a quota of 2 million cars a year on car imports from Mobilia. That quantity appears as the vertical line labelled Quota. Because the quantity of cars supplied by Mobilia is restricted to 2 million, the price of a car in Farmland increases to $6,000. Importing cars is profitable because Mobilia is willing to supply cars at $2,000 each. There is competition for import quotas.

REVIEW QUIZ

1 What are the tools that a country can use to restrict international trade?
2 What do international trade restrictions do to the gains from international trade?
3 Which is best for a country: restricted trade, no trade, or free trade? Why?
4 What does a tariff on imports do to the volume of imports and the volume of exports?
5 In the absence of international borrowing and lending, how do tariffs and other international trade restrictions influence the total value of imports and exports and the balance of trade—the value of exports minus the value of imports?

ⓧ myeconlab   **Study Plan 32.3**

We're now going to look at some commonly heard arguments for restricting international trade and see why they are almost never correct.

The Case Against Protection

FOR AS LONG AS NATIONS AND INTERNATIONAL trade have existed, people have debated whether a country is better off with free international trade or with protection from foreign competition. The debate continues, but for most economists, a verdict has been delivered and is the one you have just seen. Free trade promotes prosperity for all; protection is inefficient. We've seen the most powerful case for free trade in the example of how Farmland and Mobilia both benefit from their comparative advantage. But there is a broader range of issues in the free trade versus protection debate. Let's review these issues.

Three arguments for restricting international trade are

- The employment argument
- The infant-industry argument
- The dumping argument

Let's look at each in turn.

The Employment Argument

The argument that protection saves jobs goes as follows: When we buy shoes from Brazil or shirts from Taiwan, Canadian workers in these industries lose their jobs. With no earnings and poor prospects, these workers become a drain on welfare and spend less, causing a ripple effect of further job losses. The proposed solution to this problem is to ban imports of cheap foreign goods and protect Canadian jobs. This argument for protection does not withstand scrutiny for three reasons.

First, free trade does cost some jobs, but it also creates other jobs. It brings about a global rationalization of labour and allocates labour resources to their highest-valued activities. Because of international trade in textiles, tens of thousands of workers in Canada have lost their jobs because textile mills and other factories have closed. But tens of thousands of workers in other countries have gotten jobs because textile mills have opened there. And tens of thousands of Canadian workers have gotten better-paying jobs than those of textile workers because other export industries have expanded and created more jobs than have been destroyed.

Second, imports create jobs. They create jobs for retailers that sell imported goods and firms that service those goods. They also create jobs by creating incomes in the rest of the world, some of which are spent on imports of Canadian-made goods and services.

Although protection does save particular jobs, it does so at inordinate cost. A striking example of the cost of quotas is that of the quotas on the import of textiles. Quotas imposed under an international agreement called the Multifibre Arrangement (which ended in 2005) protected textile jobs, especially in the United States. The U.S. International Trade Commission (ITC) estimated that because of quotas, 72,000 jobs existed in textiles that would otherwise have disappeared and the annual clothing expenditure in the United States was $US 15.9 billion or $U.S. 160 per family higher than it will be with free trade. Equivalently, the ITC estimated that each textile job saved cost $US 221,000 a year.

The Infant-Industry Argument

The so-called **infant-industry argument** for protection is that it is necessary to protect a new industry to enable it to grow into a mature industry that can compete in world markets. The argument is based on the idea of *dynamic comparative advantage*, which can arise from learning-by-doing (see Chapter 2).

Learning-by-doing is a powerful engine of productivity growth, and comparative advantage does evolve and change because of on-the-job experience. But these facts do not justify protection.

First, the infant-industry argument is valid only if the benefits of learning-by-doing *not only* accrue to the owners and workers of the firms in the infant industry but also *spill over* to other industries and parts of the economy. For example, there are huge productivity gains from learning-by-doing in the manufacture of aircraft. But almost all of these gains benefit the stockholders and workers of Bombardier. Because the people making the decisions, bearing the risk, and doing the work are the ones who benefit, they take the dynamic gains into account when they decide on the scale of their activities. In this case, almost no benefits spill over to other parts of the economy, so there is no need for government assistance to achieve an efficient outcome.

Second, even if the case is made for protecting an infant industry, it is more efficient to do so by subsidizing the firms in the industry, with the subsidy paid out of taxes.

The Dumping Argument

Dumping occurs when a foreign firm sells its exports at a price below its cost of production. Dumping might be used by a firm that wants to gain a global monopoly. In this case, the foreign firm sells its output at a price below its cost to drive domestic firms out of business. When the domestic firms have gone, the foreign firm takes advantage of its monopoly position and charges a higher price for its product. Dumping is usually regarded as a justification for temporary countervailing tariffs.

But there are powerful reasons to resist the dumping argument for protection. First, it is virtually impossible to detect dumping because it is hard to determine a firm's costs. As a result, the test for dumping is whether a firm's export price is below its domestic price. But this test is a weak one because it can be rational for a firm to charge a low price in markets in which the quantity demanded is highly sensitive to price and a higher price in a market in which demand is less price-sensitive.

Second, it is hard to think of a good that is produced by a natural *global* monopoly. So even if all the domestic firms were driven out of business in some industry, it would always be possible to find several and usually many alternative foreign sources of supply and to buy at prices determined in competitive markets.

Third, if a good or service were a truly global natural monopoly, the best way of dealing with it would be by regulation—just as in the case of domestic monopolies. Such regulation would require international cooperation.

The three arguments for protection that we've just examined have an element of credibility. The counterarguments are in general stronger, however, so these arguments do not make the case for protection. But they are not the only arguments that you might encounter. There are many other newer arguments against globalization and for protection. The most common of them are that protection

- Maintains national security
- Allows us to compete with cheap foreign labour
- Brings diversity and stability
- Penalizes lax environmental standards
- Protects national culture
- Prevents rich countries from exploiting developing countries

Maintains National Security

The national security argument for protection is that a country must protect industries that produce defence equipment and armaments and industries on which the defence industries rely for their raw materials and other intermediate inputs. This argument for protection does not withstand close scrutiny.

First, it is an argument for international isolation, for in a time of war, there is no industry that does not contribute to national defence. Second, if the case is made for boosting the output of a strategic industry, it is more efficient to achieve this outcome with a subsidy to the firms in the industry that is financed out of taxes. Such a subsidy would keep the industry operating at the scale judged appropriate, and free international trade would keep the prices faced by consumers at their world market levels.

Allows Us to Compete with Cheap Foreign Labour

With the removal of tariffs in Canadian trade with Mexico, people said we would hear a "giant sucking sound" as jobs rushed to Mexico. Let's see what's wrong with this view.

The labour cost of a unit of output equals the wage rate divided by labour productivity. For example, if a Canadian auto worker earns $30 an hour and produces 15 units of output an hour, the average labour cost of a unit of output is $2. If a Mexican auto assembly worker earns $3 an hour and produces 1 unit of output an hour, the average labour cost of a unit of output is $3. Other things remaining the same, the higher a worker's productivity, the higher is the worker's wage rate. High-wage workers have high productivity. Low-wage workers have low productivity.

Although high-wage Canadian workers are more productive, on the average, than low-wage Mexican workers, there are differences across industries. Canadian labour is relatively more productive in some activities than in others. For example, the productivity of Canadian workers in producing financial services and telephone systems is relatively higher than their productivity in the production of metals and some standardized machine parts. The activities in which Canadian workers are relatively more productive than their Mexican counterparts are those in which Canada has a *comparative advantage*. By engaging in free trade, increasing our production and exports of the goods and services in which we have a comparative advantage and decreasing our production and increasing our imports of the goods and services in which our trading partners have a comparative advantage, we can make ourselves and the citizens of other countries better off.

Brings Diversity and Stability

A diversified investment portfolio is less risky than one that has all the eggs in one basket. The same is true for an economy's production. A diversified economy fluctuates less than an economy that produces only one or two goods.

But big, rich, diversified economies such as those of Canada, the United States, Japan, and Europe do not have this type of stability problem. Even a country such as Saudi Arabia that produces only one good (in this case, oil) can benefit from specializing in the activity at which it has a comparative advantage and then investing in a wide range of other countries to bring greater stability to its income and consumption.

Penalizes Lax Environmental Standards

Another argument for protection is that many poorer countries, such as Mexico, do not have the same environmental policies that we have and, because they are willing to pollute and we are not, we cannot compete with them without tariffs. So if they want free trade with the richer and "greener" countries, they must clean up their environments to our standards.

This argument for trade restrictions is not entirely convincing. A poor country is less able than a rich one to devote resources to achieving high environmental standards. So if free trade helps a poor country to become richer, it will also help that country to develop the means to improve its environment.

But there probably is a case for using the negotiation of free trade agreements such as NAFTA to hold member countries to higher environmental standards. There is an especially large payoff from using such bargaining to try to avoid irreversible damage to resources such as tropical rainforests.

Protects National Culture

The national culture argument is that free trade in books, magazines, movies, and television programs means U.S. domination and the end of local culture. So, the reasoning continues, it is necessary to protect domestic "culture" industries from free

international trade to ensure the survival of a national cultural identity.

Protection of these industries is common and takes the form of nontariff barriers. For example, local content regulations on radio and television broadcasting and in magazines is often required.

The cultural identity argument for protection has no merit. Writers, publishers, and broadcasters want to limit foreign competition so that they can earn larger economic profits. But many of the creators of so-called American cultural products are not Americans but the talented citizens of other countries, ensuring the survival of their national cultural identities in Hollywood! Also, if national culture is in danger, it isn't clear that preventing competition is the best way of restoring it to health. Competition among cultures might be a source of strength.

Prevents Rich Countries from Exploiting Developing Countries

Wage rates in some developing countries are indeed very low. Do we, by trading with these countries, exploit them and their workers?

By trading with developing countries, we increase the demand for the goods that these countries produce and, more significantly, we increase the demand for their labour. When the demand for labour in developing countries increases, the wage rate also increases. So, rather than exploiting people in developing countries, international trade improves their opportunities and increases their incomes.

We have reviewed five arguments in favour of protection and seen that they all have flaws and leave the case for free international trade a strong one.

Why Is International Trade Restricted?

Why, despite all the arguments against protection, is trade restricted? There are two key reasons:

■ Tariff revenue
■ Rent seeking

Tariff Revenue Government revenue is costly to collect. In the developed countries such as Canada, a well-organized tax collection system is in place that can generate billions of dollars of income tax and sales tax revenues. This tax collection system is made possible by the fact that most economic transactions are done by firms that must keep properly audited financial records. Without such records, the revenue collection agencies (for example, Canada Revenue Agency) would be severely hampered in the work. Even with audited financial accounts, some proportion of potential tax revenue is lost. Nonetheless, for the industrialized countries, income taxes and sales taxes are the major sources of revenue and the tariff plays a very small role.

But governments in developing countries have a difficult time collecting taxes from their citizens. Much economic activity takes place in an informal economy with few financial records. So only a small amount of revenue is collected from income taxes and sales taxes in these countries. The one area in which economic transactions are well recorded and audited is in international trade. So this activity is an attractive base for tax collection in these countries and is used much more extensively than in the developed countries.

Rent Seeking   Rent seeking is the major reason why international trade is restricted. Rent seeking is lobbying and other political activity that seeks to capture the gains from trade. Free trade increases consumption possibilities *on the average*, but not everyone shares in the gain and some people even lose. Free trade brings benefits to some and imposes costs on others, with total benefits exceeding total costs. It is the uneven distribution of costs and benefits that is the principal source of impediment to achieving more liberal international trade.

Think about our example of trade in cars and grain between Farmland and Mobilia. In Farmland, the benefits from free trade accrue to all the producers of grain and to those producers of cars who would not have to bear the costs of adjusting to a smaller car industry. Those costs are transition costs, not permanent costs. The costs of moving to free trade are borne by those car producers and their employees who have to become grain producers.

The number of people who gain will, in general, be enormous in comparison with the number who lose. The gain per person will therefore be rather small. But the loss per person to those who bear the loss will be large. Because the losses that fall on those who bear them are large, it pays those people to incur considerable expense to lobby against free trade. On the other hand, it does not

pay those who gain to organize to achieve free trade. The gain from trade for any one individual is too small for that individual to spend much time or money on a political organization whose goal is to achieve free trade.

Winners—free traders—and losers–anti-free traders—each in pursuit of their self-interest, weigh benefits against costs and choose their best actions. But because only the anti-free traders have enough at stake, they will do more political lobbying than the free traders.

Compensating Losers

If, in total, the gains from free international trade exceed the losses, why don't those who stand to gain from free trade offer to compensate those who stand to lose so that everyone votes for free trade?

The main answer is that there are serious obstacles to providing direct and correctly calculated compensation. First, the cost of identifying the losers from free trade and of estimating the value of their losses would be enormous.

Second, it would never be clear whether a person who has fallen on hard times is suffering because of free trade or for other reasons, perhaps reasons that are largely under the control of the individual. Third, some people who look like losers at one point in time may, in fact, end up gaining. The young auto worker that loses her job in Windsor and becomes a computer assembly worker in Ottawa resents the loss of work and the need to move. But a year or two later, looking back on events, she counts herself fortunate. She has made a move that has increased her income and given her greater job security.

Despite the absence of explicit compensation, those who lose from a change in protection do receive some compensation. But compensation is not restricted to the losers from changes in trade policy. In Canada (and in all the other rich industrial countries) elaborate schemes are in place to ensure that people who suffer from economic change receive help during their transition to new activities.

Two major forms of compensation in Canada arise from interprovincial fiscal transfers and employment insurance. Interprovincial fiscal transfers result in tax dollars collected in the rich and expanding regions of the country being spent in the

When the United States and Canada negotiated the Canada–U.S. Free Trade Agreement (the predecessor of NAFTA), U.S. President Ronald Reagan (hand outstretched on the right) and Prime Minister Brian Mulroney (maple-leafed figure on the left), were able to go only as far as their national self-interested rent seekers would allow them to go in dismantling tariffs and other barriers to free trade between the world's two largest trading partners.

Cartoon by Alan King, *The Ottawa Citizen,* Canwest News Service. Reprinted by permission of Alan King/*The Ottawa Citizen.*

poorer regions. Employment insurance provides compensation for workers who lose their jobs regardless of the reason for the job loss. Jobs lost because of changes in international protection are included among those for which benefits are paid.

But because we do not explicitly compensate the losers from free international trade, protectionism remains a popular and permanent feature of our national economic and political life.

Protection to Avoid a Trade Deficit

In our review of the arguments for protection, we did not consider the idea of limiting imports to help a country to achieve an international trade surplus or avoid a deficit. But this argument is sometimes heard.

Today, Canada has a surplus in its international trade. But many countries have deficits and the United States is the largest deficit nation. Some people say that because China floods the United States with cheap goods, China is a major source of the U.S. deficit. So limiting imports from China is justified as a way of limiting the deficit. In the next section, you will see what determines a country's international trade balance and why a deficit doesn't justify protection.

REVIEW QUIZ

1 Can we save jobs, develop new industries, or restrain foreign monopoly by restricting international trade?

2 Can trade protection help to achieve national security goals, or better protect the environmental and national culture?

3 What is the main argument against international trade restrictions?

4 What are the two main reasons for imposing tariffs on imports?

5 What type of country benefits most from the revenue from tariffs? Provide some examples of such countries.

6 If international trade restrictions are costly, why do we use them? Why don't the people who gain from trade organize a political force that is strong enough to ensure that their interests are protected?

7 Why don't we have free trade and compensate the people who lose from it?

myeconlab   **Study Plan 32.4**

The Balance of International Payments

SO FAR IN THIS CHAPTER, WE'VE LOOKED AT balanced trade between countries. We're now going to see what makes trade unbalanced—why countries have international deficits and surpluses. When a country has an international deficit, it must borrow from the rest of the world. And when a country has an international surplus, it must lend to the rest of the world. Let's look at the scale of Canada's international trading and borrowing and lending and at the way in which we keep our records of these transactions. These records are called the balance of payments accounts.

Balance of Payments Accounts

A country's *balance of payments accounts* record its international trading, borrowing, and lending. There are in fact three balance of payments accounts:

1. Current account
2. Capital account
3. Official settlements account

The *current account* records payments for imports of goods and services from abroad, receipts from exports of goods and services sold abroad, net interest paid abroad, and net transfers (such as foreign aid payments). The *current account balance* equals exports minus imports, net interest payments, and net transfers. The *capital account* records foreign investment in Canada minus Canadian investment abroad. The *official settlements account* records the change in official Canadian reserves. *Official Canadian reserves* are the government's holdings of foreign currency. If Canadian official reserves increase, the official settlements account balance is *negative*. The reason is that holding foreign money is like investing abroad. Canadian investment abroad is a minus item in the capital account and in the official settlements account. (By the same reasoning, if official Canadian reserves decrease, the official settlements account balance is *positive*.)

The sum of the balances on the three accounts always equals zero. That is, to pay for a current account deficit, we must either borrow more from abroad than we lend abroad or use our official reserves to cover the shortfall.

Table 32.1 shows the Canadian balance of payments accounts in 2004. Items in the current account and capital account that provide foreign currency to Canada have a plus sign; items that cost Canada foreign currency have a minus sign. The table shows that in 2004, exports plus net transfers exceeded imports plus net interest payments and the current account had a surplus of $29 billion.

What do we do with our current account surplus? We lend it to the rest of the world. The capital account tells us by how much. We borrowed $62 billion (foreign investment in Canada) but made loans of $88 billion (Canadian investment abroad). Thus our net foreign lending was $26 billion. A statistical discrepancy arises because of illegal and hidden transactions, which in 2004 was –$6 billion.

The sum of our current account balance, capital account balance and statistical discrepancy is the change in our official reserves. In 2004, reserves decreased because our current account balance of $29 billion plus the capital account balance of –$26 billion and the statistical discrepancy of –$6 billion was –$3 billion. When our reserves decrease, we record

TABLE 32.1   Canadian Balance of Payments Accounts in 2004

Current account	Billions of dollars
Imports of goods and services	–437
Exports of goods and services	+491
Net interest payments	–50
Net transfers	+25
Current account balance	+29
Capital account	
Foreign investment in Canada	+62
Canadian investment abroad	–88
Capital account balance	–26
Statistical discrepancy	–6
Official settlements account	
Official settlements account balance	+3

Source: Statistics Canada, CANSIM tables 376–0001 and 376–0002.

the official settlements balance as a positive number. Why? Because a decrease in our reserves is like borrowing from the rest of the world.

The numbers in Table 34.1 give a snapshot of the balance of payments accounts in 2004. Figure 32.8 puts that snapshot into perspective by showing the balance of payments between 1984 and 2004. Because the economy grows and the price level rises, changes in the dollar value of the balance of payments do not convey much information. To remove the influences of growth and inflation, Fig. 32.8 shows the balance of payments as a percentage of nominal GDP.

As you can see, the capital account balance is almost a mirror image of the current account balance. The official settlements balance is very small in comparison with the balances of these other two accounts. A large current account deficit (and capital account surplus) emerged during the 1980s but declined after 1993. By 1996 we had a small surplus and after two more years of deficit, the early 2000s saw an increasing current account surplus.

You can understand the balance of payments and the way the accounts are linked together if you think about the income and expenditure, borrowing and lending, and bank account of an individual.

Individual Analogy Joanne's income from her job in 2005 was $25,000 and she has $10,000 worth of investments that earned her an interest income of $1,000 in that year. Joanne's current account shows an income of $26,000. Joanne spent $18,000 on consumption goods and services. She also bought a new house, which cost her $60,000. So Joanne's total expenditure was $78,000. Her income minus her expenditure is –$52,000 ($26,000 minus $78,000). This amount is Joanne's current account deficit.

To cover her $52,000 deficit, Joanne has to use the money that she has in the bank or take a loan. Joanne took a mortgage of $50,000 to help buy her house so her capital account surplus was $50,000. With a current account deficit of $52,000 and a capital account surplus of $50,000, Joanne is still $2,000 short. She got that $2,000 from her bank account. Her cash holdings decreased by $2,000.

Joanne's income from work is like a country's income from exports. Her income from investments is like a country's interest income from foreigners. Her purchases of goods and services, are like a country's imports. Joanne's mortgage—borrowing from someone else—is like a country's borrowing from the rest of the world. The change in her bank account is like the change in the country's official reserves.

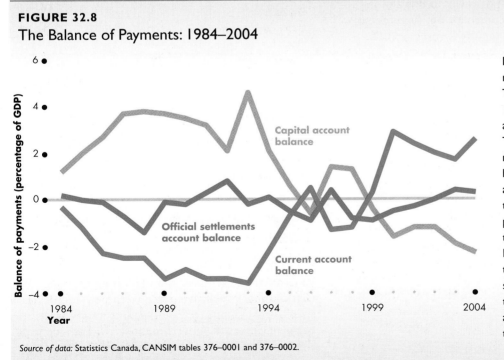

FIGURE 32.8
The Balance of Payments: 1984–2004

During the 1980s, a large current account deficit arose. That deficit decreased after 1993 and by the early 2000s an increasing surplus arose. The capital account balance mirrors the current account balance. When the current account balance is negative, the capital account balance is positive—we borrow from the rest of the world. Fluctuations in the official settlements account balance are small in comparison with fluctuations in the current account balance and the capital account balance.

Source of data: Statistics Canada, CANSIM tables 376–0001 and 376–0002.

Borrowers and Lenders, Debtors and Creditors

A country that has a current account deficit and that borrows more from the rest of the world than it lends to it is called a *net borrower*. Similarly, a *net lender* is a country that lends more to the rest of the world than it borrows from it.

From 1999 through 2004, Canada was a net lender. But most years, Canada has been a net borrower. And most countries are net borrowers.

A net borrower might be going deeper into debt or might simply be reducing its net assets held in the rest of the world. The total stock of foreign investment determines whether a country is a debtor or creditor. A *debtor nation* is a country that during its entire history has borrowed more from the rest of the world than it has lent to it. It has a stock of outstanding debt to the rest of the world that exceeds the stock of its own claims on the rest of the world. A *creditor nation* is a country that has invested more in the rest of the world than other countries have invested in it.

Canada is a debtor nation. Should we be concerned that Canada is a net borrower and debtor nation? The answer to this question depends on what we do with the funds that we borrow. If borrowing finances investment that in turn generates economic growth and higher income, borrowing is not a problem. If borrowing finances consumption, then higher interest payments are being incurred, and as a consequence, consumption will eventually have to be reduced. In this case, the more the borrowing and the longer it goes on, the greater is the reduction in consumption that will eventually be necessary.

Current Account Balance

The current account balance (in Table 32.1) is the sum of exports minus imports, net interest income, and net transfers. Exports minus imports equals net exports and fluctuations in net exports are the main source of fluctuations in the current account balance.

You are about to discover that net exports do not depend on our competitiveness in international markets. Instead, they depend on the government budget and private saving and investment. To see how, look at Table 32.2[1].

---

[1]If you've studied macroeconomics, you learned about the National Income Accounts in Chapter 20.

TABLE 32.2   Net Exports, the Government Budget, Saving, and Investment

	Symbols and equations	Canada in 2004 (billions of dollars)
(a) Variables		
Exports*	X	493
Imports*	M	438
Government expenditures	G	282
Net taxes	NT	302
Investment	I	234
Saving	S	269
(b) Balances		
Net exports	X − M	493 − 438 = 55
Government sector	NT − G	302 − 282 = 20
Private sector	S − I	269 − 234 = 35
(c) Relationship among balances		
National accounts	$Y = C + I + G + X - M$	
	$= C + S + NT$	
Rearranging:	$X - M = S - I + NT - G$	
Net exports	X − M	55
Equals:		
Government sector	NT − G	20
Plus		
Private sector	S − I	35

Source of data: Statistics Canada, CANSIM tables 380–0002 and 380–0022.

* The national income accounts' measures of exports and imports are different from the balance of payments' accounts measures by small amounts.

Part (a) lists the national income variables that we need, with their symbols. Part (b) defines three balances. We've just defined net exports. The *government sector balance* is equal to net taxes minus government expenditures on goods and services. If that number is positive, the government sector has a surplus that is lent to the other sectors; if that number is negative, the government sector has a deficit that must be financed by borrowing from the other sectors. The government sector balance is the sum of the balances of the federal, provincial, and municipal governments. The *private sector balance* is equal to saving minus investment. If saving exceeds investment, a private sector has a surplus and it is lent to other sectors. If investment exceeds saving, borrowing from other sectors finances a private sector deficit.

Part (b) shows the values of these balances for Canada in 2004. Net exports were a surplus of $55 billion. The government sector had a surplus of $20 billion. And the private sector had a surplus of $35 billion.

Part (c) shows the relationship among the three balances. From the national income accounts, we know that real GDP (Y) is the sum of consumption expenditure (C), investment (I), government expenditures (G), and net exports ($X - M$). It also equals the sum of consumption expenditure (C), saving (S), and net taxes (NT). Rearranging these equations tells us that net exports ($X - M$) is the sum of the government sector surplus ($NT - G$) and the private sector surplus ($S - I$). In Canada in 2004, the government sector had a surplus of $20 billion and the private sector had a surplus of $35 billion. The government sector surplus plus the private sector surplus equals net exports of $55 billion.

The Twin Deficits

You've seen that net exports equals the sum of the government surplus and the private surplus. And net exports plus debt interest (and other small transfers) equals the current account balance. What is the relationship over time between the current account balance and the government budget balance? How do these balances fluctuate over time? Figure 32.9 answers this question. It shows the government budget (the red line) and the current account balance (the blue line).

You can see that, with an important exception during the early 1980s, there is a tendency for the current account to go into a deeper deficit when the government budget goes into a deeper deficit. Because of the tendency for the government budget deficit and the current account deficit to move in the same direction they have been called the *twin deficits*.

Why are the two deficits linked? They are linked because capital is highly mobile in today's world. If the Canadian government increases expenditures or lowers taxes, total spending in Canada rises. But with the economy at or near full employment, the extra

FIGURE 32.9
The Twin Deficits

The current account balance and the government budget balance move in similar ways and look like twin deficits. But this relationship broke down during the early 1980s when the private sector surplus swelled.

Source of data: Statistics Canada, CANSIM tables 376–0001 and 380–0007.

goods and services demanded are sucked in from the rest of the world. Imports increase. Capital flows in to pay for those imports. Saving and investment don't change. This relationship broke down during the early 1980s because Canada was in recession and investment decreased relative to saving.

REVIEW QUIZ

1 What types of transactions do we record in the balance of payments accounts?

2 What transactions does the current account record? What transactions does the capital account record? What transactions does the official settlements account record?

3 What determines the current account balance?

myeconlab **Study Plan 32.5**

The North American Free Trade Agreement

THE NORTH AMERICAN FREE TRADE AGGREEMENT came into effect on January 1, 1994. It was the outgrowth of an earlier Canada–United States Free Trade Agreement, which was signed in 1988 and came into effect on January 1, 1989. Both agreements were struck only after years of intense negotiations and, on the Canadian side of the border, an intense political debate. First, let's look at the terms of the Canada–United States Free Trade Agreement and at the progress made in achieving freer trade between two of the world's largest trading partners.

The Terms of the Canada–United States Agreement

The main terms of the Canada–United States Free Trade Agreement are:

- Tariffs to be phased out through 1999
- Nontariff barriers to be reduced
- Free trade in energy products, with energy resource sharing in times of national shortage
- More freedom of trade in services
- Future negotiations to eliminate subsidies
- Creation of dispute-settling mechanisms

Removal of Tariffs Scheduled tariff cuts began on January 1, 1989 and were completed on January 1, 1998. But tariff protection remains in place and an atmosphere of tension prevails in many areas. Agriculture remains effectively protected with new tariffs that have replaced old quotas. And a series of *countervailing duties* has been introduced to offset the effects of domestic subsidies. Further, several *antidumping duties* have also been introduced in cases in which it is alleged that products are being exported at a price below the cost of production.

Nontariff Barriers Nontariff barriers such as government procurement policies of buying local products are removed by the agreement. Subsequent to entering into the free trade agreement, Canada and the United States took on additional obligations as members of the WTO that require the removal of agricultural quotas. Many agricultural quotas have been removed but they have been replaced with tar-

iffs. So despite the free trade agreement, we remain a long way from achieving free trade in agricultural products.

Energy Products Free trade in energy products existed before the free trade agreement but the agreement ratified the intent to maintain that arrangement. The agreement that scarce energy resources will be shared in times of national shortage became a controversial one. In effect, what the energy sharing clause amounts to is an agreement that governments will not intervene in energy markets to prevent firms from selling their energy to the other country.

Trade in Services International trade in services has expanded more quickly than trade in manufactured goods in recent years. The free trade agreement, recognizing this factor and seeking to facilitate further expansion of trade in services between the United States and Canada, incorporates two principles: the *right of establishment* and *national treatment*. The right of establishment means that American firms have the right to set up branches in Canada and Canadian firms have the right to set up operations in the United States. National treatment means that each country will treat the goods and firms and investors of the other country as if they were operating within its own borders.

Future Negotiations on Subsidies In both the United States and Canada, there are many subsidies, especially on agricultural products. The presence of subsidies causes problems and makes it legitimate under the agreement for the country importing subsidized goods to impose countervailing duties. As we have just noted, several such duties have been imposed.

Dispute-Settling Mechanisms The Free Trade Agreement included two dispute-settling mechanisms: one to settle disputes relating to all aspects of the agreement, and the other to deal with applications of countervailing duties and antidumping laws in either country. For example, the United States has applied for and received permission to impose countervailing duties on Canadian exports of durum wheat, lumber products, poultry, and live hogs. In each case, the United States accuses Canada of subsidizing these industries unfairly so that Canadian exports are cheaper than the prices at which U.S. producers can supply these goods.

The Extension of the Agreement: NAFTA

The North American Free Trade Agreement (NAFTA) is an agreement among Canada, the United States, and Mexico that has six objectives. They are to

1. Eliminate trade barriers
2. Promote conditions of fair competition
3. Increase investment opportunities
4. Protect intellectual property rights
5. Create an effective dispute resolution mechanism
6. Establish a framework for the expansion of the agreement to include other nations in the hemisphere

Effects of the Free Trade Agreement

Working out the effects of an agreement as complex as NAFTA is difficult, and there is no general consensus on what the effects have been. The theory that you have studied in this chapter predicts that the removal of tariffs will produce an increase in the *volume* of international trade. That is, the theory predicts that Canadians will increasingly specialize in those activities at which they have a comparative advantage and Mexicans and Americans will specialize in a different range of activities and that the three countries will exchange a larger volume of goods and services.

As predicted, trade among the three countries has increased. During the first five years of NAFTA, Canada's trade with the United States increased by 80 percent and Canada's trade with Mexico doubled.

The trade expansion that followed the entry of Mexico in 1995 was especially dramatic. Mexico's exports increased by 31 percent (in U.S. dollar value) in 1995 and by 21 percent in 1996, compared with increases that averaged less than 15 percent a year during the two years before the agreement. But trade expansion with Mexico has not been in one direction. Mexico's imports also increased following the agreement by 23 percent in both 1996 and 1997.

During the 1990s, Canada's exports expanded from less than 30 percent of total production to 36 percent, and Canada's imports have increased from 27 percent to 34 percent of total expenditure.

Canada greatly increased its exports of advertising services, office and telecommunications equipment, paper, and transportation services. And its imports of meat and dairy products, communications services, clothing, furniture, and processed foods and beverages also increased by a large percentage.

These huge changes in exports and imports brought gains from increased specialization and exchange. But they also brought a heavy toll of adjustment. Thousands of jobs were lost in the declining sectors and new jobs were created in the expanding sectors. The amount of job destruction in the years following the free trade agreement was historically high and the unemployment rate rose for three successive years. Only during the Great Depression did the rate of job destruction exceed that of the late 1980s and early 1990s. To what extent a high rate of labour market turnover was caused by the free trade agreement is unclear and controversial. But the net outcome of NAFTA appears to be strongly positive. More than a million new Canadian jobs were created between 1994 and 1999.

REVIEW QUIZ

1 Describe the main features of the Canada–U.S. Free Trade Agreement of 1988.
2 What effect has NAFTA had on nontariff barriers?
3 What effect has NAFTA had on trade in services?
4 How has the volume of trade among Canada, the United States, and Mexico changed during the period since NAFTA was established?

myeconlab **Study Plan 32.6**

◆ You've now seen how free international trade enables all nations to gain from trade. By producing goods in which we have a comparative advantage and trading some of our production for that of others, we expand our consumption possibilities. Placing impediments on that trade decreases the gains from trade. By opening our country up to free international trade, the market for the things that we sell expands and their relative prices rise. The market for the things that we buy also expands, and their relative prices fall.

Reading Between the Lines on pp. 778–779 looks at the softwood lumber dispute between the United States and Canada. This dispute provides a clear example of the economic cost of restricting international trade.

Tariffs in Action: Lumber

TELEGRAPH–JOURNAL, OCTOBER 20, 2005

Retaliation in softwood lumber dispute not advised

Retaliating against the United States over its refusal to accept legal defeat in the softwood lumber dispute would hurt Canada more than the Americans, a Canadian forest industry spokesman says.

Instead, Canada should get more active in U.S. politics by advancing the interests of the mass of American homeowners and other lumber consumers against a small group of protectionist corporations, Carl Grenier, general manager of the Free Trade Lumber Council, said Wednesday.

"Sabre-rattling makes some people feel good, especially when it's against the U.S.," Mr. Grenier, whose group represents companies accounting for about 40 per cent of Canadian lumber shipments to America, told the Economic Club of Toronto. ...

A better approach is to "transform what has been a fight between U.S. producers and Canadian producers of softwood lumber into a fight between U.S. producers and consumers."

And although it might seem attractive to find new markets for Canadian exports—especially oil and gas for which "other customers are lining up at the pump"—Mr. Grenier noted that the North American Free Trade Agreement originated from the failure of the Trudeau government's 1970s Third Option strategy of trade diversification.

"For the foreseeable future, most of our trade eggs will stay firmly in the U.S. basket."...

Reprinted with permission from The Canadian Press.

Essence of the Story

■ It is not in Canada's interest to retaliate against the United States for the U.S. tariff on softwood imports from Canada.

■ Instead, Canada should appeal to the self-interest of American homeowners and other lumber consumers.

■ While it might seem attractive to find new markets for Canadian oil and gas exports, we must remember that NAFTA had its origin in the failure to diversify trade when Pierre Trudeau was prime minister.

■ The reality is that our trading future is with the United States.

Economic Analysis

■ The United States has imposed a 27 percent tariff on imports of Canadian lumber.

■ The tariff damages Canada, but it also damages the United States.

■ Figure 1 shows the U.S. market for lumber.

■ The demand curve of U.S. buyers of lumber is D.

■ There are two supply curves: the supply curve of the Canadian producers, S_C, and the supply curve of U.S. producers, S_{US}. We'll assume that Canada can supply any quantity at a price of $100 per load.

■ With no tariff, the quantity of lumber bought in the United States is QC_0. Of this amount, QP_0 is produced in the United States and the rest is imported from Canada, as shown by the arrow in Fig. 1.

■ Now the United States puts a 27 percent tariff on the import of lumber. Canadian lumber is now supplied to the U.S. market at the original supply price, $100, plus the tariff, $27, so the supply curve of lumber from Canada shifts to become S_C + *tariff*.

■ With the tariff, the quantity of lumber bought in the United States is QC_1. Of this amount, QP_1 is produced in the United States and the rest is imported from Canada, as shown by the arrow in Fig. 1.

■ The tariff decreases U.S. consumption and imports and increases U.S. production.

■ Figure 2 shows the winners and the losers in the United States.

■ The winners include U.S lumber producers, who gain additional producer surplus, which is shown by the blue area in Fig. 2.

■ Another winner is the U.S. government, which collects additional revenue, shown by the purple area in Fig. 2.

■ The sum of the blue, purple, and grey areas is the loss of consumer surplus that results from the tariff.

■ A deadweight loss arises—the decrease in consumer surplus exceeds the increase in producer surplus plus the tariff revenue—regardless of whether Canadian lumber producers receive a subsidy.

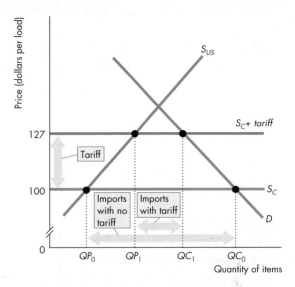

Figure 1 Tariffs and imports

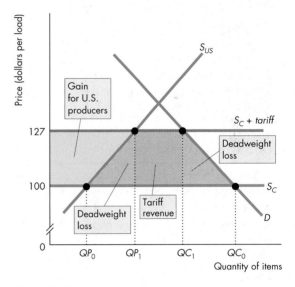

Figure 2 Winners and losers

SUMMARY

KEY POINTS

Patterns and Trends in International Trade
(p. 756)

- Large flows of trade take place between countries, most of which is in manufactured goods exchanged among rich industrialized countries.
- The volume of Canadian international trade is about 40 percent of total production.

The Gains from International Trade (pp. 757–762)

- When opportunity costs diverge, comparative advantage brings gains from trade.
- By increasing its production of goods in which it has a comparative advantage and then trading some of the increased output, a country can consume at points outside its production possibilities frontier.
- In the absence of international borrowing and lending, trade is balanced as prices adjust to reflect the international supply of and demand for goods.
- The world price balances the production and consumption plans of the trading parties. At the equilibrium price, trade is balanced.

International Trade Restrictions (pp. 763–766)

- Countries restrict international trade by imposing tariffs and nontariff barriers, such as quotas and VERS.
- International trade restrictions raise the domestic price of imported goods, lower the volume of imports, and reduce the total value of imports and exports by the same amount.

The Case Against Protection (pp. 767–771)

- Arguments that protection is necessary to save jobs, to protect infant industries, and to prevent dumping are weak.
- Arguments that protection is necessary for national security, allows us to compete with cheap foreign labour, makes the economy diversified and stable, penalizes lax environmental standards, protects national culture, and prevents exploitation of developing countries are flawed.

- Trade is restricted because tariffs raise government revenue and because protection brings a small loss to a large number of people and a large gain per person to a small number of people.

The Balance of International Payments
(pp. 772–775)

- A country's international transactions are recorded in its balance of payments accounts.
- The net exports surplus is equal to the government sector surplus plus the private sector surplus.

The North American Free Trade Agreement
(pp. 776–777)

- NAFTA is an agreement among Canada, the United States, and Mexico, which began in 1994 and grew from a previous Canada–U.S. agreement.
- Under NAFTA, trade has expanded more rapidly than before the agreement.

KEY FIGURES AND TABLE

KEY TERMS

PROBLEMS

Go to **myeconlab** for solutions to odd-numbered problems and additional exercises.

1. The table provides information about Virtual Reality's production possibilities.

TV sets (per day)		Computers (per day)
0	and	36
10	and	35
20	and	33
30	and	30
40	and	26
50	and	21
60	and	15
70	and	8
80	and	0

   a. Calculate Virtual Reality's opportunity cost of a TV set when it produces 10 sets a day.
   b. Calculate Virtual Reality's opportunity cost of a TV set when it produces 40 sets a day.
   c. Calculate Virtual Reality's opportunity cost of a TV set when it produces 70 sets a day.
   d. Using the answers to parts (a), (b), and (c), sketch the relationship between the opportunity cost of a TV set and the quantity of TV sets produced in Virtual Reality.

2. The table provides information about Vital Sign's production possibilities.

TV sets (per day)		Computers (per day)
0	and	18.0
10	and	17.5
20	and	16.5
30	and	15.0
40	and	13.0
50	and	10.5
60	and	7.5
70	and	4.0
80	and	0

   a. Calculate Vital Sign's opportunity cost of a TV set when it produces 10 sets a day.
   b. Calculate Vital Sign's opportunity cost of a TV set when it produces 40 sets a day.
   c. Calculate Vital Sign's opportunity cost of a TV set when it produces 70 sets a day.

   d. Using the answers to parts (a), (b), and (c), sketch the relationship between the opportunity cost of a TV set and the quantity of TV sets produced in Vital Sign.

3. Suppose that with no international trade, Virtual Reality in problem 1 produces and consumes 10 TV sets a day and Vital Sign in problem 2 produces and consumes 60 TV sets a day. Now suppose that the two countries begin to trade with each other.

   a. Which country exports TV sets?
   b. What adjustments are made to the amount of each good produced by each country?
   c. What adjustments are made to the amount of each good consumed by each country?
   d. What can you say about the terms of trade (the price of a TV set expressed as computers per TV set) under free trade?

4. Suppose that with no international trade, Virtual Reality in problem 1 produces and consumes 50 TV sets a day and Vital Sign in problem 2 produces and consumes 20 TV sets a day. Now suppose that the two countries begin to trade with each other.

   a. Which country exports TV sets?
   b. What adjustments are made to the amount of each good produced by each country?
   c. What adjustments are made to the amount of each good consumed by each country?
   d. What can you say about the terms of trade (the price of a TV set expressed as computers per TV set) under free trade?

5. Compare the total quantities of each good produced in problems 1 and 2 with the total quantities of each good produced in problems 3 and 4.

   a. Does free trade increase or decrease the total quantities of TV sets and computers produced in each case? Why?
   b. What happens to the price of a TV set in Virtual Reality in each case? Why does it rise in one case and fall in the other?
   c. What happens to the price of a computer in Vital Sign in each case? Why does it rise in one case and fall in the other?

6. Compare the international trade in problem 3 with that in problem 4.

   a. Why does Virtual Reality export TV sets in one case and import them in the other case?
   b. Do the TV producers or the computer producers gain in each case?
   c. Do consumers gain in each case?

7. The figure depicts the world market for soybeans. With free trade, what is the world price of soybeans, the quantities exported and imported, and the balance of trade?

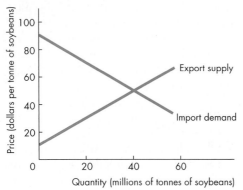

8. If in problem 7, a tariff of $20 per tonne is imposed on imported soybean, what is the world price of soybeans, the quantity of soybean imports, the price in the importing country, and the tariff revenue?

9. The Silecon, whose currency is the grain, conducted the following transactions in 2002:

Item	Billions of grains
Net exports of goods and services	250
Borrowing from the rest of the world	−60
Lending to the rest of the world	200
Change in official reserves	−10

What are the current account, capital account, and official settlements balances?

10. Spin, whose currency is the wheel, conducted the following transactions in 2002:

Item	Billions of wheels
Net exports of goods and services	20
Borrowing from the rest of the world	4
Lending to the rest of the world	24
Change in official reserves	0

What are the current account, capital account, and official settlements balances?

CRITICAL THINKING

1. Study *Reading Between the Lines* on pp. 778–779 and then answer the following questions:
   a. Why did the United States impose a tariff on lumber imports from Canada?
   b. What are the effects of the tariff on lumber?
   c. Who are the winners and who are the losers from the tariff on lumber?
   d. Modify the figures on page 779 to show the effects of a Canadian subsidy to lumber producers on the consumer surplus, producer surplus, and deadweight loss in the United States.

WEB EXERCISES

Use the links on ⓧ myeconlab to work the following exercises.

1. Visit the Web site of the World Trade Organization and obtain information about the latest round of trade talks on freeing trade in agricultural products.
   a. What is the argument for ending agricultural subsidies in rich countries?
   b. Why is the European Union so opposed to dismantling farm subsidies?
   c. Why do you think Australia and New Zealand have ended farm subsidies?
   d. What is Canada's position of farm subsidies? What accounts for Canada's position?
2. Obtain information to write a NAFTA report card on agriculture. Then answer the following questions:
   a. What does NAFTA seek to achieve in agriculture trade?
   b. What has NAFTA achieved to date?
   c. What are the obstacles to greater gains for North American trade in agricultural products?
   d. Would you vote to maintain NAFTA? Why or why not?
   e. Would you vote to expand NAFTA to include other countries? Why or why not?

Expanding the Frontier

Economics is about how we cope with scarcity. We cope by making choices that balance marginal benefits and marginal costs so that we use our scarce resources efficiently.

These choices determine how much work we do; how hard we work at school to learn the mental skills that form our human capital and that determine the kinds of jobs we get and the incomes we earn; and how much we save for future big-ticket expenditures. These choices also determine how much businesses and governments spend on new capital—on auto assembly lines, computers and fibre cables for improved Internet services, shopping malls, highways, bridges, and tunnels; and how intensively existing capital and natural resources are used and therefore how quickly they wear out or are used up. Most significant of all, these choices determine the problems that scientists, engineers, and other inventors work on to develop new technologies.

All the choices we've just described determine two vital measures of economic performance:

- Real GDP
- Economic growth

Real GDP is determined by the quantity of labour, the quantity of capital, and the state of technological knowledge. And economic growth is determined by growth in the quantity of labour, capital accumulation, and technological advances.

Economic growth, maintained at a steady rate over a number of decades, is the single most powerful influence on any society. It brings a transformation that continues to amaze thoughtful people. Economic growth that is maintained at a rapid rate can transform a society in years, not decades. Such transformations are taking place right now in many Asian countries. These transformations are economic miracles.

The three chapters in this part studied the foundations of aggregate supply, the miracle of rapid economic growth and the forces that shape our capacity to produce goods and services, and the gains from international trade and the national balance of payments. Chapter 30 explained how labour market equilibrium determines potential GDP and derives the aggregate supply curves. Chapter 31 studied the process of economic growth in the fast-growing economies of Asia and Canada. It explained how growth is influenced by technological change and the incentives that stimulate it. Chapter 32 explained how all nations can benefit from free international trade, reviewed the free trade versus protection debate, and explained the source of a nation's international deficit.

The global economy is big news these days. And it has always attracted attention. On the next pages, you can meet the economist who first understood comparative advantage, David Ricardo. And you can meet one of Canada's leading international economists, Dan Trefler of the University of Toronto.

783

Gains from International Trade

THE ECONOMIST

David Ricardo *(1772–1832) was a highly successful 27-year-old stockbroker when he stumbled on a copy of Adam Smith's* Wealth of Nations *(see p. 54) on a weekend visit to the country. He was immediately hooked and went on to become the most celebrated economist of his age and one of the all-time great economists. One of his many contributions was to develop the principle of comparative advantage, the foundation on which the modern theory of international trade is built. The example he used to illustrate this principle was the trade between England and Portugal in cloth and wine.*

The World Trade Organization (WTO) and its predecessor, General Agreement on Tariffs and Trade, were established as a reaction against the devastation wrought by beggar-thy-neighbour tariffs imposed during the 1930s. But the WTO and the goals that it pursues are also triumphs for the logic first worked out by Smith and Ricardo.

THE ISSUES

Until the mid-eighteenth century, it was generally believed that the purpose of international trade was to keep exports greater than imports and pile up gold. If gold was accumulated, it was believed, the nation would prosper; if gold was lost through an international deficit, the nation would be drained of money and impoverished. These beliefs are called *mercantilism*, and the *mercantilists* were pamphleteers who advocated with missionary fervor the pursuit of an international surplus. If exports did not exceed imports, the mercantilists wanted imports restricted.

In the 1740s, David Hume explained that as the quantity of money (gold) changes, so also does the price level, and the nation's *real* wealth is unaffected. In the 1770s, Adam Smith argued that import restrictions would lower the gains from specialization and make a nation poorer. Thirty years later, David Ricardo proved the law of comparative advantage and demonstrated the superiority of free trade. Mercantilism was intellectually bankrupt but remained politically powerful.

Gradually, through the nineteenth century, the mercantilist influence waned and North America and Western Europe prospered in an environment of increasingly free international trade. But despite remarkable advances in economic understanding, mercantilism never quite died. It had a brief and devastating revival in the 1920s and 1930s when tariff hikes brought about the collapse of international trade and accentuated the Great Depression. It subsided again after World War II with the establishment of the General Agreement on Tariffs and Trade (GATT).

But mercantilism lingers on. The often-expressed view that the United States should restrict Chinese imports and reduce its deficit with China and the fear that NAFTA will bring economic ruin to Canada are modern manifestations of mercantilism. It would be interesting to have David Hume, Adam Smith, and David Ricardo commenting on these views. But we know what they would say—the same things that they said to the eighteenth-century mercantilists. And they would still be right today.

THEN

In the eighteenth century, when mercantilists and economists were debating the pros and cons of free international exchange, the transportation technology that was available limited the gains from international trade. Sailing ships with tiny cargo holds took close to a month to cross the Atlantic Ocean. But the potential gains were large, and so was the incentive to cut shipping costs. By the 1850s, the clipper ship had been developed, cutting the journey from Boston to Liverpool to only $12\frac{1}{4}$ days. Half a century later, 10,000-ton steamships were sailing between North America and England in just 4 days. As sailing times and costs declined, the gains from international trade increased and the volume of trade expanded.

NOW

The container ship has revolutionized international trade and contributed to its continued expansion. Today, most goods cross the oceans in containers—metal boxes—packed into and piled on top of ships like this one. Container technology has cut the cost of ocean shipping by economizing on handling and by making cargoes harder to steal, thereby lowering insurance costs. It is unlikely that there would be much international trade in goods such as television sets and DVD players without this technology. High-value and perishable cargoes such as flowers and fresh foods, as well as urgent courier packages, travel by air. Every day, dozens of cargo-laden 747s fly between every major North American city and to destinations across the Atlantic and Pacific oceans.

Dan Trefler, whom you can meet on the following pages, is one of Canada's the most distinguished international trade economists. He has contributed to our understanding of the effects of international trade and trade policy on economic growth and development and today's global trading arrangements.

785

Dan Trefler is the J. Douglas and Ruth Grant Canada Research Chair in Competitiveness and Prosperity at the University of Toronto's Rotman School of Management. Born in Toronto, he was an undergraduate at the University of Toronto and a graduate student at Cambridge University and the University of California, Los Angeles.

Professor Trefler is a Research Fellow at the Canadian Institute for Advanced Research and a Research Associate at the National Bureau of Economic Research. He also serves on the Ontario Task Force on Competitiveness, Productivity, and Economic Progress. He was the winner of the Canadian Economics Association's Rae Award for Excellence in Research and is a co-editor of the Journal of International Economics.

Professor Trefler's research is broad but focuses on policy levers for promoting Canadian competitiveness.

Dan Trefler

Michael Parkin and Robin Bade talked with Dan Trefler about his work and the light that it sheds on international trade issues such as offshoring and NAFTA.

Dan, what attracted you to economics?

Throughout my life, including when I was a teenager, I've been interested in how social systems work and what makes some societies so much more successful than others.

Economics offers one of several perspectives on that question. What is so nice about the economic perspective is that it tries to combine a whole bunch of nifty theories about what makes a society successful with evidence-based data-driven analysis that is often lacking in other approaches.

So why is it that Africa has done so poorly over the years? We often use very vague terms like colonial heritage or poor institutions, but if you gave me a large-scale database to analyze the problem, I'd be like a pig at the trough, delighted to really think about it.

Why did you decide to focus on international economics?

In part, because of a profound interest in development economics, which is so tightly linked to international trade. But more specifically, as a young man just starting out in economics, the hot topic of the day was the 1988 General Election which was fought on the issue of should Canada have a free trade agreement with the United States, after more than 100 years of protectionism.

Who has had the greatest influence on your development as an economist?

Again, as a teenager I was thinking about society in political science and sociological terms until I read a book by Che Guevara (now back in fashion), who said that if you really want to understand society you have to understand economics. The best place to think about that is to be doing things like reading the *Wall Street Journal*, and from there it was downhill. I was completely entranced by the economic approach.

Why should Canadians care about international trade?

Because it is where little things make a big difference. I think most of us would like to think that we have solutions to all of society's problems, which are magic bullets. In fact, the way to make Canada an even greater place is to make it even a little bit more productive, say 10 to15 percent more productive. Even a 10 percent increase in our productivity would generate for us upwards of $100 billion in revenue to play with. With $100 billion, think of what you could do. You could, if you're a new conservative, eliminate all corporate taxes, which would cost maybe about $25 billion. If you were very left leaning, you could pour huge amounts of money into single moms, natives, immigrants, and male high school dropouts—the four poorest groups in our country.

> " *Little things make a big difference. ... Even a 10 percent increase in our productivity would generate for us upwards of $100 billion in revenue to play with. ... Interntional trade is one of the biggest drivers of productivity.* "

You would have plenty of money left to drive an agenda for children if you were so inclined; lots of money left for redistributing to our have-not provinces like Newfoundland. You could run every single one of these things that I've mentioned at a cadillac level of service or delivery with $100 billion.

So worrying about productivity is really worrying about how we're going to feed our social agenda. And then that's where trade comes in. International trade is one of the biggest drivers of productivity, and it does so in two ways. First, it pressures our companies to become more innovative than they ever have been; and second, it supports our companies by providing them with the possibility of accessing larger markets, say like the U.S. market or the Chinese market.

So I think about international trade as a way of pressuring firms to be more competitive and in supporting them in entering the foreign markets.

Let's talk about the aspect of international economic activity that scares most people: offshoring. First, is it really new, or has it been around a long time? Or, what is new about it?

You know I read recently in the back of a news magazine an advertisement saying "offshore your personal life." They provided dating services for people!

We hear a lot of hype around offshoring. There are two aspects of it that are new. One is that the pace at which we are seeing manufacturing rise in low-wage countries like China is really breathtaking. That's both wonderful and scary. It's wonderful for these poor countries, which are suddenly finding themselves to be more affluent. It's a little scary for Canadian workers in the manufacturing sector.

The other aspect that is really fundamentally new and we've never seen it before is the tradability of services. The idea that somebody sitting in, say, Bangalore, India, is providing services to us is truly remarkable. And it speaks to the word "globalization" in a way that I think no other statement does. Nothing like that has ever been seen in history.

How big is the offshoring of services?

The Bangalore example turned out to be the exception to the rule. First of all, offshoring is not that large. There are different ways of doing the accounting, but if you think about offshoring of services, which is not all of offshoring, it accounts for only about 10 percent of our international trade. It's a small amount though it is growing fast and that's why people are so interested in it.

The second aspect of offshoring of services is that 85 percent of it goes to other rich countries, like the United States, so only a small portion of it is with countries like India. But that is changing rapidly. So right now, it's not important. Where we'll be in the future, that's another question.

What are the effects of offshoring on unemployment and wages?

The unemployment rate fluctuates for reasons that have very little to do with international trade. That is very obvious if you just plot the data.

Offshoring does have an impact on wages, but much less of an impact than people think. There is a small group of people out there, maybe less than 5 percent of the population, who has been hammered by international trade, seeing their jobs displaced and wages absolutely collapse under the weight to Chinese competition. That is the exception.

The interesting thing about offshoring of services is what impact it will have on wages because now we're seeing international trade affecting the wages of the very skilled. That is something new. That is not something we've ever seen before. It is too early to say for sure what the impacts are but the early research suggests that it will have a very large impact on wages and a moderate impact on employment.

Let's now turn to another big source of discussion and concern: NAFTA. What is the latest tally on its benefits and costs?

NAFTA was my teething grounds in economics—I spent years and years studying it. There are many aspects of it that interest people. Let's start with the narrowest and simplest and that is its affect on employment, wages, and productivity. NAFTA has had a large effect on displacing workers. That is, the shipping of workers from low value-added activities, activities that were once protected, into higher value-added activities. Some workers were definitely displaced. And it hurts if you're unemployed for six months, looking for a new job. That's a big hit.

There's been absolutely no affect of the free trade agreement on wages, which to me was a big surprise since I was expecting that we would be competing with labour from south of the Mason-Dixon Line in the United States.

The surprise has been the huge impact on productivity and that impact has been upward of 6 percent for manufacturing as a whole, which is a very, very large number. The idea that a single government policy like liberalizing trade could have such a big impact on productivity is to me remarkable and a testament to what government can do when it puts its mind to it.

> *The surprise has been the huge impact [of NAFTA] on productivity ... upward of 6 percent for manufacturing as a whole.*

> *Become informed so you know exactly why you're demonstrating.*

Now there is also a larger issue about what is sometimes called the "Trade and ..." agenda, which deals with things like the environment and sovereignty issues where we retain our rights over water and so on. Those have turned out so far to be a non-issue.

What advice do you have for a student who is just starting to study economics? Is economics a good subject in which to major?

Economics works extremely well with the social sciences. It works with sociology, it works with political science, and it's starting to work with areas that are more surprising, which is psychology and the natural sciences; we're getting an increased insight in that area. What advice do I have? It would be to read a lot. Becoming knowledgeable is the best way to have fun.

What would you suggest students read?

Read books, read books. People all around you are writing books that are acceptable to very general audiences. Go out and read some books on neuroscience and economics, or sociology and economics, or political science. If you're interested in economic development, read books about the new institutionalism. If you're interested in international trade, read Helpman's *The Mystery of Economic Growth* or Jared Diamond's *Guns, Germs, and Steel*. Or if you're interested in something more historical, read David S. Landes, *The Wealth and Poverty of Nations*.

What can a student do to make a difference?

When it comes to international trade, it's very important to know that you have a huge impact through activism, that you can do it through going out there and demonstrating on the lines every time there is an international trade agreement. But it's important to become informed so that you know exactly why you're out there demonstrating.

You can also make a difference through consumer activism—that is things like eco-labelling, insisting on it or making the effort to try to find out where the goods that you use are produced, or even something simple like going to Second Cup or Starbucks and saying "what you're doing for fair trade in coffee is not nearly enough, you could do a lot more."

CANADIAN
ECONOMY
DATABASE

The following data tables provide a description of some of the main features of the Canadian economy from 1926 to 2001.

You can make graphs of these data by using *Economics in Action* on the Parkin–Bade Web site. To do so, open the table of contents page for *any* chapter, click on Data Graphing and then click on Canada Historical.

These data are updated annually on the Parkin–Bade Web site.

Sources

CANSIM series: Statistics Canada, Ottawa

HSC series: Statistics Canada, *Historical Statistics of Canada*, Second Edition, F. H. Leacy (ed.), Ottawa, 1983.

HSC(1) series: The MacMillan Company of Canada Limited, *Historical Statistics of Canada*, M.C. Urquhart (ed.), Toronto, 1965.

A break in a series is indicated by [b].

Variables

1. Real GDP
HSC series F55 and CANSIM series v1992292. The data for 1926–1960 are F55 multiplied by the 1961 ratio of v1992292 to F55.

2. Real consumption expenditure
HSC series F33 and CANSIM series v1992262. The data for 1926–1960 are F33 multiplied by the 1961 ratio of v1992262 to F33.

3. Real investment
HSC is F55 minus the sum of F33, F34, and F51 plus F52; CANSIM series is v1992292 minus the sum of v1992262, v1992268, 1992282 plus v1992286. The data for 1926–1960 are *HSC* multiplied by the 1961 ratio of CANSIM to *HSC*.

4. Real government expenditure
HSC series F34 and CANSIM series v1992268. The data for 1926–1960 are F34 multiplied by the 1961 ratio of v1992268 to F34.

5. Real exports
HSC series F51 and CANSIM series v1992282. The data for 1926–1960 are F51 multiplied by the 1961 ratio of v1992282 to F51.

6. Real imports
HSC series F52 and CANSIM series v1992286. The data for 1926–1960 are F51 multiplied by the 1961 ratio of v1992286 to F52.

7. Real net exports
Real exports *minus* real imports.

8. Potential GDP
Real GDP trends and authors' assumptions and calculations.

9. Fluctuations around potential GDP
Percentage deviation of real GDP from potential GDP.

10. Real GDP growth rate
Annual percentage change in real GDP.

11. GDP deflator
HSC series K172 and CANSIM series v647710 and v3860248. The data for 1961–1980 are v647710 multiplied by the 1981 ratio of v3860248 to v647710. The data for 1926–1960 are K172 multiplied by the 1961 ratio of the above calculation to K172.

12. CPI
Statistics Canada, CANSIM series v737344.

13. Inflation rate
Annual percentage change in the GDP deflator.

14. Inflation rate
Annual percentage change in the CPI.

15. Labour force
CANSIM series v21051 and v2461098.

16. Labour force participation rate
CANSIM series v21051, v21056, and v2461245.

17. Average weekly hours
HSC series E128, E129, E130, E131, E132, E133, E134, E135; Statistics Canada, CANSIM series v2461119 and v2641490, and authors' calculations.

18. Unemployment rate
HSC series D127, D132, and D491 and CANSIM series v2461224.

19. Long-term interest rate
HSC(1) series H605, *HSC* series J475, and Bank of Canada series B14013.

20. Short-term interest rate
HSC series J471 and Bank of Canada series B14060.

21. Federal government revenues
HSC series H18 and CANSIM series v499985.

22. Federal government outlays
HSC series H34 and CANSIM series v500016.

23. Federal government surplus(+)/deficit(-)
HSC series H18 and H34 and CANSIM series v499985 and v500016.

24. Gross federal debt
CANSIM series v151537.

25. M1
Bank of Canada series B2033.

26. M2+
Bank of Canada series B2037.

27. M1 velocity
Series 1 multiplied by series 11 divided by series 25.

28. M2+ velocity
Series 1 multiplied by series 11 divided by series 26.

29. Exchange rate
HSC series J562 and CANSIM series v37426.

30. Current account
HSC series G83 and CANSIM series v114421.

Year		1926	1927	1928	1929	1930	1931	1932	1933	1934	1935
Real GDP (billions of 1997 dollars)	1	61.2	67.0	73.1	73.4	70.3	61.4	55.0	51.3	57.6	62.1
Real consumption expenditure (billions of 1997 dollars)	2	35.6	39.8	43.6	46.3	44.3	42.2	38.9	37.9	39.9	41.6
Real investment (billions of 1997 dollars)	3	12.4	14.5	16.3	14.4	12.7	4.2	1.0	0.0	2.8	4.5
Real government expenditures (billions of 1997 dollars)	4	10.0	10.5	10.6	11.9	13.0	13.8	13.3	11.2	11.9	12.4
Real exports (billions of 1997 dollars)	5	12.1	12.2	13.8	13.0	11.3	10.1	9.4	9.5	10.7	11.8
Real imports (billions of 1997 dollars)	6	8.9	9.9	11.1	12.1	11.0	8.8	7.6	7.2	7.7	8.2
Real net exports (billions of 1997 dollars)	7	3.2	2.3	2.7	0.9	0.3	1.3	1.8	2.2	3.0	3.5
Potential GDP (billions of 1997 dollars)	8	62.0	63.8	65.7	67.7	69.7	71.8	73.9	76.1	78.4	80.8
Fluctuations around potential GDP (percentage)	9	−1.2	5.0	11.3	8.5	0.8	−14.5	−25.6	−32.6	−26.6	−23.2
Real GDP growth rate (percent per year)	10	—	9.5	9.1	0.4	−4.3	−12.7	−10.4	−6.7	12.1	7.8
GDP deflator (1997 = 100)	11	8.7	8.6	8.5	8.6	8.4	7.9	7.1	7.0	7.1	7.1
CPI (1992 = 100)	12	10.9	10.8	10.8	11.0	10.9	9.8	8.9	8.5	8.6	8.7
Inflation rate (GDP deflator percent per year)	13	—	−1.1	−0.6	1.1	−2.5	−6.2	−9.3	−1.7	1.4	0.3
Inflation rate (CPI percent per year)	14	0	−0.9	0	1.9	−0.9	−10.1	−9.2	−4.5	1.2	1.2
Labour force (millions)	15	3.7	3.8	3.9	4.0	4.1	4.2	4.2	4.3	4.3	4.4
Labour force participation rate (percentage)	16	57.8	57.9	58.0	58.1	58.2	58.3	58.2	58.0	57.9	57.8
Average weekly hours (hours per week)	17	—	—	—	—	—	—	—	—	—	—
Unemployment rate (percentage)	18	2.9	1.8	1.7	2.9	9.1	11.6	17.6	19.3	14.5	14.2
Long-term interest rate (percent per year)	19	4.9	4.6	4.5	4.9	4.7	4.6	5.1	4.6	4.0	3.6
Short-term interest rate (percent per year)	20	—	—	—	—	—	—	—	—	2.5	1.5
Federal government revenues (billions of dollars)	21	0.4	0.4	0.5	0.5	0.4	0.3	0.3	0.3	0.4	0.4
Federal government outlays (billions of dollars)	22	0.4	0.4	0.4	0.4	0.4	0.4	0.5	0.5	0.5	0.5
Federal government surplus (+)/deficit(−) (billions of dollars)	23	0	0.1	0.1	0	−0.1	−0.1	−0.2	−0.1	−0.1	−0.2
Gross federal debt (billions of dollars)	24	2.8	2.8	2.7	2.7	2.6	2.7	2.9	3.1	3.2	3.5
M1 (billions of dollars)	25	—	—	—	—	—	—	—	—	—	—
M2+ (billions of dollars)	26	—	—	—	—	—	—	—	—	—	—
M1 velocity (GDP/M1)	27	—	—	—	—	—	—	—	—	—	—
M2+ velocity (GDP/M2+)	28	—	—	—	—	—	—	—	—	—	—
Exchange rate (U.S. dollars per Canadian dollar)	29	1.00	1.00	1.00	1.00	1.00	0.96	0.88	0.92	1.01	0.99
Current account balance (billions of dollars)	30	0.1	0	0	−0.3	−0.3	−0.2	−0.1	0	0.1	0.1

1936	1937	1938	1939	1940	1941	1942	1943	1944	1945	1946	1947	1948	1949	
64.8	71.3	71.9	77.2	88.1	100.8	119.5	124.3	129.2	126.3	123.0	128.2	131.4	136.4	1
43.5	46.2	45.6	46.9	50.3	53.7	55.1	56.7	60.8	66.9	74.4	79.6	77.7	82.1	2
4.0	8.3	8.8	11.3	6.4	0.5	−20.7	−29.9	−38.0	−19.0	9.5	19.5	23.6	23.4	3
12.5	12.6	14.1	15.0	26.5	38.3	80.2	87.7	100.7	69.3	32.8	24.7	23.4	25.9	4
14.2	14.5	13.1	14.4	16.4	21.6	19.3	26.8	25.9	25.2	21.2	21.0	21.7	20.4	5
9.3	10.3	9.6	10.3	11.5	13.3	14.3	17.0	20.2	16.0	14.8	16.7	15.0	15.4	6
4.8	4.2	3.4	4.1	4.9	8.3	5.0	9.8	5.7	9.2	6.3	4.4	6.7	5.0	7
83.2	85.7	88.2	90.9	93.6	97.3	101.1	105.1	109.3	113.7	118.3	123.2	128.2	133.6	8
−22.1	−16.7	−18.5	−15.0	−5.8	3.6	18.2	18.2	18.2	11.1	3.9	4.1	2.4	2.1	9
4.4	10.0	0.8	7.4	14.1	14.4	18.6	4.0	4.0	−2.2	−2.7	4.3	2.5	3.8	10
7.4	7.6	7.6	7.5	7.9	8.5	8.9	9.2	9.4	9.7	10.0	10.8	12.2	12.7	11
8.8	9.1	9.2	9.2	9.5	10.1	10.5	10.7	10.8	10.9	11.2	12.3	14.0	14.5	12
3.3	2.6	0	−0.9	4.7	7.9	4.5	3.5	3.1	2.5	2.9	8.8	12.3	4.3	13
1.1	3.4	1.1	0	3.3	6.3	4.0	1.9	0.9	0.9	2.8	9.8	13.8	3.6	14
4.5	4.5	4.6	4.6	4.6	4.5	4.6	4.6	4.5	4.5	4.8	4.9	5.0	5.2	15
57.6	57.5	57.4	57.2	56.6	55.4	56.5	58.0	57.4	56.2	55.0	54.9	54.6	54.4	16
—	—	—	—	—	—	—	—	—	44.1	42.7	42.5	42.3	42.2	17
12.8	9.1	11.4	11.4	9.0	4.1	2.7	1.4	1.2	1.4	b3.4	2.2	2.3	2.8	18
b3.0	3.2	3.1	3.2	3.3	3.1	3.1	3.0	3.0	2.9	2.6	2.6	2.9	2.8	19
0.9	0.7	0.6	0.7	0.7	0.6	0.5	0.5	0.4	0.4	0.4	0.4	0.4	0.5	20
0.5	0.5	0.5	0.6	0.9	1.5	2.3	2.8	2.7	3.0	3.0	2.9	2.8	2.6	21
0.5	0.5	0.6	0.7	1.3	1.9	4.4	5.3	5.2	5.1	2.6	2.2	2.2	2.4	22
−0.1	0	−0.1	−0.1	−0.4	−0.4	−2.1	−2.6	−2.6	−2.1	0.4	0.7	0.6	0.1	23
3.5	3.6	3.6	3.7	4.0	5.0	6.6	8.8	11.8	14.9	17.9	17.7	17.2	16.9	24
—	—	—	—	—	—	—	—	—	—	—	—	—	—	25
—	—	—	—	—	—	—	—	—	—	—	—	—	—	26
—	—	—	—	—	—	—	—	—	—	—	—	—	—	27
—	—	—	—	—	—	—	—	—	—	—	—	—	—	28
1.00	1.00	0.99	0.96	0.90	0.90	0.90	0.90	0.90	0.91	1.00	1.00	1.00	0.97	29
0.2	0.2	0.1	0.1	0.2	0.5	0.1	0.7	0.1	0.7	b0.3	0.0	0.4	0.2	30

Year		1950	1951	1952	1953	1954	1955	1956	1957	1958	1959
Real GDP (billions of 1997 dollars)	1	146.7	154.1	167.8	176.5	174.3	190.7	206.9	211.7	216.6	224.8
Real consumption expenditure (billions of 1997 dollars)	2	87.5	88.2	94.4	100.9	104.6	113.6	122.1	126.6	131.2	138.5
Real investment (billions of 1997 dollars)	3	27.8	26.2	23.4	26.0	21.8	29.3	37.5	38.0	35.2	38.0
Real government expenditures (billions of 1997 dollars)	4	27.9	36.4	44.8	46.2	44.4	45.4	46.6	45.8	47.2	46.8
Real exports (billions of 1997 dollars)	5	20.3	22.2	24.7	24.5	23.6	25.4	27.3	27.5	27.4	28.5
Real imports (billions of 1997 dollars)	6	16.8	18.9	19.5	21.2	20.2	22.9	26.5	26.2	24.4	26.9
Real net exports (billions of 1997 dollars)	7	3.5	3.3	5.2	3.3	3.4	2.5	0.7	1.3	3.0	1.6
Potential GDP (billions of 1997 dollars)	8	139.1	145.0	151.1	157.6	164.4	171.5	179.0	186.9	195.3	204.1
Fluctuations around potential GDP (percentage)	9	5.5	6.3	11.0	12.0	6.0	11.2	15.5	13.3	10.9	10.2
Real GDP growth rate (percent per year)	10	7.6	5.0	8.9	5.1	−1.2	9.4	8.4	2.4	2.3	3.8
GDP deflator (1997 = 100)	11	13.0	14.5	15.1	15.1	15.3	15.4	16.0	16.3	16.6	16.9
CPI (1992 = 100)	12	14.9	16.4	16.9	16.7	16.8	16.8	17.1	17.6	18.0	18.3
Inflation rate (GDP deflator percent per year)	13	2.4	11.3	4.4	−0.2	1.6	0.6	3.7	2.1	1.5	2.0
Inflation rate (CPI percent per year)	14	2.8	10.1	3.0	−1.2	0.6	0	1.8	2.9	2.3	1.7
Labour force (millions)	15	5.2	5.2	5.3	5.4	5.5	5.6	5.8	6.0	6.1	6.2
Labour force participation rate (percentage)	16	53.7	53.7	53.5	53.1	52.9	52.9	53.5	54.0	53.9	53.8
Average weekly hours (hours per week)	17	42.3	41.7	41.5	41.3	40.7	41.0	41.0	40.4	40.2	40.7
Unemployment rate (percentage)	18	3.6	2.4	2.9	3.0	4.6	4.4	3.4	4.6	7.0	6.0
Long-term interest rate (percent per year)	19	2.8	3.2	3.6	3.7	3.1	3.1	3.6	4.2	4.5	5.0
Short-term interest rate (percent per year)	20	0.6	0.8	1.1	1.7	1.4	1.6	2.9	3.8	2.3	4.8
Federal government revenues (billions of dollars)	21	3.1	4.0	4.6	4.7	4.4	4.7	5.5	5.4	5.1	5.8
Federal government outlays (billions of dollars)	22	2.9	3.8	4.6	4.7	4.7	4.8	5.2	5.5	6.0	6.3
Federal government surplus (+)/deficit(−) (billions of dollars)	23	0.2	0.2	−0.1	0	−0.2	−0.1	0.3	−0.1	−0.8	−0.4
Gross federal debt (billions of dollars)	24	16.7	16.7	16.8	17.4	17.6	17.6	18.7	18.0	18.0	19.7
M1 (billions of dollars)	25	—	—	—	4.2	4.4	4.8	4.8	4.8	5.4	5.2
M2+ (billions of dollars)	26	—	—	—	—	—	—	—	—	—	—
M1 velocity (GDP/M1)	27	—	—	—	6.3	6.1	6.1	6.9	7.2	6.6	7.3
M2+ velocity (GDP/M2+)	28	—	—	—	—	—	—	—	—	—	—
Exchange rate (U.S. dollars per Canadian dollar)	29	[b]0.95	0.95	1.02	1.02	1.03	1.01	1.02	1.04	1.03	1.04
Current account balance (billions of dollars)	30	−0.3	−0.5	0.2	−0.4	−0.4	−0.7	−1.3	−1.4	−1.1	−1.4

1960	1961	1962	1963	1964	1965	1966	1967	1968	1969	1970	1971	1972	1973	
231.3	245.2	262.4	276.3	294.2	312.9	333.7	343.5	360.2	378.3	389.8	405.9	428.0	457.8	1
143.3	152.7	160.4	167.0	175.7	185.8	194.9	202.0	210.7	220.5	224.6	236.7	253.0	270.0	2
37.3	34.1	36.7	39.0	44.4	51.0	56.2	52.2	53.6	59.4	56.8	61.2	65.6	75.9	3
47.9	64.0	67.4	69.3	72.3	76.8	83.8	90.5	95.8	99.0	106.2	110.5	113.7	117.5	4
29.7	39.0	40.8	44.4	50.5	52.8	60.0	66.3	74.3	80.3	87.8	91.9	99.8	109.8	5
26.9	38.5	39.3	40.0	45.1	51.1	58.0	61.2	67.4	76.2	75.0	80.0	91.4	104.7	6
2.8	0.5	1.5	4.4	5.4	1.7	2.0	5.2	6.9	4.1	12.7	11.9	8.3	5.1	7
212.0	248.3	262.2	275.0	290.4	306.4	325.8	337.0	355.9	373.4	389.6	406.5	426.8	451.8	8
9.1	−1.2	0.1	0.5	1.3	2.1	2.4	1.9	1.2	1.3	0.1	−0.2	0.3	1.3	9
2.9	2.8	7.0	5.3	6.5	6.4	6.6	2.9	4.9	5.0	3.0	4.1	5.4	7.0	10
17.1	16.8	17.0	17.4	17.9	18.5	19.4	20.3	21.1	22.2	23.1	24.3	25.7	28.2	11
18.5	18.7	18.9	19.2	19.6	20.0	20.8	21.5	22.4	23.4	24.2	24.9	26.1	28.1	12
1.3	0.4	1.4	2.0	2.9	3.6	4.9	4.5	4.1	4.8	4.4	4.8	5.9	9.7	13
1.1	1.1	1.1	1.6	2.1	2.0	4.0	3.4	4.2	4.5	3.4	2.9	4.8	7.7	14
6.4	6.5	6.6	6.7	6.9	7.1	7.4	7.7	7.9	8.2	8.4	8.6	8.9	9.3	15
54.2	54.1	53.9	53.8	54.1	54.4	55.1	55.5	55.5	55.8	55.8	56.1	56.5	57.5	16
40.7	40.5	40.3	40.1	40.1	40.0	39.7	38.9	38.5	37.9	37.3	37.1	37.2	36.6	17
7.0	7.1	5.9	5.5	4.7	3.9	3.6	4.1	4.8	4.7	5.9	6.4	6.3	5.6	18
5.1	5.0	5.1	5.1	5.1	5.3	5.7	6.0	6.7	7.6	7.9	7.0	7.2	7.6	19
3.2	2.8	4.0	3.6	3.7	4.0	5.0	4.6	6.3	7.1	6.1	3.6	3.5	5.4	20
6.2	6.6	6.7	7.0	8.0	8.8	9.6	10.5	11.7	13.9	14.9	16.5	18.8	21.9	21
6.6	7.1	7.6	7.7	8.1	8.6	9.8	11.0	12.2	13.2	15.1	17.2	19.6	21.8	22
−0.3	−0.5	−0.9	−0.7	−0.1	0.2	−0.2	−0.5	−0.5	0.7	−0.2	−0.7	−0.9	0.1	23
20.4	20.9	22.8	24.5	26.2	26.8	27.7	29.8	32.0	34.4	35.8	39.9	43.8	46.2	24
5.5	5.9	6.1	6.3	6.7	7.1	7.7	8.4	8.9	9.7	9.9	11.0	12.7	14.6	25
—	—	—	—	—	—	—	—	32.2	35.6	38.9	43.8	49.8	58.0	26
7.2	6.9	7.3	7.6	7.8	8.1	8.4	8.2	8.5	8.7	9.1	9.0	8.6	8.8	27
—	—	—	—	—	—	—	—	2.4	2.4	2.3	2.2	2.2	2.2	28
1.03	0.99	0.94	0.93	0.93	0.93	0.93	0.93	0.93	0.93	0.96	0.99	1.01	1.00	29
−1.2	−1.1	−1.2	−0.9	−0.5	−1.8	−1.7	−1.4	−1.1	−2.1	0.5	−1.0	−2.4	−2.1	30

Year		1974	1975	1976	1977	1978	1979	1980	1981	1982	1983
Real GDP (billions of 1997 dollars)	1	474.7	483.3	508.4	526.0	546.8	567.6	579.9	600.3	583.1	598.9
Real consumption expenditure (billions of 1997 dollars)	2	283.5	294.3	309.4	318.0	327.5	335.0	340.7	344.8	336.1	344.9
Real investment (billions of 1997 dollars)	3	84.9	84.5	91.6	91.7	92.4	106.8	103.2	112.4	71.9	83.6
Real government expenditures (billions of 1997 dollars)	4	124.7	132.6	134.5	140.4	142.5	143.6	148.3	150.3	154.3	155.9
Real exports (billions of 1997 dollars)	5	104.8	96.1	103.6	110.1	121.0	125.4	126.6	128.9	126.9	134.4
Real imports (billions of 1997 dollars)	6	115.3	111.8	118.8	118.4	121.9	130.4	126.3	129.5	108.6	119.4
Real net exports (billions of 1997 dollars)	7	−10.5	−15.7	−15.3	−8.3	−0.9	−5.0	0.4	−0.6	18.2	14.9
Potential GDP (billions of 1997 dollars)	8	466.0	481.5	504.9	525.7	547.1	560.7	569.1	587.3	604.9	623.2
Fluctuations around potential GDP (percentage)	9	1.8	0.4	0.7	0.1	−0.1	1.2	1.9	2.2	−3.6	−3.9
Real GDP growth rate (percent per year)	10	3.7	1.8	5.2	3.5	4.0	3.8	2.2	3.5	−2.9	2.7
GDP deflator (1997 = 100)	11	32.5	35.9	39.3	42.0	44.8	49.3	54.2	60.1	65.1	68.7
CPI (1992 = 100)	12	31.1	34.5	37.1	40.0	43.6	47.6	52.4	58.9	65.3	69.1
Inflation rate (GDP deflator percent per year)	13	15.2	10.7	9.5	6.8	6.6	10.0	10.1	10.8	8.5	5.4
Inflation rate (CPI percent per year)	14	10.7	10.9	7.5	7.8	9.0	9.2	10.1	12.4	10.9	5.8
Labour force (millions)	15	9.6	10.0	10.5	10.8	11.2	11.5	11.9	12.2	12.3	12.5
Labour force participation rate (percentage)	16	58.3	58.8	61.5	61.8	62.6	63.6	64.2	65.0	64.4	64.7
Average weekly hours (hours per week)	17	35.7	35.2	35.3	35.3	35.7	35.7	35.1	34.6	34.4	34.5
Unemployment rate (percentage)	18	5.4	7.1	7.1	8.0	8.4	7.5	7.5	7.6	11.1	11.9
Long-term interest rate (percent per year)	19	8.9	9.0	9.2	9.8	10.1	10.9	13.3	16.3	15.9	12.7
Short-term interest rate (percent per year)	20	7.8	7.4	8.9	7.4	8.6	11.5	12.7	17.8	13.9	9.3
Federal government revenues (billions of dollars)	21	29.0	30.9	34.5	35.3	36.7	42.0	49.1	63.4	65.1	67.4
Federal government outlays (billions of dollars)	22	28.4	35.4	38.7	43.5	48.2	52.5	60.8	71.7	83.6	91.0
Federal government surplus (+)/deficit(−) (billions of dollars)	23	0.6	−4.5	−4.2	−8.2	−11.4	−10.4	−11.8	−8.3	−18.5	−23.6
Gross federal debt (billions of dollars)	24	49.1	55.1	61.9	69.7	82.4	100.5	110.6	127.7	144.5	173.1
M1 (billions of dollars)	25	16.2	18.3	19.7	21.2	23.5	25.0	26.9	27.8	27.0	29.5
M2+ (billions of dollars)	26	70.0	81.5	94.5	110.7	127.3	149.0	174.8	201.0	218.6	235.4
M1 velocity (GDP/M1)	27	9.5	9.5	10.2	10.4	10.4	11.2	11.7	13.0	14.0	14.0
M2+ velocity (GDP/M2+)	28	2.2	2.1	2.1	2.0	1.9	1.9	1.8	1.8	1.7	1.7
Exchange rate (U.S. dollars per Canadian dollar)	29	1.02	0.98	1.01	0.94	0.88	0.85	0.86	0.83	0.81	0.81
Current account balance (billions of dollars)	30	−4.5	−8.3	−7.5	−7.4	−9.4	−9.8	−7.1	−15.0	2.3	−3.1

1984	1985	1986	1987	1988	1989	1990	1991	1992	1993	1994	1995	1996	1997	
633.8	664.1	680.1	709.1	744.3	763.8	765.3	749.3	755.8	773.5	810.7	833.5	847.0	882.7	1
359.5	377.3	391.4	407.7	425.3	439.9	444.9	437.9	444.6	452.6	466.3	475.9	488.2	510.7	2
95.5	103.0	107.6	121.3	133.7	143.1	128.3	114.9	110.6	114.4	126.4	132.5	133.6	162.9	3
158.1	165.8	168.5	171.1	179.1	185.3	192.5	198.4	199.8	199.7	199.0	197.3	194.3	191.9	4
159.1	166.7	173.9	179.0	195.0	196.9	206.1	209.8	224.9	249.2	280.9	304.7	321.8	348.6	5
139.8	151.5	162.4	171.1	194.1	205.5	209.7	214.9	224.9	241.5	260.9	275.9	290.0	331.3	6
19.3	15.3	11.5	7.9	0.9	−8.6	−3.5	−5.1	−0.1	7.8	20.0	28.9	31.8	17.3	7
642.1	661.4	681.5	702.7	725.5	739.4	751.0	761.5	772.9	788.5	807.5	831.0	859.0	890.7	8
−1.3	0.4	−0.2	0.9	2.6	3.3	1.9	−1.6	−2.2	−1.9	0.4	0.3	−1.4	−0.9	9
5.8	4.8	2.4	4.3	5.0	2.6	0.2	−2.1	0.9	2.3	4.8	2.8	1.6	4.2	10
70.9	73.1	75.4	78.8	82.4	86.1	88.8	91.5	92.7	94.0	95.1	97.2	98.8	100.0	11
72.1	75.0	78.1	81.5	84.8	89.0	93.3	98.5	100.0	101.8	102.0	104.2	105.8	107.6	12
3.3	3.1	3.0	4.6	4.5	4.5	3.2	3.0	1.3	1.4	1.1	2.3	1.6	1.2	13
4.3	4.0	4.1	4.4	4.0	5.0	4.8	5.6	1.5	1.8	0.2	2.2	1.5	1.7	14
12.7	13.0	13.3	13.5	13.8	14.1	14.2	14.3	14.3	14.4	14.6	14.7	14.8	15.1	15
65.0	65.5	66.0	66.4	66.8	67.2	67.1	66.5	65.7	65.4	65.2	64.9	64.7	64.9	16
34.5	34.7	34.7	34.1	34.7	35.1	34.6	33.9	33.4	33.8	34.3	34.0	34.2	34.2	17
11.3	10.6	9.7	8.8	7.8	7.5	8.2	10.3	11.2	11.4	10.3	9.4	9.6	9.2	18
13.5	11.7	10.4	10.7	10.9	10.8	11.9	10.8	9.9	8.9	9.4	9.0	8.1	7.0	19
11.1	9.5	9.0	8.2	9.4	12.0	12.8	8.9	6.5	4.9	5.4	7.0	4.3	3.2	20
73.5	80.2	88.6	97.3	106.6	113.7	120.9	125.8	130.1	128.7	131.9	140.3	148.0	162.6	21
102.2	112.3	114.4	120.6	128.9	138.5	151.5	161.2	164.4	167.2	165.9	172.4	166.1	160.1	22
−28.7	−32.2	−25.8	−23.3	−22.4	−24.8	−30.6	−35.4	−34.4	−38.5	−34.0	−32.1	−18.1	2.5	23
209.3	250.5	284.0	318.3	349.9	380.0	406.6	444.6	476.1	514.4	557.6	595.9	634.9	651.1	24
30.1	31.2	33.5	37.5	39.3	40.4	40.9	42.0	45.0	49.3	55.8	59.4	66.7	78.0	25
252.0	277.7	306.2	341.6	374.2	426.7	477.0	518.0	548.3	571.3	582.1	604.4	631.1	636.6	26
14.9	15.6	15.3	14.9	15.6	16.3	16.6	16.3	15.6	14.8	13.8	13.6	12.5	11.3	27
1.8	1.7	1.7	1.6	1.6	1.5	1.4	1.3	1.3	1.3	1.3	1.3	1.3	1.4	28
0.77	0.73	0.72	0.75	0.81	0.84	0.86	0.87	0.83	0.78	0.73	0.73	0.73	0.72	29
−1.7	−7.8	−15.5	−17.8	−18.3	−25.8	−23.1	−25.6	−25.4	−28.1	−17.7	−6.1	4.6	−11.4	30

Year		1998	1999	2000	2001	2002	2003	2004
Real GDP (billions of 1997 dollars)	1	918.9	969.8	1,020.5	1,038.7	1,070.8	1,092.4	1,124.4
Real consumption expenditure (billions of 1997 dollars)	2	524.8	544.8	566.7	579.5	600.7	619.4	640.6
Real investment (billions of 1997 dollars)	3	165.1	175.6	190.6	180.1	185.5	206.1	220.0
Real government expenditures (billions of 1997 dollars)	4	197.2	204.1	210.6	220.6	227.7	234.8	241.8
Real exports (billions of 1997 dollars)	5	380.4	421.0	458.6	445.0	449.3	439.8	461.7
Real imports (billions of 1997 dollars)	6	348.1	375.2	405.7	384.9	390.7	406.7	439.6
Real net exports (billions of 1997 dollars)	7	32.3	45.8	52.9	60.1	58.6	33.1	22.1
Potential GDP (billions of 1997 dollars)	8	926.3	963.0	999.5	1,034.6	1,063.3	1,095.7	1,128.9
Fluctuations around potential GDP (percentage)	9	−0.8	0.7	2.1	0.4	0.7	−0.3	−0.4
Real GDP growth rate (percent per year)	10	4.1	5.5	5.2	1.8	3.1	2.0	2.9
GDP deflator (1997 = 100)	11	99.6	101.3	105.5	106.7	107.8	111.3	114.7
CPI (1992 = 100)	12	108.6	110.5	113.5	116.4	119.0	122.3	124.6
Inflation rate (GDP deflator percent per year)	13	−0.4	1.7	4.1	1.1	1.0	3.3	3.1
Inflation rate (CPI percent per year)	14	0.9	1.7	2.7	2.6	2.2	2.8	1.9
Labour force (millions)	15	15.3	15.6	15.8	16.1	16.6	17.0	17.2
Labour force participation rate (percentage)	16	65.1	65.6	65.9	65.9	66.9	67.5	67.6
Average weekly hours (hours per week)	17	34.0	34.2	34.5	33.8	33.5	32.9	33.3
Unemployment rate (percentage)	18	8.4	7.6	6.9	7.2	7.7	7.6	7.2
Long-term interest rate (percent per year)	19	6.2	6.6	7.1	7.1	7.0	6.5	6.1
Short-term interest rate (percent per year)	20	4.7	4.7	5.5	3.9	2.5	2.9	2.3
Federal government revenues (billions of dollars)	21	167.5	177.7	195.7	193.9	191.6	196.2	207.3
Federal government outlays (billions of dollars)	22	163.7	171.9	179.3	184.5	184.3	195.6	199.5
Federal government surplus (+)/deficit(−) (billions of dollars)	23	3.8	5.8	16.4	9.5	7.3	0.6	7.8
Gross federal debt (billions of dollars)	24	645.7	648.4	648.2	644.9	640.5	629.6	628.8
M1 (billions of dollars)	25	86.0	92.6	106.2	119.0	133.0	143.6	161.4
M2+ (billions of dollars)	26	629.6	652.4	691.0	736.5	791.4	828.3	867.1
M1 velocity (GDP/M1)	27	10.6	10.6	10.1	9.3	8.7	8.5	8.0
M2+ velocity (GDP/M2+)	28	1.5	1.5	1.6	1.5	1.5	1.5	1.5
Exchange rate (U.S. dollars per Canadian dollar)	29	0.67	0.67	0.67	0.65	0.64	0.71	0.77
Current account balance (billions of dollars)	30	−11.4	2.6	29.3	25.1	21.1	18.4	28.8

GLOSSARY

Above full-employment equilibrium A macroeconomic equilibrium in which real GDP exceeds potential GDP. (p. 519)

Absolute advantage A person has an absolute advantage if that person is more productive than another person. (p. 42)

Aggregate demand The relationship between the quantity of real GDP demanded and the price level. (p. 513)

Aggregate hours The total number of hours worked by all the people employed, both full time and part time, during a year. (p. 491)

Aggregate planned expenditure The expenditure that households, firms, governments, and foreigners plan to undertake in given circumstances. It is the sum of planned consumption expenditure, planned investment, planned government expenditures on goods and services, and planned exports minus planned imports. (p. 541)

Aggregate production function The relationship between the quantity of real GDP supplied and the quantities of labour and capital and the state of technology. (pp. 508, 739)

Allocative efficiency A situation in which we cannot produce more of any good without giving up some of another good that we *value more highly*. (p. 39)

Automated Clearing Settlement System (ACSS) A system through which all payments not processed by the LVTS are handled. (p. 596)

Automatic fiscal policy A change in fiscal policy that is triggered by the state of the economy. (p. 570)

Automatic stabilizers Mechanisms that stabilize real GDP without explicit action by the government. (p. 574)

Autonomous expenditure The sum of those components of aggregate planned expenditure that are not influenced by real GDP. Autonomous expenditure equals the sum of investment, government expenditures, exports, and the autonomous parts of consumption expenditure and imports. (p. 543)

Autonomous taxes Taxes that do not vary with real GDP. (p. 570)

Autonomous tax multiplier The magnification effect of a change in autonomous taxes on equilibrium expenditure and real GDP. (p. 572)

Balanced budget A government budget in which revenues and outlays are equal. (p. 565)

Bank rate The interest rate that the Bank of Canada charges the chartered banks on the reserves it lends them. (p. 660)

Barter The direct exchange of one good or service for other goods and services. (p. 590)

Base period The period in which the CPI is defined to be 100. (p. 498)

Below full-employment equilibrium A macroeconomic equilibrium in which potential GDP exceeds real GDP. (p. 518)

Big tradeoff The conflict between equity and efficiency. (pp. 10, 115)

Budget deficit A government's budget balance that is negative—outlays exceed revenues. (p. 565)

Budget surplus A government's budget balance that is positive—revenues exceed outlays. (p. 565)

Business cycle The periodic but irregular up-and-down movement in production and jobs. (p. 448)

Canadian interest rate differential A gap equal to the Canadian interest rate minus the foreign interest rate. (p. 619)

Capital The tools, equipment, buildings, and other constructions that businesses now use to produce goods and services. (p. 4)

Capital accumulation The growth of capital resources, which includes human capital. (p. 40)

Capital consumption The decrease in the capital stock that results from wear and tear and obsolescence. (p. 469)

Central bank A public authority that supervises financial institutions and markets and conducts monetary policy. (p. 595)

Ceteris paribus Other things being equal—all other relevant things remaining the same. (p. 13)

Chain-weighted output index An index that uses the prices of two adjacent years to calculate the real GDP growth rate. (p. 474)

Change in demand A change in buyers' plans that occurs when some influence on those plans other than the price of the good changes. It is illustrated by a shift of the demand curve. (p. 62)

Change in supply A change in sellers' plans that occurs when some influence on those plans other than the price of the good changes. It is illustrated by a shift of the supply curve. (p. 67)

Change in the quantity demanded A change in buyers' plans that occurs when the price of a good changes but all other influences on buyers' plans remain unchanged. It is illustrated by a movement along the demand curve. (p. 65)

Change in the quantity supplied A change in sellers' plans that occurs when the price of a good changes but all other influences on sellers' plans remain unchanged. It is illustrated by a movement along the supply curve. (p. 68)

Chartered bank A private firm, chartered under the Bank Act of 1992 to receive deposits and make loans. (p. 593)

Classical growth theory A theory of economic growth based on the view that real GDP growth is temporary and that when real GDP per person increases above subsistence level, a population explosion brings real GDP back to subsistence level. (p. 743)

Comparative advantage A person or country has a comparative advantage in an activity if that person or country can perform the activity at a lower opportunity cost than anyone else or any other country. (p. 42)

Competitive market A market that has many buyers and many sellers, so no single buyer or seller can influence the price. (p. 60)

Complement A good that is used in conjunction with another good. (p. 63)

Consumer Price Index (CPI) An index that measures the average of the prices paid by urban consumers for a fixed "basket" of the consumer goods and services. (p. 498)

Consumption expenditure The total payment for consumer goods and services. (p. 467)

Consumption function The relationship between consumption expenditure and disposable income, other things remaining the same. (p. 536)

Contractionary fiscal policy A decrease in government expenditures or an increase in taxes. (p. 577)

Core inflation A measure of inflation based on the CPI excluding the eight most volatile prices–the prices of fruit, vegetables, gasoline, fuel oil, natural gas, mortgage interest, inter-city transportation, and tobacco—and also excluding changes in indirect taxes—taxes such as GST, HST, and provincial sales taxes. (p. 656)

Cost-push inflation An inflation that results from an initial increase in costs. (p. 635)

Crawling peg A policy regime is one that selects a target path for the exchange rate with intervention in the foreign exchange market to achieve that path. (p. 624)

Credit union A cooperative organization that operates under the Co-operative Credit Association Act of 1992 and that receives deposits and makes loans to its members. (p. 593)

Cross-section graph A graph that shows the values of an economic variable for different groups in a population at a point in time. (p. 18)

Crowding in The tendency for expansionary fiscal policy to increase investment. (p. 683)

Crowding out The tendency for an expansionary fiscal policy action to decrease investment. (p. 683)

Currency The coins and Bank of Canada notes that we use today. (p. 591)

Currency appreciation The rise in the value of one currency in terms of another currency. (p. 613)

Currency depreciation The fall in the value of one currency in terms of another currency. (p. 613)

Currency drain ratio The ratio of currency to deposits. (p. 597)

Currency union A merger of the currencies of a number of countries to form a single money and avoid foreign exchange transactions. (p. 624)

Current account A record of exports minus imports and interest payments paid to and received from abroad. (p. 457)

Cyclical surplus or deficit The actual surplus or deficit minus the structural surplus or deficit. (p. 575)

Cyclical unemployment The fluctuations in unemployment over the business cycle. (p. 496)

Deflation A negative inflation rate—a process in which the price level is falling. (p. 455)

Demand The relationship between the quantity of a good that consumers plan to buy and the price of the good when all other influences on buyers' plans remain the same. It is described by a demand schedule and illustrated by a demand curve. (p. 61)

Demand curve A curve that shows the relationship between the quantity demanded of a good and its price when all other influences on consumers' planned purchases remain the same. (p. 62)

Demand for labour The relationship between the quantity of labour demanded and the real wage rate when all other influences on firms' hiring plans remain the same. (p. 709)

Demand for money curve The relationship between the quantity of money demanded and the interest rate when all other influences on the amount of money that people wish to hold remain the same. (p. 602)

Demand-pull inflation An inflation that results from an initial increase in aggregate demand. (p. 633)

Depository institution A firm that takes deposits from households and firms and makes loans to other households and firms. (p. 593)

Depreciation The decrease in the capital stock that results from wear and tear and obsolescence. (p. 469)

Desired reserve ratio The ratio of reserves to deposits that banks wish to hold. (p. 597)

Direct relationship A relationship between two variables that move in the same direction. (p. 20)

Discouraged worker A person who does not have a job, is available for work, and is willing to work but who has given up the effort to find work. (pp. 453, 490)

Discretionary fiscal policy A policy action that is initiated by an act of Parliament. (p. 570)

Disposable income Aggregate income minus taxes plus transfer payments. (pp. 515, 536)

Dumping The sale by a foreign firm of exports at a lower price than the cost of production. (p. 768)

Dynamic comparative advantage A comparative advantage that a person or country possesses as a result of having specialized in a particular activity and then, as a result of learning-by-doing, having become the producer with the lowest opportunity cost. (p. 45)

Economic growth The expansion of production possibilities that results from capital accumulation and technological change. (pp. 40, 447)

Economic growth rate The percentage change in the quantity of goods and services produced from one year to the next. (p. 476)

Economic model A description of some aspect of the economic world that includes only those features of the world that are needed for the purpose at hand. (p. 12)

Economic theory A generalization that summarizes what we think we understand about the economic choices that people make and the performance of industries and entire economies. (p. 12)

Economic welfare A comprehensive measure of the general state of economic well-being. (p. 476)

Economics The social science that studies the choices that we make as we cope with *scarcity* and the *incen-tives* that influence and reconcile those choices. (p. 2)

Efficiency wage A real wage rate that is set above the full-employment equilibrium wage rate and that balances the costs and benefits of this higher wage rate to maximize the firm's profit. (p. 720)

Employment-to-population ratio The percentage of people of working age who have jobs. (p. 490)

Entrepreneurship The human resource that organizes the other three factors of production: labour, land, and capital. (p. 4)

Equation of exchange An equation that states that the quantity of money multiplied by the velocity of circulation equals GDP. (p. 638)

Equilibrium expenditure The level of aggregate expenditure that occurs when aggregate planned expenditure equals real GDP. (p. 544)

Equilibrium price The price at which the quantity demanded equals the quantity supplied. (p. 70)

Equilibrium quantity The quantity bought and sold at the equilibrium price. (p. 70)

Excess reserves A bank's actual reserves minus its desired reserves. (p. 597)

Expansion A business cycle phase between a trough and a peak—a period in which real GDP increases. (p. 448)

Expansionary fiscal policy An increase in government expenditures or a decrease in taxes. (p. 577)

Exports The goods and services that we sell to people in other countries. (pp. 468, 756)

Factors of production The resources used to produce goods and services. (p. 3)

Federal budget The annual statement of the outlays and revenues of the government of Canada, together with the laws and regulations that approve and support those outlays and revenues. (p. 564)

Final good An item that is bought by its final user during the specified time period. (p. 466)

Financial innovation The development of new financial products—new ways of borrowing and lending. (p. 601)

Firm An economic unit that hires factors of production and organizes those factors to produce and sell goods and services. (p. 45)

Fiscal policy The use of the federal budget to achieve macroeconomic objectives such as full employment, sustained long-term economic growth, and price level stability by setting and changing taxes, making transfer payments, and purchasing goods and services. (pp. 459, 515, 564)

Fixed exchange rate A policy regime in which the value of the exchange rate is decided by the government or central bank and the unregulated forces of demand and supply are blocked by direct intervention in the foreign exchange market. (p. 623)

Flexible exchange rate A policy regime in which the value of the exchange rate is determined by demand and supply with no direct intervention in the foreign exchange market by the central bank. (p. 623)

Flow A quantity per unit of time. (p. 469)

Foreign currency The notes, coins and bank deposits in the currency of another country. (p. 612)

Foreign exchange market The market in which the currency of one country is exchanged for the currency of another. (p. 612)

Foreign exchange rate The price at which one currency exchanges for another. (p. 612)

Frictional unemployment The unemployment that arises from normal labour turnover—from people entering and leaving the labour force and from the ongoing creation and destruction of jobs. (p. 495)

Full employment A situation in which the quantity of labour demanded equals the quantity supplied. At full employment, there is no cyclical unemployment—all unemployment is frictional, structural, and seasonal. (p. 496)

GDP deflator One measure of the price level, which is the average of current-year prices as a percentage of base-year prices. (p. 474)

General Agreement on Tariffs and Trade An international agreement signed in 1947 to reduce tariffs on international trade. (p. 763)

Goods and services All the objects that people value and produce to satisfy their wants. (p. 3)

Government budget deficit The deficit that arises when the government spends more than it collects in taxes. (p. 457)

Government budget surplus The surplus that arises when the government collects more in taxes than it spends. (p. 457)

Government debt The total amount of borrowing that the government has undertaken. It equals the sum of past budget deficits minus the sum of past budget surpluses. (p. 567)

Government expenditures Goods and services bought by the government. (p. 468)

Government expenditures multiplier The magnification effect of a change in government expenditures on goods and services on equilibrium expenditure and real GDP (p. 570)

Great Depression A decade (1929–1939) of high unemployment and stagnant production throughout the world economy. (p. 446)

Gross domestic product (GDP) The market value of all final goods and services produced within a country during a given time period. (p. 466)

Gross investment The total amount spent on purchases of new capital and on replacing depreciated capital. (p. 469)

Growth accounting A method of calculating how much real GDP growth results from growth of labour and capital and how much is attributable to technological change. (p. 739)

Growth rate cycle downturn A pronounced, pervasive, and persistent decline in the growth rate of aggregate economic activity. (p. 486)

Growth recession A situation in which the growth rate of real GDP remains positive but slows so that real GDP falls below potential GDP. (p. 448)

Human capital The knowledge and skill that people obtain from education, on-the-job training, and work experience. (pp. 3, 707)

Imports The goods and services that we buy from people in other countries. (pp. 468, 756)

Incentive A reward that encourages or a penalty that discourages an action. (p. 2)

Induced expenditure The sum of the components of aggregate planned expenditure that vary with real GDP. Induced expenditure equals consumption expenditure minus imports. (p. 543)

Induced taxes Taxes that vary with real GDP. (p. 573)

Infant-industry argument The argument that it is necessary to protect a new industry to enable it to grow into a mature industry that can compete in world markets. (p. 767)

Inferior good A good for which demand decreases as income increases. (p. 64)

Inflation A process in which the price level is rising and money is losing value. (p. 455)

Inflation rate The percentage change in the price level from one year to the next. (p. 500)

Inflationary gap The amount by which real GDP exceeds potential GDP. (p. 519)

Instrument rule A decision rule for monetary policy that sets the policy instrument at a level that is based on the current state of the economy. (p. 659)

Interest The income that capital earns. (p. 4)

Interest rate The amount received by a lender and paid by a borrower expressed as a percentage of the amount of the loan. (p. 604)

Interest rate parity A situation in which the interest rates on assets in different currencies are equal when exchange rate changes are taken into account. (p. 622)

Interest-sensitive expenditure curve The relationship between aggregate expenditure plans and the real interest rate when all other influences on expenditure plans remain the same. (p. 667)

Intermediate good An item that is produced by one firm, bought by another firm, and used as a component of a final good or service. (p. 466)

International crowding out The tendency for an expansionary fiscal policy to decrease net exports. (p. 683)

Inverse relationship A relationship between variables that move in opposite directions. (p. 21)

Investment The purchase of new plant, equipment, and buildings and additions to inventories. (p. 468)

Job rationing The practice of paying a real wage rate above the equilibrium level and then rationing jobs by some method. (p. 720)

Job search The activity of looking for an acceptable vacant job. (p. 719)

Keynesian A macroeconomist who regards the economy as being inherently unstable and requiring active government intervention to achieve stability. (p. 688)

***k*-percent rule** A rule that makes the quantity of money grow at a rate of *k* percent a year, where *k* equals the growth rate of potential GDP. (p. 671)

Labour The work time and work effort that people devote to producing goods and services. (p. 3)

Labour force The sum of the people who are employed and who are unemployed. (pp. 452, 488)

Labour force participation rate The percentage of the working-age population who are members of the labour force. (p. 490)

Labour productivity Real GDP per hour of labour. (pp. 707, 739)

Land All the gifts of nature that we use to produce goods and services. (p. 3)

Large Value Tranfer System (LVTS) An electronic payments system that enables financial institutions and their customers to make large payments instantly and with sure knowledge that the payment has been made. (p. 596)

Law of demand Other things remaining the same, the higher the price of a good, the smaller is the quantity demanded of it. (p. 61)

Law of diminishing returns As a firm uses more of a variable input, with a given quantity of other inputs (fixed inputs), the marginal product of the variable input eventually diminishes. (pp. 709, 740)

Law of supply Other things remaining the same, the higher the price of a good, the greater is the quantity supplied of it. (p. 66)

Learning-by-doing People become more productive in an activity (learn) just by repeatedly producing a particular good or service (doing). (pp. 45, 707)

Lender of last resort The Bank of Canada stands ready to make loans to banks when the banking system as a whole is short of reserves. (p. 595)

Linear relationship A relationship between two variables that is illustrated by a straight line. (p. 20)

Liquidity The property of being instantly convertible into a means of payment with little loss in value. (p. 592)

Long-run aggregate supply curve The relationship between the quantity of real GDP supplied and the price level in the long run when real GDP equals potential GDP. (pp. 508, 713)

Long-run macroeconomic equilibrium A situation that occurs when real GDP equals potential GDP— the economy is on its long-run aggregate supply curve. (p. 517)

Long-run neutrality The proposition that in the long run, a change in the quantity of money changes the price level and leaves all real variables unchanged. (p. 691)

Long-run Phillips curve A curve that shows the relationship between inflation and unemployment when the actual inflation rate equals the expected inflation rate. (p. 646)

Lucas wedge The accumulated loss of output that results from a slowdown in the growth rate of real GDP per person. (p. 451)

M1 A measure of money that consists of currency held outside the banks plus demand deposits at chartered banks that are owned by individuals and businesses. (p. 591)

M2+ A measure of money that consists of M1 plus personal savings deposits, and nonpersonal notice deposits at chartered banks plus all types of deposits at trust and mortgage loan companies, credit unions, caisses populaires, and other financial institutions. (p. 591)

Macroeconomic long run A time frame that is sufficiently long for real GDP to return to potential GDP so that full employment prevails. (p. 508)

Macroeconomics The study of the performance of the national economy and the global economy. (p. 2)

Macroeconomic short run A period during which real GDP has fallen below or risen above potential GDP. (p. 509)

Margin When a choice is changed by a small amount or by a little at a time, the choice is made at the margin. (p. 11)

Marginal benefit The benefit that a person receives from consuming one more unit of a good or service. It is measured as the maximum amount that a person is willing to pay for one more unit of the good or service. (pp. 11, 38)

Marginal benefit curve A curve that shows the relationship between the marginal benefit of a good and the quantity of that good consumed. (p. 38)

Marginal cost The opportunity cost of producing one more unit of a good or service. It is the best alternative forgone. It is calculated as the increase in total cost divided by the increase in output. (pp. 11, 37)

Marginal product of labour The additional real GDP produced by an additional hour of labour when all other influences on production remain the same. (p. 709)

Marginal propensity to consume The fraction of a change in disposable income that is consumed. It is calculated as the change in consumption expenditure divided by the change in disposable income. (p. 538)

Marginal propensity to import The fraction of an increase in real GDP that is spent on imports. (p. 541)

Marginal propensity to save The fraction of an increase in disposable income that is saved. It is calculated as the change in saving divided by the change in disposable income. (p. 538)

Market Any arrangement that enables buyers and sellers to get information and to do business with each other. (p. 46)

McCallum rule A rule that makes the growth rate of the monetary base respond to the long-term average growth rate of real GDP and medium-term changes in the velocity of circulation of the monetary base. (p. 670)

Means of payment A method of settling a debt. (p. 590)

Microeconomics The study of the choices that individuals and businesses make, the way these choices interact, and the influence governments exert on them. (p. 2)

Minimum wage A regulation that makes the hiring of labour below a specified wage rate illegal. (p. 721)

Monetarist A macroeconomist who believes that fluctuations in the quantity of money are the main source of economic fluctuations. (p. 688)

Monetary base The sum of the Bank of Canada notes outside the Bank of Canada, chartered banks' deposits at the Bank of Canada, and coins held by households, firms, and banks. (p. 597)

Monetary policy The attempt to control inflation and moderate the business cycle by changing the quantity of money and adjusting interest rates and the exchange rate. (pp. 459, 515, 606)

Money Any commodity or token that is generally acceptable as the means of payment. (pp. 46, 590)

Money multiplier The ratio of the change in the quantity of money to the change in the monetary base. (p. 600)

Money price The number of dollars that must be given up in exchange for a good or service. (p. 60)

Money wage rate The number of dollars that an hour of labour earns. (p. 709)

Multiplier The amount by which a change in autonomous expenditure is magnified or multiplied to determine the change in equilibrium expenditure and real GDP. (p. 546)

National saving The sum of private saving (saving by households and businesses) and government saving. (p. 469)

Natural rate of unemployment The unemployment rate when the economy is at full employment. There is no cyclical unemployment; all unemployment is frictional, structural, and seasonal. (pp. 496, 508)

Negative relationship A relationship between variables that move in opposite directions. (p. 21)

Neoclassical growth theory A theory of economic growth that proposes that real GDP per person grows because technological change induces a level of saving and investment that makes capital per hour of labour grow. (p. 745)

Net exports The value of exports minus the value of imports. (pp. 468, 756)

Net investment Net increase in the capital stock—gross investment minus depreciation. (p. 469)

Net taxes Taxes paid to governments minus transfer payments received from governments. (p. 468)

New growth theory A theory of economic growth based on the idea that real GDP per person grows because of the choices that people make in the pursuit of profit and that growth can persist indefinitely. (p. 747)

Nominal GDP The value of the final goods and services produced in a given year valued at the prices that prevailed in that same year. It is a more precise name for GDP. (p. 473)

Nominal interest rate The percentage return on an asset such as a bond expressed in terms of money. (p. 665)

Nontariff barrier Any action other than a tariff that restricts international trade. (p. 763)

Normal good A good for which demand increases as income increases. (p. 64)

North American Free Trade Agreement An agreement, which became effective on January 1, 1994, to eliminate all barriers to international trade between the United States, Canada, and Mexico after a 15-year phasing-in period. (p. 764)

One-third rule The rule that, with no change in technology, a 1 percent increase in capital per hour of labour brings, on the average, a one-third of 1 percent increase in real GDP per hour of labour. (p. 740)

Open market operation The purchase or sale of government of Canada securities—Treasury bills and government bonds—by the Bank of Canada from or to a chartered bank or the public. (p. 660)

Operating band The target overnight loans rate plus or minus 0.25 percentage points. (p.660)

Opportunity cost The highest-valued alternative that we give up to get something. (p. 10)

Output gap Real GDP minus potential GDP. (p. 451)

Overnight loans rate The interest rate on overnight loans that members of the LVTS (big banks) make to each other. (p. 658)

Payments system The system through which banks make payments to each other to settle transactions by their customers. (p. 595)

Phillips curve A curve that shows a relationship between inflation and unemployment. (p. 644)

Policy conflict A situation in which the government and the Bank of Canada pursue different goals and the actions of one make it harder for the other to achieve its goals. (p. 692)

Policy coordination A situation in which the government and the Bank of Canada work together to achieve a common set of goals. (p. 692)

Positive relationship A relationship between two variables that move in the same direction. (p. 20)

Potential GDP The value of production when all the economy's labour, capital, land, and entrepreneurial ability are fully employed; the quantity of real GDP at full employment. (pp. 447, 497)

Preferences A description of a person's likes and dislikes. (p. 38)

Price level The average level of prices as measured by a price index. (pp. 455, 474)

Production efficiency A situation in which the economy cannot produce more of one good without producing less of some other good. (p. 35)

Production function The relationship between real GDP and the quantity of labour employed when all other influences on production remain the same. (p. 706)

Production possibilities frontier The boundary between the combinations of goods and services that can be produced and the combinations that cannot. (p. 34)

Productivity curve A relationship that shows how real GDP per hour of labour changes as the amount of capital per hour of labour changes with a given state of technology. (p. 739)

Productivity growth slowdown A situation in which the growth rate of output per person sags. (p. 447)

Profit The income earned by entrepreneurship. (p. 4)

Property rights Social arrangements that govern the ownership, use, and disposal of resources or factors of production, goods, and services that are enforceable in the courts. (p. 46)

Provincial budget The annual statement of the outlays and revenues of a provincial government, together with the laws and regulations that approve and support those outlays and revenues. (p. 564)

Purchasing power parity The equal value of different monies. (p. 622)

Quantity demanded The amount of a good or service that consumers plan to buy during a given time period at a particular price. (p. 61)

Quantity of labour demanded The number of labour hours hired by all the firms in the economy. (p. 709)

Quantity of labour supplied The number of labour hours that all households in the economy plan to work. (p. 711)

Quantity supplied The amount of a good or service that producers plan to sell during a given time period at a particular price. (p. 66)

Quantity theory of money The proposition that in the long run, an increase in the quantity of money brings an equal percentage increase in the price level. (p. 638)

Quota A quantitative restriction on the import of a particular good, which specifies the maximum amount that can be imported in a given time period. (p. 766)

Rational expectation The most accurate forecast possible, a forecast that uses all the available information, including knowledge of the relevant economic forces that influence the variable being forecasted. (p. 641)

Real exchange rate The relative price of the GDP baskets of goods and services in two countries. (p. 671)

Real GDP The value of final goods and services produced in a given year when valued at constant prices. (pp. 447, 473)

Real gross domestic product (real GDP) The value of final goods and services produced in a given year when valued at constant prices. (pp. 447, 473)

Real interest rate The percentage return on an asset expressed in terms of what money will buy. It is the nominal interest rate adjusted for inflation and is approximately equal to the nominal interest rate minus the inflation rate. (p. 665)

Real wage rate The quantity of goods and services that an hour's work can buy. It is equal to the money wage rate divided by the price level and multiplied by 100. (pp. 492, 709)

Recession A period during which real GDP decreases—the growth rate of real GDP is negative—for at least two successive quarters. (pp. 448)

Recessionary gap The amount by which potential GDP exceeds real GDP. (p. 518)

Relative price The ratio of the price of one good or service to the price of another good or service. A relative price is an opportunity cost. (p. 60)

Rent The income that land earns. (p. 4)

Reserve ratio The fraction of a bank's total deposits that are held in reserves. (p. 597)

Reserves Cash in a bank's vault plus the bank's deposits at the Bank of Canada. (p. 593)

Saving The amount of income that households have left after they have paid their taxes and bought their consumption goods and services. (p. 468)

Saving function The relationship between saving and disposable income, other things remaining the same. (p. 536)

Scarcity The state in which the resources available are insufficient to satisfy people's wants. (p. 2)

Scatter diagram A diagram that plots the value of one variable against the value of another. (p. 19)

Seasonal unemployment Unemployment that arises because the number of jobs available has decreased because of the season. (p. 496)

Self-interest The choices that you think are best for you. (p. 5)

Settlements balances rate The interest rate that the Bank of Canada pays banks on their reserve deposits at the Bank of Canada. (p. 660)

Short-run aggregate supply curve A curve that shows the relationship between the quantity of real GDP supplied and the price level in the short run when the money wage rate, other resource prices, and potential GDP remain constant. (pp. 509, 713)

Short-run macroeconomic equilibrium A situation that occurs when the quantity of real GDP demanded equals the quantity of real GDP supplied—at the point of intersection of the *AD* curve and the *SAS* curve. (p. 516)

Short-run Phillips curve A curve that shows the tradeoff between inflation and unemployment, when the expected inflation rate and the natural rate of unemployment remain the same. (p. 644)

Slope The change in the value of the variable measured on the *y*-axis divided by the change in the value of the variable measured on the *x*-axis. (p. 24)

Social interest Choices that are the best for society as a whole. (p. 5)

Stock A quantity that exists at a point in time. (p. 469)

Structural surplus or deficit The budget balance that would occur if the economy were at full employment and real GDP were equal to potential GDP. (p. 575)

Structural unemployment The unemployment that arises when changes in technology or international competition change the skills needed to perform jobs or change the locations of jobs. (p. 496)

Subsistence real wage rate The minimum real wage rate needed to maintain life. (p. 744)

Substitute A good that can be used in place of another good. (p. 63)

Supply The relationship between the quantity of a good that producers plan to sell and the price of the good when all other influences on producers' plans remain the same. It is described by a supply schedule and illustrated by a supply curve. (p. 66)

Supply curve A curve that shows the relationship between the quantity supplied and the price of a good when all other influences on producers' planned sales remain the same. (p. 66)

Supply of labour The relationship between the quantity of labour supplied and the real wage rate when all other influences on work plans remain the same. (p. 711)

Targeting rule A decision rule for monetary policy that sets the policy instrument at a level that makes the forecast of the ultimate policy target equal to the target. (p. 659)

Tarrif A tax that is imposed by the importing country when an imported good crosses its international boundary. (p. 763)

Taylor rule A rule that sets the overnight rate in response to only the current inflation rate and the current estimate of the output gap. (p. 670)

Technological change The development of new goods and of better ways of producing goods and services. (p. 40)

Terms of trade The quantity of goods and services that a country exports to pay for its imports of goods and services. (p. 758)

Time-series graph A graph that measures time (for example, months or years) on the *x*-axis and the variable or variables in which we are interested on the *y*-axis. (p. 18)

Tradeoff A constraint that involves giving up one thing to get something else. (p. 9)

Trend The general tendency for a variable to move in one direction. (p. 18)

Trust and mortgage loan company A privately owned depository institution that operates under the Trust and Loan Companies Act of 1992. (p. 593)

Unemployment A state in which a person does not have a job but is available for work, willing to work, and has made some effort to find work within the previous four weeks. (p. 452)

Unemployment rate The percentage of the people in the labour force who are unemployed. (pp. 452, 489)

Velocity of circulation The average number of times a dollar of money is used annually to buy the goods and services that make up GDP. (p. 638)

Voluntary export restraint An agreement between two governments in which the government of the exporting country agrees to restrain the volume of its own exports. (p. 766)

Wages The income that labour earns. (p. 4)

Wealth The market value of all the things that people own—the market value of their assets. (p. 469)

Working-age population The total number of people aged 15 years and over. (p. 488)

World Trade Organization An international organization that places greater obligations on its member countries to observe the GATT rules. (p. 763)

INDEX

Note: Key terms and the pages on which they are defined are **bolded**. References to "*f*" denote a figure and "*t*" denote a table.